Jazz Styles

History & Analysis

Eighth Edition

Mark C. Gridley
Heidelberg College
Tiffin, Ohio 44883

With Contributions
by David Cutler

Prentice Hall

Upper Saddle River, New Jersey 07458

Library of Congress Cataloging-in-Publication Data

Gridley, Mark C.
Jazz styles : history and analysis / Mark C. Gridley.—8th ed.
p. cm.
Includes bibliographical references and index.
ISBN 0-13-099282-8
1. Jazz—Analysis, appreciation. 2. Style, Musical. 3. Jazz musicians. I. Title.

ML3506.G74 2003
781.65—dc21

2001058796

VP, Editorial Director: Charlyce Jones Owen
Senior Acquisitions Editor: Christopher Johnson
Editorial Assistant: Evette Dickerson
AVP, Director of Production and Manufacturing: Barbara Kittle
Senior Production Editor: Harriet Tellem
Prepress and Manufacturing Manager: Nick Sklitsis
Prepress and Manufacturing Buyer: Ben Smith
Art Director, Interior Design: Nancy Wells
Cover Design: Ximena Tamvakopoulos
Line Art Supervisor: Guy Ruggiero
Marketing Manager: Chris Ruel
Marketing Assistant: Scott Rich
Photo Research: Diana Gongora
Director, Image Resource Center: Melinda Reo
Manager, Rights and Permissions: Zina Arabia
Interior Image Specialist: Beth Boyd-Brenzel
Cover Image Specialist: Karen Sanatar
Image Permission Coordinator: Tara Gardner
Cover Art: *A Concerted Effort* by Darryl Daniels.
Darryl Daniels is renowned for his colorful, sylized paintings, including his signature "Jazz Collection" series. An award-winning artist, his work has been exhibited in galleries, on numerous recordings, and publications. Visit the artist's website at www.darryldaniels.com

Portions of pages 63–67 originally appeared in *Jazz Educators Journal,* Vol. XVI (1984), No. 3, pp 71–72, as "Why Is Louis Armstrong So Important?" Portions of pages 306–311 originally appeared in *Popular Music and Society,* Vol. IX (1983), No. 2, pp. 27–34, as "Clarifying Labels: Jazz, Rock, Funk and Jazz-Rock." Portions of pages 36–47 originally appeared in *The Black Perspective in Music,* Vol. 12 (1984), No. 1, pp. 44–56, as "Towards Identification of African Traits in Early Jazz." Portions of pages 158–162 originally appeared in *Popular Music and Society,* Vol. IX (1984), No. 4, pp. 41–45, as "Why Have Modern Jazz Combos Been Less Popular Than Swing Big Bands?" Portion of pages of 186–189 originally appeared in *Tracking: Popular Music Studies,* Vol. 2 (1990), Issue 2, pp. 8–16, as "Clarifying Labels: Cool Jazz, West Coast and Hard Bop." All of the above are reproduced here by permission of their respective editors. The "(Meet the) Flintstones Theme" is used on the *Demonstration CD* by permission of Barbera-Hanna Music (copyright 1960 and 1967), composed by William Hanna, Joseph Barbera and Hoyt Curtin. Reproduction and performance without permission of Barbera-Hanna Music is forbidden.

The book was set in 10/12 New Caledonia by Clarinda Co., and printed and bound by Courier, Westford. The cover was printed by Phoenix Color Corp.

Prentice Hall

Printed in the United States of America
10 9 8 7 6 5 4 3 2 1

ISBN 0-13-099282-8

Prentice-Hall International (UK) Limited, *London*
Prentice-Hall of Australia Pty. Limited, *Sydney*
Prentice-Hall Canada Inc., *Toronto*
Prentice-Hall Hispanoamericana, S. A., *Mexico*
Prentice-Hall of India Private Limited, *New Delhi*
Prentice-Hall of Japan, Inc., *Tokyo*
Pearson Education Pte. Ltd., *Singapore*
Editora Prentice-Hall do Brasil, Ltda., *Rio de Janeiro*

Contents

Part III Modern Jazz: The Early 1940s to The Early 1960s

Part IV Modern Jazz: The Early 1960s To The Early 2000s

Tables and Special Boxed Features

Tables

Special Boxed Features

Preface to the Eighth Edition

The goal of the eighth edition of *Jazz Styles* was to give the reader a broader and more current picture of jazz while maintaining the same style and structure that has proven so effective in earlier editions. To reach this goal we have undertaken several significant additions to this edition, all of them came from the requests of students and professors familiar with earlier editions. The major additions are:

1) A new chapter dealing with contemporary jazz
2) A new concluding chapter
3) New photos of Wynton Marsalis, John Zorn, Steve Turre, Joe Lovano, Bobby McFerrin, Cassandra Wilson, and Fats Waller

The contemporary jazz chapter (chapter 17) updates this text with a discussion of various jazz styles and performers from around 1980 to the present. With so many diverse approaches and phenomenal players coming to prominence in the last twenty years or so, it would be impossible to describe all developments and trends. This chapter presents some of the most important innovations, balancing musicians from different "camps." Though by no means comprehensive, this chapter should give students a firm foundation in many of the issues important to contemporary jazz while introducing some of the major players of the era.

The final chapter (chapter 18) poses several questions: *What is jazz?* (with some possible new conclusions to complement chapter 2); *Why hasn't jazz become more popular?; What next?*. While some possible solutions are suggested for each query, no definite conclusions are drawn. Instead, these questions are intended to serve as springboards for discussion and an opportunity for students to synthesize the material they have studied throughout the course of the text.

In fact, both new chapters pose several questions in addition to presenting a substantial amount of new information. For example, Chapter 17 briefly discusses the controversies that surround two prominent contemporary jazz musicians, as well as their contributions. It then asks what defines the jazz tradition–the way the music sounds, or the manner in which it is approached? This type of discussion has been present in just about every jazz circle from the earliest days of the music. The debate is not closed here, just propounded. Perhaps, in the jazz tradition, the asking of the question is more important than finding a conclusive answer.

****

Adding to an already outstanding text was an exciting, but daunting task. I'd like to thank many people for their contributions. First, I am grateful to Mark Gridley for writing such a comprehensive and significant text. Not only did he provide an exquisite backdrop for the contributions found here, but he composed a text that I have personally used and enjoyed in classes over the past several years.

Several people helped in the research, writing, and editing process of my contributions here. I am greatly indebted to those who freely shared their suggestions and comments about the writings with me: Joe DeFazio, Scott Garlock, Rob Hudson, Lee Heritage, John Wilson, Joe Rishel, Tom Blobner, Bryon Holly, and Jeremy Frantz. I'd also like to thank my colleagues at Duquesne University who have been so supportive in my taking on this project, especially Ed Kocher, David Stock, Jessica Wiskus, Lynn and Bill Purse, and Sister Carole Riley, as well as my colleagues, mentors, and friends Don Freund, Sven-David Sandstrom, Claude Baker, Fred Sturm, Amy Cutler, and In-Sil Yoo. Chris Johnson, from Prentice Hall, was incredibly helpful and friendly throughout this project. A special thanks goes to my mother, Dr. Tina Cantrell, who spent countless hours editing my writing. Most of all, I'd like to thank my students, who have made the research and teaching of jazz an incredibly gratifying experience.

David Cuttler
Duquesne University
June, 2002

Preface to the Seventh Edition

This book was written to help listeners increase their appreciation and enjoyment of jazz. The book and its accompanying *Jazz Styles Demonstration CD* give readers a peek into how jazz musicians put together performances and how their methods have differed from style to style. There is discussion of how jazz originated, and the *Jazz Classics CD* provides examples of the roots, the earliest recordings, and many major styles that developed later. Styles are described in ways that should help the reader get more out of listening to them. The music is presented roughly in chronological order, and the historically minded reader can use that order to examine major currents in the history of jazz. This particular book was intended, however, more as a description of the styles themselves rather than a decade-by-decade chronicle of the changing jazz scene.

This text was designed as a smorgasbord of information so readers would have a flexible reference source. Chapters can be skipped without doing serious damage to an introductory course in jazz appreciation or a single-semester course in jazz history. Numerous deletions and rearrangements in this book's contents have supplied workable sequences for hundreds of jazz courses since the first edition appeared in 1978.

Because of space limitations, this book deals almost exclusively with American instrumental jazz, and coverage is neither comprehensive nor encyclopedic. For more comprehensive coverage, see (a) "Supplementary Reading" (page 407), (b) the books that are footnoted throughout the text, and (c) the bibliographies and discographies that appear in the *Instructor's Resource Manual for Jazz Styles, Seventh Edition* (write College Marketing, Prentice Hall, 1 Lake Street, Upper Saddle River, NJ 07458) and *How To Teach Jazz History* (write the International Association of Jazz Educators, Box 724, Manhattan, Kansas 66502). With space limitations in mind, however, the book was designed to devote proportionally more pages to music that developed since 1940. This is because, given that the first jazz recordings were not made until 1917, about three-fourths of recorded jazz history has occurred since 1940, and this is music that occupies the lion's share of available recording, nightclub, and concert fare encountered by today's readers. Another reason for this allocation of space is that much of the music discussed here in reference to the 1960s—John Coltrane and Chick Corea, for instance—provided foundations for the dominant styles of the 1970s, 80s, and 90s, as that which is discussed here regarding the 1930s—such as Count Basie and Lester Young, for instance—provided foundations for the dominant styles of the 1940s and 50s.

No technical knowledge of music is required to understand the contents of this book, and the text's vocabulary has proven to be comprehensible for high school students as well as college students. Past editions have been used effectively in high schools and community colleges as well as universities. Many instructors have successfully taught their courses from this book without devoting any attention to technical terms. Other instructors have used the "Elements of Music" Appendix (pages 364–393) and the *Demonstration CD* to introduce basic technical concepts at the beginning of their course before they discuss selected jazz styles.

Though the book was originally conceived as a text for nonmusicians, previous editions have also been used as the basic text in jazz history courses for music majors. This occurred because of (a) the "For Musicians" Appendix (pages 415–431) that provides notations illustrating basic musical principles (chord changes, modes, comping, walking bass, ride rhythms, etc.) and because (b) the book is especially concerned with detailing the ways styles sound and how they can be differentiated in terms of preferred instruments, tone quality, melody, harmony, rhythm, and approaches to improvisation. Supplements of musical notation are referenced in footnotes throughout the text as well as in the sections devoted to technical references (page 410 and pages 412–414).

HOW TO USE THIS BOOK

Music appreciation courses have been in existence far longer than jazz history courses. Since the 1960s, colleges have been extending the means by which nonmusician students can expand their appreciation of music. In addition to traditional approaches that teach listening skills by exposure to the forms and sounds of classical music, new courses also teach listening skills and multicultural awareness by introductory classes in jazz, rock, and world music. Some college curricula allow humanities elective credits to be earned by completing courses in jazz history. The *Jazz Styles* books, compact discs, and instructor's manuals are particularly useful for this type of course. With the *Demo CD* and the *Jazz Classics CD*, the *Jazz Styles* textbook can serve as the core of a self-paced course of study in which the reader/listener becomes familiar with basic principles of music listening. The sights and sounds of jazz can be enjoyed apart from the presentations made by the instructor. The *Jazz Styles* materials can supplement and complement classroom experiences. Technical concepts that otherwise require lecture/demonstrations by professional musicians can be learned by pairing the CDs with the accompanying text pages. The contents of the *Demo CD* can be used as reinforcement of classroom lecture/demonstrations because it provides a handy source of review materials. Several professors have required that their students learn the contents of the *Demo CD* outside of class, thereby saving class time to learn other topics. No matter what approach is taken to using this textbook and its CDs, every individual and class is encouraged to listen to as much recorded and live jazz as possible. **The book will be an effective guide only if accompanied by repeated listening to pivotal selections and extensive listening to a variety of styles.**

Adapting the Book for Different Courses

This book was originally conceived in an omnibus format whose organization was intended to provide a flexible reference for learning about jazz. Sample syllabi for different class schedules and various approaches to introducing jazz are provided in the *Instructor's Resource Manual* that is available from Prentice Hall sales representatives. The next five paragraphs outline approaches that have proven successful in schools where previous editions of this book have been required.

The text provides the essentials for a course in **UNDERSTANDING JAZZ** if it is accompanied by several carefully conceived, in-class demonstrations by musicians plus a well-chosen collection of recordings. A bare minimum collection might begin with this book's compact discs and a number of the albums footnoted in the text. The in-class demonstrations might follow the guidelines described in "Getting the Most From a Drumming Demonstration and Live Rhythm Section" in *How To Teach Jazz History* (Mark C. Gridley, IAJE Press, 1984/1997; available from the International Association of Jazz Educators, Box 724, Manhattan, Kansas 66502; phone 913-7768744). Other helpful strategies are demonstrated in "Teaching Jazz History to Nonmusicians" (1984 NAJE Convention Cassette #37, available from IAJE, at above address or email: IAJE@ksu.ksu.edu). Previous editions of the text have been used in this way at several colleges. These sections of the book provided the key components: Elements of Music Appendix (364–393), chapter 2 (What Is jazz?), chapter 3 (Appreciating Jazz Improvisation), and chapter 4 (Origins of Jazz). Much emphasis was placed on the listening guides that appear throughout the text. Instructors usually supplemented that material with selected portions of styles chapters. The portions that give readers the most insight into how jazz is made are the nonbiographical units that appear at the beginnings of chapters 5, 6, 9, 14, and 16.

The text provides the essentials for a historically organized **INTRODUCTION TO JAZZ STYLES.** Again, a basic collection of records is essential. The bare bones of such a collection could be taken from the *Jazz Classics CD* for *Concise Guide to Jazz* (available from Prentice Hall as ISBN 0-13-088792-7) and the *Smithsonian Collection of Classic Jazz.* The skeleton of the course is described in the "styles" chapters: chapter 5 (Early jazz), chapter 6 (Swing), chapter 9 (Bop), chapter 10 (Cool), chapter 11 (Hard Bop), chapter 14 (Avant-Garde/Free Jazz), and chapter 16 (Jazz/Rock). Instructors frequently preface their styles sequence with appendix materials (Elements of Music) and the introductory chapters (What Is Jazz; Appreciating Jazz Improvisation). They frequently supplement with more specialized chapters, such as those devoted to Duke Ellington and Miles Davis, for instance.

The text provides the essentials for a course concerned primarily with **MAJOR FIGURES IN JAZZ:** Louis Armstrong (covered in chapter 5), Duke Ellington (chapter 7), Charlie Parker/Dizzy Gillespie (chapter 9), Miles Davis (chapters 12 and 16), and John Coltrane (chapter 13). For those who wish to explore more than just the top five or six figures, the text also covers such other giants as Jelly Roll Morton (chapter 5), Earl Hines (chapter 5), Count Basie (chapter 8), Lester Young (chapter 8), Lennie Tristano (chapter 10), Ornette Coleman (chapter 14), Charles Mingus (chapter 14), Bill Evans (chapter 15), Sun Ra (chapter 14), and Stan Kenton (chapter 10), to name just a few.

For a course in **THE HISTORY OF JAZZ,** the text can be used intact, though minor juggling of contents will make the final chapters more chronological. For example, the main treatment of Miles Davis (chapter 12) runs from the 1950s to the late 1960s; so the instructor may wish to postpone coverage of its second half until after covering parts of other chapters that deal with the early 1960s: John Coltrane (13), Avant-Garde (14), and Bill Evans (15). Similarly, the instructor may wish to postpone the final two-thirds of chapter 15 (Bill Evans, Herbie Hancock, Chick Corea & Keith Jarrett) until the 1970s have been covered, because the bulk of its material overlaps the same span and then spills into the 1980s with its updates on Herbie Hancock and Chick Corea. Before attempting to be perfectly chronological, instructors are encouraged to note that coverage of Charles Mingus in chapter 14 runs from the 1940s to the 1970s, as does that of Sun Ra. Also note that chapter 14's coverage for the Art Ensemble of Chicago, Anthony Braxton, and the World Saxophone Quartet overlaps the same time period as chapter 16's coverage of jazz-rock. Incidentally, to do justice to the course title of "jazz history," the instructor will need more than merely the brief recorded examples contained in the *Smithsonian Collection of Classic Jazz,* the *Jazz Classics CD* for *Jazz Styles,* and the *Jazz Classics CD* for the *Concise Guide to Jazz.* A good start would be a sampling of recordings that are footnoted for each chapter and/or the *Small Basic Collection* presented before chapter 1.

At several schools, jazz styles and history are introduced by instrument rather than by era. For example, the history of major influences on jazz styles of trumpet playing is treated separately from the history of major influences on piano styles. Each instrument is treated separately until all the instruments have been covered through all of jazz history. For the convenience of those schools, most of the era chapters in *Jazz Styles* are organized by instrument. Students need merely pull out the particular section of each chapter that deals with the instrument of the week. After all chapters have been scanned for that instrument, the next instrument can be investigated in a similar fashion. Some schools also have entire courses devoted to the study of styles for improvising on just one instrument. At least one professor requires *Jazz Styles* to be read by students in courses called "jazz trumpet," "jazz trombone," "jazz saxophone," "jazz piano," "jazz bass," and "jazz drums."

This text has also been used in courses called "American Music," "Contemporary Music," "Twentieth Century Music," "Popular Music in America," "African American Music," and "Black Music." The last third of the text is used in many courses called "Rock," "The History of Rock and Roll," and "Jazz/Rock Foundations." The "Elements of Music" appendix is used in numerous music appreciation courses. The "For Musicians" appendix is used in many courses in "jazz theory" and "Introduction to Jazz Styles," "Jazz Survey," and "Jazz Perspectives." Additionally, a number of band directors require their ensemble members to read the book, listen to the CDs, and learn where their own performance repertory fits in the large picture of jazz history.

Teaching Strategies

A number of professors have said that this book has too much information in it, and, in particular, that it is impossible for them to cover some chapters, such as Ellington and Coltrane, in a single-semester college course. These professors are correct. However, if they are unduly frustrated by this, they are overlooking two considerations. First is that **this book, like most good textbooks, is intended to be merely a resource, not a rigid syllabus for a particular course. It was never intended to be studied line by line, cover to cover by novice listeners in a single-semester jazz appreciation course.** The second consideration is that part of **a teacher's job is to make judicious choices from the assortment of information offered in a textbook and then guide students to a comprehensible sampling that is suitable for them.**

Instructors need to be aware that students are often confused and frustrated in courses where professors do not routinely follow a detailed syllabus that tells what textbook pages, terms, and musicians the students are expected to learn. Textbooks tend to be overwhelming when students assume that they must learn everything in them. Helpful teachers tell their students what not to be overly concerned with. A few examples will clarify this. Whereas some teachers consider sidemen names to be superfluous, others believe that familiarity with every musician in the Ellington chapter is essential for a minimum understanding of the music. Some teachers feel that to know John Coltrane was an important post-Parker saxophonist is sufficient. Other teachers consider an appreciation of Coltrane's McCoy Tyner-Jimmy Garrison-Elvin Jones rhythm section also to be essential. And some teachers want students to remember not only that Coltrane had roots in the styles of Coleman Hawkins, Lester Young, Charlie Parker, and Sonny Stitt, but also that Coltrane influenced such current giants as David Liebman and Michael Brecker. Some teachers believe that a basic introduction to jazz involves learning to discriminate soprano from tenor saxophone timbre. Other teachers feel that such a skill exceeds reasonable expectations for nonmusician students. Whereas some teachers feel that students should be able to recognize the sound of a 12-bar blues before receiving a passing grade in an introductory course, other teachers are more concerned that their students remember the birthplaces of famous musicians. Some teachers believe that an immersion in the sounds of jazz is sufficient and students need not acquire knowledge about how it is made. Regardless of a teacher's philosophy of education, students benefit from being told what that philosophy is. They also welcome knowing what pages to read and what they will be expected to remember.

A number of profs have said their students ask them what names are important among the many names appearing in *Jazz Styles.* Resourceful profs tell their less motivated students to learn approximately the ten to twenty names that receive the most page space. More-motivated students can do fine if they skip all but the boldfaced names.

Here is a rule of thumb for using a book that mentions a large number of important musicians. Hold students responsible for familiarity with only the musicians whose work they have extended opportunity to hear. For example, if your music library or listening lab lacks the classic Miles Davis recordings *Steamin', Cookin', Workin', Relaxin'*, and other Prestige recordings with Philly Joe Jones, it would not be reasonable to hold students responsible for Jones. If your library lacks the *Jazz Classics CD* for the *Concise Guide to Jazz* or the *Smithsonian Collection of Classic Jazz* that have examples of Art Tatum, Coleman Hawkins, Clifford Brown and Ornette Coleman, it might not be reasonable to hold students responsible for those four artists. All are missing from the *Jazz Classics CD* for *Jazz Styles.*

Students have reported several different ways to use the tables of musician names that appear in most styles chapters. One way is to use them for keeping track of what is covered in class. Whenever the professor discusses a particular musician and plays examples of the music, students turn to the table and put a check mark next to that musician's name. Students also use the tables to help classify new musicians they hear on the radio or see in concert. When they hear someone new, they look up that name. This helps them remember the new name by classifying it in a familiar way. Students know that if they like the sound of one player in that style, others from that same table may also be enjoyable and worth seeking on recordings.

The strategy that some professors use to choose textbooks is to seek one that will serve as a skeleton of knowledge to be fleshed out in lecture. This differs from the strategy of finding a book that can serve as a smorgasbord to be trimmed down. Instead of giving students a book having more than they will need, these professors prefer to give students a book having less than they need. These professors might wish to assign the *Concise Guide to Jazz,* the abridged version of *Jazz Styles.* By comparison with *Jazz Styles,* it contains about half the number of pages, 10 chapters, a fifth the number of musician profiles, and about a fortieth the number of musician names and tune titles. It retains important appendix items from *Jazz Styles* such as the Elements of Music, the Guide to Album Buying, and the Glossary. It also retains most of what is in the *Jazz Styles* chapters on What Is Jazz and Appreciating Jazz Improvisation. It comes with a *Demonstration CD* adapted from the Jazz Styles *Demo CD* and an optional CD containing 21 historic recordings that are analyzed in listening guides. The contents of the *Jazz Classics CD* for the *Concise Guide to Jazz* is balanced across jazz history. However, it can also serve as a complement to the *Jazz Classics CD* for *Jazz Styles* and the *Smithsonian Collection of Classic Jazz* because it duplicates only five selections from those compilations.

A strategy that some professors use when choosing a textbook is to find a reference work that allows inquiring students to go beyond what can be covered in class. They want their students to have something to refer to whenever more information is sought about music that they hear in class or on the radio. *Jazz Styles* is exhaustively indexed to serve precisely such a function. It also has tables listing the prominent names by style and era. Numerous footnotes steer the reader to the best sources for hearing the important musicians and reading about them.

Here is an example of the flexibility that *Jazz Styles* recently offered a professor who was willing to glean relevant material from the resources in the text rather than assuming the course must rigidly follow the book. For a one-semester course in jazz and rock that students took as a music appreciation elective, the instructor first introduced some "how to listen" ideas, by way of in-class demonstrations of instruments and analysis of song forms (as explained in the Elements of Music Appendix and chapter 3). Then an African retentions sequence (as explained in chapter 4) was presented, moving smoothly to jazz-rock, because jazz-rock has more Africanisms than other jazz styles and because the course title was "Jazz and Rock." Both instructor and students were already familiar with Spyro Gyra, so its style became a good jumping-off place, and they analyzed one of their favorite recordings by that band. Joe Zawinul's "Birdland" was another handy point of departure because some students had heard the popular Manhattan Transfer version and could connect it to the Count Basie riff band style they heard in "One O'Clock Jump." (These are found together at the beginning of the *Jazz Classics CD.*) Then an assortment of pop music was presented (James Brown, Ray Charles, the Jacksons, and various Motown recording artists), and its African connections were outlined via chapter 4 (Origins of Jazz) and chapter 16 (Jazz-Rock). The explanations for African connections and origins of jazz/rock were keyed to the chart of parallel streams that appears in chapter 16. Much of the sequence was done according to suggestions found in the "Demonstrating African Connections" chapter of *How To Teach Jazz History* (IAJE Press, 1984/1997). Then, for the remainder of the course, a few key jazz styles such as swing and bop were introduced, and discussion was offered for only a few essential figures (Louis Armstrong, Duke Ellington, Count Basie, Charlie Parker, Dizzy Gillespie, Miles Davis, and John Coltrane).

Acknowledgments

I remain deeply grateful to many people who took time out of their own busy schedules to provide ideas and feedback for past editions of this book and its abridged edition, the *Concise Guide to Jazz.* Since 1971, Harvey Pekar has been sharing his penetrating stylistic insights, historical perspective, and discographical knowledge. He was always willing to discuss controversies, direct me to new perspectives, and allow me to include his observations when I prepared my manuscripts. Every chapter in this text reflects his input. Since the very first manuscript in 1973, John Richmond has continued to be a source of counsel in my jazz history research. I also remain indebted to Chuck Braman for his help on the first five editions because the results survive in this new one.

I remain indebted for the detail and accuracy in Bill Anderson's updating 552 footnotes of albums and books and editing the 52-page discography in the *Instructor's Resource Manual.* His dedication takes much of the pain out of my revision tasks.

This edition reflects extensive critiques performed on earlier editions by Morris Holbrook, Karl Koenig, Victor Schonfield, and Joel Simpson. Holbrook and Koenig allowed me to include their own words in my rewrites. Wallace Rave conceptualized the original analyses for Chapter 4's section on What is African and What Is European About Jazz, as Koenig did for the brass bands origins of New Orleans jazz. As in the previous three editions, Carl Woideck supplied critiques that helped improve this edition's accuracy and clarity.

For the new coverage of acid jazz, the following people provided their knowledge and guidance: Rob Hoff, David Miyares, Dan Poletta, Chris Hovan, Bob Belden, Wayne "DJ Smash" Hunter, Jarrad Hoffman, Gilles Peterson, Chris Bangs, Randy Norfus, Carlo Wolff, Harvey Pekar, and Ed Stephens.

For the new coverage of singers, the following people shared their observations and allowed me to use them: Iris Sharp, Fred Sharp, Gary Pildner, Bob Fraser, Nan O'Malley, George Gridley, Chad Gearig, Grant Cook, and Tom Inck.

I thank Elaine Hopkins and Ruth Wahlstrom for their generosity and creativity in proofreading and editing new sections on vocal blues, women singers, smooth jazz, and acid jazz. I appreciate the helpful suggestions kindly provided by Jackie Warren and Ed Harrington, who proofread piano comping music on pages 424, 425, and 429.

Many consultants were involved in the research, preparation, and editing of the listening guides. A few of the biggest contributors are singled out here. Anita Clark helped edit almost all the listening guides. Assistance for analysis of "Masqualero" came from Bob Belden, Rick Helzer, Bart Polot, and the composer himself, Wayne Shorter. Assistance for "Jitney #2" was provided by David Such and Franck Amsallem. "Surucucu" was prepared with the assistance of the performer on the recording, Joe Zawinul, and the composer of the piece, Wayne Shorter. Dan Levinson, Karl Koenig, and others contributed to the prefatory remarks for "Dixie Jazz Band One-Step." Willa Rouder proofread "You've Got To Be Modernistic." Andrew White provided a transcription of John Coltrane's "The Promise." Bill Dobbins provided a transcription of Chick Corea's "Steps." Jerry Sheer helped verify electronic instruments on "Birdland."

This edition reflects research done for all previous editions and the kindness of hundreds of musicians who shared their observations, memories, and opinions with me. For a complete listing, see the Acknowledgments sections for the previous editions. The accuracy of coverage in this book is due in part to the cooperation of many musicians whose music is discussed on its pages. Unfortunately several of them passed away before seeing the finished product. Over the past twenty-five years, the following players helped by means of conversations, proofreading, and/or correspondence: Benny Goodman, Stan Kenton, Bill Evans, Wayne Shorter, Joe Zawinul, Eric Gravatt, Herbie Hancock, Tony Williams, Joe Venuti, Al McKibbon, Dizzy Gillespie, Paul Smith, Richard Davis, Bob Curnow, Jimmy Heath, Jaco Pastorius, Red Rodney, Jimmy Giuffre, Andrew White, Bud Freeman, Gerry Mulligan, Maynard Ferguson, Billy Taylor, Eddie Vinson, George West, Paul Motian, Ken McIntyre, William Parker, Barry Martyn, Don Sickler, Dave Berger, Richard Sudhalter, Val Kent, Mel Lewis, Ernie Krivda, Mike Lee, Bob Fraser, Fred Sharp, Chuck Wayne, Abe Laboriel, Gene Lees, Airto Moreira, Bill Kirchner, Gunnar Biggs, John Klayman, Mal Barron, Bill Dobbins, and Harold Battiste.

I am grateful to the many professors and their students who took time to tell me how previous editions worked for their classes. A few of the more recent evaluations came from:

Billy Barnard	University of Minnesota at Duluth
Bill Dobbins and Mark Flugge	Eastman School of Music
Gary Scott	Cuyahoga Community College
David Joyner	North Texas State University
Lewis Porter	Rutgers University
Tom Everett and Jim Cox	Harvard University
Jeff Stout	Berklee College of Music
Mark Harvey	Massachusetts Institute of Technology
Jay Busch and Wallace Rave	Arizona State University
Warren Gaughan	Warren Wilson College
Paul Evoskevich	College of St. Rose-Albany, New York
Justin DiCiccio	LaGuardia High School for the Performing Arts and Manhattan School of Music
Steve Gryb	Barry University
Grant Wolf and Don Bothwell	Mesa College
David Kay	University School-Pepper Pike, Ohio
Paul Ferguson and Jack Schantz	Cleveland State University
Robin Dinda	Fitchburg State College
Ed Flanagan	Temple University
Gene Parker, David Jex, Joe Palmer, Lee Heritage	University of Toledo
Curt Wilson	Texas Christian University
Lindsey Sarjeant	Florida Agricultural and Mechanical University
Carroll Dashiell and George Broussard	East Carolina State University
Terry Steele	Slippery Rock State University
John Joyce	Tulane University
Rick Helzer	San Diego State University
John Harding	University of North Carolina at Charlotte
Leonard Feather	UCLA
Howard Mandel	New York University
Alan Hood	Miami University
Bart Polot	University of Michigan

Supplements

SUPPLEMENTS FOR USING THIS BOOK

Several sources of material supplement this edition of *Jazz Styles: History and Analysis.* First is the *Demonstration CD,* which contains 73 minutes of audio demonstrations for instrument sounds (guitar vs. banjo, trumpet vs. fluegelhorn, clarinet vs. soprano sax, ride cymbal vs. crash cymbal, walking bass, etc.), and musical concepts (blue notes, swing eighth-note patterns, A-A-B-A song form, 12-bar blues chord changes, etc.). The CD illustrates the contents of the Elements of Music Appendix and Chapter 3: "Appreciating Jazz Improvisation." There are 171 audio demonstrations. The CD format is available separately as ISBN 0-13-099283-6. A one-hour video version of the *Demonstration CD,* called *Listening to Jazz* (Prentice Hall, 1992), was prepared by Steve Gryb. It is available as ISBN 0-13-532862-4. Phone 800-947-7700 to order any of these supplements.

The second main supplement is the *Jazz Classics CD* (available separately as ISBN 0-13-099348-4), containing 26 selections of historic jazz recordings, at least one for each chapter, totalling 90 minutes of music and narration. The pieces on it have corresponding listening guides in this textbook. (Performers include West African folk musicians, American Gospel singers, the Original Dixieland Jazz Band, Louis Armstrong, Earl Hines, James P. Johnson, Count Basie, Duke Ellington, Johnny Hodges, Ben Webster, Charlie Parker, Dizzy Gillespie, Lennie Tristano, Stan Getz, Miles Davis, Bill Evans, Cannonball Adderley, John Coltrane, McCoy Tyner, Elvin Jones, Cecil Taylor, Wayne Shorter, Herbie Hancock, Tony Williams, Chick Corea, Joe Zawinul, and others.) Note that very few of its selections are in the *Smithsonian Collection of Classic Jazz* (SCCJ). Therefore the *Jazz Classics CD* can serve equally well as a SCCJ substitute or supplement.

The third supplement to *Jazz Styles: History and Analysis* is the 76-minute *Classics CD for Concise Guide to Jazz* (Prentice Hall, 2001; ISBN 0-13-088792-7; phone 800-947-7700). Only four of its selections duplicate SCCJ contents. Therefore it serves equally well as a substitute or a supplement to the SCCJ and the *Jazz Classics CD.* It includes: "Dixie Jazz Band One-Step" (1917) by the Original Dixieland Jazz Band, "West End Blues" (1928) by Louis Armstrong & Earl Hines, "Sobbin' Hearted Blues" (1925) by Bessie Smith & Louis Armstrong, "Taxi War Dance" (1939) by Count Basie & Lester Young, "Back in Your Own Back Yard" (1938) by Billie Holiday & Lester Young, "Tiger Rag" (1933) by Art Tatum, "Body and Soul" (1939) by Coleman Hawkins, "Harlem Airshaft" (1940) by Duke Ellington, "I've Got It Bad" (1961) by Johnny Hodges, "Ko-Ko" (1945) by Charlie Parker & Max Roach, "Things to Come" (1946) by the Dizzy Gillespie big band, "Dexter Digs In" (1946) by Dexter Gordon, Bud Powell & Max Roach, "Subconscious-Lee" (1949) by Lee Konitz & Lennie Tristano, "Two Bass Hit" (1958) by John Coltrane & Cannonball Adderley, "Blue in Green" (1959) by Miles Davis, John Coltrane & Bill Evans, "Gertrude's Bounce" (1956) by Clifford Brown & Sonny Rollins, "Cloning" (1987) by Ornette Coleman & Don Cherry, "Your Lady" (1963) by John Coltrane, McCoy Tyner, Jimmy Garrison & Elvin Jones, "Solar" (1961) by Bill Evans, Scott LaFaro & Paul Motian, "Captain Marvel" (1968) by Chick Corea, Stanley Clarke, Joe Farrell, Flora Purim & Airto Moreira, and "Birdland" (1977) by Joe Zawinul, Wayne Shorter & Jaco Pastorius.

The fourth category of supplements includes a 183-page *Instructor's Resource Manual* (with a 71-page discography) and a *Test Item File* of 1000 exam questions in hard copy and in computer disc form. These are available only to instructors.

Notes with Information about Recordings

Footnotes citing recordings are designed to provide information necessary for obtaining examples discussed in the text and/or to note further recordings by the artists discussed. They indicate the most recently available issue of a cited recording. The currently available format is compact disc (CD) unless otherwise indicated as LP (33 1/3 rpm long-playing record) or AC (audio cassette). Since manufacturers have discontinued most LPs in favor of CDs or audio cassettes, most of the listed LPs are out of print; CD equivalents have been listed when available. The development of the compact disc has led to many jazz reissues. In addition, CDs have appealed to libraries and schools because of their smaller size, ease of accessibility to portions of a selection, and improved resistance to deteriorating sound quality. Because many libraries and stores have moved to CDs exclusively, this book provides information on CD availability for most cited recordings. It lists LPs or audio cassettes only when a CD format was not available when we went to press.

A Small Basic CD Collection

The Jazz Classics Compact Disc for Jazz Styles. Prentice-Hall: ISBN 0-13-099348-4, 1917–1977.
Jazz Classics Compact Disc for Concise Guide to Jazz. Prentice-Hall: ISBN 0-13-088792-7, 1917–1987.
(The above two CDs are not available in music stores; phone 800-947-7700 for mail order.)
Smithsonian Collection of Classic Jazz. Smithsonian: RI 0010, 1916–1981 (phone 800-863-9943 for mail order)
Masters of Jazz, Vol. 1: Traditional Jazz Classics. Rhino: 72468, 1923–1992.
Masters of Jazz, Vol. 2: Bebop's Greatest Hits. Rhino: 72469, 1945–1954.
Masters of Jazz, Vol. 3: Big Bands of the '30s & '40s. Rhino: 72470, 1931–1947.
Louis Armstrong, *The Hot Fives & Hot Sevens, Vol. 3.* Columbia: CK 44422, 1927–1928.
Louis Armstrong and Earl Hines, Vol. 4. Columbia: CK 45142, 1928.
The Legendary Sidney Bechet. RCA Bluebird: 6590-2-RB, 1932–1941.
Bix Beiderbecke, Vol. 1: Singing the Blues. Columbia: CK 45450, 1927–1928.
Duke Ellington: *The Blanton-Webster Band.* RCA Bluebird: 5691-2-RB, 3CD set, 1940–1942.
Count Basie. *The Complete Decca Recordings.* Decca Jazz/GRP: GRD3-611, 3CD set, 1937–1939.
Coleman Hawkins. *Body and Soul.* Victor Jazz: 09026-68515-2, 1939–1956.
Benny Goodman. *Carnegie Hall Concert.* Columbia: G2K 40244, 2CD set, 1938.
Roy Eldridge. *Little Jazz.* Columbia: CK 45275, 1935–1940.
Dizzy Gillespie: The Complete RCA Victor Recordings. RCA Bluebird: 07863-66528-2, 2CD set, 1937–1949.
Charlie Parker. *Yardbird Suite: The Ultimate Charlie Parker Collection.* Rhino: 72260, 2CD set, 1945–54.
Bud Powell. *Jazz Giant.* Verve: 829 937-2. 1949–1950.
Best of Thelonious Monk: The Blue Note Years. Blue Note: 95636, 1947–1951.
Miles Davis. *The Complete Birth of the Cool.* Capitol: 94550, 1948–1950. (with Gerry Mulligan and Lee Konitz)
Woody Herman. *The Thundering Herds.* Columbia: CK 44108, 1945–1947.
Lee Konitz. *Subconscious Lee.* Fantasy: OJCCD-186-2, 1949. (with Lennie Tristano)
Stan Kenton. *New Concepts of Artistry in Rhythm.* Capitol: 92865, 1952.
Stan Getz. *The Roost Quartets.* Roulette: 96052, 1950–1951.
Dave BrubecK. *Jazz at Oberlin.* Fantasy: OJCCD-046-2, 1953.
Sonny Rollins. *Sonny Rollins Plus 4.* Fantasy. OJC-243-2, 1956 (with Clifford Brown)
Art Blakey. *A Night at Birdland, Vols. 1 & 2.* Blue Note: 46519/46520, 2CDs, 1954. (with Horace Silver)
Charles Mingus. *Mingus Ah Um.* Columbia: CK 40648, 1959.
Ornette Coleman. *The Shape of Jazz to Come.* Atlantic: 1317-2, 1959.
Albert Ayler. *Spiritual Unity.* ESP DISK: 1002, 1964.
Miles Davis. *Kind of Blue.* Columbia: CK 64935, 1959. (with Cannonball Adderley, John Coltrane, Bill Evans)
John Coltrane. *Giant Steps.* Atlantic: 1311-2, 1959.
Bill Evans. *Sunday at the Village Vanguard.* Fantasy: OJCCD-140-2, 1961.
John Coltrane. *Live at Birdland.* Impulse/GRP: GRD-198, 1963. (with McCoy Tyner, Elvin Jones)
Miles Davis. *Sorcerer.* Columbia: CK 65680, 1967. (with Wayne Shorter, Herbie Hancock, Tony Williams)
Miles Davis. *Bitches Brew.* Columbia C4K 65570, 4CD set, 1969–70. (with Joe Zawimul, John McLaughlin)
Chick Corea. *Now He Sings, Now He Sobs.* Blue Note: 90055, 1968.
Cecil Taylor. *Silent Tongues.* Freedom: FCD-741005, 1974.
Keith Jarrett. *Staircase.* ECM: 78118-21090-2, 2CD set, 1976.
Weather Report. *I Sing the Body Electric.* Columbia: CK 46107, 1971–1972.
Many of these recording may not be in your local music store. See page 400 for mail order sources.

Chapter One

Tenor Saxophonist Lester Young. Photo courtesy of Frank Driggs.

Introduction

Jazz includes many different streams of music. They can be played by almost any combination of instruments. They can evoke almost any mood. Some are light and happy. Some are heavy and serious. Some make you want to dance. Some make you think. Some are smooth and predictable. Some are agitated and full of surprises.

Jazz can be heard in many different places. It is often presented as serious music in concert halls. Some jazz is played in ballrooms for dancers. There is jazz in background music on the radio. Much jazz is played in night clubs where people listen while they drink and talk with their friends.

Jazz is unique for two very special aspects: a) its provocative rhythms and b) its insistence that performers create their parts as they play them. Each jazz performance represents a new and original creation. Hearing live jazz is exciting not only for the way it makes us feel but also for the realization that we are following the musical thinking of the musicians at the very moment they are inventing their music. They are taking us along with them while they make up fresh sounds. This is akin to the impossible situation of seeing a finished painting as we watch the artist apply paint to the canvas, *at the same time* as we watch one manufacturer produce the canvas and another manufacturer produce the paints themselves.

Jazz has an impressive reputation. It is so interesting that it is played and analyzed in hundreds of colleges. Almost every high school and college has at least one jazz band. Though it originated in America, jazz is so compelling that musicians on every continent have played it, and today there is no city without it. The sounds of jazz have influenced the development of new styles in popular music and the work of symphonic composers. Jazz is so sturdy that the old styles are still being played, and new styles are always being developed. In fact, jazz is regarded as a fine art, not just a passing fad.

This book is organized historically, though it is not really about the history for its own sake so much as the styles themselves. The styles are presented chronologically because that is the easiest way to organize them. Since history and evolution of styles will be touched by your study, here are a few ideas to keep in mind. First of all, the central figures did not create their innovations entirely by themselves. Rather, their work reflects the influence of other players, as well as chance occurrences that were combined, modified, and developed in original ways. A stream of styles might emanate from the talent and hard work of a few musicians who devised the freshest approaches. However, jazz history cannot accurately be described as a single stream evolving from Dixieland directly to swing, and from swing directly to bop and so forth. Nor can approaches used in playing a given instrument be traced to a narrow line of innovators, each of whom is the sole influence on the next—a prominent saxophonist from the 1930s influencing his successor in the 1940s, who in turn influenced another successor in the 1950s, for example. There is no neat line of succession, with each subsequent style rendering the previous ones obsolete. Usually many different styles of jazz coexist, no matter which ones are in vogue with a particular audience at any given time.

Another idea to keep in mind when studying history is that the evolution of jazz cannot accurately be considered a series of "reactions," as though musicians became collectively angry and then suddenly fought a style by inventing another to oppose it. Many historians are fond of believing this. But the truth is that most musicians just find their own favorite way of playing. Often it is an existing style they like. They modify it to suit their tastes and capabilities. Sometimes they combine different approaches until the proportions please them. Many players stick with that style for good; others change their styles when they become bored with them.

Most of all, keep in mind that the more of jazz history you delve into, the more opportunities you have for discovering additional styles to enjoy. It is also good to know that the more we hear, the more skilled we will become as listeners. Then we can extract more pleasure from the sounds. Though some of the subtle aspects are not immediately evident to us, most are accessible after we exert some effort to find out what is going on. In other words, jazz offers a set of pleasures that deepen with understanding. The rewards are guaranteed—you will delight in the surprises that jazz improvisations offer. Incidentally, studying jazz can also lead you to other kinds of music you might enjoy. There is another advantage, too. As you become better at listening to jazz, you will also notice more of the subtle aspects in other kinds of music.

NOTE: See pages 364–393 for a quick orientation to musical terms.

Chapter Two

Dizzy Gillespie 1947. Photo by William Gottlieb.

What Is Jazz?

Many different kinds of music have been called "jazz." So it is no surprise that people cannot agree about how to define it. Different people use different ways to decide whether a given performance should be called "jazz." Not all listeners focus on the same aspects. For example, some call it "jazz" if saxophones and drums are used. Some consider only how it makes them feel ("swinging"). Some decide it must be jazz if it is made by performers who have a reputation for jazz. Some won't call any music "jazz" unless they know that part of it is being composed as it is being performed. Another problem frequently occurs because people attempt to define jazz only by what they have heard called "jazz." Though it may include everything they themselves have heard called "jazz," this might omit other kinds of music that have been called "jazz" by different people. Moreover, some people use the term to designate all sorts of American popular music associated with the 1920s because that period was dubbed "The Jazz Age." Despite these problems, there are two elements that most jazz styles have in common—improvisation and jazz swing feeling.

◇IMPROVISATION

To improvise is to compose and perform at the same time. Instead of saying "improvise," many people say *ad lib*, *ride*, or *jam*. This means that jazz musicians make up their music as they go along. A great deal of jazz is spontaneous. It is not written down or rehearsed beforehand. This is like the impromptu speaking all of us do every day when we talk "off the cuff." We use words and phrases we have used before. But now we improvise by using them in new ways and new orders that have not been rehearsed. A lot of originality can result. This is significant because being original is very important to jazz musicians. They try to be as spontaneous as possible. In fact, they try to never improvise the same way twice. Some of the spirit and vitality associated with jazz may be due to the spontaneity of improvisation. Several versions of a tune made during the same recording session may be entirely different because of this.

For most people, improvisation is an essential element of jazz, and musicians occasionally say "jazz" when they mean "improvise." For example, in a music publisher's brochure describing big band arrangements, a note might be included saying, "only the tenor saxophone part requires jazz." Or a musician's contractor might phone a player requesting that he play "jazz trumpet chair" in a big band, meaning the player will be the only trumpeter required to improvise.

Improvisation is essential to jazz. If you are not very familiar with jazz, however, you might not be able to tell what has been written or memorized beforehand from what is being improvised. One clue is that if part of a performance sounds improvised, it quite often is. Improvised parts sometimes sound more casual and less organized than the written or memorized parts. The problem with using that clue, however, is that the best improvisations are so well constructed that they sound almost like written melodies.

Another clue comes from knowing about a routine that most jazz musicians use. The players begin with a tune they all know. First they play it once all the way through. The melody is played by the horns, the accompaniment by the piano, bass, and drums. Then the piano, bass, and drums continue to do what they did before. But this time, the horns make up and play new melodies of their own. They improvise their own melodies to the tune's accompaniment chords. The way the chords progress in that accompaniment guides the notes they choose for their new melodies, which we call improvisations. In other words, when the melody of the piece itself ends, what follows is improvised. Then it is all improvised until that same melody begins again. This kind of improvisation distinguishes jazz musicians from most pop musicians who merely decorate a tune by changing some of its rhythms or adding notes to it.

Even though improvisation is the main emphasis in jazz, not everything is spontaneous. Most jazz bands use arrangements of some sort. In large jazz ensembles where the players are seated with written arrangements in front of them, a player is usually improvising when he stands up to solo; otherwise, the music is coming from the written parts. And, of course, any lines played by several players in unison must have been prepared beforehand. In the next chapter, we will examine a few of the common practices that indicate what parts in a jazz performance are usually worked out in advance.

◇SWING FEELING

Next, we will consider different views regarding what jazz is. Some views allow music that bears no jazz swing feeling to be called jazz. Some views allow nonimprovised music to be called jazz. As a foundation for describing jazz swing feeling, let's discuss a few elements which contribute to swing feeling in performances of both jazz and nonjazz styles.

If music makes you want to dance, clap your hands, or tap your feet, it has the effect we call a *swinging* feeling. This effect can be created by almost any kind of music, not just jazz. Music that keeps a relatively steady beat and is performed with great spirit seems buoyant. In that sense, many nonjazz performances can be described as swinging. But to specify the unique ways in which an effective jazz performance swings, we must outline both the general characteristics of swinging and those characteristics specific to jazz swing feeling.

Swing is a rhythmic phenomenon which results from several easily defined factors and a few subtle, almost indefinable factors. This is solely a rhythmic concept. Musicians can play out of tune with each other yet still swing. For the sake of our discussion here, note also that the term "swing" should not be confused with its use as a label for an era in American popular music that began during the 1930s and continued until the late 1940s (swing era, swing bands, King of Swing, etc.). It is also not to be confused with its occasional use as a synonym for jazz itself.

Swing in the General Sense

One of the easily defined factors causing swing feeling is **constant tempo.** This helps us distinguish it from kinds of symphonic music where conductors are free to vary the tempo while playing a piece. A steady beat is nearly always kept in jazz pieces. It brings a certain momentum that is essential to swing feeling. Much of the excitement in jazz comes from musicians in the band tugging against this very solid foundation by playing notes slightly before or after the beat.

Another easily defined element of swing feeling is **cohesive group sound.** This is achieved when every member's playing is precisely synchronized with that of every other member. The different members need not be playing the same rhythms in unison, but each player must execute the rhythms of his part with great precision in relation to the beat and the sounds of the other instruments. A group cannot swing if its members are not playing closely together.

Saying that a performance swings means that the group is keeping a steady tempo and its rhythmic parts are synchronized. But to call music "swinging" also indicates that the performance conveys a **rhythmic lilt.** This property is also sometimes referred to as a good rhythmic groove. In fact, verbs derived from the nouns "swing" and "groove" are commonly applied to the sound of jazz: "The band is swinging tonight." "That pianist is really grooving." To a certain extent, swinging simply denotes pleasure. A swinging performance is like a swinging party. Both are very enjoyable.

The **spirit** with which a group plays contributes to swing feeling. Jazz has a reputation for being highly spirited music. In fact, the word "jazzy" is sometimes used instead of the word "spirited." To "jazz up" and to "liven up" are often used interchangeably, and some people call clothes "jazzy" if they are gaudy or extraverted.

Music that swings, then, has constant tempo, cohesive playing, and is performed with rhythmic lilt and spirit. Listeners may be inclined to describe a good performance of any kind of music as swinging if it conveys a feeling of life and energy that compels the listener to respond. This description of swinging applies not only to jazz, but also to lilting performances of polkas, waltzes, flamenco music, Gypsy music, marches, bluegrass, rock, and classical music. This general sense of swing can describe the feeling achieved by a good performance of almost any music that bears constant tempo, cohesive group sound, lilt, and spirit.

Swing in the Jazz Sense

For music to swing in the way peculiar to jazz, more conditions have to be met. One is **an abundance of syncopated rhythms** (see pages 366–367 for more explanation). "Syncopating" means accenting notes that occur just before or just after a beat. Think of syncopation as being off-beat accenting or the occurrence of stress where it is least expected. Jazz swing feeling requires precisely such off-beat accents. The tension generated by members of a band tugging at opposite sides of the beat is essential to jazz swing feeling. Playing slightly after the beat can lend music a soulful or laid back feeling, and syncopations are especially good at providing this. Jazz musicians exaggerate this tendency more than classical musicians, and, if a classical musician were presented with a written syncopation, he would play it slightly earlier than would a jazz musician. Because rhythm is a matter of timing, we must remember that a player's degree of jazz swing feeling is tied to the success with which he times his syncopations. This means that when a player's quality of swing feeling is appraised, his sense of timing is valued more than his tone quality, note selection, and melodic imagination.

Another factor contributing to the special kind of swing feeling found in jazz is the **swing eighth-note pattern.** This is difficult to explain in a brief introduction and best described in the appendix for nonmusicians on pages 368–369. If you have not already read that section, you might find it useful to study now.

Another component of jazz swing feeling is not actually a rhythmic element. Jazz historian Harvey Pekar suggests that swing requires a continuous rising and falling motion or the alternation of more and less activity in a jazz line that provides **alternation of tension and relaxation in the listener.**

Swing in the jazz sense requires the properties that comprise swing in the general sense (constant tempo, cohesive playing, rhythmic lilt, and spirit) plus syncopation, swing eighth-note patterns, and the continuous alternation of tension and relaxation. As with swing in the general sense, jazz swing feeling exists in the ear of the beholder. **Listeners disagree about whether a given performance swings** at all, and, if so, how much. Note also that **there are several different types of jazz swing feeling.**

◇DEFINING JAZZ: FOUR VIEWS[1]

1) For many people, music need only **be associated with the jazz tradition** to be called jazz. Defining jazz in this way is circular. According to this approach, jazz can be anything that anyone ever called "jazz." In other words, the meaning of the term resides in the use to which the term has been put. In the view of these people, to know what jazz is, we merely go by how the word is used. Many individuals say that jazz cannot be defined. They just use the term, and then whatever they used it for becomes its meaning. So if someone calls a particular kind of music jazz, that particular kind of music really *is* jazz. In fact, some people apply the term to almost any music that displays characteristics that have ever been associated with anything ever called jazz. For example, music might be called jazz just because it has a bluesy flavor, or just because it uses instruments that have been associated with jazz, such as saxophones and drums, or just because it has "jazzy rhythms," or just because it displays manipulations of pitch and tone quality associated with jazz. (See chapter 4 for discussion of buzzings, roughnesses, blue notes, drops, doits, scoops, smears, and bends.) This means that a given performance might fall into the jazz category even though it uses no improvisation and conveys no swing feeling. When people use the term that loosely, they rarely distinguish between jazz and other kinds of music to which we might best apply the term "jazz-like."

2) For many other people, a performance need only **convey jazz swing feeling** in order to be called jazz. These people tend to say, "Jazz is a feeling more than anything else," or "Jazz is not what you play but how you play it."

3) For some people, a performance need only **be improvised** in order to qualify as jazz. Note, however, that if we define jazz this way, we overlook characteristics that can distinguish jazz from other kinds of music that also employ improvisation, such as rock, and the music of India and Africa.

4) The most common definition for jazz requires that a performance **contain improvisation and convey jazz swing feeling.**

Much music can be sorted according to the two categories of swing feeling (the general sense and the jazz sense) and the four approaches to defining jazz. The next few paragraphs illustrate these definitional approaches by highlighting kinds of music in which one or more of the critical properties are absent.

Applications of the Four Definitions

If we adhere to our fourth definition of jazz (i.e., it must be improvised and project jazz swing feeling), then what can be said about "jazz" performances in which the music doesn't seem to be improvised? For example, there are historically significant solos on alternate versions of the same record that differ very little from each other. This suggests that the later versions are not improvised, even if the first one was. Some concert music written and performed by famous jazz musicians also falls into this category. If we define jazz rigidly and insist that *some* improvisation is *always* required, then such performances can *not* be jazz. This may seem an odd conclusion in the case of pieces by bandleaders well known for performing jazz, but it is both logical and useful. In fact, a category for such works already exists: *swinging concert music.* And this term not only saves the marriage of jazz and improvisation, but it also creates a category for a musical tradition that, though *deriving* from jazz, might be kept *separate*. Yet for those of us who would be outraged to find someone calling our favorite "jazz" solo or "jazz" concert work anything other than "jazz," our first definition (association with the jazz tradition) is most appropriate because it would allow such improvisationless performances to be called "jazz."

Our fourth definition (it must be improvised and swing) is useful because it *excludes* music that does not swing and that jazz musicians do not ordinarily consider jazz, such as George Gershwin's symphonic piece "Rhapsody in Blue." This distinguishes it for those people who would consider the piece "jazz" merely because it has bluesy melodies and jazzy rhythms—see the first definition. Controversy surrounds our fourth definition because it excludes some music that is called "jazz" by most listeners. Among the troublesome examples are a) pieces you will study in the chapter called "1960s and 70s Avant-Garde" because they do not convey jazz swing feeling (for instance, Cecil Taylor's "Jitney #2" in the *Jazz Classics CD*), b) some of the concert music mentioned in the Duke Ellington chapter because it is neither swinging nor largely improvised (for instance "Transblucency" in the *Jazz Classics CD*, and c) recreations of jazz instrumentals, sung with lyrics by groups such as the Manhattan Transfer because, despite the swinging, the singers are not improvising.[2]

We could also apply this reasoning to classifying the very popular piano solos of George Winston. Most jazz musicians agree that Winston does not swing, and Winston himself refuses to call his music jazz. However, his albums are often found in the "jazz" bins of music stores, and many listeners call him a "jazz pianist." Winston's music qualifies as jazz by our third definition (must be improvised), but not by our second (must swing) or our fourth (must swing and be improvised). Perhaps his music could be considered jazz in the same flexible sense of the term that is outlined in our first definition. This is the flexible sense that allows people to consider "jazz" the music in the famous movie with Al Jolson called *The Jazz Singer,* even though it is about a vaudeville singer who neither improvises nor swings. (See pages 329–330.)

◇IS JAZZ POPULAR?

Now that we have considered a few definitions of jazz, let's examine five ways to answer the question of whether it is popular music.[3]

1) If "popular" means something liked by a large portion of the population, jazz does not qualify because jazz represents only about three percent of radio airplay and album sales.

2) If "popular" means "of the common people," jazz does not qualify as popular music. Unlike most folk musicians and blues players, jazz musicians represent a highly versatile and specially trained elite whose level of sophistication is not common to the population at large. We will learn more about this in the next chapter.

3) Some jazz is "popular music" in the sense that it is functional music or "utilitarian" because it constitutes dance music, film music, and party music. But for the most part, jazz fits none of those qualifications. It is not *primarily* utilitarian in nature. Instead, it is appreciated for its esthetic and intellectual rewards, and it is approached with some effort.

4) Some jazz can be considered "popular music" because it possesses an easy accessibility. But much jazz, especially the post-1930s styles, does not qualify in this way because it requires a cultivated taste.

5) The term "jazz" was once applied so loosely that it denoted syncopated popular music as a whole. We can find illustrations for this in the 1920s, when Al Jolson's movie about a vaudeville singer was titled *The Jazz Singer.* The confusion was furthered by the Neil Diamond remake of that movie. We must also remember that fiction writer F. Scott Fitzgerald dubbed the 1920s "The Jazz Age." So today many people think jazz is only music of "The Roaring Twenties," with musicians playing in speak-easies and wearing red-and-white striped clothing. Partly because of that situation, the term "jazz" is still frequently confused with popular music as a whole, long after it began acquiring a much narrower meaning. For instance, today many people still lump jazz with rock, and vice versa. Even now some people use the term "jazz" to designate almost every popular style that is not "classical" music. "Jazz" has been applied to the folk music of Peter, Paul & Mary, the folk rock of Bob Dylan, the popular singing of Isaac Hayes, the written piano music of George Gershwin, and the minimalist compositions of Philip Glass and Steve Reich.

In summary, much jazz fails to qualify as popular music by any of the above definitions of the term "popular." It warrants the label of "art music." But to be prepared for arguments, we must remember that some jazz is popular music according to some conceptions of "popular music," and some jazz is popular music according to all of the above conceptions.

CHAPTER SUMMARY

1) Jazz involves i mprovisation and swing feeling.
2) Though most jazz groups use arrangements that are preset in some regard, a substantial portion of each performance is usually spontaneous.
3) Swing feeling is achieved by spirited performances of many different kinds of music which employ steady tempo.
4) Jazz swing feeling is like swing feeling in the general sense, but it also has an abundance of syncopated rhythms, swing eighth-notes, and a continuous rise and fall of tension.
5) Some people use the term jazz very loosely, applying it to anything they ever heard called jazz or anything that reminds them of anything they think it is.
6) For some people jazz is a feeling more than anything else, jazz swing feeling.
7) Some people believe that improvisation is the central requirement of jazz.
8) Most of what is called "jazz" contains improvisation and swing feeling.
9) Some jazz is "popular music" because people use it as party music, film music, and dance music.
10) Jazz is not particularly popular by comparison with most other kinds of music, as evidenced by its three-percent market share.
11) For most people, jazz is a cultivated taste and not easily accessible. This makes it art music rather than popular music.

NOTES

1. For a lengthy examination of these issues, see Mark Gridley, Robert Maxham, and Robert Hoff, "Three Approaches to Defining Jazz," *Musical Quarterly*, Vol. 73, No. 4 (1989): 513–531. Reprinted and updated in Lewis Porter (ed.), *Jazz: A Century of Change: Readings and New Essays* (Schirmer, 1997).
2. By our first definition (association with elements in the jazz tradition) and our second definition (jazz swing feeling), Manhattan Transfer's first recording of Joe Zawinul's "Birdland" would qualify as jazz because of its jazzy rhythms and swing feeling. However, Weather Report's original version of "Birdland" would qualify more clearly because of its improvisation and swing feeling (fourth definition) and because of its use of saxophone (an element associated with the jazz tradition, a criterion of our first definition).
3. For a more detailed documentation of these points, see Mark C. Gridley, "Is Jazz Popular Music?" *The Instrumentalist*, Vol. 41, No. 8 (March 1987): 19–22, 25–26, 85.

Chapter Three

Chick Corea, Dave Holland, Wayne Shorter. Photo by Ray Avery.

Appreciating Jazz Improvisation

Jazz can be a lot of fun to listen to. But some people miss that fun because they let themselves be intimidated. They think that getting more out of listening to jazz requires that they engage in a difficult learning process. They believe jazz can be enjoyed only by listeners who have deep technical knowledge. It is true that we get more out of listening if we know more about how jazz is made. But learning about jazz is not difficult. Some styles sound chaotic to everyone at first. But they become more coherent each time we rehear them. Much of the real substance in jazz is subtle. We can enjoy it deeply once we begin noticing the subtleties. This book will point them out.

Reading this book is very different from reading most other books. This book doesn't work if you merely read it. **This book works only if you combine your reading with a lot of jazz listening**. This book will not be very helpful unless you also attend concerts and listen to recordings. It only works if you find examples of what you are studying. **You are not really learning until you actually *hear* what the book is talking about**. A good rule of thumb is to never read more than about five paragraphs without listening to a corresponding selection on your tape or disc. **You need to hear a good example of the music in order for the text to mean anything**. Choose your selections from the recordings that came with your book and the recordings that are cited in it. Visit a well-stocked record collection in your library or at a friend's place. Some college radio stations broadcast jazz that can also help you. A few regions even have community public radio stations that broadcast jazz for you. Buying or borrowing recordings that are cited in this book's "Small Basic Collection" can be very useful. Having at least one good album for each chapter would be ideal.

◇LISTENING TECHNIQUES

Before beginning this chapter, study the *Demonstration CD,* hereafter termed *Demo CD,* and pages 364 to 393. You should also return to that material once in a while throughout your study of this book. The more jazz you hear, the more meaningful the demonstrations will be. The more familiar the demonstrations, the more you will recognize in the jazz you hear. Also keep in mind that there is so much material on the *Demo CD* that you should not try to absorb it all at one sitting. Try to space your listening sessions over several days. Some students have found that about a half hour a day is enough to digest on the first time around.

Most of this chapter describes traditional approaches to making jazz. Therefore it is helpful to have a few ways to find the sounds you are reading about. Here are three sources that should be easy to find on most campuses and in most libraries: *The Smithsonian Collection of Classic Jazz* (hereafter referred to as SCCJ), the *Jazz Classics CD* for *Jazz Styles* by Gridley (your book), and the *Jazz Classics CD* for the abridged edition of this book, *Concise Guide To Jazz* by Gridley. Locate a few of the following selections before you begin studying this chapter:

1) "Blue Seven" by Sonny Rollins (SCCJ)

2) "Bikini" by Dexter Gordon (SCCJ)

3) "Gertrude's Bounce" by Clifford Brown *(Concise Guide to Jazz CD)*

4) "Dexter Digs In" by Dexter Gordon *(Concise Guide to Jazz CD)*

5) "Pent-Up House" by Sonny Rollins (SCCJ)

Jazz fans use a number of different strategies when they listen. Grab one of the selections listed above, and try listening to it by each of these next strategies.

Listen to the performance in a relaxed way first. Absorb the overall experience. Don't worry about trying to pick out anything in particular. It will still be there whenever you come back to listen again. Listen to the piece this way three or four times. Soon you will find that you are almost able to hum along with some of it.

Next, begin acquainting yourself with the basis of the music. The accompaniment is the best place to start. Pick out the sound of the bass. In traditional approaches to jazz combo playing, the bass part will be the steadiest. This makes it the easiest part to follow. Ignore the other sounds, and follow the bassist's part through the entire performance. You might want to do this several times. Like magic, the bass part will become clearer each time you rehear the performance.

After you have become good at finding and following the bass part, try to pick out the sound of the cymbals. Then try to follow the steady rhythm that is played on the cymbals and coordinated with the bass part. As you listen, you will begin to notice extra notes that come before and after the beat. Such decorations can be fascinating to follow. They make the music more exciting and they give an accompanist's work a more personal touch. Listen to the performance several more times, focusing only on the bass and cymbals.

Once you have become accustomed to the music's steady foundation in the bass and cymbals, listen for the chords. These sounds may come from a piano or a guitar. You will notice the harmony, and you will also notice that the chords are played in very rhythmic ways. The harmony helps guide the improvisations. The rhythmic ways in which the chords are played prods the soloists and helps make the band swing.

By now, you already will have heard the solo lines several times, even if you were trying to ignore them. So it is time to consider the ways that many jazz fans rotate their attention among the various activities that are occurring in the combo performance.

1) **Hearing the improvised lines of a jazz soloist as melodies in themselves should help you enjoy much jazz**. Experienced listeners get as much pleasure from hearing their favorite improvisations as most people get from hearing their favorite songs. Many listeners pay close attention as the improvisations are unfolding. They want to notice when the line becomes particularly melodic. Then they can have the satisfaction of hearing a new song being composed. Some jazz improvisers strive to invent lines that are as catchy as the melodies in pop tunes and classical pieces. On the other hand, many improvisers tend toward more elaborate lines. Some passages in their improvisations are more melody-like than others. There are gems of inspired melody hidden in many improvisations just waiting to be discovered by attentive listeners. We need to remember, however, that melody is more important in some styles than others. For instance, in some avant-garde and jazz-rock fusion performances, the music emphasizes instead the variations in mood, sound qualities, and rhythms. Sometimes the mood alone may be the most prominent aspect.
2) **One way a lot of jazz fans listen is to imagine layers of sound, one on top of another, all moving forward in time**. Each layer can represent the sound of a different instrument. Once you become skilled in visualizing separate sounds, you will begin to notice relationships between sounds. Try to imagine a graph of the solo line. The horizontal side of the graph represents time passing. The vertical dimension represents highness and lowness of pitch. Your graph can be embellished by colored shapes and textures representing the accompanying sounds of piano chords, drums, cymbals, bass, and so on. (See Figure 3.1 below for possible visualizations of the ways tones change.)
3) **Some people hum the original tune to themselves while listening to the improvisations which are guided by its chord changes**. Try to synchronize the

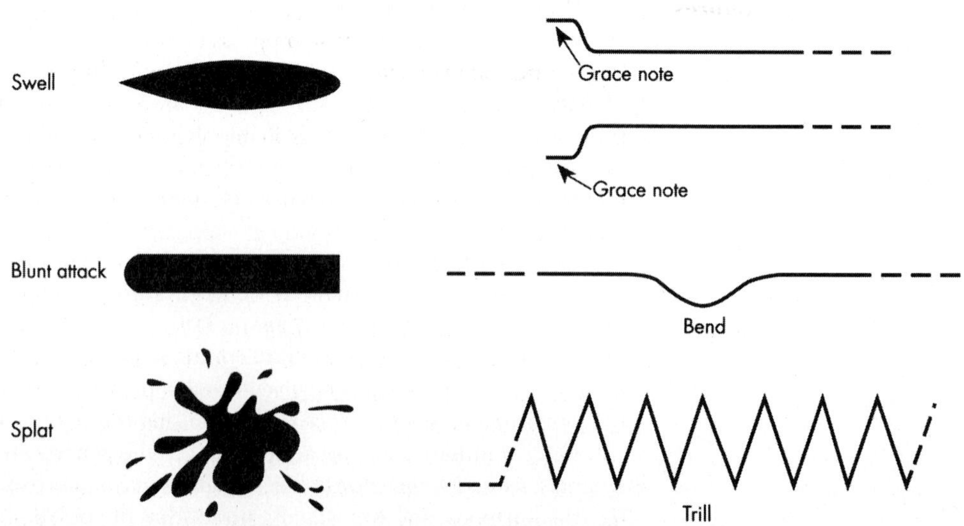

FIGURE 3.1 Possible visualizations of tone perceptions. In most, pitch and volume go up and down, time goes left to right.

beginning of your humming with the beginning of a solo improvisation. Then keep the same tempo as the performer. Snatches of the original tune might turn up in the improvisation, and you will begin to recognize the chords in the accompaniment more clearly. You will also become aware of two compositions based on the same chord changes: the original tune and the improvised melody. As you become more aware of how they go together, your appreciation of jazz will deepen considerably.

4) **Try listening to every note in a soloist's improvisation**. You might not be able to detect each note in fast passages, especially those of saxophonist John Coltrane or pianist Oscar Peterson. But with repeated listening and close concentration, eventually you should be able to hear every note. Do not be discouraged if this temporarily proves difficult. Even professional musicians need repeated listenings before they can account for every note in some improvisations. Your ears will get better and better the more you listen.

◇CHORD PROGRESSIONS AND TUNE CONSTRUCTION

To improvise is to compose and perform at the same time. Jazz musicians make up their music as they go along. Much of this chapter outlines unwritten rules and guidelines that all jazz musicians know. These guide the improvisations in situations such as jam sessions where musicians do not know each other and have not rehearsed. They help musicians piece together performances spontaneously. And they continue to guide improvisations long after rehearsals.

Most jazz is guided by musicians agreeing beforehand to maintain a given tempo, key, and progression of accompaniment chords. They then invent and play their own melodies and accompaniments in a way that is compatible with those chords. Frequently, the agreed-upon harmonies are borrowed from a familiar melody, and the melody itself is played before and after the improvisations. This is easy because jazz musicians tend to know many of the same tunes in the same keys. Though the original melody is often kept in mind by the improvisers, rarely are the improvised lines actually variations on the original melody. A progression of accompaniment chords is all the improvised melodies and the original melody have in common. (Listen to the *Demo CD* Track 33 for an explanation and demonstration.) Performances are facilitated because standard chord changes for these tunes are followed, and traditions regarding the sequence of melody and improvisations are adhered to. In the next few paragraphs, we will examine those traditions.

Blues Chorus

When a jazz group plays a twelve-bar blues, the melody is usually played twice. Then the soloists improvise over the progression of chords in its accompaniment. **One complete twelve-bar progression of chords is called a blues chorus**. (This is explained in detail on pages 375–382 and the *Demo CD* Track 19.) Each soloist usually improvises for several choruses. When one soloist ends an improvisation, another soloist takes over. The chords continue to progress in an unvarying cycle, even if a musician misses an entrance or overlaps into someone else's chorus. In that way, the whole group stays together. That particular progression of chords and the tempo at which it is played are the glue that holds the music together. After all the solos, the group concludes by playing the melody twice more.

A-A-B-A

Some tunes are written in the form of four sections that are eight measures each. (This is demonstrated on the *Demo CD* Track 33. The concept of "measure," also known as "bar," is explained on pages 364–366.) This is called a thirty-two bar form. The most common arrangement for such pieces is comprised of two sections of music. One section is called the A-section. The other is called the B-section, bridge, release, inside, second strain, or channel. The A-section is played twice in succession. Then the B-section is inserted, followed by the A-section again. The sequence is **A-A-B-A**, and thousands of tunes have been organized this way. You might recall the format if you hum the melody to the

Christmas carol "Deck the Halls" or the theme song for the "Flintstones" television program. The same format is used for "Cottontail" (in the *Jazz Classics CD*).[1]

When jazz musicians play an A-A-B-A tune, they usually play its melody once before and once after the solo improvisations. Each solo adheres to the tune's chord progression. A repeating sequence of A-A-B-A is followed over and over again without interruption. The cycle continues A-A-B-A-A-A-B-A-A-A-B-A. What musicians signify by the term **chorus** is one playing through of a chord progression. The length of a solo is measured by the number of choruses the soloist improvises. In a jam session, each soloist ends on the last measure of a given chorus and is immediately followed by another soloist starting on the first measure of the next chorus. If a soloist stops improvising in the middle of a chorus—usually at the end of an eight-measure section—another player immediately takes up where the previous player left off. The A-A-B-A form continues unchanged in its cycle.

Trading Fours, Trading Eights

Soloists sometimes alternate eight-measure sections with each other. One musician improvises on the first eight measures, another on the second eight, and so on. This is called *trading eights.* The same thing is done with four-measure sections and is called *trading fours.* (Listen to the fourth chorus of "Lester Leaps In" in the SCCJ. Pianist Count Basie and tenor saxophonist Lester Young trade fours within the tune's thirty-two bar A-A-B-A construction.)

In jazz styles of the 1940s and 1950s, it is common for drummers to trade fours or eights with the rest of the group. A soloist, accompanied by the rhythm section, plays for four (or eight) bars. Then the entire band drops out while the drummer improvises alone for the same number of bars. This pattern repeats over and over so that various soloists are trading fours (or eights) with the drummer. The form of the tune and its tempo are maintained throughout that sequence, even though no chords or melodies are played during the drum solos. Adherence to that format allows the entire band to begin playing again, precisely after four (or eight) measures because each musician is silently counting the beats and thinking of the chords that are progressing while he is not playing.

Absence of Steady Tempo

When you are listening to improvisations and trying to detect the form of an underlying chord progression, watch for three different manipulations which might throw off your counting. First is an **absence of steady tempo**. This is not commonly found in jazz, but introductions and endings sometimes employ it. Ballad melodies sometimes also receive this treatment the first time they are played. (Miles Davis uses it for the beginning melody statement on his famous 1964 recording of "My Funny Valentine.") Jazz musicians use the term **rubato** to indicate such absence of steadiness in tempo.[2]

Aside from the infrequent occurrence of rubato, a passage within an improvisation might sound as though its tempo increased simply because of an increased amount of activity. Or, a passage might sound as though the tempo is decreasing simply because of a decreased amount of activity. Most of these situations can be deceiving because, after the theme statement, each chord is in effect for the same amount of time, yet it sounds like it is not. In other words, the chords change at the same rate. **Only the density of musical activity is changing**, not the tempo for the passage of the chords that guide improvisation. It is often difficult to differentiate a true rubato, in the jazz sense of the term, from an alteration in density (what you might call "pseudo rubato"), and some performers, notably post-1960 stylists, use both techniques. But it should not be too difficult to learn to detect two other manipulations: double-timing and half-timing.

Double-Timing

When a member of a band starts playing as though the tempo were double its original rate, we say that the musician is **double-timing**. This results from doubling the rate of notes without doubling the amount of time each chord is in effect. (This is demonstrated on the *Demo CD* Track 35.) (Listen to Coleman Hawkins depart from the ballad tempo feeling of the melody in his "Body and Soul" in *Jazz Classics CD* for *Concise Guide to Jazz* and SCCJ or to Charlie Parker similarly doubling the pace of notes on "Embraceable You" in SCCJ.) To create double-time feeling, a soloist might switch from improvising eighth notes to improvising sixteenth notes. A bassist, for example, can create double-time feeling by playing eighth notes where he would ordinarily play quarter notes. He plays two notes on each beat instead of playing only one, and his walking bass pattern might now best be characterized as "running bass." The result is a feeling that the tempo has doubled, even though there is no change in the amount of time each chord's harmony is in effect. This can deceive the listener who is trying to follow the improvised solo line in relation to its underlying progression of accompaniment chords because twice as many sounds now occur on each beat. The solution is to concentrate harder on humming the original melody while listening to the improvisation. You might also tap your foot at the original tempo to help keep your place.

Half-Timing

The opposite of double-timing is **half-timing**. In half-timing, we halve the number of notes that are played without halving the rate at which the chords change. The tempo remains the same, but the note values become twice as long. The tempo seems to be slower, half as fast as the absolute rate at which chords are passing. As with double-timing, the chords remain in effect for the same amount of time, regardless of the pace that is perceived. (Listen to the *Demo CD* Track 36.)

Half-timing is rare, but double-timing is quite common. During the 1950s and 1960s, improvisations on ballads were often played in double-time. After the piece's melody was played once in its original tempo, solo improvisations followed, nearly always in double-time. It almost conveyed the impression that improvisers wanted to swing hard and were impatient with the slowness of the original tempo. Chords progressed in these performances at the same absolute rate during solos as during the tune itself, but the improvisations seemed twice as fast as the tune.

Quadruple-Timing

Double-timing is also common in Latin American jazz because the beat in that music is usually subdivided into eighth notes instead of quarter notes. (These terms are explained on pages 365–367.) Rock music of the 1960s is often performed in double-time, and some is actually in quadruple-time. **In quadruple-time the beat is sounded in four equal parts (sixteenth notes).** Young dancers during the early 1960s often requested "fast music" when in fact they did not want up-tempo performances at all. They wanted music performed in a double-time or quadruple-time feel. To the dancers, it was "fast."

Stop-Timing

The **stop-time solo break** is another manipulation that often leads the listener to believe mistakenly that the tempo has changed. Its name "stop-time" implies that the tempo stops when all group members except the soloist stop playing. Actually, however, the tempo is maintained along with the amount of time each chord's harmonies are in effect. We perceive the tempo as suspended as though "the time has stopped" because everyone except the soloist has stopped playing. (On "Lester Leaps In," on the SCCJ, listen to the second A-section and the final A-section of Lester Young's second solo chorus. He has a stop-time solo break in the first two measures of each.)

Stop-time solo breaks are especially effective as springboards to launch solo choruses. Often, groups finish the opening melody statement with a two-measure break for the first soloist. Many tunes end with a long note held for four or eight beats, and this "empty space" in the melody furnishes a good opportunity for a solo break. In other words, a combo might stop playing during the last two measures of a thirty-two-bar tune, giving the soloist a two-measure break to launch his improvisation. If the piece is a twelve-bar blues, the solo break takes place in the eleventh and twelfth measures (explained and illustrated on the *Demo CD* Track 34).

Beginning and Ending a Piece

Other standard alternatives are also available to aid unrehearsed performances. For example, if a band of horns (trumpet, saxophone) and rhythm section (piano, bass, and drums) wants to include an **introduction**, the performers have at least four stock alternatives:

1) Use the final four or eight measures of the tune, and let the rhythm section rework and play it without the horns.
2) Have the rhythm section play a common four- or eight-measure chord progression and improvise a line compatible with it. (Listen to Count Basie's four-measure introduction to "Lester Leaps In" in SCCJ.)
3) Use an introduction that the entire group knows (from a famous recording of the tune, for example), thus including the horns in addition to the rhythm section.
4) Let the rhythm section play a one-, two-, or four-bar figure (called a *vamp*) over and over until the hornmen feel like starting the tune. (Listen to the beginning of Basie's "Taxi War Dance" on the *Jazz Classics CD.*)

Endings are handled in similar ways. A few of the standard alternatives include:

1) End immediately at the end of the melody itself, with no extra notes.
2) Improvise a *ritard* for the last three or four bars, and then sustain the final chord. (Listen to the ending used by Louis Armstrong and Earl Hines on "Weather Bird" in SCCJ.)
3) Rest or sustain a chord while a soloist takes a cadenza (an improvisation out of context), then follow it with a sustained chord.
4) Repeat the last four bars of the tune, thus creating a tag, and then sustain the tune's final chord.
5) Use a well-known ending.
6) Let the rhythm section play a vamp followed by a final chord.
7) Have the rhythm section improvise some common progression and end with it.

Once a progression has begun, its chords and its tempo remain in charge of the situation. Even strangers can play with each other and be instantly compatible. Musicians from different style eras can also play with each other without much conflict because the tempo and chord progression hold things together.

Exceptions to the Rules

Although the time is usually played as written, before and after the improvised solos, **jazz performers occasionally omit the melody statement**. For example, the 1945 Don Byas-Slam Stewart recording of "I Got Rhythm" (in SCCJ) does not have a return to the melody at the end. Charlie Parker does not completely state the melody in either of his 1947 Dial recordings of "Embraceable You" (in SCCJ). Coleman Hawkins departs considerably from completing an opening melody statement in his 1939 recording of "Body and Soul" (in SCCJ) and never states the melody at the end, either. Miles Davis once recorded a twelve-bar blues improvisation without a melody and, quite understandably, called it "No Line." (Many examples are included in the *Demo CD.*)

During the 1960s and 1970s, much jazz departed from the tradition of improvising within fixed chord progressions and preset chorus lengths. Ornette Coleman and Cecil Taylor popularized such practices. Such music is often called "free jazz" because improvisers are free from the requirement to follow preset chord changes. (Listen to the excerpts of Coleman's *Free Jazz* album and Taylor's "Enter Evening" from his *Unit Structures* album in SCCJ.)

Beginning in the 1960s, **John Coltrane and his disciples recorded pieces whose melodies had chord progressions in their accompaniment but whose improvisations were not based on those progressions**. These improvisations were accompanied by extensively repeated, two-chord patterns. Coltrane's improvisations on "My Favorite Things" exemplify this approach.

◇SKILLS POSSESSED BY THE IMPROVISER

Spontaneous music is not totally spontaneous creation. Extensive preparation is required. A musician must undergo much training before he can improvise coherent lines with jazz swing feeling. Some of this training is formal, but most is informal. Jazz players spend years practicing their instruments and learning tunes and the chord changes that accompany them.

Near-effortless command of an instrument is the constant goal of a jazz player because the ability to play any musical idea that comes to mind depends partly on instrumental proficiency. It is not unusual for a player to practice by himself for more than two hours a day, and some average more than four hours a day, five to six days per week. In other words, they play every spare minute. In addition to practicing scales and exercises, the jazz musician invents, collects, and develops phrases he might later use during improvisation. He tries out rhythmic variations of his favorite phrases. He practices to achieve fluency in different keys, in different registers of his instrument, and in different tempos and rhythmic styles.

To adequately respond to the harmonies produced by accompanists, **a jazz improviser must be well acquainted with harmony. Most jazz soloists know the piano well** because the piano keyboard provides a means for seeing and hearing relationships between melody and harmony at the same time.

To respond in a split second to his accompanists, the improvising soloist must have **an extremely quick and keen ear for pitch and rhythm**. This ability also helps him imagine a note or phrase and immediately play it. Jazz musicians are so quick to perceive and respond to subtle nuances in style and group direction that they can usually play a respectable performance the first time they work with an unfamiliar group.

Most jazz musicians have remarkably good memories for sounds. The average jazz improviser is able to hear a note or phrase once and then remember it and play it back. In fact, you can often hear an improviser incorporate phrases from the solo that immediately preceded his.

A jazz musician has to **remember hundreds of tunes and chord progressions**. He must be as familiar with pop tunes and jazz standards as he is with his native language, perhaps more so. The convenience of knowing many of the same tunes helps musicians play together without rehearsal.

Another helpful skill is that of **recognizing chord progressions** quickly. Many jazz musicians can play a tune from memory after hearing it only a few times, and they often improvise solos compatible with the tune's chord progression after hearing it only once or twice.

Even though improvisation is their primary skill, most jazz musicians can also read music. Basically, **the skills of reading and writing music** can be described as four levels:

1) **The ability to read music** accurately if allowed to practice or look it over ahead of time. Many people call that "reading music."

2) **The ability to play a piece of music correctly the first time it is seen**. This is called "sight-reading." Musicians call it "reading." When musicians say someone

"reads," they usually mean he is capable of sight-reading. This skill is possessed by all symphony orchestra musicians and by most jazz musicians. It is not a common skill among pop singers or rock or country and western musicians. The ability to sight-read saves rehearsal time because it is easier to learn a new piece by reading it than by trial and error ("by ear"). Some people go so far as to say that a player "is not a real musician unless he reads music." That latter attitude may be a bit severe, though, because there are players who are instrumentally proficient and compositionally creative but unable to sight-read music.

3) The **ability to make up an original tune and correctly notate it**: "writing music" or "composing." Actually, the act of making up a tune is "composing"; notation is more specialized. But the term "writing music" usually refers to the process of making up a tune, not necessarily to writing it down for musicians to play. Many people who are said to "write" music actually cannot write down their ideas. In other words, there are composers who cannot read or write music. Pop singers and rock musicians often make up songs and then pay a skilled musician to write them down for copyright, sales, and publication. (The singers and rock musicians often teach songs to each other by ear instead of placing sheet music in front of each other.)

4) The highest level of music reading and writing is **the ability to listen to someone else's music and then correctly notate it.** This skill is possessed by people who write down jazz solos they hear on records.

During the 1950s and 1960s, it was rare to find rock groups or country groups who could quickly notate their own work or sight-read someone else's. Some pop singers can read music, but most are unable to sight-read. But it is common for jazz musicians to both compose and notate their own tunes. **Nearly all jazz improvisers are also composers**. Most jazz musicians occasionally write down their improvisations in the form of tunes. Few of the tunes become famous in jazz history, but all serve as vehicles for improvisation. Some jazz players have written every tune on every album they have recorded. It is not unusual to find a jazz saxophonist or pianist who has written more than one hundred original tunes. Though many of them never write a memorable tune, some become so good at writing that they are more important as tune writers or band arrangers than as improvising players.

◇INSTRUMENT ROLES

To help follow the music in a jazz performance, you might try to divide the sounds into the functions they serve. For these reasons, we describe what the band members do in terms of solo roles and accompanying roles. The manner in which musicians fill these roles has been relatively standardized since the 1930s. Once you become familiar with them, you will appreciate how they sound within each style and era. With that frame of reference, you can also begin distinguishing innovations. Most of the chapters in this book describe styles by stressing departures that were made from the ways the musicians filled those roles. Particularly since 1960, certain jazz groups have made innovations in the use of instruments. So the best way to familiarize yourself with the basic roles is by listening to the selections that are cited in your reading, not by grabbing a jazz recording at random.

Jazz is partly an ensemble art. The soloist and accompanists combine to form an ensemble which attempts to play as a single unit. The soloist role can be assumed by any melody instrument, though saxophones and trumpets are the most common. The accompanists are usually classified as members of a *rhythm* section. This consists of musicians who play string bass or electric bass guitar (see Figure 3.2), drums (see Figure 3.3, page 20), and an instrument that plays chords, such as a piano or guitar.[3] The rhythm section is a group of players who improvise together to accompany and inspire the soloist. They provide a springboard for his lines and can make or break his effectiveness. The following discussion is intended to clarify the role of each instrument in the rhythm section.

Bass

The bassist improvises his part in the rhythm section by plucking a string once per beat and occasionally adding embellishments. Many bassists play the second and fourth of every four notes harder than the first and third. This helps create swing feeling. The bass pattern often rises and falls as though the music is walking up and down a staircase. This timekeeping style is called **walking bass**. Good walking bass lines make musical sense by themselves. In fact, some soloists consider walking bass to be the most essential sound in the rhythm section. They would play without drums or chording instrument before they would play without walking bass. (Listen to the demonstrations of walking bass on Track 23 of the *Demo CD.* Listen to Miroslav Vitous play this way on "Steps" in the *Jazz Classics CD,* and see page 426 for notations of typical bass lines. Listen to the *Demo CD* Track 32 to hear how a jazz combo sounds with and without bass.)

How does the bassist know what notes to play if he is improvising his part? The bassist selects his notes from important notes in the accompaniment chords that are guiding the solo improvisation. Sometimes the bassist's notes are not the same as the chord notes, but they lead into the chord notes or complement the chords. In other words, the bassist keeps the beat, provides a low-register component for the group sound, generates a buoyant quality in the effect of the music, and clarifies the progression of chords by playing its most important notes.

FIGURE 3.2 Jimmy Blanton, Jaco Pastorius. String bass, also known as acoustic bass, bass viol, or upright bass (left).

Photo Courtesy of Frank Driggs.

Electric bass guitar, also known as Fender bass or electric bass (right). Though it looks like a guitar, the electric bass can be differentiated from the solid body electric guitar by having four instead of six tuning pegs, one for each string.

Photo by Randy Nortus.

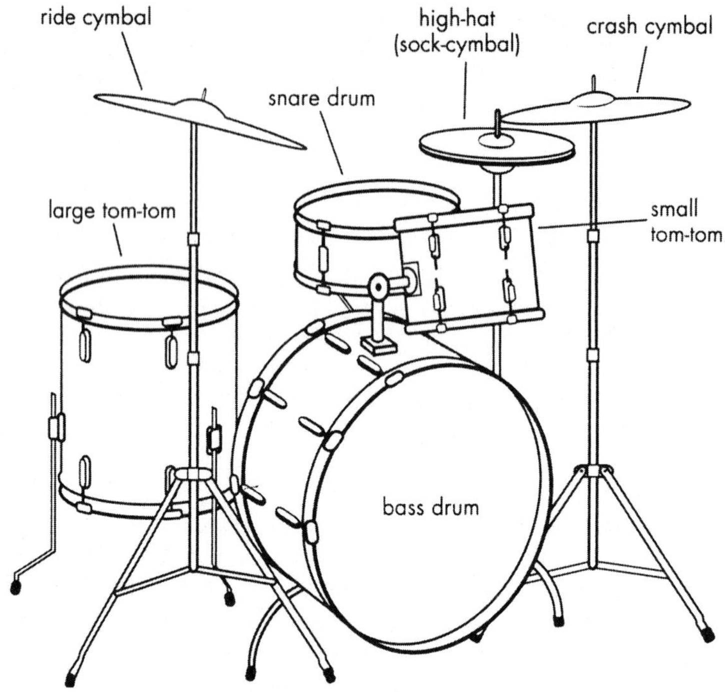

FIGURE 3.3 Audience view of drum set.

Some bassists employ a variety of techniques in their work. Occasionally a bassist will pluck two strings at the same time. That is called a **double-stop**. Or he might strum his four bass strings as though a guitar. In symphony orchestras, the bass sound is usually extracted by a bow drawn across the strings similar to a saw cutting wood. This technique is called **arco**, not to be confused with plucking, which is **pizzicato** ("pitts-a-cah-toe"). Though most jazz bassists are capable of it, they do not use the bow very often. (Listen to the *Demo CD* Tracks 21 and 22 to hear arco contrasted with pizzicato.)

Some bassists fill in silences with musical remarks that sound almost like they were talking with the rest of the group. This technique is sometimes called "broken time." In some post-1960 groups, making these musical remarks became more important than stating the beat. In some bands, the bassist is often involved in intricate counterplay and musical conversations. Accompaniment rhythms also became more varied, once bassists were freed from playing exclusively walking style. (Listen to Scott LaFaro on the first four choruses of "Solar" in the *Jazz Classics CD.*) After the 1950s, bassists also played melody more often than they traditionally had. During the 1970s, it also became common for bassists to play prewritten theme statements in unison with horns.

Piano

The pianist improvises chords in a syncopated fashion to provide harmonies and rhythms for complementing and supporting the soloist. These chords are usually played in the middle of the piano keyboard, creating notes in a pitch range that is easy to hear. (See pages 424–425 for notations of typical piano accompaniments.) What the pianist is doing is called **comping**. This is short for ac**comp**anying. The pianist uses both hands to play the chorded rhythms behind a soloist. However, **when taking his own solo, he uses his left hand to comp while his right hand plays melodic lines**. (For a narrated illustration, listen to the *Demo CD* Tracks 20, 29, 31–33. Then listen to Chick Corea comp for himself in "Steps" on the *Jazz Classics CD.*)

Comping is an improvised activity intended to enhance the solo line. Sometimes it inspires the soloist, suggesting chords and rhythms for his improvisation. Comping also involves responding instantaneously to changes in direction taken by a soloist. When the direction of a soloist's improvisation suggests a particular sequence of chords, the pianist must follow suit, even if that progression is not standard for the piece and was not discussed ahead of time. The pianist has a very difficult task because he must be inventive when he comps, without getting in the soloist's way. Sometimes the pianist may stop playing if he feels that the soloist would sound better without piano accompaniment. Comping must not clash with the work of the bassist or conflict with the drummer's kicks and prods, either. The members of the rhythm section are providing an accompaniment for the ever-changing melodic and rhythmic directions of the soloist's improvisation. Ideally, the pianist and drummer will kick and prod the soloist in a fashion that is integrated. They also underscore rhythms in written melodies and ensemble figures.

Drums

The drummer uses his right hand to play rhythms which provide both regular pulse and swing feeling. These rhythms are played on a cymbal suspended on the right side over the drum set (see Figures 3.3 and 3.4). Such a cymbal comes to occupy the role of **ride cymbal** if it is capable of producing a certain quality of "ping" and its sound sustains properly. The timekeeping rhythms played on it are called **ride rhythms**. Occasionally they consist of one stroke per beat *(ching, ching, ching, ching)*, played in unison with the walking bass. But they are usually more complicated, for example, *ching chick a ching chick a ching chick a ching* OR *ching ching ching chick a ching* OR *ching chick a ching chick a ching chick a chick a ching*, etc. (See page 430 for notations.) The drummer may play ride rhythms on other parts of his set, too. In fact, before the ride cymbal came into common use, ride rhythms were played on the snare drum and high-hat cymbals. Note also that the drummer might play ride rhythms on another cymbal suspended to his left, and the drummer's right hand is not limited to playing the ride cymbal. He can use it to play any of his instruments. The ride cymbal just gets more of its attention.

Drummers frequently interrupt timekeeping patterns to make other, more colorful sounds. The *crash cymbal* is often struck by the drummer's right hand, after a fill, while ride rhythms are interrupted. By comparison with the ride cymbal, the crash cymbal makes a splashier tone color, and its sound disappears more quickly. (Ride and crash cymbal sounds are compared on the *Demo CD* Track 4. They are abundant in the drumming of Elvin Jones on "The Promise" and Tony Williams on "Masqualero" in the *Jazz Classics CD.*) Other colorations can be extracted from the *small tom-tom,* suspended over the bass drum, and the *large tom-tom,* sitting on the floor to the player's right. (See Figures 3.3 and 3.4, and listen to tom-toms on the *Demo CD* Tracks 6 and 7.)

The drummer's left hand is free to accent and color the group sound by striking his *snare drum,* on a stand close to his lap (see Figure 3.4). The snare drum has a crisp, crackling sound. The sounds made by striking the snare drum are often called "fills" because they fill in a musical gap left by the soloist. In addition to "fills," the snare drum is used to provide an undercurrent of activity that seems to be "chattering" while the band is playing. (Listen to the narrated demonstration on the *Demo CD* Tracks 5, 8, 31, and 32. Then listen for these sounds from Roy Haynes on "Steps" in the *Jazz Classics CD.*)

Accentuating the swing feeling achieved by the bassist's emphasis of the second and fourth beats in each measure, the drummer plays those same beats by pressing his left foot on a pedal which closes two cymbals together, making a "chick" sound. This apparatus is called a *high-hat* or *sock cymbal.* (See Figure 3.5, and listen to the *Demo CD* Track 2.) The high-hat will produce a "chick" sound if the pedal is depressed and held in closed position

FIGURE 3.4 Drums.

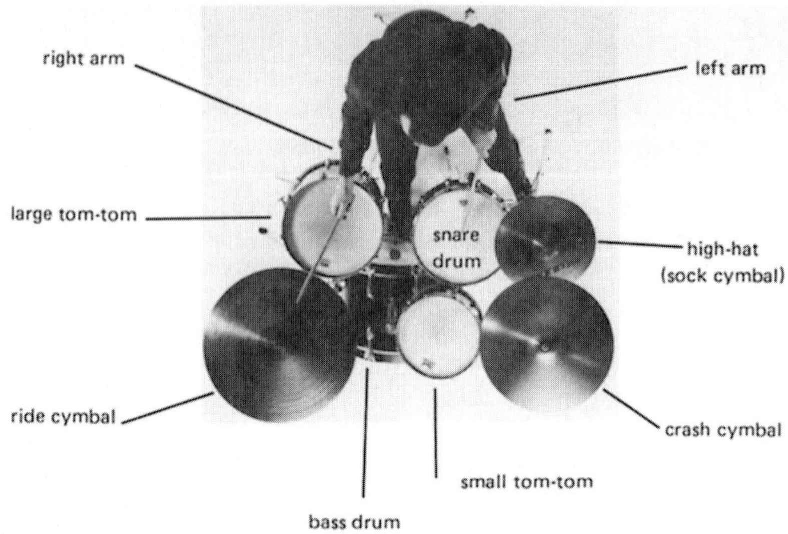

for a second. It can then be opened and closed again for another "chick" sound. A "ching" sound can be achieved by bringing the cymbals together just long enough for them to strike each other, then releasing them to resonate. All this is done by means of the high-hat's foot pedal. Sounds can also be extracted from the high-hat by sticks, wire brushes, or mallets. Each implement produces different sounds (see Figure 3.6). The high-hat cymbals can be struck when they are closed or open. Each cymbal in the unit can also be struck independently. Any part of any cymbal can be struck; each part produces a different sound (demonstrated on the *Demo CD* Tracks 3 and 4).

The drummer uses his right foot to press a pedal which, in turn, causes a mallet to strike the bass drum (see Figure 3.7). The drummer sometimes plays the bass drum lightly on every beat, and he also uses it for accents.

A drummer can be recognized on a record by the particular instruments he plays and the characteristic ways in which he strikes them. No two drummers have the same cymbal sound, and each drummer has his own personal way of tuning the drums and cymbals. By means of adjustment bolts, drummers tighten the plastic or animal hide striking surfaces (drumheads). In addition, some drummers attach gauze and tape to their drumheads to selectively deaden the sound. They tune cymbals by critical placement of tape on the underside. To produce a "sizzle" sound, they often drill holes in a cymbal and attach rivets that vibrate against the cymbal when the cymbal is struck; another technique that achieves a sustained hiss is to hang a large key chain across the top of the cymbal. It bounces when the cymbal is struck and keeps vibrating.

Cymbals on a bandstand often appear old and dirty. This is because few drummers polish their cymbals. The cymbal's sound will be changed if any part of its surface is removed, whether it be dirt, corrosion, or the brass itself. Many drummers actually let new cymbals age to provide a desired tone quality.

Even though they are marketed in various brands, thicknesses, and diameters, cymbal manufacturing is not sufficiently standardized to guarantee perfect cymbals for every drummer. No two are alike, even among the same make and model. Drummers spend years searching for cymbals which give them the particular sound they desire. Many drummers collect

FIGURE 3.5 Open high-hat, closed high-hat (hear on *Demo CD* Track 2).

cymbals, using certain ones for certain jobs, depending on the sound that is desired. When required to play on someone else's drum set, a jazz drummer often removes its cymbals and uses his own.

The drummer can create a huge variety of sounds, depending on what drum or cymbal he strikes, how hard he strikes it, and what part of the surface is struck. Striking the center of the cymbal creates a sound different from that produced by striking halfway to the edge which, in turn, is unlike striking the edge itself. The sound also varies according to what means are used to initiate it: sticks, wire brushes, mallets, and bare hands all produce different effects. (Listen to drummer Max Roach on Charlie Parker's "Ko-Ko" in the *Classics CD* for *Concise Guide to Jazz* and SCCJ. Roach plays snare drum with wire brushes for the introduction. Then he switches to playing ride cymbal with a drum stick for accompanying the solos. Roach can also be heard contributing spontaneous interjections by striking his snare drum with a drum stick and by striking the bass drum with a mallet that is mounted on a foot pedal.)

What has just been summarized is the basic drum set, "drum kit," or "set of traps." Most drummers also carry additional instruments such as extra cymbals, tom-toms, and Latin American percussion instruments. Until the 1960s, many drummers also had a cowbell (without its clapper) and a wood block (illustrated on the *Demo CD* Track 10).

The public often considers drummers merely to be timekeepers for a band. Though this is true in some bands, throughout jazz history drummers have also added sounds and rhythms that make music more colorful and exciting. Many of these colorful sounds do make the tempo explicit. However, the point here is that much jazz percussion work does not consist merely of timekeeping patterns. It consists of decoration for the band's sound. In other words, **the drummer acts as a colorist in addition to acting as a timekeeper**. In fact, some bands have employed drummers exclusively for coloristic playing instead of timekeeping. Instead of "drummer," the designation "percussionist" is frequently used to describe that role. (Listen to Dom Um Romao play in this manner on "Surucucu" at the end of the *Jazz Classics CD*.)

The drummer not only keeps time and colors the group sound, but he also **kicks and prods the soloist** in ways that relate to rhythms the pianist and bassist are using. The jazz drummer plays figures that underscore rhythms in the band arrangements. By the mid-1960s, the conception of jazz drumming had changed so much that the sounds made by drummers in some groups were in the forefront as much as melody instruments. The amount of interplay between drummers and other group members began to equal the amount of interplay previously expected only among the other instruments. (Listen to Elvin Jones play in this manner on "Your Lady" on the *Jazz Classics CD* for the *Concise Guide to Jazz* and

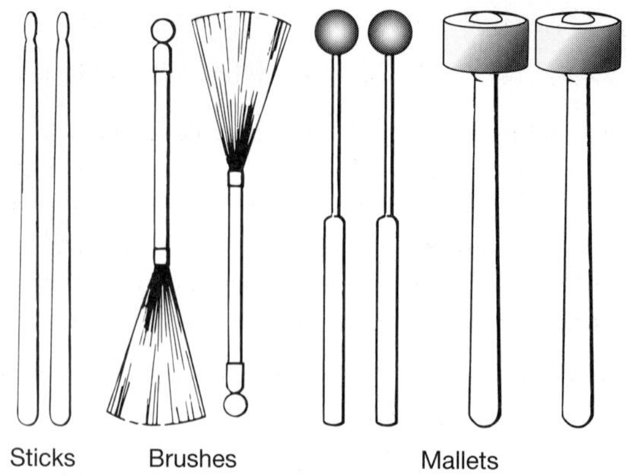

Figure 3.6 Sticks, brushes, mallets. (Listen to *Demo CD* Tracks 11–15 for examples.)

"The Promise" on the *Jazz Classics CD.*)[4] In addition, **by his own playing, a drummer can control the loudness level, sound texture, and mood of a combo's performance,** much as a conductor does with a symphony orchestra. (Listen to Tony Williams play in this manner on "Masqualero" on the *Jazz Classics CD.*)[5]

The 1970s saw a large number of combos using two or more drummers.[6] In some performances, all the drummers would function as colorists. However, in most performances, one player would be explicitly stating the beats on a standard drum set while the other colored the group sound using auxiliary percussion instruments. (This is evident on "Surucucu" on the *Jazz Classics CD.*)

Soloist

The jazz soloist learns to be aware of a number of important events while he is improvising. Although he cannot possibly be conscious of all of them all the time, he does manage to respond intuitively to most of them. Much successful jazz improvisation is largely the result of ultra-high-speed intuition. Here are **a few things the improvising soloist tries to do**:

1) *Remember the chord changes common to the tune he is playing.*[7]
2) *Create phrases compatible with the chord changes.*[8]
3) *Edit* his work so that each improvisation represents a clear musical statement.

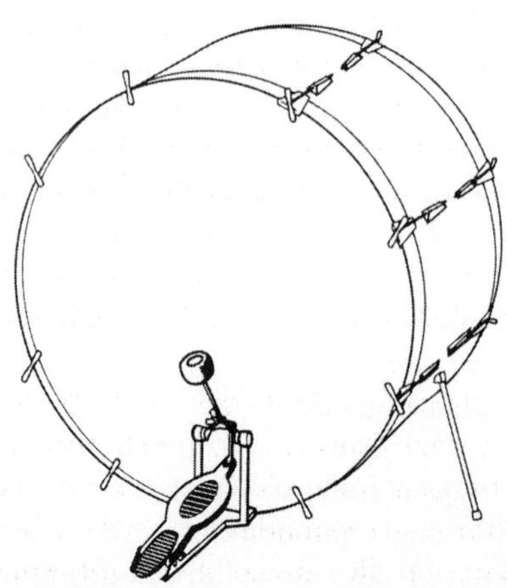

Figure 3.7 Bass drum—foot pedal.

4) *Think ahead* so that the phrases will fit together well.

5) *Remember what he has played* so that self-duplication does not occur.

6) *Swing* with the tempo of the piece. Incidentally, if you have been told that the rhythm section keeps time for the band, you might assume that steady tempo would not be maintained without a rhythm section. That is not true at all. Much jazz was originally dance music. So you might say that the rhythm section was keeping time to make the beat obvious for dancing. The improvising soloist keeps time to himself. The ability to keep perfect time enables a soloist to swing without a rhythm section or in spite of a bad one.

7) *Respond to the rhythmic figures of his accompanists* so that a creative interaction will occur instead of a monologue.

8) Keep loudness at a level which will *project* beyond the sound of the band and out to the audience.

9) *Play in tune and with the desired tone quality.*

10) *Remember how long he has been soloing* so that he can stop before he uses the time left for other soloists.

11) *Play in the mood of the piece.*

12) *Create something personal and original.*

This last point requires some clarification. An improviser's lines are not totally original in each and every performance. There are recurring themes in the improvisations of every jazz musician. In fact, these very themes combine with the player's own unique tone qualities and rhythmic feeling to help us identify his style. Using recurring themes is an accepted practice. Aspiring jazz musicians are advised to collect favorite "licks," those very themes and fragments which will later recur in their music and help us identify them. Most improvisers tend to play bits and pieces of lines they have played before, melodic figures they have practiced, and pet phrases of other improvisers. An improviser may actually play portions of a solo he remembers from another musician's recording. Sometimes an improviser will quote snatches of a pop tune or a classical piece. The bits and pieces that constitute a solo may not themselves be original, but the way in which they are combined often is.[9]

Jazz improvisations can be very intimate, personal creations. This is especially obvious when a soloist uses his instrument almost as an extension or substitute for his own voice. This is apparent when drummers can be seen mouthing their rhythmic figures. It is also evident when pianists and guitarists can be heard humming the lines they are playing. Pianists Keith Jarrett and Oscar Peterson are known for this, often to the distraction of their listeners. Guitarist George Benson has intentionally incorporated such tendencies into his style. He sings the same notes he is playing on guitar, and makes certain that the audience hears the mixture of his voice and his guitar. The result is a unique and compelling sound that he adds to recordings that otherwise feature only his guitar or voice.

◇ALTERNATIVES AVAILABLE TO THE IMPROVISER

Describing what an improvising soloist does must take into account the actual playing situation. Let's examine a few alternatives suggested by three different situations: playing alone, playing with chord instruments, and playing according to chord changes and steady tempo. The following descriptions are separated only for the sake of clarity. The rules listed in each category are not binding, and they are not necessarily exclusive to that category. The player probably never thinks in these terms, either. He responds intuitively to the requirements of each situation. Consider these three situations as groups of requirements that build upon each other in the order presented here. In other words, the rules increase as the adherence to musical forms and roles increases and as the number of players increases. The first situation is what has become known as "free jazz," whereas the third situation typifies improvisatory practices running from the 1930s until now.

If he is playing alone and not required to follow chord changes or keep time, he is free to play anything that comes to mind:

1) He can organize his notes in a melodic sequence or
2) just place them in a haphazard way.
3) He can use notes common to a single key,
4) switch keys occasionally, or
5) play in no key at all.
6) He can group his notes in a way that implies a tempo, or
7) use no tempo of any sort, either stated or implied.
8) He can play loudly or softly at will.

If he is playing with chording instruments such as piano and guitar, but not necessarily improvising on a tune or chord changes:

1) He must play notes which are compatible and in tune with the other sounds.
2) His notes should not make the ensemble sound cluttered—they must have clarity and balance.
3) He must sequence his notes so that they fit with what preceded them and what is likely to follow. This means paying attention to both the construction of his own line and its relationship to the lines of the other performers.
4) He must adjust the loudness of his playing in response to the group sound, though he might suddenly play louder or softer for the sake of contrast.
5) He might play melodically with such strength that he surfaces to the forefront of the ensemble sound, or
6) he might choose, at any moment, to play notes and rhythms which are subsidiary to those of another group member. Those sounds might help create an ensemble texture instead of a solo line.

If an improviser is playing according to chord changes and constant tempo:

1) His lines must reflect the direction set by the chord progression.[10]
2) He must maintain the tempo of the piece, and
3) swing in that tempo, letting the steadiness of tempo give momentum to his improvisation.

CHAPTER SUMMARY

1) Unwritten rules are followed that enable jazz improvisers to piece together respectable performances without rehearsal.
2) Musicians know many of the same tunes, and they follow common practices when performing tunes having twelve-bar blues and thirty-two-bar A-A-B-A construction.
3) Jazz musicians play the melody before and after they play improvisations that are guided by a cycle of repetitions of its accompaniment.
4) It sometimes sounds like the musicians are playing twice as fast (double-time) when they double the density of their activity or half as fast (half-time) when they halve the density of their activity, even though accompaniment chords change at the same rate throughout the performance of a given piece.
5) Jazz musicians are thoroughly trained in methods of playing their instruments, and in reading and writing music, and they know so many tunes and chord progressions that they can instantaneously respond to what each other plays when improvising.
6) Walking bass style involves playing notes that serve to keep time for the band as well as outlining the chord progression being followed by the improvisers.
7) The jazz drummer uses snare drum, bass drum, ride cymbal, and high-hat cymbals to keep time for the band as well as contribute kicks and prods that communicate with the improvising soloist.
8) Comping is the accompaniment style in which the pianist feeds chords to the improvising soloist in a flexible and syncopated way.
9) The improvising soloist keeps many considerations in mind while performing—chord progressions, logical and original construction of the solo, communication with accompanists, etc.

NOTES

1. A few of the thirty-two bar A-A-B-A pieces found on SCCJ are "Body and Soul" (once by Coleman Hawkins and once by Benny Goodman), "I Got Rhythm" (by Don Byas and Slam Stewart), "Lester Leaps In" and "Taxi War Dance" (by Count Basie with Lester Young), "I Can't Believe That You're In Love With Me" (Benny Carter), "Willow Weep For Me" (Art Tatum), "The Man I Love" (Coleman Hawkins), "Moten Swing" (Bennie Moten), and "Smoke Gets in Your Eyes" (Thelonious Monk). If you do not have access to SCCJ, and you do not have examples of any thirty-two bar A-A-B-A compositions listed on page 383, find a recording of "Honeysuckle Rose," "Undecided," "Moose the Mooch," "Roseland Shuffle," "Jumpin' at the Woodside," "Off Minor," "There Is No Greater Love," "Polka Dots and Moonbeams," "Stompin' at the Savoy," "Give Me the Simple Life," or Mel Torme's "Christmas Song" ("Chestnuts roasting on an open fire . . . "). Note that the format followed by musicians recording these tunes might not be identical to the routine described above, but at least their solos will probably adhere to the chord progression of the tune. It should not take much time or thought to determine how the musicians are handling the form. Just listen for such musical landmarks as turnarounds and bridges as described on pages 387–388 and on the *Demo CD* Track 33.
2. Classical musicians, however, call that practice "free rhythmic style," and they reserve the term "rubato" for designating the situation in which the tempo remains steady but part of the time originally occupied by some notes is robbed from them and used to extend the sound of other notes. In other words, classical musicians use the term rubato to indicate that a passage is not played exactly as written and that the relative durations of the notes are rearranged at the discretion of the performer.
3. An organ can be substituted for both the chord instrument and the bass in a band because bass lines can be played on the organ by means of foot pedals. But despite this advantage, most jazz organists actually play bass lines with the left hand, using the foot pedals for assistance. This technique restricts the organist to a single hand for playing chords underneath the solos of others. It leaves no extra hand for chording behind their own right-hand solos. The poor pianos and poor sound systems often furnished by night clubs compel many groups to bring their own portable electric piano or electric organ. Incidentally, if a band carries an organist, they don't have to pay salary for a bassist because their organist can supply bass lines.
4. Listen to the John Coltrane albums *Live at Birdland* (Impulse!/GRP: GRD-198 [A-50], 1963); and *Sun Ship* (Impulse!/GRP: IMPD-167 [9211], 1965); or the Miles Davis albums *Miles Smiles* (Columbia: CK 65682 [9401], 1966); and *Filles de Kilimanjaro* (Columbia: CK 46116 [9750], 1968).
5. Listen to the drumming on "Masqualero" on the Miles Davis album *Sorcerer* (Columbia: CK 65680 [9532], 1967) or on the *Jazz Classics CD*.
6. Listen to Weather Report, *I Sing the Body Electric* (Columbia: CK 46107 [31352], 1971–72); *Black Market* (Columbia: CK 34099, 1976); and *Sweetnighter* (Columbia: CK 64976 [32210], 1973); or Miles Davis, *Live-Evil* (Columbia: C2K 65135 [30954], 1970); and *On the Corner* (Columbia: CK 53579 [53579], 1972).
7. Occasionally, when the improviser is at a jam session or sitting in with an unfamiliar group, he may not know the chord progressions of the tune being played. He might know the melody but be unsure of some of the progressions. Or he might be requested to play a tune he once knew but whose progressions he has forgotten. In these cases, he listens to the rhythm section and determines the chord changes while he improvises. He can usually guess some of the progressions because he knows certain patterns that recur in hundreds of tunes. He can also determine the chords by listening to other soloists use them. Note, however, that he cannot always predict the chord progressions the rhythm section will play, because a tune can be harmonized in many different ways. This practice of altering chord progressions, **reharmonization**, is very common in jazz.
8. The concept of compatibility is very broad. Both the particular style and the individual player determine what notes are "compatible" with the chord changes. For example, some notes that are compatible for modern jazz of the 1940s are not compatible for jazz of the 1920s.
9. To understand the mechanics of a sound that a musical model produces and the phrases that he prefers, developing jazz musicians usually analyze, memorize, and then imitate the model's work. Once the player has mastered the techniques required to produce whatever sounds and phrases he wants, he usually develops variations of the learned imitations and mixes them with his own original ideas. The process of artistic development starting with imitation is not exclusive to jazz musicians. It has been employed by painters, writers, and composers for centuries. It may seem curious to the outsider, but the musician's practice of analyzing, memorizing, and imitating is not usually viewed as plagiarism (stealing another's idea and calling it your own), but rather as a necessary first step in the elaborate training process which jazz musicians undergo. If, however, the player never moves beyond the imitation phase and ends up living out his career sounding much like his model, he frequently elicits the dismay of music critics and, to a lesser extent, the disappointment of fellow musicians. But there are exceptions to this. Some players may be so proficient or play with such beauty that they earn admiration despite their failure to develop beyond the imitation stage. Sometimes imitation itself leads to innovation. For instance, tenor saxophonist Lester Young produced a tone quality that was unusual and highly influential for its time, partly because he was imitating the playing of Frankie Trumbauer, whose instrument was the smaller C-Melody saxophone. Almost as important to jazz history as Young was trumpeter Roy Eldridge, who created an innovative style by imitating jazz saxophonists instead of trumpeters.
10. Though jazz musicians in this situation usually play notes that fit with the underlying chords, improvisers are free to initiate lines that deviate from an otherwise strictly defined chord progression. But if the line is to sound good, the improviser's accompanists must listen and instantly follow suit. Frequently a hornman initiates the deviation, and the pianist responds with appropriate chords. Or a pianist can suggest alterations in harmony by what he plays. Then the hornman picks up the direction, and the ensemble works together with the alteration. Soloists can also play notes which are incompatible with the underlying chords, while the rhythm section maintains the preset progression. This is called playing "against the changes" or playing "outside," and it is used effectively by some soloists, including many of the saxophonists who soloed on Miles Davis records during the 1970s and 1980s.

Chapter Four

The Superior Orchestra. Photo Courtesy of William Ranson Hogan Jazz Archive, Tulane University.

Origins of Jazz

Jazz originated from styles of popular music that were blended to satisfy social dancers. It began developing during the 1890s in New Orleans, and it was fully formed by the early 1920s when it was recorded in New York, Los Angeles, and Chicago. Several different trends led to the birth of jazz. One was the practice of taking liberties with the melodies and accompaniments of tunes. This led to what we today call improvisation. Another was black Americans creating new kinds of music such as ragtime and blues. Ragtime provided some of the jazz repertory and made syncopated rhythms popular. Blues provided another portion of jazz repertory and popularized the practice of manipulating a melody note's pitch to produce a soulful effect. A third trend consisted of taking liberties with tone qualities. For instance, musicians cultivated rough and raspy sounds to add to their collection of smooth tone qualities.

A glance back at the experiences of Africans in America will help us understand how these different kinds of music came together. When African slaves were brought to America, they were not allowed to bring musical instruments. Moreover, villages and families of Africans were so thoroughly separated that many groups of slaves in America did not even have a single language in common. But they did bring their own musical tastes and a tradition of musical practices. This may explain why European music often sounded different when played in the New World by musicians of African ancestry. For example, some slaves modified European church hymns, folk songs, and dance music to fit their own tastes and traditions. Their children followed suit, and musical preferences were thereby passed down from generation to generation. In other words, jazz did not derive its similarities to African music from direct contact with African music. It acquired these characteristics secondhand, through other music that had developed by contact with African musical practices in the New World. Keep in mind also that there is much about jazz that has nothing to do with African music.[1]

◇WHY DID JAZZ ORIGINATE IN NEW ORLEANS?

Before analyzing the features of jazz in greater depth, let's first examine the setting in which it was born. We will begin with the history of ethnic diversity in New Orleans. The next three paragraphs are paraphrased from the work of James Haskins in his book *The Creoles of Color of New Orleans* (Crowell, 1975).

Ethnic Diversity and Creoles of Color

France began building New Orleans in 1718, and 147 black slaves were brought there in 1719. There were free blacks there as early as 1722. In 1763, France gave the territory of Louisiana to Spain as a gift. But Spanish rule was not firmly established until 1769, and despite Spanish rule, the language and customs there remained primarily French. In 1801, Spain ceded Louisiana back to France, but Spain continued to rule the territory until the United States bought it from France in 1803.

Significant social patterns can be traced back to that period of Spanish rule. Marriage between the different ethnic groups in Louisiana occurred more frequently at that time. Furthermore, the Spanish freed many slaves, thereby increasing the number of free blacks (there were 1,147 by 1789). Under Spanish rule, **free people of color began to be regarded as a class that was separate from the whites and the slaves, with status closer to that of whites**. Many light-skinned women of color became mistresses to white men and were set up as second families to the men in separate houses. This was common where there were more white men than white women. Sexual relations between blacks and whites prior to the mid-1800s led to a mixing of African and European traditions. The offspring from some of these unions were called *Creoles of Color.* Their ancestry was part African and part French. This distinguished them from the white Creoles, whose background was French and Spanish. Strictly speaking, Creole originally meant people speaking French and Spanish who were born in the New World. Creoles of Color were not referred to as Negro. That term was reserved for blacks who had little or no white ancestry.

Another event affected New Orleans Creoles at about this time. From 1791 to 1804, there was a slave revolt in Haiti against the white French and the Creole planters. This caused many free people of color from Haiti to move to New Orleans after, in 1809, being forced out of Cuba, where they had been given refuge. By 1810, the number of free people of color living in New Orleans had increased to 5,000. This made them the largest ethnic group there. The small white population reacted to their own minority status with fear. The whites captured business and governmental power. With that power, they began enacting laws ("black codes") and continued enacting laws for about 100 years which eroded the favored status of the Creoles of Color. These laws eventually placed Creoles of Color in the same position as Negroes. The process was slow. As late as 1830, Creoles of Color owned almost 2,500 slaves and continued to prosper in business. However, by the mid-1840s, life became so uncomfortable for them that many left New Orleans.

A sharp separation existed between the two groups of New Orleans residents who had African ancestry. Negroes lived in a racially mixed neighborhood, a large portion of which was uptown. They worked primarily as house servants and unskilled laborers. Many of the Creoles lived downtown in the area of New Orleans today known as the French Quarter. Creoles of Color were mostly well-educated, successful people—businessmen, physicians, landowners, and skilled craftsmen. They spoke French. Many owned slaves, and often required their slaves to speak French, too. Children in Creole families often received high-quality musical training. Some even travelled to Paris for study at a conservatory. The Creoles maintained a resident symphony orchestra, and supported an opera house. This reinforced the intensely musical orientation of New Orleans, a city that had three opera houses, far more than any other American city of comparable size. By comparison with residents of other regions, they took the pleasures of music and dance more seriously.

The Blues

The vocal music of the uptown blacks in New Orleans included African American work songs, devised to ease the burden of laborers, and African American religious music that was a compromise between European church music and African vocal style. Another kind of black vocal music was the cry of the street vendor, a kind of music which capitalized on expressive variations in pitch and voice quality. (Listen to the first selection on the *Jazz Classics CD.*) These sounds had evolved into a new form of music by the first decade of the twentieth century. It began as an unaccompanied solo vocal style but eventually used guitar or banjo as accompaniment. The chords in this accompaniment were originally almost incidental to the melodic line—whatever chords the singer could play. The progression of chords was simple. Sometimes only two or three different chords were used in an entire song. Lyrics and melody lines were also simple, with brief pauses between phrases and much repetition. This was the form of music we now call *the blues.* (See pages 375–384 for full explanation. Listen to the *Demo CD* for demonstration of its accompaniment chord progression. Listen to Bessie Smith sing "Sobbin' Hearted Blues" on the *Jazz Classics CD* for *Concise Guide to Jazz.*)

This social history pertains to jazz because it helps us appreciate the origins of the intensely musical orientation of New Orleans. Creoles of Color, like the white Creoles, wholeheartedly favored European music, including French wind band and European concert traditions. Meanwhile, some music played by Negroes retained aspects of African musical practices. Though many Negro musicians received musical training in the European styles, their music was generally less refined than that of the Creoles. It may have included improvisation. In summary, many European concert traditions were absorbed and maintained by Creole music, and some African traditions were preserved in Negro music.

The Need for Live Music

To help us appreciate the setting in which jazz emerged, historian-musicologist Karl Koenig encourages us to envision life at the beginning of the twentieth century. Let's follow his observations, paraphrased in the next seven paragraphs from his writings.

To understand the effects of living in an age without the electronic devices we now possess, imagine trying to amuse yourself on a night in the New Orleans area. You could not listen to any radio or television programs, records, or tapes. You could not call anyone on the telephone or visit movie theaters or video arcades. Candlelight would be needed for reading. However, you could go to the town park or square, which would be illuminated by gas lamps. There you could buy flavored ices from a vendor, exchange pleasantries with your neighbors, and take a walk in the moonlight. You could also listen and dance to the local band. In other words, there almost had to be music, *live* music. A town without a band was a very dull place to be. The social and fraternal organizations knew this, as did the newspapers and commercial establishments. Therefore sponsorship was provided for most of the local bands by churches (mostly Catholic), social and benevolent clubs, fraternal clubs (Elks, Masons, etc.), fire departments, townships, undertakers, and plantation owners.[2]

Brass Bands

The band was present at almost every social activity, most of which took place outdoors: picnics, sporting events, political speeches, or dramatic presentations at the town hall, and dances in the open-air pavilions. Dancing was the main social activity of the nineteenth century. The band played before the event and for the dance that followed. A large brass band was used so that the music could be heard in outdoor settings. Note that in the narrowest sense, a "brass band" has only brass instruments (such as cornet and trombone) plus drums and cymbals. But the early Louisiana bands also included a clarinet and later a saxophone. (These are technically known as "woodwinds," even when not constructed entirely of wood; see photographs on page 86.) When the social activity was held indoors, a large band was not needed. There the smaller "string band" was suitable. It was often comprised of cornet, violin, guitar, bass, and piano, or some combination of those instruments.

There were bands in the New Orleans area long before the Civil War. Then, during the war, occupation by Union troops exposed the city to many more. About thirty different regimental bands of the occupying forces were stationed in and around New Orleans. They were very conspicuous. They played for the many military ceremonies and for concerts of patriotic and popular music. Their presence was an additional stimulus for the band tradition in New Orleans.

Ragtime

By the end of the 1800s, **ragtime** was very popular in New Orleans. The word "rag" refers to a kind of music that was put together like a military march and had rhythms borrowed from African American banjo music. You could tell ragtime music because many of the loud accents fell in between the beats. This is called syncopation. Musicians would use syncopation on all kinds of different tunes and say they were "ragging" those tunes. So the term "to rag" came to mean giving a piece of music a distinctly syncopated or ragged-time feeling. "Ragtime" ordinarily refers to a kind of written piano music that first appeared in the 1890s. The most famous composer of this style was Scott Joplin (1868–1917). (Listen to Joplin's "Maple Leaf Rag" in SCCJ.) The term has also been used to identify an entire era of music, not exclusively written piano music. For example, between the 1890s and the 1920s, there were ragtime bands, ragtime singers, and ragtime banjo players, in addition to ragtime pianists. Many of the musicians we classify today as "jazz musicians" called themselves "ragtime" musicians. Because of this, some scholars consider ragtime to have been the first jazz style. However, ragtime was not a jazz style in the strict sense. It involved only limited improvisation, and it lacked what is today called jazz swing feeling. Instead we can say that ragtime was a forerunner of jazz. It popularized using accents before and after the beat instead of always directly on it. Today jazz musicians play "around" the beat partly because ragtime made the practice popular.

Combining Influences

During the 1890s, there were bands in almost every small town and settlement in southern Louisiana, and their music reflected several influences. It combined march music and ragtime. Moreover, these two styles were interrelated. John Philip Sousa, the famous bandleader, had included ragtime pieces in his band concerts, and ragtime pianists often performed Sousa marches in a ragtime style. Another influence was music of the Mexican bands that visited New Orleans. Musicians from these bands settled in and around New Orleans, and some became music teachers. Their music was respected and enjoyed so much that it influenced the styles of New Orleans trumpet players.

Band music influenced jazz quite directly. By the beginning of the twentieth century, New Orleanians were accustomed to hearing brass bands such as Sousa's and Arthur Pryor's, having already heard Patrick Gilmore's military bands of the Gulf Coast Command. Music for dances held in the middle 1800s was often provided by the military band that was stationed in the region. In fact, the march form was sometimes modified and used as dance music. Later, a popular dance called the "twostep" was done to march-like music. Moreover, the way the themes were organized in ragtime pieces followed the pattern found in marches. Eventually roles of various instruments were transferred from marching band to jazz band. For instance, the flute and piccolo parts from march arrangements were imitated by jazz clarinetists. In the typical marching drum part, the bass drum played on beats

Scott Joplin, the leading composer of ragtime piano music. His pieces and their syncopations influenced the development of early jazz playing styles.

Photo courtesy of New York Public Library.

one and three while the snare drum, with its sharper sound, played on beats two and four. In early jazz there is a correspondingly heavy emphasis on beats two and four. (See pages 364–366 for more explanation; listen to the "Dixie Jazz Band One-Step" in the *Jazz Classics CD* and notice its similarity to march music.)

Party Atmosphere

Other factors besides the brass band movement made New Orleans an ideal setting for the birth of jazz. New Orleans was a center of commerce because of its proximity to the mouth of the Mississippi River, a flourishing trade route for America, the Caribbean, and Europe. Because the city was a seaport, it catered to travelers from all over the world, and New Orleans maintained a cosmopolitan party atmosphere. There were numerous taverns and dance halls. One aspect of the entertainment it provided was a famous prostitution district known as Storyville. It took its name from an alderman (city councilman), Sidney Story, who drafted legislation that sectioned off a portion of the town in 1897 and limited prostitution to that area. **The reason the party atmosphere of New Orleans is important to the beginning of jazz is that it generated so much work for musicians. There was so much demand for live music that there was a continuous need for fresh material. This caused musicians to stretch styles. They blended, salvaged, and continuously revised odd assortments of approaches and material. This ultimately became jazz**. Karl Koenig has offered this as the key explanation for the origin of jazz.

Dance Music

Now let's delve a bit more deeply into what probably occurred at the time jazz was born. Ordinarily jazz is thought to have derived from blues and rags that were popular in New Orleans. However, only a few pieces in the repertory of New Orleans brass bands were rags, and—at least between 1905 and 1915—twelve-bar blues pieces were not as common as we would expect if we designated these groups as "jazz" bands. In other words, our current notion of "jazz repertory" is not really reflected in the music of the first jazz musicians.

Unlike most of today's jazz, the earliest jazz was intended mostly for dancing, not just for listening. The music's beat, form, and spirit interested dancers the most. The evolution of new dances and the overall popularity of dancing were big factors in the evolution of jazz. Dancers were not necessarily impressed by the wonders of collective improvisation or the inspirations of well-crafted solo improvisations. They responded more to new jazz rhythms.

The musicians who performed the first jazz have said that their repertory was constructed primarily to accompany dances such as the mazurka, schottische, quadrille, and one-step. These musicians, whom today we call "jazz players," were not hired specifically to play jazz.

At the beginning of the twentieth century, New Orleans parade bands and dance bands shared the same musicians and much of the same repertory. It was almost as though the musicians walked directly from the street parade into the dance hall, often putting down a brass instrument and picking up a violin. The performing groups that accompanied dances were termed "string bands" or "orchestras"—violin, guitar, bass viol, and one or two wind instruments, played by the same musicians who had paraded with trumpet and trombone. To satisfy the demands of dancers, these musicians often combined music from different sources. Sometimes they ended up creating new sounds that were very compelling rhythmically. These approaches became the core of jazz style, and their manner of playing led to the idea that jazz is not *what* you play, but *how* you play it. In other words, **jazz was an outgrowth of treatments for many kinds of music being played on the demand of dancers**. Today we call these same musicians "jazz musicians," and their music "New Orleans jazz" or "Dixieland," though some people reserve the term "Dixieland" solely for the music of white bands. **Because their audiences liked ragtime so much, the musicians adapted repertory from many sources, often syncopating ("ragging") otherwise unsyncopated pieces, often lending rhythmic vitality to pieces that lacked it.**

In parades as well as dance halls, small bands were trying to perform music originally written for large bands. Their compromises led to what became standard Dixieland style and instrumentation. In trying to fill out the sound, more activity was required of each player, so musicians improvised parts to order. They got in the habit of improvising, and, as jazz evolved, this habit changed from a necessity into a choice. In essence, the musicians in New Orleans were combining diverse materials to please people who had a taste for special kinds of musical excitement. Jazz originated directly in the instrumentation, repertory, and musical practices of brass bands and string bands that were active before the 1920s.

◇WHY DID JAZZ EMERGE NEAR THE TURN OF THE CENTURY?

There are several factors that might explain why jazz emerged when it did. (1) The intensity of musical activity in New Orleans was especially high at the beginning of the twentieth century. Karl Koenig has noted that (2) the origin of jazz coincides with the zenith of popularity for the brass concert band in America. Koenig reminds us that (3) this was a very fertile time because there was so much work for musicians, there were so many bands, plenty of motivation to play varied styles, and almost all the musicians listened to each other's music. Also, (4) because of the popularity of the ragtime style, there was incentive to "rag" music from nonrag sources. This resulted in improvising syncopations into the performance of compositions that did not necessarily bear much syncopation.

Similarly, as the twentieth century began, (5) the popularity of blues encouraged musicians to play band instruments in a bluesy way even when not playing a blues piece. This was especially common in music for a dance called the " slow drag."

Another factor is the cumulative effect of social and legal changes in Louisiana that gradually resulted in Creoles being consigned to the same low status the Negroes had. Remember that between the beginning of the 1800s and the beginning of the 1900s, distinctions between "pure" and "mixed" ancestry were increasingly ignored. All citizens with any African ancestry were consigned to the same category. Creoles were forced to give up the status they had attained during the 1700s. They had to assume the status of Negroes and mix socially and occupationally with Negroes. Though the Creoles resented this, jazz was the ultimate benefactor because this readjustment further facilitated the blending of European traditions (as represented by the Creoles) with African traditions (as represented by the Negroes).

An African Heritage of Musical Tastes

Before beginning a more detailed examination of jazz elements, we must consider some important qualifications regarding the mixing of styles. When African American ragtime and blues began affecting the performance of other kinds of music, some observers contended that the race of the musician was responsible for the particular way the music was played. For example, many listeners felt that the highly rhythmic nature of African American forms reflected a rhythmic talent that came with the race of the musician. Yet these observers overlooked the fact that most musical preferences are probably learned, not genetic. Preferences for certain African techniques were indeed passed down from generation to generation by imitation and instruction. But slaves also learned European music that was available. For example, by the mid-1800s, there were highly accomplished concert artists in the European style who had slavery backgrounds. (Conversely, by the 1920s, there were highly accomplished jazz musicians whose backgrounds were strictly European and white.) It is not reasonable to expect all music played by blacks to sound African. No one inherits desires for music of any particular region; there is no "racial unconscious" that is transmitted genetically. Remember that in New Orleans, most black and Creole musicians played European types of dance music such as mazurkas, waltzes, polkas, and quadrilles. They had to, or they would not be hired. The fact that these New Orleans musicians had African ancestry was irrelevant to the music they played. So, as you consider the next few pages of analysis, keep in mind that (1) when we speak of African traditions, we are referring only to tastes for particular ways of making music; (2) these tastes were conveyed more by American Negro culture than by Creole culture; (3) the opportunity to alter established styles, and thereby season to taste, was capitalized upon by African Americans in such highly creative ways that the result was ragtime, blues, jazz, rock, and funk music; but (4) many Americans of African descent never had such preferences, and many whites did. Incidentally, by the 1980s, African American musical styles had become the most popular in the world, not just among people of African descent, but among all races in every geographic region.

◇WHAT IS AFRICAN AND WHAT IS EUROPEAN ABOUT JAZZ?

Most innovators in jazz have been African American and, until recently, a disproportionately high percentage of jazz musicians was African American. These facts lead us to ask whether jazz contains characteristics of African music that might have filtered into it through the African American culture that produced so many of its practitioners. The question is impossible to answer, however, because African music and European music have so many elements in common and because both were available as models when jazz was forming. But it remains interesting to consider the possibilities. So now we are going to examine some features of jazz, keeping in mind African and European sources.

Improvisation

The first feature of jazz we are going to examine is improvisation, the practice of **spontaneously varying individual parts**. It has been an important element of music since the beginning of time, and only recently in history was it difficult to find in European concert music. Improvisation characterizes some African music and much jazz. Musicologists are uncertain about the extent to which African American music retained improvisatory traditions from African music. Let's first consider improvisation in music of cultures that contributed slaves to the New World. For instance, in the typical drum ensemble of Ghana, the lead drummer is in charge of giving signals. His part is more variable than any of the others, so it might be regarded as improvised. In the Mandinka drum ensemble, the senior player has leeway to improvise more than the others, but all members are allowed to slightly vary their parts as they play. Some African singing in leader-and-chorus format allows spontaneous variations in the leader's part, as in "Hunter's Dance" on the *Jazz Classics CD.* To keep this in perspective, we must note, however, that these practices come nowhere near the extent of improvisation that is found today in jazz. In the West African singing and the African American blues singing that evolved from it, improvisations did not consist of inventing elaborate melody lines as eventually became common for jazz improvisers. Instead, these singers channeled their creativity into altering the sound of a single sustained tone, varying the timing, pitch, and timbre at its beginning and ending. They also improvised by toying with the rhythms of melodies. Tones would be started a bit earlier or later. Or a given tone might be repeated several times in succession instead of being sung only once. Similarly, a tone might be started, then softened, and then pushed again by an abrupt increase in volume. Sometimes whole phrases would be placed differently in relation to the underlying beat. This is known as *rhythmic displacement.* Incidentally, these techniques are still evident in performances of gospel music by African American singers and in gospel-influenced styles of pop music, such as the singing of Aretha Franklin and James Brown. (These practices are evident in the three samples of vocal music at the beginning of the *Jazz Classics CD.*)

The reason we discuss singing at this point in a textbook about instrumental jazz is that these vocal practices are thought to have influenced the styles used by jazz musicians who played trumpet, trombone, clarinet, and saxophone. (That is why the beginning of the *Jazz Classics CD* has an instrumental demonstration by Miles Davis directly following the cry of the African American street vendor.) Individual creativity and unorthodox means for learning how to play instruments have also been suggested as roots for pitch and timbre improvisation in horn work. Some musicologists believe that demand for live music was so great in New Orleans that many unpolished amateurs were called upon to perform as professionals, and the incomplete mastery these players had over their instruments gave us the collection of raw, unorthodox sounds we now associate with New Orleans jazz. Imitation of singing style, however, is the most popular explanation among musicologists. In addition, some scholars believe that the spirit of improvisation and the stress on individuality in jazz stem from African traditions. But these traits are also found in America within non-African folk music as well. So a striving for individuality among jazz musicians could be, but is not necessarily or exclusively, an extension of African preferences or what has been called "the black esthetic."

Now let's consider what European music could have contributed to the origins of improvisation in jazz. In America there was already a well-developed European tradition for improvising by the time jazz had begun. Improvised ornaments were common in pre-twentieth-century concert music, and they have long been common in folk music and popular music. Within informal American music prior to the emergence of jazz, there are also precedents for improvisation in the form of musicians making spontaneously varied entrances. Often singers start notes whenever they feel like it instead of singing precisely in unison with the others. This is termed *heterophony,* sounding to our ears like ensemble "sloppiness." It is also notable that improvised variations were common parts of solo recital format for some keyboard artists. During the 1800s, concert pianists often improvised within the encore number of their program. And there existed a French and German keyboard tradition for improvisation called *preluding.* Some early American musicians were even required to be able to improvise a piece on demand, using phrases supplied by their audience. So it is clear that the practice of making up music as you go along is precedented in both West African and European music. Both of these traditions could have influenced the use of improvisation in jazz.

Now consider improvisation among New Orleans musicians at the beginning of the twentieth century. At least as late as 1923, the improvisational creativity of the players was directed primarily at piecing together band routines. Some routines, however, were spontaneously devised during performances, thereby qualifying as improvised. The skeletons for these routines were often provided by published arrangements that were known among musicians as "stocks." For the first few run-throughs, many of the parts were not fixed. Trombone counterlines, clarinet obbligatos, and trumpet variations of the melody were sometimes invented and performed spontaneously. Accompaniments were improvised and varied by the more adventurous and creative players. After a suitable set of parts had been worked out, the musicians frequently remained relatively loyal to them. A striving for improvisation was not as central to a jazz esthetic as it has become. The extent to which new melodies were freshly improvised during performance was limited. There was, however, a striving for personalization and individualization which did not require improvisation, at least in the sense that the term is used here. Though the seeds were planted in New Orleans, it is possible that the kind and the extent of jazz improvisation known today did not first emerge there.[3]

By the late 1920s, these improvisational tendencies had expanded to the extent of improvisation we usually expect from most jazz today. Unfortunately, we do not know why this change occurred. A few possibilities are (1) boredom with fixed routines; (2) a need to learn new material without recourse to sheet music; (3) increased interest in bravura solo excursions and emergence of the "star" system of players; (4) a continuation of European and/or African traditions for spontaneous alteration; (5) unbridled creativity; (6) longer dances necessitating stretching out the numbers, that, in turn, led to solos that give other hornmen time to rest their lips; and (7) a combination of these reasons.

Syncopation

Next let's consider **syncopation**, a rhythmic phenomenon most easily understood as accents that don't occur on a main beat. (For more technical explanation, see pages 366–369. To hear the difference between unsyncopated and syncopated playing, listen to the piano comping demonstrations on the *Demo CD* Track 20.) Syncopation is common in both African and European music, though Africa is especially known for highly syncopated music. Some syncopation in jazz is thought to derive from African American banjo music and ragtime. Some is thought to stem from the heterophony discussed above. The taste for syncopation that exists among jazz musicians might stem, in part, from musical preferences for *rhythmic contrast,* which musicologist Olly Wilson has shown to prevail among many African and African American styles of music.

Harmony

A third feature of jazz is **harmony**. Though harmony is found in African music, the chord progressions in jazz are not common to native African music. European music provided chord progressions of the type that jazz uses. (For explanation of chord progressions, see pages 369–388. To hear demonstrations, listen to Tracks 16–19 on the *Demo CD.*)

Instruments

A fourth feature of jazz is the choice of instruments. Where did the earliest jazz groups derive their **instrumentation**? The European brass band provided the model that included trumpet, trombone, clarinet, saxophone, and tuba. The black and the white fraternal bands that were plentiful in New Orleans at the beginning of the twentieth century used brass band instrumentation; and they played marches and pop tunes for parades, picnics, dances, and funerals. The region of Africa that supplied slaves for the New World did not have musical instruments that closely resembled the trumpet, clarinet, trombone, or saxophone.

What about drums? The drums of West Africa can be found in some modern jazz groups. The drums used in the earliest jazz, however, were from European-style brass bands. (See illustrations in the previous chapter.) The wood block and cowbell, two other percussion instruments used in the manner of drums, have been heard in jazz since the earliest recordings. (Listen to wood block on the *Demo CD* and in "Dixie Jazz Band One-Step" on the *Jazz Classics CD*.) They are thought to have African ancestry, though China and Turkey have also contributed forerunners for many similar instruments in the New World. (Incidentally, the way the ride cymbal is used in jazz is very similar to the way West African musicians play their atoke or karinyan, a slender, iron instrument, technically classed as a clapperless bell.)

What about stringed instruments? The earliest jazz bands frequently employed banjo (see Fig. 4.1), an African American instrument that descended from the African halam. They also employed guitar, which has a European ancestry. The bass viol was also common in early jazz, and it too came from Europe. (See illustration on page 19.)

Role of Percussion

A fifth feature of jazz is the **prominent role of percussion**. Most jazz groups include a drummer who plays a set of assorted instruments and provides almost continuous timekeeping sounds, thereby generating musical excitement. (Listen to the *Demo CD* Tracks 1–15,

FIGURE 4.1 Guitar and banjo (note that the guitar has six tuning pegs, one for each string, and the banjo has four). Guitars appear in a variety of shapes. The one pictured here is a guitar used in early jazz. Electric guitars are usually solid slabs of wood with electronic attachments embedded. Basically, a banjo is a drum with a guitar-like neck and strings. The banjo commonly used in early jazz had four strings, but some banjos have as many as nine strings.

and see pages 20–24 for illustrations and commentary.) Essentially, by adding a drummer to a string band, you have an early jazz band. Dancing to quadrilles, for example, did not require percussion. So historically, drums were an important addition to dance bands that lent them a "jazz sound." Drums are very important in much African music, too. And percussion is important in brass band music of European traditions as well as in some European folk dance music, such as Irish.

A feature related to the role of percussion in jazz is playing melodic instruments in highly rhythmic or percussive ways. Nonpercussion instruments are used in these ways in many other kinds of music, too. But the extent to which melodic instruments are used this way is outstanding in jazz. It resembles the way melody instruments are employed in Africa. Olly Wilson has called this *rhythmization.*

Roughenings, Buzzes, and Ringings

A sixth feature of jazz is the presence of **rough sounds, buzzes, and ringings**. Preferences for these kinds of sounds are thought to derive from African musical tastes and African traditions for improvising on tone quality. For instance, jazz drummers sometimes place a key chain atop the ride cymbal to create a sustained hiss or ringing sound. Some drummers insert rivets in a cymbal so that the vibration of the rivets against the cymbal creates a sizzle sound. Many jazz saxophonists cultivate a rasping tone quality. Saxophonist John Coltrane produced a wide range of sound qualities, from smooth to guttural, from full to shrieking. He can be heard in "So What" on SCCJ, "Flamenco Sketches" and "The Promise" on the *Jazz Classics CD.* Listen for the raw tone qualities of soloists on Duke Ellington's "Harlem Airshaft" and the gruff tone quality of saxophonist Ben Webster on "Cottontail" on the *Jazz Classics CD.* Compare this with the occasionally rough quality in the male lead singer's voice on "One Day." On the *Jazz Classics CD,* you can hear jazz trumpeters and trombonists play in a rough "growl" style—trumpeter Cootie Williams at the beginning of "Cottontail," and trombonist Joe Nanton on "Harlem Airshaft." Other evidence of a taste for rough sounds and buzzes is the jazz brassman's preoccupation with the tone-altering potential of mutes. (For details, see page 390, and listen to Tracks 63–68 of the *Demo CD.* Listen to Joe Oliver's muted cornet solo on "Dippermouth Blues" and Cootie Williams's on "Concerto for Cootie" in SCCJ.)

Repetition of Brief Patterns

A seventh feature of jazz is the **extensive repetition of brief patterns**. Musicians use the term *ostinato* (from the Italian word for "obstinate") to describe the brief, repetitive patterns we are discussing. Ostinato is common in many different kinds of music, but it is a distinguishing trait of African music and jazz. One example is the ride rhythm. You can hear it on the *Demo CD* Track 7, and in the West African "Hunter's Dance" at the beginning of the *Jazz Classics CD.* Another example of extensive repetition is the style of figure played by the left hand of the boogie-woogie pianist. (Listen to Meade Lux Lewis play "Honky Tonk Train" in SCCJ.) Other examples can be found in brief, repetitive bass figures common to jazz/rock fusion, as in recordings by Herbie Hancock and Weather Report from the 1970s and 1980s. There is extensive repetition of short phrases called *riffs* in some jazz styles of the 1930s and 1940s as well as in jazz-rock of the 1970s and 1980s. Both of these are illustrated at the beginning of the *Jazz Classics CD*—the riff band style in Count Basie's "One O'Clock Jump" and the jazz-rock in Weather Report's "Birdland." These characteristics came from accompaniment rhythms in folk music and march music that were popular in America at the same time. Some came from ragtime and military drumming. Using these musical devices contributes to swing feeling. The effect of these devices in African music is so similar to their effect in jazz that musicologists believe a taste for this effect was retained in African American culture, and it ultimately caused these practices to emerge in jazz. Though scholars are not unanimous about this, most consider jazz swing feeling to be an African or an African American contribution to jazz.

Joe "King" Oliver's Creole Jazz Band, 1923: Baby Dodds (drums), Honore Dutrey (trombone), Oliver (cornet), Louis Armstrong (cornet), Bill Johnson (bass viol), Johnny Dodds (clarinet), Lil Hardin (piano).

Photo courtesy of The Cleveland Press Collection/Cleveland State University Archives.

Polyrhythms

An eighth feature of jazz is **the practice of sounding different rhythms at the same time**. In particular is the sounding of some rhythms that have a basis of two pulses while sounding other rhythms that have a basis of three pulses. The combination is called a **polyrhythm**. It contributes to the swing feeling and rhythmic excitement of jazz because it creates tensions within the listener, who can neither resist following either division of pulses nor reconcile the two. (See page 369 for more explanation, and listen for moments of such rhythmic conflict in John Coltrane's "The Promise" on the *Jazz Classics CD* and in James P. Johnson's "Carolina Shout" in SCCJ.)

Much of the polyrhythmic construction in jazz comes from the inventiveness of the musicians, not necessarily from the imitation of pre-existing models. We know this to be true, for example, in some work by drummers Max Roach and Elvin Jones. (Listen to Jones on "The Promise" on the *Jazz Classics CD*.) But some polyrhythms in early jazz are thought to be borrowed from combinations of rhythms found in ragtime. Note that polyrhythms are also employed in European folk music and concert music that were present in America before jazz originated, and they are prominent in African music. If derived from ragtime, these polyrhythms in jazz have a partly African ancestry because ragtime has roots in an African American banjo tradition. Olly Wilson believes jazz musicians' preference for polyrhythmic construction reflects a tradition retained from African preference for rhythmic contrast. However, we must not overlook its long use in European music, too, even though it seems somewhat less prominent there than in African music.

The Ways Tones Are Decorated

A ninth feature of jazz is the assortment of **ways in which tones are decorated**. Some of these came to us from practices in European classical, opera, and folk music. Some came by way of West African practices. Some originated in the New World from blending and expanding European and African tendencies. We have already discussed a preference for rough timbres as our sixth feature of jazz. Now let's examine alterations of pitch. Study

Explanation of Vibrato

To understand vibrato, imagine a sustained tone as a straight line.

Now imagine the pitch of that tone oscillating, that is, becoming alternately higher and lower. The up and down motion of the line represents the slight changes in pitch which constitute vibrato.

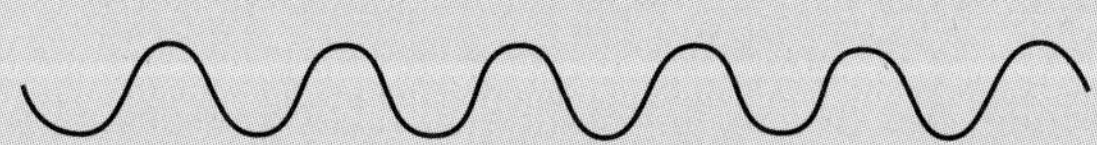

We often tend to take vibrato for granted, because it can be almost imperceptible. But if you listen carefully to sustained tones in the work of most singers, violinists, saxophonists, trombonists, and trumpeters, you will hear it.

Vibrato can be present or absent, fast or slow, regular or irregular. Many jazz singers and some jazz instrumentalists tend to start vibrato slowly and then increase its rate so that it is fastest at the end of the note.

This contrasts with the practice of musicians in symphony orchestras who tend to maintain an even rate of vibrato through a tone's complete duration. They employ different rates of vibrato for different styles of composition, however, and many use no vibrato at all.

Vibrato is considered an expressive device. It can also be a prime characteristic for differentiating styles. Early jazz players tended to use much quicker vibratos than modern jazz players. The fast vibrato was undoubtedly a characteristic contributing to the popular description of early jazz as "hot," while modern jazz of the 1940s and 50s with its slower vibrato was "cool." During the 1960s and 70s, many jazz saxophonists employed faster vibrato than was common during the 1940s and 50s. Saxophonists of the 1980s often used a regular rate of vibrato, rather than increasing it near the end of the tone. If you compare music from these periods, you will notice distinct differences in feeling, partly due to the vibrato rate.

Examples of Pitch Bends

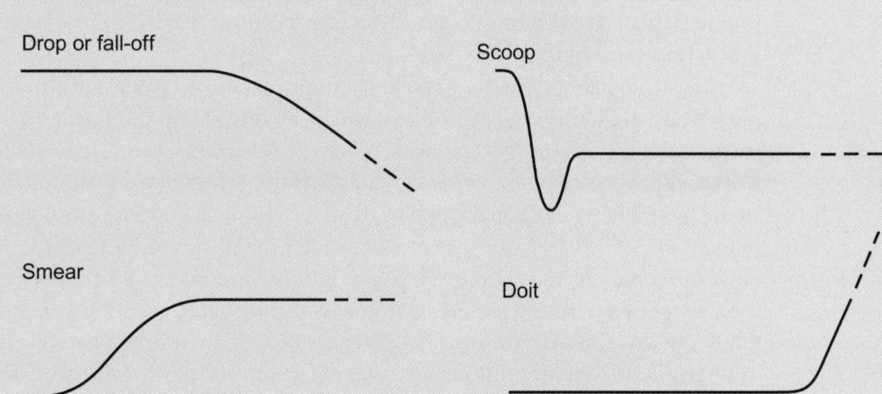

Tracks 46–58 of the *Demo CD* to understand what is meant by "pitch bending" and "pitch manipulation." Listen until you can identify the occurrence of no vibrato, slow vibrato, fast vibrato, terminal vibrato, drop, scoop, smear, and doit. Then study the first six minutes of the *Jazz Classics CD* where many examples can be found. Notice them in the music of the street vendor ("Street Cries") letting pitch fall at the end of his notes, the male gospel singer ("One Day") who toys with the pitches at the beginnings of his notes, the clarinetist ("Dixie Jazz Band One-Step") who smears the pitches at the end of his notes, and Miles Davis ("Strawberries") using his horn to imitate the street vendor by placing pitch bends in the middle of his notes. Listen to this music while you keep in mind the dimensions of sound that the jazz improviser can alter in his tone: duration, intensity, pitch (vibrato is a steady alternation of pitch), quality (roughness, for example), attack (how a note begins), and decay (how a note ends). Listen to selections 1–4 on the *Jazz Classics CD* several times. They go by quickly, but you will notice more decorations of tones each time you listen.

Blue Notes

A tenth feature of jazz is the **blue note**. This is a concept best understood by listening to the examples on the *Demo CD* Tracks 54–58 and studying the discussion on page 380. You can gain a rough idea of what the term means by imagining the piano keyboard to represent the entire selection of pitches which musicians are allowed to draw upon. Then imagine how notes would sound if drawn from finer gradations of pitch, as though produced by piano keys existing in the cracks between the ordinary arrangement of keys. The notes that come out from "between the cracks" are blue notes. European music's pitch system, as represented by the piano's seven white keys and five black keys, does not provide all the intervals needed by West African music. Thus, sometimes when Africans performed European-style music, they sang using their own intervals. The sound of these intervals in reference to our ear's expectations was "blue." This is the area of musical performance we call *intonation.* This manner of toying with the pitch of notes is an expressive device that has become a jazz tradition. Though not used by all jazz musicians—they are impossible for pianists—blue notes are common in jazz horn playing. Some of these pitches, which in formal European music constitute "playing out of tune" or "off-key," are common in jazz. They are not ordinarily considered mistakes or the result of incomplete mastery of the musician's instrument. That such "out-of-tune" playing is prominent in so many styles of jazz reflects an esthetic of pitch flexibility more than any player's lack of ability to play "in tune." In other words, the kind of out-of-tune playing found in jazz is usually intentional, and it is used as a central element of the art. This might represent a retention of African or African American musical practices. However, such "neutral" pitches, as they are technically termed, were not exclusive to African traditions. They were also present in Anglo-American and Scotch-Irish folk music that was heard in early America.

Musicologists generally believe that approaches to pitch and timbre among jazz horn players are not a direct imitation of African singing. They stem instead from imitating wide-ranging, imaginative sounds found in New World vocal idioms such as Negro field hollers, work songs, cries of street vendors, and the blues. The bluesy manipulations of pitch that are found in jazz horn work stem, in part, from imitating approaches to singing that were devised in the New World by blacks, as demonstrated in the first minute of the *Jazz Classics CD.* In New Orleans, the most bluesy interpretations of dance music were frequently associated with black musicians.[4] Some of this was perpetuated in the humorous, novelty effects ("hokum" style) used by minstrel show musicians. The tendency to playfully vary the sounds of instruments might stem in part from African traditions. However, similar musical traditions also existed in other ethnic groups in New Orleans at the same time, so these practices do not necessarily reflect exclusively African American sources.

Listening Guide for

"STREET CRIES"

Available on the *Jazz Classics CD*, side 1; "Street Cries of Charleston" also available on *The Riverside History of Classic Jazz* (Riverside: 3RBCD-005-2, 3CD set); "Fishermen, Strawberry, and Devil Crab" is also on Miles Davis, *Porgy and Bess* (Columbia: CK 65141, 1958).

This comparison illustrates traditions for expressive inflections of pitch in both African American vocal and jazz instrumental styles. First is the call of an African American street vendor advertising the blackberries he is trying to sell. This recording was made early in the twentieth century in Charleston, South Carolina. Second is an excerpt from a piece called "Fishermen, Strawberry and Devil Crab" in an instrumental version that Miles Davis made in 1958 of George Gershwin's opera, "Porgy and Bess." The opera was inspired by African American life in Charleston, including Gershwin's own scores for the musical sounds of vendors pitching their wares. As a jazz trumpeter, Davis was distinguished for his uniquely personal, very expressive tone qualities and inflections of pitch. His mastery of this tradition is conspicuous here.

CD Track	Elapsed Time	
1	0'00"	"Street Cries of Charleston" (male street vendor)
2	0'30"	"Fishermen, Strawberry, Devil Crab" (Miles Davis trumpet solo)

Call-and-Response

An eleventh feature of jazz is **call-and-response format**. One member or one section of the band offers a musical phrase that is like a question. Another member or section of the band then follows it with a new phrase that is like an answer. (At about 2'34" into "Cottontail" on the *Jazz Classics CD*, notice the "question" posed by the brass section and the "answer" offered by the sax section. Listen to the "call" of the bassist and the "response" of the horns in the theme statement of "So What" by Miles Davis in SCCJ.) This feature of jazz and African music receives considerable attention from musicologists but is not as common as most of the other features we have discussed. There is an interesting distinction, however, between the type of call and response used in West African music and that used in European music. Often the sound of the call is still in the air when the response begins. The two parts overlap. And sometimes the call begins again before the response is done, thereby overlapping once more. This causes rhythmic conflict and results in a provocative effect. It is the prominence of *overlapping* call and response, not merely call and response, that distinguishes West African and African American music from music elsewhere. (It is evident in the four excerpts sequenced together at the beginning of the *Jazz Classics CD*—West African, American Gospel, swing-era riff style, and jazz-rock fusion.)

Listening Guide for

African American Sequence on the *Jazz Classics CD*

"Hunter's Dance," a West African folk number

"One Day," an American gospel singing number

"One O' Clock Jump," a swing-era riff band number

"Birdland," a jazz-rock fusion number

These four pieces illustrate several properties that are common to West African music, African American gospel music, swing-era riff-band style, and jazz-rock fusion. Each piece demonstrates extensive repetition of brief patterns, much syncopation, an overlapping-call-and-response format, and the capacity to evoke swing feeling in the listener. By the strictest definition, none of these truly qualifies as jazz because not much is improvised. The third and fourth pieces are usually called jazz, though, because they are played by jazz bands and because they swing.

Though call-and-response format is common in many kinds of music, not just African and African American styles, the format in which the response overlaps the call is particularly noticeable in African and African American music. The following examples therefore illustrate overlapping call-and-response format, not merely call-and-response.

"Hunter's Dance" is popular peasant music made by the people of Mali, also known as the Malinke people. To obtain this music, in 1952 ethnomusicologist Gilbert Rouget journeyed to Karalo, a relatively isolated native village in the West African country of Guinea. The recording features a six-string harp-lute (dozo-konu), the voice of the man who plays it, a women's chorus accompanying him, a wooden whistle (fere), and a metal scraper (karinyan), which is a small tube of wrought iron that is slit down the middle. The karinyan is held in the left hand and struck with a nail held in the right hand, playing a rhythm similar to the jazz drummer's ride rhythm. ("Hunter's Dance" was issued in France on *Musique D'Afrique Occidental* (Vogue: LVLX 193, LP); it was released in the U.S. on *Anthology of Music of Black Africa* (Everest: 3254/3, 3LP set), and most recently on *African Tribal Music & Dances* (Legacy International: CD 328, CD, 1952).

When listening to "Hunter's Dance," notice that the rhythms of the different parts are carefully calculated to achieve a provocative effect that is peculiarly African. Also notice how the music's excitement increases as the performance evolves and more layers of activity are added.

CD Track	Elapsed Time	
3	0' 0"	repeating bass figure, obtained by plucking the strings of the dozo-konu; accompanied by a repeating rhythm on the metallic sounding karinyan
	0' 15"	melody sung by the male voice
	0' 20"	response sung by women's chorus
	0' 23"	Before the response is complete, the male voice begins to sing again (thus the expression "overlapping call and response").
	0' 27"	women's chorus responds again
	0' 28"	whistle sounds
	0' 30"	male voice returns
4	0' 37"	"One Day" was recorded in 1951 by the Angelic Gospel Singers (four women), the Dixie Hummingbirds (five men), and a pianist; reissued on the collection: *The Gospel Sound* (Columbia: C2K 57160, 2CD set, 1926–68).

As in all the pieces of this African American sequence, the music's excitement increases over the course of the performance as more parts are layered on top of each other, each part's rhythms tugging at the other's in a provocative way. Tremendous spirit and exuberance are projected by this music. Ultimately the music sounds almost like it is going to break apart in wild abandon.

Here are a few highlights. The intensity and momentum are unrelenting, and they occur without the assistance of any bass or drums. Though highly rhythmic piano accompaniment is in the background, the manner in which the singers produce their rhythms is so compelling that they could probably swing without any accompaniment at all. Male voice is in the foreground, though its sound eases in and out of the sounds of background singers answering its phrases. Notice the tendency of the male lead singer to smear up into the pitch of the main notes. This gliding through the pitch range is a very expressive device he uses expertly. Also note the raspy timbre the male singer uses for one of his phrases. This is a preference that is also common to West African singers and musicians. The entrances of the lead singer are highly syncopated, and these syncopations are timed to evoke maximum swing feeling and rhythmic conflict. The responsorial chorus provides the repeating riff in this selection. Notice that the call and response pattern doubles in rate near the end, and finally a woman's voice soars high over the.proceedings as one more element to tug at the beat and generate excitement. (A similar device is used at the end of "Birdland.")

CD Track	Elapsed Time	
5	1' 07"	"One O'Clock Jump" recorded in 1942 by the Count Basie big band. This is a riff-band piece from the swing era. The original 1937 version of it was a big hit. Excerpted here are the ninth and tenth choruses in twelve-bar blues form. Several different riffs are played against each other at the same time by different sections of the band: trombones, trumpets, and saxophones. This illustrates the principle of antiphony, literally "against sounds." Saxes play a syncopated figure, as though answering the trombone phrase. Trumpets play a different riff that is also syncopated, as though on the opposite end of a see-saw from the trombones. A timekeeping foundation is provided by piano, rhythm guitar, walking bass, and the drummer using sticks to play ride rhythms on opening and closing high hat. The overlapping of these parts generates rhythmic excitement.

"Birdland" by Weather Report, recorded in 1977 on Oberheim Polyphonic Synthesizer (Joe Zawinul), soprano sax (Wayne Shorter), bass guitar (Jaco Pastorius), drums (Alex Acuna), and tambourine (Manolo Badrena); available on Weather Report, *Heavy Weather* (Columbia: CK 65108, 1977).

6 1' 36" "Birdland" is in a style called jazz-rock fusion. This performance is excerpted from Weather Report's best-selling recording, a discoteque hit. For many years this piece continued to be copied and re-arranged by numerous ensembles, including the singing group Manhattan Transfer. Excerpted here is the chorus of the piece, the melody of which is played by sax, synthesizer, bass guitar, and voice. The chords in the accompaniment are provided by the synthesizer. Percussion accompaniment includes hand claps on beats #2 and #4, tambourine providing steady eighth notes, and the sound of open high-hat cymbal struck with drum stick on upbeats, snapped shut on downbeats. In addition to doubling the melody, bass guitar fills in the gaps between the notes and phrases of the melody. A high-pitched male voice (bass guitarist Jaco Pastorius) sustains tones over the ensemble sound, offering a countermelody.

Call-and-response format is not necessarily a distinguishing feature of improvised combo jazz. What many believe to be a call-and-response kind of communication among group members is in many instances just solo and accompaniment in which the accompaniment follows its own patterns more than it spontaneously generates fresh responses to an improvising soloist. This is revealed when we examine recordings in which the solo line is missing and we discover comping almost identical to that which occurs in the presence of improvised solo lines. Also remember that comping ordinarily derives from a repertory of learned patterns (see pages 425 and 429), not necessarily from a spur-of-the-moment response evoked by the call of another musician's sound. (Prior to the Bill Evans Trio of 1961, heard on "Solar" in the *Jazz Classics CD,* there was less spontaneous interaction among rhythm section members and less between accompanists and soloists than observers ordinarily believed.) In general, improvised lines are much more a "response" to the challenges of the chord progressions and the player's own ingenuity than to any "call" of another musician.

Some commentators have applied "call-and-response" to describe the function of the phrases that instrumentalists play to fill in a singer's pauses within the twelve-bar blues (for example, in Bessie Smith's blues pieces in SCCJ, or "Sobbin' Hearted Blues" on the *Jazz Classics CD* for *Concise Guide to Jazz*). However, careful listening reveals that the fills are not necessarily "responses" to the singer's phrases. They merely arrive in sequence with them. Often they are just improvised lines inspired only by the player's own imagination. They frequently originate from attempts to reconcile horn lines with the underlying chord progressions more than from attempts to establish a musical dialog with the singer. The term "call-and-response" is therefore not always an appropriate designation.

Responsorial singing is a pervasive trait of African music, and it is common in European-derived church music found in America. Call-and-response patterns can be found in classical music and in folk music of many ethnic groups present in America. In summary, call-and-response format can be found in some jazz, and the model for it could reflect any or all of several available sources.

CHAPTER SUMMARY

1) Jazz originated in New Orleans around the beginning of the twentieth century.
2) New Orleans was the ideal site for the birth of jazz because it was an intensely musical city with a history of rich ethnic diversity, especially French and African.
3) Jazz emerged when brass bands were at a zenith of popularity and ragtime was in such high demand that brass bands and string bands were improvising rag-like syncopations into their pieces to please dancers.
4) African American forms of music such as the blues and ragtime blended with European dance music and church music.
5) Jazz has features that reflect African musical tastes that were retained in African American music—improvisation, syncopation, rough timbres, extensive repetition of brief patterns, polyrhythms, and overlapping-call-and-response format.
6) Jazz reflects European music's instruments, chord progressions, and improvisation.
7) Blending of European and African practices resulted in blue notes and various decorations of a note by altering its pitch.

NOTES

1. See *Instructor's Resource Manual* for bibliography, discography, and lengthy discussion of the controversies.

2. Though the plantation system of labor was nonexistent in name, the plantations still operated with hired labor, and most of the plantations hired bandmasters/teachers to instruct these hired hands and to form bands. Many early jazz musicians received their musical training there.

3. The players may have done much without referring to written scores. However, the absence of notation in these situations should not be taken as evidence of improvisation any more than we would consider "improvised" the music of today's wedding bands and lounge acts that sometimes play fresh routines without notation. Research by Karl Koenig has shown that most early New Orleans jazz musicians could read music well enough to work out the notes and fingerings, though they could not necessarily sight read fast. Some could not read music, however, and most chose not to read pieces once they had been learned.

4. You might be able to detect blue notes in the Joe Oliver cornet solo on "Dippermouth Blues" in SCCJ. There are many Rex Stewart cornet solos which use blue notes on Duke Ellington records from the 1930s and 1940s. His "Boy Meets Horn" is the most famous example. Modern trumpeter Miles Davis is also particularly known for using blue notes. Listen to "Strawberries" on his *Porgy and Bess* album, excerpted in the *Jazz Classics CD*, or "Solea" on his *Sketches of Spain* album. During the 1970s, Don Ellis played on a specially made trumpet that, by the addition of an extra valve, could produce quarter tones, those "notes in the cracks." Ordinarily, trumpeters had tried to achieve the same sound by depressing their trumpet key halfway, thereby leaving a cocked valve. However, they could not depend on obtaining this result consistently. The Ellis trumpet managed a similar effect, but much more reliably.

Chapter Five

The Original Dixieland Jazz Band. Photo courtesy of the Hogan Jazz Archive, Tulane University

Early Jazz

The earliest jazz musicians took liberties with the tunes and accompaniments in their performances. Their new ideas and embellishments sometimes became more important to a performance than the tunes themselves. This trend evolved across the 1920s, and in some performances of the 1930s all that remained of the original was the tune's spirit and chord progressions. What is today called improvising was referred to by early jazz musicians as "messin' around," embellishing, "jassing," or "jazzing up."

The earliest jazz had roots in ragtime, blues, and brass band music. But after a few years, several important differences were heard:

1) Much of each performance was improvised.

2) Rhythmic feeling was looser and more relaxed, thus anticipating jazz swing feeling.

3) It generated some of its own repertory of compositions.

4) Its collectively improvised format created a more complex musical product than was typical in ragtime, blues, or brass band music.

5) The earliest jazz was even more exciting than ragtime, blues, or brass band music.

TABLE 5.1 A Few of the Many Early Jazz Musicians

TRUMPET
Buddy Bolden
Freddie Keppord
Joe "King" Oliver
Louis Armstrong
Wingy Manone
Red Nichols
Bix Beiderbecke
Tommy Ladnier
Henry "Red" Allen
Joe Smith
Bubber Miley
Charlie Teagarden
Jobbo Smith
Nick LaRocca
Paul Mares
George Mitchell
Sidney DeParis
Muggsy Spanier
Phil Napoleon
Wild Bill Davidson
Mutt Carey

DRUMS
Baby Dodds
Papa Jack Laine
Paul Borbarin
Zutty Singleton
Sonny Greer
Dave Tough
George Wettling
Ben Pollock
Andrew Hilaire
Chauncey Morehouse
Gene Krupa
Vic Berton
Ray Bouduc
Tony Sbarbaro

COMPOSER-ARRANGER
Kid Ory
Jelly Roll Morton
W.C. Handy
Clarence Williams
Fats Waller

VIOLIN
Joe Venuti

BASS
Pops Foster
Wellman Braud
John Lindsay

TROMBONE
Kid Ory
J. C. Higginbotham
Miff Mole
Jack Teagarden
Fred Robinson
Charlie Green
Jimmy Harrison
Charlie Irvis
Joe "Tricky Sam" Nonton
George Brunis
Bill Rank
Tommy Dorsey
Glenn Miller
Wilbur DeParis
Eddie Edwards
Honore Dutrey

CLARINET AND SAXOPHONE
Johnny Dodds
Sidney Bechet
Jimmie Noone
Frank Teschemacher
Benny Goodman
Albert Nicholas
Barney Bigard
Omer Simeon
Alphonse Picou
Mezz Mezzrow
Jimmy Strong
Sidney Arodin
Darnell Howard
Leon Roppolo
Buster Bailey
Don Redman
Bud Freeman
Floyd Towne
Coleman Hawkins
Jimmy Dorsey
Hilton Jefferson
Stomp Evans
Charlie Holmes
Larry Shields
Pee Wee Russell
Adrian Rollini
Don Murray
Tony Parenti
Izzy Friedman
Min Leibrook
Cecil Scott
Frankie Trumbauer
Edmond Hall
Gene Sedric
George Lewis

GUITAR AND BANJO
Lonnie Johnson
Johnny St. Cyr
Elmer Snowden
Eddie Lang
Eddie Condon

PIANO
James P. Johnson
Fate Marable
Jelly Roll Morton
Willie "The Lion" Smith
Fats Waller
Lil Hardin Armstrong
Pete Johnson
Clarence Williams
Meade Lux Lewis
Albert Ammons
Cripple Clarence Lofton
Cow Cow Davenport
Elmer Schoebel
Pinetop Smith
Jimmy Yancey
Earl Hines
Frank Signorelli
Fletcher Henderson
Joe Sullivan
Jimmy Blythe
Henry Rogas

Combo jazz began in New Orleans, and that city contributed several soloists of far-reaching significance. The best known were trumpeter Louis Armstrong and clarinetist-saxophonist Sidney Bechet. Jelly Roll Morton was the most significant composer-arranger from New Orleans, and his finest recordings were made during the 1920s in Chicago. New combinations of musicians in Chicago also made several other figures important: Pittsburgh-born pianist Earl Hines; and Bix Beiderbecke, a Davenport, Iowa–born cornetist. Chicago was additionally the home of "The Austin High Gang," which, together with The New Orleans Rhythm Kings, created a white parallel of the New Orleans combo style that today is called "Dixieland." Another important part of early jazz was an East Coast piano tradition that evolved partly from New Jersey-born James P. Johnson and continued through Fats Waller to Count Basie. Let's examine these styles now.

◇THE CHICAGO SCENE

It was in Chicago that many black New Orleans musicians were first recorded in the early 1920s. What is usually referred to as New Orleans style is not the music that was played between 1900 and 1920 in New Orleans—we have never heard that music because it was not recorded—but rather the music recorded by New Orleans musicians in Chicago during the 1920s. We know from interviews and a few early records that the earliest forms of jazz were characterized by collective improvisation, with all group members playing at the same time. These early bands featured choruses in which every player was creating phrases which complemented every other player's phrases. For many listeners, the greatest appeal of early jazz is the activity of several horn lines sounding at the same time without clashing. Musicians managed to stay out of each other's way partly because they tended to fulfill set musical roles similar to those established for their instruments in brass bands. The trumpet often played the melody. The clarinet played busy figures with many notes. The clarinet part decorated the melody played by the trumpet. The trombone would play simpler figures. The trombone's music outlined the chord notes and filled in low-pitched harmony notes. The trombone created motion in a pitch range lower than the clarinet and trumpet.

The style of the black Chicago musicians, most of whom were from New Orleans, evolved away from a strictly collective approach in favor of a style which featured more improvised solos. The skills of the improviser who was required to blend with the collectively improvised phrases of other players differed from the skills of the improviser who was required to solo dramatically. The delicate balance and sensitive interplay in collective improvisation which characterized the earliest form of jazz receded during the Chicago period of the New Orleans players. However, musicians who played Dixieland in subsequent eras tried to recapture the essence of those special skills which make successful collective improvisation possible.

The Original Dixieland Jazz Band

New Orleans jazz was first recorded in Chicago and New York, not in New Orleans. **The Original Dixieland Jazz Band** made the first recordings. This was a collection of white New Orleans musicians who organized a band in Chicago during 1916 and played in New York in 1917. They used cornet, clarinet, trombone, piano, and drums. Under the leadership of cornetist **Nick LaRocca** (1889–1961), the band recorded its first 78 r.p.m. record in 1917. They played "Livery Stable Blues" on one side and "Dixie Jazz Band One-Step" on the other. It garnered phenomenally high sales, international fame, and numerous imitators. Even during the 1990s, musicians were forming Dixieland jazz bands in the style of this group. (Listen to their "Dixie Jazz Band One-Step" in the *Jazz Classics CD.* It is the first jazz record ever issued.)[1]

Oliver's Creole Jazz Band

Joe Oliver's **Creole Jazz Band** was an all-star New Orleans group which, at various times, had most of the best black New Orleans jazz musicians in Chicago. Trumpeter **Joe Oliver** (1885–1938) had worked with several New Orleans bands, then moved to Chicago in

1918, worked with several more bands, and finally formed one of his own. Several recordings made under Oliver's leadership in 1923 are often cited as the first recording of black New Orleans combo jazz. Aside from accompaniments for singers, however, a band led by New Orleans-born trombonist Kid Ory had been the first black jazz combo to have its playing issued on record.[2] This chapter devotes considerable space to the styles of three musicians in Oliver's band: trumpeter Louis Armstrong, clarinetist Johnny Dodds, and drummer Warren "Baby" Dodds. (Listen to their "Dippermouth Blues" in SCCJ.)

The Chicago School

Chicago was the center for a very active jazz scene during the 1920s. Musicians there can be described in terms of three main categories. One was the transplanted New Orleans black musicians. Another contained their white New Orleans counterparts, among whom were the New Orleans Rhythm Kings (Friar's Society Orchestra).[3] These two groups of musicians, in turn, were influencing a third group of younger white musicians, many of whom were Chicago natives. This young white community developed what was called *The Chicago Style,* or *The Chicago School.* Its music was modeled on the New Orleans style, but sounded more hurried. Several of these musicians (Jimmy McPartland, Frank Teschemacher, and Bud Freeman) had attended the same Chicago high school, Austin High. They subsequently earned the name of *The Austin High Gang,* though their "gang" included Dave Tough, who attended Wayne High. In addition to the Austin High Gang, the white Chicago scene included other notables (see Table 5.2).

Eventually the Chicago musicians and the transplanted New Orleans musicians mixed with New York musicians. By the late 1920s, a strong New York scene had also developed. Key performers in the early combo jazz of New York included trumpeter Red Nichols, trombonist Miff Mole, and violinist Joe Venuti. Most of the original Chicagoans had moved to New York by the 1930s.

Early jazz has been identified by many labels which lack standard use. Certain labels have definite meanings for some jazz scholars and musicians, though they are not uniformly applied by everyone. Chicago jazz and New Orleans jazz are two of these terms. Ragtime, gut bucket, barrelhouse, Dixieland, classic jazz, and traditional jazz are others.

TABLE 5.2 THE NEW ORLEANS AND CHICAGO JAZZ STYLES—REPRESENTATIVE MUSICIANS

NEW ORLEANS		CHICAGO
Joe "King" Oliver	Zutty Singleton	Muggsy Spanier
Bunk Johnson	Johnny St. Cyr	Jimmy McPartland (Austin High School)
Freddie Keppard	Lonnie Johnson	Frank Teschemacher (Austin High School)
Buddy Bolden	Omer Simeon	Dave Tough
Louis Armstrong	Jelly Roll Morton	Bud Freeman (Austin High School)
Sidney Bechet	Honore Dutrey	Joe Sullivan
Jimmie Noone	Albert Nicholas	Mezz Mezzrow
Kid Ory	Barney Bigard	Eddie Condon
Baby Dodds	George Brunies	Gene Krupa
Johnny Dodds	Leon Rappolo	

Listening Guide for

"Dixie Jazz Band One-Step"

Recorded February 26, 1917, by Nick LaRocca (cornet), Larry Shields (clarinet), Eddie Edwards (trombone), Henry Ragas (piano), and Tony Spargo (drums); available on the *Jazz Classics CD.*

This record was made in New York by a group of white New Orleans musicians who had come together in Chicago the preceding year. They called themselves the Original Dixieland Jass Band (ODJB). "Dixie Jazz Band One-Step" (also known as "Original Dixieland One-Step") was on the reverse side of "Livery Stable Blues," one of the most popular discs in the first decade of recorded jazz. The piece heard here originated from a combination of ideas contributed by all the band members, though ragtime composer Joe Jordan wrote its third theme, and the sheet music for this piece lists bandleader Nick LaRocca as composer. Worldwide sales of the record it was on are said to have reached about a million copies by the late 1930s.

This is the first instrumental jazz recording ever released, and music by the ODJB has continued to influence musicians, partly because this band made the first jazz records. However, there is controversy about what to call the music. First, the name for the style, as well as the piece itself, was originally "jass," not jazz. Second, the music on this recording might not qualify as jazz if we define jazz as music that has improvisation and swing feeling. We don't know whether any of the music was freshly improvised for this particular recording session, but we do know that most of the ODJB's music was worked out in advance, despite the spontaneity of its sound. For instance, the embellishments were recreated almost intact for most performances, though they are likely to have been improvised when this arrangement was first devised. Regarding its quality of swing, the feeling of this music does not have the easy rise and fall of tensions that we associate with swing feeling of later jazz. However, the ODJB's music is loaded with syncopations that evolved from ragtime, and it is highly spirited.

The roles that the different instruments assume on this recording were associated with what is known today as New Orleans, Chicago, or Dixieland style jazz. We can consider this record to be an example of music that was popular in New Orleans during this period because most of the fashions heard here were already common in New Orleans ragtime bands by 1917. So even though it was the first to be recorded, the ODJB was not necessarily the first or "The Original" band of its kind, as its name implies.

Though it often sounds as if a larger band is playing, this performance was constructed by only five instruments: cornet, clarinet, trombone, piano, and drums. The clarinet is most evident, and the piano is least evident, almost inaudible. The cornet and trombone sounds frequently blend so closely that you may have difficulty distinguishing them, though many trombone smears are conspicuous. As was typical for New Orleans drummers of the period, Spargo frequently switches instruments. At various moments he can be heard playing snare drum, wood block, and cowbell. He uses the cymbal sparingly, and a cymbal crash usually signifies a climactic moment in the music, as it does in nonjazz idioms.

To prepare yourself for following the various activities in this piece, it may help to keep three things in mind. First, the music goes by very fast. So you will need to count "1234 1234 . . ."

almost as fast as you can to keep your place by counting beats. Second, you'll hear more each time you replay the recording. So don't get frustrated if it sounds like a blur the first time you listen to it. Third, the arrangement contains only three brief themes, and they are frequently repeated. So once you become acquainted with them, you will know almost all that is necessary to follow this arrangement.

Many of the different sounds are so close in their pitch range and rhythm that they blend together and disguise each other. But the more often you listen, the more distinct they will become. Your search for the separate instruments might resemble peering at a trick sketch on a comic book or cereal box. (Remember trying to identify a tiger hidden in jungle ferns where overlapping lines camouflaged its contours?) Repeated listening also allows you to get swept up in the excitement of this music. Then you can appreciate why this band was so popular.

You may find it helpful to think of the performance as a loud party in which people are talking to each other very energetically, sometimes agreeing, sometimes disagreeing, often interrupting each other. Once in a while an interrupter gets everyone's attention, and they stop to hear what he has to say. But they almost immediately return to chattering boisterously among themselves. Sometimes as one person speaks, others shout out their agreement with him, and a running commentary is happening most of the time.

To help get your counting synchronized with the music, note that the first two sounds in the performance indicate the first two beats. There is no sound on beat three or beat four. The musicians count these unsounded beats silently to themselves so they can restart their playing together on the first of the next group of four beats (henceforth termed "a measure"). Then the pattern repeats. This goes by very fast, but it is a dependable indication of the tempo for the entire piece. The third measure is occupied by a smear from the trombone that starts high, goes low, then goes back up high again, finishing on the first beat of the next measure.

The ODJB's roots in the brass band tradition are reflected in this piece's opening. The rhythm of the first four-measure sequence is called a "roll-off," a device usually played by a parade band's drummer to prepare musicians to march. Its effect is dramatic, as in a call to arms. The band stands at attention during the roll-off, then begins to march. By listening closely, you can hear the drummer playing the roll-off pattern underneath the horns. His rhythm is the same as theirs. The trombone smear in the third measure coincides with a drum roll. Like other march-style popular music of this period, this piece was also used to accompany a dance; in this case the dance was called the one-step.

The form of the performance is A - A′ - B - B′ - A - A′ - B - B′ - C - C′ - C - C′ - C - C′.

Terms to learn from the *Demo CD* before listening: eighth notes, stop-time, bass drum, snare drum, wood block, trombone smears, clarinet, and trumpet.

Elapsed Time		
0′ 00″	**First Theme**	
	First Measure:	bang . . . . bang . . . . . . silence . . . . . silence
	numbered beats:	1 . . . . 2 . . . . 3 4
	Second Measure:	bang. . . . . bang . . . . . . silence . . . . . silence
		1 . . . . 2 . . . . 3 4

Third Measure: trombone smear. . . . .

1 . . . . 2 . . . . 3 4

Fourth Measure: smear ends . . . silence . . . . . crash

1 . . . . 2 . . . . 3 4

0′ 03″ *Fifth, Sixth, Seventh, and Eighth Measures:*

Band plays a new theme, with clarinet playing around the cornet and trombone parts. The drummer plays a military snare drum rhythm as a counteractivity to the rhythms of the horn lines.

0′ 07″ **Repeat of the First Theme** (A′, 8 measures)

We call this section A′ ("ay-prime") because it is the same as A, but the end differs.

0′ 15″ **Second Theme** (B, 8 measures)

In the final two beats of A′, the trombone begins to slide up until he reaches the first beat of the second theme, called "B." The entire band joins him on that beat. Then every instrument but clarinet immediately goes silent, and all we hear is clarinet slurring from note to note during beats 2, 3, and 4. This continues through another measure and is called a "stop-time." Then the clarinetist is joined by his bandmates, all playing different lines for an additional six measures (24 beats).

0′ 23″ **Repeat of the Second Theme** (B′; "bee-prime," 8 measures)

The beginning of this eight-measure section resembles the beginning of the preceding section, but the music goes in a different direction for its final four measures, conveying a more resolved quality than the first B. For that reason we designate this strain as B′ rather than B.

0′ 30″ **A-A′-B-B′** (32 measures)

This repetition occurs with only minor alterations. Follow the listening guide from the beginning.

Third Theme (C, 16 measures)

1′ 00″ "That Teasin' Rag" composed by Joe Jordan

Trombone exchanges with clarinet in a call-and-response fashion, playfully trading descending smears; "clickety-clacking" of the drummer's sticks sound military rhythms on the wood block for the first eight measures, then alternately striking wood block and cowbell.

Trombone plays descending smears in unison with piano as a "call." Cornet and clarinet harmonize a bobbing little figure of eighth notes as a "response." This section ends with the horn parts going in different directions. A robust authoritative trombone part emerges with a repeating figure near the end. Intensity builds and then culminates with a high-pitched, descending clarinet smear.

C′ (16 measures)

1′ 16″ Note: Every other time C occurs, it ends differently. So these alternate renditions are designated C′ ("see-prime").

First beat is played by the drummer striking his cymbal for a crash. Then he plays wood block and cowbell. The trombone then briefly carries a melody of its own in the final eight measures, using a style similar to the tuba parts of march arrangements. The cornet chimes in with a sustained tone on an offbeat in the second to last measure.

1′ 32″ **C** (16 measures)

Drummer begins this section emphasizing his cowbell and uses wood block less than before. Notice the descending trombone smears. A quick, high-pitched clarinet smear ends the section.

1′ 48″ **C′** (16 measures)

Drummer begins the section with a cymbal crash, then plays patterns on wood block. He interrupts his pattern during the middle of this section and strikes the bass drum twice in succession.

2′ 03″ **C** (16 measures)

If you listen closely during the last half of this section, you will hear the piano pounding out bass patterns. This section ends with a descending clarinet smear played more hurriedly than in the first C.

2′ 18″ **C′** (16 measures)

2′ 26″ *Final Eight Measures*

Drummer is playing snare drum instead of wood block and cowbell. Then he ties up the piece with a cymbal crash.

These terms tend to be applied to solo piano styles as well as combo jazz, to include both black and white musicians, and to refer to music produced by old New Orleans and Chicago veterans as well as revivalist groups. As though this is not already confusing enough, note that the terms "ragtime" and "jazz" have frequently been used to encompass all popular music of the period, not only the jazz-related styles. The problem has worsened because novelist F. Scott Fitzgerald dubbed the 1920s "The Jazz Age." Other writers adopted the term and used it in a way that indiscriminately confused what we today call "jazz" with almost all the syncopated music that was popular in that decade.

◇PIANO

We know that jazz piano styles were evolving in places other than New Orleans prior to 1920. In fact, many outstanding jazz pianists of the 1920s were from the East Coast. Many had played unaccompanied. Early jazz piano styles evolved from ragtime. Playing ragtime did not always necessitate reading or memorizing written music. Once the style had been absorbed, skilled pianists appeared who could improvise original rags as well as embellish prewritten ones. One jazz piano style with roots in ragtime is known as *stride style.* Stride piano playing uses percussive, striding, lefthand figures in which low bass notes alternate with mid-range chords, while the right hand plays melodies and embellishments in a very energetic fashion. (This is demonstrated and explained on the *Demo CD* Track 38. It is illustrated by one of its founders in James P. Johnson's "You've Got to Be Modernistic" on the *Jazz Classics CD.*)[4]

Jelly Roll Morton

Jelly Roll Morton (1890–1941) was a pianist, composer-arranger, and bandleader from New Orleans. He was one of the first jazz pianists as well as the first important jazz composer. Morton was capable of performing in both the ragtime style and the jazz style. He perfected rhythmic techniques that altered the character of eighth-note lines so that they swung. Pianist-historian James Dapogny has pointed out that Morton used long-short, long-short patterns in playing eighth notes and that Morton alternated intensities of eighth notes so that they gave the impression of strong-weak, strong-weak (see page xxx for explanation). By doing this and reducing adornment, Morton played with a lighter and more swinging feeling than was typical of ragtime.

Morton's piano style was quite involved. He often played two or three lines at a time, much in the manner of a band. It was as though trumpet parts, clarinet parts, and trombone parts were being heard coming from a piano! Morton put a variety of themes and much activity within a single piece. Sometimes he would use stop-time solo breaks in the same manner as horns in a combo. (Stop-times are explained on the *Demo CD* Track 34.) Morton mixed ragtime with less formal, more blues-oriented New Orleans styles. (Listen to "Maple Leaf Rag" in SCCJ, and see page xxx for information on how to get James Dapogny's transcriptions and analyses of Jelly Roll Morton solos.)

The best known of Morton's several bands were a series of recording groups in Chicago called the Red Hot Peppers.[5] Morton employed many of the same New Orleans-born musicians shared by other black Chicago groups. However, under Morton's leadership, the resulting sounds were unusually well organized, though they retained the spirit of music made by less tightly run bands. The imagination of Morton's compositions and arrangements on these recordings is still respected by jazz composers and scholars. (Listen to his "Black Bottom Stomp" in SCCJ.)

In summary, Jelly Roll Morton is historically notable because:

1) He was the first important jazz composer, and several of his pieces became well known in rearranged form played by other bands—"Wolverine Blues," "Milenburg Joys," "Wild Man Blues," "King Porter Stomp."

2) He introduced arranging practices in his small-group performances that came to be imitated during the early stages of the history of big bands.

3) He was one of the first jazz musicians to blend composition with improvisation in an elaborate and balanced way that still conveyed the kind of excitement that had typified collectively improvised jazz. In this way, Morton anticipated similar contributions by Duke Ellington, Charlie Mingus, and Sun Ra.

4) He recorded piano solos that were well organized, forcefully executed musical statements with horn-like lines in them.

5) He helped bridge the gap between ragtime piano style and jazz piano style by loosening ragtime's rhythmic feeling and decreasing its embellishments.

Earl Hines

Earl Hines (1903–1983) was an early jazz pianist who significantly influenced piano playing styles of the 1930s and 1940s. Born in Pittsburgh, Hines moved to Chicago in 1924. He brought with him an assortment of different jazz techniques, all combined in the form of one catchy style. His playing began its enormous influence during the late 1920s when he recorded with Louis Armstrong and made a series of important records of his own. (Listen to Hines on Louis Armstrong's "West End Blues" on the *Jazz Classics CD.*) This impact extended during the 1930s by way of radio broadcasts and tours with the big band he led at the Grand Terrace Ballroom in Chicago from 1928 to 1939. Musicians as far away as Kansas and Texas heard his broadcasts. The Hines style affected Art Tatum, Count Basie, Teddy Wilson, and Nat Cole. Hines had an influence on modern jazz because these players, in turn, influenced

Jelly Roll Morton and his Red Hot Peppers, one of the first groups to masterfully combine improvisation and well-developed compositions without losing the spirit of New Orleans jazz. (Left to right): Andrew Hilaire (drums), Kid Ory (trombone), George Mitchell (trumpet), John Lindsay (bass), Morton (piano), Johnny St. Cyr (banjo), Omer Simeon (clarinet). Pictured here in 1926.

Photo courtesy of Duncan Schiedt.

the development of modern styles. They influenced Bud Powell, for example, the single most imitated pianist in modern jazz of the 1950s.

Much of the piano music made by Hines can be called "brassy." This is partly because of the great physical force Hines employed to strike the piano keys. In fact, the sheer force of his left-hand playing broke the large, strong, bass strings on a few pianos. (Most people cannot break those strings even by smashing a fist down on the piano's bass keys.) Even when Hines played in a flowery way, a roughness remained in his sound. Rarely was anything sustained, and nearly everything had a punching quality. These properties combined with his method of phrasing to lend a brassy quality to the sound of the piano. Because his right-hand lines sometimes sound like jazz trumpet playing, **the Hines approach earned the title of trumpet-style or horn-like.** His piano lines even seem to breathe at the moments a trumpeter would breathe. Additionally, they contained phrases and rhythms preferred by trumpeters rather than pianists. This manner stems partly from Hines having originally begun his musical training with the goal of becoming a trumpeter instead of a pianist. And it stems from what Hines did to overcome the piano's inability to be heard over loud band instruments. We must remember that he was playing long before electronic amplification came to the aid of jazz pianists. To manage the task of cutting through, he played very hard, phrased like a trumpeter, and doubled his right-hand melody lines in octaves (demonstrated on the *Demo CD* Track 41, and by Hines on "West End Blues" in the *Jazz Classics CD*).

The Hines style is the one most commonly associated with the term "trumpet-style," despite Jelly Roll Morton's having previously improvised piano passages in the manner of band instruments. This approach is historically significant because, by playing more as a horn and less in the standard piano styles, Hines paved the way for modern jazz pianists who solo with essentially the same conception that is used by jazz trumpeters and saxophonists. It is less flowery and more direct. It is less classically pianistic and more swinging. Additionally it is important to realize that the Hines approach is more flexible than the ragtime and stride approaches. Because of this, Hines had the capacity for conveying a broader assortment of musical feelings.

Earl Hines is known for a sturdy sense of tempo which persisted relentlessly despite the many interruptions in melodic flow that he made. This sense of tempo, plus his insistently percussive attack and varied syncopations, made Hines one of the most rhythmically compelling jazz pianists. (Listen to Hines on Armstrong's recording of "Weather Bird" in SCCJ.)

Hines was prone to introducing new and often jarring ideas into his solos in midflight, departing on tangents, the source of which was understood only by him. Instead of maintaining a smooth flow and consistent texture from the beginning of a piece to its end, he filled his work with surprises. In the middle of a piece, he would frequently stop a pattern, cease left-hand accompaniment, employing both hands to seemingly leap all over the keyboard before resuming any repeating pattern. On any one of his unaccompanied piano solos, he pulled a multitude of techniques into play, sometimes all in a single piece.[6] These techniques are explained and demonstrated on the *Demo CD* Tracks 37 to 42:

1) stride style
2) walking tenths (the two outside fingers of the left hand moving in scale-wise fashion, simultaneously sounding tones of about a ten-step interval apart)
3) horn-like lines
4) flowery embellishments
5) octave voicing
6) tremolo
7) stop-time solo breaks for the right hand
8) brief double-time figures
9) off-balance left-hand rhythms which are highly syncopated, seeming to come out of nowhere

Later, these techniques prominently appeared in the playing of several generations of jazz pianists. Some historians believe that Hines was the single most pervasive influence on pianists of the swing era in the 1930s, and a few consider him to be the most influential of all jazz pianists. He did not come up with most of these techniques himself, but he combined them in a way that was absorbed by others.

Fats Waller

New York-born **Fats Waller** (1904–1943) was one of the best known stride pianists.[7] Waller played with excellent technique and a bouncing swing feeling which he used to create countless lighthearted and joyful performances. Count Basie, Art Tatum, and Dave Brubeck have all cited Waller as an influence on their styles. Waller wrote hundreds of tunes, the most familiar of which are "Ain't Misbehavin'," "Honeysuckle Rose," "Squeeze Me," and "Jitterbug Waltz." During the 1970s, an entire Broadway revue was devoted to music associated with Waller. This immensely successful show was called *Ain't Misbehavin'*, and it revived interest in Waller's work. (Listen to his "I Ain't Got Nobody" in SCCJ.)

Boogie Woogie

In addition to ragtime and stride styles, early jazz pianists developed **boogie woogie**. A prime characteristic of boogie woogie is the subdivision of each beat in the left-hand figures so that, in a measure of four beats, there are actually eight pulses ("eight to the bar"). These left-hand patterns surfaced around 1912 in southern pianists. If you hear a record of boogie woogie, you will have no trouble recognizing it because the style has been revived so often it will be familiar to you. Pianist Pinetop Smith actually entitled one of his tunes "Boogie Woogie," and his own rendition of it was a hit record in 1929. An adaptation of that piece became an even bigger hit record in 1938 and again in 1943 for trombonist Tommy Dorsey's big band. The leading boogie woogie pianists include Pete Johnson, Albert Ammons, Cow Cow Davenport, and Meade Lux Lewis (listen to Lewis's "Honky Tonk Train Blues" in SCCJ). Popular pianist Jerry Lee Lewis developed much of his style from this concept. Note that some ways the word "boogie" was used during the 1970s and 1980s do not fit the meaning described here.

James P. Johnson

James P. Johnson (1894–1955) was born in New Jersey and is part of an East Coast jazz piano tradition that was developing at about the same time as combo jazz was developing in New Orleans. He was the most respected and influential of pianists who smoothed the transition from ragtime to jazz. One of the first jazz musicians to broadcast on the radio, Johnson was already a prominent figure by the time jazz began to be recorded. In 1914 he wrote "Carolina Shout," and then, when he recorded a version of it in 1921, the style behind his reputation was documented for posterity. (Listen to it in SCCJ.) Though stride style was played by other pre-1920s pianists also, Johnson is usually referred to as "the father of stride piano" because his own brand of stride style did the most to spread this approach. (An example of stride style left hand is on the *Demo CD* Track 38.) According to Johnson's biographers, Dick Wellstood and Willa Rouder, Johnson dispensed with the stiff rhythms, the broken-chord melodies and march-like bass of ragtime, while contributing a fluidity, a harmonic sophistication, and an attention to chord voicings. He perfected an orchestral

James P. Johnson, father of stride piano, pictured here in 1921 at age 27.

Photo courtesy of Frank Driggs.

Listening Guide for

"You've Got to Be Modernistic"

Composed and performed by pianist James P. Johnson, recorded January 21, 1930; available on the *Jazz Classics CD*.

James P. Johnson was among the two or three most significant pianists in the first thirty years of jazz. This recording documents one of his meatiest and most spirited performances. The virtuoso technique, staggering strength and richness displayed on this recording help us understand why an entire generation of stride-style pianists were so impressed. (For demonstration of stride style, listen to Track 38 of the *Demo CD*.)

Pay particular attention to the stride-bass style played by Johnson's left hand almost relentlessly in this performance. The tremendous momentum of the piece is partly due to the locomotive-like power of Johnson's left-hand work and partly due to his percussive forcefulness in playing the highly syncopated right-hand parts.

Johnson worked out in advance most of what is heard here, though he varied it somewhat from performance to performance, as was the practice for pianists at that time. The choruses of the trio section contain the most improvisation, and Johnson's renditions of the first and second strains contain the least.

Elapsed Time

0' 00" **Introduction**

Four measures

0' 04" **First Section** (technically termed "first strain")

16 measures (A-A'-A-B, four measures in each section)

0' 20" **Repeat of First Strain,** with some modifications

16 measures (A-A'-A-B, four measures in each section)

0' 34" **Second Strain**

16 measures (A-A-B-A, four measures in each section)

The striding left-hand figures are sporadic.

Notice the syncopation and tricky interaction of the right and left hands in the B-section.

0' 48" **Repeat of Second Strain,** with modifications

16 measures (A-A-B-A, four measures in each section)

To appreciate how rhythmically complicated the B-section is, notice how much easier it is to count "1234 2234 3234. . . " when you are listening to the other sections.

1′ 05″ **First Strain** (16 measures)

The melody is played an octave higher than before.

The striding left-hand part resumes.

1′ 19″ **Introduction to Trio Section** (four measures)

This new group of sections is termed a "trio" because it is like the central section of a march, and such sections used to be written in three-part harmony.

In each 16-measure chorus of this trio, Johnson selects a melodic idea and varies it. Some of the choruses center around syncopated riffs in the manner that became common for swing era band arrangements, a device that is central to the pieces in the African American Retentions Sequence at the beginning of this CD. And, like its effect there, the riff style here also evokes a lilting, buoyant feeling. This is some of the first piano music to "swing" in the jazz sense of the term.

1′ 23″ **The "Trio" Section**

First Chorus of Trio

Johnson repeats a single riff six times.

1′ 40″ *Second Chorus of Trio*

Johnson toys with a figure that involves firmly striking two adjacent piano keys in the high register of the piano and letting the resulting dissonance ring. These piano keys represent the "major third" and "minor third" steps of the scale, which when crushed together approximate a "blue pitch," as on the *Demo CD* Track 58.

1′ 53″ *Third Chorus*

Johnson's melody for this chorus is played in the bass range.

2′ 09″ *Fourth Chorus*

This chorus is the most rag-like of all Johnson's choruses.

2′ 24″ *Fifth Chorus*

The melody of this chorus is like the first strain.

2′ 40″ *Sixth Chorus*

Johnson bases the first eight measures on one riff, the second eight measures on another.

2′ 54″ *Seventh Chorus*

Johnson plays his right-hand chords more frequently, thereby giving the illusion that the tempo has increased.

approach to jazz piano playing, as though he were a one-man band. Many musicians feel that he was never surpassed in this style. (Listen to his "You've Got to Be Modernistic" on the *Jazz Classics CD.*) At a time when informal competitions among solo pianists were common in New York, Johnson is said to have won more contests than anyone else. His speed, precision, dexterity, and imagination amazed musicians. The force and swing of his pianistic feats are legendary. Most jazz pianists who emerged during the 1920s, such as Art Tatum and Duke Ellington, said that Johnson influenced them.

James P. Johnson is known to jazz musicians primarily as an innovative stride pianist, but much of his living was made from work as composer-conductor-pianist for stage shows, and accompanist for singers. Johnson wrote 230 popular tunes and 19 symphonic works, as well as scoring 11 musicals for the stage. In fact, the famous piece "The Charleston" was written by Johnson for a stage show called *Runnin' Wild* that was popular in 1923. So in appreciating Johnson's status in American music, we need to remember that only one aspect of his career was central to jazz history. Since so much of his time was occupied writing non-jazz works, he was not very visible in the jazz scene for some years. His jazz stature was eclipsed during the 1930s by the attention given to other players. For this reason, he has not been given his proper due, even though he continued to record jazz during the 1940s.[8]

◇LOUIS ARMSTRONG

Trumpeter **Louis Armstrong** (1901–1971) is often called the "father of jazz." In fact, musicians often refer to him as "Pops." No list of jazz greats omits him, and most start with him. Born in New Orleans, he left in 1922 to join Joe Oliver's New Orleans style band in Chicago. The band's best known piece "Dippermouth Blues" takes its title from another Armstrong nickname, a reference to his mouth being as large as a dipper. A third nickname, Satchmo, is a variation on the same idea: Satchel Mouth. Although some of Armstrong's 1940s and 1950s recordings are outstanding, his most significant are the innovative series he made in 1927 and 1928 billed as "Louis Armstrong and His Hot Five" (or "Hot Seven").[9] Some of them included his colleagues from New Orleans, trombonist Kid Ory and clarinetist Johnny Dodds. Armstrong's earliest appearances on record had displayed him involved primarily with collective improvisation, as in his 1924 playing with Clarence Williams on "Cake Walkin' Babies From Home" (in SCCJ). But on his Hot Five and Hot Seven recordings of 1925–1928, Armstrong's dramatic solo style was showcased more than his collective improvisation skills. The music that he made in those recordings became a model for the swing era that followed.

Louis Armstrong appeared in about fifty movies and sang in most of his post-1930 performances. For instance, his vocal rendition of the theme from the Broadway musical *Hello, Dolly* was #1 for one week on the popularity charts. On February 15, 1964, he displaced the phenomenally popular singing group called The Beatles. With the success of the 1988 revival of his "What a Wonderful World" (in the movie *Good Morning Viet Nam*), Armstrong demonstrated the longest run of having singles rate on the national popularity charts. He even outdistanced singers Bing Crosby and Frank Sinatra. (Crosby and Armstrong both had hits during the 1920s.) Understandably then, the post-1930s public knows Armstrong more as an entertainer than as an innovative jazz improviser. Even though they have heard his name, most people are not aware of Armstrong's monumental contributions to the history of jazz.

Armstrong was the most widely imitated jazz improviser prior to the appearance of modern saxophonist Charlie Parker in the 1940s. Armstrong's style is particularly easy to detect in three of the most prominent trumpeters of the 1930s and 1940s: Oran "Hot Lips" Page, Bunny Berigan, and Buck Clayton. His influence extended not only to trumpeters, but to saxophonists, pianists, guitarists, and trombonists. For instance, Johnny Hodges, the most influential alto saxophonist of the 1930s, said that Armstrong influenced his sax style. Players within the swing era almost universally cite Armstrong's influence. Segments of his tunes and improvisations continued to be found in the work of such post-swing era innovators as Charlie Parker and Lee Konitz.

Louis Armstrong's Historic Contributions

Let's examine a few aspects of Armstrong's work that musicians appreciated so much:

1) Armstrong showed that the New Orleans technique of collective improvisation need not be the only approach to jazz horn work. Intelligently developed solos could be improvised in a stirring manner, and the musical effectiveness of such solos need not depend much on ensemble interaction. In other words, **Armstrong was one of the**

Listening Guide for

"West End Blues"

Composed by Joe Oliver; recorded June 6, 1928, in Chicago by Louis Armstrong (trumpet and vocal), Jimmy Strong (clarinet), Fred Robinson (trombone), Earl Hines (piano), Mancy Cara (banjo), and Zutty Singleton (drums); available on the *Jazz Classics CD;* on SCCJ; and on *Louis Armstrong and Earl Hines, Vol. 4* (Columbia: CK 45142, 1928).

Terms to know from the *Demo CD* before using this listening guide: ride rhythm, legato, staccato, pitch smear, tremolo, octave voicing, stride style, double-time, 12-bar blues, chorus, vibrato, banjo, trumpet, trombone, and clarinet.

CD Track	Elapsed Time	
8	0' 00"	**Introduction**

The opening phrases in this piece are among the most famous in jazz history. Note the drama as Armstrong reaches up to his highest note, the one he sustains. Then listen to the manner in which he gradually descends to finish with a note that makes you eager to hear what follows. Notice his warm, brassy tone and his sure-footed manner. This introduction is a masterpiece that you might want to hear several times before listening to the rest of the performance.

The idea of a bravura solo style, particularly an unaccompanied solo passage like this, was common in light classical music that was popular in America around 1900. Virtuoso cornet soloists were frequently featured in band concerts at that time. In addition, the trumpet sounds of Mexican bands that visited New Orleans had impressed musicians there. When Louis Armstrong devised this stirring opening, he was drawing, either consciously or unconsciously, from that tradition in light classical music, and he was establishing a tradition in jazz.

0' 13" Full band plays a chord

0' 16" **First Chorus** (a 12-bar blues played slowly)

Melody Played by Armstrong on Trumpet

Notice Armstrong's firm, deliberate manner and quick vibrato.

Accompaniment includes:

soft, sustained trombone notes (often preceded by a smear of pitch that begins well below the ultimate note;

sustained tones of clarinet, sometimes paralleling the motion of the trumpet line (listen for the clarinet's edgy timbre and fast vibrato);

trombone and clarinet notes together indicating the chords changing underneath the trumpet; piano chords sounded in unison along with banjo chords played staccato on each beat ("chomp chomp chomp chomp. . . ")

9 0′ 50″ **Second Chorus**

Trombone Solo

The trombonist uses the high register and many smears of pitch.

Accompaniment includes:

staccato chording from banjo;

tremolo chords from piano;

slow ride rhythm played by drummer on a hand-held "Bock-A-Da-Bock" apparatus that brings together two cymbals that are each about three inches wide, played by drummer cupping the apparatus in his hand as in playing spoons.*

10 1′ 25″ **Third Chorus**

Improvised Duet Between Clarinet and Armstrong's Vocal

This chorus employs a call-and-response format, with the vocal supplying the responses. It is an early example of "scat" singing. Piano and banjo are chording in a staccato manner on each beat. The duet's last phrase is done in harmony. No percussion instruments are used here or in the next chorus.

11 2′ 00″ **Fourth Chorus**

Unaccompanied Piano Improvisation by Earl Hines

First Four Measures

Pianist's left hand is contributing legato chording in stride style while right hand improvises flowery figures.

2′ 10″ *Second Four Measures*

Style of playing by right hand switches to brash character and pounds out a double-time figure voiced in octaves. This is the famous "trumpet-style" piano playing of Earl Hines.

2′ 20″ *Third Four Measures*

Style returns to flowery character.

12 2′ 32″ **Fifth Chorus**

Trumpet Solo

First Four Measures

Sustained high note from trumpet for 16 beats. Accompaniment includes staccato chords from piano on each beat, and sustained trombone notes, and sustained clarinet notes.

2′ 45″ *Second Four Measures*

Trumpet line features double-timing.

2′ 55″ *Third Four Measures*

Horns stop playing for 12 beats while piano plays a descending sequence of chords, striking each in bell-like fashion, linking them with a glissando. Piano sustains a chord. Armstrong returns with a long, drawn-out bluesy figure played in a markedly slowed pace. It is accompanied by long tones harmonized by trombone, clarinet, and piano to form three different chords that conclude the piece.

*The Bock-A-Da-Bock cymbal apparatus is pictured as "cymbal tongs" on page 50 of *The Percussionist's Dictionary* by Joseph Adato and George Judy (Belwin-Mills, 1984; available from P.O. Box 21269, Cleveland, Ohio 44121).

first great soloists in jazz history, and, partly because of him, post-Armstrong styles usually stressed solo improvisation instead of group improvisation.

2) Armstrong was one of the first jazz musicians to refine a rhythmic conception that
   a) abandoned the stiffness of ragtime,
   b) employed swing eighth-note patterns,
   c) gracefully syncopated selected rhythmic figures, sometimes staggering the placement of an entire phrase, as though he were playing behind the beat, a technique called "rhythmic displacement." This conveyed a more relaxed feeling than ragtime, and it exhibited more variety in the ways that notes seemed to tug at opposite sides of the beat.

These rhythmic elements combined to produce one of the first jazz styles that could elicit in listeners what we today call "jazz swing feeling." None of these elements was entirely new with Armstrong. However, they were more clearly evident in his work as a finished product than in the playing of either his predecessors or other trumpeters of the 1920s.

Louis Armstrong, the most influential of all jazz musicians, and the most influential trumpeter in pre-modern jazz. Pictured here at age 26, in 1927, the year several of his classic Hot Five and Hot Seven recordings were made.

Photo courtesy of Frank Driggs.

3) Despite the numerous giants who have followed Armstrong in jazz history, few have approximated his skill and creativity as musical architects. Few had his degree of control over the general form of a solo. He calmly forged sensible lines that had both the flow of spontaneity and the stamp of finality. His improvisations are well-paced, economical statements. The organization of Armstrong's phrases suggests that he was thinking ahead, yet the phrases manage to sound spontaneous, rather than calculated.

4) He brought a superb sense of drama to jazz solo conception. His pacing was careful, allowing a solo to build tension. His double-time solo breaks were constructed to achieve maximum excitement, and his high-note endings ensured a properly timed peak of intensity and resolution of tension. (Listen to "West End Blues" on the *Jazz Classics CD,* and listen to Track 35 of the *Demo CD* for explanations of double-time.)

5) During a period when most improvisers were satisfied simply to embellish or paraphrase a tune's melody—and Armstrong himself was a master at both—Armstrong frequently broke away from the melody and improvised original, melody-like lines that were compatible with the tune's chord progressions. This became the predominant approach for jazz improvisation thereafter.

6) Armstrong's command of the trumpet was arguably greater than that of any preceding jazz trumpeter who recorded. It became a model to which others aspired. He had an enormous, brassy tone, and remarkable range. Altogether with his rhythmic and dramatic sense, he conveyed a certainty and surging power. Even during the final decades of his career, Armstrong maintained a tone quality that was unusual for its weight, breadth, and richness.

7) Armstrong popularized the musical vocabulary of New Orleans trumpet style and then extended it.

8) Armstrong's tremendously fertile melodic imagination provided jazz with a repertory of phrases and ways of going about constructing improvisations. In other words, he extended the vocabulary for the jazz soloist.

These next two contributions are less central to what made his reputation among jazz instrumentalists, but they remain significant in the broadest sense of jazz history.

9) The Armstrong singing style influenced many popular singers, including Louis Prima, Billie Holiday, and Bing Crosby. In this way, he affected American music beyond the boundaries of jazz. Armstrong's influence was so pervasive that Leslie Gourse titled a book about American jazz singers *Louis' Children.*

10) Armstrong popularized scat singing, a vocal technique in which lyrics are not used. The voice improvises in the manner of a jazz trumpeter or saxophonist. (This can be heard in his recordings "West End Blues" in the *Jazz Classics CD* and "Hotter Than That" in SCCJ.) Recent examples of the technique can be found in the work of George Benson, Al Jarreau, and Bobby McFerrin.

◇BIX BEIDERBECKE

Bix Beiderbecke (1903–1931) was a very important white trumpeter and composer from Iowa. His recordings are significant in early jazz, but he fits neatly into neither New Orleans nor Chicago style. He and Armstrong developed about the same time and became the leading trumpeters for the late 1920s and early 1930s. Beiderbecke's style gave young trumpeters an alternative to the model that Armstrong provided.

Distinguishing Cornet From Trumpet

In the early years of jazz, the cornet was much more widely used than the trumpet. The trumpet's and cornet's tones and ranges are quite similar, and many listeners cannot tell the two instruments apart. The tone color of the cornet is said to be mellow, and that of the trumpet is said to be more brilliant. Their appearance is also a confusing factor, but one distinguishing feature is the apparent length. The tubing of the cornet, although equal in length to that of the trumpet, is organized so that it looks shorter. Some old jazz cornets are especially compact and stubby.

The prime difference between trumpet and cornet, a difference that is difficult to see, is that the inside of the cornet's tubing is cone-like, whereas the trumpet's is more cylinder-like. The technical term for the inside diameter is "bore." So, it is said that cornets have a primarily conical bore and trumpets have a primarily cylindrical bore. Their mouthpieces are also slightly different, although the instruments are played in almost the same way.

Except for Nat Adderley and Thad Jones, most modern players usually use trumpet instead of cornet. Before 1927, nearly all jazz trumpeters used the cornet. The 1930s to early 40s was a period of transition between the two instruments: every band had a so-called trumpet section, but in at least two famous bands, Duke Ellington's and Fletcher Henderson's, the trumpet section sometimes contained more cornets than trumpets. This book ignores the problem and labels most cornetists as trumpeters for the following reasons: (a) most listeners cannot detect the difference in sound; (b) it is often impossible to determine from recording data whether a player was using trumpet or cornet on a particular session; (c) the only well-known player who used cornet exclusively throughout his career was Bix Beiderbecke; and (d) trumpet tone colors in jazz vary across a range that actually encompasses the pure tones of both trumpet and cornet.

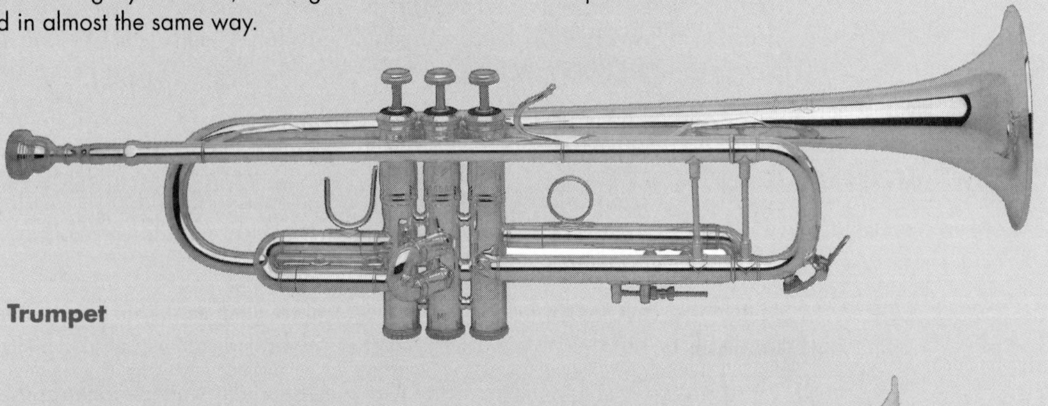

Trumpet

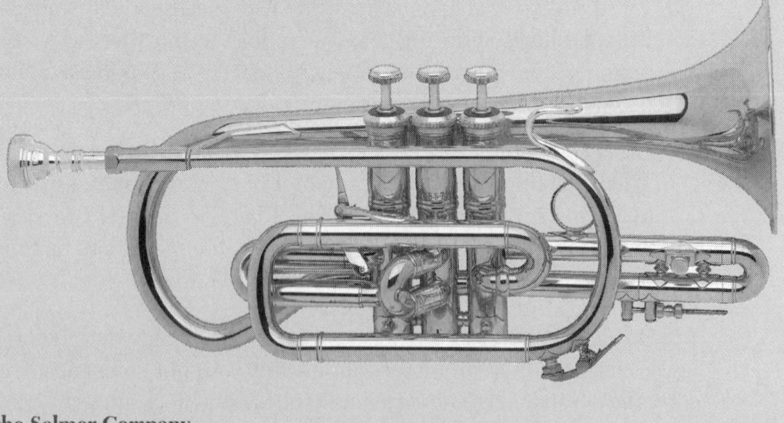

Cornet

Courtesy of the Selmer Company.

Beiderbecke first recorded in 1924 with a small group called the Wolverine Orchestra. Beginning in 1927 he became better known as a featured soloist with a much larger group—the famous Paul Whiteman Orchestra. Often considered the first great white jazz improviser, Beiderbecke influenced many trumpeters, the best known of whom were Jimmy McPartland, Red Nichols, and Bobby Hackett.

Beiderbecke was almost as original and creative as Armstrong, but he had less command over his instrument and a bit cooler sound. Beiderbecke's tone was softer, lighter weight, and less brassy than Armstrong's. His rhythmic approach was less aggressive. Like most early jazz players, he did not have pronounced jazz swing feeling when he began performing, but later he developed a swing feeling which approached that of Armstrong. Beiderbecke's attitude differs considerably from Armstrong's. He was less dramatic and more subtle. In contrast to Armstrong's assured, outgoing style, Beiderbecke was quieter and considerably more restrained. He played more in the instrument's middle register than did Armstrong, who liked high notes. Beiderbecke also paid more attention to stringing together unusual note choices and acknowledging every passing chord in the progression—something he knew well because he was also a good pianist. In this way, he anticipated trumpeter-guitarist Bobby Hackett, who also made masterful use of chord notes in his improvisations, acknowledging almost every passing chord. This approach brought acclaim to Hackett in his Beiderbecke-like solo on Glenn Miller's famous 1942 recording "String of Pearls."[10] (For comparison with Armstrong, see Table 5.3.)

Beiderbecke was also a composer who blended ragtime and jazz with the French Impressionist style of Maurice Ravel and Claude Debussy. His "Flashes," "In the Dark," and "Candlelights" are not well known, but his "In a Mist" has been orchestrated by numerous jazz arrangers. Beiderbecke's own 1927 piano recording of it is especially effective.[11] The piece is distinguished by its use of the whole-tone scale, a sound that was favored by Debussy (see piano keyboard illustration on page 145).

Beiderbecke and Trumbauer

Beiderbecke joined saxophonist **Frankie Trumbauer** (1901–1956) for several landmark recording sessions. Their 1927 recordings of "Singin' the Blues" and "A Good Man Is Hard to Find" represent two of the most relaxed, melodic, and tender performances in early jazz.[12]

TABLE 5.3 Comparing Louis Armstrong with Bix Beiderbecke

	ARMSTRONG	BEIDERBECKE
command of trumpet	virtuoso	solid
tone quality	full	bell-like
	hot	warm
	brassy	dry
range	wide	moderate
improvisatory character	outgoing	reflective
rhythmic conception	swinging	closer to ragtime
influences	Chris Kelly	Nick LaRocca
	Buddy Petit	Emmett Hardy
	Joe "King" Oliver	ragtime
birthplace	New Orleans	Davenport, Iowa

Trumbauer's instrument was a C-melody saxophone, an instrument that is a size between the alto and tenor saxophones. It is capable of a pale, light-weight tone. Trumbauer was a very precise and melodic soloist. He conveyed very relaxed feeling and employed a vibrato that was uncommonly slow for early jazz. Tenor saxophonist Lester Young, a significant figure in the beginnings of modern jazz, has said that he modeled his own light, cool tenor saxophone sound after Trumbauer's playing of the C-melody saxophone. Like Trumbauer, Young also sounded very relaxed and melodic and used a slower vibrato than his contemporaries.

The Trumbauer-Beiderbecke "Singin' the Blues" performance is one of the most heralded recordings in jazz history (listen to it in SCCJ). Many players have memorized the improvisations on it, and the Fletcher Henderson big band twice recorded the piece with a harmonized transcription of Trumbauer's solo. Jazz historians routinely cite Beiderbecke's solo for its advanced use of the tune's harmonies. The notes Beiderbecke chose for his solo go beyond the notes offered by the tune's accompanying chords and reflect a higher level of musical thinking than was common with most other improvisers of the 1920s.

◇CLARINET

Clarinet was more common than saxophone in early jazz, a situation that was reversed in modern jazz. Clarinet usually played countermelodies around the trumpet part. Clarinet solos were not usually as dramatic as the trumpet solos. Eventually, however, some clarinetists got away from a conception based on embellishment. By the late 1930s some early players and many swing era players were playing dramatic, well-paced solo lines.

Johnny Dodds

Johnny Dodds (1892–1940) was one of the leading New Orleans clarinetists who moved to Chicago. Dodds used an edgy tone and fast vibrato. With great confidence, he constructed fluid counterlines that managed an almost relentless activity for recordings by Joe Oliver's band in 1923. He had an aggressive solo style that featured swooping pitch bends that sometimes dwell on a single blue note. Many listeners call the effect of his playing "raw." (A jazz historian once said that some of Dodds's work could "curl your hair!") Listen to his work in the recording of "Dippermouth Blues" by Oliver's band and in "Struttin' With Some Barbecue" by Louis Armstrong's band (in SCCJ).

Jimmie Noone

Jimmie Noone (1895–1944) was a more polished player than Johnny Dodds and possessed a greater command of the clarinet. Some consider Noone to be the best New Orleans clarinetist. He had a dark, warm, round tone. He often played jumping staccato lines which had a lot of flash and verve. Noone was a favorite of Benny Goodman, a leading white Chicago clarinetist who went on to become the best known clarinetist in the twentieth century. (Noone made an excellent series of recordings in 1928 with pianist Earl Hines. Their "Four or Five Times" is in the revised SCCJ.)

Sidney Bechet

New Orleans clarinetist and soprano saxophonist **Sidney Bechet** (1897–1959) was one of the most highly regarded musicians in early jazz (see Figure 5.1 for a comparison of clarinet and soprano sax). He was one of the first great soloists. In addition to Armstrong, he was one of the first improvisers to display jazz swing feeling. Like Armstrong, he double-timed and created dramatic solos. Bechet had a big, warm tone with a wide, rapid vibrato. He was a very energetic, hard-driving improviser who played with broad imagination and authority. Along with Louis Armstrong, Bechet was among the earliest improvisers to devise a stirringly dramatic way of constructing solos. He and Armstrong cultivated these approaches after they had mastered the requirements of collective, nonsolo improvisation which are essential to the New Orleans tradition. (Listen to the New Orleans-style collective improvisation in their playing on "Cake Walkin' Babies From Home" in SCCJ.) In this respect, they introduced a new way for jazz hornmen to be viewed in combo format. Both men eventually became regarded primarily as soloists

FIGURE 5.1 Clarinet and soprano sax. To compare the sounds of these instruments, listen to *Demo CD* Tracks 69–70.

Photo courtesy of the Selmer Company.

instead of ensemble players. This helped make jazz into an improvising soloist's art. For at least the next four decades of jazz, collective improvisation skills remained almost exclusively the domain of rhythm section musicians, not hornmen. (See photo on page 72.)

Bechet exerted his impact on solo conception by mastering the timing of central notes and carefully using extended inflections of the note's pitch. (See pages 40–42 and *Demo CD* Track 50 for details.) Though capable of complicated, supercharged solo improvisations, Bechet's most popular solos are quite simple. Those that journalists discuss the most are slow-tempo performances that exemplify meticulous placement of a few carefully chosen notes. (Listen to "Summertime" and "Blue Horizon" in SCCJ.) The pitches of these notes are bent in manners that have been perceived as being highly sensual. "Blues drenched" is how some writers describe the sounds. The timing of these expressive devices demonstrates the command of restraint necessary for making an emotionally effective climax. This is especially evident in the ornaments Bechet employs to lead up to a central note. The scoop or smear of pitches Bechet uses to introduce a note is essential to the success of his improvisation. The long, swooping lead-in, which carries at its topmost note the precise moment for maximum dramatic effect, became standard in the vocabulary of jazz saxophonists. It was used extensively by swing era saxophonist Johnny Hodges, a Bechet disciple, and modern saxophonist John Coltrane, who followed in Hodges's footsteps.[13]

Many of Bechet's solos simply display the reworking of elementary blues phrases. The musical concepts of "bluesy" and "funky" are defined by Bechet's playing. He summarizes the instrumental equivalent of the blues singer. And, in this way, Bechet summarizes what many listeners have come to regard as the essential feeling of New Orleans style: an earthy, warm, and full sound that has searing intensity. (Listen to Bechet's "Blue Horizon" in SCCJ.)

◇TROMBONE

In ensemble improvisation, trombonists invented low harmony parts. They filled in gaps with devices similar to those of tuba and trombone in brass band music. With clarinet and trumpet filling out the middle and upper registers, trombone contributed to the combo sound in the lower range. When soloing, early trombonists tended toward a jazz trumpet

Sidney Bechet, the most famous clavinetest-saxophonist to emerge from New Orleans.
Mosaic Images–CORBIS.

conception to which they added the trombone's unique capacity for smears and slides. Rarely, however, did they play lines as intricate as those of early jazz trumpeters.

Kid Ory

Kid Ory (1886–1973) was one of the first notable jazz trombonists from New Orleans. (See photo on page 58.) His husky tone and assertive presence were an important part of several early jazz combos. He had a hard, cutting tone, and a percussive attack. His work had a boisterous air about it. Ory was also a composer and group leader. His "Muskat Ramble" (later spelled "Muskrat Ramble") became a jazz standard. (Listen to Ory on Louis Armstrong's "Struttin' With Some Barbecue" in SCCJ.)

Jack Teagarden

Jack Teagarden (1905–1964) was from Texas, and he ultimately became one of the most loved and best known of all jazz trombonists. He paid close attention to producing and maintaining a smooth, full tone which was prettier than that of most other premodern trombonists.[14] His work projected a thoughtful, relaxed quality, even though some of his favorite phrases were technically demanding. Teagarden's unique feeling and well-formed phrases were an inspiration to the trombonists of modern jazz. His style was possibly as important to jazz trombone history as Armstrong's was to jazz trumpet history. Teagarden's career was long and productive, running from the 1920s until his death in 1964. (Listen to his solos on the Red Nichols version of "Dinah" in SCCJ-R.)

◇RHYTHM SECTION

The front line of most early jazz combos included trumpet, clarinet, trombone, and occasionally, saxophone. The rhythm section was made up of several instruments which might include guitar, banjo, tuba, bass saxophone, string bass, piano, and drums. No bands had all these instruments playing at the same time, but most drew some combination from that collection. It was not unusual for early jazz combos to be without string bass, and many early jazz recordings were made without drums. Some groups substituted tuba for string bass, and in many groups the bassists alternated brass bass with string bass. Eventually many tuba players learned to play string bass, and by the late 1930s, most had abandoned the tuba. Some groups used bass saxophone (see Figures 5.2 and 5.3). Groups often included both guitar and banjo, though some had only one of these. Usually one player alternated between the two instruments. Piano was absent from some recordings and replaced banjo and guitar on others, though usually both piano and banjo or guitar were used.

Role of Banjo, Guitar, and Bass

The banjo and guitar were often strummed on each beat. The tuba, bass sax, or string bass frequently played on only the first and third of every four beats. This is called "two-beat style" because they played on only two beats out of every four. Prior to 1927, string bass was often bowed instead of plucked. (See page 19 for illustration of string bass.) Walking bass and two-beat style consist of longer tones when bowed than the staccato sound ordinarily produced when the bass strings are plucked.[15]

Role of Piano

Sometimes the pianist played chords in unison with the guitar or banjo, sometimes embellishments instead. In many groups, the pianist created countermelodies while the front-line instruments were playing melodies or countermelodies of their own. Stride style was another approach (*Demo CD* Track 38). Comping, as illustrated on the *Demo CD* Track 20, was only sporadically heard during this era.

FIGURE 5.2 Baritone saxophone—Bass saxophone.
Photo courtesy Dan Morgan/Straight Shooter Photography.

FIGURE 5.3 Tuba.
Photo courtesy of the Selmer Company.

Role of Drums

Early jazz drummers are poorly heard on records because early studio equipment was not well suited to recording drums. At that time, records were made by playing into acoustic recording horns. (See page 79.) The small end of the horn was connected to a cutting needle which made grooves in a cylinder or a disc. Any loud sound, especially a blow to the bass drum, could literally knock the needle off the cutting surface. Many recordings during this period consequently represent working bands minus their drummers. Many of the recordings that do employ drummers either omit most drum equipment entirely or muffle it so much that drum sounds are almost inaudible. We are often left with little more than the clickety clicking sound that is made by drum sticks striking a small wood block that has been hollowed out to increase resonance (heard on *Demo CD* Track 10). This was one of the only sounds drummers were ordinarily allowed to produce during the recording sessions in which engineers were apprehensive about the mechanical effects of loud sounds. (However, you can detect a number of different rhythm instruments in "Dixie Jazz Band One-Step" on the *Jazz Classics CD.*)[16]

The drumming style described above represents only one sample in a range of sounds commonly generated by the earliest jazz drummers, though it was particularly convenient in adapting to the restrictions of early recording situations. Light, staccato sounds were also produced by striking a cowbell or the shell of the bass drum instead of the drum head that usually receives the blow. These sounds were also employed in some early record dates, but, at that time, aggressive use of the snare drum and bass drum was generally limited to band engagements. A large cymbal or gong was sometimes used to signal a dramatic height in the music. Some jazz combo drummers of the 1920s also had orchestra and theater band experience, and so they brought along some of their orchestral approach when devising their combo performances. When playing on the light-sounding instruments, however, many of the earliest drummers chose patterns from military drumming and ragtime drumming, not necessarily from the tradition of orchestral drumming in which the percussionist only embellishes or reinforces other instrumental activity. The 1917–1923 drumming heard in recordings uses more military than orchestral concepts. (If you have a keen enough ear, you might be able to detect these military patterns played on snare drum by Tony Sbarbaro with the Original Dixieland Jazz Band in their 1917 "Dixie Jazz Band One-Step" on the *Jazz Classics CD.*)

Although we do not know exactly how he sounded, we do know what kind of instruments the early jazz drummer played. He did not have a high-hat. He had a floor cymbal apparatus which enabled him to strike a cymbal with a foot pedal, but it did not allow him to achieve the "chick" sound possible with the high-hat. He also had a bass drum, almost marching band size, two to three times as large as that which became popular during the mid-1960s. A snare drum mounted on a stand and a cymbal suspended above the set were also at his disposal. Wood block and cowbell were attached to the bass drum.

There are significant similarities and differences between the roles assumed by the earliest jazz drummers and those assumed by drummers in later styles. For example, on some of the earliest recordings, horn lines often existed without drum accompaniment. That these lines could exist and often did exist without drum accompaniment is especially important when combined with the observation that, on some of the pieces in which drum lines were present, drum lines constituted an additional instrument line rather than the timekeeping or "swing machine" function that drums provided for some later styles. The earliest jazz drummers could also perform in timekeeping style and often did. However, the point here is an additional one: **the earliest jazz drummers often devised lines of**

activity bearing rhythmic and melodic contours that were distinctly different from the contours of lines being contributed by their fellow musicians. The practice of playing an independent line of activity was suppressed in swing, the primary jazz style of the 1930s. It enjoyed a resurgence, however, in bop, the primary modern jazz style of the 1940s. In modern jazz, this independent line of activity has sometimes been termed "chatter," and it provides a layer of boiling sounds that increases the excitement of the combo performance. The use of this activity continued throughout the 1950s and 1960s, increasing in density and importance. It has been an accepted practice for all modern drummers of the 1970s and 1980s. The rhythms used by the modern drummers were not those of ragtime, but the spirit in which they were played is analogous to the conception shown by the earliest jazz drummers.

Another important comparison can be made between early jazz drumming and later styles. The earliest drummers sometimes changed loudness, rhythm, and/or instrument for each successive soloist. Many of their accompaniment patterns, however, usually remained patterns rather than deriving spontaneously from rhythmic ideas heard in the improvised solo lines they accompanied, as later occurred in modern drumming. Spontaneous interaction between soloist and accompanist was limited.[17]

"Baby" Dodds

New Orleans drummer **Warren "Baby" Dodds** (1898–1959), brother of clarinetist Johnny Dodds, has been credited with pioneering the use of the ride rhythm. He played it on the snare drum. Later in jazz history, ride rhythms were played on the high-hat. By the 1950s and 1960s, they had become the primary timekeeping rhythms, and drummers played them on the ride cymbal. (Listen to the *Demo CD* Tracks 3, 11, 12, and 13 for examples.)

"Zutty" Singleton

Arthur "Zutty" Singleton (1898–1975), another leading New Orleans drummer, was among the first to use wire brushes to strike his drums. Brushes did not totally replace sticks, but they offered a lighter, softer sound, as well as the capacity to produce sustained sounds if dragged across and around a drum head or cymbal. Zutty also pioneered the practice of striking the bass drum on every beat. Many drummers had struck the bass drum primarily on the first and third or every four beats. Singleton can be heard playing brushes on Louis Armstrong's 1928 recordings of "St. James Infirmary" and "Tight Like This." He can be heard playing a suspended cymbal on "Skip the Gutter." And, on "No, Papa, No," Singleton can be heard briefly playing ride rhythms on a cymbal, thereby predating, by about a decade, the sound that was to characterize modern jazz timekeeping style.[18] Drummers George Wettling and Sid Catlett were influenced by Singleton. Catlett played a transitional role in jazz by helping jazz drum conceptions move from early jazz to modern jazz.

Guitar: Eddie Lang and Lonnie Johnson

During the 1920s, most guitarists confined themselves to timekeeping, or, they used simple, chorded solos when they played exposed parts. Guitar was generally ignored as a jazz solo voice until the late 1930s, partly because of the limited loudness that guitarists could generate before the electric amplification of the instrument became common. But two significant guitar soloists did record: Philadelphia-born **Eddie Lang** (1902–1933) and New Orleans-born **Lonnie Johnson** (1899–1970). Lang's work can be heard in recordings by violinist Joe Venuti, and in recordings made by the Beiderbecke-Trumbauer team, such as "Singin' the Blues" (in SCCJ). Good examples of Johnson's music exist in combo recordings with Louis Armstrong, such as "Hotter Than That" (in SCCJ), and a few moments with Duke Ellington, such as the 1928 Okeh version of "The Mooche."

The guitar styles developed by Johnson and Lang contrast markedly. Johnson was a bluesier player than Lang. A favorite means for creating the earthy flavor in his work was to let a tone ring while he glided up to desired pitch. Both men were well organized in their solos, but, in his execution, Lang projects an almost classical conception. (It is notable that he was first trained as a classical violinist.) His technique was excellent, and his lines were executed more cleanly than Johnson's. Listen to the counterlines which Lang improvises delicately under the horn lines in "Singin' the Blues" (in SCCJ). Their construction and execution is almost like that of classical chamber music. Although both players are historically significant, Lang has been the more influential of the two.

◇VOCAL BLUES

The "blues" refers to several different kinds of music. The first is a folk music developed in America by African slaves and their descendants. Because it was not written and it was developing before the invention of the recording machine in 1877, we really don't know how all its roots and developmental stages sounded. Researchers believe it originated from other vocal idioms such as (1) field hollers, which slaves devised from highly varied pitches and rhythms for the purpose of communicating among themselves while working in fields; (2) ballads, which come partly from European traditions for songs that tell stories; and (3) music devised for dances, such as the ring shout. Performing the blues involves some of the same techniques used by singers and musicians who play stringed instruments in Senegal and Gambia, the northern parts of West Africa. For example, the earliest recorded blues have enormous variety in the ways notes are sung. In particular, what might sound like moans and wails may indicate merely the vocabulary of drops and scoops of pitch in vocal music of the parent culture. (See page 42.) Or what may sound to us like odd starting and stopping points in the phrases probably reflects the rich variation of rhythms common to the music that influenced the blues. Creatively toying with the rhythms and pitches in the melody notes was commonplace. The effect of these manipulations became known as "bluesy" or "soulful." Twentieth-century recordings of Son House, Tommy Johnson, Charley Patton, and Robert Johnson provide us with an indication of how the nineteenth-century precursors sounded.[19]

In the beginning, blues was a form of unaccompanied solo singing. As it evolved, singers began to accompany themselves on the guitar or banjo. The earliest accompaniments did not necessarily use chords or chord progressions. Accompaniments often had only one note at a time or two notes played together. Eventually singers began to use chords. At first they used only whatever chords they already knew. They didn't necessarily learn a set of harmonies that would, in turn, dictate the notes they were allowed to use in the melody, as jazz musicians later did. Usually only a few chords were employed. There was much repetition in the accompaniment and in the lyrics. As the blues developed, the pattern of words and the rhythms of words in the lyrics began to become more and more standardized. By about 1910, a rhyme scheme had been adopted that had its own rhythm. (See the example of paired couplets in iambic pentameter for "Fine and Mellow," in the Elements of Music Appendix page xxx. Listen to Bessie Smith sing "Sobbin' Hearted Blues" on the *Jazz Classics CD* for *Concise Guide to Jazz.*) Underneath that rhyme scheme, a given progression of accompaniment chords also became standardized. It was similar to one in church hymns. (See Elements of Music Appendix pages xxx–xxx and *Demo CD* Track 19 for explanation and illustration.) This pattern of chords, in turn, set the pace for the twentieth-century tradition of blues performances that had no singing. Instrumental blues, as it has been called, evolved as its own idiom. (Listen to the trumpet, trombone, and piano solos on "West End Blues" in the *Jazz Classics CD.*)

Bessie Smith (1894–1937) was the most famous early blues singer. She had enormous talent and influenced generations of singers, both inside and outside the field of jazz. Though most significant for her blues contributions, she also sang other forms of pop tunes and was part of the vaudeville entertainment scene at large. She recorded with some of the best jazz musicians, including Louis Armstrong, James P. Johnson, and Benny Goodman. Smith outsold all other African American recording artists in the 1920s. (Listen to her "St. Louis Blues" and "Lost Your Head Blues" on SCCJ and "Sobbin' Hearted Blues" on the *Jazz Classics CD* for *Concise Guide to Jazz.*)

Known as "The Empress of the Blues," Smith had a voice so powerful that it could be heard over the sound of a band, even without using a microphone. It had a weighty quality that added to the unusual intensity of her effect. She had excellent intonation and breath support. Her manner was very aggressive and hard hitting. She played with the pitch and size of her sound to extract maximum bluesiness. Smith's songs were quite simple, and most were similar. The content was earthy and soul stirring. Her lyrics frequently recalled love affairs gone sour and feelings of self-pity and revenge accompanying such disappointments. In a straightforward manner her huge voice delivered these sentiments with seriousness and insistence.[20]

When trumpeters, clarinetists, saxophonists, and trombonists began playing jazz, they sometimes imitated the scoops and drops of pitch that blues singers used. They also decorated their songs with rhythmic displacements and tone qualities that had been demonstrated by blues singers. These nuances of rhythm, inflections of pitch, and varied timbres

Bessie Smith, Empress of the Blues.

Photo courtesy of Frank Driggs.

allowed instrumentalists to spice up bland melodies by making their rhythms less even and regular and the tone qualities and pitches of melody notes more flexible. Occasionally instrumentalists also picked tunes that had first been introduced by blues singers.

Many blues singers, not just Bessie Smith, hired jazz musicians to accompany them. At the end of the century, jazz musicians were still finding employment in blues bands, and many jazz bands routinely featured a blues singer. So you see that the blues tradition contributed to jazz in at least four respects: (1) providing a model for novel sounds, (2) offering a standard set of accompaniment harmonies, (3) furnishing part of the jazz repertory, and (4) giving work to instrumentalists. After jazz and blues had both become recognizable forms, blues continued to change over the years, parallel to, but usually separate from the course of development that jazz followed. Its progress occasionally overlapped with jazz, however. Eventually blues became a major part of popular music in America and provided one of the roots for rock and roll. Jazz, on the other hand, became more complicated, less popular, and some of it was considered art music, instead of popular music.

◇POPULAR APPEAL

The earliest jazz had a wide appeal, especially to youthful audiences and particularly to social dancers. This roughly parallels the kind of popularity enjoyed by rock during the 1950s and 1960s. But it contrasts dramatically with public response to modern jazz of later eras. Whereas modern jazz recordings rarely penetrated the pop charts, the Original Dixieland Jazz Band had several records hover near the top of the popularity charts, and jazz giants such as Louis Armstrong, Jelly Roll Morton, and Bix Beiderbecke were known to a wide public.

Like much rock and roll of the 1950s, New Orleans and Chicago styles of the 1920s are often perceived as happy music. Traditionally they have been used as entertainment to set a mood of cheer and frivolity. Though scholars and musicians often take the music quite

Ma Rainey, a well-known blues singer, and the jazz musicians she employed as accompanists.

Photo courtesy of Frank Driggs.

FIGURE 5.4 Recording by playing into acoustic recording horns. This was the method before the advent of electric microphones.

Photo courtesy of William Ransom Hogan Jazz Archive, Tulane University.

seriously, the public associates the sound with images of exciting parties in the "Roaring Twenties." Unlike the solemn view often ascribed to modern styles, the earliest styles are usually perceived as lighthearted and fun, though many of the early classics possess masterful construction and great depth of emotion.

New Orleans and Chicago styles did not just live and die with the 1920s. Their popularity has had its ups and downs since the decade ended, but the music has persisted because demand for it has remained. For instance, there was a revival of interest in New Orleans combo jazz during the 1940s, and several players who had left music returned to careers in performing. The music at New Orleans's Preservation Hall, since 1962, has been so popular that they have always had to have several bands on hand so that one could be on tour and at least one could be in residence. For many years it has been common to find a few good Dixieland bands in every major U.S. city. In addition, many regions of America sport yearly festivals of traditional jazz.

CHAPTER SUMMARY

1) The first forms of jazz resulted from blending improvisational approaches to ragtime, blues, spirituals, marches, and popular tunes.
2) The first jazz bands used the instruments of brass bands: trumpet, clarinet, trombone, tuba, drums, and (occasionally) saxophone.
3) The earliest jazz was not recorded. We can only infer how it sounded on the basis of recordings made by New Orleans players after they had moved to Chicago.
4) The first jazz group to record was the Original Dixieland Jazz Band in 1917.
5) Chicago was the jazz center of the world during the 1920s, comprised of
   a) all-star black groups such as Oliver's Creole Jazz Band which had moved from New Orleans,

b) white bands from New Orleans such as the New Orleans Rhythm Kings,
c) Chicago-born imitators of the New Orleans Rhythm Kings such as the Austin High Gang.

6) One of the most historically significant New Orleans natives to first record in Chicago was pianist-composer-bandleader Jelly Roll Morton.
7) Morton was the first great jazz composer. Several of his tunes became standards: "Wolverine Blues," "King Porter Stomp," "Milenburg Joys."
8) Morton devised a piano style that featured horn-like lines and long-short, strong-weak eighth-note patterns that swung more than ragtime.
9) Morton blended New Orleans improvisational approaches with elaborately arranged, prewritten passages.
10) The single player who stands above all others in jazz history is New Orleans-born trumpeter Louis Armstrong.
11) Armstrong possessed a large tone, wider range, and better command of the trumpet than most early players.
12) Armstrong's improvisations were especially well constructed.
13) Armstrong was one of the first combo players to effectively demonstrate solo improvisation instead of retaining the New Orleans tradition of collective improvisation.
14) Armstrong is possibly the most influential of all trumpeters, having been imitated by saxophonists, trombonists, and pianists as well as by trumpeters.
15) Next to Armstrong, Bix Beiderbecke was the most influential brass player of the 1920s, and he was harmonically more advanced than Armstrong.
16) In addition to a cool, thoughtful style, Beiderbecke was a composer in the tradition of French Impressionists Maurice Ravel, and Claude Debussy.
17) Soprano saxophonist-clarinetist Sidney Bechet helped move jazz horn conception from collective improvisation techniques to a dramatic solo style.
18) Bechet influenced Johnny Hodges and John Coltrane, especially in the expressive timing of ornamentations which precede important notes.
19) Earl Hines helped take jazz piano conception from a traditionally pianistic orientation to a horn-like conception.
20) Hines influenced numerous other piano greats, including Teddy Wilson, Art Tatum, and Nat Cole.
21) The stride piano tradition of James P. Johnson was continued by Fats Waller, who, in turn, became the principal influence on Count Basie.
22) Vocal blues originated before jazz, then influenced jazz by offering novel sounds and new repertory.
23) Blues singers often hired jazz musicians for their bands.
24) Bessie Smith was the most famous blues singer from the 1920s.

NOTES

1. Original Dixieland Jazz Band, *The 75th Anniversary* (RCA Bluebird: 07863-61098-2,1917-21). For more about this band and this period of jazz history, see Martin Williams, *Jazz Masters of New Orleans* (Macmillan, 1970; DaCapo, 1979), Nat Shapiro and Nat Hentoff, *Hear Me Talkin' to Ya* (Rinehart, 1955; Dover, 1966); Mezz Mezzrow, *Really the Blues* (Random House, 1946; Citadel, 1990); Gunther Schuller, *Early Jazz* (Oxford, 1968); and Max Harrison, Charles Fox, and Eric Thacker, *The Essential Jazz Records, Vol. 1: Ragtime to Swing* (Mansell, 1984; DaCapo, 1988).

2. *Louis Armstrong and King Oliver* (Milestone: 47017 (Gennet/ Paramount), 1923–24); *King Oliver's Jazz Band* (Smithsonian: 2001(Okeh), 2LP set, 1923); Kid Ory's recordings from 1922 are on *Steppin' on the Gas: Rags to Jazz, 1913–1927* (New World: 269, LP, 1913–27). For more about Oliver, see Laurie Wright, *King Oliver* (Storyville, 1987).

3. *The New Orleans Rhythm Kings* (Milestone: 47020, 1922–23).

4. Stride style left-hand consists of playing a bass note on the first and third beats and a mid-range chord on the second and fourth beats of each measure. Listen to a dissected example on the *Demo CD* Track 38. Together, the two hands produced music which you might imagine as a small orchestra with a driving rhythm section. This style is very demanding for the pianist. Listen to James P. Johnson's "You've Got to Be Modernistic" on the *Jazz Classics CD.*

5. For more about Morton, see Alan Lomax, *Mister Jelly Lord* (University of California Press, 1973), and listen to Jelly Roll Morton, *The Pearls* (RCA Bluebird: 6588-2-RB, 1926–38). His "Mamanita" and "The Pearls" are on *Jazz Piano* (Smithsonian: 7002 (RD-039), 4CD set, 1924–78).

6. *Louis Armstrong & Earl Hines* (Columbia: CK 45142, 1928); *The Earl Hines Collection: Piano Solos, 1928–1940* (Collector's Classics: COCD-11, 1928–40). "Blues in Thirds," "Chimes in Blues," and "Fifty-Seven Varieties" are on *Jazz Piano* (Smithsonian). See Stanley Dance, *The World of Earl Hines* (Scribner's, 1977; DaCapo, 1983); Gunther Schuller, *The Swing Era* (Oxford, 1989), 263–291; and Richard Hadlock, *Jazz Masters of the Twenties* (Macmillan, 1965; DaCapo, 1988).

7. See *Turn on the Heat: The Fats Waller Piano Solos* (RCA Bluebird: 2482-2-RB, 2 CD set, 192741). See Paul S. Machlin, *Stride: The Music of Fats Waller* (Twayne, 1985); and Maurice Waller and Anthony Calabrese, *Fats Waller* (Schirmer, 1997).

8. See Scott E. Brown and Robert Hilbert, *James P. Johnson: A Case of Mistaken Identity* (Scarecrow, 1986).

9. Listen to "Struttin' with Some Barbecue" and "Hotter Than That" on SCCJ, and see Scott Reeves's analysis of the solo on "Hotter Than That" in his *Creative Improvisation,* 2nd ed. (Prentice-Hall, 1995). Gunther Schuller provides transcriptions and analyses for several of Armstrong's best solos of the 1920s in *Early Jazz* (Oxford, 1968). More from this period can be heard on a number of Armstrong albums: *Hot Fives & Sevens, Vol. 1* (Columbia: CK 44049, 1925–26); *Vol. 2* (Columbia: CK 44253, 1926–27); *Vol. 3* (Columbia: CK 44422, 1927–28); *Vol. 4* (Columbia: CK 45142, 1928). Gunther Schuller provides transcriptions and analyses for several Armstrong solos of the 1930s and 1940s in *The Swing Era* (Oxford, 1989), 158–197. For more about Armstrong's life, see Max Jones and John Chilton, *Louis* (Little, Brown, 1971; DaCapo, 1988); Gary Giddins, *Satchmo* (Doubleday, 1988); and Armstrong's autobiography: *Satchmo: My Life in New Orleans* (Prentice-Hall, 1954: DaCapo, 1986).

10. See Glenn Miller, *The Popular Recordings* (RCA Bluebird: 9785-2-RB, 3CD set, 1938–42).

11. *Bix Beiderbecke, Vol. 1: Singin' the Blues* (Columbia: CK 45450, 1927–28).

12. *Bix Beiderbecke, Vol. 1: Singin' the Blues* (Columbia: CK 45450); *Bix Beiderbecke, Vol. 2: At the Jazz Band Ball* (Columbia: CK 46175, 1927–28). See the biography, Richard M. Sudhalter, P.R. Evans, & W.D. Myatt, *Bix: Man & Legend* (Schirmer, 1974).

13. Hodges preferred to preface an important note with a gradual smearing of pitches, whereas Coltrane usually selected a rapid, scale-like sequence to sweep up to that central tone. (Listen to Coltrane play soprano and note his attention to such prefaces to his high notes in "The Promise" on the *Jazz Classics CD.* Listen to the exquisite timing and very sensual results in the Johnny Hodges rendition of "Prelude to a Kiss" on the *Jazz Classics CD.*) Hodges's pre-1940 playing also displayed some of the double-timing and ebullience of Bechet. For an example of Hodges's double-timing, listen to his solo on Duke Ellington's 1940 recording of "In a Mellotone" in SCCJR. For close comparison of the two soprano sax styles, play Bechet's "Really the Blues" (1938), then Hodges's "Jeep's Blues" (1938); and Bechet's "When It's Sleepy Time Down South" (1941), then Hodges's "Empty Ballroom Blues" (1938). The Hodges numbers are on Duke Ellington, *The Duke's Men: Small Groups, Vol. 2* (Columbia/Legacy: C2K 48835, 2 CD set, 1938–39). The Bechet numbers are on *The Legendary Sidney Bechet* (RCA Bluebird: 6590-2-RB, 1932–41). Hodges later slowed down and smoothed out considerably, but retained the smoothness of tone and soulful inflections of pitch learned from Bechet. During the 1960s, the soprano sax was revived by modern saxophonist John Coltrane, who called one of his compositions "Blues to Bechet." Then during the 1980s, the instrument reached its widest audience in the hands of saxophonist Kenny G, whose records sold millions of copies. See also John Chilton, *Sidney Bechet* (Oxford, 1987).

14. Jack Teagarden, *King of the Blues Trombone* (Columbia Special Products: JSN 6044, 3LP set, 1928–40). For biography, see Jay D. Smith and Leonard F. Guttridge, *Jack Teagarden: The Story of a Jazz Maverick* (Cassell, 1960; DaCapo, 1976).

15. SCCJ provides examples for these techniques. A two-beat style tuba part can be heard in portions of "Potato Head Blues" (1927) by Louis Armstrong. Walking bass alternating with two-beat style can be heard on "Black Bottom Stomp" and "Dead Man Blues" (both 1926) recorded by Jelly Roll Morton, available on SCCJ. A bass saxophone can be heard playing in this rhythm role on Frankie Trumbauer and Bix Beiderbecke's "A Good Man Is Hard to Find" (1927) on *Bix Beiderbecke, Vol. 2: At the Jazz Band Ball.* See Figure 5.2 for a bass saxophone illustration. For more about early bass, see George M. Foster, *Pops Foster: The Autobiography of a New Orleans Jazzman* (University of California Press, 1971).

16. Listen to Warren "Baby" Dodds play wood block with Oliver's Creole Jazz Band on "Dippermouth Blues" (1923) in SCCJ, and Listen to Tony Sbarbaro play it on the Original Dixieland Jazz Band's "Margie" (1920) or "Home Again Blues" (1921) (see footnote 1). See pages 413–414 for information on how to get an illustrated history of premodern drumming. For more about these techniques, see Larry Gara, *The Baby*

Dodds Story (Contemporary, 1959), and listen to *Baby Dodds Talking and Drum Solos* [Footnotes to jazz, Vol. 1] (Folkways: 2290, 1946), available on cassette by special order from Smithsonian/Folkways; phone 800-410-9815.

17. All these examples can be found on *Louis Armstrong and Earl Hines, Vol. 4* (Columbia: CK 45142), or *Louis Armstrong & Earl Hines 1928* (Smithsonian: 2002, 2LP set).

18. The foregoing discussion will be almost meaningless unless you hear the sounds. Listen to the playing of Baby Dodds on "Dippermouth Blues" in SCCJ and that of Zutty Singleton with Louis Armstrong on "West End Blues" in SCCJ. In those examples, Dodds plays wood block and Singleton plays a pair of small, hand-held cymbals. (Wood block is demonstrated on *Demo CD* Track 10.) It would also be helpful to sample recordings that are not contained on SCCJ. For instance, Singleton can be heard on other Armstrong recordings of 1928: "My Monday Date" and "Sugar Foot Stomp" (see footnote 17). Dodds is best heard on the recordings that Oliver's Creole Jazz Band made for the Gennett company, not those made for Okeh. Oliver's recordings for Gennett are available on *Louis Armstrong and King Oliver* (Milestone: MCD-47017-2,1923). The 1923 "I'm Going to Wear You Off My Mind" has particularly distinct wood block playing, in which Dodds's accompaniment rhythms show considerable variety, seeming to constitute a response to the rhythms of the solo lines. This might, however, have been worked out ahead and not be purely improvised for this particular recording. Tony Sbarbaro can be heard on the 1917 recording of "Dixie Jazz Band One Step" by the Original Dixieland Jazz Band on the *Jazz Classics CD*. After a passage of snare drum, bass drum, and cymbals, he plays wood block and cowbell. This combination can also be heard in the 1918 recording of "Clarinet Marmalade." Note that most all of Sbarbaro's instruments can be heard in these recordings, Sidney Bechet, the most famous clarinetist-saxophonist to emerge from New Orleans, despite what has been said about drummers not having entire drum sets in the studio. The ODJB recordings for Victor have been reissued on *The 75th Anniversary* (RCA Bluebird: 07863-61098-2, 1917–21).

19. *The Roots of the Blues* (New World: 80252-2, 1959) has field recordings and compares African and African American sources for blues singing style. New World records can be found in many libraries and ordered from 701 Seventh Ave., NY, NY 10036; phone 212-302-0460. *Legends of the Blues, Vol. 1* (Columbia: CK 46215, 1925-65) has Bessie Smith, Robert Johnson, Leadbelly, Lonnie Johnson, and others. *Roots of Robert Johnson* (Yazoo 1073) has Charley Patton, Son House, and others.

20. Bessie Smith, *The Collection* (Columbia: CK 44441, 1923-33); Smith, *The Complete Recordings, Vol. 2* (Columbia C2K 47471, 2CD set, 1924–25). For biography, see Chris Albertson, *Bessie* (Stein & Day, 1972).

Chapter Six

Benny Goodman, 1936   Photo courtesy of Duncan Schiedt

Swing

During the 1930s, a new style of jazz emerged. It ultimately became the most popular kind of jazz in the twentieth century. This style began gradually during the late 1920s and continued into the 1940s. Over this period, jazz began to swing more because musicians adopted swing eighth-note patterns and a looser, less stiff rhythmic feeling. (For demonstration of swing eighth-note patterns, see pages 364–369 and *Demo CD* Track 44.) **Most jazz from the 1930s and early 1940s is called "swing music," and this time in history is now known as "the swing era." Much of its music was played by bands of ten or more musicians, and so it is also called "the big band era."** Partly because of its rhythmic properties, swing-style jazz attracted millions of dancers. It also produced several excellent big bands. A few soloists with these bands went on to influence the development of modern jazz.

Let's examine how swing-style jazz differs from early jazz.

1) The preferred instrumentation for swing was **big band** rather than combo, and greater use of written arrangements therefore occurred during the swing era.

2) **Saxophones** were more common in swing.

3) **Bass viol** appeared more often in swing.
4) **High-hat** cymbals were used more.
5) Collective improvisation was rare in swing.
6) Overall **rhythmic feeling was smoother.**
7) Swing musicians usually showed a **higher level of instrumental proficiency** in terms of speed, agility, tone control, and playing in tune.

Big Band Instrumentation

Big bands were made up of ten or more musicians whose instruments were grouped into three categories called "sections": rhythm, brass, and saxophone. The rhythm section was usually comprised of piano, guitar, bass viol, and drums. The brass section was, in turn, divided into trumpet section and trombone section. The saxophone section was separate from "the brass section" even though saxophones are also made of brass. Saxophones are technically classified with the "woodwind" instrument family because they originated from instruments traditionally made of wood (clarinet, flute, and oboe). They are also played in the manner of traditional wooden instruments. Incidentally, the sax section was often called the "reed section" because most saxophonists also played clarinet, and both sax and clarinet have cane reeds attached to their mouthpieces. This label was retained in later decades, even when saxophonists began alternating flute, a non-reed instrument.

The alto and tenor saxophones were the most frequently used saxes in the big bands. By the late 1930s, most bands were also using the baritone saxophone. (See Figure 6.1, and listen to the tenor and baritone sax solos on "Cottontail" on the *Jazz Classics CD.*) The soprano and bass saxophones were not common. (To learn how the different saxophones sound, listen to *Demo CD* Tracks 72–73. To hear them playing together, listen to "Harlem Airshaft" and "Cottontail" on the *Jazz Classics CD.*)

The sax section contained from three to five musicians. By the late 1940s, two altos, two tenors, and a baritone had become the standard make-up. The leader of the sax section, an alto saxophonist, sat in the middle. The baritone saxophonist sat on one end, the tenor saxophonist on the other. Saxophonists did not usually play only one instrument. Some, for instance, were required to alternate clarinet with alto and baritone saxophones.

The trumpet section varied from two to five musicans. Three was the standard number during the late 1930s and early 1940s. The lead trumpeter usually sat in the middle. The trombone section ranged from one to five musicans, two to three being standard. The lead trombonist was in the center. (Trumpet and trombone are demonstrated on *Demo CD* Tracks 59 and 78. Combinations of these instruments can be heard on "Cottontail" on the *Jazz Classics CD.*)

Big Band Arrangements

With the growth of big bands came an increase in the use of written arrangements. These had not been as necessary with small combos. As bands became bigger, it was more difficult to improvise a respectable performance, though some bands did succeed in playing without written arrangements. Eventually, however, musicians had to learn to read and write arrangements to have a big enough repertory on hand. A newcomer had much less difficulty adapting to a band that used written arrangements rather than memorized routines.

The compositional devices employed in most of the arrangements were simple. Melodies were played by the entire band in unison or in harmony. (Listen to the saxes and trumpets play the melody together in "Cottontail" on the *Jazz Classics CD.*) Then jazz improvisation followed, accompanied both by the rhythm section and by figures scored for other members of the group. (Sax improvisation is accompanied by rhythm section and brass figures in the bridge sections of the second and third choruses in "Cottontail.") The melodies and accom-

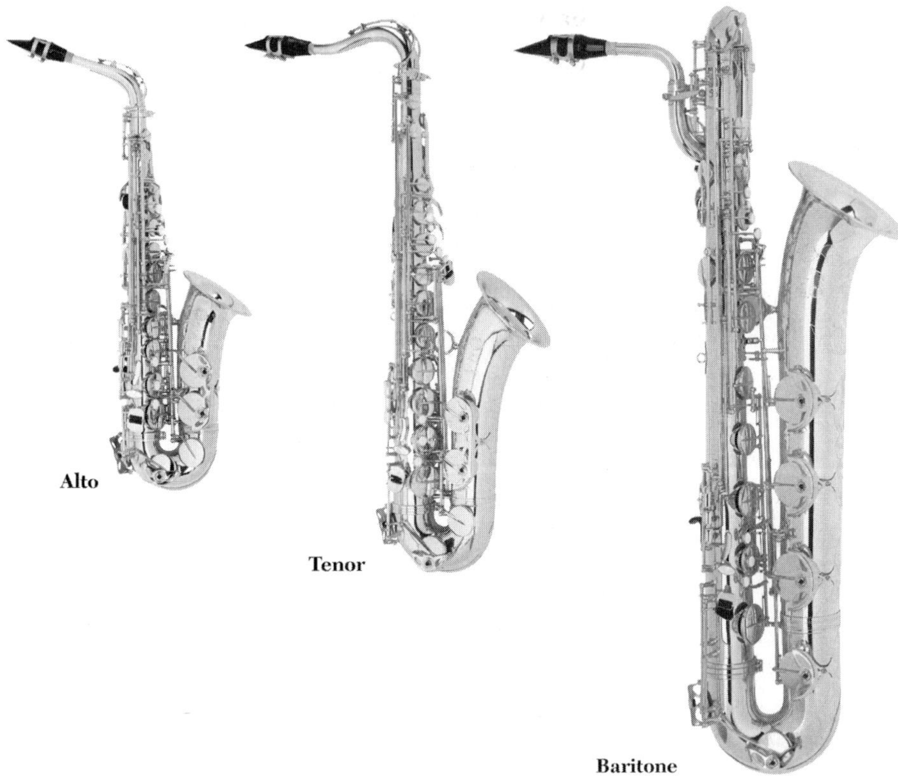

FIGURE 6.1 Saxophones. Alto (on left), tenor (middle), and baritone saxophone (on right). Listen to *Demo CD* Tracks 72–74 to compare the sounds of these instruments.
Courtesy of the Selmer Company.

panying figures were taken up in turn by one section of the band and then another. Saxes might state the A-section, brass state the bridge, and so forth. In addition to pop tune melodies, arrangements often contained variations on those themes. Some of the variations were as good as improvised solos (as in in the fifth chorus of "Cottontail"). These were offered as passages for one section of the band to play while another accompanied them or remained silent. Sometimes portions within the passages were passed back and forth. This sounded as though one section of the band posed a question and another section answered it. This technique is called *call-and-response,* question and answer, or responsorial style. (Notice it in the sixth chorus of "Cottontail" on *Jazz Classics CD* Track 19 and the end of "One O'Clock Jump" on the *Jazz Classics CD* Track 5.)

Short, simple, phrases called *riffs* were used by some big bands as essential elements of their style. At times, different riffs were assigned to various sections of the band and played against each other. Such *antiphonal* (an-TIFF-on-ull) activities could swing a band buoyantly and give jazz improvisation a good send-off. Sometimes entire arrangements were based on such riffs. (Listen to Count Basie's "One O'Clock Jump" on Track 5 of the *Jazz Classics CD*. Listen to the fifth and sixth choruses of "Lester Leaps In" in SCCJ.)

The Rhythm Section

The rhythm section was usually comprised of piano, guitar, bass viol, and drums. The propulsive rhythmic quality in most swing era recordings is partly due to the sound of the guitarist percussively strumming a chord on each beat. This is known as *rhythm guitar style* (demonstrated on *Demo CD* Track 88). This role of **rhythm guitarist** remained an essential part of Count Basie's band until guitarist Freddie Green died in 1987, but it had disappeared from most other big bands during the late 1940s. Although the banjo had been present

TABLE 6.1 A FEW SWING-STYLE MUSICIANS

COMPOSING ARRANGING

Fletcher Henderson
Eddie Durham
Benny Carter
Sy Oliver
Don Redman
Duke Ellington
Billy Strayhorn
Eddie Sauter
Will Hudson
Budd Johnson
Edgar Sampson
Jimmy Mundy
Deane Kincaide

DRUMS

Jo Jones
Sid Catlett
Chick Webb
Gene Krupa
Sonny Greer
Cozy Cole
Louis Bellson
Buddy Rich
Dave Tough
Jimmy Crawford
Ben Thigpen

TROMBONE

Lawrence Brown
Dicky Wells
Trummy Young
Jimmy Harrison
Benny Morton
Vic Dickenson
Joe "Tricky Sam" Nanton
Bill Harris
J. C. Higginbotham
Jack Jenney
Tommy Dorsey

BANDLEADERS

Duke Ellington
Count Basie
Bennie Moten
Benny Carter
Chick Webb
Andy Kirk
Jay McShann
Cab Calloway
Benny Goodman
Jimmy Dorsey
Glenn Miller
Charlie Barnet
Boyd Raeburn
Woody Herman
Stan Kenton
Gene Krupa
Artie Shaw
Fletcher Henderson
Lionel Hampton
Bunny Berigan
Harry James
Earl Hines
Billy Eckstine
Jimmie Lunceford
Luis Russell
Claude Thornhill

TRUMPET

Roy Eldridge
Cootie Williams
Bunny Berigan
Harry James
Buck Clayton
Charlie Shavers
Frankie Newton
Henry Red Allen
Oran "Hot Lips" Page
Harry "Sweets" Edison
Rex Stewart
Harold "Shorty" Baker
Jonah Jones
Taft Jordan
Jabbo Smith
Herman Autrey

CLARINET

Artie Shaw
Benny Goodman
Barney Bigard
Woody Herman
Buster Bailey
Jimmy Hamilton

GUITAR

Django Reinhardt
Charlie Christian
Eddie Durham
Oscar Moore
Irving Ashby
Al Casey

PIANO

Art Tatum
Teddy Wilson
Billy Kyle
Mary Lou Williams
Milt Buckner
Count Basie
Duke Ellington
Nat Cole
Erroll Garner
Clyde Hart
Johnny Guarnieri
Jay McShann
Mel Powell
Jess Stacy

BASS

John Kirby
Walter Page
Jimmy Blanton
Israel Crosby
Wellman Braud
Milt Hinton
Slam Stewart

VIBRAHARP

Red Norvo
Lionel Hampton
Adrian Rollini
Tyree Genn

SAXOPHONE

Chu Berry
Coleman Hawkins
Johnny Hodges
Benny Carter
Willie Smith
Herschel Evans
Dick Wilson
Ben Webster
Lester Young
Georgia Auld
Don Byas
Russell Procope
Illinois Jacquet
Hilton Jefferson
Tab Smith
Flip Phillips
Pete Brown
Buster Smith
Tex Beneke
Jerry Jerome
Boomie Richman
Vido Musso
Ernie Caceres
Earl Bostic
Joe Thomas
Budd Johnson
Jimmy Dorsey

in early-style bands, it dropped out of sight during the 1930s. Tuba had preceded string bass in some bands, but had been abandoned by the mid-1930s. Before the guitar and string bass became firmly established, guitarists had often been required to alternate guitar and banjo, while bassists alternated tuba (also called brass bass) and string bass (also called bass viol or bass fiddle).

The **pianist** in the rhythm section occasionally played melody instead of just chords and embellishments. Comping was not the common accompaniment style during the swing era, though Count Basie did use it. Pianists of the swing era used stride style or played a chord on every beat or every other beat. They did not necessarily improvise new rhythms to flexibly fit those of the solo line, as did their successors in modern jazz.

Bass

Bassists were usually assigned timekeeping duties. The sound of the bassist was heard on the first and third of every four beats, *two-beat style,* or on every beat, *walking style* (demonstrated on the *Demo CD*). Bassists during the swing era remained in the background, auditorily as well as visually. Bass features were very rare until the 1950s and remained relatively infrequent thereafter. In the next chapter, we will mention how Duke Ellington's bassist **Jimmy Blanton** originated melodically conceived pizzicato bass solos. But bassists in this era were usually felt more than they were heard. Some dancers and attentive listeners detected a difference in a band's rhythmic feeling when there was a weak bassist or no bassist at all. However, those same listeners rarely knew the cause for the difference.

When musicians discuss this period, three bassists besides Jimmy Blanton are also mentioned: **Walter Page**, **Slam Stewart** (1914–1987), and **Milt Hinton** (1910–2000). (For more about Page, see the Count Basie chapter.) Hinton made his reputation playing with Cab Calloway's big band during the 1930s, but he continued to be in demand for a variety of jazz settings through the 1990s. Known for his sure sense of tempo and huge tone, Hinton acquired a nickname of "The Judge" because, once he set the tempo for a piece, he was remarkably firm and authoritative in maintaining it.[1] Slam Stewart was a good timekeeper and a responsive accompanist, especially for the melodic flights of pianist Art Tatum, whom he often accompanied. Stewart is best known, however, as an inventive soloist. He is notable for a solo technique in which he bowed his bass while humming the same notes. The combination of voice and bass produced a rough-textured and original tone color. He humorously slid from note to note in his solos, but always managed to make a lot of melodic sense. Historically, Stewart's solo playing moved jazz bass a step away from the role of mere timekeeper.

Drums

The majority of drummers who played with big bands during this period tended to limit themselves to making the beat obvious for dancers and lending swing feeling to the band. These priorities were higher than doing as the earliest jazz drummers had done and creating a separate line of rhythmic activity that coexisted with the melodic rhythms of the horns. With the exception of striking cymbals and gongs for dramatically timed effects, many of the big band drummers played lengthy passages without doing much more than stating each beat on the bass drum and reinforcing this with a simple timekeeping pattern played on the snare drum with wire brushes or on a closed high-hat with sticks. Sometimes the second and fourth beats of each measure were emphasized by striking the snare drum with sticks. (This rhythm is called a "back beat.") Deviations from these patterns usually constituted simple embellishments of the beat or busy patterns that were quickly played when the horns were pausing between ensemble phrases. Swing drummers tended not to play new and provocative rhythms that ran counter to the horn lines. Listeners had to wait until modern jazz developed during the 1940s before they could hear drummers again offering a parallel line of activity instead of just keeping time. Listeners also had to wait to hear a substantial amount of interaction between improvising soloist and accompanying drummer. For the most part, swing drumming was quite conservative and not very light or swinging. It was not until the late 1930s that a lighter and more graceful sound was heard from big band drummers. And, even then, it was only heard in the few bands that were lucky enough to boast such drummers as Jo Jones and Dave Tough.

Jazz drumming authority Denny Brown has pointed out that the nature of the 1930s big band style restricted the jazz drummer's activity. It was decreased from the amount of rhythmic freedom that combo drummers had. The riff-based format used by big bands discouraged swing drummers from playing complex rhythmic patterns because such complexity might conflict with the melodic rhythms of the written horn parts. Brown contends that the 1930s swing era originated the idea that a jazz drummer should only be felt, not heard. Exceptions to this rule are notable, however, and **Gene Krupa's** popularity during this period might stem partly from his violating the norm. Brown suggests that Krupa's playing forecast aspects of modern drumming by being heard and by including patterns that responded to horn lines as well as building excitement. Some of Krupa's accompaniments are like solos. In that respect they are a continuation of the methods of the earliest jazz drummers and a contrast to the typical approach of swing drummers.[2]

During the late 1930s, a contrast to the Krupa style was offered by Count Basie's drummer **Jo Jones**. In place of Krupa's loud and insistent pounding of the bass drum on each beat, Jones often omitted bass drum playing altogether. In contrast to striking his high-hat while it was closed, Jones continued a ride rhythm on it while it was continuously opening and closing. He let the cymbals ring, thereby making a sound pattern that was less abrupt, more sustained (demonstrated on the *Demo CD* Track 2). This technique, together with an unusually close coordination with the bassist, projected a more flowing feeling than other rhythm sections produced during the swing era. Jones also gave each beat more equal treatment than his contemporaries had done. The feeling Jones conveyed, and the precision with which he played, evolved into the modern jazz drummer's tendency to play timekeeping rhythms on a suspended cymbal that is now known as the *ride cymbal*. (It is also notable that Jones steered clear of cowbell and wood block, which make sounds that today help us identify the corny aspects of premodern jazz drumming. For more about this, see chapter 3, and listen to the *Demo CD* Track 3. Listen to Jones in "Taxi War Dance" on the *Jazz Classics CD* and "Lester Leaps In" on SCCJ.)

Bandleaders

Some of the best swing bands were led by Fletcher Henderson, Count Basie, Duke Ellington, Jimmie Lunceford, and Benny Goodman.[3] Following this discussion are entire chapters devoted to Ellington and his musicians and Basie and his musicians. The Henderson and Ellington bands bridged the gap between the styles of early jazz and the swing approach. Each had begun in the early 1920s and had grown larger and more sophisticated by the late 1930s.

Many great early jazz and swing era improvisers worked with **Fletcher Henderson** (1897–1952) between the early 1920s and late 1930s (see Table 6.2). Henderson's was an all-star band. His style represented one major stream of big band jazz; Ellington's represented another. In his arrangements, Henderson pitted saxes against brass. He also perfected techniques of block voicing, in which the melody is the top voice of a series of chords, and each note in a chord is assigned to a different instrument or combination of instruments. It produced a thicker sound than if the line were not harmonized. Ellington used block voicing too, but he added an assortment of other special techniques that made his sound unique (discussed in the next chapter). Part of Henderson's arranging reputation resulted from the use of his work by the phenomenally popular band of Benny Goodman.[4] (Get SCCJ, and listen to Henderson's band play Henderson's arrangement of "Wrappin' It Up," later recorded by Goodman, and Don Redman's arrangement of "The Stampede." Redman was equally important.)

TABLE 6.2 MUSICIANS PROMINENT IN THE FLETCHER HENDERSON BANDS

TRUMPET	TROMBONE	SAXOPHONE AND CLARINET
Louis Armstrong	Jimmy Harrison	Coleman Hawkins
Rex Stewart	Charlie Green	Chu Berry
Roy Eldridge	Dicky Wells	Don Redman
Tommy Ladnier	J. C. Higginbotham	Benny Carter
Cootie Williams	Benny Morton	Ben Webster
Joe Smith		Russell Procope
Bobby Stark		Hilton Jefferson
Henry "Red" Allen		Buster Bailey
Emmett Berry		
DRUMS	**BASS AND TUBA**	
Sid Catlett	John Kirby	
Kaiser Marshall	June Cole	
	Ralph Escudero	
	Israel Crosby	

Jimmie Lunceford (1902–1947) led an excellent big band that was noted for its quality of swing feeling and well-disciplined musicianship. The consistency and balance of sound projected by each section of the band was matched only by their smooth, even swing feeling. Lunceford's band had exciting solo improvisers, and it could generate musical moments of "white heat" (the title of a lively feature number).[5] Its place in jazz history was earned for this special touch and the effect it had on dancers as well as fellow musicians.

During the 1930s and 1940s, **Benny Goodman** (1909–1986) led the most well-known big band that was jazz-oriented. His big band had a very hard-driving effect and showcased its leader's swinging, technically impressive clarinet playing. He influenced almost every jazz musician who played clarinet after him. (Listen to Goodman's clarinet solos on Red Nichols's band version of "Dinah" in the Revised SCCJ.)[6] His name was so high so often on the popularity charts that he ranks above all but five other artists making recordings between 1890 and 1954. This means that Goodman was one of the most popular figures in the music industry as a whole, not just in jazz. Today he ranks with Louis Armstrong and Dave Brubeck as one of the best known musicians in all of jazz history. In addition to his impact as a clarinetist, he may be responsible for influencing the course of jazz by the exposure he provided for other outstanding improvisers. His small combos were especially effective for bringing wide recognition to such swing era stand-outs as pianist Teddy Wilson, guitarist Charlie Christian, and vibraharpist Lionel Hampton. (Listen to Goodman's trio play "Body and Soul" and his sextet play "I Found a New Baby" in SCCJ.)[7]

Trombone

Many of the leading trombonists in early jazz were also prominent trombonists in the swing era. Their styles became more refined, and they were found more often in big bands than in Dixieland-style combos. Jack Teagarden and Tommy Dorsey were among this group.

(See the preceding chapter for coverage of **Jack Teagarden**.) **Tommy Dorsey** (1905–1956) led a tremendously popular series of dance bands during the 1930s, 40s, and 50s, as well as co-leading others with his saxophonist brother, Jimmy Dorsey.[8] He is best known among musicians because he developed a method of playing trombone which produced an extremely smooth, clear tone. His mastery of the instrument, his consistently polished manner, and his high-register work became the model for a string of highly skilled trombonists who had glossy tones and meticulous technique. **Lawrence Brown** was another standout of the era, though we treat his style in the Ellington chapter because he was known primarily to Ellington fans. The swing era spilled into the decade of the 1940s and produced an important trombonist who did not already have a reputation in early jazz. **Bill Harris** (1916–1973) was probably the most original and influential of the brass soloists featured in the Woody Herman big band of the 1940s. Harris is a transitional figure in the development of modern jazz trombone, emerging before J. J. Johnson. He had a broad, thick tone and quick vibrato which remained for the duration of each tone. Harris played with pronounced authority and employed good high range, by 1940s standards. Harris's well-constructed solos made use of staccato, punching figures in addition to slides and smears.[9]

Trumpet

Trumpeter **Roy Eldridge** (1911–1989) was one of the most advanced improvisers of the swing era. (Listen to his work with Benny Carter on "I Can't Believe That You're In Love With Me" in SCCJ.) He is often considered a link between swing and modern jazz. Eldridge had a fiery, aggressive style and unprecedented mastery over the trumpet. His imaginative choice of notes and sax-like lines bridged the gap between the style of Louis Armstrong and the modern approach pioneered by Dizzy Gillespie. Eldridge also creatively varied the size, texture, and vibrato of his tone. Sometimes it was clear and warm, at other times brittle and edgy. His high-register playing had a sweeping scope. In that register, he gave his entrances a rhythmic feeling which suggested modern jazz inflections to come.[10]

Roy Eldridge demonstrated that long, sinewy lines were possible on the trumpet. These, though easy to execute on saxophone, do not lend themselves to the mechanics of the trumpet. Eldridge's influence caused modern trumpeters to cultivate greater instrumental facility and to improvise in more intricate and unpredictable ways than their early jazz counterparts. His conception also extended the average phrase length used by improvising trumpeters. Eldridge's influence extended into the 1950s because trumpeter Dizzy Gillespie built his own influential modern style upon the foundation of Eldridge's bristling high-register work, unorthodox choice of notes, and saxophone style of phrasing. (Listen to Eldridge's solos in Gene Krupa's band version of "Rockin' Chair" in SCCJ.)[11]

One of the most famous swing era trumpeters was **Bunny Berigan** (1908–1942). Berigan based his style on Louis Armstrong's. Berigan was a very proficient trumpeter with a clear tone and remarkably clean articulation. His relaxed, assured style of playing was characterized by a fullness and consistency of tone from the lowest to the highest registers. His 1937 solo on "I Can't Get Started" was so well loved that it made this tune a standard in the repertory of trumpet players.[12] Berigan's improvisation in Tommy Dorsey's band recording of "Marie" was so impressive that it was transcribed and included in subsequent arrangements for other bands.

Saxophone

The man generally considered to be the first important jazz tenor saxophonist is **Coleman Hawkins** (1904–1969). Prior to his arrival on the jazz scene in the 1920s, the saxophone was considered little more than a novelty. Hawkins's supercharged playing on it brought recognition to the horn. His command of the instrument and his deep, husky tone became a model for other saxophonists. As a result, tenor sax became one of the most pop-

Roy Eldridge, the most daring trumpeter of the 1930s. Eldridge often improvised in the manner of a saxophonist by using long, swooping, scale-like lines. He also liked to dart into the high register and make his sound explode like fireworks.

Photo courtesy of Frank Driggs

ular instruments in jazz. In fact, it symbolizes jazz for many people. (Listen to his solo on Lionel Hampton's band version of "When Lights Are Low" in SCCJ.)

More than most other premodern saxophonists, Hawkins demonstrated great interest in chord progressions. He loved to play over complex chord progressions, such as those in his famous rendition of "Body and Soul" (on *Jazz Classics CD* for *Concise Guide to Jazz* or SCCJ.)[13] Often he seemed less interested in devising new melodies than in investigating the chord progressions that could be added to a tune's original accompaniment. Because of his attitude, some listeners consider Hawkins to be more of a harmonic improviser than a melodic improviser.[14]

Hawkins was a featured soloist with the Fletcher Henderson band from 1923 to 1934. He worked mostly with small groups thereafter. Though primarily associated with the swing era, he was also a respected figure at modern jazz sessions of the 1940s. His playing lacked the smoothness and fluid swing that typified modern jazz soloists, but his skill with difficult chord progressions helped him adjust to newer styles. Hawkins was one of the most intense and consistent saxophone soloists in jazz history. (Listen to his 1943 recording of "The Man I Love" in SCCJ.) A surging energy continued to flow unabated from his horn for decades. His influence was not limited to his swing era contemporaries. Such modern tenor saxophonists as Sonny Rollins and John Coltrane were also influenced by him. Hawkins, Coltrane, and Lester Young (discussed later) were the most influential tenor saxophonists in jazz history.

Coleman Hawkins, the first important tenor saxophonist to play jazz. Often referred to as "father of tenor saxophone," he had a robust style and showed sophisticated harmonic development in his solo improvisations. Shown here at age 45 in 1947.

Photo courtesy of Duncan Schiedt

Don Byas (1912–1972) was more advanced than most swing tenor saxophonists and could hold his own with many modern players of the late 1940s. (Listen to his "I Got Rhythm" in SCCJ.) Byas had fire, enviable command of the saxophone, harmonic sophistication, and melodic daring. He loved to double-time and run through every note in each chord. More significant was his tendency to add new chords to a tune, and to use both the original and new chords in his improvisations. He had derived this method from pianist Art Tatum. The richness of his lines easily matches that of later saxophonists. Though he had much of the huskiness in tone possessed by Hawkins, Byas swung more easily than Hawkins, perhaps because the ideas that Byas devised were less varied in their rhythms. Byas's style was widely appreciated by fellow saxophonists, and it became the primary model for two distinguished modern players: Lucky Thompson and Benny Golson.

Benny Carter (b. 1907) and Johnny Hodges were the most influential alto saxophonists of the swing era. Hodges will be discussed in the next chapter, but we will briefly examine Carter here. (Listen to Carter's "I Can't Believe That You're In Love With Me" in SCCJ.) The first elements of Carter's playing that usually strike listeners are the precision of his execution and the glow of his tone quality. His sound is rich and luxurious. His solos flow with grace and lightness. There is a striking neatness and order with which Carter plays his eighth notes. They are very even and well-measured. Carter devised intelligently conceived solos that are oriented in an obvious way to the changing harmonies of his accompaniment. He was also a good trumpeter, clarinetist, and a top-notch arranger.[15]

Piano

Art Tatum (1910–1956) is among the most widely admired pianists in jazz history. (Listen to Tatum's "Tiger Rag" on the *Jazz Classics CD* for *Concise Guide to Jazz* or "Willow Weep for Me" and "Too Marvelous For Words" in SCCJ.) Even when compared with all the very fast, imaginative pianists who have emerged since the 1940s, Tatum still stands above with his impressive technical facility and unceasing energy. His style combined a variety of techniques. In his improvisations and the ways he decorated pop tunes, Tatum was unpredictable. He indulged his impulses and pursued musical tangents, frequently interrupting the direction of his own lines. He often employed stride-style left hand as well as horn-like lines. (Horn-like lines are illustrated on *Demo CD* Track 40.) Tatum's playing was quite flowery, with long, fast runs which sometimes overlapped each other. He was a master at spontaneously adding and changing chords during his performance of pop tunes. This is termed *chord substitution.* Sometimes Tatum was found to be changing keys several times within a phrase and still managing to gracefully resolve the harmonic motion. (He had an enviable capacity for neatly getting out of precarious positions within the adventure of his improvisations.) Modern jazz musicians adopted both his chord substitutions and his methods of changing keys in mid-solo.

Rhythmically Tatum was also very inventive. His left-hand rhythms were full of surprises. He is also known for changing the piece's rhythmic feeling in mid-solo, sometimes leaving the intent listener dangling on an unresolved pattern while Tatum pursued another tangent. His right-hand playing sometimes seemed to throw showers of notes upon the listener. The rhythms in these showers were often odd combinations, not merely strings of eighth notes and sixteenth notes. But despite their complexity, Tatum's runs have been memorized by hundreds of pianists, and they have been used to decorate solos in performances by jazz pianists and popular pianists alike.

Art Tatum's impact on jazz history was enormous. His astounding mastery of the keyboard became a pinnacle for which other jazz pianists aspired. His practice of changing keys within a single phrase and adding chords were absorbed by tenor saxophonist Don Byas and modern saxophonist Charlie Parker. Tatum also influenced two highly innovative pianists who played pivotal roles during the early days of modern jazz: Bud Powell and Lennie Tristano (discussed in upcoming chapters). Both Powell and Tristano, in turn, went on to influence numerous pianists of the 1950s who further extended Tatum's impact.[16]

Art Tatum, Earl Hines, and **Teddy Wilson** (1912–1986) were the most outstanding pianists in the swing era. (Listen to Wilson's work with Benny Goodman on "Body and Soul" in SCCJ.) Like Tatum and Hines, Wilson also contributed to the development of modern jazz.[17] **Wilson lightened the sound of jazz piano playing and removed some of the weightiness that was found in piano styles of early jazz and swing. He replaced it with a fleet smoothness and streamlined quality.** Listeners are particularly impressed by the grace and evenness with which Wilson improvised even the fastest passages. It was as though equal attention were focused on every note, no matter how brief. His work could be dazzling.[18]

Like Tatum, Wilson is often mistaken for the type of pianist who usually plays in cocktail lounges and is therefore referred to as a "cocktail pianist." This is partly due to the pleasantness of his style. Both Tatum and Wilson influenced many cocktail pianists but do not themselves fall into this category. Melodic ideas, variety, swing, and refinement distinguish Wilson and Tatum from the multitudes of less-gifted pianists who have incorporated aspects of their styles.

Techniques of Earl Hines were especially evident in the early 1940s work of **Nat Cole** (1917–1965) and Erroll Garner. Cole was one of the first pianists to incorporate spare, hornlike lines in his playing. His lines exhibit a lightness that was not typical of the heavy-handed and flowery styles of premodern jazz. Cole also perfected a style of accompanying in which chords are played as brief, syncopated bursts. This eventually became known as *comping* (demonstrated on *Demo CD* Track 20). In 1939, Cole formed a trio comprised of piano, guitar and bass.[19] Most of his hit records of 1943 to 1949 were made with that group. The trio featured pleasant chord voicings that had a modern ring to them. The musicians closely coordinated their parts so that much of the music's rhythm was played in unison by piano, and guitar, with bass lines that tightly corresponded. Highly syncopated introductions and endings were devised, and cheerful little interludes often joined the various sections of each composition. Most of each piece was worked out in advance, but there was usually room for well-paced solos whose construction was logical and easy to follow. The overall effect was light and subtle, with a snappy kind of swing feeling.

Nat Cole had a more pervasive influence than most people realize. Modern pianists Oscar Peterson, Bill Evans, and Horace Silver have all cited him as an influence on their own musical thinking. Peterson has said that Cole was the main source of his own jazz piano style and that he tried to create as tightly knit a trio technique as Cole's. For several years, Peterson led a successful piano-guitar-bass trio that played in a style that was similar to Cole's. Evans has said that he was impressed by the way Cole could take a melodic idea and develop it over the course of an improvisation. (Similar remarks have since been made about Evans himself.) Cole's piano style received less and less attention after he became one of the most popular singers in recording history. His piano playing is often overlooked because of that.

Erroll Garner (1923–1977) is a unique figure in jazz piano history because he does not fit neatly into either the swing era or the bop era and because he originated a relatively unorthodox style. (Listen to "Fantasy on Frankie and Johnny" in SCCJ.) He attained recognition at a time when swing had already peaked and modern jazz had already been launched. Garner had a simple, swinging style that was easy to follow. His piano trio interpretations of popular songs, including his own composition "Misty," made him one of the best known of all jazz musicians to record during the 1950s. His greatest popularity occurred during the 1950s, even though his style was rooted in the swing era of the 1930s. And though Garner played in a swing style, he recorded with saxophonist Charlie Parker, who was the most significant figure in the creation of modern jazz. Garner influenced several important modern pianists, including George Shearing and Ahmad Jamal.[20]

The origins of Garner's approach are far flung. The sound of Earl Hines is suggested by Garner's octave-voiced right-hand lines and his pounding approach. Garner's melodic sense, however, is much simpler than Hines's, and he showed nowhere near the quantity of rhythmic surprises that typified Hines. It is notable that Garner's style evolved over the years, but he never relaxed his eighth-note conception to the streamlined feeling that was employed by modern pianists or by such advanced swing pianists as Teddy Wilson and Nat Cole. Several aspects of Garner's approach have assumed trademark quality for his name. One is that his left hand played a chord on each beat as a rhythm guitarist might, but each chord was played ever so slightly after the beat rather than directly on it. Another is a skillful use of loudness changes. (This is a trait that Ahmad Jamal might have learned from Garner.) A third prime aspect of Garner's style is a flowery manner that seems to almost drip with its extensive use of tremolo and grace notes.

Some of Garner's playing is richly orchestral, and it is harmonically like the French Impressionistic music of Claude Debussy and Maurice Ravel. Garner often voiced his melodies chordally instead of letting melody notes sound by themselves. This has led jazz historian

Harvey Pekar to feel that Garner's historical impact may have been to get pianists to think more in terms of chordal playing. Pekar suggests that, through a concern with chordal playing and impressionism, Garner may have begun a stream of styles which ran from Ahmad Jamal to Red Garland, and from Garland to Bill Evans and McCoy Tyner. Pekar also notes that Garner's regular statement of the beat with his left hand influenced—possibly through Jamal—Red Garland. Garner, however, played on each beat, whereas Garland punctuated just every other beat.

Milt Buckner (1915–1977) influenced pianists of the 1940s through his use of block chording, or the so-called *locked-hands style.* This is a method of voicing a chord and making the top note of it the melody note.[21] Buckner created piano solos that were like the four-, five-, and six-part horn voicings in band arrangements of the 1930s and 1940s. It was as though each finger played the part that a saxophone would ordinarily play. This contrasts to a style in which one hand plays a single melodic line while the other occasionally plays chords. In locked-hands style, the pianist uses both hands as though they were locked together, all fingers striking the piano keyboard at the same time. During the late 1940s and early 1950s, Lennie Tristano, George Shearing, Ahmad Jamal, Oscar Peterson, and others used this technique. Red Garland and Bill Evans used it in the late 1950s. During the 1960s, many pianists, including McCoy Tyner, made extensive use of block chording. Each pianist's particular approach to block chording became a signature for his style.

To briefly review jazz piano history up to this time, remember that **James P. Johnson**, Willie "The Lion" Smith, and other early pianists **had contributed the stride style. Earl Hines was a pioneer in playing horn-like lines. Meade Lux Lewis**, Pinetop Smith, Cow Cow Davenport, and others **introduced boogie woogie. Tatum had explored reharmonization.** And now **Milt Buckner had added locked-hands style** to the list of alternatives that were available for pianists to select.

Guitar

During the swing era, guitar was beginning to be viewed as more than a timekeeping member of the rhythm section. Prior to the emergence of Django Reinhardt, most jazz guitarists had played brief, chorded solos which were technically quite modest by comparison with piano and horn solos. That changed with the appearance of Charlie Christian and Django Reinhardt. **Charlie Christian** (1916–1942) mastered what was then the almost unexplored world of electric guitar. (Listen to Christian with the Benny Goodman sextet on "Blues Sequence From Breakfast Feud" in SCCJ.) His long, swinging, single-note-at-a-time lines gave solo guitar the stature of a jazz horn.[22] Some of his phrasing had the fluid swing and freshness of his model, tenor saxophonist Lester Young (see chapter 8). Christian is cited as an influence by almost all modern jazz guitarists who matured before the jazz-rock era. His style provided the foundation for that of Wes Montgomery, who was the single most influential jazz guitarist of the 1960s. This extended Christian's impact long past the 1940s and well into the 1990s. George Benson, for instance, was one of many contemporary players to be influenced by Montgomery and later became a significant influence himself.

Django Reinhardt (1910–1953) was a Belgian Gypsy guitarist who was based in France, played mostly within Europe, and visited America only once. However, his recordings were available in America, and he was held in high esteem by American guitarists, especially during the swing era. Reinhardt had a technical command of his guitar that rivalled the speed attained by players of less difficult instruments. Reinhardt's playing was ornate and flamboyant, with a prominent vibrato.[23] He combined the spirited flavor of Gypsy music with the equally spirited sound of jazz. (Listen to his 1934 version of "Dinah" in SCCJ-R.) His lines could have the intelligence of a master composer or be merely a sequence of flourishes.

To examine these two important guitarists in more depth, let's contrast their approaches, element by element.

1) Christian's pace within solos was usually steady, whereas Reinhardt's was uneven and marked by sporadic flashiness.
2) Christian's lines were horn-like, whereas Reinhardt's were more pianistic.
3) Most of Christian's recordings were made with amplified hollow-body guitar, whereas most of Reinhardt's were made on unamplified hollow-body guitar.
4) Christian's tone was usually round and soft, whereas Reinhardt's possessed a bite and was often metallic sounding.
5) Christian drew more from blues tradition, whereas Reinhardt drew from Gypsy music and the French Impressionist composers Maurice Ravel and Claude Debussy.
6) Christian used long patterns of swing eighth notes, whereas Reinhardt used somewhat jumpier sequences, with interruptions for drawn-out pitch bends.
7) Christian preferred eighth-note lines, whereas Reinhardt often leaned more toward triplet and sixteenth-note lines.
8) Christian used very little vibrato, whereas Reinhardt employed vibrato as a key element in his approach.[24]

Singers

Billie Holiday, (1915–1959) is the most influential singer associated with jazz since the early 1930s. Many vocalists began their careers imitating her. Some devoted albums to tunes they first heard Holiday sing. Nicknamed "Lady Day," she is also the singer most frequently cited by jazz musicians when asked what music they would take to a desert island. This is quite an endorsement because most jazz musicians prefer instrumental music and rarely name a vocal recording among their favorites.

Holiday did not possess the power of Bessie Smith, the deep, rich voice of Sarah Vaughan, or the speed and range of Ella Fitzgerald. Yet why is she so revered? First, she was original and fresh. Second, the depth and sincerity of emotion that she communicated are unparalleled. She made lyrics come alive. Holiday conveyed the song's meaning as though speaking directly to you. The agony she portrayed in sad songs could tear your heart out. Her renditions of "Gloomy Sunday," "Strange Fruit," and a tune she herself co-authored, "God Bless the Child," had intense effects on listeners.[25,26] On the other hand, some of her late 1930s recordings convey a carefree spirit of joy unmatched by her contemporaries.[27] No matter the mood, her tender, knowing delivery grabbed you right away. (Listen to her "She's Funny That Way" on SCCJ and her "Back in Your Own Back Yard" on the *Jazz Classics CD* for *Concise Guide to Jazz*.)

A third reason for Holiday's stature is jazz flavor. Though she was not really a blues singer—her repertory was mostly pop and show tunes—Holiday often formed her tones as a jazz hornman, with a whine that had blues flavor. Like jazz instrumentalists, she did not always give songs a straight reading, even though she had excellent diction. Instead, she varied her delivery creatively. One of the ways Holiday transformed songs was by manipulating their rhythms. Her method of intentionally delaying the arrival of certain words and phrases is almost indistinguishable from rhythmic displacements used by trumpeter Louis Armstrong, one of her main influences. (Listen to her "She's Funny That Way" on SCCJ.) This caused an engaging syncopation and swing feeling. The combination of her bluesy inflections, jazzy accents, and improvising gave jazz flavor to her music.[28]

Billie Holiday, the most influential singer in jazz after the early 1930s.
©Bradley Smith/CORBIS

Holiday toured and recorded with many of the top jazz musicians of the time, including Artie Shaw, Benny Goodman, and Count Basie. Her 1938 recording sessions with Teddy Wilson, Lester Young, and members of the Basie band produced some of the most poignant and swinging recordings of the era.[29] Her 1937 recording of "Carelessly" reached the #1 position on the popularity charts, and she had thirty-five other recordings reach the top twenty by 1945. She was prolific during the 1940s and 50s as well. During the 1930s, she had a range of about an octave and a half, and a light, clear voice quality which she could make sound warm. After the 1930s, Holiday's range became more limited, and her tone became more raw. (Listen to her 1952 "These Foolish Things" in SCCJ.) Some listeners like her work of the 1930s the most. Others find her late recordings of the 1950s to be even more emotionally compelling.[30] Not only did her life story inspire a popular movie (*Lady Sings the Blues*, 1972), but her recordings continue to sell today, more than forty years after her death.[31]

Ella Fitzgerald (1918–1996) is considered by many to be the most outstanding non-operatic singer of the twentieth century. She had near-flawless technique. Listeners were impressed by her grace and lilt. Mastery of swing eighth notes and perfect timing of syncopations

Ella Fitzgerald, the most outstanding nonoperatic singer in the twentieth century and a leading popularizer of scat singing.
Courtesy of The Jazz Image

gave her singing the rhythmic effect achieved by the best swing era hornmen. Delivered with such bounce and lightness, her phrases actually swung more than those of some modern trumpeters and saxophonists.

First achieving prominence in the mid-1930s, Fitzgerald had a #1 hit in her 1938 rendition of "A-Tisket-A-Tasket" with the Chick Webb Band.[32] With this group she recorded, toured and, for several years after Webb died, served as leader. By 1955, thirty-four of her other records had risen to popularity positions within the top twenty. Albums of her concert appearances climbed to high positions on the popularity charts during the 1960s and again in the 1980s.[33]

Ella Fitzgerald's tone was pure and supple. Her command spanned the unusually wide range of three and a half octaves. Singing in tune proves difficult for many singers, but not for Fitzgerald. Her pitch was accurate, no matter the register or tempo of the material. Her articulation was exquisite. A remarkable agility conveyed an effortless feeling. She gave every note a lift. Her overall manner achieved great presence and warmth.[34] Her combination of spirit and ease imparted a bright touch even to ballads, as though she were never really sad. A youthful quality always pervaded her work, even when she was in her seventies. Not inclined to the melodramatic attitude of so many other singers, Fitzgerald's effect is often called "cheerful," "exuberant," or "ebullient." Many consider her creative peak to be the 1950s and 60s, yet she was still giving remarkable performances during the 1970s and 80s.

Though she did not invent it, Fitzgerald was **scat singing**'s best known practitioner. Among the modern scat singers who followed, almost all cite her work as their first inspiration. Contained within her scat devices were stock phrases from late swing and early bop improvisers. On some recordings she functions as a horn, using nonsense syllables exclusively, no lyrics.[35] Fitzgerald was quite melodic in her scats. This was due in part to (1) basing portions of her passages on set routines rather than completely fresh improvisations in every performance and (2) improvising more around the melody of the original tune than from the chords of its accompaniment.[36]

Despite her scat singing's historic visibility, that work represents only a small fraction of her output. Fitzgerald gets high marks from listeners who like a singer to stick to the melody as written. Some of the greatest pop tune composers were eager to have her perform their songs because her readings were so true to their original intent. So, in addition to her exalted position in jazz, she also had a large following among pop music listeners.[37]

Popular Appeal

Before we can answer the question of whether jazz itself was popular during the swing era, we first need to decide which definition of jazz to use. (Review Chapter 2 for ways to define jazz.) If music can be called "jazz" solely by its association with the jazz tradition, the swing era was a great period for jazz. And if music can be called "jazz" whenever it swings, this era clearly marks a peak for jazz. But if we employ a strict definition and require jazz to be improvised, the matter becomes sticky. In examining the extent of appeal generated by swing-style jazz, we need to comment briefly on the style and size of bands, and to make some distinctions between big bands that emphasized improvisation and big bands that did not.

Though big bands were prevalent during the swing era, big band style does not necessarily mean swing style. There were also jazz-oriented big bands before and after the swing era. Many of these sounded very different from swing bands. Big band style doesn't necessarily mean jazz style, either. In the 1930s and 1940s, ten to sixteen musicians was the standard size of bands for many types of popular music. After that, the standard size decreased to about three to eight musicians.

Also during the swing era, journalists and musicians distinguished between bands that emphasized jazz improvisation and those that did not. For example, the very popular Glenn Miller big band was a swinging band. It had a handful of hit records that contained brief jazz improvisations. But the Miller band emphasized pretty arrangements and vocals more than improvised jazz solos. Therefore, despite its swinging qualities, the band was sometimes classified as a *sweet band* (as in the popularity polls conducted by *Down Beat* magazine in 1940 and 1941). This distinguished it from the *hot band* or *swing band* classification. Bands such as Count Basie's and Duke Ellington's fell into these categories because they had more solo improvisations.

With these distinctions in mind, note that this textbook discusses only the most jazz-oriented bands and soloists from the 1930s and 1940s big band scene. During the swing era, there were many big bands, though most were not primarily concerned with jazz improvisation. Some of the jazz improvisations that historians have heralded were well known by the public. But most were not. In other words, swing fans were far from unanimous in their awareness and appreciation of jazz improvisation. For jazz groups of later eras, improvisation was the primary focus of each performance. But for most big bands of the swing era, even the jazz-oriented ones, improvisation was not necessarily a first priority.

A few other points should be considered before the era is described as a successful period for jazz:

1) A significant portion of swing era hits contained vocals, and many of those that did not have singing were at least based on songs that listeners had previously learned by way of a vocal rendition. This alerts us to consider that *jazz improvisation might not have provided the primary appeal of the pieces. The popularity of those pieces might just reflect the same appeal that songs have had throughout history.*

2) Most of the swing era hits that were jazz-oriented contained only a few solo improvisations, often only one.

3) The amount of improvisation in most swing era hits was small, sometimes only sixteen measures, rarely more than a thirty-two bar chorus.

4) The construction of improvised solos in most hits was melodically conservative.

The big band sound, the context for the improvisations, and the tunes being improvised upon were certainly popular during the swing era. And some listeners no doubt focused primarily on the improvised solos themselves. But *for a large portion of the public, the improvisations were incidental, perhaps inconsequential, segments of the performances.* Jazz historians, being jazz fans themselves, like to believe that the adulation of the swing big bands was directed mostly at jazz qualities of the music. It is more likely, however, that most fans were more entranced by the overall effect of big band music and its rhythm than by the inspiration and skill with which solo improvisers devised their lines. Traditionally in most kinds of music only a small segment of the audience has been attracted by nuances of form and innovations of method. There may have been no greater love for the qualities of jazz improvisation during the swing era than in other eras, though more improvisers were in the public eye during the swing era.

Certain jazz musicians were as well known to the general public during the swing era as rock stars are today. For instance, Benny Goodman, Count Basie, and Duke Ellington were household words during the 1930s and 1940s. The public knew them as leaders of dance bands more than as jazz musicians. Still, they were better known than the jazz giants of later eras. Even some of their soloists were well known and not just by jazz buffs. The big bands, famous and not so famous, employed hundreds of jazz musicians. This made it easier at that time for musicians to find work as performers. Unfortunately, however, most of the jobs with big bands did not include extensive opportunities to improvise because these groups worked largely from written arrangements. Opportunities to improvise were generous in smaller combos, yet steady employment in jazz combos was difficult to find.

Like rock combos since the 1950s, *one of the most important functions for swing bands of the 1930s and 1940s was to provide dance music.* Jazz functioned as dance music more during the swing era than it did thereafter. Another similarity with popular rock combos is that swing era big bands usually used elaborate costumes, showy staging, and most of them routinely featured several singers. The visual appeal of the performance, including the personality and looks of the singers, was a primary attraction for a sizable portion of the audience. Only occasionally during the swing era were jazz musicians given paid opportunities to perform just for listening, as later became customary. In summary, the popular success of jazz bands during the swing era was partly a result of their appeal to the eyes and feet of fans instead of to the ears alone.

CHAPTER SUMMARY

1) Swing differs from early jazz in
   a) more use of written arrangements
   b) less emphasis on ragtime-like compositions
   c) less collective improvisation and more solo improvisation
   d) less use of tuba and more use of string bass
   e) more swing feeling, achieved by increased use of swing eighth-note patterns
   f) increased use of high-hat cymbals
   g) replacement of banjo with guitar
   h) big band rather than small-group instrumentation
   i) saxophone becoming the predominant instrument
2) Important big bands were led by Fletcher Henderson, Duke Ellington, Count Basie, Benny Goodman, and Jimmie Lunceford.
3) The most influential saxophonists were Coleman Hawkins, Lester Young, Benny Carter, and Johnny Hodges.
4) The most influential pianists were Art Tatum and Teddy Wilson.
5) Tatum possessed phenomenal speed and was known for spontaneously changing keys and chords in pop tune accompaniments.
6) Wilson was known for his grace and his streamlining of jazz piano style.
7) Nat Cole influenced modern jazz piano style by reducing left-hand activity and making right-hand lines more horn-like.
8) Pianist Milt Buckner perfected the technique of harmonizing melody lines in a block-chord "locked-hands" fashion.
9) Roy Eldridge paved the way for modern jazz trumpeter Dizzy Gillespie by improvising fiery, saxophone-like lines on trumpet.
10) Django Reinhardt and Charlie Christian were the most prominent guitarists of the swing era.
11) Billie Holiday and Ella Fitzgerald were the most prominent singers to be associated with jazz in the swing era.

NOTES

1. See the autobiography: Milt Hinton & David Berger, *Bass Line* (Temple, 1988). Listen to Hinton's feature numbers with Cab Calloway's big band: "Ebony Silhouette" (1941) on *Jammin' for the Jackpot* (New World: 217, LP, 1929–41); "Pluckin' the Bass" on *Cab Calloway and His Orchestra: 1939–40* (Classics: 595, 1939–40). Notice his accompaniment work in Lionel Hampton's band version of "When Lights Are Low" on SCCJ.
2. See page 413 to get Denny Brown's history of premodern drumming.
3. All the big bands mentioned in this chapter can be heard on *Big Band Jazz: From the Beginnings to the Fifties* (Smithsonian: 2202, 4CD set, 1924–56; contents listed in *Instructor's Resource Manual for Jazz Styles*), and some are also on *Big Band Renaissance* (Smithsonian: 108). Henderson is well represented on Fletcher Henderson, *A Study in Frustration* (Columbia/Legacy: C3K 57596, 3CD set, 1923–38). After the Smithsonian compilations, the next best is *Masters of Jazz, Vol. 3: Big Bands of the '30s & '40s* (Rhino: 72470, 1931–1947). Most important bands and musicians from this era can also be heard on SCCJ, and the Basie and Ellington bands are represented on the *Jazz Classics CD*. All the pianists in this chapter, except Milt Buckner, can be heard on *Jazz Piano* (Smithsonian: 7002 [RD-039], 4CD set, 1924–78).
4. Henderson's arrangements can be heard on Goodman's recordings of "King Porter Stomp," "Wrappin' It Up," "Blue Skies," "Down South Camp Meeting," "Sometimes I'm Happy," "Japanese Sandman," and "When Buddha Smiles." For more about his and other important bands of the era, see Gunther Schuller, *The Swing Era* (Oxford, 1989); Stanley Dance, *The World of Swing* (Scribner's, 1975; DaCapo, 1979); George T. Simon, *The Big Bands*, 4th ed. (Schirmer, 1981); Nathan W. Pearson, *Goin' to Kansas City* (University of Illinois, 1987); and Nat Shapiro and Nat Hentoff, *The Jazz Makers* (Grove, 1957; DaCapo, 1979).
5. *Jimmie Lunceford and His Orchestra, 1930–1934* (Classics: 501 [Decca/Victor]); Listen to "Lunceford Special" on SCCJ or "Organ Grinder Swing" in SCCJ-R; or on Jimmy Lunceford, *For Dancers Only* (Decca Jazz/GRP: GRD-645, 1935–37). A wider sampling ("Stratosphere," "Uptown Blues," and "Organ Grinder Swing") is available on *Big Band Jazz* (Smithsonian: 2202, 4CD set).
6. Benny Goodman, *Sing, Sing, Sing* (RCA Bluebird: 5630-2-RB, 1935–38 big band); *The Complete RCA Victor Small Group Recordings* (Victor Jazz: 09026-68764-2, 3CD set, 1935–39).
7. Several of the players Goodman spotlighted also led their own swing bands at one time or another: 1) trumpeter Bunny Berigan; 2) trumpeter Harry James (1916–1983) continued to lead big bands for decades after the end of the swing era; 3) trumpeter Cootie Williams (see chapter 7 for discussion); 4) vibraharpist Lionel Hampton (b. 1909); see page 146 for illustrations of the vibraharp (Listen to his "When Lights Are Low" on SCCJ); 5) drummer Gene Krupa (1909–1973): his drum solos helped emancipate jazz drummers from their restricted role of being merely timekeepers (Listen to his "Rockin' Chair" on SCCJ).

   For more about Goodman, see Bruce Crowther, *Benny Goodman* (Apollo, 1988); Russell D. Connor, *Benny Goodman: Listen to His Legacy* (Scarecrow, 1988); James Lincoln Collier, *Benny Goodman and the Swing Era* (Oxford, 1989); Ross Firestone, *Swing, Swing, Swing* (Norton, 1994); and Gunther Schuller, *The Swing Era* (Oxford, 1989), 3–45.
8. *Yes Indeed!* (RCA Bluebird: 9987-2-RB, 1939–45); *The Best of Tommy Dorsey* (RCA Bluebird: 07863-51087-2, 1935–45).
9. Harris solos on "Bijou," "Northwest Passage," "Apple Honey," and "Woodchopper's Ball" on Woody Herman, *The Thundering Herds* (Columbia: CK 44108, 1945–47).
10. Roy Eldridge, *After You've Gone* (Decca Jazz/GRP: GRD605, 1943–46); *Roy Eldridge with the Gene Krupa Orchestra: Uptown* (Columbia: CK 45448, 1940–42). Listen to his blazing solo on the 1941 "After You've Gone" with Gene Krupa's band. For transcription and analysis of his solo on "I Can't Believe That You're in Love With Me" (on SCCJ), see Gunther Schuller, *The Swing Era* (Oxford, 1989), 458–60.
11. To detect the Eldridge character in Gillespie's earliest playing, listen to Eldridge's solo on the Gene Krupa band recording of "After You've Gone," then listen to Gillespie's playing on the Cab Calloway recording of "Pickin' the Cabbage" on *Cab Calloway and His Orchestra 1939–1940* (Classics: 595).
12. Bunny Berigan, *The Pied Piper* (RCA Bluebird: 07863-66615-2, 1934–40).
13. *Body and Soul* (Victor Jazz: 09026-68515-2, 1939–56); *Classic Tenors* (Signature/CBS: AK 38446, 1943).
14. For technical analysis of Hawkins, see Schuller, *The Swing Era* (Oxford, 1988), 426–50. For a transcription and analysis of his solo on "Body and Soul," see Stuart Isacoff, *Solos for Jazz Tenor Sax* (Carl Fischer, 1985; order from Carl Fischer Music Store, 54 Cooper Square, NYC, NY 10003). See also biographies: *John Chilton, The Song of the Hawk* (Univ. of Michigan, 1990); and Burnett James, *Coleman Hawkins* (Hippocrene, 1984).
15. Benny Carter, *Cosmopolite: The Oscar Peterson Verve Sessions* (Verve 314 521 673-2 [MGV8226], 1952, 1954). Also see Morroe Berger, Edward Berger, and James Patrick, *Benny Carter: A Life in American Music, Vols. 1 & 2* (Scarecrow, 1982).
16. For a transcription and analysis of Tatum's "The Man I Love," see John Rodby, *Solos for Jazz Piano* (Carl Fischer, 1989; order from Carl Fischer Music Store, 54 Cooper Square, NYC, NY 10003). For Joseph Howard's four-volume analysis of Tatum's style, see page 413. See also John Mehegan, *Jazz Improvisation, Vol. 3* (Watson-Guptill/Amsco, 1964), and Gunther Schuller, *The Swing Era* (Oxford, 1989), 476–502. See also James Leser, *Too Marvelous for Words: The Life and Genius of Art Tatum* (Oxford, 1995).
17. When Wilson chose to create horn-like lines, he refined the best of Earl Hines. Wilson's work on the 1936 "Blues in C-Sharp Minor" provides an excellent demonstration of his precisely executed, intelligently conceived horn lines. This can be heard on Roy Eldridge, *Little Jazz* (Columbia: CK 45275, 1935–40). For analysis of his style, see John Mehegan, *Jazz Improvisation, Vol. 3* (Watson-Guptill,1964). For a comparison with Tatum's style, see Schuller, *The Swing Era* (Oxford, 1989), 502–513.
18. Teddy Wilson, *Piano Solos* (Affinity/Charly: CDAFS 1016, 1934–1937).
19. Nat King Cole, *Hit That Jive, Jack* (Decca Jazz/GRP: GRD-662, 1936, 1940–41); "The Man I Love" (1944) and "Blues in My Shower" (1947) on *Jazz Piano* (Smithsonian: 7002 [039], 4CD set); and *Best of the Nat Cole Trio: Instrumental Classics* (Capitol Jazz 98288, 1944–49). For transcriptions and analyses, see Schuller, *The Swing Era*, 816–825.

20. For a transcription and analysis of Garner's solo on "I'll Remember April," see John Rodby, *Solos for Jazz Piano* (Carl Fischer, 1989; order from Carl Fischer Music Store, 54 Cooper Square, NYC, NY 10003). For more about Garner's life, see James M. Doran, *Erroll Garner: The Most Happy Piano* (Scarecrow, 1985).

21. Buckner is heard on "Royal Family" on Lionel Hampton, *Swingsation* (Decca Jazz/GRP: GRD-9922, 1942–47).

22. Charlie Christian, *Genius of the Electric Guitar* (Columbia: CK 40846 [CL 652], 1939–41); *Benny Goodman Sextet Featuring Charlie Christian* (Columbia: CK 45144, 1939–41).

23. Django Reinhardt, *Souvenirs* (London: 820 591-2, 1935–39); *Djangologie U.S.A.* (DRG/Swing: CDSW-8420/CDSW-8424, two 2CD sets, 1936–37); *Peche a la Mouche: The Great Blue Star Sessions* (Verve: 835418-2, 2CD set, 1947 & 1953). For more about his life, see Charles Delaunay, *Django Reinhardt* (Cassell, 1961; DaCapo, 1982).

24. For transcriptions and analyses of Christian and Reinhardt solos, see Fred Sokolow, *Solos for Jazz Guitar* (Carl Fischer, 1988; available from Carl Fischer Music Store, 54 Cooper Square, NYC, NY 10003). For biography, see Peter Broadbent, *Charlie Christian* (Hal Leonard, 1997). For more Reinhardt transcriptions, see Stuart Isacoff, *Django Reinhardt* (Amsco, 1978).

25. "Gloomy Sunday" and "God Bless the Child" are on *The Quintessential Billie Holiday, Vol. 9* (Columbia: CK 47031, 1940–42). Holiday liked this rendition of "Gloomy Sunday."

26. "Strange Fruit" is on *The Complete Commodore Recordings* (Commodore/GRP: CMD2-401, 2CD set, 1939, 1944). This compilation also contains a selection Holiday listed as being among her own favorite recordings: "Fine and Mellow." See her lyrics for it on page 382. Watch her perform it on *The Sound of Jazz* television show (available on videocassette; see page 401).

27. Holiday's most cheerful material is on *The Quintessential Billie Holiday, Vol. 5* (Columbia: CK 44423, 1937–38).

28. "Lover Man" (*The Complete Decca Recordings,* GRD2-601, 2CD set, 1944–50) brings together all these elements and constitutes the definitive Holiday recording for some fans. This compilation also contains "Good Morning Heartache" and a rendition of "God Bless the Child" recorded later than the one cited in footnote 25.

29. The most delightful of the recordings with Basie's musicians, particularly Lester Young and Buck Clayton, are on *The Quintessential Billie Holiday, Vol. 5* (Columbia: CK 44423, 1937–38).

30. *Lady in Satin* (Columbia: CK 40247, 1959) is a favorite album among listeners who like late-period Billie Holiday.

31. For biography, see Billie Holiday with William Dufty, *Lady Sings the Blues* (Penguin, 1956, 1992); John Chilton, *Billie's Blues* (Quartet, 1975); Stuart Nicholson, *Billie Holiday* (Northeastern University Press, 1995); and Leslie Gourse, ed., *The Billie Holiday Companion: Seven Decades of Commentary* (Schirmer, 1997).

32. "A-Tisket-A-Tasket" is on *The Best of Ella Fitzgerald* (Decca Jazz/GRP: GRD-659, 1935–55).

33. *The Complete Ella in Berlin: Mack the Knife* (Verve: 314 519 564-2 [4041], 1960). The Berlin concert was particularly exciting, and it contains moments many fans remember best: During her performance of "Mack the Knife," Fitzgerald forgot some of the words but proceeded to invent several swinging choruses of new ones, all without missing a beat or losing any momentum.

34. Many Fitzgerald fans are impressed with the warmth and presence conveyed by her renditions of "Spring Can Really Hang You Up the Most" and "Cry Me A River" on *Clap Hands, Here Comes Charlie!* (Verve: 422 835646-2, 1961).

35. "Flying Home" on Charlie Parker, *Jazz at the Philharmonic 1949* (Verve: 314 519 803-2) has Fitzgerald singing entirely without words, recreating horn parts from a band version.

36. "Perdido" and "How High the Moon" on Charlie Parker, *Jazz at the Philharmonic 1949* (Verve: 314 519 803-2) show Fitzgerald making up new lyrics and improvising fresh scat lines. On her improvisation in "How High the Moon," she quotes a number of other tunes. Incidentally, her exciting 1960 version of this tune has a number of set routines interwoven among tune quotes [see *The Complete Ella in Berlin: Mack the Knife* (Verve: 314 519 564-2, 1960)].

37. Among Fitzgerald's most popular albums are *Ella Fitzgerald Sings the Cole Porter Songbook* (Verve: 314 537 257-2 [4001], 2 CD set, 1956); *Ella Fitzgerald Sings the George and Ira Gershwin Songbooks* (Verve: 314 539 759-2 [V-29-5], 3CD set, 1958–59); *Ella Fitzgerald Sings the Rodgers and Hart Songbook* (Verve: 314 537-258-2 [400-2], 2CD set, 1956). For biography, see Stuart Nicholson, *Ella Fitzgerald: A Biography of the First Lady of Jazz* (Macmillan, 1993; DaCapo, 1995).

Chapter Seven

Photo courtesy of Cleveland Press Collection/Cleveland State University Archives

Duke Ellington

Duke Ellington (1899–1974) was **the most creative and prolific composer-arranger in jazz history, and he led the most stable and longest-lived big band.** Many musicians and historians feel that his band was the best of all jazz groups and the most interesting of swing bands. Ellington wrote more than two thousand compositions as well as many arrangements and rearrangements for them, beginning before 1920 and continuing until his death in 1974. His compositional fertility depended partly upon contributions by the musicians in his bands. Ellington chose musicians who had substantial and distinctive styles; together they made up an all-star unit that ran from the early 1920s to the early 1970s. Some of his men remained for twenty to thirty years at a stretch. Ellington often incorporated their ideas into his melodies. Many of their improvisations were so good that they also became permanent parts of the band's arrangements, as though composed. Ellington appreciated the musical personalities in his band so much that he wrote each part for a particular player. He imaginatively mixed and matched their work with his own. The collaborative result was a breadth and depth of repertory superior to every other jazz band. Recording more than any other, Ellington's band and its leader's compositions can be heard in hundreds of 78 r.p.m. recordings, long-play albums, and compact discs.

Pianist

During the first three decades of his career, Ellington performed often in the stride-style tradition of pianist James P. Johnson. Thereafter, he usually performed in his own original style which, though still quite percussive, was more economical than the stride style. (Listen to his solo in the fourth chorus of "Cottontail" on the *Jazz Classics CD.*) His playing sparkled and popped with unerring swing feeling, and Ellington became distinguished for unusual harmonies and voicings. (Listen to his improvised accompaniments on "Transblucency" on the *Jazz Classics CD.*) As an accompanist, Ellington was highly praised by his sidemen. They particularly liked the way his accompaniments were spare and complementary. His comping was full of spirit, and his timing and taste were near perfect.

Composer

Ellington wrote many tunes, often in collaboration with his sidemen. Some of these became popular songs when lyrics were added, and a few were hits when recorded by singers apart from the Ellington band. Among his best-known songs are "I'm Beginning to See the Light," "Solitude," "Mood Indigo," and "Don't Get Around Much Anymore."[1] Nearly all jazz musicians have played at least one Ellington tune during their careers. More musicians have devoted entire albums to his music than to any other jazz composer's. During the 1980s, an entire Broadway revue, *Sophisticated Ladies,* was devoted to Ellington's music.

Ellington also wrote hundreds of three-minute instrumentals, a few of which we will study in this chapter. (These instrumentals averaged three minutes because that was the standard length for one side of a 78 r.p.m. record.) **Some of his short instrumentals paint musical portraits of famous personalities** such as the great stride pianist Willie "The Lion" Smith ("Portrait of the Lion") and the comedian Bert Williams ("Portrait of Bert Williams"). **Others paint musical pictures of places** such as "Warm Valley" and "Harlem Airshaft," or sensations such as the combination of blue and translucency, "Transblucency" (both are on the *Jazz Classics CD*).

Duke Ellington's 1942 band, the mobile laboratory for explorations in varied tone colors and the multilayered weaving of improvisation and composition. Left to right: Otto Hardwicke, Juan Tizol, Harold Baker, Ray Nance (directly behind Ellington, who is seated at the piano), Harry Carney (directly behind Betty Roche), Rex Stewart, Johnny Hodges (alto sax), Ben Webster (tenor sax), Chauncey Haughton, Joe "Tricky Sam" Nanton (trombone), Wallace Jones (trumpet), Lawrence Brown (trombone), and Sonny Greer (drums).

Photo courtesy of Frank Driggs

Ellington also wrote many longer pieces, and **he is widely acclaimed for having taken jazz into the format of "extended works,"** as these longer pieces are termed. (His "Creole Rhapsody" is in SCCJ, and his "Diminuendo in Blue and Crescendo in Blue" is in the revised SCCJ.) His most respected long work is "Black, Brown, and Beige," a fifty-minute tone parallel to the history of the American Negro.[2] Some of his longest works were film scores; a favorite of musicians and critics is his music for *Anatomy of a Murder,* the Otto Preminger movie starring Jimmy Stewart.

Arranging Style

One of Ellington's greatest skills as an arranger was that of **capitalizing on the uniquely personal sounds of individual players.** Most arrangers occasionally showcase particular musicians, and in doing so they write parts that are well suited to the performer's talents as well as writing accompaniments that complement those talents. Ellington did this, too; but he also went much further. When writing for a group of instruments, he did not write parts anonymously assigned to the instruments (lead trumpeter, second trumpeter, third trumpeter, etc.), as most arrangers do. Ellington instead **wrote parts suited to the peculiar sounds and capabilities of each player in his band** (Cat Anderson, Cootie Williams, Rex Stewart, etc.). Each one of Ellington's musicians had a highly individual sound. So, even when they were not playing solos, their own unique way of sounding each pitch was considered before giving them a particular part to play. For example, if a chord were scored for three trumpets, Ellington remembered the particular tone quality that each of his trumpeters ordinarily produced for each note in that chord. He then distributed the parts of the chord among the musicians to create the overall color he wanted for that chord. In addition, sometimes he would have one trumpeter use a mute, another player without mute, and a third player sound his note with an odd tone quality that was unique to his own playing style. Ellington scored this way for saxes and trombones, too. This is one reason that when other musicians perform Ellington's arrangements, the music never sounds like Ellington's band.

Another notable skill employed by Ellington is what we call **voicing across sections of the band.** This technique departs from the way most arrangers, including Ellington, routinely write passages that pit the sound of one section of the band, such as the saxes, against another section of the band, such as the brasses (as in "Cottontail" on the *Jazz Classics CD*). By contrast, Ellington often wrote passages to be played by combinations of instruments drawn from *different* sections of the band. The most famous example can be heard in his 1930 recording of "Mood Indigo."[3] There he combined clarinet with muted trumpet and muted trombone, thus voicing instruments from three different sections of the band: trumpet section, trombone section, and reed section. In his 1940 recording of "Concerto for Cootie" (in SCCJ), he required the bassist to play notes in unison with the horns. This was unusual because bass was a member of the rhythm section, assigned primarily to timekeeping roles, and it rarely played melody parts. (Listen to *Demo CD* Track 27, for examples of melody lines played in pizzicato bass style.)

Another unique method employed by Ellington was placing a **wordless vocal** in an arrangement. Sometimes called *instrumentalized voice,* this became identified with Ellington, and he was applauded for its use in his 1927 recording of "Creole Love Call"[4] and his 1946 recording of "Transblucency" (on the *Jazz Classics CD*).[5]

Other unique sounds that became associated with Ellington originated with his jobs. For instance, he often played for floor shows at New York night clubs, which needed exotic "jungle sounds." Partly to satisfy the club's demand for exotic sounds, and partly because of his own admiration for New Orleans jazz, he scored for the **growl style** associated with trumpeter Bubber Miley and trombonist, Joe "Tricky Sam" Nanton. (For examples, listen to *Demo CD* Track 81, the beginning of "Cottontail" on the *Jazz Classics CD,* and "East St. Louis Toodle-O" in SCCJ.) For the same reasons, he liked to use clarinets in a wailing manner. He

Listening Guide for

"Transblucency: A Blue Fog You Can Almost See Through"

Composed by Lawrence Brown and Duke Ellington; recorded July 9, 1946; available on the *Jazz Classics CD* and on Duke Ellington, *Black, Brown and Beige* (RCA Bluebird: 6641-2-RB, 3CD set 1944–46).*

This recording is included to provide a fuller picture of Ellington's talents than what is conveyed by "Cottontail" and "Harlem Airshaft." "Transblucency" exemplifies Ellington's practice of painting musical pictures, in this case the combined impression of translucency and the color blue. The composition was developed from "Blue Light," an earlier Ellington band number containing a twelve-bar blues theme composed by Lawrence Brown, the trombonist who performed it. This piece displays Ellington's imagination for unique blends of tone colors. Here he combines instrumentalized voice (wordless vocal) with instruments drawn from different sections of the band (voicing across sections). The result is a facet of Ellington's repertory that is not hard-driving or wild. It is pretty and might remind you of opera more than jazz.

This performance allows us to explore controversies about how jazz is defined. To call this a "jazz" recording stretches the conventional definition in two ways. First, it demonstrates Ellington's practice of constructing pieces in which the only improvisation of consequence lies in the accompaniment. Second, the piece is unusual because swing feeling is elicited here only by accompaniment rhythms, and only quite subtly.

Unlike most of Ellington's pieces, "Transblucency" does not use his entire band. Though he assigns the melody to his saxes in the fifth chorus, Ellington otherwise dispenses with everyone except clarinetist Jimmy Hamilton, trombonist Lawrence Brown, and bassist Oscar Pettiford. In a few choruses, the voice of Kay Davis is added as an instrument. Piano chording can sometimes be heard faintly in the background.

CD Track	Elapsed Time	
26	0' 00"	**Introduction** Piano flourishes by Ellington. At the end of the piano phrases, the bass ever so slightly anticipates the down beat of the first chorus by playing a string of triplets.
27	0' 04"	**First Chorus** Slow, 12-bar blues. The melody line is harmonized, clarinet on the lowest notes, cup-muted trombone on the middle notes, and voice on the highest notes. Piano occasionally fills in the pauses between phrases and provides counteractivity underneath sustained tones. Pizzicato bass tones provide timekeeping. Note the triplets played just before the first and third beats of

*The score and parts for "Transblucency" are available from King Brand Classic Editions, P.O. Box 580, Keyport, New Jersey 07735.

selected measures. This bass style is called "decorative-two" because, of the four beats in the measure, it emphasizes only two, sometimes decorated by preceding notes. Bass is joined by piano in some of the decorations here.

28 0' 38" **Second Chorus**

Muted trombone plays the melody, accompanied by bass playing in a decorative-two style. Notice the absence of piano.

0' 47" *Fifth Measure*

Trombone is joined by voice and clarinet in harmony, and then the three instruments continue together. Bass accompaniment alternates between decorative-two and walking style.

1' 12" *Twelfth Measure*

A piano flourish introduces the next chorus.

29 1' 14" **Third Chorus**

Clarinet and voice duet, accompanied by walking bass and piano chording. The harmony created by the two sounds, clarinet and voice, occasionally seems to create a third sound. Ellington has assigned pitches so cleverly that their combination has generated additional pitches, technically termed "heterodynes."

1' 47" *Final Two Measures*

As the melody instruments end their phrase, Ellington improvises a melodic little phrase which he plays twice.

30 1' 51" **Fourth Chorus**

Sax section softly plays the flowing melody in unison while voice provides a countermelody. Piano chording accompanies softly on each beat.

2' 27" *Twelfth Measure*

Piano re-enters percussively, as though splashing bright colors on the subdued portrait.

31 2' 35" **Ending**

2' 44" Vocal, trombone, and clarinet join piano.

A marching of piano chords, then a high-register piano chord is emphatically sounded. Its ringing concludes the piece, accompanied by a very soft, arco bass note.

employed unusual voicings for his clarinets, and his musicians played them very intensely. The effect was stirring. Years after he finished his work at these floor shows, Ellington continued to employ these exotic sounds, and they contributed to his group's reputation as a "hot band."

Clarinet

Clarinetists **Barney Bigard** (1906–1981) and his successor Jimmy Hamilton provided pivotal voices in the Ellington sound. (Listen to *Demo CD* Track 69 to familiarize yourself with the sound of the clarinet.) Both men doubled on tenor saxophone in the band, but their

Listening Guide for

"Cottontail"

Recorded May 4, 1940 by Duke Ellington big band (5 saxes, 3 trumpets, 3 trombones, piano, guitar, bass, and drums). Available on the *Jazz Classics CD,* on SCCJ-R; and on Duke Ellington, *The Blanton-Webster Band* (RCA Bluebird: 5659-2-RB, 3CD set, 1940–42).*

"Cottontail" is Ben Webster's new tune using the progression of accompaniment chords from George Gershwin's "I Got Rhythm." Ellington wrote the arrangement. The "melody in harmony" that Webster and Ellington wrote for the sax section to play as the fifth chorus has some of the melodic and rhythmic character of a modern jazz improvisation. It remains one of the band's most famous passages. Its popularity with musicians rivals that of Webster's often-quoted solo on this recording. When it is performed, this "saxophone soli," as it is termed, has all the saxophonists standing up together.

CD Track	Elapsed Time		
14	0' 00"	**First Chorus**	
		A	Melody stated by alto sax, baritone sax, muted trumpet, and trombone.
	0' 07"	**A**	Melody repeated with trombone and trumpet figures punctuating over guitar, bass, and drums accompaniment.
	0' 15"	**B**	Saxes ask musical questions, muted trumpet (Cootie Williams) answers them.
15	0' 25"	**Four-Measures Interlude**	
			This consists of a brief conversation between the sax section and brass section with rhythm accompaniment.
16	0' 29"	**Second Chorus**	
		A-A	Improvised tenor sax solo (Ben Webster) with rhythm accompaniment.
	0' 44"	**B**	Tenor sax talks for a while with the brass section.
	0' 53"	**A**	Brass depart, leaving tenor to continue improvising with rhythm section accompaniment.
	1' 00"	**Third Chorus**	
		A-A	Tenor continues improvisation accompanied by rhythm section.
	1' 16"	**B**	Brass return to talk more with tenor sax.
	1' 25"	**A**	Brass depart and tenor finishes his improvisation accompanied by rhythm section.

*The score and parts for "Cottontail" are available from King Brand Classic Editions, P.O. Box 580, Keyport, New Jersey 07735.

Track	Time	Section	Description
17	1' 32"	**Fourth Chorus**	
		A-A	Brass play alone, accompanied by rhythm section.
	1' 48"	**B**	Improvised baritone sax solo (Harry Carney) accompanied by rhythm section.
	1' 56"	**A**	Improvised piano solo accompanied by rhythm guitar, bass, and drums.
18	2' 03"	**Fifth Chorus**	
		A-A-B-A	Sax section plays the whole chorus accompanied by rhythm section.
19	2' 34"	**Sixth Chorus**	
		A-A	Brass section shouts questions, and sax section answers, accompanied by rhythm section.
	2' 51"	**B**	Brass section joins saxes with rhythm section steaming forward.
	2' 58"	**A**	Alto sax, baritone sax, muted trumpet, and trombone play the melody to its end with rhythm section accompaniment.

best-known contributions were their solo improvisations on clarinet. Bigard was from New Orleans, and he brought the expressive, soulful approach of his hometown music to Ellington's sophisticated conception of big band style. His long, legato lines swooped and darted through the band sound. Bigard played with the band from 1928 to 1942. Some of his best improvisations are found in Ellington's 1940 recording of "Harlem Airshaft" (on the *Jazz Classics CD*). You might also enjoy studying his improvisation on "Clarinet Lament," a 1936 performance that Ellington built around Bigard.[6]

Jimmy Hamilton (1917–1994) is an original improviser with a style less intense than Bigard's. His sound is well manicured and lighter than that of most swing era clarinetists. Hamilton's conception is precise and articulate, with a cool, floating quality that suggests modern jazz. He was with the band from 1943 to 1968, and Ellington featured him extensively during the 1950s. (Listen to his duet with wordless vocal on "Transblucency" on the *Jazz Classics CD* as well as the albums he recorded with Ellington.)[7]

Trumpet

Bubber Miley (1903–1932) and **Cootie Williams** (1910–1985) were known for their *growl style of trumpet playing and the unorthodox use of rubber plunger mutes.* (See the illustration on page 390, *Demo CD* Track 67, and the beginning of "Cottontail" on the *Jazz Classics CD* Track 14.) Miley was one of Ellington's leading soloists from 1924 to 1929. His style furnished a playful voice for such classic Ellington recordings as the 1927 "Creole Love Call" and "East St. Louis Toodle-O."[8]

Like Bubber Miley, Cootie Williams was also influenced by the bluesy New Orleans style. From that tradition, Williams cultivated ways to spontaneously alter the size, shape, and quality of instrument sounds and achieve a vast range of musical effects. Williams was Miley's successor in the Ellington band, and he served as Ellington's main trumpet soloist. He played with the band from 1929 to 1940, rejoining in 1962 and remaining until Ellington's death in 1974. Ellington composed his 1936 "Echoes of Harlem" and his 1940 "Concerto for Cootie" to feature Williams. (Listen to "Concerto for Cootie" in SCCJ. You can also hear Williams on "In A Mellotone" in SCCJ.)

Some of Cootie Williams's most inventive playing was captured in Ellington's 1940 recording of "Harlem Airshaft." (Study the listening guide in this chapter while you listen to the piece on the *Jazz Classics CD.*) His work on this number demonstrates his unique mastery of wide-ranging techniques for colorfully altering pitch and tone quality. (See pages 40–42 for explanation and illustrations of tone quality and pitch manipulation techniques, and listen to *Demo CD* Tracks 50–53 for examples of the doit, smear, drop, and scoop.) Williams is very calculating in the way he reaches notes, but his sound projects a great naturalness rather than cold calculation. His solos on this piece combine a diversity of techniques reminiscent of the searing sensuality and peaks of raw excitement in blues singing. Another Williams asset is a keen sense of rhythm. Sometimes his notes are so well timed and percussively executed that the listener might assume Williams to be a drummer. In these regards, Miley and Williams helped Ellington create a more New Orleans-like sound than was common to other New York bands of the same era. Incidentally, it is no coincidence that Ellington's "jungle style" was developed during the 1920s when New Orleans-born clarinetists Sidney Bechet and Barney Bigard and bassist Wellman Braud all played with the band.

Ellington had distinctive trumpet soloists besides Miley and Williams. But the only one to achieve much fame outside the Ellington band was **Clark Terry** (b. 1920), a leading brass soloist in the band from 1951 to 1959. One of the first Ellington sidemen to show the influence of modern jazz, Terry invented a unique style that bridged the gap between the swing era approaches and the new bop style of Dizzy Gillespie. He displayed seemingly effortless command over his horn, no matter how fast or intricate a figure he chose to improvise. He had a talkative, swinging style that is easy to recognize. It spontaneously unfolded catchy melodic lines and conveyed an enthusiasm that seemed to bubble through every note. (See footnote 7.)

Clark Terry also helped popularize the fluegelhorn, a kind of oversized cornet that is played in much the same manner as cornet and trumpet. (See page 112, and listen to *Demo CD* Track 60.) Most players stress the instrument's naturally soft, dark tone quality, but Terry achieves a brassy edge, combined with a distinct fullness that is round and vibrant. No other brass player sounds like Clark Terry. (A large portion of his solos on Ellington records feature his fluegelhorn, not his trumpet.)

Saxophone

Johnny Hodges (1907–1970) was the best known of Ellington's sidemen (see page 115). He often played position of lead alto, the saxophonist whose parts contain the melody notes instead of the harmony notes. This layer leads the other saxophonists in timing and interpretation of written sax parts. His solos and his style in leading the sax section were a vital part of the Ellington sound from 1928 until 1970 (with an absence from 1951 to 1955). Nearly every Ellington album features Hodges, and he was such a consistent player that almost all these recordings contain representative examples. Hodges produced such an unusually deep, lush tone that his recorded alto sax has sometimes been mistaken for tenor saxophone. (Listen to "Prelude to a Kiss" in the *Jazz Classics Cassette/CD.*) He is particularly known for a remarkable way of gliding from note to note so gradually and smoothly that it sounds almost as if his instrument were equipped with a slide, like a trombone. This technique is called *portamento,* but jazz musicians generally refer to it as *smearing*. Hodges used it to great effect in playing ballads. Ellington wrote numerous pieces to take full advantage of this well-known Hodges approach.[9]

An exquisite sense of timing was crucial to the Hodges style. Hodges was a master of subtlety with his inflections of pitch, and his syncopations were especially well timed. Pre-1942 Hodges often displayed flashy double-timing like Sidney Bechet, his primary influence. But after the mid-1940s, Hodges tended to lay back very deliberately, no matter what the tempo. Hodges is possibly the most influential jazz alto saxophonist to come out of the swing era (see Table 7.2), and he is one of few jazz saxophonists to ever have hit

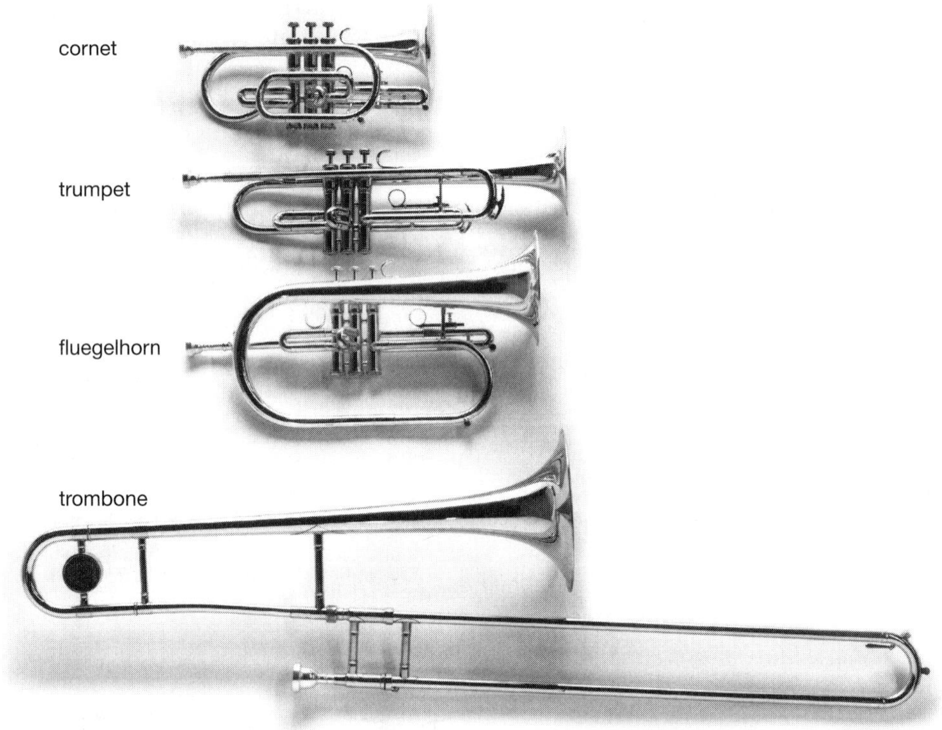

FIGURE 7.1 Listen for the fluegelhorn on *Demo CD* Track 60, where you will have the opportunity to compare its sound with that of the trumpet.

Photo: Dan Morgan/Sharp Shooter, Courtesy of the Selmer Company

records. He is particularly known for a romantic approach to ballad playing that has pervaded American music so much that hundreds of saxophonists are imitating it without even knowing who Johnny Hodges was. (His work on "Prelude to a Kiss" typifies that side of his talents.)[10]

Aside from Hodges, Benny Carter was the most widely respected jazz alto saxophonist of the swing era. Perhaps we can learn more about both styles by comparing them. Both players had rich, full-bodied tones, but they had different rhythmic styles. Carter tended to divide the beat precisely and evenly into legato eighth notes. Hodges had a more natural rhythmic feel. The placement of notes in relation to the beat was far less obvious in Hodges's playing. Though Carter and Hodges both imparted a luxurious feel to their playing, Carter was more obvious in his constructions, Hodges more subtle. Hodges had a strikingly original way of placing accents. His accenting set him apart from most swing and early jazz players. Despite its originality, he made it sound easy and natural. Both Hodges and Carter swung easily, but Carter had more of a classical feeling to his rhythmic conception. (Get SCCJ and compare Carter on "I Can't Believe That You're in Love with Me" with Hodges on "In a Mellotone.")

Harry Carney (1910–1974) is usually considered the father of jazz baritone saxophone playing, which almost puts him in a class with Coleman Hawkins, the father of the jazz tenor saxophone, a soloist who influenced Carney. No other baritone saxophonist has been able to match the size and strength of Carney's mammoth, rich sound. (Listen to *Demo CD* Tracks 72–74 to hear differences in sound among alto, tenor, and baritone saxophones. Listen to Carney improvise the bridge of the fourth chorus in "Cottontail" on the *Jazz Classics CD.*)

TABLE 7.1 A Few of the Musicians Most Significant to Ellington

CLARINET AND SAXOPHONES	TRUMPET	TROMBONE
Willie Smith	Louis Metcalf	Joe "Tricky Sam" Nanton
Rudy Jackson	Bubber Miley	Lawrence Brown
Barney Bigard	Arthur Whetsol	Juan Tizol
Jimmy Hamilton	Cootie Williams	Britt Woodman
Russell Procope	Rex Stewart	Quentin "Butter" Jackson
Otto Hardwicke	Taft Jordan	Tyree Glenn
Johnny Hodges	Ray Nance	Buster Cooper
Harry Carney	Willie Cook	
Ben Webster	Cat Anderson	
Paul Sears	Clark Terry	
Paul Gonsalves	"Shorty" Baker	
Harold Ashby	Johnny Coles	
	Money Johnson	

DRUMS	PIANO	BASS
Sonny Greer	Duke Ellington	Aaron Bell
Louis Bellson	Billy Strayhorn	Billy Taylor
Sam Woodyard		Wellman Braud
Rufus Jones		Jimmy Blanton
		Oscar Pettiford
		Jimmy Woode
		Ernie Shepard
		Wendell Marshall

Carney's ensemble playing in Ellington's sax section often vied with that of Hodges himself. It provided a very solid foundation, often as important as that of the band's bassist. Inspired by Carney's playing, Ellington occasionally wrote in a way that gave baritone sax the lead. Carney also played clarinet and bass clarinet, each of which, in his hands, became a strong, thick-toned voice in the Ellington ensemble. Although primarily an ensemble player, Carney occasionally received feature numbers, including "Serious Serenade," "Frustration," and "Chromatic Love Affair."

Ellington's most outstanding soloists on the tenor saxophone were **Ben Webster** (1909–1973) and **Paul Gonsalves** (1920–1974). Webster played with the band from 1940 to 1943, then again in 1948 and 1949. Before Webster began full-time in 1940, Ellington had no major tenor sax soloist. But thereafter, he always featured someone in that position, and it was Gonsalves from 1951 to 1974. Though some of Webster's style was inspired by Coleman Hawkins and Johnny Hodges, Webster should not be viewed as derivative. He established his own distinctive approach. His improvisations were frequently so tuneful that the listener might assume they were not improvised, but prepared for the written arrangement. In fact, the sense of completeness in Webster's phrases has so greatly affected musicians that Webster phrases are sometimes quoted by other improvisers.

TABLE 7.2 A Few of the Many Saxophonists Influenced by Johnny Hodges

Tab Smith	Willie Smith	Woody Herman
Louis Jordan	Ben Webster	Eddie Vinson
Earl Bostic	Bobby Plater	John Coltrane
Johnny Bothwell	Charlie Barnet	Jan Garbarek

Webster provided a model for how to play ballads. One trademark was delaying, ever so slightly, the delivery of crucial notes in a phrase—sometimes giving the listener a sense of suspense that was resolved when those crucial notes were finally sounded. His playing gives the listener an overall impression of being laid back. Together with his richly textured, breathy tone, and slow, marked vibrato, Webster used his delayed deliveries to create a very sensual effect. Some of his work in this vein resembles the way a crooner delivers the tones of a love song. Consistent with his sense of drama, Webster was known for changing the character of the music within a single solo by transforming his sound from smootth and soothing to hoarse and rasping. Like other Ellington soloists, Webster seemed capable of making his manipulations of tone and timing at least as important as the choice of notes themselves. Sometimes Webster made listeners hear the rush of air in his breath, not just the saxophone tone that it ordinarily energized. Partly because of the carefully marked vibrato that accompanied it, listening to that rush of air by itself could be an intimately moving experience. In fact, Webster's style is often described as romantic.[11] Apart from Coleman Hawkins and Lester Young, Ben Webster was the most influential tenor saxophonist of the swing era, and he influenced saxophonists in eras as far-flung as the 1940s and the 1970s.[12]

Paul Gonsalves (1920–1974) was Ellington's main soloist during the 1950s, 60s, and 70s. He began as a disciple of Ben Webster but also showed hints of the Don Byas approach. Despite these roots, Gonsalves's style was unique, particularly in a very unusual and fluid conception for medium- and up-tempo playing. He had a soft, diffuse tone without edge, but despite the softness of his tone, his playing had an intense urgency to it. Moreover, Gonsalves's choice of notes was so unusual that it is amazing he could deliver them as fluently as he did. And his solos invariably had substance. Though he was relatively unknown to all but Ellington band fans, Gonsalves ranks among the originators in the history of jazz tenor styles. His solos lent Ellington's music an excitement and a modern character without detracting from the warmth and sincerity that had traditionally been such prime traits of the Ellington sound. Gonsalves played with Ellington from 1951 until his death in 1974.[13]

Trombone

Trombonist **Joe "Tricky Sam" Nanton** (1904–1946) was **master of the growl style.** From 1926 until 1946, Nanton gave Ellington a provocative sound to use in arrangements. His most common mute was the rubber suction cup from a plumber's plunger, which he used to open and close the bell of the trombone. An additional mute, alternately termed a *pixie mute* or a *buzz mute,* was secured inside the trombone to lend a buzz to the horn's tone. With his plunger and his unorthodox blowing, Nanton came very close to pronouncing words with his trombone ("ya..ya"). (Listen to him in "Harlem Airshaft" on the *Jazz Classics CD* and see pages 390–391.)[14]

Lawrence Brown (1907–1988) was one of the first trombonists of the swing era to play with a very smooth, large, consistent sound. His tone added a great deal of body to the sound of Ellington's trombone section. As a soloist, Brown could also play quite aggressively.

Johnny Hodges, Duke Ellington's star soloist, the most widely imitated alto saxophonist of the swing era. Even modern giants like John Coltrane were influenced by his style.

Photo by Lee Tanner/The Jazz Image.

Ellington wrote "Blue Cellophane" and "Golden Cress" as features for Brown. (Listen to his muted work on the *Jazz Classics CD's* "Transblucency," for which Brown himself composed a theme.)

Drums

There have been only a few drummers in the long history of the Ellington band: Sonny Greer (1919–1951), Louis Bellson (early 1950s), Sam Woodyard (mid-1955 to 1966), and Rufus Jones (1968–1973). Others played briefly with the band but remained relatively unknown. Ellington's drummers have performed a relatively unobtrusive role in creating the band's sound. Although all were swinging drummers, none were as historically significant as Jo Jones with Count Basie, Max Roach with Charlie Parker, Elvin Jones with John Coltrane, or Tony Williams with Miles Davis. All Ellington drummers were primarily timekeepers. There are four eras of this role in the band, reflecting Ellington's incorporating the strengths of four different drummers.

The classic tradition of **Sonny Greer** (1903–1982) lasted for more than half of the band's fifty-year history. Ellington's first drummer, Greer used drumming techniques in the manner of early jazz drummers. He kept time on the snare drum with sticks and brushes, often switching instruments for a new chorus or to accompany a new soloist. (Listen to how hard he swings on "Cottontail" on the *Jazz Classics CD.*) During the 1940s, he sometimes moved his timekeeping rhythms to high-hat. And, in a few isolated instances near the end of his tenure with the band, he played ride rhythms on the ride cymbal. Though simple in style and technique, Greer was dramatic in presentation. His equipment included tympani, gongs, vibraharp, and wood blocks. (Wood block is demonstrated on *Demo CD* Track 10, vibraphone on *Demo CD* Track 97.) Listen to his work in "Echoes of Harlem," for which he devised exceptionally adept accompaniments.

A new era began in 1951 when Greer left and **Louis Bellson** (b. 1924) joined Ellington. In his two-year stay, Bellson changed the technique and technology of Ellington drummers. Like a bop drummer, Bellson kept time primarily with his ride cymbal, using his left hand to play musical punctuations on his snare drum. Blessed with enviable technique, he was a precise and tasteful accompanist.

Bellson also added a second bass drum and small tom-tom to his drum kit. (See pages 20 and 22 for illustrations.) Ellington took advantage of Bellson's capabilities by giving him solos. The recording of Bellson's solo on his own composition "Skin Deep" in *Hi-Fi Ellington Uptown* furnished a means for demonstrating sound quality in high-fidelity equipment that was just then becoming popular.[15] The piece became a crowd-pleasing part of Ellington's repertory. Bellson's showmanship revitalized the band's appeal when all big bands were experiencing a declining audience size and Ellington was particularly low due to the temporary loss of Lawrence Brown and Johnny Hodges. After Bellson left, his successors on the drum throne were required to perform the often-requested "Skin Deep." They also employed the modern timekeeping techniques that Bellson used.

Replacing Bellson was **Sam Woodyard** (1925–1988), Ellington's drummer of eleven years. Woodyard supplied a special spark to the band. His style was hard-swinging and unrelenting. Woodyard's approach was not complicated or flashy. He established a groove. Then, by playing so hard and so passionately, he musically challenged the band members to swing equally hard. The records Ellington made with Woodyard have an insistence in their swing feeling that is unmatched by his records from any other period. (See footnote 7.) For many Ellington fans and a number of Ellington's musicians themselves, Woodyard was the all-time favorite drummer for the band.

The Bellson-Woodyard contributions to Ellington's style were expanded by **Rufus Jones** (b. 1936) between 1966 and 1973. In addition to fulfilling the traditional duties for his position, Jones was notable for also devising original rhythms to fit music that Ellington composed on his world tours during this era.[16] In generating African, Latin American, and oriental flavors for Ellington's suites, Jones played rhythms that were new to the Ellington sound.

Bass

Over his long career of bandleading, Ellington had several outstanding bassists. (Note Oscar Pettiford's work on "Transblucency" in the *Jazz Classics CD.*) The greatest standout among them was Jimmy Blanton (1918–1942), who played with the band from 1939 to 1941. With his impressive instrumental proficiency and musical imagination, Blanton shattered traditional conceptions of jazz bass playing. **His cleanly executed solos showed that, in the hands of a virtuoso, the string bass can contribute more to a band than timekeeping.** Though Blanton's sound was also a powerful component of Ellington's intensely swinging rhythm section, Blanton is best known for the ways Ellington capitalized on his talents for solo improvisation. (His walking swings hard in "Harlem Airshaft" and "Cottontail" on the *Jazz Classics CD.*) **Ellington spotlighted Blanton in melodic roles, and he arranged parts for Blanton's bass that were like horn parts.** In the 1940 "Jack the Bear," Blanton played solo melodies, and he played in unison with ensemble horn lines. During the same year, he also played in unison with horns in "Concerto for Cootie," and he soloed on "Sepia Panorama."[17] Blanton profoundly shaped the next twenty years of jazz bass

Listening Guide for

"Harlem Airshaft"

Recorded July 22, 1940 by Duke Ellington big band; available on the *Jazz Classics CD,* and on Duke Ellington, *The Blanton-Webster Band* (RCA Bluebird: 5659-2-RB, 3CD set, 1940–42).*

CD Track	Elapsed Time	
20	0' 00"	**Introduction**
		Four Measures
		The brass instruments call in harmonized, sustained tones, and the saxes respond with an active figure. Then, while they are silent, you can hear a full rhythm section sound with prominent rhythm guitar, walking bass, and Sonny Greer using brushes on snare drum for timekeeping. Ellington inserts a brief piano fill.
	0' 05"	*Four Measures*
		Saxes now have the lead. Listen to their harmony. Notice more piano fills.
	0'10"	*Four Measures*
		Now the trombones take the lead for about a measure and a half with the baritone saxophone coming in with a response at the end of that second measure. Trombones instantaneously return for two measures of punching figures.
21	0' 15"	**First Chorus**
		(The remainder of the piece follows a repeating, thirty-two bar A-A-B-A form.)
		A Saxes play a simple melody in unison while muted trumpets repeat a more complex background figure in harmony as an answering embellishment.
	0' 25"	**A** Repeat the above.
	0' 35"	**B** Saxes take the foreground by playing a harmonized part in the high register, alternating their calling with trombonist Joe "Tricky Sam" Nanton responding in plunger-muted growl style. Then saxes tie it up with a quick, little, low-register figure at the end of the bridge.
	0' 45"	**A** Repeat of A, but this time with a tie-it-up figure from the trumpets to get ready for the upcoming stop-time. Sonny Greer ends the figure by striking a cymbal, then quickly grabs it to prevent ringing. (The sound and timing of this technique are effective for closing a musical idea in an abrupt way.)

*The score and parts for "Harlem Airshaft" are available from King Brand Classic Editions, P.O. Box 580, Keyport, New Jersey 07735.

22 0' 55" **Second Chorus**

A *First Four Measures*

The rhythm section stops playing. This creates a four-measure stop-time break. The saxes use it to play a high-register, harmonized part with sustained tones. This evokes a suspended feeling, partly because the rhythm section is no longer stating each beat, and partly because there is suddenly very little movement in the sax sound. Then Sonny Greer uses sticks to play rolls and rim shots, "breaking things up," to enhance the band's transition from the suspension to a rough and tumble trumpet solo by Cootie Williams.

23 1' 00" *Second Four Measures*

Cootie Williams opens his trumpet improvisation by percussively stating the same note repeatedly in an off-the-beat fashion. He creates excitement by using the high register and by shaking his tones as they end. Notice the sax activity underneath Williams.

1' 06" **A** Same strategy as for the first A-section. Williams continues with more repeated and shaken high notes, and Greer uses cymbal clasp to end this section of the piece.

1' 16" **B** Sax part becomes more intricate, repeating a climbing figure while Williams continues his improvisation against sax lines. Greer's cymbal clasp ends this section, too.

1' 25" **A** Same strategy as for the first and second A-sections. Notice how Williams dramatically slides down from his last high note. Listen to Greer's activity. It almost constitutes another line added to those of Williams and the saxes.

24 1' 35" **Third Chorus**

A Trombones play a harmonized melody in the foreground while clarinetist Barney Bigard improvises around it, and saxes play yet another series of interjections underneath. Pay attention to Bigard's swoops and the New Orleans flavor of his playing. Imagine having to invent all those lines and colorations to spontaneously embroider the trombone and sax parts without clashing. This is not an ordinary jazz solo.

1' 45" **A** Same formula as for the first A-section.

1' 54" **B** Trumpets join trombones to repeat a sustained tone while Bigard continues his improvisation and answers them. Saxes make periodic interjections. Listen to Bigard's shake at the end of the bridge.

2' 04" **A** Same formula as for the first A-section. Notice Bigard's blue notes. Drummer Sonny Greer becomes louder, striking high-hat while it is in partially opened position.

25 2' 14" **Fourth Chorus**

(Though it starts softly, this chorus gets louder and louder, gradually raising excitement for the climax.)

A Band softly plays a syncopated, low-register melody while Bigard's solo from the previous chorus overlaps into the first three measures of this one, with him entering the clarinet's lower register. Listen to the rhythm guitar and Jimmy Blanton's driving bass sound. They are easier to hear now that the band has quieted down. Cootie Williams begins a muted trumpet solo where Bigard leaves off. Williams starts softly, but, as he proceeds, note how he changes the size and texture of his tone.

2' 23" **A** Pay attention to the finish of his solo in which Williams taps out the last four notes in the manner of a drummer.

2' 33" **B** The arrangement builds excitement by increasing loudness, adding instrumental activity, and going higher in register. The band calls, and Bigard repeatedly climbs out of the ensemble sound in response. The brass sound becomes clearer. Note the relationship between Bigard's improvised figures and the composed ones being played by the rest of the band. It all fits together despite the spontaneity.

2' 43" **A** Saxes call, and the brass answer repeatedly. A high level of excitement is reached. Bigard is improvising throughout the sounds of several written themes. Saxes repeat a new riff of their own. Bigard enters the high register. Brass begin repeating a new riff of their own. The several levels of competing activity threaten to result in chaos by becoming more and more active at the end, but it all is resolved just in time to prevent an explosion. It ends with the brass sustaining a chord and the baritone sax sounding a low note at the finish.

styles. For instance, the idea of voicing pizzicato bass with horns was later used in arrangements by Thad Jones. It became common in modern jazz of the 1970s and 1980s, especially in jazz-rock fusion bands. Few musicians who use the technique today realize that Ellington had been using it as early as 1940.[18]

Diversity of Ellington's Music

Diversity and breadth characterized Ellington's music. The pieces in Ellington's repertory were filled with variety, and the lack of repetition within each piece is striking. When compared with the arrangements used by most swing bands, Ellington's possessed a larger number of different themes and rhythmic figures. Accompanying figures also reflected a greater assortment than was customary. (Listen to "Harlem Airshaft" on the *Jazz Classics CD,* and note the interweaving parts and numerous layers of activity.) In addition, Ellington's repertory was also diverse. It was so varied that we can summarize it as a number of separate books.[19]

1) An impressionistic book with arrangements that place more emphasis on orchestral colors and shading than on swinging. Examples from his pre-LP work include "On a Turquoise Cloud" and "Transblucency" (on the *Jazz Classics CD*). From his LP work, examples include portions of *Anatomy of a Murder* and *Paris Blues.*

2) A book of romantic ballads. Examples from his pre-LP work include "Daydream," "Prelude to a Kiss," and "Sophisticated Lady." Examples from his LP work include the albums *Ellington Indigos* and *At the Bal Masque.*

3) An exotic book. Examples from his pre-LP work include "Caravan," "Flaming Sword," and "Bakiff." Examples from his LP work include entire albums such as *Latin American Suite* and *Togo Brava Suite.*

4) A concert book in which each piece is a long work with much less improvisation than was usually found in his music. Examples in his pre-LP work include "Reminiscing in Tempo," "Black, Brown, and Beige," and "Deep South Suite." Examples in his LP work include *Such Sweet Thunder, Suite Thursday,* and *A Drum Is a Woman.*

5) A book of concertos in which each piece frames the style of one Ellington sideman. Examples from his pre-LP period include "Clarinet Lament" (Barney Bigard), "Echoes of Harlem" (Cootie Williams), and "Boy Meets Horn" (Rex Stewart). Examples from his LP work include "Cop-Out" (Paul Gonsalves) and "Lonesome Lullaby" (Ray Nance).

6) A book of music for sacred concerts, a context that brought Ellington to present new shows and use choirs, new vocal soloists, organ, and dancers. It inspired writing for different moods, such as that of prayer. It also inspired extensive lyrics (Duke Ellington's *Concert of Sacred Music* and *Second Sacred Concert*).

7) A book of swinging instrumentals, each with jazz solos, catchy ensemble themes, and punching accompaniment figures. These are evident throughout Ellington's career: "Rockin' in Rhythm" from the 1930s, "Main Stem" and "Cottontail" (on the *Jazz Classics CD*) from the 1940s, "Launching Pad" from the 1950s.

The vastness of Duke Ellington's contributions becomes all the more evident when you have explored a few hundred selections and then realize that Ellington also composed several operas, a couple of ballets, and about ten musical shows. We should also remember that the style of the Ellington band never really fell into any fixed category—early jazz, swing, or modern. It was always unique. Various editions of the band did portray a somewhat different character because of changes in personnel and repertory, but Ellington created a jazz classification that was practically his own. And, not only did the band present a very colorful and richly diverse repertory, it maintained creative energy for more than four decades.

Ellington's Influence

The influence of Ellington's music was also vast. Other big bands were influenced by his writing style as early as the 1930s.[20] There was an echo of Ellington in the work of several outstanding arrangers of the 1950s and 1960s.[21] Revivals of Ellington's work were frequent during the 1980s and 1990s. Avant-garde bands and composers of this period also drew upon Ellington for inspiration.[22] Ellington's piano style influenced a number of players, including the highly individualistic modernists Thelonious Monk and Cecil Taylor.

CHAPTER SUMMARY

1) Duke Ellington is among the most significant of all figures in jazz history.[23]
2) As a pianist, Ellington derived his approach from the stride style of James P. Johnson, though he also devised an original style with which he set the pace and mood for his pieces and ornamented the solos of his musicians.
3) Ellington was outstanding as a bandleader, maintaining a large ensemble from the early 1920s until his death in 1974, with many musicians remaining for more than twenty years at a stretch.
4) Ellington composed more than two thousand pieces, frequently in collaboration with his musicians.
5) A few of Ellington's pieces became popular songs, such as "Satin Doll," "Mood Indigo," and "I'm Beginning to See the Light."
6) Some of Ellington's pieces represent pioneering efforts in jazz for exceeding the brief time limit that was standard. Among his "extended works" is "Black, Brown, and Beige," a tone parallel to the history of the American Negro.

7) As an arranger, Ellington was distinctive for
   a) using a diversity of themes within a single piece
   b) voicing across sections
   c) using wordless vocals
   d) writing parts particularly for the unique capabilities of each musician
   e) mixing improvised parts with prewritten parts
8) From 1939 to 1941, Ellington showcased bassist Jimmy Blanton, who revolutionized traditional concepts of the bassist's role by playing melody lines by himself and with the horn sections of the band.
9) Ellington's most famous saxophonists were Johnnyy Hodges and Ben Webster.
10) Ellington featured brass players who were masters of the growl style: trumpeter Cootie Williams and trombonist Joe "Tricky Sam" Nanton.
11) During the 1950s, Ellington featured saxophonist Paul Gonsalves and trumpeter Clark Terry.

NOTES

1. Not all of Ellington's pieces represent exclusively his own ideas. Often Ellington incorporated or developed a phrase or countermelody he had heard improvised by one of his musicians. Many works were written by Ellington's musicians or in collaboration with them: for instance, with Bubber Miley, "East St. Louis Toodle-o" and "Black and Tan Fantasy"; with Johnny Hodges, "I'm Beginning To See The Light" and "Don't Get Around Much Anymore"; with Ben Webster, "Cottontail"; with Otto Hardwicke and Lawrence Brown, "Sophisticated Lady." Trombonist Juan Tizol wrote "Caravan," "Bakiff," "Conga Brava," and "Perdido," a melody often mistakenly credited to Ellington. Barney Bigard adapted ideas of New Orleans clarinetist Lorenzo Tio and ended up contributing one strain for Ellington's "Mood Indigo." From 1939 until 1967, Ellington worked closely with pianist-composer-arranger **Billy Strayhorn** (1915–1967). The two men collaborated on countless pieces, and their styles were so similar that most listeners and even the band members themselves rarely knew which of them contributed the larger portion of any particular arrangement. (And, upon later listening, sometimes Strayhorn himself could not recognize what aspects of a piece were his and what came from Ellington.) However, there are several pieces usually credited just to Strayhorn, the most famous of which is "Take the 'A' Train," which replaced "East St. Louis Toodle-o" as the band's theme. Musicians are especially fond of Strayhorn's ballads "Chelsea Bridge" and "Lush Life," the last of which he wrote while still in high school.
2. *Black Brown, and Beige* (RCA Bluebird: 6641-2-RB, 1944–46).
3. *The Best of Early Ellington* (Decca Jazz/GRP: GRD-660, 1926–31); *The OKeh Ellington* (Columbia: C2K 46177, 2CD set, 1927–30). For technical analyses of Ellington's work, see Schuller, *Early Jazz* (Oxford, 1968), 318–357; and Schuller, *The Swing Era* (Oxford, 1989), 46–157.
4. *Early Ellington* (RCA Bluebird: 6852-2, 1927–34).
5. See footnote 2.
6. Get the *Jazz Classics CD* and listen to Bigard's work while you study this chapter's listening guide for "Harlem Airshaft." Musicians may also wish to study the written parts and score transcribed by David Berger and available through King Brand Classic Editions (P.O. Box 580, Keyport, NJ 07735). Berger and King Brand have also made available the score and parts for "Clarinet Lament." Also see Bigard's autobiography, *With Louis and the Duke* (Oxford, 1986).
7. *Ellington at Newport* (Columbia: CK 40587 [CL 934], 1956); *Festival Session* (Columbia: PC 36979, LP, 1959). See *Instructor's Resource Manual* for more examples.
8. Miley co-authored both. Listen to "East St. Louis Toodle-o" in SCCJ. Its title (sometimes spelled "todalo") is pronounced "toad-el-low," to indicate a kind of dance that imitates the low, tired, dragging walk that the term originally referred to; it is not a farewell expression.
9. Listen to Hodges play "Passion Flower" on *Jive at Five* (New World: 274, LP, 1927–46) or *Passion Flower* (Victor jazz: 07863-666162, 1940–46).
10. Hodges not only influenced premodern players, he also had an impact on such modern saxophonists as Eddie Vinson, John Coltrane, and Eric Dolphy. Listen to Coltrane's recording of "Theme for Ernie," on John Coltrane, *Soultrane* (Fantasy: OJCCD-021-2 [Prestige 7142], 1958) in which his ballad style recalls the fullness of sound and timing of ornaments that Hodges refined. Even as recently as the 1970s and 1980s, there was a continuation of the Hodges influence: for example, saxophonist Jan Garbarek cited Hodges as a source for his own style.
11. After studying "Cottontail" on the *Jazz Classics CD,* a good place to continue listening to Webster is Ellington, *The Blanton-Webster Band* (RCA Bluebird: 5659-2-RB, 3CD set, 1940–42). To sample the rasping side of his musical character, listen to "Raincheck," "Mainstem," and "Blue Serge." For the crooning side, listen to "All Too Soon" and his obbligato behind the muted brass in the second chorus of "I Don't Know What Kind of Blues I've Got."
12. Webster influenced Charlie Ventura, Paul Gonsalves, Eddie "Lockjaw" Davis, Archie Shepp, Lew Tabackin, Bennie Wallace, and Scott Hamilton, to name a few.
13. Listen to "Take the 'A' Train" on *Ellington Uptown* (Columbia: CK 40836 [CL 830], 1950–51), and the Gonsalves solos on *Ellington at Newport, Duke Ellington and His Orchestra Live at Newport 1958* (C2K 53584 [8072], 2CD set), *Cosmic Scene* (CBS: 467179 2 [1198], 1958), and *Festival Session.* Also see footnote 7.
14. Listen to Nanton's work on SCCJ on "Blue Serge" and "Harlem Airshaft" (also on the *Jazz Classics CD*). For explanation of his methods, see Al Grey and Mike Grey, *Plunger Techniques* (Second Floor Music, 1987; available from Second Floor Music, 130 West 28th Street, NYC, NY 10001).
15. *Ellington Uptown* (Columbia: CK 40836 [CL 830], 1950–51).
16. *Far East Suite* (RCA Bluebird: 07863-66551-2 [LSP 3782], 1966); *Latin American Suite* (Fantasy: OJCCD-469-2 [8419], 1968); *Afro-Eurasian Eclipse* (Fantasy: OJCCD-645-2 [9498], 1971); *The Ellington Suites* (Fantasy: OJCCD-446-2 [Pablo 2310-762], 1959, 1971–72) has "The Queen's Suite" and the "Goutelas" and "UWIS" suites.
17. These are on *The Blanton-Webster Band* (RCA Bluebird: 5659, 3CD set, 1940–41).
18. Listen to Blanton's work on "Concerto for Cootie" on SCCJ and on "Pitter Panther Patter" on Duke Ellington, *Solos, Duets and Trios* (RCA Bluebird: 2178-2-RB, 1932–67), or *Jive at Five* (New World: 274, LP, 1927–46).
19. See *Instructor's Resource Manual* for a list of albums containing each example.
20. Charlie Barnet's and Woody Herman's bands imitated the Ellington band, and many other bandleaders had hits when they recorded Ellington pieces.
21. Gil Evans, Charles Mingus, George Russell, Clare Fischer, Sun Ra, Lalo Schifrin, Thad Jones, Toshiko Akiyoshi, to name a few.
22. James Newton, Anthony Davis, The World Saxophone Quartet, and others.
23. For more about Ellington's life, see his autobiography, *Music Is My Mistress* (Doubleday, 1973; DaCapo, 1976); Stanley Dance, *The World of Duke Ellington* (Scribner's, 1970; DaCapo, 1980), Mercer Ellington, *Duke Ellington In Person* (Houghton-Mifflin, 1978); Mark Tucker, *Ellington: The Early Years* (University of Illinois, 1991); Tucker, ed., *The Duke Ellington Reader* (Oxford, 1993); David Hadju, *Lush Life: A Biography of Billy Strayhorn* (Farrar Straus Giroux, 1996); and James Lincoln Collier, *Duke Ellington* (Oxford, 1987).

Chapter Eight

© Bettmann/Corbis

The Count Basie Bands

Count Basie (1904–1984) led one of the most swinging big bands in jazz history. When compared with all others from the swing era, Basie's never seemed out of breath nor the least bit frantic. Basie led a big band almost continuously from 1937 until his death. Every edition of the band had at least two players who made important contributions to jazz history. Some editions had four or five.

Basie the Pianist

Basie was originally a stride-style pianist, first inspired by Fats Waller. (For explanation of stride style, listen to the *Demo CD* Track 38. For examples of Fats Waller, listen to *SCCJ*.) Basie's manner was unique among jazz pianists. It was very light and extremely precise. His choice of notes was near perfect, and his impeccable sense of timing was equivalent to a good drummer's. In fact, Basie originally began his musical career as a drummer, not a pianist. Succinct and compact statements are hallmarks of Basie's style. When he soloed, he artfully used silence to pace his lines. The sound of his piano playing usually set the mood and tempo for each piece. Then, sometimes, the entire selection went by without the audience hearing more from Basie than a few "plink plink" interjections.

Basie's Rhythm Section During the Late 1930s to Early 1940s

Basie led the first rhythm section in jazz history that consistently swung in a smooth, relaxed way. That famous rhythm section consisted of Basie himself (piano), Freddie Green (rhythm guitar), Walter Page (string bass), and Jo Jones (drums). Before reading about their

Count Basie Band, perhaps the best of swing era big bands. Its rhythm section style and the innovative sax style of Lester Young bridged the gap between swing and modern jazz. They are pictured here at the Famous Door, in 1938, with (from left to right): Walter Page (bass), Jo Jones (drums), Freddie Green (guitar), Count Basie (piano), Bennie Morton (trombone), Herschel Evans (tenor sax), Buck Clayton (trumpet with cup mute), Dicky Wells (hidden), Earle Warren (alto sax), Ed Lewis (hidden), Harry "Sweets" Edison (trumpet), Jack Washington (playing alto, with his baritone sax at side), Lester Young (tenor sax).

Photo courtesy of Frank Driggs

virtues, review the *Demo CD* to familiarize yourself with the sounds of *walking bass, bass drum, high-hat cymbals, wire brushes,* and *ride rhythms*. Then listen to the final one third of *Demo CD* Track 88 to familiarize yourself with *rhythm guitar*. The virtues of the Basie rhythm section are evident in their "Taxi War Dance" on the *Jazz Classics CD.* Listen to it while you read the following outline.

Among the special qualities of the Basie rhythm section were:

1) An excellent sense of tempo.

2) The ability to keep time and swing consistently without using a hard-driving, pressured approach.

3) Quiet, relaxed playing, which conveyed a feeling of ease.

4) Placing a fairly even amount of stress on each beat instead of pushing every other beat.

5)Emphasis on buoyancy rather than intensity.

Bassist **Walter Page** (1900–1957) contributed:

1) A supple walking bass sound. (He is considered one of the first masters of the walking style.)

2) A strong, articulated sound with life in it, not the dead thud common to many premodern bassists.

3) Playing each beat evenly.

4) Balancing his sound to mesh smoothly with piano, bass, and guitar.

Guitarist **Freddie Green** (1911–1987) was noted for:

1) His crisp strokes on unamplified guitar that sounded his rhythm chords with unerring steadiness and propulsive swing feeling.

2) His close coordination with bass and drums.

The style of drummer **Jo Jones** (1911–1985) was distinguished for:

1) Precise playing without any stiffness. Jones offered a loose, assured manner.

2) Quieter bass drum playing than was common in the swing era. Jones sometimes omitted bass drum entirely, sometimes using it only for off-beat accents.

3) Quiet use of wire brushes on high-hat.

4) Ride rhythms played on high-hat continuously as the apparatus was opening and closing. Jones let his cymbals ring prominently between strokes, thereby creating a sustained sound that smoothed the timekeeping pattern instead of leaving each stroke as an abrupt sound. Jones also maintained this conception when using sticks to play ride rhythms on a separate suspended cymbal (also known as a "top cymbal").

The Basie rhythm section was noted for achieving a balance among the sounds of its members. The four parts were so smoothly integrated that one listener was inspired to compare the effect to riding on ball bearings. If you listen carefully to recordings of the band, you will notice that it is unusual for one member to dominate. Guitar, bass, and drums are all carefully controlled to avoid disturbing the evenness and balance of sound.

In Basie's chordal interjections, jazz piano had the lightness, bounce, syncopation, and flexibility of what became known as **comping.** Though he did not invent it, Basie is so thoroughly associated with comping that he might as well have. His comping was very sharp and lively. Basie comped so well and with such relaxed swing feeling that he provided the most-used model for it. (To further understand comping, listen to the *Demo CD* Track 20.) To elevate Basie's comping to its proper place in history, note that even by the mid-1940s many excellent jazz pianists had not learned to comp, though Basie had been doing it for over ten years. They continued in the predominant styles of the 1920s and 1930s, accompanying by 1) stride style, 2) playing a chord on each beat in the manner of a rhythm guitarist, or 3) playing flowery countermelodies and embellishments. But by the end of the 1940s, the evolution of jazz had been permanently nudged along by Basie's example, and comping had become central to modern jazz.

Arrangements

During the 1920s and 1930s there was a thriving jazz scene in Kansas City, Missouri.[1] A number of significant jazz musicians, including Basie, worked there. Though associated with "Kansas City style jazz," few were born there (see Table 8.1). Their music was not as glossy or elaborate as that of their New York counterparts; it was lighter and more relaxed. This accounts, at least in part, for its exceptional swing feeling.

Kansas City style was not based on the interweaving lines of the collectively improvised New Orleans style. Arrangements in this style were based instead on short musical phrases called *riffs* that are repeated again and again. Riffs serve two functions. Sometimes they are theme statements, and sometimes they are backgrounds for improvised solos. A few of these riffs were written down, but many were created spontaneously during a performance ("off the top of someone's head"), learned by ear, and kept in the heads of the players. Arrangements of this kind are called **head arrangements**, and they are basic to the Kansas

TABLE 8.1 MUSICIANS OF THE 1930S KANSAS CITY SCENE (BIRTHPLACES IN PARENTHESES)

Count Basie (New Jersey) pianist-bandleader	Buddy Tate (Texas) saxophonist
Gus Johnson (Texas) drummer	Pete Johnson (Missouri) pianist
Walter Page (Missouri) bassist-bandleader	Charlie Parker (Kansas) saxophonist-composer
Lester Young (Mississippi) saxophonist	Jay McShann (Oklahoma) pianist-bandleader
Buck Clayton (Kansas) trumpeter	Budd Johnson (Texas) saxophonist-composer
Andy Kirk (Kentucky) bandleader-saxophonist	Hot Lips Page (Texas) trumpeter
Herschel Evans (Texas) saxophonist	Jo Jones (Illinois) drummer
Eddie Durham (Texas) guitarist-arranger-trombonist	Jesse Stone (Kansas) pianist-arranger-bandleader
Buster Smith (Texas) saxophonist	George Lee (Missouri) saxophonist-pianist-bandleader
Bennie Moten (Missouri) pianist-bandleader	Harlan Leonard (Missouri) saxophonist-bandleader
Mary Lou Williams (Georgia) pianist-composer-arranger	

City *riff band style.* (Follow the listening guide on page 133. For a best-selling example of this by a big band, listen to the final strains of "One O'Clock Jump" at the beginning of the *Jazz Classics CD.*)[2]

Lester Young

Many of the best jazz trumpeters and saxophonists of the 1930s and 1940s played with Count Basie at one time or another. Basie's most notable soloist during this period was tenor saxophonist **Lester Young** (1909–1959). This musician was so good that he was nicknamed "Pres" (or "Prez"), an abbreviation for "president of tenor saxophone players." Young played lines which were fresher and more smoothly swinging than those of any previous improvisers. His light tone, slow vibrato, and buoyant phrases served as a model for modern jazz saxophonists and an entire subcategory of modern jazz that was called "cool jazz." Not only did he influence other saxophonists, but he also influenced guitarist Charlie Christian and trumpeter Miles Davis. Some musicians liked his work so much they copied and performed his solos note for note in their own improvisations (see Table 8.4).

To explore Lester Young's improvisatory style, let's compare it with Coleman Hawkins's. (See Table 8.3.) **Young offered a clear alternative to the heavy tone, fast vibrato, and complicated style of Coleman Hawkins.** Often, where Hawkins seemed to be chugging, Young seemed to be floating. Hawkins made improvisation sound like hard work. Young made it seem easy, like talking. Whereas Hawkins accented hard and often directly on main beats, Young was more subtle. Furthermore, Young tended to accent off-beats and lightly stress portions of beats that made his lines swing gracefully. Young's playing was not as intricate as Hawkins's, but his melodic ideas were at least as advanced. He just made them sound easier. (Listen to Young play what he came to consider one of his own best solos: "Taxi War Dance" on the *Jazz Classics CD.*)[3]

Young's approach contrasted with Hawkins's preference for running through the set of notes contained in each chord (musicians call this "arpeggiating"). Instead of playing every note in every chord, as Hawkins often did, Young was more cool and concise. In fact, **Young sometimes purposely ignored the notes in the chords or chose others which, when**

Listening Guide for

"Taxi War Dance"

Recorded March 19, 1939 by Count Basie big band; available on the *Jazz Classics CD,* on *SCCJ;* and on *The Essential Count Basie, Vol. 1* (Columbia: CK 40608, 1936–39). This piece has no theme. The performance consists of improvisations and riffs over the chord progression of "Willow Weep For Me."

CD Track	Elapsed Time	
33	0' 00"	**Introduction**
		Four Measures
		Basie's boogie-woogie left-hand figure with no bass, guitar, or drums accompaniment.
	0' 04"	*Four Measures*
		Trumpets punctuate in unison with piano as a set-up for the piece, all the while trombones are "walking" underneath them, and Jo Jones has begun playing ride rhythms.
34	0' 09"	**First Chorus**
		A Tenor saxophonist Lester Young opens his improvisation by quoting the first line of "Ol' Man River." Listen to Freddie Green playing rhythm guitar, Walter Page playing walking bass lines, and Jo Jones playing ride rhythms on opening and closing high-hat. Basie stops his boogie-woogie figures and moves to comping.
	0' 18"	**A** In the first four bars Basie returns to his boogie-woogie piano figures under Young's solo. After that, Basie returns to comping. Notice how Young's lines relate to these changes in accompaniment patterns.
	0' 27"	**B** Continuation of Young with rhythm section accompaniment.
	0' 37"	**A** Continuation (This is a good example of Basie's big band functioning as a combo, something they were particularly distinguished for).
	0' 45"	**Two-Measure Introduction to the Next Chorus**
		A return to the brass figure that originally opened the piece. Basie's boogie-woogie piano figure is also included. The walking trombones are missing, however.
	0' 47"	**Second Chorus**
		A Trombonist Dicky Wells improvises a solo. He is very melodic and sounds like he is poking fun. Pay attention to how he bases his solo on simple phrases to be developed by repetitions and slight alterations. Note how clear and logical his lines are.
	0' 57"	**A** Solo continues with rhythm section accompaniment, again returning to a small combo performance.

1' 05" **B** Continuation.

1' 14" **A** Continuation.

36 1' 23" **Third Chorus**

A *First Four Measures*

Band returns, Basie abandons comping for patterned figures. Trombones call and trumpets respond.

1' 27" *Second Four Measures*

Tenor saxophonist Buddy Tate begins a solo improvisation. He can be distinguished from Lester Young by having a coarser tone that is darker and has faster vibrato. Tate's execution is less poised and has less swinging rhythmic feeling.

1' 32" **A** Repeat of layout for first A-section.

1' 41" **B** Piano solo by Basie. Notice his light touch, use of the piano's upper register, and impeccable timing.

1' 50" **A** *First Four Measures*

Trombones call and trumpets respond.

1' 55" *Second Four Measures*

Tate solos with a rapid pattern repeated.

37 1' 59" **Fourth Chorus**

A *First Four Measures*

Basie plays a boogie woogie figure underneath ensemble figures by trumpets and trombones.

2' 04" *Second Four Measures*

Tenor saxophonist Lester Young returns with a light feeling. He improvises in his instrument's upper register.

2' 09" **A** *First Four Measures*

2' 13" Repeat of the pattern used in the first A-section, but this time Young enters his solo space early by using a bit of the four-measure lead-in to get started.

Second Four Measures

Young completes his solo, remaining with upper register tones.

2' 17" **B** Basie solos in the upper register, playing lightly and staccato.

2' 27" **A** *First Four Measures*

Trombones call, and the trumpets respond with a simple, syncopated figure which uses alternation of muted and unmuted sound in rapid succession.

2' 31" *Second Four Measures*

Lester Young improvises by rapidly alternating his tone quality.

38 2' 36" **Ending**

Two Measures

Stop-time solo break for Count Basie.

2' 38" *Two Measures*

Stop-time solo break for Lester Young (this is called "trading two's").

2' 40" *Two Measures*

Walking bass unaccompanied.

2' 42" *Two Measures*

Sticks on drums unaccompanied.

2' 44" *Two Measures*

Brass play a tie-it-up figure, and Jo Jones strikes a cymbal and grabs it abruptly to prevent it from ringing. This technique effectively closes up the sounds and provides a dramatic means for ending a performance.

combined with the chord tones, altered the effect of both the tone and the chord. (Musicians refer to such notes as "color tones" because they have the capacity to alter the "color" of the sound, much as voicing alters the "color" of a chord.) And even when he played a solo using many notes, the result was not as densely packed as a typical Hawkins solo.[4]

Young concerned himself with only a core of melodic material. He didn't incorporate afterthoughts into his phrases, as Hawkins was prone to do. He practiced deliberate restraint. He could pace a solo so well that it seemed an integral part of the written arrangement. His gift for improvising new, easily singable melodies is unsurpassed in jazz history. There is an overriding sense of continuity in Young's improvisations that is very satisfying. Young possessed a musical storytelling talent which surfaced in nearly every improvisation.[5]

The advanced level of Young's conception was evident in his easy swing and in his placement of phrases that seemed unhindered by turnarounds and bridges. (Listen to *Demo CD* for illustrations of chord progression organization, and see pages 380–388 for more explanation.) Young often transcended the phrasing style of many premodern players who had organized lines around the two- and four-bar sequences of chord progressions. The internal logic of his lines took precedence over strict adherence to the underlying harmonies and the way they were blocked out. He improvised long lines which had a fresh, expansive feeling unlike the crowded feeling that we often get from improvisations of other soloists.

Young's playing was strongest during the late 1930s. His first recordings were probably the best of his entire career. When he left Basie in 1940, his tone began to darken, his vibrato quickened, and the crispness of his execution decreased. He changed his style. His playing seemed to lose energy steadily until his death in 1959. Yet Young's work remained intelligent and swinging all those later years. In fact, his loyalty to storytelling-type improvisations increased. But after 1940, he seemed unable to jump into his solos with the animation and freshness of his early work.

Kansas City Five; Jones-Smith, Inc.

Several of the most significant recordings in jazz history were made by small combinations of Basie band members. Variously called the Kansas City Five, Six, or Seven, depending on how many musicians were used, these combos often included the Basie rhythm section plus Lester Young, Buck Clayton, and Dicky Wells. Their 1939 recordings, such as "Dickie's Dream" and "Lester Leaps In," are combo classics. One set omitted Basie, added Eddie

TABLE 8.2 A Few of the Many Musicians Who Have Been Important to Basie

TRUMPET	SAXOPHONE	COMPOSER-ARRANGER
Carl Smith	Don Byas	Eddie Durham
Hot Lips Page	Lester Young	Andy Gibson
Buck Clayton	Herschel Evans	Dicky Wells
Harry "Sweets" Edison	Jack Washington	Buck Clayton
Shad Collins	Tab Smith	Buster Harding
Emmett Berry	Earle Warren	Don Redman
Clark Terry	Buddy Tate	Jimmy Mundy
Thad Jones	Wardell Gray	Don Kirkpatrick
Joe Newman	Lucky Thompson	Ernie Wilkins
Al Aarons	Illinois Jacquet	Thad Jones
Sonny Cohn	Serge Chaloff	Frank Foster
Snooky Young	Paul Gonsalves	Frank Wess
Wendell Culley	Eddie "Lockjaw" Davis	Neal Hefti
	Frank Foster	Quincy Jones
	Eric Dixon	Benny Carter
	Jimmy Forrest	Billy Byers
	Billy Mitchell	Chico O'Farrill
	Frank Wess	Sammy Nestico
	Marshall Royal	Al Grey
	Charlie Fowlkes	
	Bobby Plater	
	Paul Quinichette	

DRUMS	BASS	TROMBONE
Jo Jones	Walter Page	Dicky Wells
Shadow Wilson	Eddie Jones	Benny Morton
Sonny Payne	Buddy Catlett	Vic Dickenson
Gus Johnson		Al Grey
Louis Bellson		Henry Coker
Harold Jones		Curtis Fuller
Butch Miles		Benny Powell
Rufus Jones		

GUITAR
Freddie Green

Durham on guitar, and featured some of the all-time best playing of Lester Young and trumpeter Buck Clayton ("Good Mornin' Blues," "Pagin' The Devil," "I Want A Little Girl").[6] Another of these combos included drummer Jo Jones and trumpeter Carl Smith and was given the group name Jones-Smith, Inc. The recordings they made in 1936, including "Shoe Shine Boy" and "Lady Be Good," are masterpieces.[7]

Basie after the 1940s

After the 1940s, Basie retained many elements of his rhythm section style. His own piano style remained constant, and guitarist Freddie Green was still with him, playing in the same style he originated. Basie's post-1940s drummers kept time more on the ride cymbal

Tenor saxophonist Lester Young (soloist) and drummer Jo Jones (accompanist). Both men contributed to the smoothly swinging music of Count Basie's band in the 1930s.

Photo by Robert Asen Courtesy of Scott Asen

TABLE 8.3 COMPARISON OF COLEMAN HAWKINS WITH LESTER YOUNG

	COLEMAN HAWKINS	LESTER YOUNG
tone quality	warm dark-colored heavy-weight full-bodied	cool light-colored light-weight hollow
rate of vibrato	medium to fast	slow
swing feeling	early jazz style	more relaxed and graceful than Hawkins
intricacy of solos	much	less than Hawkins
tunefulness of improvisations	little	much
came to prominence with	Fletcher Henderson (1923–34)	Count Basie (1936–44)
influenced	Herschel Evans Chu Berry Dick Wilson Ben Webster	Charlie Parker Wardell Gray Stan Getz Lee Konitz Sony Stitt Woody Herman band's "Four Brother's" sound and West Coast Style players (see Table 8.4)

Listening Guide for

"Lester Leaps In"

Recorded September 5, 1939 by Lester Young (tenor sax), Buck Clayton (cup-muted trumpet), Dicky Wells (trombone), Count Basie (piano), Freddie Green (guitar), Walter Page (bass), Jo Jones (drums); available on *SCCJ;* and on *The Essential Count Basie, Vol. 2* (Columbia: CK 40835, 1939–40). This piece consists of riffs and improvisations over the chord progression to "I Got Rhythm." A transcription and analysis of Young's solo is available in Scott Reeves, *Creative Jazz Improvisation, 2nd ed.* (Prentice-Hall, 1995).

Elapsed Time		
0' 00"	**Four-Measure Piano Introduction**	
0' 3"	**First Chorus**	
	A-A	Muted trumpet, trombone, and tenor saxophone play a single four-measure melodic figure four times with rhythm section accompaniment (a typical riff band device).
0' 19"	**B**	Count Basie piano solo, very lean, just indicating the moments during which chords change. He allows plenty of space for us to hear bass and drums.
0' 27"	**A**	The three horns state original theme (that same riff) two more times.
0' 35"	**Second Chorus**	
	A-A-B-A	Lester Young tenor sax solo accompanied by drummer Jo Jones playing ride rhythm on opening and closing high-hat. Notice Basie's comping and Page's walking bass.
1' 06"	**Third Chorus**	
	A	Young and Basie improvise counterpoint around each other.
1' 14"	**A**	Rhythm section creates stop-time solo breaks for Young during first six measures. Rhythm section resumes normal timekeeping patterns for last two measures while Young keeps on improvising.
1' 22"	**B**	Young continues solo with rhythm section accompaniment.
1' 30"	**A**	Rhythm section creates more stop-times for Young.
1' 37"	**Fourth Chorus**	
	A	Basie solos the first four measures, Young does the second four.
1' 41"	**A**	Basie solos the first four measures, Young does the second four.
1' 55"	**B**	Basie solos the first four measures, Young does the second four.
2' 01"	**A**	Basie solos the first four measures, Young does the second four. (This is called "trading fours.")

2' 09"	**Fifth Chorus**	
	(This chorus uses another typical riff band device.)	
	A	*First Four Measures*
		Ensemble calls, "Bop bop bop-bop baah!"
2' 12"		*Second Four Measures*
		Young responds with improvisation.
2' 17"	**A**	*First Four Measures*
		Ensemble calls, "Bop bop bop-bop baah!"
2' 21"		*Second Four Measures*
		Basie responds with improvisation.
2' 25"	**B**	Basie continues his improvisation.
2' 33"	**A**	*First Four Measures*
		Ensemble calls, "Bop bop bop-bop baah!"
2' 36"		*Second Four Measures*
		Young responds with improvisation.
2' 40"	**Sixth Chorus**	
	A	*First Four Measures*
		Ensemble calls, "Bop bop bop-bop baah!"
2' 44"		*Second Four Measures*
		Basie responds with improvisation.
2' 49"	**A**	*First Four Measures*
		Ensemble calls, "Bop bop bop-bop baah!"
2' 53"		*Second Four Measures*
		Basie responds with improvisation.
2' 56"	**B**	Basie continues his improvisation.
3' 04"	**A**	Ensemble calls, "Bop bop bop-bop baah!" Then the band members collectively improvise a closing by simultaneously playing different lines in Dixieland style.

than on the high-hat, and they played far more fills than Jo Jones had. However, his drummers were not performing in contemporary styles after the 1940s. They kept to what worked best for the Basie big band approach.

For thirty years, the Basie band had the unusual distinction of being almost the only big band that swung while playing softly. Some of the music written for the band during the 1950s and 1960s capitalized on the band's skill with dynamic contrasts: loud passages which instantaneously get soft; soft passages interrupted momentarily by very loud chords; passages which rise and fall in volume so gradually that one wonders how it is possible. The

TABLE 8.4 A Few of the Many Saxophonists Influenced by Lester Young

Charlie Parker	Zoot Sims	Richie Kamuca
Brew Moore	Lee Konitz	Al Cohn
Paul Quinichette	Warne Marsh	Jerry Jerome
Dave Pell	Dexter Gordon	Don Lanphere
Bob Cooper	Gene Ammons	Jimmy Giuffre
Bill Perkins	Sonny Stitt	Buddy Collette
Wardell Gray	Stan Getz	John Coltrane
Allen Eager	Herbie Steward	Hank Mobley

band maintained precision and balance at a variety of loudness levels, all without losing the unrelenting drive that is expected of jazz performances. Moreover, the band did this without sounding mechanical. In fact, it projected a warm and supple feeling.

Count Basie's band always placed more emphasis on simplicity and swing feeling than on complexity and colorful sounds. Simple, catchy riffs were the rule, even during the 1950s and 1960s when sophisticated composers and arrangers were writing for the band. Basie had previously run the band much as an oversized combo, with more emphasis on swinging solo improvisations than fancy arrangements. That approach contrasted with the highly polished, well-arranged style of Jimmie Lunceford and the elaborate embroidery of written music and improvisation that occurred in Duke Ellington's band. However, Basie's emphasis on the oversized combo format decreased somewhat during the 1950s and more so thereafter. On the other hand, the group achieved a very high level of polish, and it became known as a swinging showcase for glossy ensemble sound like Lunceford's band of twenty years earlier. (See *Instructor's Resource Manual* for a discography of this period.)

CHAPTER SUMMARY

1) Count Basie was a Fats Waller-derived stride pianist with a light, precise touch, and impeccable sense of tempo.
2) Count Basie's accompaniment style constituted one of the first examples of comping.
3) Count Basie was one of the few pianists to make silence almost as important as the notes he played.
4) The 1937–1940 Basie rhythm section set the pace for modern methods of timekeeping and accompanying.
5) Basie's band played in the Kansas City style, using riffs, simple figures which were played repeatedly atop pop tune and 12-bar blues accompaniments.
6) Tenor saxophonist Lester Young offered a light-toned alternative to the deep, heavy sound of Coleman Hawkins.
7) Young was very melodic and fresh in his improvisations. He became the major model for hundreds of modern jazz saxophonists, as well as an entire subcategory of modern jazz called "cool jazz."
8) Basie always stressed simplicity and swing instead of complex arrangements, and he retained the same unhurried feeling throughout his bandleading career.

NOTES

1. For more about Kansas City style, see Nathan Pearson, *Goin' to Kansas City* (University of Illinois Press, 1987); Gunther Schuller, *Early Jazz* (Oxford, 1968), 279–317; and Schuller, *The Swing Era* (Oxford, 1989), 222–262.
2. Many riff-based pieces that band members at first identified only by numbers were eventually given names and composer credits. Count Basie's "One O'Clock Jump" and "Jumpin' at the Woodside" are best-selling examples, available in the anthology: *Big Band Jazz: From the Beginnings to the Fifties* (Smithsonian: 2202, 4CD set, 1924–56). Listen to this style on "Moten Swing," as recorded by the Bennie Moten band in 1932 and available on SCCJ. The piece is a thirty-two measure A-A-B-A form that is based on the chord progression to a song called "You're Driving Me Crazy." This recording will also give you a peek into Kansas City jazz history because Count Basie had been a member of both Moten's band and the Blue Devils, led by bassist Walter Page. These two groups eventually fused to become Basie's first Kansas City band.
3. In the opening to "Taxi War Dance," Young plays notes that purposely clash with the notes of Basie's boogie-woogie figure; then the harmonic conflict resolves when Basie comes out of the boogie-woogie figure. Another clever Young solo is his improvisation on Basie's "Jive at Five" (1939) available on *Jive at Five* (New World: 274, LP, 1927–46) and Count Basie, *The Complete Decca Recordings 1937–39* (Decca Jazz/GRP:GRD3-611, 3CD set, 1937–1939). This particular solo is especially intriguing because it foreshadows the fluffy tone and melodic approach Stan Getz was to display eight years later.
4. For a transcription and analysis of Young's solo on "Lester Leaps In," see Scott Reeves, *Creative Jazz Improvisation, 2nd ed.* (Prentice-Hall, 1995). The solo is nearly all eighth notes, but the sequences are clear despite the number of notes and surprises they contain. They are free of the many twists and turns which typify Hawkins's improvisations. For comments about 251 Lester Young recording sessions and transcriptions of solos, see Frank Büchmann-Møller, *You Got to Be Original, Man!: The Music of Lester Young* (Greenwood, 1990).
5. His clarinet solos on the 1938 "I Want a Little Girl" and "Pagin' the Devil" illustrate his "storytelling" talent quite well. They are available on Lester Young, *"The Kansas City Sessions"* (Commodore Jazz/GRP: GRD-402,1938, 1944). Also outstanding in this regard is his tenor sax solo on "Pound Cake" (1939), available in *The Essential Count Basie, Vol. 1* (Columbia: CK 40608, 1936–39).
6. Available on Lester Young, *"The Kansas City Sessions"* (Commodore Jazz/GRP: GRD-402, 1938, 1944).
7. Available on *The Essential Count Basie, Vol. 1* (Columbia: CK 40608). For a transcription and analysis of Young's solo on "Lady Be Good," see Schuller, *The Swing Era* (Oxford, 1989), 230–235.

To listen to more Basie performances, see *Big Band Jazz* (Smithsonian: 2202), *Big Band Renaissance* (Smithsonian: 108), and Count Basie, *The Complete Decca Recordings* (Decca Jazz/GRP: GRD3-611, 3CD set, 1937–39).

To read more about the Basie band and its musicians, see *Good Morning Blues: The Autobiography of Count Basie As Told to Albert Murray* (Random House, 1985); Stanley Dance, *The World of Count Basie* (Scribner's, 1980; DaCapo, 1985); Lewis Porter, *Lester Young* (Twayne, 1985); Dave Gelly, *Lester Young* (Hippocrene, 1984); Lewis Porter, ed., *The Lester Young Reader* (Smithsonian, 1991); Buck Clayton, *Buck Clayton's Jazz World* (Oxford, 1986); Dicky Wells, *Night People* (Crescendo, 1971; Smithsonian, 1991); Frank Büchmann-Møller, *You Just Fight for Your Life: The Story of Lester Young* (Praeger, 1990); Luc Delannoy, *Pres: The Story of Lester Young* (University of Arkansas Press, 1993); and Chris Sheridan, *Count Basie: A Bio-Discography* (Greenwood, 1986).

Chapter Nine

Charlie Mingus, Roy Haynes, Thelonious Monk, Charlie Parker. Photo by Bob Parent, courtesy of Don Parent

Bop

During the 1940s, a number of adventuresome musicians showed the effects of studying the advanced swing era styles of saxophonists Coleman Hawkins and Lester Young, pianists Art Tatum and Nat Cole, trumpeter Roy Eldridge, guitarist Charlie Christian, and the Count Basie rhythm section. "Early jazz" and other pre-1940 styles are today referred to as the "classic period." The new styles which emerged after 1940 were classified as modern jazz. These first "modern" musicians were alto saxophonist Charlie Parker, pianist Thelonious Monk, and trumpeter Dizzy Gillespie. Their music was called bebop, or just "bop." By the middle 1940s, bop had inspired a legion of other creative musicians including trumpeter Miles Davis and pianist Bud Powell. By the late 1940s, Parker and Gillespie had also influenced the music in several big bands, including Woody Herman's. This chapter will discuss the solo and combo styles of these musicians and the big bands of Herman and Gillespie.

Modern jazz did not burst upon the jazz scene suddenly. It developed gradually through the work of swing era musicians. Parker and Gillespie themselves began their careers by creating swing-style improvisations. Then they expanded on swing styles and gradually incorporated new techniques; their work eventually became a different style, but its swing era roots remained evident. Rather than being a reaction *against* swing styles, modern jazz developed smoothly *from* swing styles.

Bebop was considerably less popular than swing, and it failed to attract dancers. However, it did contribute impressive soloists who continued to gain disciples for the rest of the century. The first bop soloists contributed a new vocabulary of musical phrases and distinctive methods of matching improvisation to chord progressions. This became the most substantial system of jazz for the next forty years. Even during the 1990s, musicians frequently evaluated new players according to their ability to play bop. Mastery of this style was considered the foundation for competence as a jazz improviser.

◇BOP CONTRASTED WITH SWING

Bop differed from swing in a number of performance aspects:

1) Preferred instrumentation for bop was the small combo instead of big band.
2) Less emphasis was placed on arrangements in bop.
3) Average tempo was faster in bop.
4) Clarinet was rare in bop.
5) Display of instrumental virtuosity was a higher priority for bop players.
6) Rhythm guitar was rare.

Bop differed from swing in a number of stylistic respects:

1) Bop improvisation was more complex because it contained
   a) more themes per solo,
   b) less similarity among themes,
   c) more excursions outside the tune's original key, and
   d) a greater scope of rhythmic development.
2) Melodies were more complex in bop.
3) Harmonies were more complex in bop.
4) Bop tunes and chord progressions projected a more unresolved quality.
5) Accompaniment rhythms were more varied in bop.
6) Comping was more prevalent than stride style and simple, on-the-beat chording.
7) Drummers played their timekeeping rhythms primarily on suspended cymbal, rather than snare drum, high-hat, or bass drum.
8) Surprise was more highly valued in bop.
9) Bop was a more agitated style than swing was.

Bop improvisations were composed mostly of eighth-note and sixteenth-note figures which seemed jumpy, full of twists and turns. The contours of the melodic lines were jagged; there were often abrupt changes of direction and large intervals between the notes. The rhythms in those lines were quick and unpredictable, with more syncopation than any music previously common in Europe or America.

Bop players took a cue from Lester Young and often began phrases in the middle of eight-bar sections, continuing them through the turnarounds, past the traditional barriers of the eighth bar (twelfth bar in the blues). Bop performers more often overcame the tendency of premodern improvisers to stop phrases at or before *turnarounds*. (See pages 387–388 for nontechnical explanation of turnarounds or page 416 for examples.) They planned ahead further and mastered the improvisation of extended lines which reflected a tune's underlying chord progression less and less.

◇BOP HARMONY

By contrast with the earliest jazz musicians, bop musicians did more than embellish a song. As a starting point for their improvisations, they retained only the chord progressions that had accompanied a song.[1] Then they often enriched a progression by adding new chords. (See third example under "Chord Progressions for the Twelve-Bar Blues" on page 415.) When jazz musicians add chords or change chords in a given progression, they call it *substitution* or reharmonization because new chords are substituted in place of the old ones. Art Tatum had previously added and replaced chords underneath existing melodies. In fact, his reharmonization of "Tea For Two" is well known among jazz musicians. Coleman Hawkins had loved to improvise on complicated chord progressions and invent solo lines whose construction implied that chords had been added. His recording of "Body and Soul" demonstrates this. In these ways, Tatum and Hawkins had set the stage for the wide use of these techniques in bop style. Some bop lines implied chords which were not originally in a tune's accompaniment; these lines were sometimes played against a tune's original harmonies to achieve purposely clashing effects. In other cases, the pianist and bassist instantaneously changed chords and chord progressions to fit the new harmonic directions implied by an improvised line.

Bop players also altered existing chords. They often based their lines more on the alterations than on the fundamental tones. So, by comparison with their predecessors, bop musicians not only used more chords, they used richer chords and created lines that drew from the enrichments. The most common alteration was the *flatted fifth* (also known as the lowered fifth or raised eleventh). It soon became identified as much with modern jazz as the lowered third and lowered seventh were identified with premodern jazz. Today all three intervals are basic to the character of jazz. (Dizzy Gillespie's 1945 arrangement of "Shaw Nuff" ends on a flatted fifth.)

Because bop musicians liked to improvise on difficult chord progressions, they sometimes wrote original progressions themselves. But a more common practice was to improvise on popular song progressions that were challenging. "All the Things You Are" served this purpose. "Cherokee" also became a favorite because the progressions in its bridge are unusual.[2]

◇CHARLIE PARKER

The musician who contributed most to the development of bop was alto saxophonist **Charlie Parker** (1920–1955). Jazz musicians and historians feel that he is the most important saxophonist in jazz history. Many musicologists consider Parker one of the most brilliant musical figures in the twentieth century. Going beyond the advances made by Lester Young, Coleman Hawkins, and Art Tatum, he built an entire system that was conveyed in his improvisations and compositions. The system embodied

1) new ways of selecting notes to be compatible with the accompaniment chords;
2) new ways of accenting notes so that the phrases have a highly syncopated character;
3) methods for adding chords to existing chord progressions and implying additional chords by the selection of notes for the improvised lines.

Parker astonished other musicians with his tremendous fertility of melodic imagination, unprecedented mastery of the saxophone, and the dizzying pace with which he was able to improvise.[3] Parker's solos were densely packed with ideas. During his improvisations, his mind seemed to be bubbling over with little melodies and paraphrases of melodies. It was

TABLE 9.1 A Few of the Many Bop Style Musicians

TRUMPET

Dizzy Gillespie
Fats Navarro
Howard McGhee
Miles Davis
Kenny Dorham
Red Rodney
Benny Harris
Sonny Berman
Freddie Webster
Conte Candoli
Clark Terry
Idrees Sulieman
Benny Bailey

TROMBONE

J.J. Johnson
Kai Winding
Bennie Green
Frank Rosolino

BASS

Oscar Pettiford
Ray Brown
Tommy Potter
Curly Russell
Nelson Boyd
Al McKibbon
Gene Ramey
Red Callender
Teddy Kotick
Chubby Jackson
Eddie Safranski

SAXOPHONE

Charlie Parker
Dexter Gordon
Lucky Thompson
Stan Getz
Wardell Gray
Allen Eager
Herbie Steward
Brew Moore
Gene Ammons
Sonny Stitt
Flip Phillips
James Moody
Charlie Ventura
Zoot Sims
Al Cohn
Ernie Henry
Leo Parker
Sonny Criss
Serge Chaloff
Don Lanphere
Charlie Rouse
Sonny Rollins
Phil Urso
Boots Mussulli

VIBRAHARP

Milt Jackson
Teddy Charles
Terry Gibbs

DRUMS

Kenny Clarke
Max Roach
Joe Harris
Tiny Kahn
Don Lamond
Roy Haynes
Osie Johnson
Denzil Best

PIANO

Bud Powell
Thelonious Monk
Al Haig
Dodo Marmarosa
Joe Albany
Walter Bishop, Jr.
Duke Jordan
George Shearing
Oscar Peterson
Billy Taylor
Hank Jones
Argonne Thornton (Sadik Hakim)
Hampton Hawes
John Lewis
Todd Dameron
Ahmad Jamal

GUITAR

Arv Garrison
Tal Farlow
Bill DeArango
Jimmy Raney
Johnny Collins
Barry Galbraith
Chuck Wayne
Barney Kessel
Billy Bauer
Johnny Smith

COMPOSER-ARRANGER

Gil Fuller
George Russell
Neal Hefti
Dizzy Gillespie
Charlie Parker
Thelonious Monk
Todd Dameron
John Lewis
Shorty Rogers
Ralph Burns
Gil Evans
Gerry Mulligan

Charlie Parker (alto sax) and Miles Davis (trumpet), two of the most influential men in modern jazz. Parker devised the bop approach, and Davis went on to develop cool, modal, and jazz-rock approaches. Pictured here in 1947 when Parker was 27 and Davis was 21.

Photo by William P. Gottlieb

as though he had so much energy and enthusiasm that he could barely contain himself. This led to interspersing his solos with double-time and quadruple-time figures. Even in ballad renditions, he tended to ornament slow lines with double-time figures. (For a demonstration of double-timing, listen to the *Demo CD* Track 35.) In other words, he played fast, and he played a lot of notes. It is no coincidence that soon after Parker's mid-1940s recordings appeared, there was an increase in the average tempo, an increase in double-timing, and an increase in the average amount of melodic ideas in the improvisations of other modern jazz musicians. Though this trend had already begun during the swing era, it was also partly a function of the new example set by Parker.

Parker's timbre departed from standard swing era models. In place of the lush, sweet tone preferred by Johnny Hodges and Benny Carter, Parker used the dry, biting tone preferred by Kansas City saxophonist Buster Smith, an early model for Parker. Though Parker's tone had considerable fullness, it possessed a lighter color than Hodges' tone. In place of the pronounced vibrato of Hodges and Carter, Parker used the slower, narrower vibrato preferred by Smith, and Parker was less prone to dwell on a few choice notes than Hodges. By comparison with Hodges, Parker sounded more hurried. As opposed to an easygoing romantic, Parker sounded like a modern composer improvising at lightning speed.[4]

Parker's Sources

Parker's improvisations were inspired by many sources. An adequate analysis of his techniques is beyond the nontechnical scope of this book, but we should note that Parker's improvisatory techniques echo the methods that are routinely employed by classical composers.[5] Though we will not be able to recognize examples of the techniques if we do not know them, we might notice other sources for his improvisations because they draw upon familiar material. Parker interspersed his lines with phrases from highly varied sources. He drew from materials as far-flung as the solos of Louis Armstrong and Lester Young and the melodies of blues singers and early jazz hornmen. He selected phrases from pop tunes and traditional melodies, themes from opera and classical music.[6]

Parker's Tunes

Parker wrote a sizable body of tunes, and their character set the flavor for bop as much as his improvisations did. Though not melody-like in the pop tune sense, they were catchy lines in a jazz vein. Most were accompanied by chord progressions borrowed from popular songs. Many used accompaniments of the twelve-bar blues chord progression. Their phrases were memorized and analyzed by hundreds of jazz soloists. His "Now's the Time," "Billie's Bounce," and "Confirmation" were played at jam sessions for decades after he introduced them. This was the musical language of bop.

Parker's Impact

Parker's impact on jazz was immense. Bop trumpeter Dizzy Gillespie cites Parker as a primary influence on his own style, and bop pianist Bud Powell modelled some of his lines on those of Parker. Methods of improvisation devised by Parker were adopted by numerous saxophonists during the 1940s and 50s (see Table 9.2). Parker's tunes and phrases were even heard in the earliest recordings of Ornette Coleman and Albert Ayler, leaders of the avant-garde in the 1960s. Jazz clubs were named for Parker—Birdland in New York and Birdhouse in Chicago. Parker's melodic inventiveness is so stunning that bop singer Eddie Jefferson performed Parker's "Billie's Bounce" and "Parker's Mood" with lyrics which had been written for the melodies and the improvisations. During the 1970s, a group called Supersax began using five saxes and rhythm section to play harmonized transcriptions of Parker solos. Supersax was able to treat his solos as compositions because catchy ideas are so abundant in Parker's improvisations.

◇DIZZY GILLESPIE

Dizzy Gillespie (1917–1993) was the first and most important bop trumpeter. Like Louis Armstrong and Roy Eldridge before him, Gillespie was his era's virtuoso instrumentalist. He was particularly noted for unprecedented agility and command of his instrument's highest register. But unlike Armstrong's and Eldridge's, Gillespie's proficiency was unmatched thereafter. Note, however, that only part of Gillespie's impact stemmed from his awe-inspiring command of the trumpet. Great instrumental proficiency was necessary for bop improvisation on all instruments. Gillespie's stirring musical ideas were responsible for much of his influence. By the time he first recorded with Parker, he had absorbed the saxophone-style lines of Roy Eldridge's approach, and Gillespie had devised his own brand of bop which bristled with excitement.

Dizzy Gillespie's harmonic skills were startling, and he flaunted them. His phrases were full of surprises and playful changes of direction. He could daringly go in and out of keys within a single phrase, always managing to resolve the unexpected at the next chord. He often zoomed

TABLE 9.2 **A Few of the Many Saxophonists Influenced by Charlie Parker**

Phil Woods	Lou Donaldson	Sonny Rollins
Charlie Mariano	Davey Schildkraut	Ornette Coleman
Sahib Shihab	Sonny Stitt	Albert Ayler
Ernie Henry	James Moody	Wardell Gray
Sonny Criss	Jackie McLean	Dexter Gordon
Charlie McPherson	Cannonball Adderley	Art Pepper
Frank Strozier	Eric Dolphy	Bud Shank
Jimmy Heath	John Coltrane	Joe Farrell

Dizzy Gillespie invented the first modern approach to jazz trumpet playing, and he pioneered bop compositional style. He is seen here in 1947 at age 30.

Photo by William P. Gottlieb

up to the trumpet's high register during the middle of a phrase and still managed to connect the melodic ideas logically. Sometimes he interspersed quotes from non-jazz pieces, such as Bizet's opera *Carmen* or the pop tune "We're in the Money." He often used the quote as a point of departure for developing his own phrases. Gillespie built tension by going higher and higher with syncopated notes played staccato, and then resolved the tension by coming down with legato lines. Moreover, Gillespie's lines made sense even when he played rapid cascades of notes.

Like Eldridge, Gillespie occasionally would toy with a single note, playing it again and again, each time in a different way, creating different rhythmic patterns and using changes in loudness and tone color to achieve variety in his sound. One of Gillespie's methods is especially reminiscent of Eldridge. He could make the trumpet tone brittle and then crack it resoundingly in a burst of high notes. Also like Eldridge, he could channel all his terrific energy into a ballad, using his exceptional skill with harmony and his fertile imagination to mold a unique, personal creation.[7]

Gillespie's Impact

Gillespie exerted sweeping influence on modern jazz. His pet phrases became stock clichés for two generations of jazz trumpeters; these phrases can also be heard in the playing of pianists, guitarists, saxophonists, and trombonists. During the 1940s, he influenced numerous trumpeters.[8] Some of these players originally derived their styles from premodern sources, but they incorporated some of Gillespie's devices upon hearing him. Though only a year or two older than several of them, Gillespie influenced them as a classic model rather than a mere contemporary. Though Gillespie did not drastically alter his trumpet style after 1947, he continued to perform regularly and remained active until his death in 1993.

Gillespie also made lasting contributions to modern jazz as a composer.[9] His "Groovin' High" and "A Night in Tunisia" became jazz standards that are still played. After being recorded with lyrics, they gained wider audiences in the 1980s. Afro-Cuban music was one of Gillespie's special interests, and he explored it in his big band numbers "Manteca," "Cubano Be," and "Cubano Bop." These pieces are among the earliest appearances of Latin American music in modern jazz.[10]

After co-leading a combo with Charlie Parker and leading a few small bands of his own, Gillespie began a series of bop big bands[11] that kept going through most of the late 1940s. He formed others sporadically thereafter. His combos and big bands saw a flow of powerful players, many of whom—Milt Jackson and John Coltrane, for example—went on to lead significant groups of their own.

In summary, Gillespie contributed

1) a model of unparalleled trumpet mastery;
2) a body of original compositions;
3) a string of high-quality combos and big bands featuring numerous jazz stars-to-be;
4) the use of Afro-Cuban music in jazz;
5) a new vocabulary of phrases and ways of matching solo notes to accompanying chords.

◇THELONIOUS MONK

The emphasis of bop was on improvisation, but there were a few outstanding bop composers. **Thelonious Monk** (1917–1982) was a pianist and composer whose melodies were unorthodox and whose chord progressions severely challenged improvisers. Monk's compositions influenced the flavor of much modern jazz, and his jazz piano style influenced a number of pianists (see Table 9.3). Several musicians have devoted entire albums to his music, and a few touring bands have constructed their repertories primarily from his compositions. Monk's "Straight, No Chaser," "Well, You Needn't," and "'Round Midnight" became jazz standards.

Thelonious Monk, the first bebop composer and pianist. Monk's tunes became standard repertory for generations of jazz musicians who liked his unorthodox rhythms and harmonies. Shown here in 1947 at age 30.

Photo by William P. Gottlieb

TABLE 9.3 A Few of the Many Pianists Influenced by Thelonious Monk

Randy Weston	Andrew Hill	Karl Berger
Herbie Nichols	Bud Powell	Chick Corea
Cecil Taylor	Misja Mengelberg	Dollar Brand
Mal Waldron	Anthony Davis	Geri Allen

Monk's tunes have a logic and symmetry all their own. Unlike the tunes of many composers, his are so perfectly structured and concise that they cannot withstand tampering. Monk was expert at placing accents in irregular order—his "Rhythm-n-ing" is exceedingly difficult to play properly because of its odd accents. He was especially skilled in ending phrases on the least expected notes, yet making the piece sound as though those phrase endings had been expected all along—his "Off Minor," for instance. Monk employed simple compositional devices with very original results. His "Straight, No Chaser" involves basically only one idea played again and again, each time in a different part of the measure and with a different ending. The shifting accents reflect a craftsmanship which can produce depth in simplicity. The melody is an ingenious invention set atop the twelve-bar blues chord progression.[12]

Monk's Piano Style

As a pianist, Monk was a curious mixture. His use of stride piano techniques suggests Fats Waller. Some of his horn-like lines are reminiscent of Earl Hines. In some voicings, Monk's playing suggests Ellington's, though Monk conveys more blunt starkness. Monk's style also resembles Ellington's in the percussive way both men strike the piano keys, the dark and rough tone quality they extract from the piano, and the way that both men sometimes allow notes to ring long after the keys are struck. Monk also likes the lower register, another Ellington similarity.

Monk's comping was not like conventional bop comping style. Nor was it like the light and bouncing approach that evolved from Count Basie's methods. It resembled more of a declamation than the springy chording provided by most modern pianists. It assumed more the character of a bop drummer's snare drumming than a guitarist's chording. Monk's comping seemed to be setting up spaces framed by resounding punches. Note also that Monk often stopped comping for long passages, leaving the soloist to improvise with only bass and drums accompaniment.

Monk was one of the most original of all jazz improvisers. In fact, his inventions sound so different from other styles that some listeners feel it is misleading to classify his style as swing or bop. They would rather see his music in a category of its own. His lines often display jagged contours, and the construction for some of his improvisations is quite playful. For example, he loved to insert a whole-tone scale abruptly into his line (see Figure 9.1). In his harmonies, Monk is particularly known for combinations of tones that clash resoundingly with each other. It has been playfully said that Monk could make an in-tune piano sound out of tune. Combined with an uneven rhythmic style, these harmonic characteristics made his music quite jarring.

Monk's music conveys a sense of unsettling deliberation. He uses notes so sparingly that silence is almost as important as sound. (Listen to his "Bags' Groove" solo on SCCJ.) The agonizing care he devotes to choosing each individual note and rhythm precludes the long, horn-like improvisations generated by most other pianists. His music is not smooth. His piano

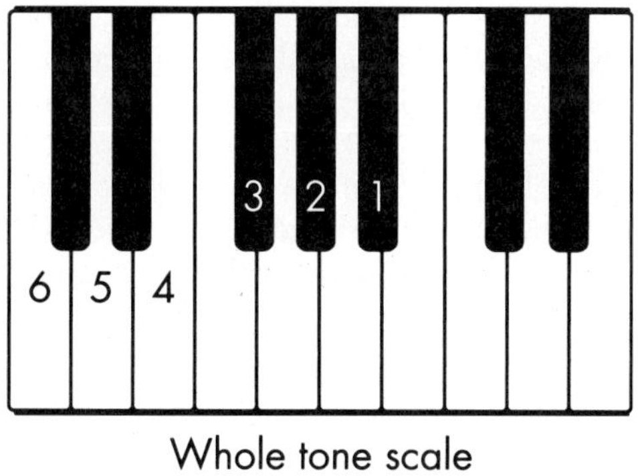

FIGURE 9.1 Piano keyboard illustration of a whole-tone sequence of the kind Monk was likely to insert in his improvisations.

improvisations convey a sense that he is struggling to decide on every note, and then reaches that decision just barely in time to play it. Nothing is produced casually or routinely. Each phrase is played very emphatically, and with much consideration for its maximum rhythmic effect. Monk's approach is very intense and percussive. He often strikes a note or chord several times in a row, as though knocking on a door. In fact his rhythms are so pronounced and jaunty that his music does not evoke the easy rise and fall of tensions associated with most jazz lines. In the perceptions of many listeners, Monk's music swings, but for others there is insufficient relaxation and grace to allow more than a rudimentary hint of swing feeling.[13]

◇TADD DAMERON

Pianist **Tadd Dameron** (1917–1965) was one of the foremost composers in bop. His work covered a broad range—from the bop melody "Hot House," to his simple but catchy line, "Good Bait," to a pretty song that he scored for wordless vocal in the manner of Duke Ellington ("Casbah"). His "Hot House" and "Lady Bird" became standards among jazz instrumentalists.[14]

Much of Dameron's most distinctive work appeared in the form of arrangements for medium-sized bands. Dameron was good at getting a big band sound from a smaller group of instruments. His arrangements had voicings with the thick textures and rhythmic style of bop piano. Using the strong, clear-toned lead of a trumpeter like Fats Navarro, Dameron would then assign melody notes in a block-chord fashion to alto sax, tenor sax, trombone, and baritone sax. The range of the voicing might encompass three octaves.[15]

◇JOHN LEWIS

Several of the most imaginative writers in bop were associated with the Dizzy Gillespie big band. One was **John Lewis** (1920–2001), who contributed "Two Bass Hit" and "Toccata for Trumpet and Orchestra." He also wrote hundreds of other pieces in a variety of contexts, ranging from ballet music to film scores, with instrumentations ranging from jazz combos to symphony orchestras. (Listen to his "Django" in SCCJ.) A special interest for Lewis was combining classical music with jazz. This idiom is called **Third Stream music.**[16] It usually consists of mixing the instrumentation and forms of classical music with jazz improvisation and jazz swing feeling. The term was coined by Gunther Schuller, a composer whose "Concertino for Jazz Quartet and Orchestra" was written for the Modern Jazz Quartet, Lewis's group.[17]

Modern Jazz Quartet and Milt Jackson

In 1952, John Lewis and three other musicians from Dizzy Gillespie's bands formed The Milt Jackson Quartet. After several personnel changes, it became the **Modern Jazz Quartet**—vibraharpist **Milt Jackson** (1923–1999), pianist Lewis, bassist Percy Heath, and drummer Connie Kay. Together they produced a delicate sound so polished and dignified that listeners likened it to classical chamber music.[18] A substantial part of this character was due to the style of their vibraharpist. Despite the mechanical and percussive nature of the vibraharp, Jackson managed to extract a warm, gentle sound and project remarkable presence. This was done partly by Jackson's bluesy, melodic phrasing. Much of the effect was achieved by his careful regulation of the vibraharp's tremolo speed and his fondness for a particularly slow rate of tremolo (see Figure 9.2). He often adjusted the tremolo rate while playing, just as saxophonists adjust vibrato and blowing pressure for expressive purposes. Jackson's graceful, relaxed style meshed with Lewis's light touch on the piano and his gift for understated melody. The group created a cool kind of bop and became one of the best known

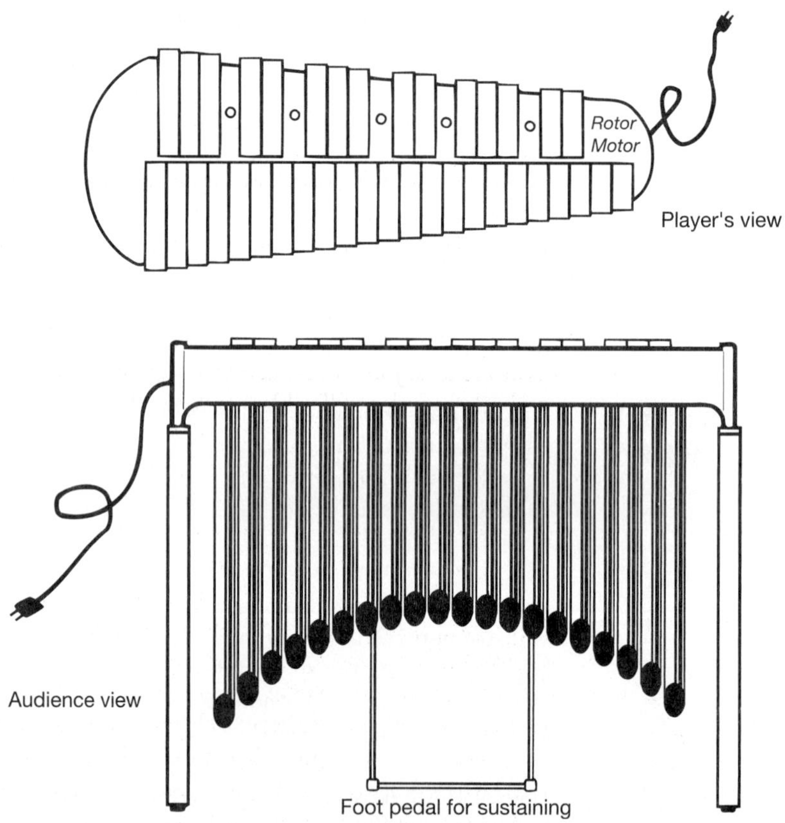

FIGURE 9.2 Vibraharp. To most people, the vibraharp (also called the vibraphone or vibes) looks like a marimba or a big xylophone with tubes hanging under its keys. The vibraharp is played similarly to the marimba and xylophone, but it is constructed differently. Its keys are metal; those of the xylophone and marimba are wooden. The vibraharp's resonating tubes are like those of the marimba, but each tube contains a disc that twirls by means of an electric motor. The twirling discs enable the sound of ringing keys to project and sustain. The discs give the vibraharp sound a wavering character, an even pulsation called a tremolo. The sound reaches our ears in alternating pulses (wuh . . . wuh . . . wuh . . .). Tremolo is not to be confused with vibrato. Tremolo is an alternation of loudness, whereas vibrato is an alternation of pitch. Some vibraharps allow the player to control the rate of tremolo by means of a dial attached to the rotor motor. All vibraharps allow the player to start and stop sustaining the sound by means of a foot pedal.

bands in modern jazz. Jackson, Lewis, Heath, and Kay played together regularly until the fall of 1974 and then regrouped occasionally thereafter for tours and recordings.[19]

◇BASS

Few bop bassists could approximate the tone quality, agility, or imagination of Duke Ellington's Jimmy Blanton, though most walked effectively underneath the piano and horn parts.[20] Three bop bassists in particular, though, did learn Blanton's ideas and used them for developing their own styles—**Oscar Pettiford** (1922–1960), **Charles Mingus** (1922–1979), and **Ray Brown** (b. 1926). (For examples of horn-like bass lines, listen to the *Demo CD* Track 27.) Pettiford was present at many of the earliest bop sessions, having co-led an important band with Dizzy Gillespie in 1943.[21] The earliest recorded Mingus solos are especially significant because they are among the first on record to go beyond Blanton and incorporate bop melodic concept.[22] And it is not just their historical position and style that is notable, but also their quality. Mingus extracted a large, percussive sound from his bass, and his solos exude strength and sureness. The Mingus improvisations were developed in a compositionally sensible way that was forceful and emphasized every note. Moreover, he continued to evolve new styles for the bass and went on to become one of the top avant-garde composer-bandleaders in the 1950s and 1960s. Ray Brown was widely known because he received consistent and extensive exposure in tours and recordings with the very popular Oscar Peterson trios of 1951 to 1966. Long viewed as the most swinging modern bassist, he is widely regarded for his big tone, unrelenting drive, and melodic solos.[23]

◇DRUMS

Jo Jones and Sid Catlett are the swing drummers whom bop drummers cite most frequently as influences. Jones eliminated bass drum playing in some contexts and recorded some of the earliest examples of flexible interaction between soloist and drummer. (Listen to his work on Benny Goodman's rendition of "I've Found a New Baby" in SCCJ.) Catlett kept time with a more swinging feeling than was common to drummers in the 1930s. He was one of the few drummers who was able to play equally well with bands from both the swing and bop eras.

Kenny Clarke and Max Roach

The advances made by Jones, Catlett, and others became crystallized in the playing of bop drummers **Kenny Clarke** (1914–1985) and **Max Roach** (b. 1925). Their styles advanced from swing approaches in at least three respects. First, they **increased the frequency and spontaneity of kicks and prods,** those sounds that deviate from timekeeping rhythms. (When these extra sounds were extracted from the bass drum, they were called **bombs**.) Bop drummers were not merely timekeepers. The kicks and prods were developed for spontaneously accenting and coloring solo lines of horns and piano. These sounds served at least two important purposes: a) communication between the drummer and the solo improvisers they were accompanying; b) "chatter," the assortment of pops and crashes that provide an energetic layer of activity that increased the excitement of the band sound. (Listen to Roy Haynes accompany Chick Corea on "Steps" on the *Jazz Classics CD.*)

A second advancement was made when **Kenny Clarke and Max Roach took a cue from Jo Jones and altered the manner of timekeeping on the bass drum by playing more gently, "feathering" the bass drum instead of pounding it.** This practice became standard for at least one generation of jazz drummers beyond its originators. However, it is difficult to detect in recordings because not all the drummers' instruments were equally well recorded.

A third advancement occurred in the choice of percussion instrument used for timekeeping. In swing style, drummers reinforced the tempo by striking the bass drum and by playing a timekeeping rhythm on snare drum or high-hat. In the bop era, Kenny Clarke and Max Roach extended ways in which Jo Jones and Dave Tough had already been getting away from these devices. During the late 1930s, Jones had occasionally played ride rhythms on a single cymbal, as in Count Basie's 1937 recording of "One O'Clock Jump," and Dave Tough had already been playing ride rhythms on a large cymbal that was not part of his high-hat apparatus. (Listen to the *Demo CD* for demonstrations, and see page 430 for notations of the rhythms.) Kenny Clarke is generally credited with influencing the widespread adoption of **playing timekeeping rhythms on a cymbal suspended over the drum set.**

Bop differed not only in the instruments on which timekeeping rhythms were played, but also in the way the rhythms were executed. Modern drummers continued the sustained cymbal sound popularized by Jo Jones. However, they did this on neither the opening and closing high-hat nor a single cymbal of the high-hat apparatus. They kept time on a large, thick, heavy cymbal which allowed them to extract a "ping" that would sustain until the next "ping." In other words, Jo Jones had smoothed out the manner for playing timekeeping rhythms, and bop drummers extended this to achieve an even more continuous (legato) sound. Bop drummers also emphasized snapping the high-hat shut sharply on the second and fourth beats of each measure. (For demonstrations, listen to the *Demo CD*.)[24]

◇PIANO

Concepts of rhythm section playing did not advance as rapidly as those of solo playing. In fact, some pre-1947 Gillespie and Parker recordings contain bop-style melodies and improvisations which are accompanied by swing-style pianists, bassists, and drummers. However, bop pianists eventually mastered **comping,** a technique of spontaneous chording that flexibly interacts with the improvised solo lines. This accompaniment technique had been demonstrated by Count Basie as early as the mid-1930s. (For demonstrations, listen to the *Demo CD*). Swing piano styles began to take advantage of the widening use of string bass. Pianists placed less emphasis on the left hand for supplying chorded or single-note bass lines. By the time bop was well underway, pianists had almost entirely abandoned the left hand's bass functions that were so common in stride, boogie woogie, and swing piano; a new left-hand style evolved which was to characterize jazz piano for several decades.

Bud Powell

Bud Powell (1924–1966) is the most imitated of all bop pianists. Powell crafted his approach from Art Tatum's, with other borrowings from the styles of Billy Kyle and Nat Cole. Atop these foundations, Powell incorporated the style and phrases of Charlie Parker and Dizzy Gillespie. The result was one of the first modern jazz piano styles.[25]

Powell de-emphasized the activity of the left hand. In that way he departed from the stride tradition and the "chomp, chomp, chomp, chomp" style of chording used by many swing pianists. This served to lighten the way pianists had begun playing, even more than the streamlining that had already been introduced by Teddy Wilson and Nat Cole. In place of the striding left-hand figures, **Powell's left hand inserted brief, sporadically placed two- and three-note chords that reduced his statement of harmony to the barest minimum.** Sometimes the chords sustained for a few beats. Sometimes there was no sound from the left hand at all. This comping style became the standard means that modern pianists used to suggest the chords underlying their own solo lines. This development was almost as significant within the history of solo piano conception as the emergence of comping had been for rhythm section pianists who were accompanying horn solos. In other words, **the breakthrough that Count Basie had made in lightening the manner in which a pianist supplied chords and support for an improvising soloist was paralleled by the way Powell lightened the manner in which a pianist accompanied his own solo lines.**

In his prime, Bud Powell had the speed and dexterity to create piano solos that almost matched the high-powered inventions of Parker and Gillespie. He mastered the erratically syncopated rhythms of bop and charged through his solos with terrific force. He employed the horn-like lines of Earl Hines and Nat Cole plus the florid ideas of Art Tatum. **Powell was**

the model for hundreds of pianists during the 1940s and 1950s, as James P. Johnson had been during the 1920s and Earl Hines had been after Johnson.

Al Haig

Though Powell lived until 1966, he was only sporadically active throughout most of his career. Of the other excellent players, another favorite of bandleaders was pianist **Al Haig** (1922–1982). Traveling with some of the top groups, including Parker's and Stan Getz's, Haig was a very sought-after pianist and made numerous recordings. His flowing solos and tasteful comping made him a top figure on the bop scene. Haig never seemed at a loss for ideas. His touch was light and clean. In some ways he resembled Teddy Wilson. Haig could play hard, driving pieces or slow, pretty ballads. On occasion he could be quite flowery, but usually he was a very direct, swinging player.

George Shearing

Two bop pianists who found much larger audiences than Haig or Powell were **George Shearing** (b. 1919) and Oscar Peterson. Shearing became known primarily for the group sound he perfected: soft, polished ensemble statements voiced for piano, guitar, vibraharp, bass, and drums, whereas Peterson's reputation was established in a trio format with bass and guitar or drums. Shearing has probably the cleanest, lightest piano sound in bop. His music sounds so refined that it has been called "polite bop." In addition to playing single-note lines and octave-voiced lines, he helped popularize the locked-hands style heard in Milt Buckner's playing of the mid-1940s, though Shearing's voicings differ from Buckner's. Shearing brought a very sophisticated harmonic conception to jazz piano. In his combo, Shearing often arranged his pieces so that each note of the melody was harmonized by his right hand on the piano, and played in unison with the vibraharp while the guitar played it one octave below with Shearing's left hand sounding the same note on the piano. Bass and drums underscored critical figures and kept time. Individual solos followed, framed by ensemble fills and endings, all well rehearsed and precisely performed. Everything swung and was well controlled.[26]

Oscar Peterson

Oscar Peterson (b. 1925) is one of the most widely envied pianists in jazz history. His extraordinary pianistic facility and endurance enable him to take tempos so fast that bassists and drummers can barely keep up with him. Peterson's ballad style is full and orchestral. He sweeps the entire keyboard with a command which amazes other pianists. Peterson has a distinctive style originating from the approaches of Nat Cole, Bud Powell, and Art Tatum. He also has incorporated the funky, gospel-flavored figures popularized by Horace Silver. Peterson has probably generated more swing feeling than any other jazz pianist from the bop era, and his concert and club date recordings are filled with sizzling renditions of pop tunes and jazz standards. He has been one of the most popular pianists in jazz, and his trios, particularly those with bassist Ray Brown, attained the status of a jazz institution. Many pianists count Peterson among their first influences. Peterson has remained a formidable force on the modern jazz scene since the late 1940s. His surging power and vitality never have seemed the least bit diminished.[27]

◇CLARINET

The clarinet has not been an important instrument in modern jazz. One of the most popular instruments during the swing era, it became one of the least popular during the bop era. Only a handful of clarinetists attempted to play bop on the instrument, and none of them gained appreciable recognition.[28]

◇GUITAR

Guitar disappeared as a member of the rhythm section during the bop era, but it returned as a solo instrument. Though bop was first pioneered as a style on saxophone and trumpet, it was soon assimilated by players of other instruments. Guitarists were among the last to learn bop style, and they did not improvise with the originality of Parker and Gillespie. Jimmy Raney and Tal Farlow were the most outstanding bop guitarists, and they were more visible during the late 1940s and early 1950s than during the developmental period of the mid-1940s.[29]

◇TRUMPET

Dizzy Gillespie was the leading trumpeter at the beginning of the bop era. But by the late 1940s, Miles Davis and Fats Navarro were so good at the new style that they also had imitators. When Charlie Parker and Gillespie separated, **Miles Davis** became Parker's new trumpeter. Davis and Parker recorded together from 1945 to 1948, and sporadically after that time.[30] In these recordings, Davis displayed elements of both Gillespie's and Parker's styles, though he used a lighter, softer tone and played less in the high register than Gillespie. (See pages 217–219 for more.) Even as early as 1945, Davis was important as an original and gifted improviser. Evidence of this is found in his combo recordings with Parker and the impact they had on the styles of trumpeters Shorty Rogers, Chet Baker, and Jack Sheldon. (See the next chapter for more about these Davis disciples.)

Fats Navarro (1923–1950) was the trumpeter most often mentioned as a match for Gillespie. Gillespie's wide range, speed, and instrumental proficiency were almost equalled by Navarro. In addition to that, Navarro had a fuller, brassier tone which he used more smoothly than Gillespie. His tone was a bit clearer and more even; Navarro was not as prone to alter its size or color. However, Navarro did not have Gillespie's rhythmic imagination and daring. As a consequence, his work was more even and had fewer surprises. Another significant difference was that Navarro used vibrato more than Gillespie or Davis, and this element became an essential aspect in the style of Navarro's influential disciple Clifford Brown. The Navarro style was spread more directly to far more trumpeters by way of Brown.[31] So the third generation Brown disciples who are prominent today are actually fourth generation Navarro disciples.

◇TROMBONE

Bop style was so instrumentally demanding that it is surprising the style could be played on so difficult an instrument as the slide trombone. But there were several trombonists in the earliest days of bop, and a number of outstanding masters had emerged by the 1950s (see next chapter for details).

J. J. Johnson

J. J. Johnson (1924–2001) is the musician most prominently identified with playing bop on the trombone, though he rarely improvised lines as complicated as Parker's or Gillespie's. Johnson's lines were often simple and tune-like; many of his solos are quite singable. Incidentally, this gift for melody was not restricted to jazz improvisation. Johnson was very active as a composer. His jazz albums from the 1950s and 1960s are filled with originals he penned, and he spent most of the 1970s writing and arranging music for movies and television instead of playing jazz.

J. J. Johnson departed from several traditions of jazz trombone playing by having an unprecedented command over the instrument and by

1) using very little vibrato;
2) producing a smooth, consistent sound rather than the guttural tone quality that many premodern trombonists favored. Johnson attacked each note cleanly and maintained consistent size and quality throughout its duration;
3) avoiding the dependence on wide, drawn-out slurs and rips which typified many early players. When Johnson used inflections at all, they were clipped, and they ornamented his main tones in a well-manicured way;
4) playing with a rhythmic regularity and evenness that lent his music a bounce and a smooth swing feeling, especially evident in his eighth-note lines.

Many earlier players had given their trombones a highly extroverted role in jazz by using a choppy melodic style, rough tone, and extensive pitch inflections. Johnson, on the other hand, brought subtlety to the instrument's role and increased its politeness. Consistent with this stance, Johnson's choice of mute was not the rubber plunger favored by growl-style

Listening Guide for

Charlie Parker's "Ko-Ko"

Recorded November 26, 1945 by Charlie Parker (alto sax), Dizzy Gillespie (cup-muted trumpet and piano), Curley Russell (bass), Max Roach (drums).

This is the most widely acclaimed improvisation of Charlie Parker on record. Almost all of this recording contains spontaneous work. The piece has no theme, and we never hear the theme to "Cherokee," the pop tune from which "Ko-Ko"'s progression of accompaniment chords was borrowed. Most of what we hear is a saxophone solo guided by those chords in their 64-measure A-A-B-A format. The only written parts are the brief figures played together by trumpet and sax at the beginning and end.

The solo style and accompaniment style typify bebop. Parker's improvisation is filled with fast, intricate phrases and abrupt changes of direction. It is well constructed and melodic. Listeners might not perceive those virtues, however, unless they speed up their hearing and attend to each note in Parker's line. Max Roach's accompaniment often contains a commentary on Parker's solo that consist of sudden "kicks" from the snare drum and "bombs" from the bass drum. Timekeeping is provided mostly by walking patterns played by the bassist and ride rhythms made by the drummer striking the ride cymbal with his drum stick. The piano comping is by trumpeter Dizzy Gillespie, not a full-time pianist. Gillespie feeds the chords to Parker and that's about all.

CD Track	Elapsed Time	
33	0' 00"	**Introduction**
		Alto sax and cup-muted trumpet play in unison, accompanied by drummer playing timekeeping rhythms on the snare drum by use of wire brushes.
	0' 06"	improvised trumpet solo in a cup mute
	0' 13"	improvised alto sax solo
	0' 19"	Sax and trumpet play a harmonized figure that ties up the introductory remarks.
	0' 22"	Explicit timekeeping rhythms stop while a figure is played by trumpet with sax playing it an octave lower.
		Charlie Parker Alto Saxophone Solo
34	0' 26"	**First Chorus** (A-A-B-A)
		sax solo improvisation following the chords to "Cherokee"; timekeeping by bassist walking, pianist comping, and drummer striking ride cymbal with drum stick in a steady pattern
	0' 38"	*Second A-Section*
	0' 50"	*Bridge*
	1' 03"	*Last A-Section*
		Notice the kicks and bombs from the drums.

	1' 16"	Second Chorus (A-A-B-A)
	1' 29"	*Second A-Section*
	1' 41"	*Bridge*
		many kicks from snare drum
	1' 54"	*Last A-Section of Second Solo Chorus*
35	2' 07"	**Drum Solo by Max Roach**
		Ending
	2' 29"	muted trumpet figure with alto sax an octave below it, no bass or piano, just drums accompaniment
	2' 36"	muted trumpet improvisation, accompanied only by cymbals and drums
	2' 49"	highly syncopated figure played in harmony by trumpet and sax, with the final two notes underscored by drums
	2' 52"	Piece ends with a very brief note (a "stinger") played by drummer crisply snapping shut his high-hat in unison with a note from the bass.

players. It was a cup mute that made his already dark, subdued sound even more gentle and clean. (For an example of this sound, listen to the *Demo CD* Track 79.) Johnson narrowed the emotional range of the jazz trombone while taking on the quick pace and increased complexity of bop. In other words, he streamlined jazz trombone conception.[32]

◇TENOR SAXOPHONE

Bop tenor saxophonists drew their styles from two primary sources: Lester Young and Charlie Parker, and several secondary sources including Coleman Hawkins, Don Byas, and others. Some preferred to play the phrases of Lester Young almost unmodified, while others merely adopted the phrases of alto saxophonist Charlie Parker and played them on tenor sax. The most original players mixed several sources with their own ideas.[33]

Dexter Gordon

Dexter Gordon (1923–1990) was the first tenor saxophonist to be recognized as a bop player. His was one of the least stereotyped bop tenor styles. Though some of his melodic ideas recalled Lester Young, Gordon's tone was deep, dark, and full, not light or hollow like Young's. He used the entire range of the tenor but had a special love for its low register. Although his style was quite aggressive, his work conveyed great ease. There was a sense of authority and majesty about his work. Perhaps the most melodic of all bop tenors, he was known for his well-paced solo improvisations that are logical, soulful, and muscular. He used a large variety of melodic devices to create his lines. His phrase lengths and rhythms were varied, and he combined bop clichés with his own inventions. Gordon loved to quote from pop tunes and bugle calls. More than any other bop tenor, Gordon was known for developing his solos by making firm statements and following through on them. This tendency increased in his playing during the 1960s and 1970s. In his later years, he offered phrase after phrase of complete musical ideas, well rounded and meaty. Gordon was a favorite player for many tenor saxophonists who were later called *hard bop.* Gordon had a strong recording career from the 1940s into the 1980s, and his playing displayed depth and swing for over four decades. (Listen to his "Bikini" in SCCJ and "Dexter Digs In" on the *Jazz Classics CD* for the *Concise Guide to Jazz.*)[34]

Sonny Stitt

For flowing, powerfully swinging solos, few modern saxophonists could compete with **Sonny Stitt** (1924–1982). His instrumental speed and precision awed other players. His notes were played with a lilt and crispness, the evenness of which was unmatched. Stitt's playing had a consistently logical construction and rarely lacked continuity. During the late 1940s and early 1950s, Stitt was second only to Charlie Parker as the leading bop alto saxophonist, and his recordings with Bud Powell placed him in the highest rank of bop tenor saxophonists.[35] Stitt was not as much of an originator as Dexter Gordon, but he influenced and inspired many modern saxophonists with his own style.[36] **Stitt inspired many players partly because he had enviable command of the saxophone and played with great ease and an unusually high level of precision and consistency. He also systematized a set of patterns which characterized bop approaches to improvisation. These patterns became formula for countless players in the mainstream of modern jazz.** It was much easier to learn these patterns than to learn the less predictable and rhythmically more complex inventions of Parker. In essence, Stitt formalized a mixture of Parker, Lester Young, and his own ideas into a homogeneous method that satisfactorily handled the entire range of tempos and common bop chord progressions.

Stan Getz

Stan Getz (1927–1991) was one of the most distinctive tenor saxophonists to emerge during the 1940s. Unlike most bop tenors, he did not rely heavily on Lester Young's ideas, and he used few of Parker's and Gillespie's pet phrases. He developed an original melodic

Stan Getz, one of the original "Four Brothers," the most distinctive of the "cool style" tenor saxophonists, and a pioneer of bossa nova.

and rhythmic vocabulary instead. His phrasing and accenting were less varied and syncopated than Parker's or Gillespie's. At times, pre-twentieth century classical music seems to have influenced him more than bop.[37] Getz played in a style rhythmically more like Lester Young's than Parker's. Getz did not usually sound as relaxed as Dexter Gordon, but he was just as melodic as Gordon. His improvisations were less like bop melodies than like melodies in classical music. Some were quite pretty. That aspect of his style fit well with his light, fluffy tone and graceful approach to the sax. Some historians believe his roots in swing era style are more evident than his bop roots. Many listeners categorize the Getz style as *cool jazz,* not bop. (See the next chapter for more about cool jazz.)

Getz was one of the few bop musicians to become popular with the general public. One of the prettiest pieces the Woody Herman big band recorded was "Summer Sequence" by Ralph Burns. It was rearranged several times during the late 1940s. One segment often lifted out was "Early Autumn," a feature for Getz.[38] Other Getz hits also took the form of slow, pretty pieces. His 1952 "Moonlight in Vermont" with guitarist Johnny Smith was quite popular. His 1962 "Desafinado" with guitarist Charlie Byrd was a major event in the popularization of *bossa nova,* a cross between Brazilian music and jazz. His 1964 recording of "Girl From Ipanema," with its vocal by Astrud Gilberto, became one of the best-selling records in jazz history.[39] During the 1980s, Getz was playing as well as in the 1940s, with remarkable verve and imagination. Moreover, he was hiring accompanists who reflected styles several generations removed from bop. (Listen to Getz on "No Figs" on the *Jazz Classics CD.*)

◇BIG BANDS

A number of big bands were influenced by bop during the 1940s. Though most played primarily in swing era styles, a few had substantial libraries of bop-style arrangements.[40] The best was led by Dizzy Gillespie, whom we have already discussed. A swing-style clarinetist-saxophonist named **Woody Herman** (1913–1987) led one of the best known bop-influenced big bands, a favorite among musicians. Toward the end of the 1940s, Herman employed a number of outstanding modern soloists and composer-arrangers (see footnote 38). His most historically significant personnel featured four saxophonists who all had roots in the style of Lester Young and were then assimilating bop styles—baritone saxophonist Serge Chaloff and tenor saxophonists Stan Getz, Zoot Sims, and Herbie Steward. (Listen to Chaloff and Getz on Lennie Tristano's "No Figs" on the *Jazz Classics CD.*) Though often considered part of "cool jazz" that was identified somewhat later, they were at an early peak of their creativity during the late 1940s, when bop was in full bloom. This particular Herman band has historically been termed "The Four Brothers Band" because it featured these four saxophonists and they often played a piece written for them by Jimmy Giuffre called "Four Brothers."

Woody Herman

The Four Brothers Band was only one of many high points in Woody Herman's career. In 1939, his band recorded "Woodchopper's Ball," a riff-based, twelve-measure blues that became a big hit. Herman also had a number of other hit records during the swing era, many as a vocalist. Then he not only survived the decline of big bands but spent the rest of his life leading a steady stream of excellent bands that often featured distinctive modern players whose styles were far removed from the swing styles—there were John Coltrane disciples among his saxophonists of the 1970s and 1980s. Throughout their history, his bands steered clear of ambitious and exotic orchestral conceptions. They always retained a looseness that was identified with Herman's band style. Herman liked his music to be swinging and direct. In fact, he edited out any passages in his men's pieces that he considered elaborate or unswinging. Herman deserves credit for his staying power as well as his allegiance to a simple and unpretentious big band style. Known for diversity and adaptability, Herman's "herds" (as they have been affectionately called) were long a mainstay of the jazz scene.

Listening Guide for

"Four Brothers"

Composed and arranged by Jimmy Giuffre;* Recorded December 27, 1947 by the Woody Herman big band (five trumpets, three trombones, four saxophones, rhythm guitar, piano, bass, and drums); available on *Big Band Jazz* (Smithsonian: 2202, 4CD set, 1924–56); and on Woody Herman, *The Thundering Herds,* Columbia: CK 44108, 1945–47).

"Four Brothers" remained one of the most frequently requested numbers in Woody Herman's repertory since its first recording was released. Swing style and bop style are both evident in this arrangement. Lester Young's approach had helped spawn the evolution from swing to bop, and it is echoed here in the saxophone improvisations as well as the composed melody lines. Most of the improvised solos here differ sufficiently from swing style to be regarded as bop. Listeners also perceive this music as bop-flavored because some of the written syncopations were chosen from the favorite rhythms of Dizzy Gillespie and Charlie Parker.

There is no introduction. The performance begins directly on the first A-section of a thirty-two bar A-A-B-A form. The pace is rapid. So if you wish to keep your place by counting beats, be prepared to count "1234 2234 . . . " quickly. To identify the beats, you might synchronize your counting with the notes of the walking bass line or the ride cymbal.

Elapsed Time		
0' 00"	**First Chorus** (32 measures)	
	A	Three tenors and one baritone saxophone (the "four brothers") state the theme in harmony. Their line is almost all eighth notes. Accompaniment comes from rhythm guitar, piano, bass, and drums. Brass figures punctuate the pauses when the saxophonists take a breath.
0' 08"	**A**	Same as first A-section, except for the ending that prefaces the bridge.
0' 17"	**B**	New theme played by same saxophonists. Brass punctuations fill the pauses.
0' 26"	**A**	Same as first A-section.
0' 35"	**Second Chorus**	
	A-A	Improvised solo by tenor saxophonist Zoot Sims. Piano, guitar, bass, and drums accompany lightly. Brass punctuate sparingly.
0' 53"	**B**	Improvised solo by baritone saxophonist Serge Chaloff.
1' 02"	**A**	Chaloff continues.

* The score and parts for this performance are available as item #7009276 from Hal Leonard Publishers, 7777 West Bluemound Road, Milwaukee, WI 53213.

1' 10" **Third Chorus**

A-A Improvised tenor saxophone solo by Herbie Steward.
Sustained saxophone harmonies provide a soft background.

1' 27" **B** Improvised tenor saxophone solo by Stan Getz.
Trombones and saxes accompany with notes that are mostly two beats long.

1' 36" **A** Getz continues his solo.
Final four measures have sustained trombone and baritone saxophone harmonies sounding softly in the background. That background indicates the progression of chords guiding the improvisation. Each chord lasts two beats.

1' 44" **Fourth Chorus**

A Trumpets play a new figure in the upper register. Saxes answer them with a fresh line in unison that extends to the end of the A-section. Brass "kicks" fill in the pauses. Drum fills are scattered throughout.

1' 53" **A** Trumpets play their figure from the preceding A-section an octave higher. Saxes answer with a new unison line that extends to the eighth measure. Trumpets play a "tie-it-up" figure in the final measures.

2' 02" **B** Woody Herman clarinet solo. Notice his full, rich tone and his bent pitch ornaments. His choice of solo notes clearly delineates the movement of chords.
Accompaniment includes the saxes softly playing mid-register chords on the off-beats, providing a syncopated rhythm underneath the clarinet solo. Sharply executed, staccato punctuations come from loud brass and snare drum.

2' 11" **A** Trumpets and trombones play a loud, syncopated phrase in unison with the snare drum. Saxes answer with a phrase of mostly eighth notes that extends almost to the end of the A-section.

2' 20" **Fifth Chorus**

A Saxes and brasses play a simple "shout" figure loudly in harmony. This adds to the excitement because it is the first time the saxes and brasses have played a figure together. Drummer fills in the pauses.

2' 29" **A** Repeat of A.

2' 36" **B** Saxes play a syncopated figure in harmony.

2' 47" **A** Repeat of A.

2' 55" **Ending**

Two Measures

Stop-time solo improvisation by Getz, answered by a "kick" from the brass and rhythm section.

2' 58" *Two-Measures*

Stop-time solo improvisation by Sims, answered by a "kick" from the brass and rhythm section.

3' 00" *Two Measures*

Stop-time solo improvisation by Steward, answered by a "kick" from the brass and rhythm section.

3' 02" *Two Measures*

Stop-time solo improvisation by Choloff, answered by two "kicks" from the brass and rhythm section.

3' 04" *Four Measures*

Stop-time with saxes playing a long, pre-written string of eighth notes in harmony.

3' 10" *Four Measures*

Entire band plays a chord. Brasses continue sustaining it while saxes play a bluesy figure that departs from tempo. Then saxes sustain their final note to rejoin the brasses. Snare drum fills finish the piece.

◇SINGERS

The best known singer to emerge from the bop era was **Sarah Vaughan** (1924–1990). Recording with the top instrumentalists, including Dizzy Gillespie, Tadd Dameron, and Clifford Brown, she achieved a position of respect among musicians that sustained throughout her long career. Like Ella Fitzgerald, she also had a large following outside of the jazz audience. "Nature Boy" and "It's Magic" were hits for her in 1948; then her "Broken Hearted Melody" became a million-seller in 1959.

Vaughan's tone quality was darker and more richly textured than Billie Holiday's and Ella Fitzgerald's. As the years passed, her pitch range deepened into tenor and almost baritone range. (Listen to her "My Funny Valentine" in SCCJ.)

Vaughan's voice control is a source of envy among singers. She showed none of the abruptness or lost tone quality and pitch control that typify most pop singers when they shift registers. She could glide through several octaves seamlessly. Like opera singers, she favored a quick and prominent vibrato, and she milked every note for its last vibration. Also as in opera, she emphasized the maximum drama that could be extracted from each phrase.

Vaughan, a professional pianist with a working knowledge of modern harmony, was an accomplished scat singer. But like other jazz singers, she rarely performed scat improvisations. Instead, she usually chose to sing the original words. The focus of her creativity was in recasting the rhythms and embellishing the pitches. These departures exceeded mere ornamentation, but they did not take the liberties that constitute scat singing.

Straight readings of tunes were not Vaughan's routine practice. She improvised extensively with the timing of words, as though the lyrics were elastic and could be stretched to occur almost anywhere in relation to the passing beats. At the same time she also played with the enunciation of the words and their tone's pitch and timbre. The effect is exceedingly sensual. She drew us in by toying with almost every phrase. The result was that each of her renditions became an intimate experience. Ballad performances account for her greatest achievements. The slow-paced tunes were excellent vehicles for her mastery of nuance. She luxuriated in the depth and richness of her voice and took listeners along in this celebration of sound for its own sake.

Most singers lose tone and energy as they age. Yet Vaughan's tone quality, range, and technique actually increased over the years. Her performances were impeccable during all phases of her career, with her greatest virtuosity displayed during her final twenty years.[41]

Sarah Vaughan, the best known singer associated with bop. Noted for recasting melodies by seamlessly changing their pitches and rhythms, she extracted the maximum drama and sensuality from each phrase.

◇POPULAR APPEAL

With the advent of bop, the status of jazz began to resemble that of classical chamber music more than that of American popular music. It became an art music in the sense that its performance required highly sophisticated skills and it was only appreciated by a relative elite. Jazz had always required special skills because of its demand for so much spontaneous creativity, and, as far as American popular music went, it had long been in the elite. Yet bop crystallized those tendencies, removing jazz even further from the mainstream of American popular music, and turning it into a fine art music. It is important to note, however, that like all jazz styles, bop had fans who could not follow every note and chord but loved it anyway. Most jazz appeals to thousands of fans who like its sound but who lack understanding of its structure and historical significance. Fans proportionally include far more musicians than fans of pop, rock, and country music, but even musician-fans do not technically understand what every improviser does. Musicians have a greater appreciation for the underlying complexities in the music, but that appreciation must be coupled with an attraction to its sound before they will spend time and money to hear it. *Knowledge of musical techniques will increase a listener's appreciation for the music, but no understanding is necessary for a listener to enjoy jazz—modern or any other style.*

Bop was not nearly as popular as swing had been. When Charlie Parker died in 1955, he was an obscure figure compared to Benny Goodman, whose name was a household word. And yet Parker was musically a more significant force in jazz than Goodman. Several swing records sold more than a million copies, yet no bop instrumentals ever came close to that mark of popularity. There are several possible explanations for this. Many not only touch on the differences between swing and bop, they also constitute observations which help explain the historically low popularity of jazz as a whole.

Visual Appeal

One account for why bop was less popular than swing is that bop players presented a more serious appearance, one perhaps less inviting to all but the most devoted jazz fans. **Bop did not have as much visual appeal as swing.** Most swing bands carried singers; many also featured dancers and showy staging. Bop combos, on the other hand, rarely featured singers, dancers, or showy staging. To appreciate modern jazz, people had to listen instead of watch.

Singers

Another factor affecting bop popularity is that, by comparison with swing, **bop had a scarcity of singers.** The bop listener was rarely offered song lyrics or the looks and personality of the singer delivering them. More than ever before, jazz fans now had to follow melodies without words. This made jazz more abstract and less enjoyable. Singers have traditionally been more popular than instrumentalists. Perhaps people like music with lyrics more than they like purely instrumental music because when someone sings a song, it is as though the singer is talking directly to you. This occurs because lyrics are in a language common to both performer and listener. Jazz instrumentals, on the other hand, are in a "language" known to only a tiny portion of the listening public. In addition to offering familiarity in the form of words, vocals offer familiarity in the sound source itself. The human voice produces a sound far more familiar to listeners than that of any instrument. And, because of this greater familiarity, music made with the voice can be expected to achieve greater popularity than music made with instruments.

Complexity

Listeners have historically shown that they like relatively uncomplicated music. Furthermore, they like music to be fairly predictable. They especially like themes that they can sing along with, remember, and hum by themselves. **In comparison to swing, bop is neither uncomplicated nor predictable, and the written melodies in many bop performances are difficult to follow.** A sizable percentage of bop tunes are so complicated that, even if listeners became familiar with them, it is unlikely that they could sing along with them.

It is essential to note that when we say "bop is complicated and unpredictable," we are talking about accompaniment styles as well as solo styles. The point is important when explaining popularity because relatively simple accompaniments backed even the most complicated swing era improvisations. Piano, guitar, bass, and drum parts were relatively simple, and they followed fairly predictable patterns that were quite steady. On the other hand, rhythm section accompaniment in bop style was less regular and therefore less predictable. Then as the 1940s progressed, drummers began to break up their timekeeping patterns and cultivate more and more musical surprises. Therefore, the decreasing popularity that was associated with the development of jazz styles during the 1940s might be explained partly by the increasing complexity of solo improvisations and the decreasing predictability of accompaniment rhythms.

Danceability

Danceability was another problem for bop. **People chose not to dance to bop.** Bop combos sometimes played for dances, but they were invited to do this far less often than they were hired to play strictly for listening. This is curious. People could have danced to bop. It had a steady beat and great rhythmic vitality. But somehow, this was not enough. Here are a few ideas that might account for this situation:

1) Perhaps bop's faster tempos scared away some dancers.
2) Perhaps the beat was not stated simply enough. It had to be made extremely obvious, as it was in most swing band performances.
3) Perhaps arrangements provided insufficient repetition to make dancers feel comfortable.
4) Perhaps dancers wanted singable melodies in their ears before they felt like dancing.

Abstract Sounds

The next four explanations are all part of the idea that **jazz improvisation is too abstract for the average listener** to enjoy.First, most bop melodies and improvisation resembled little or nothing that the average listener had heard before. **The less familiar a piece sounds, the more abstract it is to the listener.** It is harder to follow when it does not resemble a familiar pattern. The harder it is to follow, the more abstract the listener perceives it to be. And, as a rule, the more abstract something is, the less popularity it receives.

Where's the Melody?

Another aspect making bop abstract is **the barely detectable relation between an improvisation and the melody that originally came with that improvisation's chord progression.** This could upset the listener who expected jazz improvisation to consist merely of variation on a familiar theme, in the manner that singers toy with melodies or popular instrumentalists "interpret" current songs. This problem could be especially acute to the listener who asks "Where is the melody?" because he has not learned that in jazz the improvisation itself is the melody. Nonthematic improvisation had been done in jazz at least as early as the 1920s by Louis Armstrong and Sidney Bechet. But it was more abundant and drastic in bop.

Relationship Between Improvised Lines and Chord Changes

Jazz scholar Harvey Pekar has suggested a third aspect of bop that makes it abstract. He observes that **it is extremely difficult for the inexperienced listener to follow the relationship between improvised lines and chord changes in a typical bop performance.** His argument implies that listeners expect to hear particular relationships between notes in a solo line and the notes in the accompanying chord, and that listeners will notice the presence or absence of these expected relationships. As support for this argument, we find that Charlie Parker and Dizzy Gillespie are especially known for stretching the conventional ties between solo notes and accompanying notes and that Parker and Gillespie were less popular than their predecessors. In other words, the relationship between melody notes and accompaniment notes sounded unfamiliar to those who heard bop, and that lack of familiarity decreased the amount of popularity that bop had.

Packaging

A fourth element of abstractness that might account for bop's low popularity is the **relative absence of formal packaging for improvisation and the greater length and amount of solo improvisations.** To begin appreciating this, first note that the most common size for jazz groups during the swing era was the ten- to sixteen-piece big band, but the most common size for bop was the four- to six-piece combo. Also note that big bands, no matter the era, tend to use more elaborate arrangements than combos. Arrangement style that typified swing era, big band performances used simple riffs to frame improvisations and accompany them. They also interrupted long improvisations, providing reference points especially effective for listeners who might otherwise be overwhelmed by the newness and unpredictability offered by jazz improvisation. In the swing format, then, improvisations were made somewhat comprehensible because the listener was required to cope only briefly with the unexpected. The riffs that accompanied the improvisations were simple and familiar, and there was a return to familiar material after each improvisation. In the bop format, on the other hand, musicians usually preset only the introduction, the theme, and the ending. Sandwiched between the theme and the ending was uninterrupted solo after solo. In other words, improvisation was less and arrangement was more in swing-era big bands than in bop combos. When improvisation must stand by itself because accompaniment is minimal, it is more difficult to grasp than when it is frequently interrupted and framed by familiar material. Bop was accordingly less popular than swing.

Another packaging asset available in swing format is that big bands use much of the same music in live performances as in broadcasts and recordings. This is because using written arrangements allows reproducibility that a dependence upon improvisation does not allow. Remember that both the accompaniments and the solos are improvised fresh in every bop combo performance, but rehearsed arrangements provide most of the accompaniment in swing big band performances. This is relevant to popularity because the listener who had been exposed to the music ahead of time would find greater familiarity (hence, less abstractness) in a swing performance than in a bop performance of the same tune by the same musicians. The smaller amount of repetition in the bop performance would therefore present greater listening difficulty and, hence, less popularity for bop than for swing.

There is at least one problem with these explanations, however. They require that we assume jazz fans actually follow every note in the improvisations. Yet a sizable portion of swing fans probably follow only the prewritten parts, and a sizable portion of bop fans probably grasp only the overall feeling of the music.

Commercially Successful Bop

Further support for these arguments comes when we look at those few bop combos that did achieve commercial success: the George Shearing Quintet, the Modern Jazz Quartet, and the Charlie Ventura Boptet. All three groups used formats that frequently interspersed tightly arranged, well-rehearsed ensemble statements among the improvisations. All offered a greater proportion of simpler, more singable melodies than most other bop combos used. All played many well-known songs. The Boptet had the additional asset of singers Jackie Cain and Roy Kral, and the Modern Jazz Quartet generally produced improvisations that were simpler and easier to follow than in other bop combos. Two points are being made here. First, despite the generally low popularity of bop, a few groups and a few records did become commercial successes. Second, the music within those successes has some of the same features we have outlined for explaining the popularity of swing. In addition, note that Charlie Parker's best-selling records were those he made of well-known songs with written orchestral accompaniments, and the greatest hits for Stan Getz have been recordings of singable themes such as "Moonlight in Vermont," "Desafinado," and "Girl From Ipanema." As a final consideration, combine these two observations: the Getz recording of "Girl From Ipanema" contains a vocal, and it represents the largest selling record in the Getz career.

After considering the preceding arguments, you can see that differences in **the amount of popularity enjoyed by different styles of music can be partly explained by differences in performance practices and differences between the ways each style treats basic elements of music.** In comparing the relative popularity of bop with swing, these performance practices are relevant: appearance, amount of improvisation, repetition, the amount of packaging for improvisation, and presence of words in the music. The musical elements of melody, harmony, and rhythm are also treated differently in the two styles. Bop offered higher, faster, more complex playing. Bop featured more variety of rhythms in

The Modern Jazz Quartet: pianist John Lewis, vibraharpist Milt Jackson, bassist Percy Heath, and drummer Kenny Clarke. Formed from members of Dizzy Gillespie's big band, this group became associated with "cool jazz" because it played soft jazz that was polished and restrained.

Photo by Bob Parent, courtesy of Don Parent

melody lines and in accompaniments. Bop used richer chords, more chord changes, and a more elaborate relationship between the notes of the melody and the notes of the accompanying chords. Throughout jazz history, the differences between jazz and popular music have echoed the same differences that are noted here between bop and swing. Therefore, because jazz has traditionally been less popular than most other forms of American music, its low popularity is probably due, in part, to these same differences in performance practice and use of musical elements.

Modern jazz continued the jazz tradition of influencing American popular music and symphonic music, but it seemed to carve its own sturdy path for musicians and a small audience of nonmusicians. Bop became parent of a series of other modern styles which were also less popular than swing. Jazz did not regain its popularity until the 1970s when a jazz-rock fusion brought millions of new fans.

CHAPTER SUMMARY

1) Bop differed from swing by using smaller bands, richer chords, more chord changes, faster playing with more surprises and drier, more biting tone qualities.
2) The originators of bop included alto saxophonist Charlie Parker, trumpeter Dizzy Gillespie, and pianist Thelonious Monk.
3) Parker wrote numerous tunes based on popular songs and twelve-bar blues chord progressions that became standard repertory for generations of jazz musicians.
4) Gillespie devised a very unorthodox trumpet style and led a string of combos and big bands.
5) Monk played piano in a very spare manner filled with unusual rhythms and harmonies and wrote tunes rendered difficult by their odd accents and chord progressions.

6) The ideas of Tatum, Parker, and Gillespie surfaced in the piano style of Bud Powell, who was widely imitated and who significantly altered jazz piano style by reducing the activity of the left hand.
7) Tenor saxophonist Dexter Gordon extended the deep, dark-toned, swing era style and mixed it with bop approaches and his own unique lyricism.
8) Tenor saxophonist Stan Getz blended Lester Young, bop, and classical music to create an original style and became the most popular player on his instrument.
9) Pianists John Lewis and Tadd Dameron were important bop composers, and Lewis continued writing for the Modern Jazz Quartet long after the bop era.
10) Modern Jazz Quartet vibraharpist Milt Jackson devised a warm, swinging style by way of a slow tremolo rate, intelligently constructed bop lines, relaxed delivery, and funky melodic figures.
11) Bop drummers differed from swing drummers by increasing the frequency and spontaneity of kicks and prods, feathering the bass drum instead of pounding it, playing timekeeping rhythms on a suspended cymbal, and snapping the high-hat shut sharply on the second and fourth beats.
12) Bop styles and their offshoots were less popular than swing styles because they used fewer popular tunes, they had fewer singers, less predictability, and more complicated solos and accompaniments.

NOTES

1. "Indiana," "What Is This Thing Called Love," "Whispering," and "How High the Moon" respectively provided chord progressions for the bop compositions "Donna Lee," "Hot House," "Groovin' High," and "Ornithology." The chord progression of George Gershwin's "I Got Rhythm" was used so much that musicians abbreviated "I Got Rhythm chord changes" to "I Got Rhythm changes," which in turn was abbreviated to "Rhythm changes" or just "Rhythm." Pieces on SCCJ based on Rhythm changes include "Shaw Nuff," "Crazeology" (also known as "Little Benny" or "Bud's Bubble"), and the improvisations of Don Byas and Slam Stewart on "I Got Rhythm" and "Cottontail" on the *Jazz Classics CD* are also based on Rhythm changes. This chord progression is demonstrated on the *Demo CD* Track 33.

2. Listen to Charlie Parker's solo improvisations on "Ko-Ko" on *Jazz Classics CD* for *Concise Guide to Jazz* or SCCJ. The introduction alternates between brief bits of composed material and improvised trumpet and sax breaks, accompanied by timekeeping from brushes on snare drum. The piece has no main theme. Most of the performance is improvisation, guided by repetitions of the accompaniment harmonies to "Cherokee," an A-A-B-A form that is 64 measures long. The ending is constructed of a brief trumpet improvisation and a "tie-it-up" figure played in unison by trumpet and sax.

3. Sample Parker's extraordinary speed and inventiveness on "Ko-Ko" on *Jazz Classics CD* for *Concise Guide to Jazz*, SCCJ, or *Bebop* (New World: 271, LP anthology, 1945–56), or on "Bird Gets the Worm" on *The Genius of Charlie Parker* (Savoy/Devon: SV-0104, 1945–48).

4. Listen to "Embraceable You" on SCCJ or on *Bebop* (New World: 271, LP). This is based on a thirty-two bar A-B-A-C song by George Gershwin, and it became one of Parker's most acclaimed improvisations. Notice that Parker engages in much quadruple-timing while the rhythm section remains in the accompaniment style of a ballad. The improvisation is rich with complex and unpredictable ideas. Compare Parker's dense style with the Coleman Hawkins solo on "Body and Soul" (on the *Jazz Classics CD* for *Concise Guide to Jazz* and SCCJ). Parker and Hawkins were both interested in playing densely packed solos. They also sequenced the notes to indicate every chord that occurred as well as other chords that might fit the progression, even though their accompanists did not necessarily sound all those chords. Both men were doing more than merely double-timing. They were quadruple-timing. It is also notable that even though Parker has the Kansas City tone color and rhythmic swing feeling of Lester Young, he leans more toward Hawkins's preference for complex improvisation than Young's preference for singable melody.

5. The best sources for studying Parker's musical thinking are Thomas Owens, *Charlie Parker: Techniques of Improvisation* (University Microfilms, 1974; see page 413 to order by phone) and Carl Woideck, *Charlie Parker: His Music and Life* (University of Michigan Press, 1996). Eight Parker solos are transcribed and analyzed in Stuart Isacoff, *Solos for Jazz Alto Saxophone* (Carl Fischer, 1985; available by mail from Carl Fischer Music Store, 54 Cooper Square, NY, NY 10003). Transcriptions and analyses of Parker's solos on Gillespie's "Shaw Nuff" (1945) and on Parker's own "Now's the Time" (1953) are in Scott Reeves, *Creative Jazz Improvisation, 2nd ed.* (Prentice-Hall, 1995; available from Jamey Aebersold, P.O. Box 1244, New Albany, IN 47150; phone 800-456-1388). Parker's solo on "Ko-Ko" is transcribed in John Mehegan, *Jazz Improvisation, Vol. 2* (Watson-Guptill/ Amsco,1962). More transcriptions are in Stan Ayeroff, *Charlie Parker* (Amsco, 1979; available from Aebersold) and Jamey Aebersold and Ken Slone, *Charlie Parker Omnibook* (Atlantic Music, 1978; available from Aebersold).

6. To detect the influence of Lester Young, listen to Parker's 1940 recordings with Jay McShann that were collected on *Early Bird* (Stash: ST-CD- 542, 1940–44). To hear Parker's similarity to Young and to Hawkins, listen to Parker's 1943 recordings, made on tenor sax, collected on *The Complete Birth of the Bebop* (Stash: ST-CD- 535, 1940–46). To hear the similarity to blues singers and early jazz hornmen, listen to "Parker's Mood" on SCCJ or on *Bebop* (New World: 271, LP). For more about Parker, see Robert Reisner, *Bird: The Legend of Charlie Parker* (Citadel, 1962; DaCapo, 1975).

7. A masterpiece of this kind was his 1945 "I Can't Get Started" solo found on SCCJ; transcribed and analyzed in Stuart Isacoff, *Solos for Jazz Trumpet* (Carl Fischer, 1985; available by mail from Carl Fischer Music Store, 54 Cooper Square, NY, NY 10003). *The Complete RCA Victor Recordings* (RCA Bluebird: 07863-66528-2, 2CD set, 1937–49) contains "Night in Tunisia," "Manteca," "Woody 'n' You," "Cubano Be," "Cubano Bop," plus Gillespie's solos with bands of the late 1930s. For more about Gillespie, see the autobiography, Dizzy Gillespie, *To Be Or Not To Bop* (Doubleday, 1979; DaCapo, 1985).

8. Howard McGhee, Red Rodney, Benny Harris, Conte Candoli, Kenny Dorham, Fats Navarro, Miles Davis, Thad Jones, and Clark Terry are among the many trumpeters affected by Gillespie's style of the 1940s. His influence did not end in the 1940s. Chuck Mangione's earliest recorded trumpet improvisations in the 1960s contained Gillespie phrases. Trumpeter Jon Faddis appeared during the 1970s, often quoting Gillespie recordings of the 1940s, note for note. Arturo Sandoval also appeared in the 1970s, showing a mastery of the Gillespie melodic vocabulary.

9. Gillespie wrote "Birks Works," "Emanon," "Groovin' High," "Blue 'n' Boogie," "Salt Peanuts," " Woody 'n' You," "Con Alma," "A Night in Tunisia," and other tunes, as well as original compositions and arrangements for his own big bands. See next footnote.

10. These are on Dizzy Gillespie, *The Complete RCA Victor Recordings* (RCA Bluebird: 07863-66528, 2CD set, 1937–49).

11. Listen to Gillespie's big band play his "Things to Come" on *Jazz Classics CD* for *Concise Guide to Jazz; Big Band Jazz* (Smithsonian: 2202); *Bebop* (New World: 271, LP); or Dizzy Gillespie, *Shaw Nuff* (Musicraft: 70053, 1945–46).

12. "Off Minor" and "Straight, No Chaser" are on *Genius of Modern Music, Vols. 1 and 2* (Blue Note: 81510/81511); *The Best of Thelonious Monk: The Blue Note Years* (Blue Note: 95636). Monk rerecorded these tunes for other companies, but the Blue Note renditions are his first versions. Monk's "Misterioso" (found on SCCJ) is another masterpiece of simplicity. A continuous sequence of notes, it has no rests, no sustained tones, just legato eighth notes. These notes are not arranged in the bop manner, either. They are smooth alternations of low and high notes. Pairs of notes, in the interval of a sixth, move up and down a scale, never stopping to rest. All are set atop a twelve-bar blues accompaniment. A large portion of Monk's compositions are in thirty-two-bar A-A-B-A form—"Epistrophy" and "'Round Midnight," for example. "'Round Midnight," is his most frequently played ballad. Although Monk's prettiest melody, it is not conventional. Some measures contain four different chords. The tune does not even start on the first beat of the chord progression. It begins on the second beat and fits four notes into the space of that single beat. A Monk

solo version of "'Round Midnight" is on *Jazz Piano* (Smithsonian: 7002[039]). For biographies, see Leslie Gourse, *Straight, No Chaser: The Life and Genius of Thelonious Monk* (Schirmer, 1997), and Thomas Fitterling, *Thelonious Monk, His Life and Music* (Berkeley Hills, 1977).

13. Listen to Monk play "Criss Cross," "Evidence," and "I Should Care" on SCCJ. For greater understanding of similarities and differences among pianists discussed here, compare renditions of "Tea for Two" on Art Tatum, *I Got Rhythm, Vol. 3* (Decca Jazz/GRP: GRD-630, 1935–44); Bud Powell, *The Genius of Bud Powell* (Verve: 827901-2, 1950–51); and Thelonious Monk, *Criss Cross* (Columbia: CK 48823, 1963). Monk's innovative rhythmic conceptions are summarized in the way he recast the melody. For transcriptions of Monk solos, see Stuart Isacoff, *Thelonious Monk* (Consolidated Music, 1978; available from Jamey Aebersold).
14. Listen to Dameron's 1948 "Lady Bird" on SCCJ. Miles Davis borrowed its chord progression for his own "Half Nelson." Saxophonist John Coltrane and Dameron recorded an entire album of Dameron tunes in 1956, including the ballads "On a Misty Night" and "Soultrane" (Tadd Dameron, *Mating Call,* Fantasy: OJCCD-212-2 [Prestige 7070], 1956). In the 1980s an all-star New York group called Dameronia formed to perform and record Dameron's compositions and arrangements.
15. *The Complete Blue Note and Capitol Recordings of Fats Navarro and Tadd Dameron* (Blue Note: 33373, 2CD set, 1947–49). The influence of Dameron's arranging concepts turned up in later work by Benny Colson, Gigi Gryce, and Sun Ra.
16. For Third Stream music, listen to *Mirage* (New World: 216, LP), *The Birth of the Third Stream* (Columbia CK 64929), and see Gunther Schuller, *Musings* (Oxford, 1986), 114–124.
17. The Third Stream concept was not new with Lewis or Schuller nor was it unique to their era. The idea of combining jazz and classical music has influenced bandleaders and composers in every era of jazz: Paul Whiteman in the 1920s; Artie Shaw in the 1930s; Duke Ellington and John Lewis, beginning in the 1940s; and Charles Mingus, Gunther Schuller, Stan Kenton, John Lewis, George Russell, Jimmy Giuffre, Miles Davis, and Gil Evans beginning in the 1950s. The Don Ellis big bands of the 1960s and 1970s also explored Third Stream techniques.
18. *The Artistry of the Modern Jazz Quartet* (Prestige: 60-016-2, 1952–56); *Django* (Fantasy: OJCCD-057-2, 1953–54).
19. Jackson is a fluid, clear-thinking improviser with a very fertile imagination. His refinement of bop phrasing is a significant contribution which should not be viewed solely in light of jazz vibraharp literature. Listen to his work on "Django," on SCCJ, and study its transcription and analysis in Scott Reeves, *Creative Jazz Improvisation, 2nd ed.* (Prentice-Hall, 1995). Also listen to Jackson's solos on Thelonious Monk's "Evidence" and "Criss Cross" on SCCJ.
20. Present on more bop recordings than any other bassist was Curly Russell (1917–1986). He was not known as a soloist but was widely regarded as an accompanist. Tommy Potter (1918–1988) and Al McKibbon (b. 1919) also appeared often in the accompanist role with many important bop groups.
21. Listen to Pettiford in a solo role with Coleman Hawkins on his 1943 "The Man I Love" (on SCCJ) and in an accompanying role on Duke Ellington's 1946 "Transblucency" (on the *Jazz Classics CD*). Pettiford's solos and compositions have considerable exposure on Lucky Thompson, *Tricotism* (Impulse!/GRP: GRD-135 [ABC 111], 1956).
22. Parker and Gillespie melodic style appears in Mingus solos on "Mingus Fingers" (1947) with Lionel Hampton's band on *Jazz in Revolution* (New World: 284, LP), or *Hamp! The Legendary Decca Recordings of Lionel Hampton* (Decca Jazz/ GRP: GRD2-652). See chapter 14 for more about Mingus.
23. Brown first gained wide recognition when the Gillespie band featured him on "Two-Bass Hit" (1947), found on Dizzy Gillespie, *The Complete RCA Victor Recordings* (RCA Bluebird: 07863-66528-2, 2CD set, 1937–49). Brown solos on pianist Dodo Marmarosa's "Mellow Mood" (1946) on *Jazz Piano* (Smithsonian: 7002 [039]) and *Jazz in Revolution* (New World: 284, LP, 1940–49); and on "Soon" on Oscar Peterson, *The Trio* (Verve: 314 539 063-2, 1961).
24. Most of this discussion will mean nothing without hearing the sounds it describes. So have a drummer demonstrate all these practices in person for you, and listen to recordings of the drummers mentioned. All can be heard on SCCJ: Jo Jones on Count Basie's "Doggin' Around," "Taxi War Dance," and "Lester Leaps In," and Benny Goodman's "I've Found a New Baby" and "Breakfast Feud"; Sid Catlett on Dizzy Gillespie's "Shaw Nuff"; Kenny Clarke on Miles Davis's "Boplicity" and Tadd Dameron's "Lady Bird"; Max Roach on Parker's "Klactoveesedstene" and "Ko-Ko" and on Sonny Rollins's "Blue Seven" and "Pent-Up House."
25. Powell also wrote: "Tempus Fugit," "Parisian Thoroughfare," "Celia," "Dance of the Infidels," and "Hallucinations" (also known as "Budo"). Listen to Powell's "Somebody Loves Me" (1947) on SCCJ; "Night in Tunisia" (1951) on SCCJ-R; "Tempus Fugit" (1949), "Un Poco Loco" (1951), and "Polkadots and Moonbeams" (1953) on *Jazz Piano* (Smithsonian); and get *The Complete Bud Powell on Verve* (Verve: 314 521 669-2, 5CD set) and *The Complete Blue Note and Roost Recordings* (Blue Note: 30083, 4CD set). See a transcription and analysis of "Un Poco Loco" from the Blue Note set in John Rodby, *Solos for Jazz Piano* (Carl Fischer, 1989). More transcriptions are in Clifford Jay Safane, *Bud Powell* (Consolidated Music, 1978); "Nice Work If You Can Get It" from *The Bud Powell Trio Plays* (Roulette: 93902, 1947–53) in John Mehegan, *Jazz Improvisation, Vol. 2* (Watson-Guptill/Amsco, 1962); and an analysis of Powell's concepts in Mehegan, *Jazz Improvisation, Vol. 3* (Watson-Guptill/Amsco, 1964). For biography, see Francis Paudras, *Dance of the Infidels* (DaCapo, 1998).
26. An excellent sampler is *George Shearing; Jazz Masters 57* (Verve: 314 529 900-2, 1949–54). Note that Shearing also achieved a successful integration of Latin American elements and bop. Armando Peraza played auxiliary percussion with him from 1954 until 1964. For an interview with Shearing, see Len Lyons, *The Great Jazz Pianists* (Quill, 1983), 93–101. For technical discussion of Shearing's techniques, see John Mehegan, *Jazz Improvisation, Vol. 3* (Watson-Guptill, 1964).
27. A sample of Peterson's hottest playing is on *At the Concertgebouw* (Verve: 314 521 649-2, 1958). Also listen to Oscar Peterson's 1952 studio rendition of "Night and Day" on *Jazz Piano* (Smithsonian: 7002 [039]). See John Mehegan's transcription of Peterson's solo on "I've Got the World on a String" in *Jazz Improvisation, Vol. 2* (Watson-Guptill, 1962) and "Joy Spring" in *Jazz Improvisation, Vol. 4* (Watson-Guptill, 1965). See transcription and analysis of Peterson's solo on "All the Things You Are" from *Tenderly* (Verve: 2046 [Clef 696], LP, 1950) in John Rodby, *Jazz Solos for Piano* (Carl Fischer, 1989). For more about Peterson, see Gene Lees, *Oscar Peterson: The Will To Swing* (Prima, 1991).
28. Tony Scott, Stan Hasselgard, and Buddy DeFranco played bop on the clarinet, but their efforts did not catch on. Listen to DeFranco on "No Figs" on the *Jazz Classics CD*.

29. Other bop guitarists became known during the 1950s and 1960s; among them were Kenny Burrell, Wes Montgomery, Grant Green, and Pat Martino. Tal Farlow and Pat Martino remained excellent performers in the 1990s.

30. Counting alternate takes and recordings for both Savoy and Dial record companies, Davis recorded more than one hundred selections with Parker. For transcriptions and analyses of Davis's solos from this period on "Klactoveesedstene" and "Bird of Paradise," see Stuart Isacoff, *Solos for Jazz Trumpet* (Carl Fischer, 1985; order from Carl Fischer Music Store, 54 Cooper Square, NY, NY 10003).

31. Listen to Navarro on Tadd Dameron's 1948 recording of "Lady Bird" on SCCJ. For a wider sampling, get *The Complete Blue Note and Capitol Recordings of Fats Navarro and Tadd Dameron* (Blue Note: 33373, 2CD set, 1947–49), Fats Navarro, *Nostalgia* (Savoy/Denon: SV-0123 [12001], 194–647), and *Fats Navarro Memorial* (Savoy/Denon: SV-0181 [12001], 1946–47). See page 413 for information on how to get Miles Davis, Fats Navarro, and Clifford Brown solo transcriptions and analyses by David Baker.

32. Listen to *The Eminent J. J. Johnson, Vols. 1 & 2* (Blue Note: 81505/81506, 1953–55), and *Trombone Master* (Columbia: CK 44443, 1958–60). For more about Johnson, see David Baker, *J.J. Johnson: Trombone* (Shattinger, 1979); and Ira Gitler, *Jazz Masters of the Forties* (Macmillan, 1966; DaCapo, 1982), 137–48. For transcriptions of Johnson's own favorite improvisations, see John Leisenring and Hunt Butler, *J.J. Johnson Solos: 13 Personal Favorites* (Jamey Aebersold, 1989).

33. It is possible to classify bop tenor saxophonists in several ways, including the amounts of Lester Young's and Charlie Parker's styles that are detectable. The easiest approach lies in the dimension of tone. Bop tenor saxophonists preferred either light-weight, light-colored tones or heavy-weight, dark-colored tones. Though there are gradations within these categories, it might be helpful to first describe players in terms of the two extremes, and then form your own descriptions to refine your perceptions. The light-toned players include Stan Getz, Herbie Steward, Allen Eager, Brew Moore, and several players of a somewhat later style (West Coast): Buddy Collette, Bill Perkins, Bob Cooper, Richie Kamuca, and others. The heavy-toned players include Dexter Gordon, Gene Ammons, Lucky Thompson, Wardell Gray, Sonny Stitt, and others.

34. Listen to "Dexter Digs In" on the *Classics CD* for *Concise Guide to Jazz* and Dexter Gordon, *Dexter Rides Again* (Savoy/Denon: SV-0120, 1945–47). For bio, see Stan Britt, *Dexter Gordon: A Musical Biography* (DaCapo, 1989); and Ira Gitler, *Jazz Masters of the Forties* (Macmillan, 1966; DaCapo, 1982).

35. Though he made more than one hundred albums under his own name, Stitt recorded some of his best solos with others, including Dizzy Gillespie ("The Eternal Triangle" on *Sonny Side Up*, Verve: 314 521 426-2 (MGV 8262), 1957), Bud Powell ("All God's Chillun" on *Sonny Stitt/Bud Powell/J.J. Johnson*, Fantasy: OJCCD-009-2 [Prestige 7024], 1949–50), and Gene Ammons ("Blues Up and Down" on Gene Ammons and Sonny Stitt, *Boss Tenors* (Verve: 837 440-2 (MGV 8426), 1961). For transcriptions of his solos on the albums: *Stittsville, Sonny Side Up,* and *Soul Electricity*, see Gary Keller, *Sonny Stitt: Improvised Tenor Saxophone Solos* (Studio PR, 1985; available from Aebersold).

36. Frank Foster, George Coleman, Joe Henderson, and John Coltrane are among the saxophonists who have cited Stitt as an influence. Stitt provided the main model for the mid-1950s style of Coltrane; see chapter 13 for more about this.

37. Briefly in 1946, Getz performed in a bop style like Dexter Gordon, as on Getz's "Opus de Bop," "And the Angels Swing," "Running Water," and "Don't Worry About Me" on *Opus de Bop* (Savoy/Denon: SV-0118 [12114], 1946–47). Before and after that, he favored an original style. Listen to Getz in Lennie Tristano's "No Figs" on the *Jazz Classics CD.*

38. Woody Herman, *Keeper of the Flame* (Capitol: 98453, 1948–50); *Thundering Herds* (Columbia: 44108, 1945–47). See also William D. Clancy, *Woody Herman: Chronicle of the Herds* (Schirmer,1994); Woody Herman, *Woodchopper's Ball* (Dutton, 1990); Gene Lees, *Leader of the Band* (Oxford, 1995).

39. *Jazz Samba* (Verve: 314 521 413-2, 1962); *Getz/Gilberto* (Verve: 314 521 414-2, 1964). Do not let the emphasis on Getz's slow, pretty pieces lead you to overlook his exciting medium- and up-tempo style: *Stan Getz at Storyville* (Roulette: 94507, 1951); *Stan Getz Quartets* (Prestige: OJCCD–121-2, 1949–50); and *Stan Getz and J.J. Johnson at the Opera House* (Verve: 831 272-2, 1957).

40. For bop-influenced big bands, listen to *The Bebop Revolution* (RCA Bluebird: 2177); *Jazz in Revolution* (New World: 284, LP); *Big Band Jazz* (Smithsonian: 2202); *Big Band Renaissance* (Smithsonian: 108); *Mirage* (New World: 216, LP); also chapter 10, footnotes 10–12, and chapter 11, footnotes 41–47.

41. *Sarah Vaughan* (Emarcy: 814 641-2, [MG 36004], 1954); *Sarah Vaughan with Michel Legrand* (Mainstream 703 [361], 1972). For biography, see Leslie Gourse, *Sassy: The Life of Sarah Vaughan* (Macmillan, 1993; DaCapo, 1994).

Chapter Ten

Gerry Mulligan, Larry Bunker, Chet Baker, Lee Konitz   Photo courtesy of William Clayton

Cool Jazz

The term "cool jazz" refers to modern jazz that tends to be softer and easier to follow than the bop of Charlie Parker and Dizzy Gillespie. "Cool jazz" avoids roughness and brassiness. Many of the musicians whose work has been called "cool" were influenced by Lester Young and Count Basie. For instance, Stan Getz and Miles Davis are often called "cool," and both were inspired by Young. The Modern Jazz Quartet's subtle, chamber music-like qualities have also been called "cool." Incidentally, this term has not been widely embraced by jazz musicians. In fact, some players have been annoyed to hear it used to describe their music. It suggested that their playing conveyed a lack of passion. Despite this, "cool jazz" is a widely used designation. We borrow it to help organize this book by providing a place to describe the music of several significant composers and instrumentalists.

Journalists and record companies used the term "cool jazz" extensively during the 1950s. They also gave a disproportionate amount of attention to the output of white musicians based in California at that time. Therefore, many people have the impression that all West Coast jazz of the 1950s is cool jazz or vice versa. In reality, however, the label has not been limited to the work of musicians who belong to any particular race or geographic region, and the California jazz scene of the 1950s had a number of different styles in addition to cool jazz.

Listening Guide for

"No Figs"

Composed and arranged by Lennie Tristano; Recorded January 10, 1950 by Buddy DeFranco (clarinet), Kai Winding (trombone), Lee Konitz (alto sax), Stan Getz (tenor sax), Serge Chaloff (baritone sax), Billy Bauer (guitar), Lennie Tristano (piano), Eddie Safranski (bass), Max Roach (drums); available on the *Jazz Classics CD;* also available on *The Bebop Era* (Columbia: CK 40972, 1942–51).

With the exception of Tristano, Konitz, and Bauer, these musicians did not usually work together. This recording combined performers who had received the highest number of votes in various categories ("best pianist," "best alto saxophonist," etc.) of a popularity poll run in 1949 by the jazz magazine *Metronome.*

"No Figs" is included as an example of cool jazz, particularly the unique modern styles of composer-pianist Lennie Tristano and his best known student, Lee Konitz. A number of different styles have been called "cool," but Tristano's was one of the first. His was also among the few modern styles not closely tied to bop. This selection was chosen because it is one of the only recordings that brings together Tristano, Konitz, and the eminent tenor saxophonist Stan Getz. We heard Getz in Woody Herman's "Four Brothers," a performance that combined the influence of Lester Young and bop. Getz has been tagged variously as "cool" or "bop," though his style is so unique that it deserves a category of its own. Coincidentally, "No Figs" also features baritone saxophonist Serge Chaloff, another one of the original "four brothers." (Like Chaloff, the remaining soloists here, clarinetist Buddy DeFranco and trombonist Kai Winding, are not ordinarily classified as "cool." Most jazz historians classify them as bop.)

The performance begins with clarinet, alto sax, tenor sax, baritone sax, and guitar, accompanied by piano comping, walking bass, and drums. Guitar is used here as a melody instrument instead of providing chordal accompaniment. The drummer is using brushes to play timekeeping rhythms on the snare drum while snapping shut his high-hat sharply on the second and fourth beats of each measure. His close coordination with walking bass provides a steady and buoyant foundation.

"No Figs" is based on the chord progression of "Indiana," with a form that can be described roughly as thirty-two bar A-B-A-C. (We could describe it as A-B-A-B′ because the second "B" repeats portions of the first "B," but "C" is used here for the sake of simplicity.) This performance is comprised of four choruses. No soloist plays for an entire chorus, and Konitz solos only during the last eight measures of the first chorus. The opening theme statement runs through the first three eight-bar sections of "Indiana"'s form, designated here as A, B, and A. Then the improvisation by Konitz occupies the fourth section, C. Getz and Winding split a chorus. Then DeFranco and Chaloff split another. Tristano solos for the first half of the fourth chorus, and then the theme and ending occupy the second half.

CD Track	Elapsed Time	
46	0'00"	**Theme** (A-B-A of the "Indiana" chord progression) A butterfly-like effect is created by complicated lines of triplets and sixteenth notes played in various harmonies and unisons by clarinet, alto sax, tenor sax, baritone sax, guitar, and piano. Notice how instrument sounds appear, disappear, and reappear in different combinations, some in harmony, some in unison. After the initial flurry of notes, a simpler line emerges with longer notes, less harmony, more unisons and octaves. Then the butterfly-like effect returns, followed again by the simpler line.
47	0'29"	**Lee Konitz Alto Sax Improvisation** (the 8-measure C-section) Konitz confines himself to the upper register of his instrument. Notice his soft tone and legato phrasing. He begins his solo in a very smooth manner, using mostly eighth notes. Then he bases his phrases on triplets and ends his solo with a crisp burst of sixteenth notes. To appreciate how much jazz alto saxophone timbres vary, contrast the Konitz sound here with the Johnny Hodges sound on "Prelude to a Kiss."
48	0'43"	**Stan Getz Tenor Sax Improvisation** (16 measures, A–B) *Getz's* improvisation exemplifies *his own light and graceful* approach. His solo has a lyric singing quality. This improvisation is filled with pretty melodies, though the fluidity is occasionally interrupted with bursts of notes forming phrases that mimic the Tristano-Konitz style. Like Konitz, Getz also stays in the upper register. This makes his tone sound like Konitz's even more than would be expected from their mutual allegiance to Lester Young's lightweight, dry timbre. Notice that Getz's solo contains a larger variety of rhythms than Konitz used. To appreciate how much tenor saxophone timbres vary, contrast the Getz sound here with Ben Webster's on "Cottontail" and John Coltrane's on "Flamenco Sketches."
49	1'03"	**Kai Winding Trombone Improvisation** (16 measures, A–C)
50	1'25"	**Buddy DeFranco Clarinet Improvisation** (16 measures, A–B)
51	1'47"	**Serge Chaloff Baritone Sax Improvisation** (16 measures, A–C)
52	2'08"	**Lennie Tristano Piano Improvisation** (16 measures, A–B) Almost all of Tristano's solo is in quadruple-time and has the same character as the introduction that he wrote for this piece. He accents the final note of each phrase ending. Most of his notes are harmonized, making his line sound as though played in locked-hands style.
53	2'29"	**Theme** (8 measures, A)
54	2'42"	**Ending** (8 measures, C) The line is in quadruple-time, first by the piano alone, then joined by saxes, guitar, and clarinet, with the low-pitched sound of the baritone sax becoming prominent at the end. No bass or drums.

The January 10, 1950 recording session that produced "No Figs," heard on the *Jazz Classics CD*. Pete Rugolo conducts and pianist-composer Lennie Tristano plays with the all-stars. Getz, Konitz, Bauer, and Tristano are often tagged "cool jazz" style. The remaining musicians here are more closely tied to bop style. (Gillespie's solo is not heard on the *Jazz Classics* version of this performance.)

Photo by Herman Leonard, courtesy of Bob Asen—Metronome Collection

Some historians distinguish cool jazz from bop, and much of the music mentioned in the second half of this chapter is indeed simpler, softer, and more melodic than the improvisations of Charlie Parker and Dizzy Gillespie. What has been called "cool jazz" also displays somewhat greater emphasis on countermelodies and preset arrangements. Note, however, that **a substantial amount of music called "cool" is not distinguishable from bop.** A solution to this labeling dilemma might be to use "cool bop" to designate some of the softer, less agitated variants. Listeners do tend to perceive some of this music as subdued and understated, even if its rhythms, harmonies, and melodic contours derive from bop.

Here is one more example of how involved the labeling can get: The music of pianist-bandleader George Shearing, which was discussed in the preceding chapter and is considered "cool" by some and "bop" by others, has sometimes been termed "polite bop."

LENNIE TRISTANO AND LEE KONITZ

Lennie Tristano (1919–1978) was a pianist, composer, and bandleader who **created a modern jazz alternative to bop** during the late 1940s. At that time, it was the most substantial alternative available. Though rarely a public performer since then, he impressed his students so much that they carried on his style. (Listen to Tristano's "No Figs" on the *Jazz Classics CD,* "Crosscurrent" in SCCJ, or "Subconscious Lee" on the *Jazz Classics CD* for *Concise Guide to Jazz* and in SCCJ-R.)

In devising a style of his own, Lennie Tristano began by learning the work of the great masters. Art Tatum and Lester Young were particularly important influences. In developing his mastery of piano playing, Tristano learned how to play Art Tatum's difficult and impressive runs. Another piano playing technique that Tristano perfected was improvising in the locked-hands style, something we first encountered when studying the swing era and Milt Buckner. The eighteenth-century composer Johann Sebastian Bach was also important to him. Tristano regarded Bach so highly that he required his students to practice Bach compositions and to learn to improvise in that style. He treated the music of Lester Young with similar reverence, requiring his students to learn Young's solo improvisations by carefully listening to recordings.

Tristano's music differed from bop in many ways. The pet phrases of Charlie Parker and Dizzy Gillespie did not find their way into his improvisations, though his work was equally complex. Sometimes several chord changes occurred in a single measure. Tristano favored long phrases, and his lines were less erratic than Parker's or Gillespie's. The contours of Tristano lines were smoother and less jumpy, and his choice of notes was original. Tristano's lines often seemed composed of notes that were a step or a half-step away from the notes in the chords. They often created an unresolved feeling. Moreover, his lines were not melodic in the pop-tune sense or the bop sense, and his phrases did not swing in the customary bop manner. Instead, his impact tended to be very tight, on top of the beat, with less pronounced syncopation and rhythmic variety than Parker or Gillespie used. Tristano's improvisations were characterized by long strings of uninterrupted eighth notes, interspersed with patches of cleanly executed sixteenth notes. Some recalled Tatum's lines, without as much lightness and bounce. The result was a high-density, virtuosic piano sound, with almost no relaxation of the tension that was built up. Tristano's playing was almost severe in its intensity.

Most of Tristano's output is historically significant, and two performances—"Intuition" and "Digression"—were particularly precedent-setting.[1] As part of their training process during the mid-1940s, Tristano and his musicians had practiced improvising collectively without preset melodies, tempo, meter, or chord progressions. (See pages 364–378 for explanations of these terms.) Then, in 1949, they allowed a sample of this to be recorded. These performances were truly free of preset form, though much of the music conveyed a feeling of steady tempo and consistent key. In other words, **Tristano and his colleagues recorded collectively improvised "free" jazz, long before Ornette Coleman and Cecil Taylor were to become famous for it.**

Tristano made very few recordings during his career—the equivalent of about seven albums. His records remain collector's items because they did not sell well. Today they are quite rare. Tristano's force on the jazz scene was partly felt through the teaching that was his primary occupation from 1951 to his death in 1978. Jazz insiders are familiar with his work and accord him significant respect. Most players after the 1950s, however, perceived him as an underground figure, or they are altogether unaware of him. He influenced a number of excellent jazz musicians,[2] but like Tristano himself, most of them also remain unknown to the majority of jazz musicians and fans. Bill Evans and Cecil Taylor are well-known exceptions, and the Tristano legacy continued because Evans, in turn, influenced Herbie Hancock, Chick Corea, and Keith Jarrett.[3]

Tristano's most talented students during the 1940s were alto saxophonist **Lee Konitz** (b. 1927), tenor saxophonist Warne Marsh (1927–1987), and guitarist Billy Bauer. Together with bass and drums, Tristano joined his students and made recordings which still dazzle other musicians. (Listen to "No Figs" on the *Jazz Classics CD,* "Subconscious Lee" on the *Jazz Classics CD* for *Concise Guide to Jazz,* "Crosscurrent" in SCCJ, and "Subconscious Lee" in SCCJ-R.)

In the late 1940s, the Lee Konitz saxophone style constituted a new sound in jazz. Konitz's command of the alto saxophone astonished fellow musicians.[4] In fact, players often argued about whether Konitz or Parker had the most speed and agility. These two saxophonists were in a class by themselves, outplaying all others. In addition, it is historically important to remember that **Konitz developed and maintained his own Tristano-inspired style at a time when most other young alto saxophonists were imitating Charlie Parker.**

The Konitz style was almost totally unrelated to Parker's.[5] Konitz played with a dry, airy tone that was soft in texture and light in weight. He employed a slow vibrato and preferred to use the alto saxophone's high register instead of its deeper tones. His sound is the alto saxophone equivalent of Lester Young's sound on tenor. This was a historic departure from the warm, syrupy lushness of alto saxophonists Benny Carter and Johnny Hodges. It also departed from the biting, bittersweet sound of Charlie Parker. Also, Konitz was not inclined to sprinkle his improvisations with quotes from pop tunes as Parker did. Konitz also differed from Parker in rhythm and articulation, rarely using staccato. His syncopations were less plentiful than Parker's. Almost all his lines were legato and not percussive at all. The overall effect of the Konitz style typified "cool jazz." (Compare the Konitz solo on "No Figs" with the Hodges solo on "Prelude to a Kiss" on the *Jazz Classics CD.*)

During the late 1940s and early 1950s, most of Konitz's solo work consisted of lines in the style of Tristano's densely packed piano improvisations. Then during the middle 1950s, especially after 1954, Konitz gradually changed his style. The most obvious difference was that he slowed his playing. He also used more ways to construct his phrases. He made more frequent use of silence and occasionally imparted a bluesy flavor to his work. His manner lost some of its snap and freshness as well as speed and agility. With his new style, Konitz occasionally performed on tenor instead of alto saxophone, and he was not as fleet.[6] Among listeners who knew only his earlier work, many found this style difficult to recognize as belonging to Konitz. He toured and recorded for many years after changing his style, thereby giving jazz fans an extended exposure to this additional sound. With this alternative, Konitz became an influence on new generations of saxophonists in the 1970s and 1980s.

BIRTH OF THE COOL

In 1949 and 1950, trumpeter **Miles Davis** and arranger Gil Evans organized recording sessions of a nine-piece band known today as the Miles Davis Nonet or Birth of the Cool band.[7] The group was created by abbreviating Claude Thornhill's big band.[8] The nonet included Lee Konitz, who had been a member of the Thornhill band, and baritone saxophonist Gerry Mulligan, who had played and arranged for Thornhill. Like Davis, they employed lightweight tone qualities and preferred a subdued effect. Though the nonet used a standard rhythm section of piano, bass, and drums, a departure from custom was made by filling out the instrumentation with French horn and tuba. No tenor saxophone or guitar was used, though a trombone was included. (Listen to "Boplicity" in SCCJ.)

⋄WEST COAST STYLE OF THE 1950s

The sound and feeling of the Birth of the Cool sessions was similar to work by several groups of predominantly white jazz musicians centered in Los Angeles during the 1950s. The influence of Konitz and Davis was evident there in saxophone and trumpet styles, respectively. Moreover, arrangers sometimes put together bands that placed tuba and French horn in melodic roles, as in the Birth of the Cool band. Though much of this West Coast jazz was indistinguishable from bop, some performances felt more like the Count Basie-Lester Young combo recordings of the 1930s than the Charlie Parker-Dizzy Gillespie collaborations of the 1940s. Some of the music was especially subdued and understated, precisely those qualities that journalists associated with Lester Young and the term *cool jazz*. Frequently the music featured solo improvisations that were smoother and more tune-like than bop improvisations. In addition, more emphasis was placed on composition and arrangement.

A recording session for the 1950 "Birth of the Cool" band led by trumpeter Miles Davis. Alto saxophonist Lee Konitz and baritone saxophonist Gerry Mulligan are seated at his left. Notice the tuba in the foreground.

Courtesy of Frank Driggs

A number of other jazz styles were flourishing in California at this time, but journalists specified only this particular group of styles as "West Coast jazz." Journalists and record companies often neglected the other styles. This accidentally conveyed the impression that cool was the only style of significance in California during the 1950s. Rather than using the blanket term "West Coast jazz," they could have done better by choosing a more specific designation such as "West Coast Cool Jazz." They also could have acknowledged that some of the playing by even the coolest of these musicians was hard swinging and hot. This textbook uses "West Coast" to designate only the musicians who played this particular collection of cool jazz styles because historians usually mean a West Coast brand of cool jazz when they say *West Coast Style*.[9]

Many of the musicians associated with West Coast cool jazz first came to the Los Angeles area in big bands. Several such groups had disbanded there during the demise of the big band boom in the 1940s. The most notable of these were led by Stan Kenton and Woody Herman (see Table 10.2). Some of their musicians settled in California to earn livelihoods in the commercial music industry, especially in the studios that developed there to satisfy the need for background music in films. After settling, many of these players sporadically returned to those big bands for tours and recordings. Eventually the television industry also employed a considerable number of these men. Commercial music provided their livelihoods, and jazz became a part-time occupation for all but a tiny few.

Big Bands

Every style and era in jazz has been represented at least once in a large-ensemble format known as a "big band." Leaders of these bands often offer styles in addition to the one in vogue at the time of their formation. Sometimes they sample idioms that span several decades. Pianist-arranger **Stan Kenton** (1912–1979) led the best known succession of big bands in modern jazz, and he presented repertories that spanned several eras and featured numerous styles.[10] Kenton's name first became well known during the 1940s while he was leading a big band in the swing era style. The idioms of his subsequent bands were sometimes labeled "big band bop." At one time, Kenton dubbed his music *progressive jazz*. And then, during the 1970s, portions of his repertory tapped jazz-rock. Despite all these labels and shifts in flavor, Kenton's contributions and the styles of his musicians are linked most closely to cool jazz. They are linked particularly with the West Coast, where he was based for many years and where so many of his musicians settled during the 1940s and 1950s (see Tables 10.1 and 10.2). Kenton acknowledged Claude Thornhill, father of the cool style for

TABLE 10.1 A Few West Coast Style Musicians of the 1950s

ALTO SAX
- Art Pepper
- Bud Shank
- Herb Geller
- Lennie Niehaus
- Paul Desmond

BARITONE SAX
- Gerry Mulligan
- Bob Gordon

GUITAR
- Howard Roberts
- Barney Kessel
- Jim Hall

PIANO
- Hampton Hawes
- Claude Williamson
- Russ Freeman
- Pete Jolly
- Vince Guaraldi
- Andre Previn
- Dave Brubeck

BASS
- Red Mitchell
- Red Callender
- Leroy Vinnegar
- Buddy Clark
- Carson Smith
- Howard Rumsey
- Curtis Counce
- Joe Mondragon
- Monty Budwig

DRUMS
- Mel Lewis
- Shelly Manne
- Larry Bunker
- Chico Hamilton

COMPOSER-ARRANGERS
- Gerry Mulligan
- Dave Brubeck
- Shorty Rogers
- Dave Pell
- John Graas
- Jimmy Giuffre
- Bill Holman
- Marty Paich

TRUMPET
- Chet Baker
- Conte Candoli
- Jack Sheldon
- Shorty Rogers
- Stu Williamson
- Carl Perkins

TROMBONE
- Bob Brookmeyer
- Frank Rosolino
- Bob Enevoldsen
- Milt Bernhart

TENOR SAX
- Bill Perkins
- Richie Kamuca
- Bob Cooper
- Jack Montrose
- Buddy Collette
- Dave Pell
- Bill Holman
- Jimmy Giuffre
- Zoot Sims

TABLE 10.2 **A Few of the Many West Coast Style Players Who Played with the Woody Herman and Stan Kenton Big Bands. (The two bands used many of the same musicians. Most were white. Most were good sight readers. Most played in similar styles.)**

KENTON	HERMAN
Lee Konitz	Bill Perkins
Art Pepper	Richie Kamuca
Bud Shank	Shorty Rogers
Lennie Niehaus	Jimmy Giuffre
Bill Holman	Conte Candoli
Richie Kamuca	Stan Levey
Conte Candoli	Shelly Manne
Jack Sheldon	Red Mitchell
Mel Lewis	Stu Williamson
Stan Levey	Zoot Sims
Shelly Manne	
Bob Cooper	
Frank Rosolino	
Stu Williamson	
Milt Bernhart	
Zoot Sims	

big band, as a major influence on his own approach to band writing. Kenton's featured musicians drew liberally from the cool jazz styles of Lester Young, Miles Davis, and Lee Konitz; Konitz himself played with the band for more than a year.

Kenton is one of the few jazz musicians besides Louis Armstrong, Benny Goodman, and Duke Ellington to become widely known by the American public. However, his name, unlike Ellington's or Armstrong's, represented a huge collection of different composers, arrangers, and soloists. Kenton created a composing and arranging style which owed much to Claude Thornhill, Fletcher Henderson, and Benny Carter. He is well known for the compositions and arrangements he originated himself, particularly in recordings of "Eager Beaver" and "Artistry in Rhythm," his band's theme song.[11] He also developed a piano style that was influenced partly by Earl Hines.

Kenton created a distinctive band style that is immediately recognizable. Though he did record ordinary arrangements of numerous pop tunes, and he did turn out a large body of dance music, the most impressive work he presented was nonswinging concert music which vividly exposed rich, modern harmonies. Two and three moving parts were sometimes presented simultaneously. The weighty pieces differ from the dance-band tradition of big band jazz. A classical feeling was common in his music. In fact, the musicianship of his players was very high, with ensemble precision and tuning sometimes approaching the sterling standards of symphony orchestras. Usually performed without vibrato, his brass and saxophone parts had a dry quality that has sometimes been termed "transparent." Some pieces featured trumpet parts which were high-pitched, loud, and often block-voiced as five-note chords. These sounds were combined with saxophone passages written in long strings of sixteenth notes which came up from the low range of the ensemble like fountains or descended like waterfalls.

Though Kenton's performances usually ranged from the softest to the loudest of sounds, Kenton earned a reputation for leading the loudest big band. This was partly due to the preponderance of brass instruments. It was not unusual to find five trumpets and five trombones in a Kenton band at the same time as Duke Ellington was carrying only four trumpets and three trombones. Additionally, some Kenton trombonists doubled on tuba, and one version of his band carried an entire section of mellophoniums (trumpet-French horn hybrids specially made for Kenton). The saxophone section was occasionally called upon to augment the band's massiveness by employing the unusual combination of two baritone saxophones.

Another trademark of the Kenton band sound was its glossy trombone tones. The ensemble frequently featured harmonized parts for five trombones that were performed very smoothly and lightly, no matter how loud. For more than three decades, Kenton's trombone soloists invariably preferred high-register work, and they graced the beginnings of many tones with long, climbing smears. They used a meticulously controlled vibrato which was initially slow and then quickened dramatically near the tone's end. Their approach was extroverted, but in the well-manicured way of Tommy Dorsey, rather than the rough, guttural way of earlier jazz trombonists.

To help put the Kenton band sound in perspective, a comparison with Count Basie might be helpful. Just as the feeling projected by the Basie band can be described as easygoing and swinging, the feeling projected by the Kenton band can be described as serious and intense, with an emphasis on massiveness. Much of the Kenton repertory is solemn and weighty. It is essentially twentieth-century concert music scored for trumpets, trombones, and saxophones plus rhythm section. Some of the material also required French horns, tuba, strings, and Latin American percussion instruments. The band's character was based more on elaborate arrangements than on the simplicity and swing feeling associated with Basie. Remember that the Basie band of the late 1930s functioned much as a big combo. Solo improvisation was primary, and many of the ensemble backgrounds were almost incidental to the music. Kenton's approach contrasts with Basie's because its effect was frequently similar to that of a brass choir, not a big jazz combo. The Kenton bands usually emphasized composition over improvisation. In fact, some solo improvisations were not solos in the conventional sense but embellishments of the ensemble sound. For example, the Kenton band sometimes intentionally overpowered a soloist in a loud ensemble sound, thereby turning the solo line into an ensemble line that was almost indistinct.

It was not as a pianist or composer that Kenton left his greatest mark. His major contributions to jazz history were his skill at public relations and his motivation and talent for finding and leading creative modern musicians and composers. Lying behind this contribution is the important fact that because of his band's great popularity during the 1940s—"Tampico" and "Artistry in Rhythm" were million sellers—Kenton became financially free enough to invest in musical experiments. He channeled this freedom into hiring relatively unknown writers and commissioning ambitious compositions which had little chance of commercial success.[12] Improvisers had enjoyed these kinds of opportunities throughout jazz history, but composers had not. In addition, Kenton employed hundreds of musicians who otherwise may not have received much exposure. He must also be credited with tenacity and durability. Though he began leading bands in 1941, when the big band era was still flourishing, he continued into the 1960s and 1970s, long after big bands went out of fashion. Moreover, he was one of the founders of the college stage band movement, spawning today's enormous jazz education establishment. Jazz in schools perpetuated the big band tradition in jazz after regularly touring big bands disappeared from the jazz scene upon the deaths of Kenton, Basie, Ellington, Woody Herman, Buddy Rich, Harry James, and Don Ellis.

Trumpet

A number of good trumpeters have been associated with West Coast cool jazz of the 1950s and 1960s (see Table 10.1). Chet Baker and Shorty Rogers are probably the best known. Baker has the more impressive recording career as a soloist, while Rogers is better known for his writing and bandleading.

When naming "cool jazz" trumpeters, journalists usually list Miles Davis first and **Chet Baker** (1929–1988) next.[13] Unlike most white West Coast players, Baker did not gain his first wide exposure with the big bands of Stan Kenton or Woody Herman. Though he had played briefly with Charlie Parker, his largest initial exposure came from his membership in the Gerry Mulligan quartet of 1952 and 1953. From there, he toured and recorded prolifically with a variety of rhythm sections until his death in 1988.

Baker is widely admired among musicians, regardless of the idiom or era being discussed. His solos swing in an easy manner, and most of his playing projects a mellow mood. His tone quality is soft, not brassy. In fact, during the 1960s he stopped playing the trumpet temporarily and spent some of his career playing the mellower-sounding fluegelhorn (see photo on page 112).[14] As an improviser, Baker had a talent for being able to pick just the right few notes, and to invest isolated notes and phrases with especially affecting tone qualities. Some of Baker's best work conveys a poignant sense of striving to catch something just beyond his reach, a struggle to overcome obstacles. Often, when he finally plays that perfect note, it attains a delicate balance of fragility and triumph. A master at generating long phrases, Baker never seemed at a loss for melodic ideas, and the tuneful quality of his solos always made them sound fresh.

Shorty Rogers (1924–1994) was a trumpeter-composer-arranger based in Los Angeles during the 1950s and 1960s. He had played trumpet and written for the Woody Herman and Stan Kenton bands. With his own combos and big bands, sometimes called the Giants, he produced music that extended writing styles he had developed in his earlier compositions. His recordings of these pieces featured various combinations of the best jazz musicians living in the Los Angeles area at the time.[15] In isolated recordings, he also anticipated developments that later became better known in association with other musicians. Recordings he made with Jimmy Giuffre and vibraharpist Teddy Charles[16] are historically significant because they were the first after Lennie Tristano's "Intuition" and "Digression" to display improvisation not based on prearranged chord progressions. Their 1954 work predated the Ornette Coleman recordings of 1958 and 1959 which launched an entire style centered on the "free jazz" concept. Rogers also recorded pieces in which improvisation was based on modes instead of chord changes. (For explanations of modes, see pages 369–372 and 418–423.)[17] These predated the 1958 Miles Davis recording of "Milestones" and the Davis *Kind of Blue* album which launched the mode-based improvisatory styles that were popular during the 1960s and 1970s. The connection with Davis is especially intriguing because Rogers derived his trumpet style primarily from the 1940s approach of Miles Davis and, like Davis, used fluegelhorn long before it became common among trumpeters. (See page 112 for illustration of fluegelhorn.)

Saxophone

Many excellent saxophonists were associated with West Coast cool jazz (see Table 10.1).[18] They are known particularly for maintaining the tone quality and melodic ideas of Lester Young, though some also incorporated the advances of Charlie Parker. Most played with the big bands of Stan Kenton and Woody Herman at one time or another (see Table 10.2).

Saxophonist **Jimmy Giuffre** (b. 1921) was based on the West Coast from 1946 to 1960. Giuffre's output typifies the notion of cool jazz: he produced a soft, diffuse sound on all the instruments he played, and his lines were understated and melodic. Moreover, his mastery of silence and economy in solo construction is comparable to that of Count Basie and Miles Davis. Although he began as a saxophonist influenced by the Count Basie-Lester Young combo style of the 1930s, he went beyond Young. Additionally he contributed strikingly original compositions and improvisations, many of which he performed on clarinet, with a special emphasis on the instrument's lowest register. Ultimately he must be ranked as one of the most daring composers and improvisers in jazz, and rhythmically he was the most creative of the West Coast musicians. The consistency, intelligence, and coherence of even his most unorthodox lines surpassed all his colleagues. His improvisations sustain a level of originality that is higher than most modern jazz as a whole, not just West Coast jazz or cool jazz. Despite the "cool" demeanor of his work, Giuffre's sounds impart a sense of intellectual intensity and adventure that lends them a character as convincing as the most outstanding bop and post-bop performances. They have little of the tentative or easygoing feeling that is conveyed by much other music made at this time on the West Coast. Unfortunately, except for recognition as composer of the "Four Brothers" piece featured by Woody Herman's band, he is almost universally overlooked by jazz fans as well as historians, and most of his best recordings went out of print, rarely to be reissued.[19]

There were several excellent alto saxophonists associated with the West Coast scene of the 1950s (see Table 10.1), many of whom were prominently featured at one time or another with the big bands of Stan Kenton. All of them used slow vibrato and produced tone qualities that were thin-textured and light in weight, displaying a dryness we ordinarily associate with Lester Young. This contrasts with the weightier, more syrupy tone qualities of Coleman Hawkins and Johnny Hodges. Though aware of Charlie Parker's approach to melodic rhythm and phrasing, they seemed to have more in common with Lee Konitz. None of them, however, demonstrated the richness of melodic inventions we find in either Parker or Konitz. The West Coast cool saxophonists were especially simple in their improvisations. Frequently it sounded as though they were playing swing era solos spiced with a touch of bop flavoring.

The best known West Coast altoist was **Paul Desmond** (1924–1977). In surveys of musicians, Desmond ranks among the all-time favorites on his instrument. He is highly regarded for his good taste, melodic continuity, fertile imagination, and accurate intonation. Desmond received his widest exposure with pianist Dave Brubeck's quartets.[20] His quartet improvisations conveyed a sense of openness and clarity. With his soft, light, pure sound, he unfolded line after logical line. Often he created an impression that his playing was effortlessly soaring above its earthbound accompaniments.[21]

Desmond forged an instantly recognizable style that had almost nothing to do with bop—Desmond cited swing era player Pete Brown, not Charlie Parker, as his influence. And, though his tone quality closely resembled that of Lee Konitz, Desmond's style should not be considered as derivative of the Tristano-Konitz approach, either. By comparison with Konitz, he swung a bit more. Further, instead of drawing upon the complex melodic conception of Lennie Tristano as Konitz did, Desmond had his own fresh ideas, and the melodies that he improvised were less convoluted than those of the Tristano school. Though he sometimes inserted phrases from popular songs, his improvisational material was usually free of cliché. It depended instead upon original melodic invention. He was extremely economical, playing far fewer notes per solo than probably any other modern jazz saxophonist. Many of his lines are as simple and lyrical as the best popular songs. Some of his improvisations may remind listeners of themes in the classical music of Tchaikovsky and Rachmaninoff.

Desmond's playing projects a relaxed, lighthearted mood, but the construction of his improvised lines reflects care, intelligence, and inspiration. Desmond sometimes developed musical sequences by taking a phrase and repeating it in a new key to fit the next chord in his accompaniment, each time altering it or putting it in a different place relative to the underlying beat. Some of his rhythmic displacements built tension that was finally resolved by a clever turn of phrase, as though he had escaped miraculously from a self-imposed puzzle. Other times he sounded as though he were playing duets with himself, introducing a line, then answering, paraphrasing or mimicking it.[22]

Art Pepper (1925–1982) is among the best known and most original improvisers associated with the Stan Kenton bands and West Coast jazz. He fashioned a raw, plaintive style for the alto saxophone by amalgamating the approaches of Zoot Sims and Lee Konitz. Then, at the latest stage in his career, he also absorbed the influence of post-bop saxophonist John Coltrane. His was probably the hottest style to emerge from cool jazz of the white West Coast scene. In his playing is more of a cry than ordinarily found in West Coast cool saxophonists. Another central difference is his sense of urgency and rhythmic variety. Pepper pushed hard on the beat. He favored short, staccato bursts of notes, many grouped in triplets. Sometimes he tore off a double-time figure (a stream of sixteenth notes) in a tight, crisp manner. Pepper used brief, funky phrases that were abruptly stated with searing emotion. In fact, his emotionality is prized by many fans. The emotional range of his playing runs from a joyous swing feeling, particularly evident on medium- and up-tempo pieces, to despondency; on some ballad improvisations his playing is so slow it is almost as though he purposely drags to build tension.[23]

Gerry Mulligan (1927–1996) was baritone saxophonist and a primary composer-arranger in the Miles Davis nonet sessions of 1949 and 1950. (Listen to "Boplicity" on SCCJ. Mulligan contributes the first improvisation.) He also wrote for the big bands of Claude Thornhill and Stan Kenton. Mulligan used a soft, dry, light-weight tone quality whose texture has been likened to tweed cloth. By comparison with bop style, his approach was relatively uncomplicated. Rhythmically, Mulligan's improvisations were more predictable, less jarring than those of Charlie Parker and Dizzy Gillespie. His solos suggested great deliberation rather than wild exuberance. He rarely double-timed his phrases. The logic behind them was obvious, and usually they were developed quite systematically. Similarly, Mulligan's compositions were neither as complex as Lennie Tristano's nor as agitated as many bop pieces. A few are quite song-like, and they have the same gentle character projected by his improvisations. This trait, combined with his subdued tone quality, qualifies his music for the "cool" label.

In 1952, Mulligan moved to California and launched a series of piano-less quartets consisting of himself on baritone saxophone, another horn, bass, and drums. Let's take a moment to consider what it means to have a jazz group without a chording instrument. Normally a piano provides chords to the soloists. These chords act as a sort of anchor, always reminding the horn players of where they are in the harmony that accompanies the tune. In some ways the piano chords direct the flow and texture of the music. A comping pianist complicates the sound considerably. Therefore, the absence of piano in Mulligan's groups was partly responsible for the band's simple sound texture. It also highlighted the bass, which pianos often drown out. His drummers also contributed to this effect by playing conservatively, often using wire brushes instead of sticks to strike the drums and cymbals. All of these aspects together made Mulligan's band sound "cool." While on the West Coast, he also produced material with a ten-piece band in the style of the Miles Davis nonet. Trumpeter Chet Baker was his best known partner in these undertakings.[24] Though Mulligan was based on the West Coast for only about three years, his music epitomizes what journalists mean by the term "West Coast cool." Mulligan maintained his piano-less format long after returning to the New York area, and, more than thirty years later, many jazz fans still considered his music "West Coast cool."

Drums West Coast style was not known for adventuresome drumming, in either the accompaniment or solo capacity. However, one of the most novel bands to originate on the West Coast was led by drummer **Chico Hamilton** (b. 1921). Gerry Mulligan had made Hamilton the drummer in his first piano-less quartet. Then Hamilton formed a group of his own. He used an instrumentation that was even more unique: guitar, cello, bass, drums, and a hornman who played saxophones, flute, and clarinet. (Flute and cello were especially unusual to find in jazz at this time.) With tightly arranged pieces and excellent musicianship, the quintet created its own jazz style, which often resembled classical chamber music.[25] Its textures were light and pretty, and the arrangements displayed considerable variety. Sometimes several melodies sounded at the same time. This is a technique that had characterized the earliest jazz. With Hamilton's, Mulligan's, and Brubeck's groups using it, the technique had found favor again.

Chico Hamilton was one of the first modern drummers to get away from nearly always playing conventional ride rhythms as the undercurrent for a group sound. Hamilton's imagination is fertile, orchestral, and subtle. He is known for generating unusual and catchy patterns on his drums and maintaining them as consistent accompaniment figures. Instead of depending primarily on the ride cymbal and high-hat sound, Hamilton is just as likely to use a snare drum or tom-tom as the primary voice in his accompaniment pattern. Each piece features a separate rhythm pattern and percussion color. Hamilton's style is a gentle approach to creating unusual rhythmic textures instead of just defining the beat and prodding the soloists. Even when no longer based on the West Coast, Hamilton's groups continued to create a highly original brand of jazz that was full of surprises.

Guitar Several modern guitarists were associated with the West Coast scene of the 1950s (see Table 10.1). But none have come to be more revered by jazz musicians than **Jim Hall** (b. 1930). When asked to name their favorite guitarist or their biggest influence, numerous modern guitarists mention Jim Hall. Since the mid-1960s, they mention him almost as often as they mention Wes Montgomery. Though much of his reputation has been acquired since he left the Los Angeles area for New York in 1959, many fans were first introduced to Hall

The Dave Brubeck Quartet, one of the most popular small groups in jazz history (left to right): drummer Joe Morello, bassist Gene Wright, pianist Dave Brubeck, alto saxophonist Paul Desmond. Brubeck and Desmond played together from the 1940s to the 1970s. Desmond's hit tune "Take Five" still remains popular today.

Photo by Bob Parent, courtesy of Don Parent

through recordings he made with Chico Hamilton in 1955 and 1956 and with Jimmy Giuffre from 1956 to 1960.

Jim Hall extracts a mellow, soft tone from his guitar, and his sound is clear and pure, often bell-like in its resonance. His clean touch, gentle approach, and immaculate sense of pacing set him above almost all other jazz guitarists. There is nothing offhanded about what he offers his listeners. He begins his notes very precisely. The structure of his ideas displays a crystal clarity. He never overloads the listener with flashy acrobatics or a crowded sequence of notes. In his music, a sense of politeness coexists with a forceful continuity of purpose that suggests Hall knows exactly where he is going. He maintains high creative standards, placing great importance on playing only fresh ideas and avoiding well-worn patterns. Yet despite the pressure that this esthetic exerts, Hall's solos are free of the false starts that we would expect. Instead, we are treated to solos that bear an overall form that is often as good as any composed piece. Rather than beginning ideas and leaving them half-finished, Hall nearly always manages to complete each improvised idea, thereby personifying the meticulous composer as improviser. Because of the limitations such a strategy places on an improviser, Hall is possibly the slowest guitar soloist in jazz. This does not mean that he is not *able* to play fast, flashy lines. It means only that he chooses notes so judiciously that his pace cannot possibly be as brisk as it would be if he were performing prerehearsed patterns. Unlike many bop soloists, Hall does not ordinarily exceed the limits of his thinking and the speed of his fingers. Because he does stay within his capabilities, each note in his improvised lines is presented firmly, with a sureness of swing feeling.[26]

Piano

A number of creative jazz pianists were based on the West Coast during the 1950s (see Table 10.1). All contributed substantially to the quality of the West Coast scene, but only **Dave Brubeck** (b. 1920) achieved tremendous international fame. He performed in the San Francisco area during the 1940s and early 1950s. In the period 1955 to 1985, Brubeck ranked second in record sales among all jazz recording artists. During the 1950s and 1960s, his name became almost as synonymous with jazz as Louis Armstrong and Duke Ellington had been in the 1930s and 1940s. His fame came mostly as a bandleader and composer. Among musicians, he was universally admired as a composer, though he was not as influential as a pianist. During the 1940s he had led a series of small bands in California which employed approaches similar to the 1949–1950 Miles Davis nonet, though they began before he ever heard the Davis recordings.[27] Then, from 1951 to 1967, he teamed with California-born alto saxophonist Paul Desmond and led a quartet which, for millions of listeners, provided an introduction to jazz. (Though associated with "West Coast" jazz, Brubeck was not a California resident during the period of his greatest acclaim. His quartet members lived in the New York area.)

The rhythmic feeling in a lot of Brubeck's playing has much in common with classical music. However, Brubeck never was a classical pianist, though after launching his jazz career he briefly studied composition with the world-renowned symphonic composer Darius Milhaud. It remains a widely held misunderstanding that Brubeck was trained primarily in the classics. Perhaps listeners believe this because of the way Brubeck's music sounds. He is one of the few modern pianists who clearly avoids standard bop melodic conception and rhythmic feeling. He is unusually inventive and depends almost exclusively on original melodic lines, not the phrases that most of his contemporaries absorbed from the music of Charlie Parker, Dizzy Gillespie, and Bud Powell. He was inspired more by Art Tatum, Fats Waller, and Cleo Brown than bop. Another reason is that much of Brubeck's invention has a distinctly classical flavor. In fact, sometimes he and Desmond improvised duets that sounded like the two-part inventions of J. S. Bach, set atop jazz bass and drums. In other words, Brubeck is a modern jazz musician who does not use the bop language, and, despite his lack of classical piano lessons, he often sounds more like Bach than bop.

That Brubeck's work sounds classical may explain part of his popularity. By comparison with the jumpy, erratic character of bop style, his compositions and improvisations are much easier to follow. They possess a simple and tuneful quality. His creations are orderly, and they project a freshness and clarity that make the listener's job easy. In addition, most of Brubeck's pieces are pretty, and they convey a light and pleasant mood.[28]

Brubeck was rhythmically innovative. His interest in using meters unusual to jazz brought him a great deal of publicity and spawned trends among other jazz musicians. His quartet crafted a number of tunes and improvisations in odd meters such as three, five, and seven. (See page 364 for an explanation of "meter.") His albums *Time Out*[29] and *Time Further Out*,[30]) which explored those meters, were immensely popular. *Time Out* contained "Take Five," a funky and engaging theme by Paul Desmond that employed a simple accompaniment rhythm that was extensively repeated in meter of five. Brubeck was also rhythmically innovative in ways outside his adventures with odd meters. For example, he frequently improvised lines, sometimes in locked-hands style, that pitted his own separate rhythm (for example, in meter of three) against the pulse that was emanating from bass and drums (for example, in meter of two). By this strategy he was cleverly attempting to generate a provocative tension. However, the clashing rhythms were often not appreciated by those who were expecting the easy swing feeling that was ordinarily produced by other modern jazz pianists. Brubeck's mastery of odd meters led to respect among musicians, however, and it earned him a significant place in jazz history, even in the minds of musicians who were not especially influenced by his piano style.

Trombone

There are a number of highly talented trombonists associated with the Los Angeles jazz scene of the 1950s and 1960s (see Table 10.1). Among many jazz trombonists themselves, **Carl Fontana** (b. 1928) is the favorite trombonist in modern jazz. Though featured with Stan Kenton and Woody Herman, he was not consistently in the Los Angeles area during this period, but we will discuss him here. Trombonists are awed by his outstanding improvisations and unparalleled command of the instrument. Fontana's solos have more depth and substance than the work of almost all other trombonists. Fontana comes close to improvising with the thought and fluency of a modern jazz saxophonist. Unfortunately, Fontana has made so few recordings that little proof of his prowess exists for listeners who never had the opportunity to see him perform.[31] Perhaps as a result, the best-known trombonists in West Coast jazz are valve trombonist **Bob Brookmeyer** (b. 1929) and slide trombonist **Frank Rosolino** (1926–1978). Paradoxically, neither man truly qualifies as both West Coast and cool.

Brookmeyer lived in Los Angeles only sporadically, though his playing style could be called cool for several reasons. He uses a tone quality that is soft, not rough or brassy. His rhythmic conception is laid back, and his lines are light and melodic. These characteristics combine to sound altogether more like late-1930s Basie style than any bop style. He uses a combination of lip slurs and half-valve effects, and he follows through on all his ideas, never leaving the listener hanging. Most notable for Brookmeyer's relationship to cool jazz is his work as the other horn on numerous tours and recordings with Gerry Mulligan's piano-less quartets, especially after both men left Los Angeles and returned to New York. He also filled a similar role in Jimmy Giuffre's trio with guitarist Jim Hall. And, like such other West Coast notables as Gerry Mulligan, Shorty Rogers, and Chico Hamilton, Brookmeyer has made much of his living as a writer rather than as a performer.[32]

Frank Rosolino was based in Los Angeles throughout a sizable portion of his career, thereby qualifying for the "West Coast" designation. Yet, like Fontana's, his approach was a hot and fast bop style, not cool. Next to Fontana, Rosolino was often judged to possess the most speed and range of any trombonist during his era, and because of this he was one of the most influential trombonists in jazz. Like Fontana, Rosolino had also been a featured soloist with Stan Kenton.[33]

Popular Appeal

A few players in the "cool" category are the most popular musicians in modern jazz. Trumpeter Miles Davis and saxophonist Stan Getz were capable of consistently packing nightclubs and concert halls. The George Shearing Quintets and the Modern Jazz Quartet were also successful during the 1950s and 1960s. The Dave Brubeck Quartet and the Modern Jazz Quartet were among the first groups in jazz history that were sufficiently popular to tour regularly as concert artists, appearing routinely on college campuses and in recital halls previously devoted to presenting classical musicians. But such acclaim was achieved by only a few nonvocal jazz groups. For instance, Lennie Tristano, Lee Konitz, and Jimmy Giuffre remain among the least appreciated players in that same period, despite the wealth of their contributions. So to say that cool jazz had popular appeal is not entirely accurate. Only some recordings by some cool jazz musicians were popular, and only the names of a few cool jazz musicians garnered much notice beyond the usual small audience of musicians and fans.

CHAPTER SUMMARY

1) "Cool jazz" is a term applied to modern styles that sound subdued because they use light, dry tone qualities, little or no vibrato, low levels of volume, and avoid high notes. Some of this music is more relaxed and melodic than bop.
2) Cool jazz of the 1950s drew upon the styles of Lester Young and Count Basie of the 1930s, Lennie Tristano and Lee Konitz of the 1940s, and the arranging practices of the Claude Thornhill band that provided the model for the Miles Davis Nonet of 1949–1950.
3) Much cool jazz is indistinguishable from bop, and a few cool players were already discussed in the bop chapter: Stan Getz, George Shearing, and the Modern Jazz Quartet.
4) Pianist-composer Stan Kenton led a string of innovative big bands, some of which were influenced by Claude Thornhill's style.
5) Kenton's repertory of the 1950s contained ambitious concert works resembling twentieth-century classical music scored for brass, saxes, and rhythm section.
6) "West Coast style" refers to cool jazz played by a predominantly white community of jazz musicians based in the Los Angeles area during the 1950s, many of whom had played with the big bands of Stan Kenton and Woody Herman.
7) Gerry Mulligan, Chico Hamilton, Dave Brubeck, and Shorty Rogers were prominent West Coast bandleaders.
8) Paul Desmond, Art Pepper, Jimmy Giuffre, and Gerry Mulligan were prominent West Coast saxophonists.
9) Chet Baker and Shorty Rogers were prominent West Coast trumpeters.
10) Carl Fontana, Frank Rosolino, and Bob Brookmeyer were prominent West Coast trombonists.

NOTES

1. Lennie Tristano, *Intuition* (Capitol 52771, 1949); *Lennie Tristano/The New Tristano* (Atlantic/Rhino: 71595 [1224/1357], 1961).

2. Tristano influenced pianists Ronnie Ball, Sal Mosca, Clare Fischer, Alan Broadbent, Wally Cirillo, and Connie Crothers; saxophonists John LaPorta, Teo Macero, and Ted Brown; and trumpeters Don Ferrara and Cy Touff. For more about Tristano and Konitz, see Ira Gitler, *Jazz Masters of the Forties* (Macmillan, 1966; DaCapo, 1982), 226–261.

3. To hear the resemblance between Tristano and Evans, compare almost any Tristano piano solo with recordings that Evans made with George Russell, for example, "All About Rosie" on the anthology, *The Birth of the Third Stream* (Columbia: CK 64929, 1956–57); or the solo on "Oleo" on Bill Evans, *Everybody Digs Bill Evans* (Fantasy: OJCCD-068-2 [Riverside 1129], 1958). For a continuation of the Tristano legacy, listen to Hancock's solos on "Dolores" and "Gingerbread Boy" on Miles Davis, *Miles Smiles* (Columbia: CK 65682 [9401], 1966), and Jarrett's solos on "Shades of Jazz" on Keith Jarrett, *Mysteries* (Impulse!/CRP: GRD4-189 [9322], 2CD set, 1975–76). For the resemblance between Tristano and Cecil Taylor, listen to Lennie Tristano, *Descent into the Maelstrom* (Inner City: 6002, LP, 1953); then to anything Taylor recorded after 1960.

4. Listen to "Marshmallow" or "Ice Cream Konitz" on Lee Konitz, *Subconscious Lee* (Fantasy: OJCCD-186-2 [Prestige 7004], 1949). Some of the best Konitz solos are on *Konitz Meets Mulligan* (Pacific Jazz: 46847 [20142], 1953). See also footnote 10 below.

5. Konitz, in turn, influenced Bud Shank, Lennie Niehaus, and Art Pepper, among others, during the 1950s; then Anthony Braxton and Bob Mover, among others, during the 1970s.

6. Lee Konitz, *Ideal Scene* (Soul Note: 121 119-2, 1986).

7. Miles Davis, *The Birth of the Cool* (Capitol: 92862 [T762], 1949–50); or *The Complete Birth of the Cool* (Capitol Jazz: 94550, 1948–50).

8. Miles Davis asked arranger Gil Evans to provide the smallest instrumentation that could approximate the sound of the Thornhill big band. Listen to the original band on *Best of the Big Bands: Claude Thornhill* (Columbia: CK 46152 [32906], 1941–47); or *The Bebop Era* (Columbia: CK 40972, 1942–51).

9. The term "West Coast Style" will not be used here to indicate the entire variety of jazz styles that were active on the West Coast during the 1950s, such as bebop, hard bop, Dixieland, swing, and free jazz. For a more complete picture see Ted Gioia, *West Coast Jazz* (Oxford, 1992); Robert Gordon, *Jazz West Coast* (Quartet Books, 1986); William F. Lee, *Stan Kenton: Artistry in Rhythm* (Creative Press of Los Angeles, 1980); Red Callender, *Unfinished Dream* (Quartet Books, 1985); Barry McRae, *Jazz Cataclysm* (A. S. Barnes, 1967; DaCapo, 1985); Joe Goldberg, *Jazz Masters of the Fifties* (Macmillan, 1965; DaCapo, 1983); and the notes for *Black California* (Savoy: 2215, 2LP set, 1942–1952). The absence of discussion for the fine musicians who performed in these other styles should not be taken as a rejection of their work, but only as an indication that a brief text such as this cannot do justice to all jazz styles in all regions in all periods.

10. A favorite among musicians is *New Concepts of Artistry in Rhythm* (Capitol: 92865 [T383], 1952), featuring Lee Konitz, Conte Candoli, Frank Rosolino, and Maynard Ferguson; with arrangements by Gerry Mulligan, Johnny Richards, Bill Russo, and Bill Holman.

11. *The Jazz Compositions of Stan Kenton* (Creative World: 1078, LP, 1956); original recordings of these pieces are on *The Best of Stan Kenton* (Capitol: 31504, 1943–61).

12. For examples, listen to Johnny Richards's arrangements on *Cuban Fire* (Capitol: 96260 [T731], 1956); Robert Graettinger's compositions on *The City of Glass* (Capitol 32084 [T736], 1951); Russ Garcia's "Adventures in Emotions" on *Stan Kenton Conducts the Los Angeles Neophonic Orchestra* (Creative World: 1013 [Capitol SMAS 2424], 1965); Stan Kenton: *The Complete Capitol Recordings of the Holman & Russo Charts* (Mosaic: MD4-136, 4CD set, 1950–55); and Pete Rugolo's "Mirage" and William Russo's "Egdon Heath" in *Mirage* (New World: 216, LP, 1947–61). See also *Big Band Renaissance* (Smithsonian: RD 108, 5CD set, 1941–89). Some Kenton records may still be available by mail from Gene Norman, Suite 4A, 8400 Sunset Blvd., Los Angeles, CA 90069; phone 800-654-7029. In addition, the *Instructor's Resource Manual* for this book has a discography of Kenton albums, organized by composer-arrangers. Teachers can obtain it by calling 800-526-0485, contacting Prentice-Hall sales representatives, or by writing College Marketing, Prentice-Hall, Inc., 1 Lake Street, Upper Saddle River, NJ 07458. Scores and parts for many of Kenton's bands' arrangements are available from Sierra Music, P.O. Box 928, Port Townsend, Washington 98368 (phone: 800-255-6551).

13. *Best of the Gerry Mulligan Quartet with Chet Baker* (Pacific Jazz: 95481, 1952–53); *The Birth of the Cool, Vol. 2* (Capitol: 98935, 1951–53); *Chet Baker: The Pacific Years* (Pacific Jazz: 89292, 1952–54).

14. Chet Baker, *Lonely Star* (Prestige: PRCD-24172-2 [7449], 1965).

15. Shorty Rogers, *Short Stops* (RCA Bluebird: 5917-2-RB,1953–54).

16. Shelly Manne, *"The Three" and "The Two"* (Fantasy: OJCCD-172-2 [Contemporary 3584], 1954).

17. Teddy Charles/Shorty Rogers, *Collaboration: West* (Fantasy: OJCCD-122-2 [Prestige 7028], 1953).

18. Teddy Edwards, Wardell Gray, Dexter Gordon, and Harold Land are a few of the great bop players associated with California. For more about them, see Leonard Feather, *Encyclopedia of Jazz* (DaCapo, 1984); Ted Gioia, *West Coast Jazz;* Robert Gordon, *Jazz West Coast.*

19. An outstanding undertaking for Giuffre was a trio he led with trombonist Bob Brookmeyer and Jim Hall during an eighteen-month period in 1958 and 1959 (*The Complete Capitol & Atlantic Recordings of Jimmy Giuffre*, Mosaic: MD6-176 [Atlantic 1282/1330], 6CD set, 1954–58). Their music was light and lyrical, but also earthy and rhythmically daring. It featured close, three-way cooperation in the creation of improvised counterlines. The trio generated group improvisations that were very cohesive, original, and swinging (despite the absence of bass and drums). Another standout among Giuffre's endeavors was made after he left the West Coast for New York. On and off from 1961 to 1963, Giuffre played clarinet with pianist Paul Bley and bassist Steve Swallow. Their sound had the flavor of twentieth-century classical music, and it sometimes stemmed from improvisation that was free of preset chord progressions (*Jimmy Giuffre 3, 1961,* ECM: 78118 21438-2 [Verve V8397], 2CD set, 1961; *Free Fall,* Columbia: CK 65446, 1962). Subsequent work by Giuffre has preserved his tendency to lean toward experimentation.

20. Desmond penned the quartet's biggest hit, "Take Five." It sold more than a million copies in 1961 and has remained popular. See original in Dave Brubeck, *Time Out* (Columbia: CK 65122 [CL 1397], 1959). For more about Desmond, see Gene Lees, *Meet Me at Jim & Andy's* (Oxford, 1988), 243–65.

21. Desmond was so consistently inspired that almost every Brubeck album offers representative Desmond solos. A standout is Dave Brubeck, *Gone with the Wind* (Columbia: CK 40627 [CL 1347], 1959), especially his solo on "Georgia on My Mind." Away from Brubeck, Desmond recorded some very pleasant playing, including an orchestral album in which he paraphrased well-loved popular standards as well as improvising his own new lines: Paul Desmond, *Desmond Blue* (Victor Jazz: 09026-68708-2 [LPM 2438], 1961). His hottest playing on record is cited in the next footnote.

22. Desmond loved to play in the alto's high range, and he was one of the first jazz altoists to use notes from the extreme high register, the *altissimo* range. Examples are on "Perdido" on Dave Brubeck, *Jazz at Oberlin* (Fantasy: OJCCD-046-2 [3245], 1953).

23. Art Pepper, *Modern Art* (Blue Note: 46848 [Intro 606], 1956), with Russ Freeman; *Intensity* (Fantasy: OJCCD-387-2 [Contemporary 7607], 1960). See also the autobiography: Art Pepper, *Straight Life* (Schirmer, 1979; DaCapo, 1994).

24. See footnote 13 above.

25. Chico Hamilton, *The Complete Pacific Jazz Recordings of the Chico Hamilton Quintet* (Mosaic: MD6-175, 6CD set, 1955–59) with Jim Hall and Buddy Collette; *Gong's East* (Discovery: 70831 [Warner Bros. 1271], 1958) with Eric Dolphy.

26. Among Hall's most famous recordings are two albums of duets with pianist Bill Evans: *Undercurrent* (Blue Note: 90583 [UA 14003], 1962) and *Intermodulation* (Verve: 833 771-2 [V6-8655], 1966). The music is pretty, with much continuity and originality. The austere and thoughtful conceptions of these two musicians are about as free from redundancy and cliché as any jazz recorded. Moreover, even without bass or drums, their music is insistent and swinging. Hall is also featured on several outstanding Paul Desmond albums. *Desmond Blue* (Victor Jazz: 09026-68708-2 [LPM 2438], 1961) contains some of his most relaxed and lyrical improvisations.

27. *The Dave Brubeck Octet* (Fantasy: OJCCD-101-2 [3-239], 1946,1948–49).

28. Other musicians have been attracted to Brubeck's tunes "In Your Own Sweet Way" and "The Duke." Miles Davis recorded "In Your Own Sweet Way" on *Workin'* (Fantasy: OJCCD-296-2 [Prestige 7166], 1956), and "The Duke" on *Miles Ahead* (Columbia: CK 53225 [CL 1041], 1957). For more about Brubeck, see Len Lyons, *The Great Jazz Pianists* (Quill; Morrow; DaCapo, 1983) 102–112, and Fred M. Hall, *It's About Time: The Dave Brubeck Story* (University of Arkansas Press, 1996).

29. Dave Brubeck, *Time Out* (Columbia: CK 65122 [CL 1397/CS 8192], 1959).

30. Brubeck, *Time Further Out* (Columbia CK 64668 [CS8490], 1961).

31. Fontana's first album as a leader is *The Great Fontana* (Uptown: 27.28, 1987). He also plays solos in Supersax, *Salt Peanuts* (Capitol: ST-11271, LP, 1973), and Stan Kenton, *Cuban Fire* (Capitol: 96260 [T731], 1956).

32. Brookmeyer's best work includes his recordings with Jimmy Giuffre and Jim Hall (*The Complete Capitol & Atlantic Recordings of Jimmy Giuffre*, Mosaic: MD6-176, 6CD set, 1954–58), and his recordings with Clark Terry (*Tonight*, Mainstream: 56043, LP, 1964). A good recording with Zoot Sims has been reissued: Zoot Sims, *The Rare Dawn Sessions* (Biograph BCD 131 [Dawn 1102], 1956). Albums he made with Gerry Mulligan occasionally come back into print and are worth looking for.

33. Stan Kenton, *New Concepts of Artistry in Rhythm* (Capitol: 92865, 1952).

Chapter Eleven

Cannonball and Nat Adderley Photo by Herman Leonard, Courtesy of Scott Asen–Metronome Collection

Hard Bop

Hard bop is a term that appeared during the 1950s to designate styles that had roots in bop but were somewhat different from the earliest bop and cool styles. At this time, musicians themselves tended to refer to all these styles merely as "bop" or "bebop." Journalists, however, coined new names based on the differing characteristics of the styles: hard bop, funky jazz, mainstream, post-bop, and soul jazz. Unfortunately, the new names were applied without much consistency. The result was that both the styles and the musicians who played them were often misrepresented. A few popular pieces by key musicians came to be seen as representative of those musicians' overall contribution to jazz. This happened even when the pieces were a small and uncharacteristic fraction of the musicians' output. This was especially unfair to such versatile jazz giants as Horace Silver, Cannonball Adderley, and Art Blakey because it typecast them as purveyors of "funky jazz," for instance. This also got out of hand because the style of their "funky" hits came to be equated with the overall category of hard bop, when it was really only a subcategory.[1]

The small slice of this music that sometimes has been termed "funky jazz" was more popular than any other segment of modern jazz except for a few cool jazz styles, although it was only a minor interest of the most talented modern jazz musicians who played it. The label "funky jazz" was attached most frequently to earthy, blues-drenched, gospelish pieces by

Horace Silver and others.[2] By way of Silver, this bluesy quality influenced a number of players who earned considerable popular attention in the 1960s and 1970s. It also influenced hundreds of lesser known pianists and organists performing in taverns and cocktail lounges.[3]

In the rest of this chapter we will examine a stream of styles that coexisted with "funky jazz" and was sometimes performed by the same musicians who included funky pieces in their repertory. This stream of styles has no single, widely accepted name. The terms "post-bop" and "mainstream" were offered by some writers, but they failed to catch on, apparently because they were not sufficiently specific. "Hard bop" is the designation we use in this textbook. The sounds of most styles within this stream often differ little from the sounds of bop. But when they do differ, the following trends frequently can be observed:

1) Improvised lines are somewhat simpler than bop lines.
2) Drummers play with more activity.
3) Tone colors are darker, weightier, and rougher.
4) The forms of the compositions are less frequently identical to pop tune forms, and the chord progressions are more frequently original rather than being borrowed from pop tunes.
5) There is somewhat less of the start-and-stop quality that leaves the listener off balance.
6) There is a hard-driving feeling that pushes relentlessly, with an emphasis on consistent swinging.
7) Piano comping has more variety in rhythms and chord voicings.

These characteristics were first apparent during the early 1950s in the work of trumpeter Clifford Brown and the bands led by drummer Art Blakey.[4] Later the characteristics persisted in the music of subsequent bands which included those same men. It also survived in the music of their associates and disciples (see Tables 11.1, 11.4, and 11.5). The musicians playing with Art Blakey and Horace Silver at any given time worked within this style almost without exception through the 1980s. Some of these characteristics were also evident in bands which departed more drastically from bop traditions, such as the groups led by Miles Davis between 1955 and 1961.[5]

The sounds described here were not exclusive to any particular geographic region. Forerunners of hard bop tenor sax styles included Los Angeles-based Dexter Gordon and New York-based Sonny Stitt. Important models for trumpeters included New York-based Miles Davis and Fats Navarro. In addition, Philadelphia and Detroit (see Table 11.3) contributed many vital players, and Indianapolis contributed guitarist Wes Montgomery (see page 198), trumpeter Freddie Hubbard (discussed on page 192), and trombonist Slide Hampton (see page 203).

A second wave of players can be distinguished within the overall category of hard bop. Much of their music draws upon sources outside hard bop (discussed in later chapters) and goes beyond it by devising its own stream of styles. These players made their mark in the 1960s and derived their approaches less directly from bop than did those players mentioned above. With the notable exception of saxophonist John Coltrane, who died in 1967, the most prominent among this group were still active through the 1990s and remained models for aspiring jazz musicians. The outstanding tenor saxophonists in this second wave of hard bop musicians are Joe Henderson (discussed later) and Wayne Shorter (discussed in the next chapter). The top trumpeter is Freddie Hubbard (discussed later). The pianists are McCoy Tyner (see chapter 13), Herbie Hancock, Chick Corea, and Keith Jarrett (all discussed in chapter 15). The drummers are Tony Williams (see next chapter) and Elvin Jones

TABLE 11.1 A Few of the Many Hard Bop Style Musicians

TRUMPET
Clifford Brown
Kenny Dorham
Miles Davis
Blue Mitchell
Donald Byrd
Thad Jones
Art Farmer
Bill Hardman
Joe Gordon
Carmell Jones
Lee Morgan
Freddie Hubbard
Wilbur Harden
Tommy Turrentine
Benny Bailey
Booker Little
Nat Adderley

BARITONE SAX
Pepper Adams
Cecil Payne
Nick Brignola

ORGAN
Jimmy Smith
Jack McDuff
Richard "Groove" Holmes
Don Patterson
Jimmy McGriff
Shirley Scott

COMPOSER-ARRANGERS
Horace Silver
Benny Golson
Gigi Gryce
Oliver Nelson
Cannonball Adderley
Nat Adderley
Wayne Shorter
Bobby Timmons
J. J. Johnson
Jackie McLean
Tom McIntosh

TENOR SAX
Sonny Rollins
John Coltrane
Jimmy Heath
Frank Foster
Clifford Jordan
Teddy Edwards
Benny Golson
Billy Mitchell
George Coleman
John Gilmore
Oliver Nelson
Stanley Turrentine
Junior Cook
Booker Ervin
Joe Henderson
Wayne Shorter
Hank Mobley
Harold Land
J. R. Monterose
Tina Brooks
Yusef Lateef

TROMBONE
J. J. Johnson
Curtis Fuller
Jimmy Knepper
Jimmy Cleveland
Frank Rehak
Tom McIntosh

ALTO SAX
Cannonball Adderley
Jackie McLean
Lou Donaldson
Gigi Gryce
Frank Strozier
Phil Woods

BASS
Paul Chambers
Sam Jones
Doug Watkins
Wilbur Ware
Bob Cranshaw
Gene Taylor
Reggie Workman
Percy Heath
Jymie Merritt
Butch Warren
Larry Ridley

GUITAR
Wes Montgomery
Kenny Burrell
Grant Green

DRUMS
Philly Joe Jones
Roy Brooks
Louis Hayes
Art Taylor
Roy Haynes
Roger Humphries
Elvin Jones
Lex Humphries
Max Roach
Art Blakey
Mickey Roker
Al Heath
Ben Riley
Jimmy Cobb
Frankie Dunlop
Billy Higgins

PIANO
Tommy Flanagan
Barry Harris
Cedar Walton
Duke Pearson
Bobby Timmons
Red Garland
Wynton Kelly
Joe Zawinul
Junior Mance
Kenny Drew
Horace Parlan
Les McCann
Gene Harris
Ramsey Lewis
Horace Silver
Elmo Hope
Sonny Clark

TABLE 11.2 COMPARING STYLES OF THE 1950S

	COOL	HARD BOP
tone color	light	dark
tone weight	light	heavy
tone texture	soft	raw
melodic conception	simple	complex
overall character	relaxed cool	hard-driving fiery
principal influences	swing and bop	bop
sources for alto saxophone styles	Lee Konitz	Charlie Parker
sources for trumpet styles	Miles Davis	Dizzy Gillespie Fats Navarro Miles Davis
sources for tenor saxophone styles	Lester Young	Dexter Gordon Sonny Stitt Don Byas
sources for arranging practices	Claude Thornhill Gil Evans	Todd Dameron

(see chapter 13). You may recognize some of these names grouped here with the 1950s and 1960s for other styles that were developed in the 1970s. However, if we recall the versatility that is so common to jazz giants, it should not be difficult to comprehend, for example, Herbie Hancock's contributing significantly to hard bop during the early 1960s and then creating new styles in the jazz-rock fusion genres of the 1970s and 1980s.

Piano

There were a number of excellent pianists affiliated with hard bop (see Table 11.1). Two of the most prominent were **Tommy Flanagan** (1930–2001) and Horace Silver. Flanagan was influenced primarily by Teddy Wilson, Bud Powell, Art Tatum, and Hank Jones. He had more instrumental proficiency than almost any other hard bop pianist. His touch was very clean, his lines well conceived and effortlessly played. Yet in spite of his meticulous attention to technique, Flanagan managed to extract a warm tone from the piano. His tasteful comping, flowing solos, and polite touch provided a perfect complement to trumpeter Miles Davis, saxophonists Sonny Rollins and John Coltrane, and guitarist Wes Montgomery, whom he accompanied on many of their outstanding albums.[6] Flanagan went on to a long tenure as accompanist for singer Ella Fitzgerald and later remained active as leader of his own groups in the 1980s and 1990s.

Horace Silver (b. 1928) is one of the biggest names in hard bop because of his outstanding work as a composer and bandleader. He also developed an original and substantial piano style. By the 1960s, he had replaced bop's emphasis on long, convoluted lines with his own brief, catchy phrases. Virtuosity is not essential to Silver's style. He almost never double-times. Succinctness and clarity are far higher priorities than speed and agility. His ideas

TABLE 11.3 TWO CITIES CONTRIBUTED MANY LEADING HARD BOP PLAYERS

PHILADELPHIA	DETROIT
Clifford Brown	Thad Jones
Lee Morgan	Elvin Jones
McCoy Tyner	Hank Jones
Philly Joe Jones	Barry Harris
Jimmy Heath	Charles McPherson
Percy Heath	Roland Hanna
John Coltrane	Tommy Flanagan
Bobby Timmons	Paul Chambers
Benny Golson	Ron Carter
Bill Barron	Louis Hayes
Kenny Barron	Yusef Lateef
	Kenny Burrell
	Donald Byrd
	Billy Mitchell
	Doug Watkins
	Pepper Adams
	Curtis Fuller

unfold with a logic that is apparent even to the novice listener. Silver made considerable use of silence and employed an exacting deliberation in timing the starting and stopping points of his phrases. His improvised melodic figures are executed in a very forceful, percussive way. His solos are like his tunes—filled with simple ideas that are hummable and easy to remember. It is as though, while improvising, Silver keeps on composing at the same level of creativity and clarity that he maintains in his writing.[7]

As an accompanist, Horace Silver initially drew from bop style. By the late 1950s, however, he had perfected a new style of accompaniment. This approach used figures that sounded like prewritten setups for his soloists. This contrasted with the approach of spontaneously chording in manners that followed the shifting directions taken by the solo improvisations. In this way, the soloists in Silver's bands were supported by backgrounds similar to those in big bands, where written arrangements supply the same accompaniment figures each time the soloist improvises on that piece. The effects were twofold. There was more continuity in Silver's music than in the music produced by the comparatively informal structure of most modern groups. Yet these figures were also a restriction that limited the range of moods an improvising soloist could create. By comparison with traditional bop comping, however, Silver's accompaniment figures gave listeners something to cling to, and this may account for his greater popularity.

Horace Silver was hard bop's most prolific composer. For the Blue Note record company alone, he penned almost all the tunes on over twenty-five years worth of his bands' albums. Silver put together arrangements that were generally more elaborate than those of other hard bop groups. They often contained ensemble strains in the middle of a piece, as well as Latin American rhythms and hints of gospel music. Silver often voiced trumpet and tenor

Horace Silver, the leading composer-pianist-bandleader in hard bop. Prolific and versatile, Silver composed catchy themes and arranged them for his quintets. His music swung with an appealing crispness and bounce. Many of his pieces had a funky, gospelish quality that became widely influential.

Photo by Bob Parent. Courtesy of Don Parent

saxophone four or five scale steps apart. This was a particularly successful way to achieve a fullness that made the quintet sound as though it contained more than five musicians. In addition to using this technique, Silver often wrote bass figures and played them on the piano in unison with his bassist. These figures had an engaging quality which expanded the usually limited scope of bop bass lines. It is partly for these reasons that his quintet's identity was unlike that of any other bop or hard bop group. In addition, Silver's quintet performances were consistently swinging and polished, and they featured many of the best musicians of the 1950s and 1960s (see Table 11.4). Silver remained active in the 1990s and continued to tour and record with bands of similar style and instrumentation.[8]

Trumpet

The order of major influences on modern trumpeters begins in the 1940s with Dizzy Gillespie, then Miles Davis and Fats Navarro. However, it was the successor to these men who had the greatest impact. His name was **Clifford Brown** (1930–1956), and he drew his style largely from Navarro, with a touch of Davis. Among musicians, Brown is probably the most widely admired trumpeter since the swing era. Brown, however, is not widely known outside the inner circles of modern jazz musicians, and he was documented on recordings from only 1952 to 1956. He did not use the peculiar note choices that typified Gillespie, nor did he convey the intimate moods that distinguished Davis. By comparison with Gillespie and Davis, he played at a high level of inspiration and execution more consistently from performance to performance. Brown used a wider, more deliberate vibrato than Gillespie or Davis, something Navarro had occasionally employed. Brown's use of a slow, even, very obvious vibrato may be responsible for its renewed use by jazz trumpeters in the 1950s and 1960s. Another distinguishing mark of Brown's style is the overall contour of his solos. Jazz historian Harvey Pekar has observed that Brown's solos are similar to those of Davis because they jump into the high register less often than Gillespie's and Navarro's, and the contours of Brown's and Davis's lines are usually smoother than Gillespie's and Navarro's. Because of this, we might regard Brown's solos as cooler than most hard bop, even though his solos are not as simple as the most

TABLE 11.4 A Few of the Many Horace Silver Sidemen

TRUMPET	SAXOPHONE	DRUMS
Blue Mitchell	Hank Mobley	Roy Brooks
Art Farmer	Bob Berg	Louis Hayes
Tom Harrell	Junior Cook	Al Foster
Woody Shaw	Joe Henderson	Billy Cobham
Randy Brecker	Michael Brecker	

concise solos of Chet Baker or Miles Davis. It is evident that Brown drew upon previous styles, but he also devised a style that was distinguishable from his sources.

Let's consider several reasons that musicians were so impressed with Clifford Brown's playing. Most prominent was that Brown managed to suggest relaxation in his playing, even when executing intricate melodic figures. This has at least two possible causes: the perfection he achieved in making the trumpet obey his wishes, and his concern with simplifying bop instead of blazing new trails as Parker and Gillespie had. Brown also placed more emphasis on swinging than on generating surprise after surprise, as bop soloists often did. Tuneful improvisations were more common for him than for most of his contemporaries.[9] In these respects, Brown's work on trumpet parallels Sonny Stitt's work on saxophone. Brown refined a repertory of phrases and ways of moving gracefully through the chord progressions. Brown's style proved accessible to many other trumpeters because of these techniques, their fluid sensibility, and the easy swing feeling they produced. As with Stitt, Brown's contributions were also absorbed as stock vocabulary for hard bop players.

Clifford Brown's music projected a joyful spirit. This, together with the lilt and bounce in his lines, was contagious. He could generate long, flowing lines at furious tempos and still maintain the warmth and suppleness of his wide, glowing tone. Most other trumpeters stood in awe of Brown's dazzling speed and agility. Also, he did what is almost impossible at those frantic speeds: he kept his accurate intonation and relaxed swing feeling. His firm command of accurate articulation was unparalleled in modern jazz, and he was able to make meaty phrases come tumbling from his horn, chorus after chorus. An exuberance projected by Brown's music combined with his assured manner, pretty sound, and fertile imagination to influence an entire generation of modern trumpeters, including Donald Byrd, Bill Hardman, Louis Smith, Lee Morgan, and Carmell Jones. It inspired another group of players during the 1980s and 1990s, including Roy Hargrove, Phil Harper, Marlon Jordan, and others.

Miles Davis and Clifford Brown remained models for aspiring trumpeters to imitate long after they first became known among musicians. But by the 1970s, the majority of young trumpeters, including such notables as Woody Shaw and Randy Brecker, were imitating another model: **Freddie Hubbard.** Though his early playing drew from Clifford Brown, Miles Davis, and Chet Baker, Hubbard (b. 1938) had developed his own original approach by the early 1960s. His playing style departed from bop and was compatible with "free jazz" approaches of the 1960s and "jazz-rock" approaches of the 1970s.[10]

A number of characteristics can help us distinguish Hubbard from Brown and Davis. Although he incorporated some Davis methods of manipulating his tone quality and pitch, Hubbard steered clear of the way in which Davis gets away from the beat. Hubbard stuck close to the beat and liked to double-time. In contrast to the solemn and methodical manner of Davis, much of Hubbard's work sounds offhanded and playful. There is a looseness to his fashion that implies great creative freedom and tremendous conceptual flexibility. Instead of following through on every idea, he did not hesitate to interrupt himself if he got a new idea while he was playing an old one. His style bristles with excitement; even his ballad renditions project great verve. Like those of saxophonist John Coltrane, his improvisations exhibit a willingness to spontaneously construct and rework figures from odd combinations of notes and rhythms, not depending on stock bop phrases. In this way he was harmonically daring and impulsive. The richness and range of his imagination combined with his free manner to build a new vocabulary for jazz trumpet style.[11]

Freddie Hubbard is almost universally envied among trumpeters for his outstanding mastery of the instrument. His tone was clear and well focused. His intonation was excellent. His articulation was crisp, and he could improvise coherently at brisk tempos and sound as though he still had plenty of strength and agility in reserve. Like Brown's, Hubbard's sense of time was very precise. Hubbard also mastered a very demanding technique called a lip trill, in which, without changing fingering or shaking the trumpet, he rapidly alternated, in legato manner, intervals of a minor third, moving the bottom note in stepwise fashion. This became a trademark of his highly virtuosic style.[12]

Drums

The period in jazz history that produced hard bop also produced several innovative accompaniment styles of jazz drumming. Chico Hamilton has been discussed already in the unit about West Coast style cool jazz. Like Hamilton, several other innovative drummers were also important as bandleaders. Art Blakey and Max Roach are discussed here because their bands, not just their drumming, were at the forefront of hard bop. Philly Joe Jones is also discussed here because his contribution parallels that of Blakey in helping define the accompanying style in hard bop. Elvin Jones is not discussed until the John Coltrane chapter because, though he performed innovatively during the 1950s, his innovations were most widely showcased with Coltrane in the 1960s.

Art Blakey (1919–1991) epitomized the loosening of jazz drumming style, whereby loud, directive intrusions emerged at the forefront of the combo sound. Blakey's playing as an accompanist was so dynamic that for him to solo was almost anticlimactic. He was able to cue and underscore transitions within each piece by the figures he played and the various levels of loudness he used for them. He was often found to be directing the mood and choosing the moments during which tension was to rise or fall. His former sidemen have mentioned how he made them aware of pacing their improvisations and trying to build tension and excitement gradually over the course of their solos.[13]

For over thirty years, Art Blakey led quintets and sextets that were representatives of the hard bop style. Their music was extremely intense, hard driving, and uncompromising. Their swing feeling was unrelenting and possessed a weightiness that distinguished it from those "cool jazz" styles that also swung persistently. The list of notable musicians in Blakey's bands is immense. (Table 11.5 mentions only a few.) These players often received their first wide exposure to jazz fans while they toured and recorded with him. Many of them soon became leaders of their own groups. Ordinarily, Blakey hired individualists who were relatively young but played very well and sounded distinctive. Their compositions became Blakey's repertory. The character of those compositions, in turn, became part of the band's character.

Art Blakey, hard bop drummer and bandleader. The sound of Blakey's bands helped define hard bop. They played with hard-driving, unrelenting force, always swinging with a compelling seriousness of purpose. Blakey continued to hire the top musicians for four decades, including Clifford Brown, Horace Silver, Wayne Shorter, Freddie Hubbard, Wynton and Branford Marsalis.

Photo by Bernie Thrasher, Courtesy of Robert Asen–Metronome Collection

Max Roach made his reputation during the bop era and then continued to develop new bands and drumming approaches. He is best and most importantly recognized as the fountainhead of bebop and hard bop drumming styles, more so than Blakey or Philly Joe Jones. Roach is routinely cited for his clean touch and discreet accompanying, and because he does not flaunt his proficiency. He is known for intelligently developed solos that are often melodic, and a command of the drum set that never overshadows his musical sense. Few modern drummers have escaped his influence. (See chapter 9 for more about his playing.) He continued to lead hard bop-style bands during the 1990s. Roach is singled out for mention again in this chapter because he founded one of the great bands in hard bop. It was a quintet with Clifford Brown, which toured from 1954 until Brown's death in 1956.[14]

Philly Joe Jones (1923–1985) was among the most adventurous of rhythm section players in the 1950s. Next to Max Roach, Jones is the most widely cited influence among drummers who emerged during the 1960s. Compared with other drummers, he played more figures, and his activity was more conversation-like. His playing often sounded as though he were reacting instantaneously to the improvisations of his fellow band members by complementing them. His fills are models of originality and assured execution that are often as melodic as the horn lines they complement. His work conveyed a constant excitement. His crisp fills on the snare drum, accents on the bass drum, and splashes on the cymbal were so well conceived that they became models of how active drummers could be without disturbing the pulse.[15]

TABLE 11.5 A Few of the Many Art Blakey Sidemen

Clifford Brown	Junior Mance
Donald Byrd	Keith Jarrett
Bill Hardman	Curtis Fuller
Lee Morgan	Wynton Marsalis
Freddie Hubbard	Bobby Timmons
Woody Shaw	George Cables
Jackie McLean	Reggie Workman
Hank Mobley	Jymie Merritt
Wayne Shorter	Lou Donaldson
Benny Golson	Dave Schnitter
Johnny Griffin	Bobby Watson
Chuck Mangione	James Williams
Horace Silver	Valerie Ponomarev
Cedar Walton	Ira Sullivan

Saxophone

Cannonball Adderley (1928–1975) was one of the best improvisers to play alto saxophone after Charlie Parker died. In fact, some listeners considered Adderley to be Parker's successor, though Adderley himself felt such praise was undeserved. In a few respects, Adderley's style is like Parker's: highly fluid, supercharged, and unpredictable. However, Adderley initially derived his style not from Parker but from the swing era styles of Pete Brown and Benny Carter. Then he drew from Parker and Eddie Vinson, and his later style demonstrated advances made by John Coltrane. During his creative peak of 1957 to 1959, when he played with Miles Davis and John Coltrane, Adderley's solos were filled with little melodies. His command over the instrument vied with the virtuosity attained by Parker and Coltrane. Adderley's ability to keep up with Coltrane and sometimes surpass him was an indication of his stunning improvisational prowess.[16]

The tone quality that Cannonball Adderley extracted from the alto saxophone was so deep and full that listeners sometimes mistook it for tenor saxophone. (Listen to *Demo CD* Tracks 72 and 73 to acquaint yourself with the differences between alto and tenor sax sounds. Then listen to "Flamenco Sketches" on the *Jazz Classics CD*, and compare Adderley's sound with Coltrane's. Another excellent comparison is available in "Two Bass Hit" on the *Jazz Classics CD* for *Concise Guide to Jazz*. Some consider it to be Adderley's best solo on record.)

Together with the vibrato Adderley used, the effect of his tone was warm and glowing. He bent this huge tone with blue notes and wails, thereby creating an earthy, legato style that has been called "blues drenched."[17] Contrasting with the solemn urgency of most hard bop, Adderley's playing conveys a sense of fun. He loved to double-time, and he often incorporated snippets of pop tunes into his lines.[18] A feeling of exhilaration is present when he digs into an improvisation and starts spinning out inspired lines, with their dense activity and ever shifting directions. But Adderley was not entirely bouncy and lighthearted; he could also

Max Roach, the top drummer in bop, known for increasing spontaneous musical communication with the soloists he accompanied. Roach popularized the "chattering" in bop style drumming. Having been one of the most-recorded sidemen of the 1940s, Roach became a prominent bandleader in the 1950s and remained active in the 1990s as drummer, bandleader, and composer.

© Mosaic Images/CORBIS

evoke calm and reflection. For instance, his solos on the Davis album *Kind of Blue* sound quite reflective, and they are among the most original improvisations he recorded. (One of these is in "Flamenco Sketches" on the *Jazz Classics CD.*)[19]

On and off during the 1950s, 60s, and 70s, Cannonball Adderley co-led a series of bands with his brother, cornetist Nat Adderley. The groups enjoyed a large following and continued until Cannonball's death in 1975. Many pieces in the band's repertory constituted what journalists dubbed "funky jazz": "Jive Samba," "Work Song," "Sack o' Woe," and their biggest hit, "Mercy, Mercy, Mercy": Though most of its repertory was swinging music with little dilution of the bop style, the group was best known for its funk hits, "Mercy, Mercy, Mercy," "Walk Tall," and "Country Preacher."

There were many excellent tenor saxophonists in hard bop (see Table 11.1). Although an entire book would be required to do them justice, we will consider four stand-outs: John Coltrane, Sonny Rollins, Joe Henderson, and Wayne Shorter. John Coltrane created an original hard bop style that is well represented by recordings he made in the 1950s with the bands of Miles Davis. (Listen to him on "Flamenco Sketches" on the *Jazz Classics CD.*) We postpone our discussion of Coltrane to a special chapter because of the size and originality of his contributions, his stature in hard bop, his large body of unique compositions, his two other new saxophone styles, and his original band style. In the present chapter, we will briefly discuss Sonny Rollins. Some feel he had his creative peak during the 1950s. He remains the favorite jazz tenor for many musicians. Then we will examine Joe Henderson, a significant saxophonist-composer-bandleader who was important in new developments during a 1960s and 1970s phase of hard bop. In the following chapter, we will evaluate Wayne Shorter, whose contribution to jazz history was threefold: he played hard bop with Art Blakey from

1959 to 1964, devised new approaches to composition and improvisation in the Miles Davis quintet of 1964 to 1969, and developed jazz-rock fusion from 1970 to 1985 with a band called Weather Report.

Sonny Rollins (b. 1930) was among the most popular tenor saxophonists of the 1950s. Though he is known today for his originality, Rollins was among the first group of musicians to adopt Charlie Parker's alto sax style for use on tenor.[20] He began recording in 1949, and his name is often mentioned along with Charlie Parker, Sonny Stitt, and John Coltrane when saxophonists themselves list their favorites.

Rollins was widely admired for the way he improvised simple melodic ideas and then developed them, producing solos that possessed integrity and continuity. His clarity of mind allowed him to transcend cliché figures, even at the high speeds which ordinarily push saxophonists to use easily fingered patterns instead of original melodic ideas.[21]

During the 1950s, the Rollins timbre was hard, rough, and dry. It was not as deep or richly textured as Coltrane's. Some listeners called it "brittle." His vibrato was slow and very deliberate. Rollins differed from the majority of bop tenor saxophonists by using staccato phrasing instead of the almost exclusively legato style favored by them. He could manage a blunt attack, move to legato and back again to staccato. His phrases were delivered without ornamentation or any other kind of softening. The overall effect of his playing was abrupt and, though aggressive, it was not necessarily explosive or blistering.

Sonny Rollins is a giant in the history of improvisation. He mastered the rhythmic devices necessary to swing, and he swung whenever he wished. But he also purposely deviated from the tempo at times, as if he were inside the beat one moment and ignoring it the next. Rollins treated a piece as though its tempo, chord progressions, and melody were mere toys to be played with. He instantaneously redesigned them from moment to moment without reverence for their original flavor.[22]

Some listeners feel that Rollins's career reached its peak during the 1950s, that he did his most lyrical playing with Miles Davis[23] and his most swinging playing with Clifford Brown.[24] Regardless of whether you agree, there is no question that Rollins's recordings in the 1950s constitute landmarks in the history of tenor saxophone style.[25]

During the 1960s, Rollins streamlined his style[26] and explored less conventional approaches to improvisation.[27] During the 1970s, 80s, and 90s, Rollins usually played in a way that differed significantly from his style of the 1950s and 60s. He adopted a timbre that was broader, coarser, and more guttural. In addition, his playing had less speed and crispness of execution. Some of his lines recalled those of saxophonists associated with the popular music known as rhythm and blues. By contrast with his earlier style, his playing became simpler and funkier. Rollins retained his allegiance to lyricism, but now his roots in Charlie Parker were barely detectable. The tunes he performed were simpler, too, and their accompaniments resembled those of popular dance styles such as disco, funk, and Latin. Although Rollins occasionally returned to more bop-like playing (as with the Milestone Jazz Stars), his preferred approach during this period remained so simple and funky that it fit perfectly with the style of the Rolling Stones, the popular blues-oriented rock and roll group that used him on one of their recordings.[28] Twenty years after being the top hard bop tenor, Sonny Rollins had mastered a new style and gained a fresh audience.

Joe Henderson (1937–2001) was a tenor saxophonist who managed to gain considerable attention among musicians at a time when the mammoth specter of John Coltrane blotted out almost all tenors other than Stan Getz and Sonny Rollins. During the 1970s, Coltrane's was the most widely imitated approach to jazz tenor, with the influence of Michael Brecker joining it during the 1980s. Many players of the 1970s and 1980s incorporated selected parts of Henderson's approach. His influence was heard frequently during the 1980s and 1990s. By comparison with Rollins and Coltrane, however, Henderson influenced fewer saxophonists seeking to imitate completely a single style model.

Henderson's own origins were diverse. He had cited a number of different models, including Lester Young, Sonny Rollins, and John Coltrane. He had said that Stan Getz was his main influence, but Henderson also recalled Junior Cook (1934–1992), a saxophonist known for his recordings with the Horace Silver quintet of 1958 to 1964.[29] Like Cook, Henderson capitalized on melodic fragments in a hard, insistent way. However, he was less raw-sounding, more fluid and agile than Cook. Also, Henderson had an ability to play extremely quick figures with uncanny accuracy. Some of Henderson's solos sound free of hard bop traditions for solo improvisation. The result is a style that many choose not to call hard bop. Though rarely called "free jazz" either, it is a new approach with a feeling that differs considerably from Parker's and Coltrane's. Henderson had a vocabulary all his own. Rather than playing strings of notes that are all equal, Henderson used a wide variety of note durations. For example, he might combine eighth notes, triplets, sixteenth notes, and uneven groupings instead of playing uninterrupted eighth notes in long strings, as other saxophonists usually do. He interspersed shakes, trills, and wails in a knife-like way. These tendencies together lend his playing a speech-like effect.

Henderson often began his lines with brief figures which he then developed with many transformations, following through on each of his ideas. In many respects, these ideas do not represent a way to navigate through the chord progressions as much as they pose a sound to pit against the rhythm section's activity. He could swing conventionally or intentionally play free of the tempo by developing melodic figures that do not neatly fit with the beats beneath them. Intense, provocative lines spilled from his horn. Some contain syncopated staccato figures, alternating with churning legato phrases. Sometimes he employed well-controlled shrieks. He varied the speed of his vibrato, also. Henderson's playing conveyed the impression that he possessed a freedom to think very fast and clearly during the heat of improvising, and to play exactly what he thought, unhindered by the mechanical limitations of his instrument.[30]

Trombone

It was unusual to find trombone in hard bop groups, but there were first-rate trombone soloists playing in some bands (see Table 11.1). Incidentally, attaching the "hard bop" designation to any trombonist of the 1950s and 1960s might not be meaningful because most who played with hard bop bands had styles that differed little from bop. **J. J. Johnson** was the most prominent trombonist of the period. He had already earned a respected place among bop instrumentalists during the late 1940s and early 1950s (see chapter 9).[31] Johnson was the most visible of all trombonists in the 1950s and 1960s, not only because he was an excellent improviser but also because he recorded numerous albums as a bandleader. Johnson streamlined his style during the 1960s and put together bands that made music which felt less rushed than bop. Also, several of the tunes he wrote for these bands had a funky flavor that we tend to associate with hard bop.[32] Another trombonist, **Curtis Fuller** (b. 1934), was an equally impressive improviser, yet most of his career was spent as a sideman. Consequently, he never achieved Johnson's high level of public recognition.[33] His recordings with Art Blakey and John Coltrane are outstanding.

Guitar

There were few guitarists in the hard bop style of the 1950s, just as there had been only a few guitarists in the bop style of the 1940s. The most influential of these musicians was **Wes Montgomery** (1925–1968). Using his thumb instead of a pick, Montgomery extracted a tone from his guitar that was round and full. Some of his lines are voiced in octaves, a sound that became closely identified with him. (Listen to the *Demo CD* Track 87 for examples of guitar lines in octaves and comparison of sounds extracted by pick and finger.) Influenced by Charlie Christian, Montgomery played in a style that was relaxed and melodic. It projected an assured sense of swing and an unhurried, pleasant manner. His playing exudes naturalness, and most listeners perceive the overall effect to be warm and pleasant.

Montgomery systematically developed his solo improvisations in a way that began cool and built tension over several choruses to a climax. Then he would stop altogether or begin the process again. Frequently he began with lines made up of only a single note at a time, then voiced his lines in octaves, then, after a chorus of octaves, he concluded with a chorded solo. In this way, he made his sound successively thicker and more exciting in each chorus.

Montgomery's peak of creativity was the late 1950s and early 1960s. He is best known, however, for later recordings made for the Verve and A & M firms. For these popular albums, the studios provided preset orchestral accompaniments, over which Montgomery paraphrased pop tunes and improvised lightly. He played tastefully on these recordings, but his earlier work, available mostly on albums made for Riverside, is a far richer jazz vein.[34]

After Wes Montgomery, the best known hard bop guitarist is **Kenny Burrell** (b. 1931). Sources for Burrell's style included Charlie Christian and Oscar Moore. Burrell also drew from bop-style sax and trumpet lines[35] and from the funky melodic figures identified with pianist Horace Silver. Although he is quite versatile, Burrell is particularly well known for his soulful playing on bluesy albums made with organist Jimmy Smith. Most of these albums featured relatively uncomplicated music with which he established a swinging, easygoing mood. As a result, they attained considerable popularity.[36]

Bass

The instrumental prowess of bassists steadily grew as jazz evolved. Hard bop was marked by further milestones. When young bass players of the period asked, "Who should I be listening to?" the names **Paul Chambers** (1935–1969) and **Sam Jones** (1924–1981) were added to those of Ray Brown and Charles Mingus. Chambers became widely known through the recordings he made with Miles Davis between 1955 and 1963. Sam Jones is best remembered for his work with Cannonball Adderley's groups of 1957 to 1966.[37]

Paul Chambers produced a huge, dark sound on his bass. The notes he chose for walking formed a continuous harmonic complement. The propulsive way he delivered his notes played a crucial rhythmic role. (Listen to *Demo CD* Track 21 for bass techniques.) The phrases in his solo improvisations were bop-style and hornlike. These lines were sensible and swinging, possessing melodic and rhythmic richness. Chambers also expanded the solo potential of jazz bass playing by demonstrating a mastery over his instrument and a compositional approach to improvisation not ordinarily associated with the bass.[38]

Big Bands

During the late 1950s and through the 1960s, several big bands drew from the sound of hard bop. The three most prominent were led by trumpeters **Maynard Ferguson** (b. 1928), **Gerald Wilson** (b. 1918), and **Thad Jones** (1923–1986). The Jones band was co-led by drummer Mel Lewis, who took over sole leadership when Jones left in 1979. The Ferguson and Wilson bands began during the late 1950s. The Jones-Lewis band was formed in 1965. The groups led by Jones and Wilson were initially founded mostly for the musical enjoyment of freelance jazz musicians living in New York and Los Angeles, respectively. They began as rehearsal bands (also known as "kicks bands") and rarely performed away from home with their personnel intact. Most of the Jones-Lewis performances took place on Monday nights at a New York nightclub called the Village Vanguard. Of the three bands, only Ferguson's toured widely, sold many records, or became known much outside of relatively small markets.

Many great musicians played with these bands over the years. Ferguson's generally had the youngest and least-known musicians, whereas the earliest Jones-Lewis and Wilson groups were all-star bands. Wilson employed some of the best bop-style musicians to be found outside of New York, several of whom had become known to jazz fans long before they recorded with him. Among the musicians in the Jones-Lewis band, many already had made outstanding jazz records as bandleaders themselves. Like Jones, a few were pivotal figures from the fertile hard bop scene in Detroit (see Table 11.3).[39] Some of those same men were highly individualistic improvisers who, like Jones himself, had already made significant contributions to the explorative bands of Charles Mingus (see chapter 14).[40]

Thad Jones is often ranked as one of the best and most original trumpeters in hard bop. His improvisations were unorthodox and daring.[41] They often contained odd intervals that were not natural to the trumpet and were as difficult as they were unique. Jones was a storehouse of imagination, and Charles Mingus, among others, ranked Jones as a musical genius. He changed his instruments, too; he was one of very few modern trumpeters to frequently perform on cornet, and he also played fluegelhorn extensively (see page 112 for illustrations).

The styles of most soloists in the earliest Jones-Lewis band can best be categorized as bop or hard bop. Much of the band's music, however, had a feeling that was lighter than the weighty, solemn intensity that is projected by most hard bop. This was partly due to the style of Jones's compositions, which were often light, playful, and full of surprises. They were filled with silences which served as ventilation. They stressed soft, staccato phrases produced by sound qualities that were well-contained. They also possessed an alternation of funky unison lines with thickly voiced chordal passages. There is a pixie lightness and humor to Jones's melodic rhythms, and he often maintained a suspended feeling by using unconventional accompaniment patterns. He used frequently shifting densities, and occasionally deleted the rhythm section suddenly in the middle of a piece. Although the lines Jones wrote were often very difficult to play, his musicians executed them with finesse. The harmonies he constructed were rarely ordinary; they were rich without sounding muddy or affected. Jones occasionally wrote chords containing eight of the twelve notes in the chromatic scale (as in "Three In One"), a technique that is unusual among big band arrangers. (Sammy Nestico's writing for Count Basie, for example, is typically in four-note chords.) These practices contrast with the ordinary big band arrangers' penchant for massiveness and unceasing sound. Even when his melodies sound almost homespun ("Don't Get Sassy" and "Big Dipper"), they are placed in very thick chord voicings.[42] His melodies show a strong allegiance to the funky, blues tradition ("Big Dipper"), somewhat reminiscent of Horace Silver, though placed in a more elaborate setting. Jones's writing earned him great respect among jazz arrangers, and his pieces found their way into textbooks for jazz composers. He invented such a distinctive arranging style that listeners can often identify it by hearing only a single chord. The Jones arranging style was one of the most original to appear since Duke Ellington's.

The differences between the Jones-Lewis sound and that of other big bands in hard bop were also due partly to approaches employed by the band's bassist, **Richard Davis,** and its drummer, Mel Lewis. Davis contributed concepts to a big band setting that roughly paralleled what Charles Mingus and Scott LaFaro had given to combo settings: In addition to playing walking bass lines, Davis improvised accompaniments containing a great variety of fresh melodic and rhythmic figures that vigorously interacted with the solo and ensemble lines. (This approach was not new for Davis, who was already much admired for his innovative playing in avant-garde combos of the 1960s.) Compatible with the loosening and lightening done by Davis was the light, discreet drumming of **Mel Lewis** (1929–1990), whose style avoided the heavy, aggressive approaches of hard bop. A uniquely flexible accompanist, Lewis is well known for his unerring swing, versatility, and good taste.

Jazz big bands have traditionally been rooted in styles of eras earlier than the one at hand. In addition, solos have been routinely brief and frequently interrupted by screaming ensemble figures. The Jones band stood apart from these traditions. It offered plenty of uncluttered solo space to its improvisers and achieved a flexible interaction between the rhythm section and improvising soloists. During many moments in its performances, the band sounded like an up-to-date modern jazz combo. In this way it recalled Count Basie's big band of the 1930s, which often operated as an oversized combo.

Gerald Wilson was a respected composer-arranger long before he became identified with his hard bop big band. The Jimmie Lunceford and Duke Ellington bands were among the outstanding groups which had performed his work. In his band of the late 1950s and early 1960s, however, Wilson molded a unique new sound from several sources. He used outstanding hard bop soloists who played with the ferocity and bluesy mood which jazz fans had come to expect from the combos of Art Blakey, Horace Silver, and Cannonball Adderley. He used an original arranging style. It was spare, not intricate. It did not jump around, nor was it light and playful. It was hard and relentless. Each piece created and sustained a consistent mood. Thirdly, he emphasized depth of feeling; more often than not, that feeling was dark and serious. By comparison with all other big bands, the Wilson band achieved a groove that more closely resembled hard bop. The moods were funky and earthy, as though Wilson had created a big band equivalent to the organ/tenor sax combos that were common at inner-city taverns during the 1950s and 1960s.[43]

Another unique characteristic of Wilson's sound was a modal flavor. Brief, wailing phrases in a minor key were repeated again and again, over a propelling rhythm. The chords changed slowly, allowing soloists to build their ideas and raise tension over a longer time than bop progressions allowed. Several of the pieces in this genre were compositions Wilson adapted after they had been introduced by Miles Davis ("Milestones," "So What," "Freddie the Freeloader"). Others were Wilson originals ("Moment of Truth," "Viva Tirado") that had the raw ferocity of hard bop as well as a certain exoticism.[44]

Before the hard bop era, **Maynard Ferguson** had already achieved a reputation as trumpeter with big bands led by Charlie Barnet, Boyd Raeburn, and Stan Kenton. His lead trumpet work with Kenton from 1950 to 1952 did much to set the character of the Kenton sound as well as to establish Ferguson's own fame. During the late 1950s, he began a series of his own big bands which prominently featured his high-register trumpet playing. Though these bands continued Kenton's emphasis on loud, flashy brass, they conveyed a different feeling: they swung. In addition, they sounded funkier. The bands had a precise, fast-moving style. Unlike Kenton, Ferguson was not especially experimental. His band belted out driving ensemble passages in a no-nonsense manner, with Ferguson often soaring overhead. Their sound was filled with raw excitement. The band seemed to thrive on fast tempos and loud playing (listen to "Three Foxes," "L-Dopa," "Got The Spirit"). The repertory contained few slow or subdued arrangements.

The Ferguson band's instrumentation also differed from that of other big bands. (See chapter 6 for discussion of big band instrumentation traditions.) Unlike the Ellington, Basie, Wilson, and Jones bands of the same period, Ferguson's were more compact. Rather than the ordinary complement of three to five trombones, Ferguson carried only two. Instead of a sax section with two altos, two tenors, and a baritone, his had one alto, two tenors, and a baritone. Instead of the dark, full-bodied tone qualities associated with Wilson's and Ellington's saxes, Ferguson's had a bright, biting sound that was almost brassy. As the years passed, Ferguson continued to reduce the size of his band, until in the late 1960s, and again in the mid-1980s, he was all the way down to a small combo.

During the 1970s and 1980s, Ferguson's bands used electric instruments and funk-style accompaniments in the bulk of their performances. Considerable radio airplay was given to some of their pop tune arrangements, particularly their 1970 recording of "MacArthur Park"[45] and their 1972 recording of "Hey, Jude" (a tune by the Beatles, a British singing group). This was a bit of good fortune that little jazz had enjoyed since the 1940s. Ferguson's greatest popularity came with a 1976 recording of the theme song for the immensely popular movie *Rocky.* The album it appeared on, *Conquistador,* achieved gold-record status.[46] Following these best-selling pieces, Ferguson mined the same vein by continuing to record television and movie themes, using large amounts of orchestration and small amounts of improvisation. The band also capitalized on the popularity of jazz-rock fusion by recording Herbie Hancock's hit "Chameleon" in 1974 and Joe Zawinul's hit "Birdland" in 1978 (see chapter 16 for more about this style and these particular pieces).

Maynard Ferguson is not ordinarily considered a historically significant hard bop trumpeter. His exceptional command of brass instruments, however, has inspired many musicians of the 1960s, 70s, and 80s. This is partly because his music received such wide exposure and partly because he has an almost freakish mastery of the trumpet that extends throughout its entire range. No register is the least bit awkward for him. His facility takes him to B above double-high C. Significantly, on most nights he does not simply squeal those altissimo-register notes but actually plays them with good intonation and large tone.[47] Most big band high-note artists play few improvised solos, restricting their playing to trumpet-section lead work in order to keep their lips set specifically for those high parts. Ferguson amazes brass players not only by playing high-register lead parts, but also by improvising solos on nearly every tune. In addition to that, his endurance is as phenomenal as his range, and he can switch to trombone or French horn right in the middle of a piece, making an immediate adjustment to it. In fact, he is a master not only of the trumpet but of all the brass instruments, and he plays most of the reed instruments, too.

Popular Appeal

Like bop musicians, hard bop musicians found their music to be relatively neglected by the public. Only a few managed to extract steady livelihoods from performing jazz. The historically significant bands of Clifford Brown, Art Blakey, and J. J. Johnson were unknown except to musicians and a small population of fans. During the 1950s, Sonny Rollins and John Coltrane were well known by jazz fans but almost unknown otherwise. The few jazz pieces that found their way onto juke boxes were mostly simple, funky compositions. They were arranged with lots of very repetitive accompaniment rhythms and less improvisation than was found on most hard bop records. Some of these accounted for brief periods of success enjoyed by Cannonball Adderley and Horace Silver, especially during the 1960s and 1970s. But the highest record sales went to the organ-guitar-drums and piano-bass-drums groups of Jimmy Smith and Ramsey Lewis, respectively. These are players who musicians and critics do not ordinarily consider to be within the mainstream of jazz developments, though their music helps define funky jazz, and they fit the hard bop designation more closely than they fit any other.

Listening Guide for

"Frame for the Blues"

Composed and arranged by hard bop trombonist Slide Hampton; recorded May 1958 in New York City by the Maynard Ferguson big band (four trumpets, two trombones, alto sax, two tenor saxes, baritone sax, piano, bass, and drums); originally found on Maynard Ferguson, *Message from Newport* (Roulette: 52012, LP, 1958); reissued on *The Complete Roulette Recordings of the Maynard Ferguson Orchestra* (Mosaic MD10-156, 10CD set, 1958–62).

After the introduction, the piece follows the 12-bar blues form in a very slow tempo. "Frame for the Blues" resembles the simplicity and comfortable feeling of Count Basie's band style and the loud, sleek brass of Stan Kenton's band style. It also has earthier aspects associated with hard bop. Funky, bluesy phrases are abundant in the composition and improvisations. This piece became one of the most requested feature numbers for the Ferguson band of the 1960s. It was so well loved that more than one jazz disc jockey made it his program's theme song.

Terms and sounds to know before using this guide: trumpet, trombone, tenor saxophone, ride rhythm, ride cymbal, snare drum, wire brushes, walking bass, 12-bar blues, fall-off, triplet. All these are explained and illustrated on the *Demo CD*. Learn to keep your place by counting beats in the 12-bar blues by studying page 381. Page 367 explains the meaning of the term "triplets."

Elapsed Time

0' 00" **Introduction**

The band offers a bluesy call and then sustains the last note of their phrase. Trumpeter Ferguson answers with a bluesy figure played in the extreme high register. He ornaments his sustained tone with a fast shake and then comes down and resolves his line with bluesy, legato figures.

0' 12" Walking bass begins at the same time as the drummer starts using wire brushes to play timekeeping rhythms on snare drum. Trombones respond with a wailing phrase in their high register, played with the notes slurred together. Trumpets conclude the introduction with a string of triplets, that is, three notes on each beat.

0' 20" **First Chorus**

The melody is stated by the entire band in harmony. Accompaniment is provided quietly and discreetly from bass in two-beat style, piano tinkling, and drummer using wire brushes to play timekeeping rhythms on snare drum, while snapping his high-hat closed sharply on the second and fourth beats of each measure.

0' 52" *Ninth Measure*

Trombones play a legato line in harmony.

0' 54" *Tenth Measure*

Trombones are joined by the trumpets, descending in a bluesy string of legato triplets.

0' 59" *Eleventh and Twelfth Measures*

The drummer uses a drum stick on the ride cymbal to play triplets ("123 123 123 123 123 123 123 123"). Pianist plays chords in the same triplet rhythm. This builds excitement in anticipation of the upcoming sax solo. While the baritone saxophone plays a figure that emphasizes the downbeat, the other saxophones play a harmonized figure emphasizing the upbeats.

1' 06" **Second Chorus**

Tenor Saxophone Improvisation by Carmen Leggio

Walking bass begins.

After starting his solo, the saxophonist is interrupted by a screaming brass statement consisting of a shake by the trumpet section, a pause, then another shake and a fall-off.

1' 19" Saxophone solo re-emerges from being swallowed by the brass sounds. It is now accompanied by piano comping, walking bass, and a ride rhythm played on ride cymbal with a drum stick. Sax solo uses many of the bluesy melodic figures that are usually termed "funky." Notice how the saxophonist seems to tell a story with his solo, each note fitting a tuneful structure.

1' 46" *Eleventh and Twelfth Measures*

While the saxophonist is finishing his improvisation, loud, high-register triplets are played in unison by trumpets, occasionally undergirded by trombone chords on the upbeats and almost inaudible, low-pitched sax tones.

1' 55" **Third Chorus**

First Eight Measures

A cymbal crash begins this chorus. Then trumpets and trombones play a harmonized melodic fragment answered by increasingly louder drums and cymbals. Notice how drums underscore the brass rhythms, filling in the pauses and accenting phrase endings.

2' 03" Trumpets repeat the figure.

2' 06" While the brass take a breath, they are answered by Ferguson playing a scale-like figure far higher than theirs, then topping off a new chord and ornamenting the end of this phrase with a fall-off.

2' 17" High-register brass figures go higher and higher with Ferguson.

2' 21" The rising brass line concludes with Ferguson playing a stratospherically high note to top off the phrase. He ends his note with a brief fall-off.

2' 23" Fade-out at the ninth measure.

Trumpeter Clifford Brown and tenor saxophonist Sonny Rollins, the top hornmen in hard bop. Shown here in 1956 while members of the Max Roach-Clifford Brown Quintet.

Photo courtesy of Chuck Stewart

CHAPTER SUMMARY

1) Hard bop evolved directly from bop during the 1950s, mainly from East Coast and Midwest musicians.
2) When hard bop differs from bop, it is simpler, has more variety in accompaniment patterns, fewer pop tune chord progressions, darker, weightier tone qualities, and more emphasis on hard, unrelenting swinging.
3) Funky jazz is a subcategory of hard bop, and it is characterized by bluesy inflections of pitch and gospelish harmonies. Several pieces performed by the bands of Horace Silver and Cannonball Adderley were popular because of their funky qualities and simple, catchy melodies.
4) The most prominent figures in hard bop were pianist-composer Horace Silver, drummer-bandleader Art Blakey, and alto saxophonist-bandleader Cannonball Adderley.
5) The top tenor saxophonists in hard bop were Sonny Rollins, John Coltrane, Wayne Shorter, and Joe Henderson.
6) The top trumpeters in hard bop were Clifford Brown and Freddie Hubbard.
7) Drummers in hard bop were louder and more intrusive than their predecessors. Art Blakey and Philly Joe Jones further emancipated the drummer from the role of mere timekeeper.
8) Hard bop big bands were led by trumpeters Maynard Ferguson, Gerald Wilson, and Thad Jones.

NOTES

1. For nonfunky examples by these men, listen to Silver's "Ecaroh" on *Art Blakey: The Jazz Messengers* (Columbia: CK 65265 [CL897], 1956); "Moon Rays," on SCCJ-R; Cannonball Adderley, *Cannonball & Coltrane* (Quintet in Chicago) (Emarcy: 834 588-2 [MG20449], 1959); and the following Art Blakey albums: *A Night at Birdland, Vols. 1 & 2* (Blue Note: 46519/46520 [1521/22], 2CDs, 1954), *A Night in Tunisia* (Blue Note: 46532 [84049], 1960), *Indestructible* (Blue Note: 46429 [84193], 1964), and *Buttercorn Lady* (Emarcy: 8224712 [Limelight 82034], 1966).
2. To learn what is meant by "earthy, blues-drenched, gospelish," listen to "One Day" or "Frame for the Blues"; Avery Parrish's "After Hours" on *Jazz Piano* (Smithsonian: 7002 [039], 4CD set); Horace Silver's "The Preacher," "Sister Sadie," "Senor Blues," or "Song For My Father"; Bobby Timmons's "Moanin'"; Nat Adderley's "Work Song," "Sack o' Woe," or "Jive Samba"; Joe Zawinul's "Mercy, Mercy, Mercy"; or Lee Morgan's "Sidewinder." If you do not have access to any of these pieces, look in your school library for the multivolume *Recorded Anthology of American Music.* From the volume called *Bebop* (New World: 271, LP), listen to the funky melody line by Horace Silver called "Stop Time."
3. Pianists Gene Harris (of The Three Sounds), Ramsey Lewis, and Les McCann, and organists Jimmy Smith, Richard "Groove" Holmes, and Jack McDuff based large parts of their styles on Silver's funky devices and became quite popular as a result. Even the original stylists Bill Evans, McCoy Tyner, and Chick Corea, whose approaches were not primarily funky, demonstrated Silver's influence by making use of his funky devices.
4. Listen to Art Blakey, *A Night At Birdland, Vols. 1 & 2* (Blue Note: 46519/46520 [1521/22], 2CDs, 1954).
5. Much of Davis's work is routinely classified as "cool jazz," and this label is not limited to his 1948–1950 nonet recordings. It also is applied to his early 1950s work with Sonny Rollins, Horace Silver, Milt Jackson, and others. Even his 1959 *Kind of Blue* album is tagged "cool jazz" by some, though it more closely fits the "hard bop" or "modal jazz" category.
6. Miles Davis, *Collector's Items* (Fantasy: OJCCD-071-2 [Prestige-7044], 1956); Sonny Rollins, *Saxophone Colossus* (Fantasy: OJCCD-291-2 [Prestige-7079], 1956); John Coltrane, *Giant Steps* (Atlantic: 1311-2, 1959); Wes Montgomery, *The Incredible Jazz Guitar of Wes Montgomery* (Fantasy: OJCCD036-2 [Riverside 320], 1960). Flanagan can also be heard in two selections on *Jazz Piano* (Smithsonian: 7002 [RD-039], 4CD set), and on Rollins's "Blue Seven" on SCCJ.
7. For analysis of Silver's piano style, see John Mehegan, *Jazz Improvisation Vol. 3* (Watson-Guptill/Amsco, 1964).
8. Favorites among musicians are the Horace Silver albums: *Horace-Scope* (Blue Note: 84042, 1960); *Cape Verdean Blues* (Blue Note: 84220, 1965); and *In Pursuit of the 27th Man* (Blue Note: BN-LA054-F, LP, 1972).
9. See pages 412–413 for information on how to get Milton Stewart, *Structural Development in the Jazz Improvisational Technique of Clifford Brown* (University Microfilms, 1973). See David Baker, *The Jazz Style of Clifford Brown: A Musical and Historical Perspective* (Studio PR, 1982; available from Jamey Aebersold). Listen to "Pent-Up House" on SCCJ, and see the analysis in Scott Reeves, *Creative Jazz Improvisation, 2nd ed.* (Prentice-Hall, 1995).
10. Also, Hubbard was probably the first great brass player to draw heavily from the approach of saxophonist John Coltrane, notably in his use of pentatonic scales, quartal harmony, and chromaticism.
11. See Stuart Isacoff, *Solos For Jazz Trumpet* (Carl Fischer, 1985), for analyses of Hubbard's solos on "Blue Moon" and "On Green Dolphin Street."
12. Though he remained active into the 1990s, Hubbard's playing on albums in the 1960s as a sideman with Herbie Hancock and Eric Dolphy represents some of his most inventive work. Listen to Herbie Hancock, *Empyrean Isles* (Blue Note: 84175, 1964); Eric Dolphy, *Out To Lunch* (Blue Note: 46524 [84163], 1964); and Oliver Nelson, *Blues and The Abstract Truth* (Impulse!/GRP GRD-154 [A-5], 1961).
13. Listen to Blakey's work with Clifford Brown and Horace Silver from 1954, in which he is engaged in volatile rhythm section drumming years before such activity became common practice: *A Night At Birdland, Vols. 1 & 2* (Blue Note: 46519/46520 [1521/22], 1954).
14. Some of the tunes they recorded remained favorites among musicians of the 1980s and 1990s: Brown's "Joy Spring" and "Daahoud." For a sample of the quintet's sound, listen to "Pent-Up House" with saxophonist Sonny Rollins on SCCJ; "What Is This Thing Called Love?" on *Bebop* (New World: 271, LP); or *Clifford Brown & Max Roach* (Emarcy: 8146452 [MG 36036], 1954) which features saxophonist Harold Land.
15. Listen to the *Demo CD* Tracks 11–13 to familiarize yourself with the different sounds of instruments in the drum set and the effects of sticks and brushes. Then listen to Philly Joe Jones's work on "Two Bass Hit" and "Billy Boy" on Miles Davis, *Milestones* (Columbia: CK 40837 [CL 1193], 1958); "Budo" on *Miles and Coltrane* (Columbia: CK 44052 [CL 1020], 1955, 1958); "Tune-Up" on *Cookin'* (Fantasy: OJCCD-128-2 [Prestige 7094], 1956); and "Half Nelson" on *Workin'* (Fantasy: OJCCD-296-2 [Prestige 7166], 1956). "Two Bass Hit" is also in *Jazz Classics CD* for the *Concise Guide to Jazz.*
16. Cannonball Adderley's best solos from this period are found on Miles Davis, *Milestones* (Columbia: CK 40837 [CL 1193], 1958), and a recording of the Miles Davis group minus Davis: *Cannonball and Coltrane (Quintet in Chicago)* (Emarcy: 834 588-2 [MG 20449], 1959). One of his best is on "Two Bass Hit" in *Jazz Classics CD* for the *Concise Guide to Jazz.*
17. For some of his funkiest playing, listen to "Them Dirty Blues" on Cannonball Adderley, *Them Dirty Blues* (Landmark: LCD130-2 [Riverside 322], 1960).
18. On Miles Davis's *Milestones,* Adderley quotes the opening phrases of George Gershwin's "Fascinating Rhythm" in the beginning of his solo on "Milestones," and he transforms the first phrase of Vernon Duke's "I Can't Get Started" on his solo in "Two Bass Hit." "Two Bass Hit" is also on the *Jazz Classics CD* for the *Concise Guide to Jazz.*
19. See Stuart Isacoff, *Solos For Jazz Alto Sax* (Carl Fischer, 1985), for analyses of Adderley's solos on "On Green Dolphin Street" and "Sack O' Woe." For David Baker, *The Jazz Style of Cannonball Adderley* (Studio P/R, 1980), write Jamey Aebersold, P.O. Box 1244, New Albany, IN 47151-1244.
20. To hear the resemblance between Rollins and Parker, listen to Parker play tenor, instead of alto, as he does on "Half Nelson" (1947) on *Charlie Parker Memorial, Vol. 2* (Savoy/Denon: SV-0103 [12009], 1945–48). Then listen to Rollins with Bud Powell on *The Amazing Bud Powell, Vol. 1* (Blue Note: 81503, 1949); or with Miles Davis on *Dig* (Fantasy: OJCCD-005-2 [Prestige 7012], 1951).
21. Rollins's fastest, most fluid solos are on "I Know That You Know" and "The Eternal Triangle" on Dizzy Gillespie, *Sunny Side Up* (Verve: 314 521-426-2 [MGV 8262], 1957), during a session in which he was pre-

pared to keep up with the lightning-quick playing of fellow saxophonist Sonny Stitt.

22. Listen to his "Blue Seven" on SCCJ, or "You Don't Know What Love Is" on *Saxophone Colossus* (Fantasy: OJCCD291-2 [Prestige 7079], 1956). For analyses of the Rollins solo on "Blue Seven," see Gunther Schuller, *Musings* (Oxford, 1986), 86-97, and Scott Reeves, *Creative Jazz Improvisation, 2nd ed.* (Prentice-Hall, 1995). For David Baker, *The Jazz Style of Sonny Rollins* (Studio P/R, 1980), write Jamey Aebersold, P.O. Box 1244, New Albany, IN 47151-1244. For a technical evaluation of Rollins's career up to 1980, see Charles Blancq, *Sonny Rollins* (Twayne, 1983). Further transcriptions and analyses are in Charley Gerard, *Sonny Rollins* (Consolidated Music, 1980; available from Aebersold).
23. "Vierd Blues" and "No Line" on Miles Davis, *Collector's Items* (Fantasy: OJCCD-071-2 [Prestige 7044], 1956).
24. Listen to "Pent-Up House," on SCCJ, or *Sonny Rollins Plus 4* (Fantasy: OJCCD-243-2 [Prestige 7038], 1956), made under Rollins's own leadership while he was a member of the Clifford Brown-Max Roach Quintet. This is among the few albums Rollins himself has said he is pleased with.
25. The all-time favorite Rollins album for many musicians is *Saxophone Colossus* (Fantasy: OJCCD-291-2 [Prestige 7079], 1956); also impressive is *A Night at the Village Vanguard, Vols. 1 & 2* (Blue Note: 46517/46518, 2CDs, 1957).
26. Sonny Rollins, *The Bridge* (Victor Jazz: 09026-68518-2 [LSP-2527], 1962).
27. Sonny Rollins, *On the Outside (Our Man in Jazz)* (RCA Bluebird: 2496-2-RB [LSP 2612], 1962).
28. Rolling Stones, *Tattoo You* (Virgin: 39521 [Rolling Stones Records 16052], 1981).
29. Compare Cook's work on Blue Mitchell, *The Thing to Do* (Blue Note: 84178, 1964), with Henderson's work on Horace Silver, *Song for My Father* (Blue Note: 84185, 1964).
30. Listen to his work on Horace Silver, *Cape Verdean Blues* (Blue Note: 84220, 1965); "I Have a Dream" on Herbie Hancock, *The Prisoner* (Blue Note: 46845 [84321], 1969); and Joe Henderson, *Power to the People* (Milestone 9024, 1969; reissued on *The Milestone Years* [Milestone: 8MCD 4413-2]). For transcriptions of solos on Henderson's *Page One* (Blue Note: 84140, 1963) and *In 'n' Out* (Blue Note: 84166, 1964), see Don Siekler, *Joe Henderson: Improvised Saxophone Solos* (Studio PR, 1978; available from Aebersold).
31. See Scott Reeves, *Creative Jazz Improvisation, 2nd ed.* (Prentice-Hall, 1995) for analysis of J. J. Johnson's solo on "Aquarius." See David Baker, *J. J. Johnson: Trombone* (Shattinger, 1979; available from Aebersold).
32. J.J. Johnson, *J. J. Inc.* (Columbia: CK 65296 [CL 1606], 1960).
33. Fuller's work on these albums is representative: John Coltrane, *Blue Trane* (Blue Note: 46095 [81577], 1957); Art Farmer-Benny Colson Jazztet, *Meet The Jazztet* (Chess: 91550 [Argo 664], 1960); and Art Blakey, *Indestructible* (Blue Note: 46429 [84193], 1964).
34. Listen to his "West Coast Blues" on SCCJ-R or *The Incredible Jazz Guitar of Wes Montgomery* (Fantasy: OJCCD-0362 [Riverside-320], 1960). For transcription and analysis of Montgomery's solo on "Four On Six," see Fred Sokolow, *Solos for Jazz Guitar* (Carl Fischer, 1988; order from Carl Fischer Music Store, 54 Cooper Square, NY, NY 10003).
35. *Kenny Burrell and John Coltrane* (Fantasy: OJCCD-300-2 [New Jazz 8276], 1957).
36. Jimmy Smith, *Midnight Special* (Blue Note: 46399 [84078], 1960).
37. Notice the buoyant, hard-driving accompaniment Sam Jones provides and listen to his pizzicato solo on "Trouble On My Mind" on *Cannonball Adderley in Europe* (Landmark: LCD-1307-2 [Riverside 499], 1962).
38. Listen to Chambers introduce the melody line to "So What" with the Miles Davis band on SCCJ. Listen to his solos on John Coltrane, *Soultrane* (Fantasy: OJCCD-021-2 [Prestige 7142], 1958); and Coltrane, *Tranin' In* (Fantasy: OJCCD189-2 [Prestige 7123], 1957).
39. *The Complete Blue Note/UA/Roulette Recordings of Thad Jones* (Mosaic MD3-172, 3CD set, 1956–59); also see footnote 42.
40. Charles Mingus, *Jazzical Moods* (Fantasy: OJCCD-1857-2 [Period], 1954).
41. Listen to the Thad Jones solos on *The Complete Roulette Studio Recordings of Count Basie* (Mosaic: MD 10-149, 1959–1962) and *Big Band Renaissance* (Smithsonian: 108, 5CDs).
42. The *Complete Solid State Recordings of the Thad Jones/Mel Lewis Orchestra* (Mosaic: MD5-151, 5CD set, 1966–1969).
43. Gerald Wilson, *You Better Believe It* (Pacific Jazz: PJ34, LP, 1961).
44. Gerald Wilson, *Moment of Truth* (Pacific Jazz: 92928 [PJ61], 1962) and "Viva Tirado" on *Big Band Renaissance* (Smithsonian: 108).
45. Maynard Ferguson, *M. F. Horn* (Columbia: CGT 33660 [30466], AC, 1970).
46. Maynard Ferguson, *Conquistador* (Columbia: CK 34457, 1976).
47. *The Complete Roulette Recordings of the Maynard Ferguson Orchestra* (Mosaic: MD10-156, 10CD set, 1958–1962) and *Big Band Renaissance* (Smithsonian: 108). For biography, see William F. Lee, *MF Horn: Maynard Ferguson's Life in Music* (M.F. Music U.S.A. Inc., 1997; P.O. Box 716, Ojai, CA 93024).

Chapter Twelve

Paul Chambers, Cannonball Adderley Miles Davis, John Coltrane Photo courtesy of Frank Driggs/Magnum Photos

Miles Davis & Sidemen

Miles Davis (1926–1991) was a jazz trumpeter and bandleader who played a pivotal role in the history of modern jazz because he was deeply involved in recording and promoting several styles well before they became widespread trends. His recordings have won the near universal admiration of modern jazz musicians. Over a fifty-year period of productivity, Davis contributed a stylistically diverse body of music. Parts of this productivity defined jazz for three different generations of listeners. A significant slice of modern jazz history is documented in Davis-led recording sessions because he gathered the key innovators of the day for his bands. Unlike most artists, Davis never became limited to one particular band style. Among his most important contributions are

Contributions

1) Creating an original and substantial trumpet style. This was first evident in recordings that Davis made in Charlie Parker's band of the mid-1940s, and it influenced numerous trumpeters of the cool jazz and hard bop idioms (see Table 12.4).
2) Producing a large body of recordings which almost invariably contain distinctive, high-quality performances. Davis recordings served as textbooks for modern musicians in the way that recordings of Louis Armstrong and Lester Young had served his predecessors.

3) Making a significant change during the 1960s in his original trumpet style. In the 1980s, this variation was the basis for trumpet styles of Wynton Marsalis, Terence Blanchard, and others.

4) Being part of the first recording sessions which consolidated Claude Thornhill's and Gil Evans's orchestration style with the playing styles of Gerry Mulligan, Lee Konitz, and himself on the landmark "Birth of the Cool" recordings of 1949 and 1950. (See chapter 10, and listen to "Boplicity" on SCCJ.)

5) Pioneering "modal jazz" on the *Kind of Blue* album in 1959. (Listen to selections from this album: "Flamenco Sketches" on the *Jazz Classics CD,* "Blue in Green" on the *Classics CD* for *Concise Guide to Jazz,* and "So What" on SCCJ.)

6) Pioneering the predominant group approaches and individual instrumental styles of the 1980s with his quintet of 1965–1968. (Listen to "Masqualero" on the *Jazz Classics CD.*)

7) Pioneering jazz-rock fusion styles with an amalgamation of elements from "modal jazz," rock, and funk music on his *In a Silent Way* and *Bitches Brew* albums of 1969 (see chapter 16).

Though he did not invent entire jazz idioms himself, Miles Davis organized bands of key innovators at early moments in the development of bop, cool jazz, modal jazz, and jazz-rock fusion (see Tables 12.1, 12.2, and 12.3). Moreover, he invented an original and distinctive trumpet style that fit the sound of each of his bands. Like Duke Ellington's musicians, Davis's often produced the best work of their career while in his bands. (His sidemen speak highly about his help in their own stylistic development and his judicious editing of their music.) A feeling of intelligent, well-measured musical creation pervades most Davis recordings.

Trumpet Style

Miles Davis created an unmistakable sound. It is so easily identifiable that we can instantly recognize it, even in the crowded mix of a rock record or the background music for a movie. Davis was a uniquely creative thinker who departed drastically from the traditions of jazz trumpet playing to give us a sound so personal that to call it "Miles Davis" seems more accurate than to call it "jazz trumpet."

The uniqueness of the Davis style can be divided into at least eight components. The first two are manners of handling the trumpet sound.[1] The most obvious are his alternating pitch and tone quality at the beginnings and endings of notes. (For graphs of such pitch bending ornaments, see page 42; to hear Davis perform them, listen to "Fishermen, Strawberry, and Devil Crab" on the *Jazz Classics CD.*)[2]

TABLE 12.1 A Few of the Many Well-Known Saxophonists Who Worked with Miles Davis

Lee Konitz	Bennie Maupin	Wayne Shorter
Sonny Rollins	John Coltrane	David Liebman
Jackie McLean	Hank Mobley	Steve Grossman
Gerry Mulligan	Joe Henderson	Gary Bartz
Sonny Stitt	Sam Rivers	Cannonball Adderley
Jimmy Heath	George Coleman	Sonny Fortune

TABLE 12.2 A Few of the Many Well-Known Guitarists Who Worked with Miles Davis

George Benson	John Scofield
John McLaughlin	Barry Finnerty
Larry Coryell	Mike Stern

A second component of Davis's highly personal style is his frequent use of a Harmon mute without its stem (portrayed on pages 390–392, heard on "Flamenco Sketches" on the *Jazz Classics CD*). His Harmon-muted solos were amplified by placing the mute directly on the stage microphone (at least until the 1970s, when he attached wireless microphones directly to his horn). This technique resulted in a wispy sound that was delicate and conveyed an intimate mood. By comparison with that of other modern trumpeters, far more of his output was muted. On many of his albums, more than half of his playing is done through the Harmon mute.[3]

A third component of the Davis style is an unusually skillful timing and dramatic construction of melodic figures. Davis is a master of self-restraint. His placement of silence is at least as significant as his choice of notes, and he often lets several beats pass without playing. During the moments he is not sounding his own notes, the sound of bass, drums, and piano comes through clearly, further enhancing the mood. The effectiveness of this very lean approach also depends on the steadiness of swing feeling and overall musicality of the accompanists. Because Davis always hired the best accompanists, the silences in his own solos were filled in a highly musical, well-paced manner.[4] More than most improvisers, Davis conveyed the impression that he was editing his solos very carefully while performing them, clarifying his ideas before articulating them. In the same way that Lester Young approached improvisation with the tenor saxophone, Davis pared his thinking down to a bare core of melodic material; and like Young's solos, the best Davis improvisations seem to "tell a story."[5]

A fourth component of the Davis style can be identified by comparing rhythmic conceptions. Most modern trumpeters play swinging lines, but few seem capable of generating lines that are free from a sense of strict tempo and swing feeling, even when they play slow tunes. In the playing of Davis's contemporaries, a very precise subdivision of each beat seems to rule the passage of notes. Davis could improvise swinging melodic figures,[6] but distinguished himself by his skill in also improvising figures that imply freedom from strict tempo and swing feeling.[7]

A fifth component is an acute sensitivity in paraphrasing melodies. The Davis paraphrases of popular songs were constructed in such fresh and enticing ways that the finished products are almost new melodies.[8]

A sixth component is a mastery of economy and succinctness. Davis was not afraid to play simply. Certainly he did often play bop-style lines that were not simple. But often he constructed solos of very brief, simple phrases. Many of his improvisations on slow pieces and on blues forms were comprised of no more than a few carefully chosen notes timed so well and played so expressively that the result was quite dramatic. Sometimes the entire solo was forged from such devices, as in "Solea" on *Sketches of Spain,* "Freddie the Freeloader" on *Kind of Blue,* and "Bitches Brew" on *Bitches Brew.*

A seventh component is the cluster of traits possessed by his tone quality and preference for pitch range. During the 1940s and 1950s, Davis played with a tone quality that was lighter, softer, and less brassy than that of most other trumpeters. He used almost no vibrato, favored

TABLE 12.3 The Evolution of Modern Jazz Rhythm Section Styles Documented by Miles Davis Recordings

1950:	Pianist John Lewis, bassist Al McKibbon, drummer Max Roach on *Birth of the Cool.*
1951:	Pianist Walter Bishop, Jr., bassist Tommy Potter, drummer Art Blakey on "Conception"; "Denial"; "Paper Moon."
1956:	Pianist Tommy Flanagan, bassist Paul Chambers, drummer Art Taylor on "No Line"; "Vierd Blues"; "In Your Own Sweet Way."
1955–58:	Pianist Red Garland, bassist Paul Chambers, drummer Philly Joe Jones on *The New Miles Davis Quintet; Steamin'; Cookin'; Workin'; Relaxin'; 'Round About Midnight; Milestones.*
1959–63:	Pianist Wynton Kelly, bassist Paul Chambers, drummer Jimmy Cobb on *Someday My Prince Will Come; In Person at the Blackhawk; Miles Davis at Carnegie Hall.*
1963–68:	Pianist Herbie Hancock, bassist Ron Carter, drummer Tony Williams on many albums, including *My Funny Valentine; Sorcerer; Miles in the Sky; Nefertiti.*
1971:	Pianist Keith Jarrett, bassist Mike Henderson, drummer Jack DeJohnette, percussionist Airto Moreira on "Sivad" from *Live-Evil.*
1969–72:	Groups whose rhythm sections sometimes included two or three keyboards (Davis drew from a pool of pianists which included Joe Zawinul, Chick Corea, Keith Jarrett, Herbie Hancock, Larry Young, Harold Williams, Hermeto Pascoal, Lonnie Liston Smith, and Cedric Lawson).
1970s:	Groups whose rhythm sections sometimes included two or three guitars (Davis drew from a pool of guitarists which included Reggie Lucas, Pete Cosey, David Creamer, Dominique Gaumont, and Cornell Dupree).
1970s:	Groups including sitar and tabla. Use of instruments native to India, such as the sitar (a stringed instrument) and tabla (drums), was as unusual in jazz rhythm sections as using two and three keyboards at once.

the trumpet's middle register over its flashier high register, and rarely double-timed. By comparison with the styles of most other modern trumpeters, his was gentle. That trend was reversed, however, on some pieces he recorded during the 1960s, in which he began to reach into the high register more often. This reversal is especially evident in his albums *Miles in Europe* and *"Four" and More.* During the 1970s he developed an even more explosive side to his style, capitalizing on the trumpet's high register, and he occasionally included long bursts of notes and splattered tones. He also incorporated electronically generated echo[9] and "wah-wah" effects into his trumpet tone. Although his later solo work seemed more outgoing, he never entirely discarded his earlier manners, and his work in the 1980s occasionally displayed all these facets.

An eighth essential component is present in both his trumpet style and the concepts of sound that guided the playing of his bands. Throughout his career, Davis demonstrated an overriding concern with sound texture. Certainly he had also been interested in melodic and rhythmic aspects of his music. But above all, there was a recurring creation of a glass-like

TABLE 12.4 A Few of the Many Trumpeters Influenced by Miles Davis

Clifford Brown	Stu Williamson	Terence Blanchard
Chet Baker	Ted Curson	Terumaso Hino
Shorty Rogers	Luis Gasca	Kenny Wheeler
Jack Sheldon	Blue Mitchell	Tim Hagans
Nat Adderley	Lester Bowie	John McNeil
Charles Moore	Tom Harrell	Herb Pomeroy
Johnny Coles	Randy Brecker	Wynton Marsalis
Eddie Henderson	Mark Isham	Wallace Roney
Jim Powell	Donald Byrd	

smoothness of texture, extending from the bottom to the top of the band's sound. (This was evident as early as his "Now's the Time" solo of 1945 with Charlie Parker.) It characterized his attraction to the Claude Thornhill band sound, which drew heavily upon the concepts of French Impressionist composer Claude Debussy. This emerged in Davis's downsized version of the Thornhill band for his *Birth of the Cool* recordings of 1949 and 1950. (Compare Thornhill's "Snowfall" with the Davis nonet's "Moon Dreams.") It was evident in his *Kind of Blue* and *Bitches Brew*. In these albums, his own solos were filled with sustained tones that topped off the voicings of distinctly uncluttered accompaniment chords. Consistent with his concern for sound texture, Davis is known for suggesting chord voicings to his pianists and for choosing long notes in his solos that cap the voicings in his accompaniment so well that it sounds like part of an arrangement that presets the sound quality from bottom to top. His concern with texture also dovetails into his attraction to simplicity in the construction of solos. An ever-changing line would not provide sufficient sustained tones to mesh with accompaniment chords long enough for listeners to savor the combination as a texture. The Davis concern with texture is also manifested in his retaining arranger Gil Evans as adviser even when Evans was not directly involved in large-scale recording projects. Apparently Davis felt that it was important to have available the Evans sense of sound quality and balance, even in the work of his small combos. During the jazz-rock fusion period, Davis sometimes used two and three pianists or guitarists playing at the same time, and he hired extra percussionists. Often he told them how actively to play, when to play, and when not to play. This reflected the same concern for sound texture that he had shown earlier.

The Classic Miles Davis Quintet

Miles Davis made many of his historically significant recordings as a bandleader for the Prestige record company. Among musicians, the most discussed of these are *Steamin', Cookin', Workin,'* and *Relaxin'*. These were recorded in 1956 with tenor saxophonist John Coltrane, pianist Red Garland, bassist Paul Chambers, and drummer "Philly Joe" Jones. (For more about Chambers and Jones, see chapter 11.)[10] The style and energy at those recording sessions were particularly evident again in *Milestones,* an album Davis made for the Columbia record company in 1958, with the same musicians plus alto saxophonist Cannonball Adderley (discussed more in chapter 11). Though Miles Davis had long been linked with cool jazz, the band on these recordings sounds more like hard bop and later styles. The musicians played with blistering intensity. Their work had an unusual freshness and excitement that combined to make these among the most striking performances since the groundbreaking Parker-Gillespie records of ten years earlier. Many musicians and journalists consider these particular Davis albums to be as outstanding as the classic recordings by Louis Armstrong's Hot Five and Hot Seven of the 1920s and the Kansas City Six and Seven recordings of Count Basie and Lester Young of the 1930s.

These recordings marked the first time that many jazz fans heard tenor saxophonist John Coltrane. Though some journalists considered this portion of his career merely a development stage, Coltrane's style with Davis was so substantial and original at this time that he would qualify as a jazz giant even if he had never moved away from it and developed other approaches. (For details, see chapter 13.)

The classic quintet, with the addition of Cannonball Adderley, was responsible for a landmark event in jazz history. With their recording of the "Milestones" selection in 1958, they broke away from the tradition of guiding improvisations solely by chord progressions. Most of the tunes Davis had recorded before 1958 were pop tunes or bop compositions with frequently changing chords in their accompaniment. But instead of using frequently changing chords for their improvisations on "Milestones," the musicians used two modes. (See pages 372–374 and 385–387 for explanations of modes. See page 423 for musical notation of the modes used on "Milestones.") The first mode was in effect for sixteen measures, the second mode for another sixteen measures, followed by a return to the first for the final eight measures. The improvisers using this modal format had fewer demands placed on their attention. This represented quite a contrast with the demands placed by frequently changing chords. The players correspondingly had more energy left to direct toward piecing together interesting melodies and rhythms. After the *Milestones* album (containing "Milestones") was released, the approach used on "Milestones"—the absence of changing chords—became popular among modern jazz musicians. The momentum of this trend increased upon wide acceptance of mode-based music in the Davis album *Kind of Blue,* recorded in 1959 (discussed later in this chapter and represented by "Flamenco Sketches" on the *Jazz Classics CD*). "Milestones" soon took its place in the repertory of standard jam session tunes, next to "Cherokee," "All the Things You Are," "A Night in Tunisia," and numerous pieces based on the twelve-bar blues.

Collaborations with Gil Evans

In 1957, Davis renewed his association with arranger **Gil Evans** (1912–1988). Together they had organized the *Birth of the Cool* sessions a decade earlier. This time they put together new works in which Davis was the only soloist with a large band. Evans conducted his own arrangements for groups of brass, woodwinds, string bass, drums, and occasionally harp. The brass section included French horn and tuba in addition to trumpets and trombones. The woodwind section included flutes and clarinets in addition to saxophones; bassoon was added for the *Sketches of Spain* album. The arrangements reflected Evans's prolific imagination and high level of workmanship. With soulful and stirring playing by Davis, these efforts were captured on *Miles Ahead, Porgy and Bess,* and *Sketches of Spain.* The quality of these three albums has been matched only by the greatest Duke Ellington masterpieces.

Miles Ahead was recorded in 1957, with Davis playing fluegelhorn, a previously uncommon instrument in jazz (see photo on page 112). Although Clark Terry and Shorty Rogers had played it prior to 1957, the Davis recordings provided impetus for its ensuing popularity. By the 1970s, many jazz trumpeters were doubling on fluegelhorn, and arrangers who worked for popular singers were frequently including fluegelhorn parts in their orchestrations.

The program of *Miles Ahead* includes popular tunes and jazz tunes. The pieces are connected by brief interludes which Evans composed specially to bridge the gaps between selections. The contents span moods reminiscent of the subtle, unforced swinging of the *Birth of the Cool* recordings, lush pastels in slow tempo and moments of brassy excitement. Compared to other big band writing of the 1950s and 1960s, its character was more reflective. Here

Composer-arranger Gil Evans, age 58, conducting from the piano. Evans masterminded what many consider the best Miles Davis recording sessions: *Birth of the Cool*, *Sketches of Spain*, *Porgy and Bess*, and *Miles Ahead*. He also assisted when Davis was entering jazz-rock fusion with *Filles de Kilimanjaro*.

Photo by Bill Smith

Evans mastered the effective use of shading and contrast of both rhythmic and tonal dimensions. Like Duke Ellington, he freed himself of the formula writing which pitted brasses against saxes. He freely voiced across sections and assigned different parts of a melody to different instruments. Like Ellington, Evans managed to weave improvisations into the framework of a piece without sounding contrived or awkward. The sound of Davis fades gracefully into and out of the ensemble. There are brief passages in which Davis interpreted pop-tune themes, or in which he improvised on the chord progressions in the arrangements. In either case, the orchestration was perfectly conceived to match the mood and color of the Davis style.

In 1958, Davis recorded George Gershwin's opera *Porgy and Bess.* Gil Evans devised arrangements of sweeping colors and breathtaking drama. Davis reworked the familiar melodies so they acquired a new flavor. (Listen to "Fishermen, Strawberry, and Devil Crab," excerpted at the beginning of the *Jazz Classics CD.*)

Sketches of Spain was recorded in November 1959 and March 1960. It is nearly a classical music album because the music was almost exclusively written, except for "Solea," in which Davis developed a long modal improvisation. Because of Davis's playing, however, this album qualifies for the label of Third Stream music, instead of classical music. The best known piece on the album is from Joachim Rodrigo's "Concierto de Aranjuez" for guitar and symphony orchestra, which was restored by Evans for trumpet and wind orchestra, no strings.[11] "Will o' the Wisp" is from ballet music by Spanish composer Manuel de Falla. The remaining pieces are developments of Spanish folk themes: "Pan Piper," "Saeta," and "Solea." This album has proven to be exceedingly popular among nonmusicians, jazz fans, and jazz musicians.

Gil Evans had a long career in the field of arranging and bandleading, but he produced no other works whose quality exceeded these richly fulfilling and consistently compelling collaborations with Davis. Decades after their first release, *Sketches of Spain, Porgy and Bess,* and *Miles Ahead* continue to stand as monuments to combining orchestration and the jazz tradition. They remain all-time favorite albums among jazz musicians and music scholars.

Kind of Blue

In 1959, Miles Davis recorded one of the best-loved and most historically pivotal albums in modern jazz: *Kind of Blue.* On all but one selection, he used Cannonball Adderley, John Coltrane, pianist Bill Evans, bassist Paul Chambers, and drummer Jimmy Cobb. Bill Evans conceived most of the harmonies, as well as contributing one original composition ("Blue in Green," often mistakenly credited to Davis).[12] One reason the album is so important is that, instead of requiring that chords change frequently and bear preset durations, the band used formats in which the harmonies of a single chord or mode remained in effect for four or more measures (see page 421 for explanatory musical notation). Then the group either preset the durations, as with "So What" (available in SCCJ, the modes of which are notated on pages 422–423), or they left the durations up to the spontaneous discretion of the soloist (as in "Flamenco Sketches," on the *Jazz Classics CD*).

The final selection on *Kind of Blue* was created by an interesting improvisational technique. Instead of playing a melody and improvising on its chord changes, the sextet followed a preset sequence of five modes. Each mode served as the harmonic guide for improvisation as long as a soloist wanted to use it. Then, whenever a soloist wanted a change, he moved to the next mode. Although there were no restrictions on the duration of any mode, the soloists tended to use each mode for an even number of measures. In fact, most soloists used each mode for four measures and then moved to the next. So, despite the increased freedom allowed by this technique, the players usually chose duration patterns which typify conventional jazz improvisation.

The final selection on *Kind of Blue* is known by two different titles because many copies of the record were released with the tune titles interchanged on the second side of the album. Bill Evans's album jacket notes indicate that the piece was supposed to be called "All Blues." But after the album was released, several subsequent Davis versions of the second side's *first* selection were released under the "All Blues" title. The name that seems to have stuck for the second side's *second* selection is "Flamenco Sketches." (This appears as the final selection on the CD format.)

After *Kind of Blue* was released, many jazz musicians began using its formats instead of popular song formats. During the 1960s and 1970s, many players rejected the bop custom of using chords that changed frequently and bore preset durations. Entire performances were based on a single chord instead of a progression of different chords. Some performances contained spontaneous chord changes instead of preset changes. In summary, **the historical significance of *Kind of Blue*** was threefold: 1) it represented a set of inspired improvisations by an all-star band; 2) it was a highly palatable departure from bop-derived styles; and 3) it introduced a generation of improvisers to mode-based formats. Incidentally, it is also the most frequently cited album among recommended picks by musicians and critics.

Further historical perspective can be gained for *Kind of Blue* when we consider that at the same time it arrived, considerable attention was also being given to Ornette Coleman, a saxophonist who specialized in improvising with no preset harmonies at all. Whereas Davis was substituting long stretches of modes for rapidly changing chords, Coleman's improvisations were neither mode-based nor chord-based. Coleman spontaneously introduced a tone center and worked from that, then shifted to another and then another.

Coleman's improvisations followed only the internal logic of his melodic inventions, instead of adhering to a single key, mode, or chord progression. Unlike Davis, Coleman almost never used a pianist. Improvisation using such approaches had been recorded by others before Coleman and Davis (see Lennie Tristano, Shorty Rogers, et al. in chapter 10). But only after this work of Davis and Coleman in the late 1950s did the approach catch on with a sizable number of jazz musicians. Then, by the mid-1960s, free-form and modal approaches were mixed in the music of many bands. These related approaches became so abundant that, during the 1970s, more than half of all jazz and jazz-derived performances contained at least some modal or free-form improvisations. During that period, fewer than twenty prominent modern jazz combos played selections which fit neither modal nor free-form styles. An entire school of jazz styles embraced the practice of not presetting the harmonies for improvisation (see chapter 14). Incidentally, the music of the so-called "new age" bands in the 1980s was also largely modal.

Many of the jazz-rock fusion bands of the 1970s and 1980s combined passages of chord progression-based improvisation with passages of mode-based improvisation. Davis himself alternated among all these formats. The impact of *Kind of Blue* was immense. The Davis innovations complemented the developments associated with Coleman to lay the foundation for ways that jazz was structured in the succeeding two decades.

The 1959–63 Rhythm Section

The rhythm section Miles Davis used from 1959 to 1963 consisted of pianist **Wynton Kelly** (1931–1971), bassist Paul Chambers, and drummer Jimmy Cobb. Their work is documented in the albums *Miles Davis at Carnegie Hall, Friday Night at the Blackhawk, Saturday Night at the Blackhawk, Someday My Prince Will Come,* and in the selection "Freddie the Freeloader" on *Kind of Blue.* Their relaxed, even swing feeling and their lightness and bounce distinguished them from all others of the time. This was like the role played by Count Basie's rhythm section in the 1930s. Modern musicians of the era considered this Davis rhythm section to be among the most desirable accompanying units in jazz. Paul Chambers was already discussed in the hard bop chapter, but we will examine Kelly and Cobb here.

Wynton Kelly was a bop pianist who played with a lighter, less complicated feeling than Bud Powell used. He swung infectiously, and his accompaniments followed the melodic and rhythmic flights of the Davis hornmen so well that Kelly's bandmates could hardly help but swing too. Kelly was one of Davis's all-time favorite accompanists, and Cannonball Adderley also praised him highly. Kelly combined influences ranging from Powell to Horace Silver, and on *Someday My Prince Will Come,* he used the chord voicings of Bill Evans. In turn, Kelly himself was influential. Among the modern pianists who showed his influence are Herbie Hancock, Warren Bernhardt, and Keith Jarrett.

Jimmy Cobb (b. 1929) was a steady and swinging drummer. More conservative in his accompanying style than "Philly Joe" Jones, Cobb nonetheless contributed a far-reaching characteristic to modern jazz: **Cobb's ride rhythms were placed toward the front edge of the beat in a way that made them seem to pull the beat.** Though this aspect is subtle, it is quite significant because drummers before Cobb had traditionally played more toward the center of the beat. Tony Williams replaced Cobb in the Davis group, adopted Cobb's timekeeping technique, and played consistently on the leading edge of the beat. Williams had a correspondingly marked effect on the overall feeling of the Davis quintet. Then Williams, in turn, influenced other drummers who became prominent in the 1970s and 1980s.

The 1963–1968 Rhythm Section

In 1963, Miles Davis hired a new rhythm section comprised of pianist **Herbie Hancock,** bassist **Ron Carter,** and drummer **Tony Williams.**[13] This Davis rhythm section remained intact, at least on records, from 1963 until 1968. These musicians created a new jazz idiom. Though moments in their music resembled the sounds of hard bop and free jazz, their music

Listening Guide for

"Flamenco Sketches"

Recorded April 22, 1959 by Miles Davis Sextet; available on the *Jazz Classics CD;* also on Miles Davis, *Kind of Blue* (Columbia: CK 64935, 1959).

Suggestions for keeping your place while hearing "Flamenco Sketches" and following the modal construction

1) Remember that the first track on the second side of *Kind of Blue* has been labeled "Flamenco Sketches" on many copies of this album. So, if you hear a feeling of "ONE two three Four five six ONE two three Four five six" instead of a very slow "ONE two three four ONE two three four," you are listening to the wrong selection.
2) To begin synchronizing your counting with the record, notice that the piece starts with a bass note on the fourth beat of a measure that actually precedes the beginning of your counting. If you are to count accurately, you must say "FOUR" when that first note is sounding, then say "One" when the next bass note sounds. That note lasts three beats, so you must continue counting even though there is no clear statement of any beats until the pattern is repeated. In other words, to get you through the introduction and well synchronized with the tempo of the piece, you need to count "FOUR One two three FOUR One two three FOUR." When you say "FOUR One," you are acknowledging the bass notes. When you say "two three," you are acknowledging the middle of the measure, a time when the bass note is still ringing and no clear statement of beats is coming from the musicians. Eventually, you should be able to count "ONE two three four ONE two three four" with or without assistance from the musicians. This will become important later because bassist Paul Chambers sometimes plays figures that purposely delete the simple pattern outlined above and leave the listener to fill in the beats. You will have some assistance, though, beginning with John Coltrane's entrance, because drummer Jimmy Cobb starts using a wire brush to play ride rhythms on the ride cymbal. If you have yet to figure out where the beats are by the time you are near the end of the selection, simply listen to Cobb's playing under the final Miles Davis solo. It is almost exclusively quarter notes, one note on each beat.
3) Remember that the tempo is very slow, and that you should therefore take care to not be counting twice as fast or four times as fast as the beats are passing.
4) If your mind wanders, let the sound of mode #4 refocus your attention. It has a Spanish flavor that differs noticeably from the flavors of the other modes. It has also attracted the longest improvisations from the musicians and can therefore give you the most time to get back with it. In fact, if you lose your place and all of a sudden find yourself in the middle of that mode, you can restart your counting when that flavor disappears. The disappearance of that flavor will signal the beginning of mode #5.
5) Start counting anew when a different solo voice enters. Remember that the sequence is four measures of piano and bass introduction followed by these sounds each running five modes in sequence: muted trumpet, tenor sax, alto sax, piano, and muted trumpet.

A written transcription of Coltrane's solo on this recording is available from Andrew White, 4830 South Dakota Ave. N.E., Washington, D.C. 20017.

6) Listen carefully for the bass notes that begin the measures. If a new mode is starting, this will often be signalled by the sound of a NEW bass note on the first beat of the measure.
7) To help you anticipate each new mode within a single musician's solo, keep in mind that generally:
   a) Miles Davis lets bassist Paul Chambers lead him to each new mode. Chambers plays the important note of the mode while Davis is silent, then Davis enters with a new melodic idea to fit the mode.
   b) Coltrane tends to increase the number of notes played per beat just before beginning a new mode. In other words, if you hear Coltrane sound like he is going faster and faster, consider the likelihood that he is requesting the next mode.
   c) Adderley suggests the upcoming mode by a peculiar choice of notes in his line. The flavor of his melody line shifts when he is about to change modes.
8) Once you know where you are, if it is the beginning of a mode, count "1234 2234 3234 4234" in order to keep your place by tallying beats as they pass. Each group of four beats ("1234") accounts for one measure. You tag the measures by saying a number to yourself at the beginning of each one. If it is the first measure for the mode, you say, "ONE two three four." If it is the second measure of a given mode, you say, "TWO two three four." If it is the third measure, you say, "THREE two three four."

Eventually you should be able to follow the changing modes without referring to the guide. Your ears will tell you what mode is in effect at a given moment. The whole point of this exercise is to help you peek into what the jazz improviser is doing. By being able to identify the same sounds that the improviser is using as a basis for his solos, you will lessen the mystery of how solos are put together and how musicians manage to play well together without having to discuss their parts or use prewritten themes. The more you recognize in the sounds, the better prepared you are to go on to an appreciation of the compositional beauties present in the improvised lines. Listening for modes to change at the slow pace used by these performers should better equip you for listening to chords changing in conventional jazz pieces. The better you get at accurately anticipating chord changes, the more you will realize how the improviser's lines reflect his own appreciation of how the chords are progressing in a given piece. To a great extent, the progress of a melody line mirrors the progression of harmonies that lies beneath it in the accompanying chord changes. The improvised line reflects the flavor of the underlying chord, and a line improvised in "Flamenco Sketches" often bears the same character as the mode that is implied in that moment's accompaniment harmonies. Once you begin confidently following the music in this piece, it will be as though you are peering through a microscope. But instead of tiny things being made to appear large, ordinarily quick-paced improvisational processes have been slowed down for your calm examination.

CD Track	Elapsed Time	
55	0' 00"	**Introduction**

Four measures of mode #1. The sound of this mode is indicated by bass notes and chord voicings set in a pattern previously used by Bill Evans for his "Peace Piece." What were originally left-hand parts for pianist Evans are given here to bassist Paul Chambers. The pattern has Chambers playing on only the first and the fourth beats of each measure. Pianist Evans plays chords whose harmonies flesh out the rest of the mode's flavor.

56 0' 18" **Miles Davis Muted Trumpet Improvisation**

(with only piano, bass, and brushes on snare drum accompaniment)

mode #1	mode #2	mode #3	mode #4
four measures	four measures	four measures	eight measures

1' 44" mode #5
four measures

57 2' 03" **John Coltrane Tenor Saxophone Improvisation**

(with piano, bass, and ride cymbal accompaniment)

mode #1	mode #2	mode #3	mode #4
four measures	four measures	four measures	eight measures

3' 25" mode #5
four measures

3' 41" mode #5
one-measure introduction to next solo by piano, bass, and ride cymbal

58 3' 44" **Cannonball Adderley Alto Saxophone Improvisation**

(with piano, bass, and cymbals accompaniment)
Notice that bassist Chambers plays less predictably during this solo.

mode #1	mode #2	mode #3
eight measures	four measures	eight measures

(See page 421 for musical notations and technical names of these modes.)

5' 06" mode #4
eight measures
(Drummer Jimmy Cobb plays double-time and adds high-hat closings during the middle of Adderley's treatment of this mode.)
| mode #5
four measures

59 5' 54" **Bill Evans Piano Improvisation**

(with bass and ride cymbal accompaniment)

mode #1	mode #2	mode #3	mode #4
eight measures	four measures	eight measures	four measures

7' 33" mode #5
four measures

60 7' 50" **Miles Davis Muted Trumpet Improvisation**

(with piano, bass, and ride cymbal accompaniment)

mode #1	mode #2	mode #3	mode #4
four measures	four measures	four measures	eight measures

9' 11" mode #5
two measures

Tony Williams, a prime force in the Miles Davis rhythm section of 1963–68.

Photo by Charles Behnke

did not truly belong to either of those classifications. Hints of their new idiom were evident in some of their first recordings, for example *My Funny Valentine,* of 1964. Then, by 1965, every album they produced was filled with new concepts. In addition, these concepts were packaged in performances whose quality was so finished that it belied its freshness. The innovations of this band were performed so smoothly that many listeners, especially journalists, failed to recognize its historical significance. This music disappointed so many jazz fans who expected extensive repetition of brief rhythms, recycled jazz phrases, and funky melodies that it ranked as one of the least popular phases in the Davis recording career. Yet its innovations were at least as significant as those in Davis's better known styles. (For examples of this music, listen to their 1967 studio recording of "Masqualero" on the *Jazz Classics CD.*)

Hancock, Carter, and Williams all displayed stunning technical prowess on their instruments, creating what was probably the smoothest rhythm section sound jazz had experienced. The Hancock-Carter-Williams unit had excitement and power like the Garland-Chambers-Jones rhythm section and sensitivity and delicacy like the Bill Evans-Scott LaFaro-Paul Motian unit. (For a sample of Evans, LaFaro, and Motian, listen to "Solar" on the *Jazz Classics CD.*) These players had digested the work of their most impressive predecessors, combined it with in-depth knowledge and mastery of twentieth-century classical music (Bartok, Hindemith, Debussy, etc.), and then built upon that foundation to create something newer and more sparkling than any other combinations. (Listen to "Masqualero" on the *Jazz Classics CD,* and focus your attention solely on the piano, bass, and drum parts.) This rhythm section could play persuasively in the bop manner if it wished. It could emulate the Wynton Kelly-Paul Chambers-Jimmy Cobb style. And it could work well in the quiet, reflective manner of the Evans-LaFaro-Motian unit. But it was freer, more flexible and daring than those other units, and it came up with music that sounded like no jazz ever heard before. This unit's collective originality and creativity remained unsurpassed decades after its monumental contributions to the 1967 Davis album *Sorcerer* (from which "Masqualero" is taken). Their consolidations were so startling and so well played that it took most of jazz about twenty years to catch up, as evidenced by the wave of similarly styled bands emerging in the 1980s, such as those of Wynton Marsalis and Terence Blanchard.

Hancock, Carter, and Williams maintained an almost magical level of rapport. They were able to play cohesively at breakneck tempos[14] or, in the context of a slow piece, they could avoid explicitly stating tempo and sound instead as though someone were conducting them through gradual accelerations and decelerations.[15] (Listen to the middle section of "Masqualero" on the *Jazz Classics CD.*) Their rapport and high level of musicianship allowed them to change rhythms, textures, and moods spontaneously at any moment of a performance, at any tempo, and on any chord progression. Their versatility and lightning quick responsiveness were extraordinary. Because of this, **the Davis group of the 1960s was one of very few jazz bands that drastically varied its levels of loudness. It was also distinguished for creating a wide variety of distinctly different accompanying rhythms and chord patterns. A clear departure from bop traditions was evident in many of their performances.**

Herbie Hancock

Pianist **Herbie Hancock** combined the best qualities of an improviser: a clear conception, fertile imagination, a highly developed sense of continuity, and excellent instrumental proficiency. He had a quick, precise touch and comped briskly. Like his colleagues in the Davis group, he was also a composer, and his improvisations revealed his keen sense of compositional balance and integrity. He was able consistently to devise coherent, well-structured solos, even for pieces that provided him with only a mode, a mood, a key, and a tempo. Hancock was able to create and perform accompaniment patterns spontaneously during group improvisations that brought the music a form, direction, and substance comparable to that of an elaborate piece which had been worked out in advance.

Hancock contributed gracefully shifting rhythms and harmonies that were more advanced than the patterns used by bop pianists or by such contemporary pianists as Bill Evans and McCoy Tyner. What he invented as underpinning for the soloists often had the character of modern symphonic music. Incidentally, Hancock's superb mastery of the piano and his creative flexibility and taste as an accompanist put him in great demand as a recording pianist. Hancock appeared on more record dates than any other jazz pianist of the 1960s. (For an outline of Hancock's career and contributions, see chapter 15.)

Ron Carter

Bassist **Ron Carter** (b. 1937) had a slick, round tone. He walked with uncanny perfection and buoyancy. Both his tone and his sense of timing exhibited uniformly high quality. Carter played more toward the front of the beat than Paul Chambers did, thereby meshing with the timekeeping manner introduced by drummer Jimmy Cobb in the previous Davis band. He provided a sturdy yet responsive foundation for the quintet. Among musicians, Carter is often considered the most swinging accompanist after Ray Brown and Sam Jones. Yet despite his excellence as a timekeeper, Carter did not always restrict himself to walking. He incorporated other rhythmic figures, too. (Listen to his work at the beginning of "Masqualero" on the *Jazz Classics CD.*) He was continuously devising new ways both to underpin the group sound and to enrich the musical events that occurred around him.[16] This was no small achievement, either. Tony Williams was encircling Carter with exploding rhythmic ideas that had never been used before in jazz combos. And, at the same time, pianist Herbie Hancock was inventing new harmonies to fit these rhythms and moods, all of which had to be smoothly integrated almost at the moment they were conceived. Carter acquitted himself so well in these circumstances that Miles Davis was not the only leader who appreciated him. By the mid-1970s, Carter had been employed on more than four hundred records.

Tony Williams

Drummer **Tony Williams** (b. 1945) represented the highest level of drum technique, and he was possibly the most influential jazz drummer of the 1960s. He was very fast, and his cymbal tones were separated with crystal clarity. Williams provided a model of light, sharp sounds. His ride cymbal playing was very crisp and distinctive, and, because he used a smaller bass drum than most pre-1960s drummers, the low-register component of his drum set's sound was particularly well articulated. Williams was an extremely sophisticated rhythm section player, looser and more of a risk taker than any of his predecessors. Williams did more than kick and prod the hornmen. By the time *Filles de Kilimanjaro* was recorded in 1968, he had assumed a role so prominent that his creations often overshadowed the other sounds in the group. His was a very assertive style.[17]

Williams overflowed with imagination. He devised numerous ways to establish new moods and state the tempo. Let's mention two of them. As early as the 1964 *"Four" and More* album, he had played pieces without following the traditional custom of consistently snapping his high-hat shut on the second and fourth beats of each measure. In this way, he was keeping time only with the ride cymbal, and he was using the high-hat only for bursts of color. Then on "Freedom Jazz Dance" (in the 1966 *Miles Smiles* album) he closed his high-hat sharply on every beat, a timekeeping practice later adopted by hundreds of jazz-rock drummers. He also colored the group sound with a seemingly endless variety of cymbal splashes, snare drum fills, and imaginative rhythmic patterns distributed over all his drums and cymbals (particularly evident at the beginning and the end of "Masqualero" in the *Jazz Classics CD*). His work often departed from the dance band and marching band traditions of jazz drumming. Some of his methods stem from orchestral concepts in which percussion instruments perform melodic and texture-generating roles. Listening to the Davis recordings of this period will reveal why so many drummers were awed and inspired by Williams. Some musicians feel that Williams was the musician most responsible for instigating the florid constructions that came from the mid-1960s Miles Davis quintet. It was Williams who most often provoked the other musicians into their daring flights of nontraditional playing. (To study his contributions, listen to "Masqualero" on the *Jazz Classics CD,* and focus solely on drums and cymbals.)[18]

The 1964–1968 Compositional Style

Davis recorded very few conventionally constructed pieces after saxophonist-composer Wayne Shorter joined him in 1964. Most tunes Davis played during the 1950s fit conventional song forms.[19] **After 1964, Davis favored tunes that did not have bridges, complex turnarounds, or any section demarcations which can easily act as barriers to an unencumbered, free-flowing sound.** Most of his post-1964 recordings were made up of tunes which had fewer chord changes than those in pop standards by Richard Rodgers or George Gershwin, or jazz standards by Charlie Parker, Dizzy Gillespie, or Thelonious Monk.[20]

FIGURE 12.1 Wayne Shorter's melody lines often contain strings of notes separated by the interval of a fourth. Here is part of his "Masqualero." The notes of one phrase of the melody appear on this keyboard in numbered sequence.

The use of space in tune construction was another trait which lent the 1965–1968 recordings their distinctive flavor. Sometimes several measures of the melody were filled with silence. Quite often, trumpet and tenor would lay out while the rhythm section continued to play and generate a mood.[21] Incidentally, these differences in compositional form led to a drastic change not only in the sound of the Miles Davis bands then, but also in other groups of that period which used them.

One other important aspect of the group's compositional style was a significant lessening in the number of rapid, jumpy eighth-note figures which typified the highly syncopated lines of bop. The Davis repertory still contained pieces with some eighth notes and syncopation, but many of the post-1964 tunes were constructed of smoothly contoured lines with frequent sustained tones. By comparison with the compositional style of bop, this new style was less densely packed. These tunes had fewer intricate figures. An airy feeling was more common than a crowded feeling. This, in turn, influenced the character of improvisations the band produced. More variety was possible because of the greater freedom implied by the openness in feeling.

Nefertiti

The Davis quintet performance of Shorter's "Nefertiti," on the *Nefertiti* album of 1967, illustrates both these aspects. It is sixteen measures long, and it is all one section. There is a new chord in every measure, but the motion always has a slow, floating quality. Nothing abrupt or jumpy happens in either the melody or the chord changes. This melody's silences and sustained tones produce an effect unlike that of bop melodies. In addition, the entire performance consists of the melody being repeated again and again. This format was employed extensively by post-1968 Davis groups and spin-offs from those bands. Note that, with no improvised solos by anyone else, this version of "Nefertiti" is practically a feature for Tony Williams. The lazy, expansive feeling evoked by the performance suggests the impressionistic classical music of Claude Debussy ("La Mer," "Prelude to the Afternoon of a Faun") and Maurice Ravel ("Daphnis and Chloe"). The style of this "Nefertiti" performance places the burden of complexity on the rhythm section, quite the reverse of bop tendencies. So not only does the style of the melody differ from bop, the style of the accompaniment differs, too. It is a loose, highly active improvisation by piano, bass, and drums that alternates from walking bass and ride rhythms to moments with volatile drumming and very little internal repetition. Sometimes Carter is playing four times as many notes as a bassist would usually play. At other times, he is playing only a fourth as many as we would expect. Hancock does not always play conventional comping rhythms, either. This contrasts sharply with the almost unvarying sequences of walking bass, ride rhythms, and comping which typify bop accompaniment style. **The post-1964 Davis quintet evolved away from the bop formula of quick, jumpy melodic figures on top and stable, metronomic pulse patterns on the bottom. Shorter's writing brought stable simplicity to the top, and Williams's drumming brought super-charged rhythmic complexity to the bottom. This reversal of roles later became common in jazz-rock groups, especially in the band called Weather Report.**

The three characteristics outlined above all fit with the tremendously explorative attitude of drummer Tony Williams and the effect he had upon his fellow bandmates. He spurred them to use the new freedom that came from the nontraditional song forms and to contrive a fresh sound. This resulted in their creating phrases that were unlike those in previous jazz styles, and it nudged them to devise sound masses that evolved spontaneously and freely shifted. The result of this triumphed to carry the listener on an adventure filled with surprises.

In addition to their extraordinarily high instrumental proficiency, improvisatory freshness, and unique contributions to the development of jazz accompaniment style, Hancock, Shorter, Carter, and Williams managed to ensure that the variety of moods and rhythmic styles employed in the 1964–1968 Davis Quintet was vast. They recorded waltzes,[22] fast pieces,[23] slow-reflective pieces,[24] pieces in which a sequence of different rhythmic styles are created,[25] and pieces that anticipated jazz-rock fusion styles (see chapter 16).

Wayne Shorter

Between summer of 1964 and winter of 1970, Miles Davis employed **Wayne Shorter** (b. 1933). This man proved to be one of the most outstanding tenor saxophonists in jazz of the 1960s, and possibly the most original tenor stylist to emerge after Coltrane and concurrent to Albert Ayler. Shorter was also a composer whose work provided a foundation for the new jazz idiom that was created by the Davis band of 1965–1968. Some musicians consider Shorter to be the most important jazz composer of the 1960s and 1970s. His highly original writing and playing had already been central to the Art Blakey bands of 1959–1964, and they later became central to the work of Weather Report, an innovative jazz-rock fusion band of the 1970s and 1980s.

Shorter's creativity had several sides to it. Some musicians and fans are impressed the most by the side he showed in his work with Art Blakey. They may prefer it because his improvisatory methods with Blakey represent the closest he came to hard bop and using traditional ways of devising lines, such as basing phrases on strings of eighth notes, for example. His work was fluid and extremely intense, projecting a rawness that is common to hard bop. Some listeners find this work more emotionally compelling than his other work. Despite his links with tradition, however, Shorter's playing with Blakey was largely original, its level of inspiration consistently striking.

Tenor saxophonist Wayne Shorter and Miles Davis.

Courtesy of the Jazz Image

Many musicians and fans believe that Shorter's studio recordings of 1965–1968 with Miles Davis constitute his most impressive work. Though similar in many ways to his work with Blakey, these performances highlighted an even more unconventional and exceedingly explorative side to his talents. A softness and introspective quality were exposed here that are not as evident in his work with Blakey. Though his playing in all contexts always exhibited a highly logical quality, his thinking here was more calmly logical, as though this new setting allowed him to be less hurried and more reflective. Perhaps that was why some listeners perceived this music as cool and abstract. Incidentally, the few rare recordings that are available of him playing with this band in concert and nightclub appearances during this period reveal him wrestling passionately with dense swaths of color and rhythm that seem to be burning through the center of the band sound, not cool at all.

Despite the highly logical stance in Shorter's music, the lines were very fresh and rarely predictable. That lack of predictability intensely attracted some listeners, though it lost others. This work could be viewed within the avant-garde category because Shorter was severely stretching the boundaries of what a jazz improviser could do without totally ignoring steady pulse and preset accompaniment harmonies. By this time, he had evolved even further away from the bop approach to melody. His lines were formed from notes of many different durations, not primarily eighth notes. And his rhythms were not necessarily those associated with jazz. In this phase of his career, he did not routinely build solos from standard bop rhythmic figures that swing in obvious ways and busily fill every moment. Some of his phrases did not swing. They intentionally floated over and past the beat instead of getting down inside it. Shorter played lines of smoother contours than those of most hard bop saxophonists. His work did not have as many abrupt starts and stops, or the bobbing up and down that typified bop. His melodic approach often recalled the concise, floating themes, interspersed with long silences, that we find in music by such nonjazz composers as Maurice Ravel, Claude Debussy, and Erik Satie.

Though some listeners think they detect the influence of Sonny Rollins or John Coltrane in Shorter's earliest playing on record (1959 and 1960), the bulk of Shorter's style is most accurately viewed as original and not derivative. Any evidence of stylistic debts to the giants who preceded him has been so thoroughly transformed in his playing that to dwell upon it is unwarranted. In his recordings with Davis, Shorter's tone quality, articulation, rhythmic conception, and melodic tendencies all differ significantly from every major saxophonist who preceded him. His playing was as free of cliches as any saxophone style yet devised. Shorter had such extraordinarily high standards for originality that he usually managed to improvise solos that were free of patterns. He tried to create something entirely new upon each opportunity to improvise, and he usually succeeded.[26]

Shorter's tone quality and manner made his playing easily distinguishable from other saxophonists. Shorter had a gray tone with a broad-textured surface and soft edges. It was a hard sound, but he could temper that hardness according to the mood of the music. Until the 1970s, his tone rarely had vibrato. Though most saxophonists depend partly on vibrato as an expressive device, Shorter cultivated so many other expressive devices that listeners tended to not miss the vibrato. He made masterful use of various attacks and releases. He could slide up into the pitch of a note or strike it head on. He could release a note by carefully tapering it or by bending its pitch up or down. The note might trail off and disappear, or it might fall and then slide up to another. Though his technique was primarily legato, he sometimes gave out stark announcements consisting of brief tones.

Wayne Shorter brought an outstanding gift for melody to his solos. Listening to him improvise is like looking over the shoulder of a composer as he invents and develops themes. Not only did he invent theme after new theme, often using unusual intervals as he improvised, but he also tried to make something significant out of each kernel of melody that he invented. Shorter was a very intelligent improviser who brought a strong sense of continuity to his lines. (Listen to his solo on "Masqualero" on the *Jazz Classics CD.*) Almost every one of Shorter's solo choruses was a coherent and concise melodic statement. Moreover, he played them in a manner which was somehow graceful and ferocious at the same time. Some listeners find a bittersweet quality in his music.

Beginning in 1969, Shorter's style on studio recordings became extremely sparse. He rarely again played as fluidly or lyrically as in his 1965–1968 collaborations with Davis. This was also the time he began playing soprano saxophone. Both these changes are evident on two Davis albums, *In a Silent Way* and *Bitches Brew,* made at a time when Davis was moving into jazz-rock. Shorter continued to play both soprano and tenor saxophones with Weather Report, the jazz-rock fusion band he joined a year after leaving Davis. Shorter changed his style drastically when he joined Weather Report. Instead of long, melodic phrases, he often played short bursts of notes alternating with long silences and sustained tones. This new style meshed well with the sound of a group which depended upon unusual percussion sounds, conversational bass figures, and crackling keyboard ideas. Often Shorter let many beats pass without playing at all. Then, after playing only a note or two, he became silent again. His was a very difficult role. Instead of creating melodic improvisations, he participated in a collective effort to create undulating textures. The delicate balance achieved in the collective improvisations of Weather Report's early years is due in part to Shorter's tasteful and very disciplined sense of musical discretion. **He artfully made the difficult transition from jazz soloist in the conventional sense to ensemble improviser in the new context created by Weather Report.** (Listen to Shorter on "Surucucu" on the *Jazz Classics CD,* taken from a 1972 concert performance available in Weather Report's *I Sing the Body Electric.*)[27]

Wayne Shorter's Composing

Wayne Shorter was one of the key composers of the 1960s and 1970s. He wrote extensively for albums of his own and contributed substantially to the repertories of three historically significant groups: Art Blakey's Jazz Messengers (1959–1964), the Miles Davis Quintet (1964–1969), and Weather Report (1971–1985). Though the details are beyond the nontechnical scope of this book, **Shorter's historical significance is partly determined by the unusual ways that he makes chords move within his compositions.** Some of his tunes place chords in sequences which had never been common to jazz. His compositions are the subject of much study by musicians and scholars, and Shorter is one of the most respected of all post-bop jazz composers. His tunes are performed and recorded by hundreds of other musicians. Many feel that his writing is an even more important contribution to jazz than his saxophone playing.

Shorter was notable for supplying Weather Report with a style for one branch of its repertory: pieces that conveyed a pastoral feeling by dreamy melodies containing many silences and sustained tones, performed at a relatively slow tempo. They often resulted in a sense of suspension.[28] An historic aspect in the performance of some of these pieces is the **reversal of character traditionally assumed by jazz melody and accompaniment, respectively.**[29] The melodies here are floating and simple, whereas the accompaniments are hard driving and complex, as in the Davis quintet recording of Shorter's "Nefertiti."

Another aspect of Weather Report's music linked to the 1967 studio recording of "Nefertiti" is **the extensive repetition of melodic lines within a single rendition while continuous variation of accompaniment figures occurs.** This was not Shorter's idea; it

Listening Guide for

"Masqualero"

Recorded May 17, 1967 by trumpeter Miles Davis, tenor saxophonist Wayne Shorter, pianist Herbie Hancock, bassist Ron Carter, and drummer Tony Williams; available on the *Jazz Classics CD;* and on Miles Davis, *Sorcerer* (Columbia: CK 65680, 1967).

The melody for "Masqualero" was composed by Wayne Shorter. Like his tunes "Nefertiti" and "E.S.P.," it also features a succession of notes that are separated by the interval of a fourth (see Fig. 12.1). The second phrase of the melody has only ten notes—one pitch played three times, followed by a pitch one fourth lower that is played three times, followed by a pitch that is another fourth lower played three times, followed by a pitch that is a half-step lower. Incidentally, this particular sequence of intervals contributes to the sense of mystery that much of Shorter's music evokes.

The arrangement of "Masqualero" here is almost entirely spontaneous. Unissued live recordings of this piece by the same band only remotely resemble it. Unlike the arrangements discussed in previous listening guides, there is only a hint of preset organization here, often only the tempo and a few bass notes. The piano, bass, and drum parts were being devised while they were being performed. This recording presents pianist Herbie Hancock, bassist Ron Carter, and drummer Tony Williams in a cooperative improvisation of immense scope and invention. Played with impeccable musicianship, this performance is a stunning example of master improvisers confidently working at a high level of creativity. It is essential to remember that Hancock, Carter, and Williams are not merely accompanying trumpeter Davis and saxophonist Shorter. They are working as composers collaborating in the creation of a new piece of music. They are particularly sensitive to each other's playing, and they complement one another extremely well. This performance offers more examples of spontaneous interaction than any other piece on the *Jazz Classics CD.* The result is an extemporaneous work that takes the listener through significant changes in loudness, melody, texture, and rhythm, showing almost as much internal contrast and development as we might find in a prewritten symphonic piece. In some respects, it even evokes the drama we expect of an opera.

The musicians were free to invent melodies and transform them throughout the performance. Some solo passages are particularly melodic, as in the sax improvisation from about 5' 25" to 5' 50". The improvisers sometimes quote or paraphrase the original melody or the improvised line of a fellow band member. Occasionally they pass it around, each player echoing another's phrase (as in Hancock mimicking Davis at about 53" and at 1' 01" and Carter paraphrasing the melody at about 6' 35"). Sometimes they play the intact sequence of notes that define the mode (as in the sax solo at about 3' 43").

Many accompaniment harmonies in this performance were chosen spontaneously during the performance itself, not planned in advance. The musicians were free to create new melodies and harmonies guided loosely by the knowledge of what notes would be compatible with those provided by the bass part and the melody that occurred at the beginning of the piece. Basically, the harmonies here only give the music a start. They do not influence the course of improvised ideas as much as chord progressions in earlier styles did. Nor do the accompaniment rhythms under the melody constrain the rhythmic aspects of the music that evolves during the performance. Though steady tempo is maintained throughout the performance, the players are free to change melody, texture, and rhythmic style from moment to moment. Unlike pre-1960s jazz, central features of this piece's organization emerge and change spontaneously.

Over the course of the performance, soloists vary the extent to which they make their phrases swing. Sometimes they lock their rhythms tightly to the underlying pulse (as in the end of the trumpet solo, at about 2' 47"). The accompanists also vary in this respect. Tony Williams plays a continuous sequence of eighth notes on his ride cymbal through much of the piece, though he interrupts it sporadically to play rhythms on his snare drum and tom-toms that decorate the solo lines and change the mood of the performance. Ron Carter plays widely differing patterns on bass, never walking, though sometimes he plays the steady pattern that Wayne Shorter wrote for the piece.

Outstanding features of this performance include the remarkable freshness of the solo improvisations, the spontaneous changes in intensity (as in the steady increase from 5' 30" to 5' 50"), changes in rhythmic style (it changes most dramatically at 2' 37" and 3' 20"), and changes in texture. The music's texture thickens at about 1' 50" and thins at about 2' 12", then thickens again at about 2' 37" and thins at about 3' 20". Texture changes also occur at 6' 30" and 7'. It thickens considerably at 7' 52" and thins at 8' 18".

Probably the best way to begin appreciating this performance is to first make yourself comfortable in a place removed from anything you might find distracting. Use of a headset would be ideal. Close your eyes. Empty your mind of all thoughts and feelings except the intention to let the music take you wherever it can. Pretend that you are on an unhurried journey with trustworthy guides who promise to show you many new vistas. Then just listen. Don't be concerned with trying to identify all the sounds the first time you listen. Pursue those details in repeated listenings with this guide. The virtues of this performance are not only the beauty of the sounds themselves but also the success with which the players have improvised shifting lines and textures, as though their parts were strains of movement in a ballet with three or more dancers always in motion.

The form for most of this performance of "Masqualero" is A-B-A, sections of which are 8, 6, and 8 measures long, respectively. Though following repetitions of that form for most of the performance, the band makes a few departures from that organization. These are noted in the descriptions of the Wayne Shorter and Herbie Hancock solos.

OPTIONAL TECHNICAL INFORMATION: Musicians describe the harmonic basis of improvisations in this piece as "playing off a pedal point" and using a "modal flavor" or "modal color." This means that one note (usually in the bass register), "the pedal," dominates throughout that section, and atop it are played strings of notes that draw from one particular mode, though the musicians do not adhere exclusively to those notes.* Periodically a single chord abruptly occurs that differs significantly in flavor from the collection of chords that have maintained a given mode for a long passage. Musicians call the use of this chord "a cadence point," a moment of resolving tension and preparing for another stretch of music. Such a chord is used here to allow a few beats of separation between sections, particularly at the end of each B-section.

*For details, study the phrygian mode on page 419 of this book, and see chapter 6 in *Creative Jazz Improvisation* by Scott Reeves. Some of Shorter's improvisation from this performance is transcribed and analyzed by Reeves.

CD Track	Elapsed Time	
78	0' 00"	**Introduction** (8 measures) *Instruments: piano, bass, and drums* The proceedings begin loosely and then tighten as the horns' entrance approaches. Williams is playing complicated rhythms on the ride cymbal and rolls on his tom-toms. High-hat cymbals are vibrating against each other. Carter is playing pizzicato eighth notes and pauses, mostly irregular figures. Hancock is firmly sounding a string of chords that ascend like steps, each one ringing and separated from the next by a brief pause. Rhythmic activity in the bass and drums is so complex that the downbeat may be hard to detect. Hancock makes the rhythm clearer. His piano chords are grouped in three's; the first chord of each group is played on the downbeat.
		First Statement of the Theme (A-B-A)
79	0' 14"	*A-Section* (8 measures) The opening statement can be interpreted as a dialog between the horns and the piano. The composed melody starts with a two-bar phrase and alternates with two measures of silence. Hancock uses the silence to respond to the previous melodic statement. Trumpet and sax play three notes slurred together in harmony. Hancock responds with two quick chords, then three chords that mirror the horns' opening notes.
	0' 22"	Trumpet and sax play notes of the second phrase in octaves and unisons. The melody moves by the interval of a fourth. Horns pause again for seven beats while the piano fills in with a brief melodic phrase of harp-like tones which complements the second horn-like phrase.
	0' 29"	*B-section* (6 measures) Horns return in harmony. A brief trumpet phrase is answered by sax.
	0' 36"	Trumpet plays harmony notes beneath sax. This statement of the B-section concludes with horns, piano, and bass uniting on two chords, punctuated by drums. These two chords (termed a "cadence point") will be heard during the solos and can be used by the listener as indications for the form. Sax trails off at the end of this section.
	0' 39"	*A-section* (8 measures) Trumpet plays the first phrase alone. Hancock's chords, higher in pitch and more sharply articulated than before, lend more tension to this second statement of the A-section.
	0' 47"	Sax joins trumpet to play the second phrase of the melody, but an octave higher than before. Hancock plays a sequence of chords slurred together, echoing the rhythm of the previous two-measure melody.

First Chorus of the Miles Davis Trumpet Solo (A-B-A)

80 0' 54" *A-section* (8 measures)

Davis opens with a slow, three-note climb that is mimicked by Hancock on piano. (This follows the dialog format used in the melody statements.) Then Davis comes down from the high register with a more involved figure, and is pursued by a piano figure imitating the last few notes in that phrase.

1' 08" *B-section* (6 measures)

Piano accompanies Davis with a slowly ascending, step-wise string of notes.

1' 15" A transition occurs between 1' 15" and 1' 20". This is the "cadence point" (interruption in the harmony that has been sustaining underneath the first four measures of the B section). Williams underscores the change in harmony with his drumming before the group begins the last A-section.

1' 19" *A-section* (8 measures)

Activity lessens temporarily.

Bass is neither walking, nor playing a single repeating figure. It is playing fragmented patterns of eighth notes that do not emphasize the first beat of each measure. This lends the music a suspended feeling.

Second Solo Chorus for Miles Davis (A-B-A)

81 1' 33" *A-section* (8 measures)

Hancock alternates between a pair of chords and a contrasting rhythmic pattern.

Williams has begun a pattern of steady eighth notes played by drumsticks striking the ride cymbal.

1' 48" *B-section* (6 measures)

Exploding sounds from drums; temporary departure from steady rhythms on ride cymbal. Energy has increased accordingly, and Hancock's two chords which conclude the B-section struggle to be heard through the busy texture. This lasts until about 2' 15".

1' 58" *A-section* (8 measures)

Williams plays a slow roll on the tom-tom followed by the arrival of a high note on the trumpet.

Third Chorus of Miles Davis Solo (A-B-A)

82 2' 12" *A-section* (8 measures)

Activity softens, the mood calms, as though to prepare for another barrage. Williams returns to steady eighth notes on ride cymbal.

2' 27" *B-section* (6 measures)

Davis glosses a single tone over and over before ending his phrase. Tom-tom roll and high-register trumpet phrase begin a new adventure.

2' 37" *A-section* (8 measures)

Piano plays a repeating chorded figure in a staccato manner, which starts on the downbeat of the measure ("bump..bump-bump....bump..bump-bump..."). This rhythm persists through the next A-section, blurring the ending of this chorus and the beginning of the next (to about 3' 05"). Cymbals become louder, crashing amidst the timekeeping rhythms. These alterations in piano and percussion patterns dramatically change the music's character.

Fourth Chorus of Miles Davis Solo (A-B)

83 2' 51" *A-section* (8 measures)

Trumpet goes into the high register, squealing doit-like. Davis emphasizes the beats very prominently.

3' 06" *B-section* (6 measures)

Carter is playing fragmented figures of eighth notes in the upper register of his bass, serving as a transition between the end of the trumpet solo and the beginning of the saxophone solo. Drums and cymbals get softer, evoking a mood of anticipation.

Discrepancy in Following the Composition's Form: The band drops the final *A-section*.

3' 16" *A-section* (8 measures) **New Chorus Starts** (A-B-A)

This section is shared by Davis fading out using the original melody line and Shorter entering during the fourth measure. The music conjures a mysterious mood.

84 3' 22" **Wayne Shorter Saxophone Solo**

Shorter paraphrases the tune's melody, stretching each note until it is almost behind the beat.

Shorter begins with rhythms that do not swing in a particularly obvious manner. The rhythm section is propelling the piece, and Shorter's lines are oozing over it. Notice the remarkable continuity in the construction of Shorter's improvisation.

3' 31" *B-section* (6 measures)

Carter is sliding pitches on his bass and playing eighth-note figures interspersed by silences. He also repeats and extensively develops a single idea, interesting by itself, apart from its accompaniment value.

3' 39" Just prior to the beginning of the last *A-section* Shorter plays a long, mournful, high note on his tenor sax. (Shorter has said that the ultimate skill is achieved when a player can make a listener cry by playing just one note.)

3' 42" *A-section* (8 measures)

Carter is accompanying with a bass figure that is three beats long, setting up a pattern of accents that contrasts with the piece's underlying four-beat pulse. He continues this into the next chorus.

Second Chorus of Wayne Shorter Saxophone Solo (A-B-A)

85 3' 56" *A-section* (8 measures)

4' 03" Sax is playing syncopated tones starkly separated from each other.

4' 10" *B-section* (6 measures)

Shorter pauses at the end of this section.

4' 21" *A-section* (8 measures)

Shorter returns with a low-pitched sustained tone. His line then slowly climbs out of the low register, seeming to float past the beats instead of closely aligning with them.

Third Chorus of Wayne Shorter Saxophone Solo (A-B-A)

86 4' 35" *A-section* (8 measures)

Shorter creates a long melodic line that slides outside the harmonies of the accompaniment. Drums and cymbals are momentarily silent.

4' 49" *B-section* (6 measures)

Sax line climbs into the higher register, each note a half-step higher in pitch. Carter accompanies with a pizzicato tremolo on bass.

5' 00" *A-section* (8 measures)

Fourth Chorus of Wayne Shorter Saxophone Solo (A-B-A + 2-A)

87 5' 15" *A-section* (8 measures)

Piano ceases for the entire chorus. Notice the tension evoked by its absence.

5' 28" *B-section* (6 measures)

Drumming is highly active, louder and more dense.

5' 39" *A-section* (8 measures plus an extra 2 measures)

Shorter creates a new, more animated mood, collaborating only with bass and drums, mostly tom-toms. He selects high-pitched sax tones and seems to be having a musical conversation with drums. Shorter invents ascending phrases that logically build upon each other, each separated by silence, each higher in tension until he reaches the climax note.

This peak occurs later than the eighth measure. So Hancock waits two extra measures before he returns to complement the resolution of the tension and restart repetitions of the composition's 8-6-8 measure form.

5' 56" Departure From Composition's Form: An Extra A-Section (8 measures)

Piano resumes. Hancock plays the down beat for the first of every group of eight beats. Once again Shorter uses his device of constructing phrases which build upon each other. This time the phrases descend, and excitement descends accordingly.

The sounds of drums and cymbals soften in anticipation of the upcoming piano solo.

88 6' 11" **Herbie Hancock Piano Solo** (A-A-B-A-A)

This solo has very few bop characteristics. It often sounds more like the impressionistic piano music of twentieth-century composers Claude Debussy and Maurice Ravel.

Departure From Composition's Form: The band plays no *B-section* here.

A-Section (8 measures)

6' 25" Departure From Composition's Form: The band plays an extra *A-section* (8 measures)

Cascades of legato notes in harmony making a waterfall-like sound. It is accompanied by a roll played by drumsticks on the high-hat cymbal and very little bass activity. This creates the illusion that timekeeping has been suspended. Notice how this has dramatically changed the character of the music.

6' 39" *B-section* (6 measures)

Hancock sounds the same piano note again and again, then a new one again and again. Each one is higher pitched than the last, giving direction to the solo line.

Bass is echoing the melody.

6' 50" *A-section* (8 measures)

7' 03" Departure From Composition's Form: An Extra *A-Section* (8 measures)

Second Chorus of Herbie Hancock Piano Solo (A-B-A)

89 7' 17" *A-section* (8 measures)

Harp-like piano tones ringing, separated by silences; accompanied by steady eighth notes on ride cymbal.

7' 31" *B-section* (6 measures)

Bass is echoing the melody.

7' 42" *Last A-section* (8 measures)

Hancock plays chords on the piano in a staccato rhythmic way, re-establishing swing feeling and preparing for return of the horns. Bass repeats same note again and again (termed a "pedal tone").

90 7' 56" **Final Melody Statement** (A-B)

A-section (8 measures)

Trumpet and tenor sax return in harmony.

They are answered by piano.

Second phrase is played in octaves by trumpet and tenor sax. Piano answers by playing notes in pairs (intervals of a fourth) ascending the keyboard.

8' 10" *B-section* (6 measures)

Trumpet and saxophone exchange the phrases of the *B-section,* after which the saxophone trails off.

Ending (A-B)

91 8' 21" *A-section* (8 measures)

No horns.

8' 35" *B-section* (6 measures)

Piano, bass, and drums use the accompaniment for the *B-section* to tack on a conclusion.

Piano chords are played percussively with clashing voicings.

Williams is scattering strokes around his drum set.

8' 42" The piece concludes with a roll on the tom-tom with the piano sustaining the same chord that has been used to end previous *B-sections* (the "cadence chord").

stemmed from the manner in which the music was organized by Miles Davis and Tony Williams at the original "Nefertiti" recording session. However, Shorter's composition provided the impetus for this approach, and both Shorter and Weather Report's leader Joe Zawinul capitalized upon the approach in constructing pieces for the band.[30]

The facets described here only scratch the surface of Shorter's compositional contributions. For example, he also wrote a number of engaging themes that are waltzes. And he wrote pieces for Weather Report that possess a funky, dance-like sound.[31] To begin exploring the world of Shorter's music, keep in mind that Shorter's work for Miles Davis and Weather Report is easy to find because it is on Columbia records that were sufficiently popular to stay in print. However, do not let the convenience of this Columbia documentation allow you to overlook the richness contained in the many albums he made as bandleader for Blue Note records[32] and those made with Art Blakey for Blue Note, Riverside, and other companies. Many of the compositions that have attracted the attention of musicians and scholars lie in the Blue Note material.

Red Garland, Miles Davis, Paul Chambers, Art Taylor, Sonny Rollins, 1957.
Photo by Bob Parent. Courtesy of Don Parent

CHAPTER SUMMARY

1) Miles Davis was an innovative trumpeter and bandleader.
2) He hired key innovators of the day at three different phases of jazz history and led them to outstanding recordings that remain landmarks of those styles—cool jazz, modal jazz, and jazz-rock fusion.
3) The Davis trumpet style is unmistakable for its tone quality, expressive variations in pitch, and judicious timing of phrases. He is not afraid to play simply, and some of his most dramatic solos are constructed of very few notes.
4) Davis displayed a concern for smooth sound texture that was evident in his trumpet sound as well as his attraction to Claude Thornhill's band sound, and a particular interest in meshing with the chord voicings of his accompanists.
5) With the help of pianist Bill Evans on the *Kind of Blue* album, Davis popularized mode-based formats in modern jazz.
6) With arranger Gil Evans, Davis recorded three famous albums of Third Stream music: *Miles Ahead, Sketches of Spain,* and *Porgy and Bess.*
7) Tenor saxophonist Wayne Shorter contributed a fresh solo style to jazz.
8) Shorter's solos and compositions significantly affected the character of the Art Blakey band, the Miles Davis group, and Weather Report.
9) Shorter was influential in his compositional use of a) the interval of a fourth; b) sustained tones and silences in melody lines; c) melodic construction that suggests a dreamy, floating quality; and d) chord sequences previously unusual in jazz.
10) The Davis rhythm section of 1964–1968 included pianist Herbie Hancock, bassist Ron Carter, and drummer Tony Williams.
11) The Hancock-Carter-Williams unit was among the most skilled, gifted, and exploratory rhythm sections in jazz history.

NOTE: For more about Miles Davis, his groups and sidemen, see Jack Chambers, *Milestones: The Music & Times of Miles Davis* (DaCapo, 1998); Ian Carr, *Miles Davis: A Biography* (Morrow, 1982); Miles Davis with Quincy Troupe, *Miles: The Autobiography* (Simon & Schuster, 1989); Bill Kirchner, *The Miles Davis Reader* (Smithsonian, 1997); Gary Carner, *The Miles Davis Companion: Four Decades of Commentary* (Schirmer, 1996).

◇MILES DAVIS RECORDS

Most of Miles Davis's career is documented by just two record companies: Prestige and Columbia. To help you obtain the music, Miles Davis's Columbia recordings cited in this chapter, the Bill Evans chapter, the John Coltrane chapter, and the jazz-rock fusion chapter are listed here in chronological order. For each entry, the current catalog number is listed first; the original catalog number is in parentheses. Unless indicated "LP," all items are in the compact disc format.

Round About Midnight, Columbia: CK 40610 (CL 949), 1955–56
Miles Davis/Gil Evans: The Complete Columbia Studio Recordings, Columbia: CXK 67397, 6CD set, 1957–68
Miles Ahead, Columbia: CK 53225 (CL 1041), 1957 (with Gil Evans)
Milestones, Columbia: CK 40837 (CL 1193), 1958
Miles and Coltrane, Columbia: CK 44052, 1955, 1958
Porgy and Bess, Columbia: CK 65141 (CS 8085/CL 1274), 1958 (with Gil Evans)
'58 Sessions, Columbia: CK 47835 (32470), 1958
Kind of Blue, Columbia: CK 64935 (CS 8163/CL 1355), 1959

Sketches of Spain, Columbia: CK 65142 (CS 8271/CL 1480), 1959–60 (with Gil Evans)
Someday My Prince Will Come, Columbia: CK 40947 (CS 8456/CL 1656), 1961
Friday Night at the Blackhawk, Columbia: CK 44257 (CS 8469/CL 1669), 1961
Saturday Night at the Blackhawk, Columbia: CK 44425 (CS 8470/CL 1670), 1961
Miles Davis at Carnegie Hall: The Complete Concert, Columbia: C2K 65027 (CS 8612/ CL 1812), 2CD set, 1961
Seven Steps to Heaven, Columbia: CK 48827 (CS 8851/CL 2051), 1963
Miles Davis in Europe, Columbia: SRCS 5705 (CS 8983/CL 2183), 1963 (import)
The Complete Concert 1964: My Funny Valentine + "Four" and More, Columbia: C2K 48821, (CS 9106/CL 2306) + (CS 9253/CL 2453), 2CD set, 1964
Miles in Berlin, Columbia: CDCBS 62976, 1964 (import)
Miles Davis Quintet 1965–1968: The Complete Columbia Studio Recordings, Columbia: AC6K 67398, 6CD set, 1965–68
E.S.P., Columbia: CK 65683 (CS 9150/CL 2350), 1965
The Complete Live at the Plugged Nickel, Columbia: CXK 66955, 6CD set, 1965
Miles Smiles, Columbia: CK 65682 (CS 9401/CL 2601), 1966
Sorcerer, Columbia: CK 65680 (CS 9532/CL 2732), 1967
Nefertiti, Columbia: CK 65681 (CS 9594), 1967
Miles in the Sky, Columbia: CK 65684 (CS 9628), 1968
Filles de Kilimanjaro, Columbia: CK 46116 (CS 9750), 1968
In a Silent Way, Columbia: CK 40580 (CS 9875), 1969
The Complete Bitches Brew Sessions, Columbia: C4K 65570, 4CD set, 1969–70
Big Fun, Sony (Japan): SRCS 5713/5714 (PG 32866), 2CD set, 1969–72 (import)
Live-Evil, Columbia: C2K 65135 (30954), 2CD set, 1970
Miles Davis Live at Fillmore: Live at Fillmore East, Columbia: C2K 65139 (30038), 2CD set, 1970
Black Beauty: Miles Davis at Fillmore West, Columbia: C2K 65138, 2CD set, 1970
A Tribute to Jack Johnson, Columbia: CK 47036 (30455), 1970
Get Up With It, Columbia: COL 485256 2 (33236), 2CD set, 1970–74 (import)
On the Corner, Columbia: CK 53579 (31906), 1972
Miles Davis in Concert: Live at Philharmonic Hall, Columbia: C2K 65140 (32092), 2CD set, 1972 (import)
Agharta, Columbia: C2K 46799 (33967), 2CD set, 1975
Pangaea, Columbia: C2K 46115 (CBS/Sony 50DP 239–40), 2CD set, 1975

NOTES

1. Though original in most respects, Davis did model his sound and some of his improvisatory concept after Freddie Webster's. From Webster and from saxophonist Lester Young, he derived the attitude that the solo improviser should try to invent a countermelody that is as majestic and song-like as the original and which sounds as though it were somehow sailing above the original. Davis also shared Webster's affection for the low register, a clear, wide tone, long notes, and an overall gentleness in manner. This is evident most in his performance of slow tunes around 1945, then beginning again in 1954, particularly with his recording of "The Man I Love." This is a piece Webster had previously recorded (in May of 1945) in a similar manner. To hear this, compare Webster's tone quality, articulation, and overall manner on "You're Not the Kind" (1946) on Sarah Vaughan, *Tenderly* (Musicraft: 70057, 1946–48) or *Bebop* (New World: 271, LP, 146–56) with the Davis solo on "Now's the Time" (1945) from *The Charlie Parker Story* (Savoy: SV-0105 [12079], 1945). Davis has also cited Clark Terry and Dizzy Gillespie as inspiration for his own style. Parker's and Gillespie's influence is most evident on Davis's up-tempo improvisations from the mid-1940s. For transcription and analysis of the Davis solo on "So What" from *Kind of Blue* (also on SCCJ), see Scott Reeves, *Creative Jazz Improvisation, 2nd ed.* (Prentice-Hall, 1995; available from Jamey Aebersold, P.O. Box 1244, New Albany, IN 47150-1244). Other Davis solos are transcribed in Stuart Isacoff, *Miles Davis* (Amsco, 1979; available from Aebersold).
2. All album citations in this chapter that do not have record label and catalog numbers footnoted are Columbia recordings listed at the end of the chapter.
3. Listen to the slowest pieces on *Seven Steps to Heaven* and *Kind of Blue,* or "Summertime" on SCCJ.
4. An excellent example of this is the "Freddie the Freeloader" solo on *Kind of Blue.*
5. For examples, listen to his solos on Charlie Parker's recording "Now's The Time" (cited in footnote 1 above); his own recordings of "The Man I Love" on *Miles Davis & the Modern Jazz Giants* (Fantasy: OJCCD-347-2 [Prestige 7150], 1954); "Bags' Groove" on *Bag's Groove* (Fantasy: OJCCD-245-2 [Prestige 7109],1954); "Eighty-One" on *E.S.P.* (1965); "Sivad" on *Live-Evil* (1971); or "So What" on *Kind of Blue* and SCCJ.
6. Listen to "Freddie the Freeloader" on *Kind of Blue* or "Sid's Ahead" on *Milestones.*
7. As on the final selection of *Kind of Blue,* "Fishermen, Strawberry, and Devil Crab" on *Porgy and Bess,* or the first few measures of "My Funny Valentine" and "Stella By Starlight" on the *My Funny Valentine* album (reissued as *The Complete Concert 1964*). For transcription and analysis of the 1964 "My Funny Valentine" solo, see Stuart Isacoff, *Solos for Jazz Trumpet* (Carl Fischer, 1985; available by mail from Carl Fischer Music Store, 54 Cooper Square, NY, NY 10003).
8. As in his 1956 recording of "It Never Entered My Mind" on *Workin'* (Fantasy: OJCCD-296-2 [Prestige 7166]), his 1963 recording of "I Fall In Love Too Easily" on *Seven Steps to Heaven,* or his 1964 "My Funny Valentine" and "Stella By Starlight" on the *The Complete Concert 1964* album.
9. Electronically created echo is heard in *Bitches Brew* and side one of *Tribute to Jack Johnson.* Davis used electronic wah-wah on *Live-Evil.*
10. *Cookin'* (Fantasy: OJCCD-128-2 [Prestige 7094], 1956); *Relaxin'* (Fantasy: OJCCD-190-2 [Prestige 7129], 1956); *Workin'* (Fantasy: OJCCD-296-2 [Prestige 7166],1956); *Steamin'* (Fantasy: OJCCD-391-2 [Prestige 7200], 1956).
11. This is the same classical piece that inspired Chick Corea's "Spain," which in turn was made popular in a vocal rendition by Al Jarreau.
12. Listen to "Peace Piece" by Evans on *Everybody Digs Bill Evans* (Fantasy: OJCCD-068-2 [Riverside 1129], 1958), recorded four months before *Kind of Blue.*
13. By the summer of 1964, this rhythm section had made half of a studio album, *Seven Steps to Heaven,* and three concert albums: *Miles in Europe, My Funny Valentine,* and *"Four" and More* (reissued on *The Complete Concert 1964*). For more details about personnel, concert dates, and recording sessions, see Jack Chambers, *Milestones: The Music and Times of Miles Davis* (DaCapo, 1998); for appraisal of Davis's career, see Ian Carr, *Miles Davis* (Morrow, 1982).
14. "Walkin" on *"Four" and More* (reissued on *The Complete Concert 1964*).
15. "My Funny Valentine" on *My Funny Valentine* (reissued on *The Complete Concert 1964*), "Madness" on *Nefertiti,* and "Masqualero" on *Sorcerer.*
16. Listen to Carter's playing on "Pee Wee" and "Masqualero" (*Sorcerer*), "Freedom Jazz Dance" (*Miles Smiles*), and "Riot," "Fall," and "Nefertiti" (all on *Nefertiti*).
17. Compare Kenny Clarke's performance on the records Miles Davis made during the early 1950s with Tony Williams's playing on *Filles de Kilimanjaro* or *Miles Smiles.* You will hear a drastic difference between the two.
18. Though it took a long time to become common in jazz, the influence of the 1963–1968 Davis rhythm section style was evident later in recordings by Joe Henderson: *The Milestone Years* (Milestone: 8MCD 4413-2, 8CD set, 1967–75) which includes *The Kicker* (Fantasy: OJCCD-465-2 [Milestone 9008], 1967); *Tetragon* (Fantasy: OJCCD-844-2 [Milestone: 9017], 1967–68); *Power to the People* (Milestone: 9024, LP, 1969); *If You're Not Part of the Solution, You're Part of the Problem* (Milestone: 9028, LP, 1970); and *In Pursuit of Blackness* (Milestone: 9034, LP, 1971). Also see Joe Farrell: *Joe Farrell Quartet* (CTI/CBS: ZK 40694 [6003], 1970). The rhythm section style of *Miles In Europe* and *"Four" and More* was later heard in records by Freddie Hubbard, Jackie McLean (*Right Now,* Blue Note: 84215, 1965), and others. The Davis quintet approaches on *Miles Smiles, Miles in the Sky,* and *Nefertiti* influenced the Art Lande group of the 1970s: *Rubisa Patrol* (ECM: 1081, LP, 1976); and the Wynton Marsalis/Branford Marsalis quintet of the 1980s: *Wynton Marsalis* (Columbia: CK 37574, 1982); *Think of One* (Columbia: CK 38641, 1983); *Black Codes (From the Underground)* (Columbia: CK 40009, 1985).
19. After the departure of Bill Evans and prior to the arrival of Wayne Shorter, Davis had not explored much new territory in the area of song forms. This is revealed by the repertory on *Someday My Prince Will Come* (1961), *Friday/Saturday Night at the Blackhawk* (1961), *Seven Steps to Heaven* (1963), *Miles in Europe* (1963), *"Four" and More* (1964) (reissued on *The Complete Concert 1964*), and *My Funny Valentine* (1964) (reissued on *The Complete Concert 1964*).
20. A large number of post-1964 compositions are all A instead of A-A-B-A, A-B-A-B, or A-B-A-C. On *E.S.P.* is Shorter's "Iris," a 16-bar waltz: all A.

On *Sorcerer* is Shorter's "Prince of Darkness," 16 bars long with very few prearranged harmonies. On *E.S.P.* is his "E.S.P.," 16 bars long: all A, with important and frequent chord changes. It is played twice, as 12 bars + 4-bar turnaround, then 12 bars + 4-bar conclusion. The 4-bar sections differ, but the 12-bar sections are identical.

21. On *Miles Smiles* is Shorter's "Dolores," 38 bars long, divided into phrases of 2, 2 1/2, 3, and 3 1/2 measures. These phrases are separated by spaces in which the horns do not play. Only the rhythm section is heard. They are continuing and developing patterns they had played underneath the horns.
22. Davis's "Circle" and Shorter's "Footprints" (both on *Miles Smiles*), Hancock's "Little One" and Carter's "Mood" (both on *E.S.P.*), and Williams's "Pee Wee" (*Sorcerer*).
23. Jimmy Heath's "Gingerbread Boy," Shorter's "Dolores" and "Orbits" (all on *Miles Smiles*), Williams's "Hand Jive" (*Nefertiti*), Hancock's "The Sorcerer" (*Sorcerer*), Carter's "R.J." and Shorter's "E.S.P." (both on *E.S.P.*).
24. Shorter's "Fall" (*Nefertiti*), "Masqualero" and "Vonetta" (both on *Sorcerer*).
25. Davis's "Country Son" (*Miles in the Sky*) and the Davis-Carter "Eighty-One" (*E.S.P.*).
26. He could handle hard, raw playing, and yet his ballad work was tender. Among his most inspired and well-formed improvisations are those he contributed to Miles Davis's *E.S.P.* (1965) and *Sorcerer* (1967). Listen to his solo on "Eighty-One" from *E.S.P.* Note the middle section which is so melodic that it could be taken out of context and used as a tune. In spite of its very deliberate construction, it carries searing emotion. Listen to his improvisation on "Pee Wee" on Davis's *Sorcerer.* It is haunting in its other-worldly beauty. Listen to his solo on "Limbo" (*Sorcerer*) in which he manages a very unusual construction that hangs together with tuneful integrity despite extremely turbulent drumming all around it and the absence of piano accompaniment. Shorter's saxophone style influenced a number of players who became prominent during the 1980s, including Jane Ira Bloom, Branford Marsalis, Donald Harrison, Bill Kirchner, Tim Ries, and Bob Belden. Shorter's influence has also been acknowledged by David Liebman and Michael Brecker, two saxophonists who began receiving wide acclaim during the 1970s.
27. Also listen to his work on "Umbrellas" and "Seventh Arrow" on their first album, *Weather Report* (Columbia: CK 48824 [30661], 1971).
28. Listen to "Three Clowns" on Weather Report, *Black Market* (Columbia: CK 34099, 1976), and "Harlequin" on *Heavy Weather* (Columbia: CK 65108 [34418], 1977).
29. Such melodies as "Manolete" and "Non-Stop Home," on Weather Report, *Sweetnighter* (Columbia: CK 64976 [32210], 1977), possess clarity and simplicity, whereas the accompaniment is turbulent. (You might recall that, at least as early as the bop era, horn lines had traditionally been more complex than their accompaniments.) Weather Report's practice continued the manner in which the Miles Davis Quintet had performed Shorter's "Nefertiti" on Davis's *Nefertiti* (1967). The serene, floating quality of "Nefertiti" had also been present in co-leader Joe Zawinul's writing. This was evident at least as early as the 1969 Miles Davis recording of Zawinul's "In a Silent Way" and the 1970 Zawinul recording of "Dr. Honoris Causa" (*Zawinul,* Atlantic: 1579-2, 1970). Zawinul had been attracted by the flavor of the Miles Davis "Nefertiti" performance, and Shorter and Zawinul extended this compositional flavor when they teamed up to co-lead Weather Report.
30. Listen to "Boogie Woogie Waltz," "Manolete," and "NonStop Home" on Weather Report, *Sweetnighter.*
31. Listen to "Port of Entry" on Weather Report, *Night Passage* (Columbia: CK 36793, 1980), and "Mysterious Traveler" on *Mysterious Traveler* (Columbia: CK 32494, 1974).
32. Wayne Shorter, *Night Dreamer* (Blue Note: 84173, 1964); *Speak No Evil* (Blue Note: 46509 (84194), 1964). Sheet music for Shorter compositions is in *The World's Greatest Fakebook* (Sher, 1983); *The New Real Book* (Sher, 1988); and *Wayne Shorter Jazz Classics* (Jamey Aebersold, 1985); all available from Aebersold, P.O. Box 1244, New Albany, IN 47150-1244. Wayne Shorter, *Artist Transcriptions: Saxophone* (Third Earth Productions, 1990) is available as item #660120 from Hal Leonard Publishers, 7777 West Bluemound Road, Milwaukee, WI 53212.

Chapter Thirteen

Photo by Bob Parent, courtesy of Don Parent

John Coltrane

In the final forty years of the twentieth century, few musicians or composers affected jazz as much as saxophonist-composer-bandleader John Coltrane (1926–1967). This man's compositions and improvisational concepts were used not only by hundreds of saxophonists but also by pianists, trumpeters, and guitarists. Coltrane's quartet style was a major force during the few years the band toured, and it has continued to be influential. The immense force of Coltrane's music has inspired poetry, sculpture, and modern dance. Even a church was founded in Coltrane's name.

◇COLTRANE'S PRE-1960 STYLES

Relatively unknown in the 1940s and early 1950s, Coltrane performed in those years on tenor saxophone with a muscular style that drew upon the approaches of Lester Young, Dexter Gordon, and Sonny Stitt.[1] He could also be heard milking high notes in a very emotional way. This wailing into the high register, or "cry," became a Coltrane signature in the 1960s. Musicians who remember hearing him play during the 1940s say that his style was already distinctive even then, and that it had an extraordinary urgency. On the few recordings in which he made brief appearances as a sideman between 1951 and 1954, his playing reveals a very serious, highly intense craftsman.

Technique

Coltrane had developed a very individual style by 1955, when he first recorded with Miles Davis and started becoming known to a larger audience. By then, his roots in Sonny Stitt were evident, along with his own fresh ideas.[2] His approach was unusually vigorous. His tone was rough-textured and biting, huge and dark. Coltrane gave it a massive core and a searing intensity. It was full and penetrating in every register, from the lowest notes to the highest. He played with remarkable speed and agility. His command of the saxophone was possibly as great as any other saxophonist in jazz history. His mastery of multiphonics also expanded the repertory of techniques to which other saxophonists aspired.[3] Coltrane's domination of the tenor saxophone inspired hundreds of other saxophonists to strive for exceedingly high levels of instrumental proficiency. Like Charlie Parker before him, Coltrane caused young players to cultivate a taste for rapid, densely packed solo improvisations.

Sonny Rollins Comparison

Coltrane's playing was not captured on record very often before he joined Miles Davis. Yet his leading contemporary, tenor saxophonist Sonny Rollins, had already made a mark in the world of jazz tenor with numerous recordings. By the time Coltrane began to record more and gain recognition of his own, Rollins was already a prominent figure, though he was four years younger than Coltrane. This may partly explain the widespread misunderstanding that Rollins came first, and explain why when Coltrane became prominent—using a style drawn in part from the same sources Rollins used—some listeners thought Coltrane was influenced by Rollins. However, the two styles can be distinguished in several respects. Coltrane's tone was larger, coarser, darker, and weightier than Rollins's. By comparison with Rollins, Coltrane played with a more searing quality, improvised in less of a stop-and-go manner, and made less use of silence. Coltrane also drew much less from Charlie Parker's style.[4] Also, Coltrane projected a less light-hearted and playful feeling than Rollins. Coltrane was less tuneful in his improvisations, and he used staccato less than Rollins.

Infatuation with Chord Changes

Coltrane's pre-1960s playing showed an infatuation with chord changes. He loved to add chords to a tune's existing chord progression. For instance, Coltrane took "Tune-Up," Eddie Vinson's sixteen-measure composition, and almost doubled the original number of chords. Then he added a somewhat different melody and called it "Countdown."[5] What is most significant here is not just that he added chords to an existing progression—others had often done this before—but the challenging manner in which he chose new chords and the way he improvised solos over them. His system involved stacking distantly related chords on top of each other. Then, when he improvised solos, Coltrane devoured the chord changes, trying to acknowledge every note in every chord and every scale that might be compatible with it. This was a historically significant contribution to the evolution of jazz styles. Journalist Ira Gitler described Coltrane's furiously paced streams of notes as "sheets of sound."

A peak for Coltrane's infatuation with frequently changing chords and rapid playing was the title track on his *Giant Steps* album, recorded in 1959. As in "Countdown," the chords seldom last more than two fleeting beats, and each chord stakes out new territory. Coltrane originally wrote "Giant Steps" as an exercise to gain mastery over improvising through chord progressions in which unexpected intervals separate the roots of successive chords, and few notes are held in common from one chord to another. In other words, the chords move so frequently and leap such "giant steps" that the improviser is given almost no chance to develop an idea on a given chord or to take an idea and stretch it across common tones of successive chords. The chords in "Giant Steps" change at the same pace as the melody notes. Coltrane's quick tempo and the piece's unusual construction place exceptional demands on the improviser.

The piece met Coltrane's practice needs, and eventually it became a popular test piece for improvisers. It entered the ranks of other pieces possessing difficult chord changes, such as "All the Things You Are" and "Con Alma."

Ballad Style

Many listeners are familiar only with the hard-driving style that Coltrane preferred when improvising on medium-tempo and up-tempo pieces. However, Coltrane was also one of jazz history's outstanding players of slow, pretty melodies. When playing such pieces, Coltrane seemed to harness most of the energy he customarily released in his dense, multinoted passages and channel it into a few deep, full-bodied tones that seemed to glow. He blew through and past long tones and flawlessly slid from one interval to another, treating each with solemn respect. Like his early idol, alto saxophonist Johnny Hodges, he played ballads by maintaining an unusual depth and fullness of tone and an exquisite sense of timing for ornaments. For instance, Coltrane's frequent use of scale-wise lead-ins to dramatically timed high notes resembled the long, drawn-out smears that marked the Hodges approach. Some musicians feel that by listening to Hodges, Coltrane learned how to make the saxophone sing. (This is shown by his solo in "Flamenco Sketches" on the *Jazz Classics CD.*)[6]

Pedal Points

Coltrane popularized a number of different compositional devices in modern jazz. The pedal point is one of the best known. For example, on the *Giant Steps* album, his composition "Naima" has a single note, the *pedal point*, repeating continuously underneath the melody for the first eight measures. Then a new pedal point accompanies the second eight measures. This device achieves a drone-like effect that sustains despite shifts in the tune's harmony. It builds suspense because the listener expects a chord to change, a progression to resolve. Repeated bass notes in the pattern of pedal points became strongly identified with Coltrane's sound, especially during the 1960s. They were commonly part of the accompaniment to improvisations in pieces with Spanish and Indian flavor, a character that came to be called "modal."

◇1960s FORMATS

Though Coltrane never improvised pieces without planning the harmonies to be used, he did explore approaches which depended less on the preset movement of harmonies than bop did. These approaches can be labeled in two ways. Neither provides an accurate description, but both labels found a permanent place in the vocabulary of musicians and journalists. One is "free." The other is "modal."

Modal

The mode-based pieces and long improvisations of John Coltrane and his 1965–1967 associate, tenor saxophonist Pharoah Sanders, had a profound impact on jazz. This format was a new direction in Coltrane's career because such a harmonic basis for improvisation is as undemanding as the chord progression for "Giant Steps" is demanding. During the late 1950s, Miles Davis recorded mode-based pieces that proved highly influential.[7] However, the pieces by Coltrane and his disciples were even more influential. Before we discuss the details of these recordings, let's examine some tricky terminology.[8] A mode is a scale containing a predetermined selection of notes. Because his music was only loosely based on certain modes, Coltrane's 1960s playing was not always modal in the strictest sense of the word, only in the loose sense used by jazz musicians and journalists. In his "modal" work, Coltrane adhered to the overall harmonic orientation of certain modes, but he also employed notes outside the mode. Moreover, because much of Coltrane's and Sanders's work is merely based on repeating patterns of only two chords, it may be unnecessarily complicating the situation to call it "modal." Instead, we could just specify the two chords.

One of Coltrane's most famous "modal" performances can be heard on his 1960 album *My Favorite Things.*[9] The title track is based on a well-known melody from Rodgers and Hammerstein's Broadway show *The Sound of Music.* This proved one of Coltrane's best-selling recordings, undoubtedly due in part to the great familiarity of the tune. The performance's popularity stems also from several musical components which collectively make it easy to listen to: the minor key, the simplicity in the accompaniment harmonies, its waltz meter, and the extensive repetition of short patterns (these final two components lend a hypnotic, swaying feeling). During this period many other jazz musicians liked this particular record, so they attempted to make music that evoked soothing, meditative moods by similar methods.

The strategies used to construct Coltrane's performance of "My Favorite Things" are important because they were widely imitated. Pianist McCoy Tyner uses the tune's chord progression as a guide for accompanying Coltrane's rendition of the melody. Then improvisations are accompanied by a two-chord repeated pattern of indefinite length in the key of E minor (dorian mode), later shifted to the key of E major (ionian mode). For constructing his soprano saxophone improvisation, Coltrane draws liberally from a single scale that is compatible with Tyner's accompaniment.[10] Such a basis for improvisation signalled a striking departure in Coltrane's style because it is so simple by comparison with the chord progression for "Giant Steps." This new approach became very popular with improvising musicians. In fact, between the late 1960s and the mid-1970s, few prominent modern jazz combos played much else. Note, however, that despite the prominence of Coltrane's "modal" style and his "free jazz," his 1960s output continued to contain pop songs and twelve-bar blues pieces.[11]

Free Jazz

Coltrane was interested in the music of Ornette Coleman, the most prominent figure in "free jazz." This approach evolved away from adhering to preset progressions of chords; it also sometimes dispensed with distinctions between soloist and accompanist. (See next chapter.) In 1960, Coltrane recorded an album called *The Avant-Garde* with Coleman's group, minus Coleman. On the album, he performed three Coleman compositions. In 1965, Coltrane recorded an album called *Ascension,* in which he used an approach like Coleman's approach to the 1960 album *Free Jazz* (excerpted in SCCJ). *Ascension* employed collective improvisation with high-energy, high-density playing that departed from bop conventions of jazz phrasing and rhythmic feeling. As in *Free Jazz, Ascension* contained moments in which all the musicians improvised different lines at the same time. Coltrane took a cue from fellow saxophonist Albert Ayler and began improvising turbulent streams of notes, interspersed with saxophone sounds that resembled jangling cries and screams. (Ayler is discussed in the next chapter.)[12] This approach capitalized on the high register of the saxophone and mined the instrument's capacity for shrill, rasping sounds that often contained several different tones at once. These sequences of notes did not possess the melodic contours of conventional jazz improvisations. They did not evoke the easy rise and fall of tension and the swing feeling of earlier styles. Instead, they focused on development of mood and texture, replacing the earlier priorities of tunefulness and swing feeling.[13]

Improvisation on *Ascension* was neither totally collective nor totally free of prearrangement, nor was it atonal. (For explanation of scales, tone center, and atonality, see pages 369–373.) Careful listening will reveal a few changes of chord (or tone center) because Coltrane preset four scales for the musicians. The changes do not occur often, but they do occur, so it is not totally free of form. Collectively improvised sections are balanced in duration and texture. Brief, loosely stated ensemble passages separate the solos, which in turn receive rhythm section accompaniment. In this respect the music is also like conventional jazz. Coltrane used four other saxophonists, two trumpeters, and rhythm section. He preset the order for the solos so that no two similar instruments played back to back. This allowed a trumpet solo to follow a sax solo, for instance, rather than following another trumpet solo. Journalists have called this recording "free jazz," yet Coltrane's use of preset scales and the separation of soloist and accompanist roles renders the "free jazz" label invalid.

During the 1960s and 1970s, a number of other modern jazz musicians tried collective improvisation, with high-energy, high-density playing that contained no bop phrasing or swing feeling. Similar styles appeared sporadically during the 1970s and 1980s. Some of the impetus for this could be attributed to Coltrane because he was the most prominent bandleader to engage in this style. Note, however, that Coltrane recorded large-ensemble collective improvisation only once. He otherwise limited his use of this technique to quartet and quintet formats.

Slonimsky's and Gilmore's Influence

For a brief period during the early 1960s, much of Coltrane's work was less dense and intricate than it had been. Some of his work was quite simple and obvious in its development. He had taken a cue from the style of fellow tenor saxophonist John Gilmore, who sometimes developed solos by repeating the same rhythm with different pitches, changing the notes without changing the rhythm, sometimes placing the same rhythm at different spots in the measure, or occasionally inverting a phrase, as though peering at it from several different angles and sharing each view with the listener.[14] Coltrane also developed his solo improvisations in the logical manner he had learned from Nicolas Slonimsky's *Thesaurus of Scales and Melodic Patterns.* The book demonstrates how to vary note choices in many ways and still remain related to a fundamental chord or scale.[15] The effect of considering Gilmore and Slonimsky was to slow down and clarify Coltrane's improvisations, and devise a nonbop vocabulary.

Very soon Coltrane was back to producing high-density improvisations with very convoluted lines. But this time the twisting and turning did not reflect complex chord progressions as in his late-1950s "sheets of sound" period. Instead, these new patterns only *sounded* as complex. They were a speeded-up variant of the Gilmore and Slonimsky methods, and they were set atop relatively unchanging accompaniment harmonies. Those patterns and the formulas that Coltrane refined became common vocabulary for an entire generation of improvisers. During the 1990s, more than thirty years after he introduced them, these patterns were still considered fundamental building blocks for jazz improvisations, not just among saxophonists, but also among trumpeters, guitarists, and pianists.

THE CLASSIC QUARTET

Coltrane was a member of the Miles Davis groups on and off for almost six years, making his earliest Davis recording in 1955, his last in 1961. During this period, Coltrane also recorded with a few other leaders. Though he also recorded under his own name, he did not lead a group of his own with a consistent personnel and a sound that was uniquely identifiable until 1960, when he was no longer touring with Davis. After several different combinations of musicians, he finally settled on pianist McCoy Tyner, bassist Steve Davis, and drummer Elvin Jones. He used a number of different bassists during the 1960s, but after Steve Davis played with him on several albums in 1960 and 1961, Coltrane used Jimmy Garrison the most. Garrison was with Coltrane on most of the remaining recordings, and stayed with the saxophonist even after Tyner left in 1965 and Jones left in 1966. **The Coltrane quartet was one of the most important groups in jazz history, and some historians consider it to have been the most influential of all jazz combos.** (Listen to them play "The Promise" on the *Jazz Classics CD* and "Your Lady" on the *Jazz Classics CD* for *Concise Guide to Jazz.*)[16]

Elvin Jones

Some listeners consider **Elvin Jones** (b. 1927) the most overwhelming drummer in jazz history. He has established a position on the drums that equals the power and innovation established by Charlie Parker and John Coltrane on the saxophone. Like Parker and Coltrane, Jones is a remarkably consistent performer. He seems to play every tune as though it is his last chance. An almost superhuman energy and endurance are associated with him, and his imagination seems to match his energy.

The John Coltrane Quartet, one of the most original groups in jazz history. Left to right: McCoy Tyner (piano), John Coltrane (tenor sax), Jimmy Garrison (bass), Elvin Jones (drums), 1962.

Collection of Duncan Schiedt

Jones avoids the relative simplicity and repetition of most pre-1960 drummers. He rarely plays the obvious. In fact, in his most adventuresome work, he even avoids directly stating the first beat of each measure. His conception of the beat is a wider unit in time than had been usual with previous drummers. His timekeeping is steady but loose, filled with rhythmic subtleties. He roams through his drums and cymbals, distributing portions of triplets. He phrases in three's instead of two's and four's. He often begins his triplex division of time at the middle or end of a beat, and continues to juxtapose a staggered waltz feeling across the duration of several measures. (For explanation of triplets and waltz meter, see pages 364–367.) During all that time, he still maintains a basic meter of four and swings infectiously.

With Coltrane's group, Jones was able to play many rhythms at once and have the entire sound swell and heave like an ocean under Coltrane's playing. (This is particularly evident in his work on "The Promise" on the *Jazz Classics CD* and "Your Lady" on the *Jazz Classics CD* for *Concise Guide to Jazz.*) Jones was one of the first drummers to play polyrhythmically and still swing hard in a loose, flowing way. Earlier drummers who attempted to use polyrhythms had sounded stiff and self-consciously calculating. (For definition and explanation of polyrhythm, see page 369.)

While listening to Elvin Jones, you might get the impression that he is juggling. Things seem forever in the air, never sharply defined in exact, predictable proportions. But the different rhythms played simultaneously were not just randomly different; they were constructed to complement each other. And, in a broad sense, they fit together. It might not be obvious unless you listen carefully to four- and eight-measure sequences in their entirety. Some of his figures purposely omit a stroke or two but let you feel the missing stroke in the overall pattern. He distributes the parts of his triplets so that perhaps the first third is silent and the next two are sounded on snare drum. Or perhaps the middle member is omitted. Sometimes the first two members of a triplet will sound on the snare drum and the third on the high-hat or the bass drum. It might be because of his complexity and lack of predictability that few drummers ever managed to sound like him.

Elvin Jones, Coltrane's drummer from 1960 to 1966. Jones demonstrated how it was possible to play polyrhythmically and still swing hard in a broadly paced manner. He almost verged on freestyle, yet his oceans of sound, heaving and swelling, still carried the pulse and guaranteed a sure momentum underneath Coltrane's improvisations.

The Jazz Image

Jones wove his parts around those of his bandmates in as important a way as any front-line hornman at a Dixieland jam session.[17] The whole character of the Coltrane quartet reflected his highly interactive style. Jones played with the surging power and imagination of two or three drummers combined, and his force was absorbed quite musically into the quartet concept. In fact, Elvin Jones's style was possibly the most indispensable part of that ensemble concept.

After leaving Coltrane, Jones formed a sequence of high-quality groups which, during the late 1960s and throughout the 1970s, offered some of the rare jazz neither significantly influenced by rock or electric instruments nor predominantly modal in orientation. He usually employed two tenor saxophonists and a bassist, but no piano. He employed some of the best saxophonists playing at that time, and most of his tenor men were influenced by Coltrane.[18] The music in some of his groups almost achieved the solemn urgency that had been created by the Coltrane quartet.

McCoy Tyner

Coltrane's pianist from 1960 to the end of 1965 was **McCoy Tyner** (b. 1938). Creating an original approach from the linear style of Bud Powell, the block chording of Red Garland, and the voicings of Bill Evans and Horace Silver, he achieved a fresh approach to jazz piano. He already had been a distinctive and aggressive stylist in the Art Farmer-Benny Golson Jazztet, but went on to carve a very personal style. His was one of the most easily recognizable styles in all of jazz, and he was a prime force in jazz piano of the 1960s and 1970s. He was almost as influential as Evans and at least as influential as Herbie Hancock. Tyner's extensive use of chords voiced in fourths was widely adopted (see Figure 13.1). His extremely percussive, ringing style of comping became a model for pianists of the late 1960s and the 1970s, especially those playing in Coltrane-inspired groups. His fast solo lines also inspired numerous pianists, though few could match his imagination. The five-note (pentatonic) patterns he perfected as basis for his lines soon became stock solo vocabulary for numerous

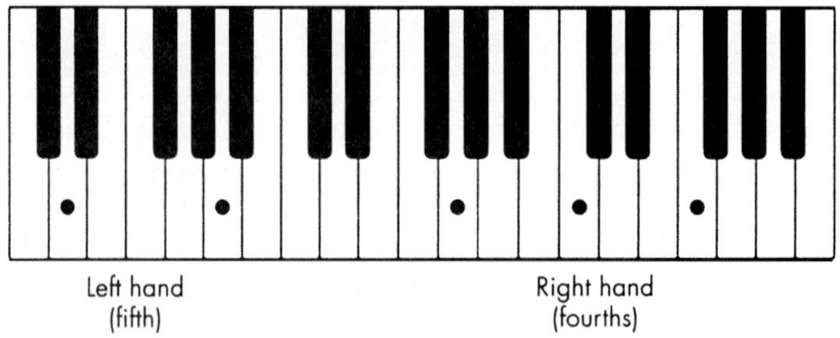

FIGURE 13.1 Piano keyboard illustration of fifths in left hand and fourths in right hand.

pianists (see Table 13.1). His originality and influence were so extensive that he even affected well-established pianists.

McCoy Tyner's playing furnished a center for the Coltrane quartet sound. It was as though he established a pivot for the seesawing of sounds that were being generated around him. His stability in this capacity was partly due to his frequent use of a loud, held note (technically called a pedal point) or a loud, held interval (usually a fifth) played with extreme force by his left hand. His right hand sounded chords in a manner that achieved a bell-like ring. His selection of notes for the chords lent them a very open quality derived from using intervals of a fourth. (See Figure 13.1, and try it out for yourself on the piano. If you strike the keys with tremendous force, you might approximate the sound of McCoy Tyner.) These clear, open-voiced chords represented more stability than was occurring in the saxophone and drum sounds around them. In most groups of this period, the bass part was the simplest and steadiest. But in the Coltrane quartet, Tyner's piano part vied with the bass part in its steadiness. (See page 418 for a technical explanation of these harmonies, and listen to Tyner play them on "The Promise" on the *Jazz Classics CD.*)

Jimmy Garrison

Jimmy Garrison (1934–1976) was an imaginative bass player who held his own within the fiercely active Coltrane quartet. He had a large, deep, rough tone quality and remarkable stamina. McCoy Tyner praised his timekeeping skill. In addition to walking, Garrison invented rhythms which countered and complemented those of Tyner and Jones. Of all the bassists Coltrane used, Garrison seemed the perfect fit because he intuitively understood the unorthodox directions that Coltrane and Jones were taking.

Occasionally, Garrison took to strumming his bass almost as though it were a guitar. His use of double stops (two strings sounding together) and his strumming have been widely imitated. He was not the first to use such techniques, but his particular handling of them

TABLE 13.1 A FEW OF THE MANY PIANISTS INFLUENCED BY MCCOY TYNER

Chick Corea	Lonnie Liston Smith	Michael Cochran
Alice McLeod Coltrane	Onaje Allan Gumbs	Joanne Brackeen
Kenny Gill	Harold Mabern	John Hicks
Bobo Stinson	Ronnie Mathews	Hal Galper
Joe Bonner	Stanley Cowell	Gil Goldstein
Bill Henderson	Hilton Ruiz	Henry Butler

might have been the stimulus behind their popularity with jazz bassists of the 1960s and 1970s. Some of Garrison's double-stopping may have had its source in Coltrane's interest in drones and in music employing two tones sustained together, five scale-steps apart. In the modal music of their native cultures, bagpipes, sitars, and tambura achieve exactly that effect. Coltrane's use of two bassists on "Olé" (on his *Olé Coltrane* album) and "India" (on his *Impressions* album) also might derive from that interest.

The Sweep

One of the most significant advances made by the 1960s Coltrane quartet was a pioneering move toward a sweeping, broadly paced organization of parts, a change in feeling that was partly due to **a departure from:**

1) explicit statement of the markers for each measure;
2) accompaniment style in which chords changed frequently;
3) dependence on simple ride rhythms and walking bass patterns; and
4) bouncing solo lines of eighth-note sequences with few sustained tones.

This new, widely imitated approach produced music which seemed to breathe more deeply and build excitement more broadly and solemnly than earlier jazz styles. (Listen for these aspects in "The Promise" on the *Jazz Classics CD.*) Phrases spanned larger units than the four- and eight-measure progressions typical of most jazz improvisation. There was more creation of a suspended feeling, which, each time it resolved, proved dramatic in effect. Much of the new feeling was directly caused by **the particular collection of techniques** that the group refined:

1) Sustained and repeating sustained tones in the bass part (pianist's left hand, bassist's plucking) which are technically termed *pedal points.*
2) Drum patterns whose basic unit occupied several measures instead of just a few beats.
3) Sustaining piano chords (sounding them loudly and letting them ring).
4) Using a single mode (or a two-chord pattern) for a long time, instead of using numerous changes in harmony.
5) Long saxophone glissandos which were carefully timed and spanned a large portion of the saxophone's pitch range:
    a) sometimes used to preface a dramatically placed high note.
    b) sometimes evoking a rhapsodic effect.
    c) sometimes snaking in and around a central idea. (These are evident in Coltrane's solos on "The Promise" on the *Jazz Classics CD* and on "Your Lady" on the *Jazz Classics CD* for *Concise Guide to Jazz.*) The rhythmic construction of these glissandos departed from swing feeling and approximated an orchestral concept in which the melody lines are not so rigidly tied to the beat.
6) Use of sustained tones in saxophone solos (allowing listeners a point of focus and relief from having to follow ever-changing melodic contours).
7) Long-term continuity of mood, as though the composition and lengthy improvisations were conceived almost in their entirety instead of being merely a sequence of tune and solos that strung together swinging phrases in jam session manner.

TABLE 13.2 A FEW OF THE MANY SAXOPHONISTS INFLUENCED BY COLTRANE

Pharoah Sanders	Pat LaBarbera	Frank Foster
Charles Lloyd	Bob Berg	Joe Henderson
Joe Farrell	Sonny Fortune	David Young
Wayne Shorter	Jan Garbarek	Harold Land
Gato Barbieri	Michael Brecker	Frank Tiberi
John Klemmer	Andrew White	Gregory Herbert
Nathan Davis	James Spalding	Bennie Moupin
Lew Tabackin	Ernie Krivda	Carlos Garnett
Robin Kenyatta	Joe Lovano	Steve Marcus
Steve Grossman	Charles B. Owens	Teddy Edwards
Billy Harper	Bob Mintzer	Steve Lederer
David Liebman	Manny Boyd	Rich Perry
John Surman	Bill Evans	Cannonball Adderley

◇COLTRANE'S IMPACT

John Coltrane exerted a striking effect on his listeners. People who hated his music fought in print with those who were impressed by it. Some felt jazz history ended with Coltrane, whereas today many feel it just started with him. Not long after Coltrane formed his own group, there were so many saxophonists imitating him that jazz journalists began complaining about a general lack of originality as vehemently as they had responded to the wave of Charlie Parker disciples who arose during the 1950s. Coltrane was the subject of numerous scholarly analyses, and the 1980s saw an increased flow of publications which evaluated Coltrane's work from a technical standpoint.[19] Saxophonist Andrew White was so inspired by Coltrane's music that he transcribed more than six hundred recorded Coltrane solos note for note. (See page 412 for information on how to get the White transcriptions, including those for "The Promise" and "Flamenco Sketches," heard on the *Jazz Classics CD*.)

Each of Coltrane's style periods caused many musicians to try the techniques that Coltrane had popularized. First it was densely packed lines and difficult chord progressions. Coltrane's manner of replacing the chord changes from standard tunes was widely adopted. Musicians began making their own chords move in the manner demonstrated by Coltrane in his "Giant Steps" and "Countdown" progressions. Then it was modal style and pedal points. After that, it was simultaneous collective improvisation and the creation of frantic turbulence that emphasized textures more than development of melodic improvised lines. Sometimes it appeared as though a large community of musicians had decided that Coltrane was their guide, and they would postpone generating their own ideas until they could see what he would do next. Even musicians already known for considerable originality felt the impact of Coltrane's work.[20]

Soprano Saxophone

About the time he formed his own groups (1960–1961), Coltrane began playing soprano saxophone in addition to tenor. (Coltrane plays soprano on "The Promise" on the *Jazz Classics CD* and "Your Lady" on the *Jazz Classics CD* for *Concise Guide to Jazz*.) Soprano saxophone had been used on recordings by Sidney Bechet, Johnny Hodges, Charlie Barnet, and Steve Lacy, but it had not caught on as a standard jazz instrument. A few years after Coltrane first recorded on it, however, the soprano saxophone had become quite popular with jazz saxophonists. By 1970, most tenor saxophonists were performing on it. Even players who were not necessarily followers of Coltrane began soprano. Such well-established jazzmen

Listening Guide for

"The Promise"

Composed by John Coltrane; Recorded October 8, 1963 at Birdland, in New York City, by John Coltrane (soprano sax), McCoy Tyner (piano), Jimmy Garrison (bass), and Elvin Jones (drums); available on the *Jazz Classics CD;* also available on John Coltrane, *Live at Birdland* (Impulse!/GRP: GRD-198, 1963).

This performance is on the *Jazz Classics CD* for several reasons that are important both historically and esthetically. It offers a succinct and representative sample for the middle period of the classic Coltrane quartet. This recording conveys how the group sounded in a typical setting because it was recorded live during a performance at Birdland, a New York nightclub. This selection clearly demonstrates the unique accompanying style of this innovative rhythm section, using its polyrhythmic approach, solemn and broadly paced kind of swing feeling, Tyner's pedal points, and Jones's complex layers of sound. (Jones's triplet patterns are conspicuous throughout the performance.) The form of the composition is typical of many Coltrane pieces from this period because it has long stretches in which only two chords alternate (musicians call them "G minor" and "C seven"). This pattern became a preferred form during the 1960s, 70s, and 80s. This particular performance is also outstanding for its distinctly melodic, five-chorus piano solo by McCoy Tyner. It catalogs many of the much-imitated methods that Tyner developed. This selection also contains a Coltrane soprano sax solo in the style that became widely imitated during the 1970s and 80s. It features his climbing, scale-like runs, his expressive bends of pitch, and dramatically timed peaks of tension. Coltrane often prefaced high notes with a very deliberate climb, and ultimately sounded as though he were squeezing the high notes out of his horn. As in the Johnny Hodges approach, the way Coltrane prefaced each important high note was almost as essential as the note itself. This is central to an impassioned effect we term "the cry." Coltrane's solo also shows his characteristic approach to working over brief figures from many different angles. This performance was also chosen because it provides many illustrations of "the sweep."

Listen for the flowing drum patterns that run throughout the accompaniment, especially the prominent use of tom-toms. The patterns used here differ considerably from the relatively unadorned timekeeping patterns we heard in previous selections on the *Jazz Classics CD*. This is the style that Elvin Jones invented.

The piece is performed in a medium tempo. There is no introduction. The performance begins with Coltrane playing the melody and the rhythm section accompanying him. Bass and drums play more densely as the performance unfolds, and the peak of intensity occurs in Coltrane's last two solo choruses. Things wind down gradually from there, though the final melody statement is so liberally ornamented it sounds like Coltrane is unwilling to restrain his creative juices and return to the theme for an ending.

The first time you listen to this, just sit back and let the sounds wash over you. The music has a sure momentum that will carry you along with it. The next several times you listen, you may begin to notice that there is a rocking back and forth motion achieved by the combination of walking bass, drummer's timekeeping patterns, and the piano accompaniment's use of two chords alternating with each other. When McCoy Tyner accompanies himself in his solo, we can hear him playing the first chord two or three times in succession, then the second chord once, sometimes twice. Then he repeats the cycle. This persists for long stretches and helps the band get into a groove. However, you will also notice that the groove is periodically interrupted by a bridge. You may begin to recognize its occurrence by the sound of a new chord (musicians call it "F seven"). It is often signalled by a loud, held bass note on piano that contrasts with the steady rocking motion that we have come to expect. The new bridge chord is in effect for eight beats, and then it begins alternating with another chord (musicians call it "D seven") that is also in effect for eight beats every time it comes along. The bridge lasts for eight measures, about 12 seconds. The drumming is more complicated and less predictable during these interruptions, though timekeeping is still maintained. Because the bridge departs from the repeating patterns, it serves to build tension that is ultimately resolved by a return to the repeating pattern. And if you lose your place, it can signal you.

Technical Note: For the accompaniment to the melody, the A-section has eight measures of a G minor chord alternating with a C seven chord (four beats each), then at 12 seconds into the piece, two measures of F seven, two measures of D seven, two of F seven again, two more of D seven. That sixteen-measure sequence repeats. Then beginning at 47 seconds into the piece, there are eight more measures of G minor alternating with C seven.

Accompaniment chords for all solo choruses follow a slightly different sequence of durations than under the melody statements. The form is 16-16-8(Bridge)-8, in which the accompaniment chords are the same for the first sixteen, second sixteen, and the final eight measures.

CD Track	Elapsed Time	
68	0' 00"	**First Chorus** (A-B-A-B-C)
		Melody Statement by Coltrane on Soprano Saxophone
		Each section lasts 8 measures, and the C-section is accompanied by the same chords as the A-section.
		Accompanying the sax, the piano plays resounding bass notes and sustained mid-range chords. They see-saw with a bass note on the first beat and a chord on the third beat of each measure.
	0' 12"	B (8 measures)
	0' 23"	A (8 measures)
	0' 34"	B (8 measures)
	0' 46"	C (8 measures)
69	0' 57"	**Second Chorus** (A-A-B-A, 8 measures in each section)
		Piano Solo Improvisation by McCoy Tyner
		This is an exceedingly melodic improvisation based on brief phrases that often seem to answer each other. Tyner plays each note very forcefully.

	1' 10"	*Second A-section*
		Piano, bass, and drums firmly establish what musicians call a "groove." This is a strong sense of swing feeling that makes you feel good. It is steady and unrushed, but not lazy. It is always going forward, as though strutting.
		The solid walking bass provides a firm frame of reference for the passage of beats. The drumming is simpler here than underneath the melody statement.
	1' 16"	Tyner is quadruple-timing the rate of notes in the line played with his right hand while he comps at a normal rate with his left hand.
	1' 23"	*Bridge*
		Drumming becomes more complex.
	1' 34"	*Last A-section*
		Tyner improvises a funky melodic idea, played in harmony by his right hand while he comps in a lower register with his left hand.
70	1' 47"	**Third Chorus** (A-A-B-A)
	1' 51"	Tyner is quadruple-timing his melody line.
	2' 00"	*Second A-section*
		Tyner improvises a funky, harmonized line.
	2' 12"	*Bridge*
	2' 25"	*Last A-section*
		Tyner improvises a funky, harmonized line.
71	2' 37"	**Fourth Chorus** (A-A-B-A)
		Tyner improvises a simple line in the high register that develops readily by continuously transforming a single idea.
	2' 50"	*Second A-section*
		A cymbal crash begins this section.
	3' 02"	*Bridge*
		Tyner uses locked hands-block chording to play an idea that includes an answer within the logic of his overall statement. Drumming activity increases.
	3' 14"	*Last A-section*
		Tyner develops a funky, harmonized line from his first idea. Drumming returns to more conventional rhythms.
72	3' 27"	**Fifth Chorus** (A-A-B-A)
	3' 33"	Tyner begins by quadruple-timing.
	3' 40"	*Second A-section*
	3' 44"	Tyner trills.
	3' 52"	*Bridge*
		Tyner begins with a funky, repeated idea that is harmonized.
	4' 00"	Tyner ends this statement with quadruple-timing.

Track	Time	Description
	4' 05"	*Last A-section*
		A cymbal crash begins this section.
		Tyner improvises a clear, simple melody line from another idea.
73	4' 17"	**Sixth Chorus** (A-A-B-A)
		Tyner uses a pattern of offering resonant bass notes as a call and a block-chorded line as a response. Drumming is more active.
	4' 30"	*Second A-section*
		A cymbal crash begins this section.
	4' 41"	A brief drum roll announces the beginning of the bridge.
	4' 43"	*Bridge*
		Cymbal crashes and tumultuous drumming occur throughout. Snare drum and tom-toms are prominent.
		Bass drum sounds are conspicuous two measures before the last A-section.
	4' 55"	*Last A-section*
		Drumming is coordinated with the drama of the piano solo.
74	5' 07"	**Seventh Chorus** (A-A-B-A)
		Coltrane Soprano Saxophone Solo
		Notice how Coltrane rises into the pitch of his first note. Drumming activity increases.
	5' 15"	Coltrane uses a scale-wise run to preface an important high note.
	5' 20"	*Second A-section*
	5' 26"	Coltrane is quadruple-timing to 5' 45". His playing is hot immediately, displaying the urgency for which he is distinguished.
	5' 33"	*Bridge*
		Coltrane is quadruple-timing. Drum sounds are churning underneath the sax sound. Loud, held bass tones are emanating from the piano.
	5' 46"	*Last A-section*
		The sax part is very forceful, and the cymbal crashes are timed as responses to Coltrane's high notes.
75	5' 57"	**Eighth Chorus** (A-A-B-A)
		Sax is quadruple-timing until 6' 08".
	6' 10"	*Second A-section*
		Coltrane plays the same note again and again, coming at it from different angles.
	6' 23"	*Bridge*
		Coltrane prefaces his high note very emotionally, then plays as though he is squeezing it out of his horn.
	6' 31"	Coltrane often reiterates a note, each time coming at it from a different angle.
	6' 36"	*Last A-section*
		Coltrane quotes and paraphrases the original melody.

76	6' 48"	**Ninth Chorus** (A-B-A-B-C) *Final Theme Statement* Oceans of percussion support Coltrane's melody line.
	7' 02"	*Bridge* Coltrane is liberally ornamenting his original melody line. Many of his main melody notes are reiterated emphatically.
	7' 13"	*Second A-section* Coltrane makes more reiterations of selected notes in restating the melody. Piano creates a rocking motion by repeating a pattern having a bass note on the first beat, a chord on the third beat.
	7' 26"	*Second Bridge*
	7' 38"	*C-section*
	7' 49"	a long roll on cymbal
	8' 00"	Tension is resolved when the piano chord sustains, cymbals ring, and the bass improvises a finish.

A written transcription of this Coltrane solo is available from Andrew White, 4830 South Dakota Ave. N.E., Washington, D.C. 20017.

John Coltrane playing soprano saxophone, the instrument he helped popularize during the 1960s. Listen to the *Jazz Classics CD* to hear Coltrane play this instrument on "The Promise."

Photo by Bill Smith

as alto saxophonist Cannonball Adderley and tenor saxophonist Sonny Rollins began recording with soprano sax. Some players adopted it almost to the exclusion of their tenors.[21] Coltrane's popularization of the instrument coincided with a practical problem that saxophonists encountered: trying to be heard over the loud rhythm sections of the 1970s. The range and tone quality of the soprano saxophone helped saxophonists cut through the sound created by the increasing numbers of drums and amplified instruments prevalent in groups of the 1970s. The attraction to soprano saxophone can be attributed partly to the attraction of players to Coltrane, partly to the practical advantages of its sound, and partly to the search for fresh sounds that has always characterized jazz musicians.

CHAPTER SUMMARY

1) John Coltrane was an innovative saxophonist, composer, and bandleader who had enormous impact on modern jazz, particularly in the 1960s.
2) He devised several original styles of saxophone playing, first inspired partly by Lester Young, Dexter Gordon, and Sonny Stitt during the 1940s, and then partly by Ornette Coleman, John Gilmore, and Albert Ayler during the 1960s.
3) Coltrane's first new style was evident in recordings he made in the Miles Davis bands of the 1950s.
4) Coltrane played such energetic, densely packed solos that his late-1950s playing was described as "sheets of sound," though he was also a remarkably restrained player of lush ballads.
5) As a composer Coltrane was known for devising progressions of chords which change frequently and in ways that severely challenge improvisers, as in his "Giant Steps."
6) Coltrane's compositions and arrangements popularized pedal points and drone notes in jazz accompaniments, as in his "Naima."
7) Coltrane's "classic quartet" used pianist McCoy Tyner, bassist Jimmy Garrison, and drummer Elvin Jones from 1961 to 1965.
8) The quartet popularized "modal" styles of improvisation in which accompaniment harmonies do not change frequently.
9) The quartet refined methods of achieving a sweeping, broadly paced organization of parts which was more dramatic and orchestral than previous improvisational styles in jazz.
10) Coltrane's albums *Ascension* and *Meditations* were influential models in "free" jazz approaches where all musicians often improvised different lines at the same time in a high-energy, turbulent manner.
11) Elvin Jones was one of the first drummers to play very polyrhythmically and still swing hard.
12) McCoy Tyner popularized voicing chords in fourths and constructing lines from five-note patterns.

NOTES

1. Listen to Coltrane's 1951 solo on "We Love To Boogie" on Dizzy Gillespie, *School Days* (Savoy/Devon: SV-0157 [Regent 6043], 1951–52), and compare it to Lester Young's solo on Count Basie's 1939 "Pound Cake" (*The Essential Count Basie, Vol. 1*, Columbia: CK 40608, 1936–39), and Young's 1945 recording of "D.B. Blues" on *The Complete Aladdin Sessions* (Blue Note: 32787, 2CD set, 1942–48). Then compare the "We Love To Boogie" solo with Dexter Gordon's work from 1947 on Gordon, *Dexter Rides Again* (Savoy/Devon: SV-0120 [12130], 1945–47). To hear the similarities with Stitt, listen to Coltrane's work on Miles Davis's recording of "Oleo" (*Relaxin'*, Fantasy: OJCCD-190-2 [Prestige 7129], 1956) with Stitt's work on "The Eternal Triangle" on Dizzy Gillespie, *Sonny Side Up* (Verve: 314 521 426-2 [MGV 8262], 1957). For more about Coltrane's career, see Lewis Porter, *John Coltrane: His Life and Music* (University of Michigan, 1998); J. C. Thomas, *Chasin' the Trane* (Doubleday, 1975, DaCapo, 1976); and C. O. Simpkins, *Coltrane: A Biography* (Herndon House, 1975, Black Classic Press, 1989).
2. Listen to *The New Miles Davis Quintet* (Fantasy: OJCCD-006-2 [Prestige 7014], 1955), then *Steamin'* (Fantasy: OJCCD-391-2 [Prestige 7200]), *Cookin'* (Fantasy: OJCCD-128-2 [Prestige 7094]), *Workin'* (Fantasy: OJCCD-296-2 [Prestige 7166]), and *Relaxin'* (Fantasy: OJCCD-190-2 [Prestige 7129]).
3. Wind instruments such as saxophone and clarinet can be coaxed to produce two or more sounds at the same time. Some of these multiphonics, to give them their technical name, sound like chords. In his "Harmonique" on *Coltrane Jazz* (Atlantic: 1354-2, 1959), Coltrane used this method to harmonize a melody note. During the mid-1960s he frequently used multiphonics for controlled screeches that helped create peaks of musical excitement. An isolated example is his solo on "Chasin' The Trane" (1961) on Coltrane, *Live at the Village Vanguard: The Master Takes* (Impulse!/GRP: IMPD-251 [A-10/A-42], 1961), and there are many instances in his albums *Meditations* (Impulse!/GRP: GRD-199 [9110], 1965); *Expression* (Impulse!/GRP: GRD-131[9120], 1967); and *Live In Seattle* (Impulse!/GRP: GRD2-146 [9202], 2CD set, 1965).
4. To hear the Parker roots in the Rollins style, listen to Parker play tenor sax on "Half Nelson" (1947) on *Charlie Parker Memorial, Vol. 2* (Savoy/Devon: SV-0103 [12009], 1945–48).
5. "Countdown" is on John Coltrane, *Giant Steps* (Atlantic: 1311-2, 1959). The written music for this piece is available, with recorded rhythm section accompaniment, on Jamey Aebersold, *A New Approach to Jazz Improvisation, Vol. 28* (Jamey Aebersold, P.O. Box 1244, New Albany, IN 47151). In his *Creative Jazz Improvisation, 2nd ed.* (Prentice-Hall, 1995), Scott Reeves discusses Coltrane's chord progression style with a transcription of the solo on "Giant Steps" (also available from Aebersold). More transcribed solos and analyses of this Coltrane period appear in Stuart Isacoff, *Solos for Jazz Tenor Saxophone* (Carl Fischer, 1985; available by mail from Carl Fischer Music Store, 62 Cooper Square, NY, NY 10003).
6. Almost every album that Coltrane made for the Prestige label contains at least one ballad. *Mating Call* (Fantasy: OJCCD-212-2 [Prestige 7070], 1956), under Tadd Dameron's leadership, has several lush ballads. John Coltrane, *Soultrane* (Fantasy: OJCCD-021-2 [Prestige 7142], 1958) features "Theme for Ernie" and "I Want To Talk About You." Slow tunes were also the format for some of Coltrane's best compositions. Listen to "Naima" from *Giant Steps*, "After the Rain" from *Dear Old Stockholm* (Impulse!/GRP: GRD-120, 1963); "Wise One" and "Lonnie's Lament" from *Crescent* (Impulse!/GRP: IMPD-200 [A-66], 1964); "Dear Lord" from *Transition* (Impulse/GRP: GRD-124 [9195], 1965); and "Ogunde" from *Expression* (Impulse!/GRP: GRD-131 [9120], 1967). SCCJ has Coltrane's "Alabama."
7. "Milestones" from *Milestones* (Columbia: CK 40837 [CS 9428/ CL 1193], 1958); "So What" from *Kind of Blue* (Columbia: CK 64935 [CS 8163], 1959), also on SCCJ.
8. If you are not familiar with the concepts of scale, mode, chord progression, or song form, you may find it helpful to study pages 369–388 before going further in this chapter. Musician readers may also wish to examine pages 418–424.
9. *My Favorite Things* (Atlantic: 1361-2, 1960).
10. Coltrane recorded several other improvisations that were based mostly on long stretches of repeating, two-chord patterns. In 1961 he recorded "Olé" on *Olé Coltrane* (Atlantic: 1373-2), and "Impressions" on *Live at the Village Vanguard: The Master Takes* (Impulse!/GRP: IMPD-251 [A-10/A-42], 1961). In 1962 he recorded *Coltrane* (Impulse!/GRP: IMPD-215 [A-21]), including "Tungi," "Miles Mode," and "Out of This World," all of which featured long passages of improvisation based on a single mode or a two-chord repeating figure.
11. For example, he recorded an entire album of blues tunes: *Coltrane Plays The Blues* (Atlantic: 1382-2, 1960). In 1964 he recorded *Crescent*, including "Bessie's Blues," and he recorded *A Love Supreme* (Impulse!/GRP: GRD-155 [A-77], 1964) with another twelve-bar blues titled "Pursuance." In concert performances he frequently included standard tunes, such as "Bye, Bye, Blackbird" and "Inch Worm."
12. Compare Coltrane's playing in the beginning of his solo on "Expression," from *Expression*, or on the middle of "Mars" on *Interstellar Space* (Impulse!/GRP: GRD-110 [9277], 1967) with Ayler's playing in the middle of "Ghosts" from Albert Ayler, *Spiritual Unity* (ESP-DISK: 1002, 1964).
13. *The Avant-Garde* (Atlantic: 90041-2 [1451], 1960); "Ascension" (Impulse: 95) has been reissued on *The Major Works of John Coltrane* (Impulse!/GRP: GRD2-113 [A-95], 2CD set, 1965). For other examples, listen to *Meditations* (Impulse!/GRP: GRD-199 [9110], 1965), and *Live In Seattle* (Impulse!/GRP: GRD 2-146 [9202], 1965).
14. The technically-inclined reader may notice the mutual use of isorhythms that is demonstrated by Gilmore on his solo in "Jet Flight" from Sun Ra, *The Futuristic Sounds of Sun Ra* (Savoy/Denon: SV-0213 [12169], 1960–61) and by Coltrane in the middle of his solo on "Impressions" (the November 5, 1961 recording on *Live at the Village Vanguard: The Master Takes*).
15. The formula for Coltrane's and Gilmore's above-cited solos may be roughly likened to alternating word order and loudnesses in repetitions of a brief sentence ("Let's go get the truck.") in this way: "Let's go get truck the." "Let's go get THE truck." "Let' s go GET the truck." "Let's go get truck THE." Then, perhaps changing to "Let's go get the CAR." "The CAR get." "Get the CAR." And so forth. If this analogy does not make sense to you, listen again to the musical passages cited in footnote 14 above, and note the ways both saxophonists develop solos by systematically reworking very brief, three- to five-note, melodic fragments.
16. Its effect was particularly notable in records by Pharoah Sanders, the Bobby Hutcherson-Harold Land groups, and those of David Liebman,

McCoy Tyner, Charles Lloyd (1966-69), John Handy (mid-1960s only), and Gato Barbieri.

17. Listen to Elvin Jones in Coltrane,"Sun Ship" (*Sun Ship*, Impulse!/GRP: IMPD-167 [Impulse 9211], 1965) and "My Lady" (*Live at Birdland*, Impulse!/GRP: GRD-198 [A-50], 1963).

18. Joe Farrell, George Coleman, Frank Foster, Steve Grossman, David Liebman, and others.

19. A few of the publications containing transcriptions and analyses of Coltrane's work: *The Music of John Coltrane* (104 compositions) (Hal Leonard Publishing, 1991); Don Sickler, *John Coltrane: Improvised Saxophone Solos* (Studio PR/Columbia Pictures Publications, 1979/1986); David Baker, *The Jazz Style of John Coltrane* (Studio PR/Columbia Pictures Publications, 1980); David Dempsey, *John Coltrane Plays Giant Steps* (Hal Leonard, 1996); Stuart Isacoff, *Solos for Jazz Tenor Sax* (Carl Fischer, 1985); Scott Reeves, *Creative Jazz Improvisation, 2nd ed.* (Prentice-Hall, 1995); Barry Kernfeld, "The Two Coltranes," *Annual Review of Jazz Studies 2* (1983): 7–66; and Lewis Porter, "John Coltrane's 'A Love Supreme': Jazz Improvisation as Composition," *Journal of the American Musicological Society 38* (Fall 1985): 593–621. The first six publications are available from Jamey Aebersold (P.O. Box 1244, New Albany, IN 47151; phone: 800-456-1388). The last two can often be found in the bound-journals section of well-stocked college music libraries and large public libraries. If you cannot find them, ask a reference librarian for assistance. For interviews with Coltrane about his methods, see Carl Woideek, ed., *The Coltrane Companion: Five Decades of Commentary* (Schirmer, 1998), pages 83–156.

    Transcriptions for most of the Coltrane solos discussed in this book, including the solos on "Flamenco Sketches" and "The Promise," heard on the *Jazz Classics CD*, are available separately from Andrew White, 4830 South Dakota Ave. N.E., Washington, D.C. 20017. White publishes over 600 Coltrane solo transcriptions.

20. Chick Corea credits Coltrane for inspiring the compositions "Litha" and "Straight Up and Down." He also cites Coltrane's *Meditations* and *Ascension* for influencing his own free-form approach used on Chick Corea, *Is* (Solid State: 18055, LP, 1969). "A Love Supreme" was recorded by jazz-rock stars John McLaughlin and Carlos Santana. "Giant Steps" was standard repertory for jazz musicians of the 1970s and 1980s.

    Coltrane had a marked influence on saxophonists during the 1960s (see Table 13.2. Along with Ornette Coleman, Coltrane became the primary model for new saxophonists to study, and several older players also incorporated his techniques in mid-career. Such established players as Frank Foster, Harold Land, Teddy Edwards, and Cannonball Adderley all demonstrated the acquisition of Coltrane techniques. Adderley absorbed some of the Coltrane approach while playing in the Miles Davis band with him during the late 1950s. (There are a few particularly Coltrane-like moments in Adderley's solo on "Fun" on Adderley, *Mercy, Mercy, Mercy,* Capitol: 29915 [ST 2663], 1966.) Coltrane's influence even showed up in Woody Herman's big band, an unlikely context because its saxophone section had been identified with the sound of Stan Getz and cool jazz. Many of Herman's players of the 1970s and 1980s have used Coltrane's methods, and the band recorded Coltrane's compositions "Naima" and "Giant Steps."

    In tallying Coltrane's disciples, note that Coltrane was rarely the only influence these players had. Woody Herman's 1970s saxophonists, for example, drew from a variety of sources, and the most outstanding players who were affected by Coltrane have shown marked individuality as well as the influence of other sources. Joe Farrell, for example, also cited Charlie Parker as a primary influence. Michael Brecker cites Coltrane as a main influence but also cites King Curtis, Junior Walker, Wayne Shorter, and David Liebman.

21. On their post-1968 Miles Davis recordings, Coltrane disciples Steve Grossman and Dave Liebman played more soprano than tenor. Saxophonist Joe Farrell, another player who absorbed portions of the Coltrane style, recorded an entire album, *Moon Germs* (CTI: 6023, LP, 1972), on soprano, and Wayne Shorter used only soprano on *Super Nova* (Blue Note: 84332, 1969).

Chapter Fourteen

Ornette Coleman, 1960 Photo by Bob Parent, courtesy of Don Parent

1960s and 1970s Avant-Garde & "Free" Jazz

The term **avant-garde** designates individuals who are ahead of their peers in developing the newest, freshest creations. All this book's chapters could justifiably contain the term "avant-garde" in their titles because they are concerned with innovators rather than imitators. Yet this is the only chapter titled "avant-garde." There are two reasons for this. First, the term has been applied in recent writing about jazz history as though it were a style unto itself. Instead of receiving original names such as Dixieland, swing, or bop, the new kinds of jazz in the 1960s and 1970s were often merely called "avant-garde," "the new thing," or "out music." Second, this book needs a chapter for several significant modern styles not given chapters of their own. So this chapter's full title probably should be "avant-garde jazz styles of the 1960s and 1970s not treated in separate chapters." Note also that there were other fine avant-garde musicians active at this time but not mentioned here because we lack the space to do them justice.

"Free" jazz is another label attached to some of the avant-garde jazz styles of the 1960s. It is most closely associated with **Ornette Coleman** and **Cecil Taylor. The term "free jazz" commonly refers to the practice of improvising music that is free of preset chord progressions.** To a certain extent, the term has also been applied to improvisation that is free from conventional practices of any kind, not just practices regarding chord progressions or tempos. A model for much of this music is a 1960 Coleman album called *Free Jazz,*[1] which contains

simultaneous collective improvisation by two bands attempting to remain free of preset key, melody, chord progressions, and meter. (The excerpt from this album that is found in SCCJ displays some, but not all, of what is later described here.)[2] But the term "free jazz" can be deceiving because very little of the music is entirely free of tempo, key, or traditional distinctions between soloists and accompanists. Moreover, a substantial portion of the music does have preset melody, organization of themes, or other structure. We will examine more of that later.

Most free jazz groups omitted piano because historically the jazz pianist had assumed a role of providing chord progressions, and restrictions created by preset chord progressions were exactly what these musicians were trying to free themselves from. Another reason for the scarcity of pianists in free jazz is that few pianists were comfortable improvising without the suggestion of chords or key. It was as though, having been the harmonic gatekeepers for so long, they could not function when such gates as chord progressions and song forms were removed. (For explanations of these traditions, see chapter 3 and the *Demo CD.*)

The next three characteristics of free jazz are incidental to freedom from preset chord progressions. They are included here because they happen to be identified more with free players than with bop or cool players. First, **many free players earned a reputation for more extensive manipulations of pitch and tone quality than had been common since early jazz.** Ultra-high-register (altissimo) playing was common, as were shrieks, squawks, wails, gurgles, and squeals. Rough, hoarse tone qualities were also common. Second, **the improvisation of textures sometimes assumed greater importance than the development of melodies. The "free jazz" label was often applied to music of high energy and dense textures which maintained turbulent activity for lengthy periods.** Some free players became so firmly identified with "energy playing" that the "free jazz" label was often attached to high-energy, nonelectronic music of any kind, not just the kind in which preset keys and song forms were absent. Third, **the free players' conception of melody displayed a loosening of bop practices.** Free jazz signalled an end to long, convoluted streams of eighth-note figures that reflected the movement of favorite chord progressions in conventional bop patterns. Phrasing was often more fragmented. Sustained tones were alternated with screeches and moans. There was an unfinished quality in many performances.

Another trend was also more common in free jazz than in bop—**the adoption of non-European musical approaches which neither rely extensively on chord progressions nor use much harmony. This includes some types of music from Africa, Indonesia, China, the Middle East, and India.** This interest led to an amalgamation of jazz with music of non-European cultures, sometimes termed **Third World music,** or just **World Music.** It manifested itself in the use of non-Western instruments and the cultivation of non-Western approaches to playing European instruments. This development might have occurred with free players because free jazz's rejection of piano and preset harmony was musically not too distant from these non-European forms of music that also did not use chord progressions or chord instruments. It resulted in a form of music that is simpler than bop. In this way, it considerably extended the range of sounds used by jazz musicians. The persistence of these elements in free music marks one of the first such lasting blends since the periodic infatuations jazz had shown with Latin American music.

◇ORNETTE COLEMAN

One of the most influential forces in jazz since the 1950s is **Ornette Coleman** (b.1930). Some consider him as historically significant as Charlie Parker.[3] Coleman is primarily an alto saxophonist, though he also plays trumpet and violin. On his 1958–1959 recordings, he displayed a soft, pure tone, and he moved from note to note in legato fashion, as if smoothly sliding along small subdivisions of pitch. His tone had neither the edge of Charlie Parker's nor the body of Cannonball Adderley's. Coleman began his notes more bluntly and used a slow vibrato. In later years, he made his tone somewhat brighter and gave it an edge. Though he seems able to play almost everything he attempts, he lacks the ultra-high-level command possessed by Parker, Adderley, and Lee Konitz. (Get SCCJ and compare Coleman's sound on "Lonely Woman" with Parker's on "Embraceable You," Adderley's on the Miles Davis "So What," and Konitz's on Tristano's "Crosscurrent.")

Coleman is one of the freshest, most prolific post-bop composers; by the mid-1970s he had already written every tune on more than twenty albums. His style is quite original, and he has an exceptional gift for melody. Some of his tunes are quite catchy. Like those of Thelonious Monk, some of Coleman's tunes sound simple, despite their unusual rhythmic and harmonic qualities. The playfulness of Coleman's tunes is also reminiscent of Monk's work.[4]

Although often called free jazz, Coleman's music actually has quite a bit of self-imposed structure. Constant tempo is usually employed. Written and memorized tunes are usually used during some portion of his performances. Moreover, there is nothing haphazard about the freedoms with which he and his sidemen play. They are limited by their own decision to listen to each other carefully, and they plan their music while they improvise. Coleman's brand of free jazz also casts instruments in conventional solo and accompaniment roles. In his trio, Coleman usually seems to be soloing while his bassist and drummer accompany. Though there is interaction, give-and-take, and mutual stimulation, there is little doubt that Coleman is the soloist. (Listen to "Congeniality" in SCCJ.)

For a trio performance to be truly free of role conventions, the three instruments would have to be undifferentiated in their roles: the absence of a solo voice would be as common as the presence of a solo voice; the drums would be accompanied by sax and bass just as often as the sax was accompanied by drums and bass. Actually, if "free" means freedom from conventional roles or song forms, there would not be any solos at all, since solos and accompaniments fulfill roles that are as conventional as constant tempo, meter, key, and chord progressions. True musical freedom can indicate the ability of a musician to play whatever is in the musician's head, regardless of its adherence to musical conventions. The problem is that this is not humanly possible. Musicians are not capable of being so "free." Musical conditioning—and the very process of learning to play an instrument—prevent so great an independence. Therefore, this extreme definition of musical freedom is not too helpful in describing free jazz, and it is clearly not a description of Ornette Coleman's music.

In short, Coleman's music is free only in some respects: it is free of preset chord progressions and their chorus lengths. Some, though not most, of his work is also free of meter and constant tempo. The music does not lack a sense of key, it is not atonal, and it is certainly not random. (See pages 369–373 for discussion of scales, modality, tonality, and atonality.) Coleman freely changes keys, but he usually stays in each one long enough for us to hear that he is, indeed, in a particular key.[5] Also, his key changes are logical and obvious; they reflect the melodic integrity of his improvised lines.

Coleman attempts a difficult task when he rejects the use of preset chord changes. Without the rise and fall of musical tension indicated by chord changes, his music still has the rise and fall of tension generated by his bassist and drummer; but that is all he has to support and inspire his creations musically. Outside of that, every measure is taxing his imagination, calling upon him to fill it with an interesting and meaningful line. But because none of those measures is supplying any organizational ideas in the form of chord changes, Coleman's improvising cannot fall back on the underlying musical motion of chord changes or on the

Ornette Coleman, alto saxophonist and the leading figure in "free" jazz. Shown in 1972 at age 42 with bassist Charlie Haden and drummer Eddie Blackwell.

Photo by Bill Smith

supportive sound of a pianist's comping. By foregoing preset chord changes, and their associated chorus lengths, turnarounds, and bridges, he has brought us an especially abstract—and challenging—form of musical experience.

Despite the freedom of his improvisational approach, Coleman's improvised lines often resemble chord progression-based lines. For Coleman, melody is primary and harmony secondary. Sometimes it may sound as though he is inventing chord progressions as he improvises lines, but this is only because the harmonic logic of those lines resembles that of chord progression-based lines we have heard elsewhere. The construction of his lines is ruled by his musical past in the same way that our perception as listeners is ruled by our past listening experiences. Coleman plays freely, but in his lines we can hear organization like that in more conventional improvisation. Some of this comes from the very melodic nature of much of his work. (In fact, Coleman has been called the supreme melodist.) The feeling of a definite key (tone center) is present in each portion of his solos, though he changes keys at will.[6] Also, part of the chord-progression feeling in Coleman's music stems from the approach taken by his bassists, especially Charlie Haden. Though Coleman's bassists follow the harmonic directions indicated by his improvisations, at times they also take the lead themselves. Coleman's line may suggest a chord progression which the bassist will complete, or vice versa. Coleman and his bassist remain alert to chord progressions that are suggested in each other's lines.

Modern jazz has been influenced by Ornette Coleman's tunes because they are so original and by his unique saxophone style because it is so emotional and melodic (see Table 14.1). But Coleman has had just as much impact through his decision to discard chord changes and his belief that an improviser can let the melody go its own way and not be directed by preset progressions of chords.

TABLE 14.1 Some of the Many Musicians Influenced by Ornette Coleman

John Tchicai	Roscoe Mitchell	James "Blood" Ulmer
Marion Brown	Jan Garbarek	Ronald Shannon Jackson
Dewey Redman	Anthony Ortega	Jamaaladeen Tacuma
Jimmy Lyons	Albert Ayler	Charlie Haden
Sonny Simmons	John Coltrane	Pat Metheny
Prince Lasha	John Carter	Joseph Jarman
Henry Threadgill	Charles Brackeen	Paul Bley
Carlos Ward	Keith Jarrett	Saheb Sarbib
Archie Shepp	Bobby Bradford	
Oliver Lake	Don Cherry	

Coleman's *Free Jazz* album of 1960 paralleled Miles Davis's *Kind of Blue* in its impact on improvisational approaches. *Kind of Blue* popularized modal approaches; *Free Jazz* contributed to more frequent use of free-form approaches. Coleman used two pianoless quartets on the album. The first included his regular quartet: trumpeter Don Cherry, bassist Charlie Haden, and drummer Eddie Blackwell. The second was made up of alto saxophonist-bass clarinetist Eric Dolphy, trumpeter Freddie Hubbard, bassist Scott LaFaro, and drummer Billy Higgins. (These names are important because all these men are giants in post-bop jazz.) The eight musicians played together, sometimes improvising all at once, never using any preset arrangement of themes, chord changes, or chorus lengths. Tone centers were evident, though they were not agreed upon in advance. (Listen to the excerpt from this album that is in SCCJ.)

Despite the album title, the music on *Free Jazz* is not entirely free. There are prearranged ensemble passages, solos with rhythm section accompaniment, and a bass duet. Some of the solos, especially Freddie Hubbard's, sound as though they were based on a preset chord progression, though the progression is suggested only by the resemblance of the improvised line to other progression-based lines. Brief themes recur in the improvisation and are passed back and forth among group members (an aspect not evident in the SCCJ excerpt). Rarely are all eight players improvising at the same time. Both bassists and both drummers play throughout most of it, but usually a single horn surfaces while the others stay out. Occasionally all the horns return to embellish the prominent voice.

Other jazz groups had recorded collectively improvised free pieces at about the same time or before Coleman's first recordings. (See chapter 10 for Tristano, Giuffre, Rogers, et al.) But these were isolated efforts, and the approach did not catch on in the main stream of jazz styles. After Coleman's *Free Jazz,* however, a number of other musicians also recorded in a similar format; some of them are discussed in this chapter.

◇DON CHERRY

Don Cherry (1936–1995) was a trumpeter, composer, bandleader, and a leading figure in free jazz. A regular member of Ornette Coleman's groups in the late 1950s and early 1960s, he played on all of Coleman's important early recordings, including *Something Else,*[7] *Change of the Century,*[8] and *Free Jazz.* Though strongly influenced by Coleman, Cherry also cited bop trumpeters Fats Navarro and Clifford Brown as influences. Consistent with this bop connection, Cherry recorded improvisations which closely follow preset chord progressions and contain phrasing and note choices that derive from bop methods.[9] However, like Coleman's, most of Cherry's recorded improvisation goes its own way spontaneously instead of relying on a preset progression of accompanying chords. Cherry's improvisations are strikingly original, filled with lines and melodic fragments which draw little from standard jazz cliche. (Listen to Cherry on Coleman's "Congeniality" and "Lonely Woman" on SCCJ.) Cherry did not ordinarily use chord instruments in his bands, and he devoted a considerable portion of his career to playing types of Oriental, Turkish, and Indian music that also omit chording instruments and chord-progression-based compositional forms.

Cherry was quite flexible as an improviser, capable of constructing logical solo lines as well as spontaneously constructing parts for collective improvisation.[10] In this way, he was a throwback to the earliest improvisers, for whom sensitivity and instantaneous flexibility were essential to making good collective music. He could improvise lines which swing and stick close to the beat. He could also play against meter, as though ignoring the beat and resisting swing. In this way, what Cherry does rhythmically is analogous to what he does harmonically. (Musicians call conventional playing "inside" and the other approach "outside.") Because many modern players are comfortable with only one of the two approaches, it is notable that Cherry is adept at both.

Since the mid-1960s, Cherry spent considerable time in Europe and devoted much of his recording to music that is not closely related to the jazz tradition. This body of music is frequently dubbed "World Music." Cherry's interests led him to compose and perform extensively in groups using such instruments as the tamboura, sitar, finger cymbals, conch horn, African finger piano, and gong. Cherry learned to play flute, bamboo flute, and assorted percussion instruments at this time. This music makes much use of drones and extensively repeated accompaniment figures. Some pieces are based entirely on chants in which the same few notes are played over and over again. For the jazz listener, there is often little in this music that distinguishes it from its non-jazz sources.[11]

◇CECIL TAYLOR

Cecil Taylor (b. 1929) is a pianist, composer, and bandleader who developed a unique and specialized style of modern jazz during the late 1950s and early 1960s. His style is not merely different, innovative, or unconventional; rather, it is **a major alternative to the main stream of modern jazz styles**. (Listen to "Enter Evening" on SCCJ, but note that it is among the most tame of all Taylor's recordings. The vast majority of his recorded music sounds wild and extremely turbulent.)

Taylor does not play with modern jazz swing feeling, and he frequently emphasizes musical textures rather than musical lines. Although quite syncopated, his rhythms tend to be played slightly ahead of or on top of the beat, and they lack the lilt and buoyancy of conventional jazz rhythmic style. As jazz scholar Harvey Pekar has noted, Taylor does not try to swing: his music is too tense to swing.

The manner in which Taylor goes about making music differs from most jazz traditions. Taylor's notes often seem to be generated in layered groups, designed to create textures of sound and sound shapes instead of singable phrases that lope along. The textures are rich in internal movement; they seem to shimmer and explode. In fact, much of Taylor's music is comprised of quick, tightly packed, staccato figures. They are played in a manner that is very percussive, with few moments of serenity. Some observers have commented that Taylor seems to "attack" the piano keyboard, and they are astounded because he has the skill to strike odd sequences of piano keys with tremendous force at a dizzying pace and not miss any. What almost universally impresses listeners is that most of his performances seem to draw on a continuous source of high energy and maintain a feverish intensity for long periods.

Pianist Cecil Taylor, the musician who created a striking alternative to all other modern jazz styles. His music emphasized dramatically changing textures instead of hummable melodies. His ideas exploded in note clusters, shimmered and popped instead of swinging. Pictured here in 1990 at age 61.

Photo by Grace Bell

Taylor began playing without preset chord progressions or constant tempo, and frequently without a bassist, during the 1960s. His earliest recordings, however, show that he once based his improvisations on familiar tunes and chord changes.[12] He often played free of the harmonic restrictions imposed by a preset progression of chords, though he did preplan what he called "unit structures." These were specific phrases and overall concepts about the architecture that the piece should assume. His preparation for performance does involve extensive rehearsal, and he does provide his musicians with musical figures to play. However, he does not always dictate the exact synchronization of parts, their timing, or tempo. In addition, he requires his musicians to improvise some passages without the guidance of preset themes, chord progressions, or chorus lengths. They are freely improvised. In other words, Taylor's music is not entirely free-form, but it is free of the preset forms that most jazz musicians use.

Some of Cecil Taylor's group performances begin with a theme loosely stated by horns and accompanied by his piano improvising in a florid, orchestral fashion. Then a collective improvisation begins in which nearly everyone participates. The emphasis is on creating textures. The style is not melodic in the pop-tune sense, the swing-era sense, or the bop sense. Some textures change gradually, others abruptly. Occasionally a preorganized ensemble portion erupts. Usually the group creates a whirlpool of sound and maintains a frantic pace.[13]

Brief portions of some Taylor improvisations are genuinely atonal. This is unusual in jazz, and in Taylor's work as well, because even the most adventuresome free-form improvisations are usually organized around tone centers, keys, modes, or shifting tone centers.[14] More than any other jazz style, Taylor's resembles the music of mid-twentieth century composers Karlheinz Stockhausen, Oliver Messiaen, and Luciano Berio. His improvisations have a hint of Thelonious Monk or Duke Ellington, but generally they sound more orchestral than jazz-like. (Listen to "Jitney #2" on the *Jazz Classics CD.*)

◇ALBERT AYLER

Tenor saxophonist **Albert Ayler** (1936–1970) was one of the most original improvisers to emerge after Charlie Parker and Ornette Coleman. His style remains one of the most unusual in jazz history. He perfected an approach that was instrumentally very demanding. Ayler's lines ran the entire range of the tenor saxophone and through at least an additional

Listening Guide for

"JITNEY #2"

Composed, arranged, and performed by pianist Cecil Taylor; recorded July 2, 1974 at the Montreux Jazz Festival in Switzerland; available on the *Jazz Classics CD,* Track 77; also available on Cecil Taylor, *Silent Tongues* (Freedom: FCD-741005, 1974).

Though many listeners report having difficulty with Cecil Taylor's music, this example should prove comprehensible to you if it is replayed several times. It is an exciting performance excerpted from one of Taylor's most widely hailed albums. His thinking on this is very clear, and we cannot be distracted or overwhelmed by the playing of additional musicians because Taylor is entirely alone here. Moreover, this performance will not require you to maintain concentration for long because Taylor plays for only three minutes and twenty-one seconds.

As in listening to most music, you might wish merely to let it wash over you the first time you hear it. Let it take you wherever it can. On successive replayings, you may become intrigued by the prospect of trying to follow Taylor's thinking as the performance unfolds. Note, however, that not all the listening strategies that you developed from previous listening guides will apply here. This music is not divided into 12-measure or 32-measure choruses with introductions, A-sections, and B-sections that you can latch onto. It does not usually follow set durations of modes or keep time, either. To make a distinction between the end of one section and beginning of another becomes impractical. Instead of following such recurring patterns, Taylor devises his own ideas and lets them recur and be transformed over the course of his performance. For instance, he uses one main statement, the first two notes, followed by a chordal answer. When Taylor reiterates that opening statement, he often repeats this pattern almost intact, though he occasionally adds one or two notes to its opening. Try to become familiar with that opening statement and then attempt to recognize recurrences among Taylor's more complicated inventions. You might be able to hear it recur in faster or slower form, and in a higher pitch range. Often Taylor will play for several seconds without referring to it in any obvious way. In fact, much of this performance is filled with cascading notes and jarring clusters of tones.

This music gives us an opportunity to ponder the way jazz can be defined. The piece contains a substantial amount of improvisation because, though it contains a few preconceived ideas, these ideas are arranged and developed spontaneously. Steady tempo is not used, however, and most listeners agree that Taylor's rhythms fail to swing in the jazz sense. The music resembles contemporary piano works by nonjazz composers such as Olivier Messiaen. Because of its nonswinging rhythmic feeling, some people do not refer to this music as jazz. They feel that "improvised concert music" is a more accurate description. On the other hand, Taylor has a history of playing within the jazz tradition, and he cites Duke Ellington, Thelonious Monk, and Lennie Tristano as important influences on his development. In fact, some people consider all of Taylor's music to be jazz because of its association with the jazz tradition.

Elapsed Time	
0'0'	the opening statement, followed by variations
	bass notes followed by mid-register chords
0' 10"	opening statement again, then echoed many times in various transformations
0' 17"	opening statement followed by quasi-broken chords, turning into runs
	more variations of the opening idea, leading to rapidly played passages, and a return to that same idea
0' 26"	opening idea again, followed by chords
0' 30" to 50"	cascades of notes that paraphrase the opening idea
0' 45"	first climax, as Taylor reaches the upper register of the keyboard
	series of repeated, broken chords played by two hands in the middle of the keyboard, tremolos scattered across the keyboard until about 56"
0' 56"	switch to single notes instead of chords
	Taylor introduces a new idea and then develops it.
1' 06"	return to opening idea
1' 08"	opening idea again
1' 09"	opening idea again
1' 12"	opening idea again
1' 15"	a new idea and several repeats of it
1' 23"	intensity begins to increase
	notes scattered all over the keyboard
1' 35"	tremolos scattered across the keyboard
1' 47" to 1' 55"	variations of the opening idea
1' 50"	Intensity still increases as heavy chords are played at slower pace.
1' 57"	a new idea
2' 05"	very rapid sprinkling of notes, lasting until 2' 39"
	cascades of notes, variations of the idea, in different keys
2' 43"	Intensity starts increasing again, in preparation for the last climax, with briefly repeated runs. High-pitched ideas occur with chorded responses in bass range.
2' 45"	Taylor is briefly melody-like until 2' 53". Then he resumes the turbulence.
3' 00"	lots of scattered tremolos; faster pace
3' 07"	quick trills are exchanged
3' 15"	Taylor plays tone clusters alternately in low then high registers.
3' 17"	Taylor pounds out a string of tone clusters, ending in the low register.
3' 21"	Taylor concludes abruptly with a restatement of the opening idea.

octave beyond the conventional "highest note." He played throughout that range with swooping, swirling legato figures, and a light, slippery tone. His sound sometimes resembled the tone of a C-melody saxophone. Ayler made moans and wails an essential part of his musical vocabulary. Much of his music was strikingly voice-like. His vibrato was sometimes slow, at other times moderately fast, but always very natural, and delivered in a driven sort of way. In his extended high register, Ayler played with the ease that good players exhibit only in the conventional midrange of the tenor saxophone. His playing often sounded like rapid, legato violin playing. These elements created an otherworldly quality. There was never anything mechanical or academic about Ayler's playing. Whether listeners enjoyed his music or not, it provided an intensely emotional experience for them.

Ayler's rhythmic conception was not like bop rhythmic conceptions. In fact, it was unlike any swinging jazz style. Like his melodic approach, his rhythmic approach had more in common with classical and folk music than with jazz. (See chapter 2 for more about different types of swing feeling.) Ayler swung in a manner that only approximated conventional jazz swing feeling. Much of his work did not swing at all. The lack of swing feeling was often caused by a continuously high level of tension, in place of the alternation of tension and relaxation that typifies bop.

Like Ornette Coleman, Ayler followed preset harmonic and rhythmic structures only loosely, and he preferred bands with no chording instrument. Ayler's bassists were some of the same gifted musicians employed by Coleman and Bill Evans. His drummers were of the "free" school, concerned little with simple timekeeping, very interested in group interaction and the creation of varied sounds and textures.[15] Like Coleman, Ayler also used a Charlie Parker tune on one of his first recordings.[16] And, like Coleman, he followed its harmonies only loosely. In other words, he acknowledged bop but did not actually play in the bop style.[17]

Ayler triggered a major style change for John Coltrane in the mid-1960s, and he had a sustained impact on numerous other saxophonists considered avant-garde during the 1970s and 1980s.[18] The close adherence to tempo that was central to bop and bop's offshoots largely disappeared in players who were affected by Ayler. His rhythmic elasticity was absorbed into the styles of many avant-garde players. A number of players drew from the combined influences of Ayler, Coleman, and Coltrane. These new players perpetuated the timbres and erratic contours associated with free jazz, even when performing pieces that followed preset chord changes and tempo.

◇CHARLES MINGUS

Charles Mingus (1922–1979) is historically significant as

1) one of the first virtuoso bass soloists to appear after Jimmy Blanton;
2) a bandleader who employed unorthodox techniques and all-star personnels; and
3) a prolific composer-arranger who
   a) created unique blends of premodern and modern jazz traditions, ranging from Jelly Roll Morton and Duke Ellington to bop and free jazz;
   b) drew from such diverse sources as Negro gospel music, Mexican folk music, and twentieth-century European concert music; and
   c) wrote distinctive melodies.

Mingus did not become widely known until the late 1950s, though he had been making highly creative recordings as a bandleader since the mid-1940s. By the late 1950s, when his work began to be issued by major record companies, he had already recorded as bassist with such modern giants as Miles Davis, Charlie Parker, and Dizzy Gillespie (for discussion of his stature as a bassist, see chapter 9). Historically significant as a bassist, Mingus is at least as significant as a composer and bandleader. Like Ellington's, his name represents an entire idiom which, though rooted in other idioms, is uniquely his own.

Mingus wrote more than one hundred fifty pieces, many of which have been rearranged and recorded several times. He explored styles as diverse as:

1) program music ("Pithecanthropus Erectus," the story of man)[19]

2) funky, bluesy, gospel-oriented music, with shouting and hand clapping ("Better Git It in Your Soul")[20]

3) Third Stream music ("Revelations")[21]

4) bop (with Charlie Parker, Dizzy Gillespie, Bud Powell, and Max Roach)[22]

5) free jazz (portions of "What Love")[23]

6) music for film (*Shadows*)

Mingus employed diverse instrumentations, including the following:

1) his own solo piano[24]

2) jazz quintets of trumpet, tenor saxophone, piano, bass, and drums[25]

3) pianoless quartet[26]

4) five trumpets, four trombones, tuba, cello, oboe, flute, six saxophones, piano, bass, and three drummers[27]

5) two trumpets, trombone, French horn, flute, bassoon, two saxophones, harp, piano, guitar, vibraharp, two basses, and drums (see footnote 21)

Throughout his career, Mingus displayed the influence of Ellington. The methods of Ellington are obvious as early as Mingus's 1946 recording of "Bedspread," made as a 78 r.p.m. single for the Four Star company. Even the style of improvisations in it shows a similarity to the Ellington approaches. Mingus has composed and recorded pieces dedicated to Ellington, such as "Duke's Choice" and "An Open Letter to Duke." Ellington-like use of plunger-muted brass playing has appeared in Mingus works. The Johnny Hodges alto saxophone style has, at the request of Mingus, been incorporated into the playing of such otherwise non-Hodges-styled saxophonists as Charlie Mariano, Jackie McLean, and John Handy. Mingus has also recorded several Ellington compositions.

Mingus is far better known for his combo recordings than for his big band material. The Mingus combo approaches are distinguished because they seldom resemble the jam session format adopted in most modern jazz concerts and recording sessions. Mingus relies heavily on the alternation of composed and improvised passages and on preset accompaniments instead of being restricted to only a unison theme statement, followed by a string of improvised solos with improvised accompaniments, and another theme statement. These sustain the listener's interest by frequently interspersing familiar material so that the listener is not required to concentrate for long periods on continuously changing improvisations. Also to Mingus's credit is that, despite the amount of planning in his performances, a looseness prevails, and a feeling of naturalness is conveyed by his music. In many performances, Mingus rejected conventional bop accompaniment patterns in favor of preset statements which broke the flow of

Charles Mingus, bassist-bandleader-composer, second only to Duke Ellington in achieving colorful integration of composition and improvisation. He drew from symphonic music and folk songs, modern jazz and avant-garde chamber music. His solo style inspired hundreds of jazz bassists, and his combo innovations influenced generations of nontraditional bandleaders. Pictured here in 1951 at age 29.

Photo by Bob Parent, courtesy of Don Parent

music by introducing stops and changes of style in mid-performance. Portions of some solos were accompanied by nothing more than hand clapping and shouting. Drumming might use a waltz pattern one moment and a conventional jazz pattern the next moment. Some passages contain many stop-time solo breaks. The tempo might be slow one moment and doubled the next. In fact, Mingus is one of the few bandleaders in jazz history to explore the gradual speeding and slowing of tempo. And, like the finished products of Jelly Roll Morton and Duke Ellington, the Mingus material rarely sounded anonymous. It could not be mistaken for an ordinary recording session run in a more conventional fashion.[28]

Mingus's unorthodox approaches to combo performance had several significant impacts. They forced improvisers away from producing purely bop-styled solos in an uninterrupted stream. They gave improvisers a varied background which, in turn, elicited more varied solos. They gave listeners brief, reassuring chunks of music in the form of figures that became familiar because they regularly recurred during the piece. This allowed listeners to latch onto something familiar amidst the flow of freshly improvised solos. This is important because, in most bop performances, familiar material was offered only at the beginning and the end of a piece. The Mingus technique of placing recurring devices *within* the piece offered listeners something that they could not ordinarily expect from other kinds of modern jazz (though this approach later became associated with bands led by former Mingus sidemen Thad Jones and Ted Curson).

To achieve a successful integration of composed and improvised music, Mingus obtained a high degree of artistic cooperation from his musicians. As a bandleader and arranger,

Mingus had a sense of what players to cast in what roles and how to pry out maximum distinctiveness in a performance. He colorfully mixed snips of improvisations with his prewritten ensemble sounds to weave unusual textures. Then, instead of thrusting their favorite phrases unthinkingly onto his music, the players were forced to appreciate his musical wishes and give those wishes higher priority than they gave their own. Players had to interpret his demands as well as contribute original twists of their own. Performance was often indistinct from rehearsal. The music amounted to a workshop endeavor in that Mingus gave his musicians sketchily written parts, dictated parts to them by playing phrases on the piano or the bass, and described in words the conceptions which he wanted converted to music. (Listen to "Hora Decubitus" on SCCJ.) [29]

◇ERIC DOLPHY

Modern jazz has known numerous virtuoso saxophonists, but **Eric Dolphy** (1928–1964) could be called virtuoso on three different instruments: flute, alto saxophone, and bass clarinet. Dolphy mastered the complete range of every instrument he played, and he capitalized on almost every sound it could produce. He even studied bird calls and mimicked them in his solos. Slides and smears connected Dolphy's notes. Sometimes his lines bounced and twittered exuberantly. Dolphy was also a composer whose pieces were as peculiar as Thelonious Monk's. Dolphy's tunes contained odd intervals and syncopations that were even more jarring than Monk's because they came at the listener much faster. Upon first hearing them, listeners often perceive Dolphy's compositions as erratic and unpredictable. Like his solo improvisations, they are so unusual that some listeners at first assumed the notes were not related to the chord changes in the accompaniment. Listeners thought that Dolphy either did not know what he was doing or was intentionally fooling people with random note choices. His style perfectly fit the "avant-garde" and "out" characterizations. Some listeners even mistook it for free jazz. Contrary to what some thought, however, Dolphy was quite sincere and thoroughly schooled. He knew exactly what he was doing, and connected every note to chords in the accompaniment. His connections were far less obvious than in earlier jazz styles. They were not so remote, however, that his playing could qualify as truly "free" jazz.

Dolphy's first well-known recordings were made with the Chico Hamilton quintet during the 1950s. He then recorded with Charles Mingus from 1960 to 1964. Many musicians regard his collaborations with Mingus to be among the most outstanding recordings in this period of jazz history. In 1961 and 1962, Dolphy toured and recorded with fellow saxophonist John Coltrane.[30]

Dolphy's 1958–1959 work with Chico Hamilton's group was rooted in bop phrasing and swing feeling.[31] His later work, however, was characterized by explosive torrents of notes that were connected by neither conventional melodic development nor bop phrasing. He could also play with swing era lushness, sometimes on the same piece that displayed the wild and jumpy side of his style.[32]

Dolphy's impact was not as extensive as Ornette Coleman's or John Coltrane's, but there were musicians after the mid-1960s who played his tunes, composed in his style, and drew upon his improvisational methods. Saxophonists and flutists were especially impressed by Dolphy's consummate mastery of his instruments and his courage to use it to invent and perform what often seemed outrageous sounds. He opened new horizons by showing that such an unorthodox manner could work.

◇FREE DRUMMERS

Several highly imaginative drummers have been associated with free jazz (see Table 14.2). They developed a style which did not rely on repetitive ride rhythms, high-hat closings, and bass drum patterns. Though much of their work did imply tempo, the rhythms they invented only sporadically stated it. All four of the drummer's limbs in this "free drumming" style

TABLE 14.2 Some of the Many Musicians Who Have Improvised Without Preset Chord Progressions

SAXOPHONISTS

Ornette Coleman
Eric Dolphy
Albert Ayler
Archie Shepp
Bill Smith
Henry Threadgill
Sam Rivers
David Murray
Oliver Lake
Anthony Braxton
Roscoe Mitchell
Joseph Jarman
John Coltrane
Dewey Redman
John Gilmore
Danny Davis
Marshall Allen
Pharoah Sanders
Sonny Rollins
Gato Barbieri
Marion Brown
John Tchicai
Jimmy Lyons
Ken McIntyre
Steve Lacy
Pat Patrick

TRUMPETERS

Bobby Bradford
Freddie Hubbard
Don Cherry
Don Ayler
Lester Bowie
Bill Dixon
Dewey Johnson
Eddie Gale Stevens
Ted Curson
Leo Smith

BASSISTS

Charlie Haden
Dave Holland
David Lee
Malachi Favors
Fred Hopkins
Jimmy Garrison
Scott LaFaro
Charlie Mingus
Buell Neidlinger
Bob Cranshaw
Henry Grimes
David Izenzon
Gary Peacock
Richard Davis
Steve Swallow
Alan Silva

PIANISTS

Lennie Tristano
Keith Jarrett
Paul Bley
Sam Rivers
Sun Ra
Cecil Taylor

DRUMMERS ASSOCIATED WITH FREE JAZZ

Milford Graves
Sunny Murray
Andrew Cyrille
Rashied Ali
Beaver Harris
Barry Altschul
Charles Moffett
Don Moye
Steve McCall
Dennis Charles
Ed Blackwell
Billy Higgins
Paul Motian

performed a function similar to the "chattering" done by bop drummers' left hands on snare drum. (For explanation of bop drumming, listen to *Demo CD.*) In other words, "chattering" came from the entire drum set. These free-style drummers were not relegating their right hands to stating a consistent timekeeping rhythm. Nor were they using their left feet to consistently snap shut their high-hat on every other beat. All four limbs were devoted to generating an undercurrent of activity that popped and crackled with ever-changing sounds. **By comparison with swing era and bop methods of rhythm section drumming, free-style produced sound patterns that were less predictable. They offered varieties of color and shading that were more extensive. This was a complete departure from the**

traditions of marching band and dance band. Free jazz drumming more closely follows an orchestral concept of percussion because it emphasizes color and shading instead of timekeeping.[33]

◇FREE BASSISTS

A number of fine bassists have been associated with free jazz (see Table 14.2). Most have played in more conventional settings, too. In this chapter we are singling out two of the best known, Charlie Haden and Dave Holland.

Charlie Haden (b. 1937) is the bassist most prominently associated with Ornette Coleman during the 1950s and 1960s. He also received wide exposure during the 1970s as a member of the Keith Jarrett Quartet, a band which drew considerable inspiration from Coleman's music. Though usually classed with free jazz musicians, Haden is known for playing that is firmly tied to movement of harmonies, a skill that is fundamental to nonfree styles. In fact, his work is usually bound more closely to jazz traditions than is the work of those he accompanies. One of his greatest contributions was to translate what free hornmen were doing into more conventional time feeling. This helped unify the group sound by anchoring the hornmen's creations when they were without feeling of formal meter. It also brought swing feeling to many musical ideas that probably would not have swung by themselves. (Listen to Haden on Coleman's "Congeniality" and "Lonely Woman" on SCCJ.)

As an accompanist, Haden constructs lines that move with unerring logic, no matter how quickly directions change in the solo lines. He manages to pick up direction that momentarily occurs in solo lines and instantaneously align himself with it. This is a skill he shares with the playing of fellow bassists Dave Holland (b. 1946) in Sam Rivers's groups and Malachi Favors (b. 1937) in the Art Ensemble of Chicago. All three bassists represent the strongest connection with conventional jazz that each of their respective groups displays. They are also distinguished by a higher level of instrumental facility than their horn-playing colleagues display. Haden, Holland, and Favors use very full, warm tones. They favor a clean, firm sound rather than the rough-hewn, explosive quality used by the hornmen they accompany. In fact, Haden makes the richness of his tone an element in his vocabulary of musical devices. He attaches more importance to single tones and the ways they can be manipulated than was the fashion with most bassists during the 1960s and 1970s. He is concerned more with sound than speed, and he is not interested in improvising bass solos in the style of hornmen. Each of his notes reflects intense deliberation. Haden contrasts with most of his contemporaries in that he is not concerned with intricacy.

Dave Holland is known for music he played with such chord-progression-based musicians as Miles Davis and Chick Corea as well as for his playing in free-form settings. No matter the setting, Holland always seems to choose the right notes and fit them together in a highly musical way that is complete and warm at the same time. He has a conception of broad scope, an imagination that rivals Scott LaFaro's, and a swinging manner of timekeeping. Holland's playing exudes strength and confidence. His tone glows with a unique color and the vibrato he gives to many long tones. Naturalness is a pervasive feeling in his style. He can take racing tempos and still swing and sound pretty. Ballads are a joy for his approach. In addition to being present in many ground-breaking recordings of Miles Davis and Chick Corea, Holland was also leader on an important record session that has been associated with avant-garde jazz: *Conference of the Birds* (see footnote 33). His work with numerous groups led by saxophonist Sam Rivers parallels the work Charlie Haden did with Ornette Coleman and Keith Jarrett; but Holland has more speed and agility than Haden and uses those abilities in ways that are not part of Haden's style. Holland can play horn-like bass solos in the bop manner as well as create action-filled textures as accompaniment in free jazz contexts.

◇CHICAGO AVANT-GARDE

A number of stylistically related black musicians from Chicago began gaining attention during the late 1950s and early 1960s. They finally received wide critical recognition during the late 1970s. The music of these players helped define avant-garde jazz for the 1960s and 1970s.[34] This stream of Chicagoans can be considered as three groups: **1) the musicians associated with Sun Ra, beginning during the 1950s; 2) the Association for the Advancement of Creative Musicians (AACM), an alliance of black players spearheaded by pianist Richard Abrams in the mid-1960s; and 3) the most well publicized of all AACM members, the Art Ensemble of Chicago and saxophonist-composer Anthony Braxton, who became well known in the 1970s.**

◇SUN RA

Sun Ra (1915–1993) was an immensely creative pianist, composer, arranger, and bandleader active as a professional musician since the 1930s. He formed his own big band during the 1950s. Like Duke Ellington's, many of Ra's principal sidemen stayed with him for twenty and thirty years at a stretch. He wrote and performed in a kaleidoscopic range of musical styles. Sun Ra's output is uniquely his own music, but its diversity is most expediently characterized by comparison with similar work of better-known musicians:

1) Some pieces resemble the chant music of Africa.
2) Some works suggest the mode-based work of John Coltrane in the 1960s.[35]
3) Some of Sun Ra's mid-1950s music almost sounds like a modern jazz version of Duke Ellington's music in the 1940s.[36]
4) Some of Sun Ra's work of the mid-1960s resembles contemporary classical music using electronically altered and synthesized sounds.[37]

Differences between Sun Ra's writing and that of conventional big bands can be summarized easily by saying that Sun Ra capitalized on the diversity that is possible with big band instrumentation and overlooked by most other bandleaders. For instance, Sun Ra:

1) used many different combinations of trumpets, trombones, saxophones, piano, bass, and drums;
2) extended the range of tone colors by adding electronic instruments (he employed electric piano and synthesizers long before rock groups made their use common);
3) made imaginative use of timpani (see Figure 14.1), celeste, xylophone, bass marimba, bells, and chimes;
4) used saxophonists who played instruments unusual in jazz, such as piccolo, oboe, bassoon, and bass clarinet (see Figure 14.2);
5) required all his sidemen to double on percussion instruments;
6) sometimes created passages by means of simultaneous collective improvisation instead of composition;
7) gave performances in which pieces were not separated, where the entire evening was an uninterrupted sequence of unusual sounds;
8) based pieces on chants instead of chord progressions.

Sun Ra's use of synthesizers and the overall conception for many of his 1960s albums, especially *Heliocentric Worlds of Sun Ra, Vols. 1 and 2*,[38] suggest the work of twentieth-

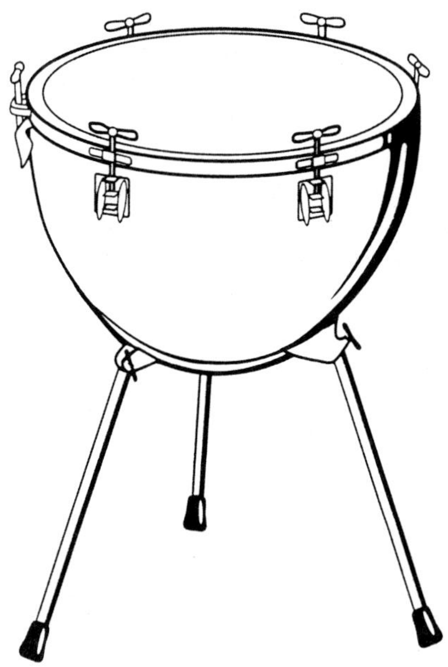

FIGURE 14.1 An instrument used in Sun Ra's band: kettledrum. (Two or more kettledrums are collectively termed timpani.)

century classical composers Edgard Varese and Krzysztof Penderecki. Central to such work is the notion that music can consist of sound by itself instead of sound in the conventional form of melody and harmony. Chunks of sound are sequenced in place of the standard ideas of melody and chord progression. When Sun Ra and his improvisers addressed themselves to this style, the result had a more natural and flowing character than similar music performed by symphony orchestra musicians.

Sun Ra was also active in the free jazz approach. Portions of his performances were collectively improvised with little apparent prearrangement (for example, *Astro Black, Magic City, Heliocentric Worlds of Sun Ra, Vol. 2*). His free jazz passages differed from those of Ornette Coleman and John Coltrane because they had more evident continuity and compositional organization. It is also important to recognize that Sun Ra succeeded artistically with free-form collective improvisation in big band contexts. This is something other leaders have not attempted. Large ensembles pose great difficulty for free jazz because of the problems musicians must overcome in considering and reacting to so many other sounds that are being improvised at the same time as their own. Sun Ra's achievement is therefore quite significant.

Sun Ra is like Duke Ellington in several ways. His fascination with widely diverse textures and his unconventional arranging methods are two similarities. He also had that rare skill of being able to oversee combinations of improvisation and composition and blend them in a unified form. Like Ellington, Sun Ra brought out the best in his sidemen who, in turn, adapted their improvisatory styles to the varying moods within his compositions.

Saxophonists **Marshall Allen** (b. 1924) and John Gilmore were Sun Ra's strongest improvisers, and both remained with the band for more than thirty years. Allen, who can play all the woodwind instruments, contributed extremely imaginative oboe and piccolo solos to Sun Ra's recordings. He also improvised free-form, high-energy alto saxophone solos that capitalized on the instrument's altissimo register and departed totally from conventional organization of pitches and jazz swing feeling. In his playing, long sequences of squeals and screeches were connected with tremendous intensity and developed organically to set the mood for Sun Ra's pieces.

FIGURE 14.2 Instruments used in Sun Ra's band (rear left to right): piccolo, flute, clarinet (bass clarinet is lying in front).
Courtesy of the Selmer Company

John Gilmore (1931–1995) is respected among knowledgeable jazz musicians, and has recorded with the noted bands of drummer Art Blakey and pianists Andrew Hill and Paul Bley. (See chapter 13 for Gilmore's influence on John Coltrane.) He stands out among post-bop saxophonists for a distinctive, hard-hitting style, and is known for a very raw, hard bop approach. He also devised an approach whereby individual notes are not as important as the overall contours and timbre of the sound. Like Albert Ayler, Gilmore refined a high-energy style of swirling legato figures that are not melodic or rhythmic. They are like extended screams and growls that help generate a mood and a sound mass.

Apart from John Gilmore, few of Sun Ra's sidemen have recorded with better known bands. One exception is trombonist Julian Priester, who worked with the band of drummer Max Roach and was part of an innovative septet led by pianist Herbie Hancock during the 1970s. Incidentally, like Sun Ra's of the early 1960s, *Herbie Hancock's group of the early 1970s used synthesizer, varied percussion sounds, piccolo, and bass clarinet, and often produced music resembling that of twentieth-century composer Edgard Varese. That Varese-like style, as practiced by Hancock and Sun Ra, resembled background music for science fiction and space travel films, and it was popularly labeled "space music."*

Sun Ra's live performances were accompanied by singing, dancing, costumes, and unusual lighting. A Sun Ra concert was a multimedia experience. This has been unusual in modern jazz, though common in rock. Though entertaining for some of Sun Ra's listeners, it was distracting for others, and his reception suffered among some musicians and critics. Listeners fail to take Sun Ra's music seriously also because Sun Ra places a humorous emphasis on philosophy, astrology, space travel, and astronomy. Another factor behind his failure to attract a wider audience is his diversity. Though it is unfair to judge any jazz musician's work on the basis of merely one album or a few live performances, it can be particularly mis-

The Sun Ra band of 1990 (pianist Sun Ra is standing at far left).

Photo by Nancy Lee

leading in judging Sun Ra's career because his output has such breadth. Unfortunately, however, many listeners dismiss him after hearing only a small slice of his music. Sun Ra remains the most controversial musician in this chapter.

Sun Ra contributed major innovations in jazz composition as well as introducing synthesizers and big band free-form improvisation to jazz. Yet despite the unusual breadth, depth, and originality of his music, Sun Ra is relatively unknown. His recordings number over one hundred, but because he produced and distributed many of his best albums himself, most of his groundbreaking recordings are not known by musicians and jazz critics.

◇THE ASSOCIATION FOR THE ADVANCEMENT OF CREATIVE MUSICIANS

The Association for the Advancement of Creative Musicians (AACM) is a Chicago-based collective of modern jazz musicians founded in the early 1960s by saxophonist Fred Anderson and pianist Muhal Richard Abrams. It organized concerts, recordings, training, and promotion for black musicians who had an affinity for jazz that was not squarely within the bop tradition. Their music was almost exclusively nonelectronic and separate from jazz-rock. Some of the AACM's music resembles Sun Ra's, Ornette Coleman's, and the work of Charles Mingus in several respects. First, **its rhythmic feeling lacks the flowing, easy character of conventional jazz and is more like the unpredictable nature of modern concert music.** Second, **solos are often freely improvised and inspired more by the mood of the piece than by standard bop patterns.** Third, **the music uses a larger assortment of accompaniment rhythms than was common to bop.** And fourth, **the proceedings display a rough quality** consistent with the Mingus concept that each performance is really a public workshop rather than a finished product.

The Art Ensemble of Chicago: Roscoe Mitchell, Joseph Jarman, Lester Bowie, Malachi Favors

The Art Ensemble of Chicago emerged during the late 1960s. The group makes music which does not follow a strict set of rules. They choose styles freely and refuse to base their music on the expectations of a particular idiom or audience. They embrace the music of the whole world as their repertory. Though they have sometimes applied conventional jazz approaches, the group has performed in a broad range of styles. Many of their approaches have not been squarely within the jazz tradition. In their work they have:

1) mimicked street bands of foreign countries,
2) performed lighthearted dramatic sketches,
3) recited poetry,
4) worn costumes and stage makeup,
5) made sounds for sound's sake instead of following traditional concepts of melody and harmony,
6) improvised without following preset progressions of chords.

Some of the Art Ensemble's music is similar to that of Ornette Coleman, Don Cherry, and Albert Ayler. Their jazz solo conceptions owe much to Coleman. Their large assortment of tone qualities and pitch bends resemble the methods of Ayler. As in the bands of Ayler and Coleman, they do not use piano. Many of their recordings dispense with the conventional jazz drum set, although all group members play percussion instruments. Timekeeping and a harmonic background are provided solely by bassist Malachi Favors, who has outstanding technique and distinctive improvisational flexibility. Without his strength and imagination, much of the group's music would be weak.

The Art Ensemble members seem to play almost every instrument, including ones that most listeners have never seen before. They collect instruments from all over the world, and their stage setting looks like a museum. To simplify the task of identifying the players, we should note that **Lester Bowie** (1941–1999) is primarily a trumpeter, **Malachi Favors** concentrates on bass, and **Joseph Jarman** (b. 1937) and **Roscoe Mitchell** (b. 1940) are primarily saxophonists. In addition to percussion instruments, Mitchell plays soprano, alto, tenor, and bass saxophones, clarinet, and flute. Jarman plays soprano, alto, tenor, and bass saxophones, clarinet, bassoon, flute, oboe, and vibraharp. Since 1970, drummer **Don Moye** (b. 1946) has also been recording with the group.

The Art Ensemble of Chicago uses musical elements that have been relatively neglected in the mainstream of modern jazz styles. The group has repackaged ideas that the originators of free jazz had pioneered, presenting them in a less frantic and more humorous way. A notable contribution is the group's practice of taking a brief melodic fragment and altering it over long stretches within a performance. Another feature is that the group sometimes offers unusual instruments and varied inflections of pitch and timbre for their own sake, instead of rapidly flowing bop lines. Strict tempo is often rejected. The group's repertory of the 1970s was distinguished by its avoidance of traditional format in which improvised solos are strung together one after another, without a storytelling quality to unify the piece. During the 1980s, however, they did record several albums that imitated traditional approaches to modern jazz.

The Art Ensemble offers simplicity and careful use of silence in place of complex chord progressions and virtuoso displays of technical prowess. In fact, the group has made more use of silence and changes in loudness than most jazz-oriented groups since Jimmy Giuffre's

The Art Ensemble of Chicago in 1973 (left to right): Roscoe Mitchell (tenor sax), Lester Bowie (trumpet), and Joseph Jarman. (The large shiny instrument in the foreground is a bass saxophone. The large instrument obscuring Jarman is a bass drum.)

Photo by Bill Smith

of the 1950s and 1960s. This puts them in direct contrast with John Coltrane's high-energy, dense-textured music of the 1960s and the loud, repetitive jazz-rock of the 1970s. The Art Ensemble is one of the first groups since the Modern Jazz Quartet to become known for exploring soft and gentle sounds.[39]

Anthony Braxton

One of the most broadly talented figures to emerge during the prominence of the AACM is **Anthony Braxton** (b. 1945). If ever there was a jazz-oriented musician whose work resists categorization, it is Braxton. He performs on almost all the woodwind instruments ever invented, yet the tone color he extracts is unlike the accepted model for each. He sometimes improvises solos with conventional modern jazz accompaniment, yet his solo lines do not resemble standard modern jazz approaches of Charlie Parker or John Coltrane.

Though he is usually classed within the jazz idiom, very little of Braxton's music swings in the jazz sense. (See chapter 2 for explanation of swing feeling.) Though sometimes suggesting atonality, Braxton's lines resemble less the truly atonal music of Arnold Schoenberg than an odd blend of Lee Konitz and Eric Dolphy. In addition, some of his unaccompanied work draws upon Oriental methods of tone alteration, timing, and motivic development. His large-scale work for symphony orchestra, however, clearly displays the influence of his favorite non-jazz composers Karlheinz Stockhausen, Krzysztof Penderecki, and John Cage.[40]

Braxton organizes groups whose instrumentation is unusual, such as two unaccompanied saxophones or just saxophone and trombone. Yet when employing big band instrumentation, his orchestrations dance back and forth between parade music, snatches of jazz history, and twentieth-century concert music.[41] Braxton seems to be tireless and blessed with endless imagination, but because his music goes far beyond jazz idioms, he should not be viewed only as a jazz musician.[42]

◇THE WORLD SAXOPHONE QUARTET

The Black Artists Group was formed in St. Louis during 1968 along organizational lines and musical views similar to those of the AACM in Chicago. Three saxophonists from this organization became prominent in the late 1970s and early 1980s: **Oliver Lake** (b. 1942), **Julius Hemphill** (1940–1995), and **Hamiet Bluiett** (b. 1940). These men recorded in numerous combinations and performed extensively on their own during that period. Their highest critical acclaim was earned when they performed in combination with Los Angeles-born saxophonist **David Murray** (b. 1955) in a group they founded in 1976 and called the World Saxophone Quartet (WSQ). Though flute and clarinets are also used, the WSQ usually has Lake and Hemphill on alto, Murray on tenor, and Hamiet Bluiett on baritone saxophone.

The WSQ drew partly from the approaches of Ornette Coleman and Albert Ayler, but placed a greater emphasis on composition. They borrowed and extended the diverse tone colors associated with free jazz players and such earlier bands as Duke Ellington's. The group was inspired by the free-form collective approaches of Coleman but achieved a greater balance of contrasts by carefully alternating prewritten parts, improvised solos, and simultaneous collective improvisations. They also achieved greater clarity of sound by performing without piano, guitar, bass, or drums.

The music of the WSQ is especially distinctive because much of it is delivered in a lighthearted manner. Diversity and activity seem the key guidelines. Sonic passages recall classical composer Igor Stravinsky's writing for woodwinds, while others suggest Ellington's

The World Saxophone Quartet of 1989 (left to right): Hamiet Bluiett (baritone sax), David Murray (tenor sax), Julius Hemphill (alto sax), and Oliver Lake (alto sax). This group extended the work of Albert Ayler, Ornette Coleman, and Eric Dolphy into the 1980s and 90s by making new music that combined avant-garde solos, collectively improvised, and prewritten passages. Each of these men was also an important bandleader and composer in his own right, active with new ideas that contrasted significantly with the most visible movements of the period, such as the second and third generations of jazz-rock fusion and the various revivals of swing, bop, and hard bop styles.

Photo by John Sobczak, Lorien Studio

Ornette Coleman's band without Coleman: Don Cherry (pocket trumpet), Charlie Haden (bass), Eddie Blackwell (drums), and Dewey Redman (tenor sax). During the mid-1970s, this personnel went by the band name of "Old and New Dreams."

Photo by Bill Smith

saxophone writing. Like the Art Ensemble of Chicago, the WSQ is significant for offering a unique refinement of free-form methods combined with numerous traditions of jazz and non-jazz sources.[43]

◇POPULAR APPEAL

The styles described in this chapter continue to be the least popular. During their earliest years, groups playing these styles were not wanted by most jazz clubs, and few record companies showed interest in recording them. The passage of almost forty years has done little to change this. Due to low demand, most of the pivotal recordings by Don Cherry, Albert Ayler, Sun Ra, and Cecil Taylor are frequently out of print, and many never sold enough copies to absorb production costs. No album by any musician discussed in this chapter ever penetrated the list of "top 200" best-selling albums in any year. Not much modern jazz is played on the radio, but the situation is especially unfortunate for free jazz. Some major cities never heard more than a few samples of free jazz during the entire decade of the 1960s. Although musicians usually blame their fate on a lack of promotion, several other styles of modern jazz have managed to sell without much promotion. This suggests that even if the avant-garde styles had been promoted, their popularity would still have been limited. The problem is that most listeners find them unswinging, harsh, and chaotic. So, ironically, this music of great innovation has received very little exposure.

CHAPTER SUMMARY

1) Free jazz improvisation does not adhere to preset progressions of chords and sometimes also dispenses with preset melody and steady timekeeping.
2) Free jazz has wider variation in pitch and tone quality than bop, and some free jazz involves lengthy collective improvisations that are loud and frenzied, in which textures are more important than melodies.
3) Prominent free saxophonists include Ornette Coleman and Albert Ayler.

4) Free jazz pianist Cecil Taylor is known for his virtuosity and his practice of improvising dense textures and turbulence.
5) Prominent bassists in free jazz include Charlie Haden and Dave Holland.
6) Trumpeter Don Cherry was Ornette Coleman's sideman in the late 1950s and early 1960s, one of the most original improvisers to appear since bop, and one of the most dedicated to World Music.
7) Free jazz drummers perfected approaches that depart from marching band and dance band traditions by generating an everchanging undercurrent of activity instead of standard timekeeping patterns.
8) Charles Mingus was an innovative modern bassist and a bandleader-composer who combined composition and improvisation while creatively altering accompaniment patterns.
9) Sun Ra and other avant-garde players from Chicago departed from bop practices of melody, chord progressions, and swing feeling, in addition to incorporating World Music.
10) Beginning in the 1950s, pianist Sun Ra's big band methods demonstrated some of the most varied voicings since Duke Ellington's.
11) Sun Ra explored collective improvisation in big band music during the 1960s and 1970s and was one of the first jazz composer-arrangers to extensively use synthesizers and electric keyboard instruments.
12) The Association for the Advancement of Creative Musicians was a Chicago-based collective founded by Richard Abrams during the 1960s.
13) The Chicagoans stressed continuity between composition and improvisation.
14) The AACM's Art Ensemble of Chicago, which gained prominence during the 1970s, consisted of trumpeter Lester Bowie, saxophonists Roscoe Mitchell and Joseph Jarman, bassist Malachi Favors, and drummer Don Moye.
15) Multi-instrumentalist Anthony Braxton is a composer and improviser of sweeping scope who does not play in bop style and whose music draws from non-Western music, the styles of Eric Dolphy and Lee Konitz, and twentieth-century symphonic music.
16) The World Saxophone Quartet was comprised of David Murray, Julius Hemphill, Oliver Lake, and Hamiet Bluiett. It demonstrated a successful integration of written passages and freely improvised parts without rhythm section accompaniment.

NOTES

1. Ornette Coleman, *Free Jazz* (Atlantic: 1364-2, 1964).
2. During the 1960s, aspects of these methods were also incorporated into the styles of John Coltrane, Albert Ayler, and a few of the groups they influenced. Coltrane's name has become prominently associated with free jazz despite the relatively small representation of these kinds of approaches in his recorded output and the fact that almost none of his music is free of preset musical organization.
3. There are numerous similarities between Parker and Coleman. A few suggest the influence of Parker on Coleman; others merely show that both men drew from similar sources. Though Coleman's timbre was unique, it resembled Parker's more than it resembled that of Johnny Hodges, Benny Carter, or Lee Konitz. Coleman's playing also had the soulfulness of Parker's and the explosions of slippery notes found in some Parker improvisations. Both had a gift for melody. Both used a lot of bluesy inflections of pitch and timbre. (On his first few recordings, all for Contemporary, Coleman's inflections and their timing resemble Parker's.) Like Parker, Coleman also liked to quote pop tunes briefly. For instance, themes from "If I Loved You," "Hawaiian War Chant," "Cherokee," and "Blues in the Night" have all been interjected in his improvisations at various times. Coleman also used a few bop phrases in his improvisation and recorded Parker's tune, "Klactoveesedstene" on *Paul Bley at the Hillcrest Club* (Inner City: 1007, LP, 1958).

   Although I disagree with the statement, I have heard Coleman called "just another bebop alto player." It is understandable how the occasional bop phrasing, steady tempo, and bluesy melodic figures in Coleman's playing might lead a listener to call him a bebop player. But though Coleman's improvisations had some flavor of bebop, they did not follow the bebop manners of navigating through the chord changes. What is remarkable about that view is that it coexists with a completely different response to Ornette Coleman's style: many people, after all, consider him a revolutionary figure. For more about Coleman and other avant-garde musicians of the 1960s, see John Litweiler, *Ornette Coleman: A Harmolodic Life* (Morrow, 1993); David G. Such, *Avant-Garde Jazz Musicians* (University of Iowa, 1993); John Gray, *Fire Music: A Bibliography of the New Jazz, 1959–1990* (Greenwood Press, 1991); A. B. Spellman, *Four Lives in the Bebop Business* (Pantheon, 1966; Limelight, 1985); Ekkehard Jost, *Free Jazz* (Universal Edition, 1974; DaCapo, 1981), 44–65; and Gunther Schuller, *Musings* (Oxford, 1986), 76–85.
4. A number of musicians have shown interest in Coleman's compositions. Pianist Keith Jarrett has written and improvised in the style of Coleman as well as dedicating a tune to him: "Piece for Ornette." Saxophonist Roscoe Mitchell titled one of his pieces "Ornette," and bassist Charlie Haden wrote a piece called "O. C."

   Though many of Coleman's pieces are simply springboards for improvisation, some have been arranged for ensembles. His "Forms and Sounds" was scored for flute, oboe, clarinet, bassoon, and French horn. His "Saints and Soldiers" and "Space Flight" were arranged for two violins, viola, and cello (*Forms and Sounds: The Music of Ornette Coleman,* RCA Bluebird: 6561-2-RB (LSC-2982), 1968). "Skies of America," which Coleman considers one of his best works, was scored for symphony orchestra (*Skies of America,* Columbia: 31562, LP, 1972).
5. To be technically accurate, it must be said that Coleman works off shifting tone centers.
6. Coleman used nine different keys in improvising on "Dee Dee" on *Ornette Coleman at the Golden Circle, Vol. 1* (Blue Note: 84224, 1965).
7. Ornette Coleman, *Something Else* (Fantasy: OJCCD-163-2 [Contemporary 7551], 1958).
8. *Change of the Century* (Atlantic 81341-2 [1327], 1959.
9. Listen to "Jayne" on Ornette Coleman, *Something Else.*
10. Listen to his work on Sonny Rollins, *On the Outside* (*Our Man in Jazz*) (RCA Bluebird: 2496-2-RB [LSP-2612], 1962). See also Jost, *Free Jazz,* 133–162.
11. Don Cherry, *Eternal Now* (Antilles: 7034, LP, 1973).
12. Cecil Taylor, *Jazz Advance* (Blue Note: 84462 [Transition], 1955); *Love For Sale* (Blue Note: 94107 [UA 4046], 1959).
13. *Trance* (Black Lion: 760220 [Debut], 1962); Taylor's most widely discussed examples of this are *Unit Structures* (Blue Note: 84237, 1966); and *Conquistador* (Blue Note: 46535 [84260], 1966). For more about Taylor, see Spellman, *Four Lives in the Bebop Business;* Jost, *Free Jazz,* 66–83; Len Lyons, *The Great Jazz Pianists* (Quill; Morrow; DaCapo, 1983), 301–311; and Gunther Schuller, *Musings,* 65–75.
14. Cecil Taylor, *Silent Tongues* (Freedom: FCD-741005, 1974).
15. Albert Ayler, *Spiritual Unity* (ESP DISK: 1002, 1964).
16. "Billie's Bounce" on *My Name Is Albert Ayler* (Black Lion: 760211 [Debut], 1963).
17. Ayler's style lived on in the playing of tenor saxophonist David Murray, whose first album, *Low Class Conspiracy* (Adelphi: 5002, LP, 1976), demonstrated that he had learned the Ayler techniques and begun to use them masterfully. Murray further honored Ayler by composing "Flowers for Albert" (*Flowers for Albert,* India Navigation: 1026, 2CD set, 1976). In listening for the Ayler connection in Murray's playing, note that after his first two albums, Murray's playing began to sound less and less like Ayler's.
18. Ayler's effect on Coltrane is especially evident on John Coltrane, *Meditations* (Impulse!/GRP: GRD-199 [9110], 1965), and *Interstellar Space* (Impulse!/GRP: GRD-110 [9277], 1967).
19. Charles Mingus, *Pithecanthropus Erectus* (Atlantic: 8809-2 [1237], 1956).
20. Charles Mingus, *Mingus Ah Um* (Columbia: CK 40648 [CL 1370/CS8171], 1959).
21. *The Birth of the Third Stream* (Columbia: CK 64929 [W127], 1956–1957); also on *Big Band Renaissance* (Smithsonian 108).
22. *The Quintet: Jazz at Massey Hall* (Fantasy: OJCCD-044-2 [Debut 124], 1953).
23. *The Complete Candid Recordings of Charles Mingus* (Mosaic: MD3-111, 3CD set, 1960–61) or *Charles Mingus Presents Charles Mingus* (Candid: CCD 79005 [8005], 1960).
24. *Mingus Plays Piano* (Impulse!/GRP: IMPD-217 [A-60], 1963).
25. *Mingus Moves* (Atlantic/Rhino: 71454 [SD 1653], 1973).
26. *Charles Mingus Presents Charles Mingus* (Candid: 79005, 1960) with Eric Dolphy, Ted Curson, and Dannie Richmond.

27. "Half-Mast Inhibition" and "Bemoanable Lady" on *Mingus Revisited* (Emarcy: 826496-2 [Mercury 20627], 1960).
28. The album Mingus made for Columbia, *Mingus Ah Um,* illustrates the varied accompaniment devices Mingus used. The version of "Fables of Faubus" in this collection switches accompanying style several times. It goes beyond the more subtle alterations in comping, bass lines, and drum fills which occur routinely in most modern jazz combo performances. "Bird Calls," from the same album, shows an integration of collective improvisation with more structured approaches. It is well managed, as is his "Ysabel's Table Dance" (1957) from Charles Mingus, *New Tijuana Moods* (Victor jazz: 09026-68591-2 [LSP-2533], 1957). For more, see *Charles Mingus: More Than a Fakebook* (prepared by Andrew Homzy, Don Sickler, and Sue Mingus; for Jazz Workshop; Hal Leonard, 1991), Brian Priestley, *Mingus: A Critical Biography* (Quartet, 1983; DaCapo, 1984), and Jost, *Free Jazz,* 35–43.
29. In the 1960 Mingus quartet with trumpeter Ted Curson and drummer Dannie Richmond, there was an exceptional level of empathy between Mingus and Dolphy. The two have an extended dialog on "What Love" that is filled with humor and flexible interaction. The conversation between Mingus's pizzicato bass and Dolphy's bass clarinet is so human that it almost makes you think words are being exchanged. It is very coherent and skillful. See footnote 23 above.
30. Dolphy solos on Coltrane's "India" and "Spiritual" on *"Live" at the Village Vanguard: The Master Takes* (Impulse!/GRP: IMPD-251 [A-10/A-42], 1961). John Coltrane, *The Complete 1961 Village Vanguard Recordings* (Impulse!/GRP: IMPD-232, 4 CD set, 1961), has better Dolphy solos from these sessions. Coltrane's *Olé Coltrane* (Atlantic: 1373-2, 1961) uses Dolphy but lists him as "George Lane" on the album jacket. Before his death in 1964, Dolphy also made a number of albums as a leader, such as *Out to Lunch* (Blue Note: 46524 [84163], 1964), but some of his best work was documented in Mingus recordings.
31. Some of his alto saxophone playing of that period sounds like Charlie Parker and Cannonball Adderley, though his main influence was fellow Californian Sonny Criss, and he was also quite familiar with Johnny Hodges, as shown in Dolphy's unaccompanied alto saxophone solo, "Tenderly," on *Far Cry* (Fantasy: OJCCD-400-2 [New Jazz 8270], 1961); and his work on Chico Hamilton, *Gongs East* (Discovery: 70831 [Warner Bros. 1271], 1958).
32. In his long duet with arco bass on the first half of "You Don't Know What Love Is" on *Last Date* (Fontana: 822226-2 [Limelight 86013], 1964), Dolphy's flute solo is so rich in tone quality, it sounds as though he savored the vibrations of each note before proceeding to the next.
33. Listen to Sunny Murray's playing on "Trance" from Cecil Taylor, *Trance* (Black Lion: 760220 [Debut], 1962), or on Albert Ayler, *Spiritual Unity* (ESP DISK: 1002, 1964); or listen to later examples of a similar style in the drumming of Barry Altschul on "Q & A" and "Interception" on Dave Holland, *Conference of the Birds* (ECM: 78118-21027-2, 1972), or on "Thanatos" and "Vendana" with bassist Holland in Chick Corea, *A.R.C.* (ECM: 78118-21009-2 [1009], 1971).
34. Much of this Chicago activity was occurring well before the first recordings of Ornette Coleman became available. We can therefore assume that much of it originated with the Chicagoans and was not derivative. However, the second wave of Chicagoans and their St. Louis relatives, the Black Artists Group, clearly derived some inspiration from Coleman and Albert Ayler. For more, see Jost, *Free Jazz,* 163–199; also see the interview with Sun Ra in Len Lyons, *The Great Jazz Pianists,* 83–92. In addition, see John F. Swed, *Space Is the Place: The Lives and Times of Sun Ra* (Pantheon, 1997; DaCapo, 1998) and Hartmut Geerken and Bernhard Hefele, *The Sun Ra Book: Omniverse Sun Ra* (S. J. Geerken, 1994); tapeography, bibliography, filmography, photos, original essays by assorted writers; available from S. J. Geerken, Wartaweil 37, D 82211 Herrsching, Germany.
35. *Nubians of Plutonia* (Evidence: 22066-2 [Saturn 406], 1959).
36. *Sun Song* (Delmark: DD 411 [Transition 10], 1956); *SuperSonic Jazz (Sounds)* (Evidence: 22015-2 [Saturn 216], 1956).
37. *Astro Black* (Impulse: 9255, LP, 1972); *The Magic City* (Evidence: ECD 22069-2 [Saturn 403], 1965).
38. *The Heliocentric Worlds of Sun Ra, Vols. 1 & 2* (ESP DISK: 1014 & 1017, 2CDs, 1965).
39. Art Ensemble of Chicago, *A Jackson in Your House* (Affinity: AFF 752 [Actuel BYG2], 1969); *People in Sorrow* (Nessa: 3, LP, 1969); *Nice Guys* (ECM: 78118-21126-2 [1126], 1978); and *Urban Bushman* (ECM: 78118-21211-2 [2-1211], 2CD set, 1980).
40. Anthony Braxton, *For Four Orchestras* (Arista: 8900, 3LP set, 1978). For background, see Graham Lock, *Forces in Motion* (Quartet; DaCapo, 1985) and Ronald Radano, *New Musical Figurations: Anthony Braxton's Cultural Critique* (University of Chicago, 1993).
41. Braxton, *Creative Orchestra Music* (RCA Bluebird: 6579-2RB [Arista 4080], 1976).
42. Examples of Braxton's work: *Three Compositions of New Jazz* (Delmark: DD 415, 1968); *For Alto* (Delmark: 420, 2LP set, 1968 solo); and *Five Pieces 1975* (Arista: 4054, LP, 1975).
43. SCCJ-R contains a version of "Steppin'" from World Saxophone Quartet, *Live in Zurich* (Black Saint: 120056-2, 1986). Of their many recordings, fans often prefer *Steppin' with the World Saxophone Quartet* (Black Saint: 120 027-2, 1978) and *Revue* (Black Saint: 120 056-2, 1980).

Chapter Fifteen

Bill Evans **Photo by Guy LeQuerrec/Magnum Photos Inc.**

Bill Evans, Herbie Hancock, Chick Corea, & Keith Jarrett

The most influential jazz pianist to emerge after Bud Powell was Bill Evans. The most widely imitated pianists after Evans were McCoy Tyner, Herbie Hancock, Chick Corea, and Keith Jarrett. All four men showed the combined influence of Powell and Evans. Each of these musicians became an important composer and bandleader in his own right. These pianists attracted large popular followings and had record sales and concert receipts that exceeded the recognition of both Powell and Evans. This chapter is devoted to the piano styles of Evans, Hancock, Corea, and Jarrett and their respective group styles.

◇BILL EVANS

Bill Evans (1929–1980)[1] played with Miles Davis for about nine months during 1958 and 1959. This exposure brought him wide attention among jazz musicians and fans. He became known particularly for his work on the important Davis album *Kind of Blue.* Shortly before his involvement with *Kind of Blue,*[2] Evans had made a trio record called *Everybody Digs Bill Evans.*[3] Its "Peace Piece" provided the basis for "Flamenco Sketches" on *Kind of Blue.* (To hear selections from *Kind of Blue,* listen to "So What" in SCCJ, "Flamenco Sketches" on the *Jazz Classics CD,* and "Blue in Green" on *Jazz Classics CD* for *Concise Guide to Jazz.* Evans arranged all of them.)

Prior to 1959, Evans displayed considerable dexterity, and his style included elements from several sources. His long, fast, smoothly contoured eighth-note lines remind us of saxophonist

Bill Evans, the most influential modern pianist after Bud Powell. Evans popularized the jazz use of harmonies based on modes and adapted the chords of French composers Maurice Ravel and Claude Debussy. He also perfected methods of "floating pulse": subtle ways of phrasing so he avoided accenting the most obvious beats. Shown here in 1960, at age 31, when he was collaborating with bassist Scott LaFaro and developing radically new approaches to jazz trio playing.

Photo by Chuck Stewart

Lee Konitz, one of his early favorites. Because Konitz derived his style from pianist Lennie Tristano, the Evans approach indirectly derives from Tristano's influence. Evans's piano solos also borrowed elements from bop pianist Bud Powell. Occasionally, Evans also used some bluesy figures which might be traced to pianist-composer Horace Silver, a far-reaching force during the 1950s. The manner in which Evans developed his ideas across a solo improvisation also reflects his debt to Nat Cole, who had also influenced Powell and Silver. In addition, Evans cited George Shearing as having opened his ears to the beauties of tone.

The Bill Evans style is unique in the history of jazz piano. His tone and conception are delicate without being fragile. On slow pieces, he sometimes creates a harp-like effect by sounding single tones and letting them ring, as though to savor each vibration. (Listen for this in his solo on "Flamenco Sketches" on the *Jazz Classics CD.*) Though he possessed considerable dexterity, his work was never flashy. Though he was physically quite strong, he usually steered clear of an aggressively percussive manner. Evans crafted his improvisations with exacting deliberation. Often he would take a phrase, or just a kernel of its character, then develop and extend its rhythms, melodic ideas, and accompanying harmonies. Then within the same solo he would often return to that kernel, transforming it each time. And while all this was happening, he would ponder ways of resolving the tension that was building. He would be considering rhythmic ways, melodic ways, and harmonies all at the same time, long before the optimal moment for resolving the idea.

An unheard, continuous self-editing occurred while Evans improvised. Evans spared the listener his false starts and discarded ideas. Though he had a creative imagination, Evans never improvised solos that merely strung together ideas at the same rate they popped into his head. The results of these deliberations could be a swinging and exhilarating experience for the listener. However, they reflected less a carefree abandon than the well-honed craftsmanship of a very serious performer working in the manner of a classical composer. "Introspective" is the adjective most frequently applied to his music.

Bill Evans refined an approach to rhythm in jazz improvisation that has been called "non-obvious pulse," "floating pulse," "phrasing across the bar line," and "de-emphasizing the beat." (For explanation of beat, meter, and rhythm, see pages 364–368.) His work was rhythmically very involved. He frequently constructed phrases without starting or stopping them on main beats. He did not necessarily accent beats that indicate the meter of the piece—the first of every four beats, in meter of four, for example. In other words, his phrases did not necessarily accent beats in ways that jazz listeners had come to expect—the manner of march and dance rhythms. Though his melodic ideas are very rhythmic, many are not obvious in terms of the beat. Evans may, for instance, stagger a melodic figure across several measures, always accenting the upbeats, never squarely accenting a downbeat. He may float past it instead. This contrasts with the rhythmic tendencies of most jazz pianists. Evans conceived his improvisations in reference to the meter and tempo of the piece. Yet listeners often could not gain a clear indication of this unless they also heard walking bass or ride rhythms as a reference. Unlike most hard bop pianists, Evans evolved away from playing strings of bouncing eighth notes that explicitly delineated each beat and formed contours that evenly rose and fell. The architecture of his lines was more complex, and tension was resolved less often. These tendencies became far more pronounced later in his career, but they were already evident in his widely acclaimed Village Vanguard sessions of June 25, 1961. (This was the last recording he made with bassist Scott LaFaro. It came to be known as the "Village Vanguard session" because it was recorded live during an appearance at that New York nightclub, and it was originally issued on an album called *Sunday at the Village Vanguard.* It is represented by "Solar" on the *Jazz Classics CD.*[4])

Despite Evans's refinement of non-obvious pulse, he did swing. In fact, many of his admirers praised his quality of swing feeling. Evans was not swinging, however, in the perceptions of listeners who were accustomed to hearing a relaxed, easily rolling line that frequently accented the first of every four beats.

Several trends in the Bill Evans style had been summarized after *Kind of Blue,* when Evans made the first of four albums with bassist Scott LaFaro.[5] Before *Kind of Blue,* he had already begun ridding himself of bop clichés, devising an original style that offered an alternative to bop-based approaches. After 1959 he rarely played lines with disconnected or staccato notes. He favored a legato style instead. Most of Evans's lines were composed of smoothly connected notes. His left hand gained importance and was soon sustaining chords in almost every measure instead of merely punctuating right-hand lines. The melodies he improvised were frequently chorded, note for note, by the locked-hands technique. He worked out methods for voicing his chorded lines in terms of modes and tight clusters of notes. (See pages 372 and 418 for more about modes.) Evans drew from the harmonies of French composers Claude Debussy and Maurice Ravel. He frequently employed chords that were composed of notes that were four scale-steps apart. (Listen for these in his accompaniments for Miles Davis on "So What" on SCCJ.) These quartal harmonies had provided the foundation for the Davis album *Kind of Blue.*

With its non-obvious pulse and modal organization of harmonies, the Evans style departed from bop traditions almost as drastically as had Cecil Taylor's. However, Evans was not

Listening Guide for

"Solar"

Composed by Chuck Wayne; recorded June, 25, 1961 at the Village Vanguard in New York City by Bill Evans (piano), Scott LaFaro (bass), and Paul Motian (drums); available on the *Jazz Classics CD;* also available on Bill Evans, *Sunday at the Village Vanguard* (Fantasy: OJCCD-140-2 [Riverside 376], 1961); and on *Bill Evans at the Village Vanguard* (Riverside: FCD-60-017, 1961).

Bill Evans had several different stylistic phases in his career. *The Jazz Classics CD* samples two of them. His piano voicings, modal thinking, and very spare solo style affected the sound of "Flamenco Sketches," a selection taken from the Miles Davis album *Kind of Blue* of 1959. "Solar" was selected to provide the clearest example of the unique approach that Evans and bassist Scott LaFaro developed for playing together. In this performance LaFaro does not walk. Moreover, his rhythms contain very little repetition. Unlike traditional bass playing that provides a very predictable foundation for the soloists, LaFaro's role here can be likened to an ever-changing counteractivity. Sometimes in fact it is not clearly subordinate to Evans but instead seems to go its own way, as in the first few choruses. Some listeners have construed it as an almost continuous musical conversation with Evans. LaFaro's accompaniment does not resemble the ways bassists had traditionally accompanied jazz pianists.

This performance of "Solar" also illustrates subtle ways of phrasing that came to characterize more and more Evans solos after the 1950s. Termed "non-obvious pulse" or "phrasing across the bar line," these approaches are particularly evident in the fifth and the seventh choruses. In the fifth chorus, almost all the accents in Evans's line are on the off-beat, and all three of his phrases are staggered across several measures. They are rhythmically displaced, never starting or clearly resolving on a strong beat. Evans seems to stretch figures out so they sound half-time, yet he sometimes comes back to a feeling that is almost double-time. The rhythms that Evans uses are so subtle in their relationship to the underlying pulse that we may have difficulty verifying the passage of beats and the beginnings of choruses if we ignore the drummer's timekeeping rhythms. Evans intentionally blurs conventional landmarks in the composition so thoroughly that this recording represents a significant departure from a jazz tradition of rhythmic obviousness. This is a new kind of jazz piano style.

The composition was written by guitarist Chuck Wayne, though it has always been mistakenly credited to Miles Davis. It is twelve measures long, but it does not follow the chord progression of a typical blues.

CD Track	Elapsed Time	
61	0' 00"	**First Chorus**

Melody Statement

Evans begins alone, playing the first phrase of the melody in octaves. Then he is joined by LaFaro and Motian, and he plays the second phrase in harmony and the remaining phrases in octaves. LaFaro improvises melody lines of his own, in the character of the "Solar" melody. LaFaro's lines occasionally incorporate phrases from the original melody and mimic Evans's lines. They also contain figures that state the pulse and outline notes in the chords.

In the first five choruses, two interweaving melodies are offered instead of the usual format in which piano melody is accompanied by walking bass. Both melodies come in and out of the foreground. Though LaFaro's lines are usually somewhat subordinate to Evans's, they are more dense, more varied, and closer to the foreground than bass parts had traditionally been.

62 0' 15" **Second Chorus**

Evans Restates the Melody

All piano phrases are harmonized. LaFaro rotates among roles as countermelody creator and beat decorator.

63 0' 30" **Third Chorus**

Evans begins his solo improvisation by voicing all his lines in octaves and not comping for himself. While Evans departs from the melody as he improvises, LaFaro paraphrases it. This amounts to a two-part invention with drums and cymbals accompaniment.

0' 43" **Fourth Chorus**

Evans and LaFaro continue to improvise counterlines to each other, LaFaro occasionally quoting the melody.

64 0' 56" **Fifth Chorus**

LaFaro moves to a less melodic and more rhythmic role. Evans phrases his own improvisational ideas in rhythmic ways that do not convey the pulse of the piece in a particularly obvious manner.

1' 09" **Sixth Chorus**

1' 22" **Seventh Chorus**

1' 36" **Eighth Chorus**

65 1' 49" **Ninth Chorus**

Beginning in the fourth measure, Evans constructs about twelve measures' worth of lines from quarter-note triplet figures.

1' 60" **Tenth Chorus**

66 2' 13" **Eleventh Chorus**

After the fourth measure, Evans stops voicing his lines in octaves and begins to play one note at a time instead. He generates solo lines with his right hand and comps for himself with his left hand. Note how soft, light, and infrequent his left hand chords are. This pattern persists until the sixteenth chorus.

2' 27" **Twelfth Chorus**

	2' 38"	**Thirteenth Chorus**
	2' 50"	**Fourteenth Chorus**
	3' 04"	**Fifteenth Chorus**
67	3' 17"	**Sixteenth Chorus** Evans paraphrases the melody, using locked-hands block chording.

generally recognized as an avant-garde figure, even though some of the music he recorded at the Village Vanguard session was avant-garde, and Miles Davis had sought his help in making his own music more advanced. We can understand why few but Davis recognized Evans's advances if we recognize that the non-obvious pulse and the modal organization of harmonies were subtle, not particularly jarring differences from the ways that most jazz had sounded before Evans. We should also keep in mind that Evans played tunes listeners recognized. For instance, he often chose pretty melodies, though they were chosen partly because they provided interesting chord progressions for inspiring improvisations. His best-known composition, "Waltz for Debby," exemplifies this aspect of his taste.[6] Moreover, Evans liked waltzes, an unusual preference for a jazz musician. Among the waltzes to which he gave his tender treatment were "Someday My Prince Will Come," "Alice in Wonderland," "Tenderly," "Skating in Central Park," and "I'm All Smiles."

Rhythm Section Innovations

During 1961, **Scott LaFaro** (1936–1961) demonstrated advances that were as historically significant as those of Jimmy Blanton two decades earlier. **LaFaro demonstrated that the bass can contribute ensemble interplay that provides a feeling of grace and freedom for the underpinnings of a group sound, and he devised a fresh conception for improvising bass solos.** LaFaro is also influential for having pioneered using more than just one or two fingers to pluck the bass strings. Previously, bassists had primarily employed only one or two fingers instead of borrowing from the technique of classical guitarists as LaFaro did. LaFaro's new technique lent added speed and allowed greater intricacy and continuity in his lines.

The idea of pianists and bassists engaging in musical conversation had been explored by Duke Ellington and Jimmy Blanton in 1940.[7] Evans and LaFaro refined this idea, and it was most dramatically apparent in their last recording together (excerpted in "Solar" on the *Jazz Classics CD*). LaFaro sometimes walked and sometimes soloed. But more often he vigorously supplied nonrepetitive figures that pitted an extra counteractivity against the sounds of piano and drums. While Evans was playing a written melody or improvising a fresh line, LaFaro contributed a great diversity of musical ideas. He would throw in melodic figures of his own. He would mimic or answer Evans. Sometimes he would underscore the figures Evans and Motian played. In addition, LaFaro often fed ideas to Evans. **LaFaro was not merely a timekeeper capable of impressive solos. He was a melodic player as important to the Evans trio as a saxophonist or trumpeter was to the standard jazz quintet.** LaFaro set the pace for a whole school of modern jazz bassists who possessed spectacular instrumental facility like his. And like LaFaro, they interacted with pianists and drummers in imaginative and highly active manners.[8]

It was partly the Evans piano style that made possible LaFaro's contributions to these new concepts of jazz trio playing. One crucial aspect was its leanness. There are more limitations

Scott LaFaro, the brilliant bassist who played with Bill Evans from 1959 to 1961. He set the pace for an entire generation of bassists who showed spectacular instrumental facility and mastered melodic-interactive approaches to accompaniment style. Shown here in 1960 at age 24.

Photo by Jim Marshall

in a Bud Powell-style trio because the pianist fills up most of the spaces with long lines of his own. Rhythmic interaction between bassist and pianist is also restricted because the bassist must focus on explicitly stating the beats and has little chance to do much else. Evans, by contrast to Powell, did not require the bassist to explicitly state each beat. The way Evans voiced chords provided another freedom for the bassist. The notes that Evans selected for his chords allowed bassists more latitude because their own notes were less likely to duplicate or clash. Incidentally, the ways Evans voiced chords for and reharmonized popular songs became models for the playing of those songs by many other musicians. **Evans provided the perfect context for the blossoming of LaFaro's new approach to bass improvisation because he left room for the bass in the forefront of the combo sound and because Evans encouraged LaFaro to capitalize on the opportunity by taking chances and trying all sorts of nontraditional techniques.**[9] This was also the manner in which Evans collaborated with LaFaro's most gifted successors, Eddie Gomez and Marc Johnson. This style allowed them more room for creativity than they experienced with other bandleaders.[10] (Listen to demonstration and explanation of this style on the *Demo CD* Track 28. Then listen to "Solar" on the *Jazz Classics CD.*)

Drummer **Paul Motian** (b. 1931) contributed an approach of great imagination and discretion to the Evans trio recordings of 1961. He decorated the combo sound and played accents which complemented the rhythms of LaFaro and Evans. Motian masterfully used wire brushes to obtain light, crisp sounds from his snare drum and cymbals. (For demonstration of typical techniques, listen to the *Demo CD.*) His highly original drum style employed contrasting sound textures and tone colors as elements of musical interest in themselves. In addition, his pioneering use of rhythmic displacement allowed him to interact more sensitively and inventively than most previous jazz drummers had done. His style of interactive coloring in the intimate trio context became a model for drummers playing in similar settings, and it contributed to the emancipation of the rhythm section. Incidentally, Motian furthered these innovations when he played with the Keith Jarrett quartet during the 1970s. On selected pieces with this later group, he nearly eliminated repetitive timekeeping patterns from his playing and was somehow able to sound free of meter while still playing within it.

The Bill Evans trio recordings of 1961 involve a great deal more than piano accompanied by walking bass and timekeeping drums and cymbals. Instead, they are composed of three continuously shifting parts which sway together. The tempo is usually steady, but it is not always made obvious by loud and clear statement of every beat. Some listeners perceive this music as Evans, LaFaro, and Motian carrying on three-way musical conversations in tempo.[11] Their musical words and phrases are both long and short, fluid and abrupt; they are not necessarily strings of eighth notes organized in the bobbing, bouncing fashion that typifies bop, nor the long, smoothly contoured eighth-note lines that typify Lennie Tristano and Lee Konitz. In other words, the group offered considerable melodic variety and considerable rhythmic variety. Swing feeling is merely one of several different rhythmic possibilities they explored.

The most historically significant contributions of the Evans-LaFaro-Motian trio recordings of 1961 were to loosen the common practices of the bop style rhythm section which had become standard during the 1940s and 1950s—walking bass, drummer playing ride rhythms and snapping shut high-hat cymbals on the second and fourth beats, pianist playing long strings of eighth notes. Though they occasionally played in conventional bop style, especially before the June 1961 sessions, their impact was to help emancipate the piano, bass, and drum roles.[12] The calm thoughtfulness, subtlety, and delicate interaction among Evans, LaFaro, and Motian provided an alternative to the more straight-ahead style of the Oscar Peterson trios, or the gospel-like orientation of other groups led during the same period by Ramsey Lewis, Les McCann, and Gene Harris (of the Three Sounds).

Herbie Hancock, the pianist and composer who made significant impacts in three different phases of modern jazz: hard bop, the mid-1960s Miles Davis Quintet, and the jazz-rock/jazz-funk genres of the 1970s and 80s. Hancock was the most in-demand accompanist among modern jazz musicians of the 1960s, and then he became the main inspiration for hundreds of young pianists during the 1970s because of his top selling *Head Hunters* and *Thrust* albums.

Guy Le Querrec/Magnum Photos, Inc.

◇HERBIE HANCOCK

Herbie Hancock (b. 1940) played with Miles Davis from 1963 to 1969 and became the most sought-after band pianist of the 1960s. Many musicians feel that Hancock's freshest work is the playing he did with Davis. (See pages 220–221 for more.) Hancock comped in a brisk manner and used a gentle, even touch. Somehow he managed to sound light and airy, yet muscular and firm at the same time. Hancock created consistently stimulating, swinging, and polished piano improvisations. His playing nearly always has a meticulous and finished quality. His execution is firm and swinging without being violent or insistent. Both his solo work and his accompanying convey politeness and sensitivity. Hancock has shown broad scope and versatility; his style is compatible with several different streams of modern jazz. He has contributed immeasurably to hundreds of records—not only those of the Miles Davis quintet. He was so impressive during the 1960s that many excellent pianists drew from his style in the process of devising their own approaches: Kenny Kirkland, George Cables, Larry Willis, Warren Bernhardt, Jim McNeely, Marc Cohen (Copland), Joey Calderazzo, Billy Childs, Kevin Hayes, Marcus Roberts, and Fred Hersh. Even Chick Corea showed Hancock's influence.

Hancock absorbed several influences while he was developing his style during the late 1950s and early 1960s. Some of his playing has the funky, bluesy figures and the rhythmic bounce that typified Horace Silver and Wynton Kelly. He was also inspired by the chord voicings and movement of harmonies perfected in the music of Clare Fischer, a prominent pianist-composer-arranger. But Bill Evans was Hancock's most significant source. The Evans use of harp-like, ringing tones surrounded by silence surfaced in Hancock's playing, as did Evans's chord voicings and mode-based thinking. Other similarities to Evans include Hancock's smooth legato lines and locked-hands style. Like Evans, he also frequently improvised passages in which accents went against the meter, and he let his ideas float free of reference to the underlying beat. In such excursions, Hancock drew from the ideas of twentieth-century classical composers Maurice Ravel, Claude Debussy, and Paul Hindemith.[13] But he did not merely imitate the music of his models. There was a tremendous sense of flexibility and openness in his improvising, resulting in a great amount of freedom and variety in his music. He extended the methods of his models and added so many original ideas that his style is instantly recognizable. (Listen to and compare the Evans work on "Solar" with the Hancock work on "Masqualero" on the *Jazz Classics CD.*)

One of Hancock's greatest contributions was to help free the pianist from the accompanying patterns that had become commonplace for hard bop pianists. In the Miles Davis quintet, where he had an almost magical rapport with his equally daring companions, Hancock mixed the impressionistic and mode-based harmonic approaches of Claude Debussy and Maurice Ravel with the polyrhythmic approaches to accompaniment devised by drummer Tony Williams. For example, his work in the *Sorcerer* album is sometimes indistinguishable from modern classical music, sprinkled with melodic fragments and suspensions. (Examples of this are in "Masqualero" on the *Jazz Classics CD.*) He could give the listener the impression of movement even when chords were not actually moving—at least as they might move in the twelve-bar blues and the popular songs of earlier eras, in which chords were treated as though their "function" were to "resolve" to another chord.

Hancock fulfilled the trends that were already occurring in the Davis group when he joined—basing improvisations on modes instead of chord changes, using chords more for their sound quality (musicians call it a chord's "color") than for their capacity to increase and decrease tension when they change. In these new contexts, there were long passages in which chords did not change, yet the amount of activity Hancock generated made up for the absence of "functional" chord changes. In the Davis quintet, Hancock coordinated with Tony Williams and bassist Ron Carter to pinpoint a mood and go with it rather than be a slave to a progression of chords. His rapport with Carter and Williams was so remarkable that he could also change a mood abruptly and then instantaneously develop rhythms and harmonies to carry it. He also allowed his improvised melodies to dictate the harmonies, rather than the reverse, which had been the standard. This marked a significant freedom associated with the groundbreaking Hancock-Carter-Williams rhythm section. All this and more can be heard in "Masqualero" on the *Jazz Classics CD.*[14]

Another measure of Hancock's creativity is his productivity and originality as a composer and arranger. By the early 1970s, he had written every tune on eight of his own albums, and he had written or co-authored many tunes on seven more. His "Dolphin Dance" is one of the most revered of all modern jazz compositions. Musicians are unanimous in their praise of the clever progression of chords and pedal points that are intertwined with its delightful melody. Hancock's "Maiden Voyage" became a staple for young musicians of the 1960s and 1970s, especially because of its modal construction (see pages 421–422 for a technical analysis). His funky, bluesy piece "Watermelon Man" became very popular, especially in Mongo Santamaria's version during the mid-1960s. The big bands of Woody Herman, Si Zentner, and Maynard Ferguson all played their own arrangements. It was performed by almost every wedding band in America whenever a funk piece was requested. By the 1980s, Hancock had captured a slice of the dance music market with numerous albums of funk music.

To survey the first fifteen years of Hancock's compositional productivity on records, it may help to group his output by idiom: 1) the lush, classical music style of "Suite Revenge" on *Death Wish,*[15] background music for the Charles Bronson movie; 2) the rock-influenced *Fat Albert Rotunda;*[16] 3) the funky, hard bop approach of *Taking Off;*[17] 4) Gil Evans-like work on *The Prisoner;* 5) writing that recalls music of Sun Ra on *Sextant*[18] and *Crossings;*[19] 6) the style of the 1960s Miles Davis Quintet on *Maiden Voyage*[20] and *Empyrean Isles;*[21] 7) the Sly Stone-influenced style of *Head Hunters*[22] and *Thrust.*[23]

Hancock did much of his creative writing after he left Miles Davis and began leading his own groups.[24] The music of Hancock's first post-Davis group capitalized on some of the advances made in the Davis groups of the 1960s. For *The Prisoner,* Hancock wrote legato passages for trumpet, trombone, and tenor saxophone employing sustained tones which had few eighth-note figures or jumpy syncopations. In accompanying the horns, Hancock, his bassist and drummer generated considerable activity in the manner that he had done with Carter and Williams in the Miles Davis quintet.

Hancock's second post-Davis band recorded the albums *Mwandishi, Sextant,* and *Crossings.* For these works, Hancock developed concepts that had been apparent on Davis albums of the late 1960s: *Nefertiti, In a Silent Way,* and *Bitches Brew.* There was extensive use of synthesizers and exotic percussion effects. In place of the busy, lightning-quick phrases of bop, Hancock frequently substituted legato lines of sustained tones that conveyed a languorous feeling. The emphasis was more on developing moods than conventional jazz swing feeling, complicated chord progressions, or intricate solo lines. In place of the standard tone colors of sax, trumpet, piano, bass, and conventional drum set, each of Hancock's seven group members was responsible for a larger assortment of sounds. His trumpeter doubled on fluegelhorn and percussion. His trombonist played tenor trombone, baritone trombone, and bass trombone. His saxophonist played alto flute, soprano saxophone, piccolo, bass clarinet, and percussion. Hancock often played electric piano, with echo and fuzz effects to alter its tone. Also, in addition to bass and drums, Hancock carried one musician who played nothing but synthesizer. Such a practice was unusual for the early 1970s, though it became common in the 1980s. Partly because he used synthesizer and it had been associated with science fiction films, Hancock's style on these albums was often referred to as "space music."

Despite the innovations and the high-level musicianship in Hancock's first two post-Davis bands, there was not enough demand for their music to pay its expenses. Partly for this reason and partly out of a stated desire to reach larger audiences, Hancock embarked on a string of styles that were less jazz-like and more in the genre that young audiences of the period wanted for dance and party music. For more than twenty years after he was forced to disband his *Mwandishi/Crossings/Sextant* band, Hancock enjoyed immense popular acclaim for styles that he devised, in part, from models within a popular black genre known as *funk music.* His first big hit came when he imitated the style of Sly Stone by creating the *Head Hunters* album, which sold over a million copies. Then, with the success of its follow-up *Thrust,* and many albums of discotheque-type dance music, Hancock was assured of selling about 200,000 copies of each new album, even when most jazz albums rarely sold more than 15,000 copies. The music had less and less jazz improvisation in it and more and more dance rhythms that were highly syncopated and repetitive. Melodies were simple and heavily rhythmic. Though much of the public routinely places it in the jazz category, Hancock himself has said that he does not consider this music to be jazz. As of this writing, his widest recognition has come from a 1983 work called "Rockit." The recording is a light-hearted construction of novel sound effects that are packaged with an engaging funk rhythm, all tightly arranged with the same sense of balance and completeness we have come to expect from Hancock. It appeared in *Future Shock,* an album selling over a million copies, which stayed on the popularity charts for more than a year.[25] As a single, "Rockit" remained in the popularity charts for nine weeks, and as a video it was one of the fifteen most popular of the year.

Funk music is not all that Hancock pursued after his innovative septet disbanded. Frequently he has regrouped the original rhythm section from the 1960s Miles Davis group to record and tour with other musicians who model their playing after the Davis quintet—Wynton and Branford Marsalis, for example. Though Hancock is no longer breaking ground in that context, these bands have consistently been of the highest quality, and they have generated considerable excitement. In summary, decades after first impressing the jazz world with his own original playing and composing, Herbie Hancock has continued to make that original style available. Furthermore, he has also expanded the breadth of his activities by adding a repertory that pleases the larger pop music audience.

◇CHICK COREA

Chick Corea (b. 1941) followed Herbie Hancock as pianist in the 1968 Miles Davis quintet. He performed with Davis from the fall of 1968 to the summer of 1970. Corea soon joined the ranks of Hancock, Bill Evans, and McCoy Tyner as the most prominent and most imitated pianist in jazz.[26] His style originated with aspects from the jazz piano approaches of Bud Powell, Horace Silver, Bill Evans, and McCoy Tyner and the classical pieces of twentieth-century composers Paul Hindemith and Bela Bartók.[27] Like Tyner, Corea voiced chords in fourths—musicians call it *quartal harmony*—and devised lines from five-note scales—musicians call them *pentatonics.* He went beyond Tyner, however, by using other advanced voicings in addition to fourths.[28] Corea may also have absorbed ideas for using fourths from Horace Silver.[29] These voicings proved especially effective for the electric piano, an instrument that was becoming popular when Corea's career was taking off. The overtones produced by the instrument make chords voiced in the manner of bop pianists sound muddy, whereas the open quality achieved by voicing in fourths is less easily muddied by the electric instrument.

Latin American music also inspired Corea's style. Early in his career, Corea had played in several bands that featured Latin American music.[30] Even in non-Latin jazz contexts, Corea's playing bears the double-time feeling of Latin American music. He plays his notes in a manner that is very even, with each one markedly emphasized. (For explanations of

Chick Corea, creator of a major post-bop piano style and a fresh approach to composing. Almost every modern pianist owns his album *Now He Sings, Now He Sobs*, and Corea's tunes have been played by thousands of musicians, including Woody Herman, Stan Getz, and Al Jarreau.

The Jazz Image

double-time and staccato, listen to *Demo CD* Tracks 35 and 45.) Corea's crisp, percussive touch enhances the Latin feeling. This is also consistent with his bright, very spirited style of comping.

In 1968, Corea summarized his vocabulary of melodic, rhythmic, and harmonic strategies in *Now He Sings, Now He Sobs,* an album of original compositions and improvisations with bassist Miroslav Vitous and drummer Roy Haynes. (This album is represented by "Steps" on the *Jazz Classics CD.*) This album inspired hundreds of pianists, and it became a staple in the record collections of modern jazz musicians.[31] In 1981, the trio regrouped and made two more albums together.[32]

On and off between 1969 and 1972, Corea led a trio with bassist Dave Holland and drummer Barry Altschul. Free-form improvisation was featured on two of their albums, *The Song of Singing* and *A.R.C.* In some settings, they were joined by saxophonist Anthony Braxton, with whom their group name became Circle.[34] This period of Corea's output reflects the influence of pianist Paul Bley, bassist Gary Peacock, and saxophonists John Coltrane, Albert Ayler, and Ornette Coleman. The music also drew from twentieth-century composers John Cage and Karlheinz Stockhausen. Corea's use of the free-form approach resulted not only in the turbulent music found on *A.R.C.* and *The Song of Singing,* but also in the serene pieces he freely improvised in his *Piano Improvisations Vols. I & II.*[34]

After Circle disbanded, Corea formed a new group with himself on Fender Rhodes electric piano (an instrument that produces a light, vibraharp-like tone), bassist Stanley Clarke, Airto Moreira—a Brazilian drummer who had played with Miles Davis together with Corea—and singer Flora Purim, Airto's wife. Airto had played auxiliary percussion with Davis, but he used a conventional drum set with Corea. The group's sound was light and happy, full of Latin American rhythms and Spanish themes. The name of the group and its first album was *Return to Forever.* Their second album was titled *Light as a Feather.*[35] These two albums became favorites among musicians, especially young players who were active during the 1970s. With this band, two of Corea's most popular tunes became known: "Spain" and "La Fiesta." Within a few years, the influence of this sound was evident in a number of jazz-rock fusion bands.

The group Chick Corea carried through the middle 1970s was strongly influenced by rock and funk music, often displaying the insistent, machine-like sound of hard rock. Corea employed rock-influenced electric guitarists—first Bill Connors, then Al Dimeola. Corea retained bassist Stanley Clarke, now playing electric bass guitar more than acoustic bass. Drummer Lenny White rounded out the group. White's style was a very full, active approach which combined aspects of the Tony Williams techniques with those of modern rock drummers, funk drummers, and Latin American percussion ensembles. Some of the group's material was orchestral, very involved, and highly imaginative. Some of it moved between rock, classical, and jazz idioms. The records made during this period sold well, and independent recording careers soon resulted for Clarke and Dimeola.[36] White and Dimeola left Corea during the summer of 1976, though the Return to Forever group name was retained for a number of Corea's subsequent projects. Thereafter, Corea appeared in a wide assortment of contexts. Al Dimeola, Stanley Clarke, and Lenny White went on to lead bands of their own, occasionally regrouping with Corea to tour and record.

Corea was a prominent composer during the 1960s and 1970s. His "Windows" and "Crystal Silence" became jazz standards. Al Jarreau's vocal rendition of Corea's "Spain" was a hit record. Like much of Horace Silver's work, many of Corea's compositions are more than merely a melody whose accompaniment chord progression provides material for solo improvisations. Some pieces have different sections, each with a distinctive rhythmic and tonal flavor. For example, "Windows," "Spain," and "Litha" are melodies and arrangements all rolled into a single package.[37] Also like Silver, Corea writes pieces that make good use of preset bass lines in the accompaniment, particularly those with a Latin American flavor.[38] In addition, many Corea compositions feature bass doubling the melody of the piano and horn parts, no matter how rapid and intricate the line. This arranging practice took advantage of the high-level instrumental proficiency of jazz bassists during the 1970s and 1980s.[39] It was widely imitated in jazz-rock groups of the 1980s and 1990s.

Corea's acoustic jazz of the 1960s and 70s did not gain a particularly wide audience. For instance, albums such as *Now He Sings, Now He Sobs*, *A.R.C.*, and *The Song of Singing* were frequently out of print for years at a time. On the other hand, his jazz-rock fusion music acquired a wide following, he became known for his use of synthesizers, and the Chick Corea Elektric Band of the 1980s managed to be among the few jazz groups known to a large audience.

◇KEITH JARRETT

After Corea left Miles Davis in 1970, pianist **Keith Jarrett** (b. 1945) took his place and performed with Davis until the winter of 1971. Like a few other Davis sidemen, Jarrett had also played with Art Blakey. But Jarrett's widest pre-Davis exposure had come as a member of saxophonist Charles Lloyd's quartet, beginning in 1966. In recordings with Lloyd, Jarrett had proven himself a powerful improviser whose talents and stature paralleled Herbie Hancock and Chick Corea. Jarrett had as much or more command of the piano as they, but more important, he had his own distinctive approach: He was a piano original. Jarrett's playing demonstrated imagination of enormous scope, and he seemed able to draw from any musical idiom and incorporate its elements in a convincing way. In Jarrett's playing were bits of Bill Evans,[40] twentieth-century classical composers Bela Bartók, Alban Berg, and Maurice Ravel, American gospel music,[41] country music, and Ornette Coleman. Innovative modern pianist Paul Bley had the most influence on him.

Listening Guide for

"Steps"

Composed by Chick Corea; recorded in March, 1968 by Chick Corea (piano), Miroslav Vitous (bass), and Roy Haynes (drums); available on the *Jazz Classics CD* Track 92; also on Chick Corea, *Now He Sings, Now He Sobs* (Blue Note: 90055, 1968).

This selection is taken from the most revered Chick Corea album, *Now He Sings, Now He Sobs.* The music represents the earliest summary of Corea's compositional and improvisational vocabulary, and it offers some of the best playing on record for drummer Roy Haynes. This album is as historically significant to Corea followers as *Sunday at the Village Vanguard* is to fans of Bill Evans.

When this recording was made, drummer **Roy Haynes** (b. 1926) had already been a favorite of jazz musicians since the 1940s. Though neglected by jazz journalists and historians, he is ranked by musicians as a peer of Max Roach and "Philly Joe" Jones. He preceded Tony Williams by decades in several of the ways he emancipated the drummer from the role of mere timekeeper. Some feel that he outshines Roach and Jones and is unsurpassed as the most creative and tasteful of modern drummers. Many would make Haynes their first choice as accompanist. *Now He Sings, Now He Sobs* contains possibly his best and most well-recorded work on record, though few listeners knew he was on it because the manufacturer failed to list personnel on the album jacket. At the time the album was recorded, bassist **Miroslav Vitous** (b. 1947) was just becoming known among musicians and had yet to attain the stature he later gained as cofounder of Weather Report, the pioneering jazz-rock fusion group. Vitous possesses phenomenal technique and a fertile imagination. (Listen to "Surucucu" at the end of the *Jazz Classics CD* for examples of Vitous performing in a freer role and using arco technique.)

Now He Sings, Now He Sobs is pivotal not just because the music is so well played and swinging, but also because its style is not really bop or hard bop. The manner of choosing notes for the lines is fresh, and so is the manner of relating the lines to the chord voicings. They are not necessarily all bop-derived.[42] By comparison with Bud Powell, Corea places his left-hand jabs in a higher pitch range, constructs them out of different intervals, and does not phrase his right-hand lines in the legato manner of a jazz saxophonist. Instead, Corea plays as though every note has a little point on it. The rhythms in the compositions and the improvised lines differ considerably from bop, too. They do not bear the same patterns of accents that typify bop style. Some of this playing also has the ring of classical music, especially that of Bartók and Hindemith. Though classical music does not swing, some of its compositional strategies and flavor were embraced by Corea. Corea's sparkling touch and the bright tone quality he extracts from the piano also remind us of classical music. Corea's higher pitch range and staccato tendencies seem to make the music dance with a snap and lightness that are not often conveyed by bop piano styles. Despite these differences, however, the music has a few bop characteristics. Most of the music keeps a steady tempo and follows chord progressions. The bassist walks, and the drummer plays ride rhythms. The pianist plays long strings of eighth-notes with his right hand and syncopated jabs of comping with his left hand. Moreover, most of the music swings with an easy rise and fall of tensions.

The *Jazz Classics CD* version of "Steps" includes the introduction, two renditions of the theme in an up-tempo, twelve-bar blues form, twenty-two choruses of piano improvisation, two more renditions of the theme, and a coda. On the original album version, a drum solo smoothly evolves from the coda and introduces a new piece, "What Was." The fade-out on the *Jazz Classics CD* version does not exclude any part of the trio performance or the form of the "Steps" composition. It merely stops before the drum solo and "What Was."

CD Track	Elapsed Time	
92	0' 00"	**Introduction**

Corea's notes here, though fast and spirited, are relatively free of steady tempo, and the ideas roam loosely through the waves of sound that comprise this section. Initially the introduction may seem confusing. However, after you have listened to the entire piece several times, you may begin to recognize fragments of ideas in the introduction that recur in Corea's solo choruses. The bass is silent, but Roy Haynes accompanies the piano with light, clicking sounds made by striking the rims and shells of his drums with his sticks, and he makes faint "ching" sounds by operating his high-hat with its foot pedal.

0' 43" Tempo begins.

93 0' 47" **First Statement of Theme**

The beginning of the twelve-bar form occurs when piano and bass sound an interval of two low-pitched notes (a fifth apart) three times in succession (bum. . . . . . bum. .bummmmmmm. .). Then the mid-register melody line begins. The piano rhythms are underscored by very light cymbal and snare drum sounds.

If you try to use the melody to help you identify the piece's 12-bar blues form, you may become confused because the melody line does not begin until the third measure of the form.

0' 57" **Second Statement of Theme**

94 1' 06" **First Solo Chorus**

You should have less difficulty determining the beginning of the solo improvisation than the beginning of the theme. The solo starts on the first beat of the first measure of the form, when walking bass and ride rhythms commence. To keep your place by counting measures, remember that the tempo is fast. Then synchronize your counting with the bass: "1234 2234 3234 . . . 11 234 12 234."

Corea comps for himself by playing three-note chords in jabbing, often syncopated ways with his left hand. Frequently he lets his right hand rest, and all we hear is the sound made by his left hand.

1' 15" **Second Solo Chorus**

In this and most subsequent choruses, Corea's lines are generally played in the piano's upper register.

1' 25" **Third Solo Chorus**

Notice how Haynes continuously varies the timekeeping rhythm that he plays on the ride cymbal.

	2' 49"	**Twelfth Chorus** Corea plays the first six measures with both hands locked together in block chord fashion. The seventh measure is played by his left hand alone, then he returns to his pattern of staccato three-note chords (usually voiced in fourths) in the left hand and long strings of eighth notes in the right hand.
	3' 46"	**Eighteenth Chorus** Corea plays long strings of eighth notes near the center of the piano keyboard.
95	3' 56"	**Nineteenth Chorus** Corea does not play any eighth notes in this chorus, but instead plays syncopated 1 1/2- and 2-beat chords for the first six measures. Then he plays block chords directly on the beat for the remainder of the chorus. This departure from the relatively steady pattern of previous choruses inspires Roy Haynes to respond with a considerable amount of crackling sounds on the drums.
	4' 13"	**Twenty-First Chorus** The last four measures are filled with chords played by both hands locked together.
96	4' 24"	**Twenty-Second Solo Chorus** The first six measures are filled with chords played by both hands locked together. The remaining measures are filled with low-pitched chords providing a transition to the return of the theme.
97	4' 36"	**Theme Statement**
	4' 43"	**Theme Statement**
98	4' 55"	**Coda**

Often Jarrett's lines project a singing quality. (Sometimes you can hear Jarrett humming the lines as he plays.) These lines have the sweep of an inspired human voice or a surging saxophone improvisation. In fact, Jarrett plays soprano saxophone at some of his concerts, and he is quite accomplished on the instrument. The long, legato sax lines he creates are mirrored by his long, legato, sax-like piano lines.

Jarrett is also a prolific and original composer. He has written mounds of material for his own albums and contributed significantly to the records of Charles Lloyd and Norwegian saxophonist Jan Garbarek. Some of his albums contain extended performances with little or no improvisation; in these pieces, the line between classical music and jazz is blurred.[43]

Keith Jarrett devised a distinctive quartet sound from 1971 to 1976 with tenor saxophonist Dewey Redman, bassist Charlie Haden (both from Ornette Coleman's band), and drummer Paul Motian, formerly of the Bill Evans trio. Jarrett's group arranged a unique combination of:

Keith Jarrett, the innovative pianist who extended the Bill Evans trio style by fusing it with music of Ornette Coleman, Paul Bley, John Coates, and his own original ideas. Jarrett also devised an original approach to unaccompanied soloing that made him one of the most sought-after concert pianists of the 1970s and 80s.

The Jazz Image

1) elements from approaches of bands led by Paul Bley and Ornette Coleman[44]
2) elements of the Bill Evans style[45]
3) extension and development of rubato style
4) long, vamp-based improvisations which were funky in Jarrett's unique way
5) World music approaches (Redman playing musette, band members using several unusual instruments such as steel drums, finger cymbals, etc.)
6) unique, non-bop timekeeping techniques used by Motian and Haden
7) group improvisations which use rubato.

During the 1970s and 1980s, Jarrett made many albums and concert appearances as an unaccompanied solo pianist. It is notable that Jarrett was one of the few pianists of that time who did not regularly play electric piano. It is also noteworthy that Jarrett's improvisations were more spontaneous than those of most jazz pianists because he rarely used prewritten melodies or preset chord progressions. His playing could be funky, earthy, and gospelish,[46] or pretty and orchestrally lush.[47] Sometimes he clearly stated a tempo. Other times he implied only a momentum. Jarrett is one of the few pianists to improvise free jazz and to show the influence of Ornette Coleman's melodic style.[48] Like Coleman, he avoids staccato phrasing, works from shifting pedal points, has a way of bursting forth with slippery streams of notes, and occasionally lends his playing a twangy flavor reminiscent of country music.

As an unaccompanied solo pianist, Jarrett created one of the first jazz sounds since the Modern Jazz Quartet's whose appeal crossed the line from jazz audiences to audiences customarily more fond of symphonic music. He is one of the first solo jazz musicians to consistently pack auditoriums throughout the United States and Europe and earn a satisfactory living as an improviser. Jarrett attracted audiences comparable to those of a nonimprovising classical virtuoso. The best illustration of the music behind this phenomenon is in his *Staircase* album. Among the explanations for this style's appeal are:

1) a rhapsodic style evoking a warm, sweeping mood
2) Jarrett's seemingly effortless control of the keyboard
3) vamp-based passages in which brief accompaniment figures repeat again and again and are easy to follow
4) the clarity of his thinking
5) the music's classical rather than jazz feeling.[49]

Jarrett's influence on jazz pianists has been slower to take hold than Herbie Hancock's and Chick Corea's. However, there are several players worth noting who recall Jarrett's sound: Bobo Stinson, Art Lande,[50] Richard Beirach,[51] and Lyle Mays (who played on numerous albums with Pat Metheny's group during the 1970s and 1980s). Other pianists, less gifted than Lande, Beirach, and Mays, have begun imitating the simplest aspects of Jarrett's style, particularly the lengthy, vamp-based improvisations which seem soothing. They have become central to a popular kind of music known as "new age," which is frequently confused with jazz because it is improvised and many of its practitioners have previously played jazz. The improvisations of these latter imitators can be distinguished from those of Jarrett because the lines are far less rich with melodic ideas, and the rhythms are much simpler. Rarely do Jarrett's imitators attain the sweeping feeling that Jarrett can elicit in the listener, nor do they play with quite the smoothness and vitality that Jarrett displays.

CHAPTER SUMMARY

1) Pianist Bill Evans came to attention during the late 1950s and became the most influential pianist since Bud Powell.
2) Though derived partly from the Tristano approach, Evans's style was original, especially in his voicings and his modal thinking.
3) With bassist Scott LaFaro and drummer Paul Motian, Evans devised a fresh approach to trio playing in which explicit statement of every beat was replaced by a highly flexible and varied group style, and the roles of soloist and accompanist were often blurred.
4) LaFaro's remarkable speed and imagination pushed jazz bass styles ahead as Jimmy Blanton's had twenty years earlier.
5) Evans influenced Herbie Hancock, Chick Corea, and Keith Jarrett, all of whom, in turn, led innovative bands and influenced many other pianists.

6) Hancock refined the Evans style, added the influence of Wynton Kelly, and raised accompanying techniques to a high level of imagination and variety while with Miles Davis.
7) Hancock led several groups of his own that played his many original compositions, including "Maiden Voyage" and "Watermelon Man."
8) Hancock's mid-1970s group, the Head Hunters, became a model jazz-rock-funk band and enjoyed very high record sales.
9) Chick Corea looked to Bill Evans as only one of many sources for his original piano style. Horace Silver, Thelonious Monk, Bud Powell, McCoy Tyner, and several classical composers also influenced Corea. His playing is more crisp and staccato than that of Hancock or Evans, and he favors Spanish themes and Latin American rhythms.
10) Corea popularized the use of fourths in compositions and piano voicings, and used them in ways that Evans and Tyner had not.
11) Corea's tunes were very popular. "Spain" and "Windows" became jazz standards.
12) Keith Jarrett showed the influence of Bill Evans—and that of Ornette Coleman—in developing his own piano style.
13) Jarrett was one of the most original composer-pianist-bandleaders of the 1970s, combining free jazz, funk, and a rhapsodic classical piano style that made him the most successful solo concert pianist in jazz history.
14) Jarrett's quartet of the 1970s mixed the methods and musicians associated with Ornette Coleman and Bill Evans and added country music, World music, and funk music in original combinations.

NOTES

1. For more about Evans, see Peter Pettinger, *How My Heart Sings* (Yale University, 1998); Win Hinkle, ed., *Letter From Evans* (back issues from 232 Hanover Pl., Cary, NC 27511); www.billevansjazz.com. For commentary about Evans, Herbie Hancock, Chick Corea, and Keith Jarrett, see Len Lyons, *The Great Jazz Pianists* (DaCapo, 1983), and the booklet that accompanies *Jazz Piano* (Smithsonian: 7002 [RD-039], 4CD set). *Jazz Piano* also presents Evans-LaFaro-Motian on "Autumn Leaves" (1959) and "Waltz for Debby" (1961, live); a live solo recording by Evans: "I Loves You Porgy" (1968). A transcription and analysis of the Evans solo on "Nardis" (*Explorations,* Fantasy: OJCCD-037-2 [Riverside 351], 1961) is in John Rodby, *Solos for Jazz Piano* (Carl Fischer, 1989; order from Carl Fischer Music Store, 54 Cooper Square, NY, NY 10003). A transcription of "Peri's Scope" (*Portrait in Jazz,* Fantasy: OJCCD-088 [Riverside 315], 1959) is in John Mehegan, *Jazz Improvisation, Vol. 4* (Watson-Guptill, 1965; Amsco, 1973).
2. Recordings with Miles Davis in 1958 include '58 *Sessions* (Columbia: CK 46835 [32470]), and most of *Miles and Coltrane* (Columbia: CK 44052, 1955, 1958).
3. *Everybody Digs Bill Evans* (Fantasy: OJCCD-068-2 [Riverside 1129], 1958); the first Evans trio record is *New Jazz Conception* (Fantasy: OJCCD-025-2 [Riverside 223], 1956).
4. Because of this famous recording and his other work, Bill Evans influenced various stages in the careers of many modern jazz pianists, especially in the jazz use of chord voicings originally identified with French Impressionist composers Maurice Ravel and Claude Debussy. Listen to the second movement of Ravel's "Sonatina" to hear one source for Evans's chord voicings. To detect the influence of the Evans voicings and manner in others, listen to Herbie Hancock on "My Funny Valentine," especially the introduction (Miles Davis, *The Complete Concert 1964*), and on "Pee Wee" (Miles Davis, *Sorcerer*); Chick Corea on Stan Getz, *Sweet Rain* (Verve: 815054-2 (V8693), 1967); Keith Jarrett on "Pretty Ballad" from *Somewhere Before* (Atlantic: 8808-2 [Vortex 2012], 1968); or Jarrett on "Ellen David" on Charlie Haden, *Closeness* (A&M/Horizon: CD-0808 [SP710], 1976).
5. A compilation of this music is *Bill Evans at the Village Vanguard* (Riverside: 60-017, 1961); or *Sunday at the Village Vanguard* (Fantasy: OJCCD-140-2 [Riverside 9376]) and *Waltz for Debby* (Fantasy: OJCCD-210-2 [Riverside 9399]).
6. On *Jazz Piano* (Smithsonian: 7002 [039], 4CD set).
7. "Pitter Panther Patter" and "Mr. J.B. Blues" on Duke Ellington, *Solos, Duets & Trios* (RCA Bluebird: 2178-2-RB, 1932–67), or *Duke Ellington 1940* (Smithsonian: 2013, 2LP set, 1940).
8. The clearest example of this style is on "Solar" on *Sunday at the Village Vanguard* (Fantasy: OJCCD-140-2 (Riverside 9376), 1961).
9. Listen to the Evans-LaFaro recordings and compare with work by the trios of Art Tatum, Bud Powell, Oscar Peterson, or Ramsey Lewis. Evans, Powell, and Peterson examples can be found on *Jazz Piano* (Smithsonian: 7002 [039], 4CD set).
10. In some passages, Evans's bassists do not emphasize all four beats of each measure but instead concentrate only on the first and third. (Listen to "All of You" on *Sunday at the Village Vanguard.*) LaFaro's playing often seemed to decorate the first and third beats and let the second and fourth beats pass. Even though four beats are present, only two are emphasized; musicians would say the music is "in two" or "two-beat style." What LaFaro did here is called a "decorative two feel."
11. An example of this is "Solar" on *Sunday at the Village Vanguard.*
12. A vivid illustration of this influence is provided by listening to the rhythm section style of pre-1963 Miles Davis records, such as *Milestones* (1958) or *Miles Davis at Carnegie Hall* (1961); then listening to Bill Evans, *Sunday at the Village Vanguard* (1961), before listening to the rhythm section on any 1963–67 Davis albums, particularly "All of You" in *The Complete Concert 1964,* "Circle" on *Miles Smiles* (1966), or "Pee Wee" on *Sorcerer* (1967). The difference between pre- and post-1963 styles reflects the influence of the 1961 Evans trio concepts.
13. The Evans influence can be heard in Hancock's playing on Miles Davis, *The Complete Concert 1964.* And, at times, the Tristano-like approach that Evans used in constructing lines is also evident in Hancock's work, as on solos with Davis in "The Sorcerer" (*Sorcerer*), "Agitation" (*E.S.P.*), and "Orbits" (*Miles Smiles*). The flexible and intelligent interaction between Hancock, Ron Carter, and Tony Williams on "Pee Wee" (*Sorcerer*), and between Hancock, Buster Williams, and Al Heath on "He Who Lives in Fear" (Herbie Hancock, *The Prisoner,* Blue Note: 46845 (84321), 1969) recalls the sensitive interaction in the 1961 recordings of Bill Evans, Scott LaFaro, and Paul Motian. For catalog numbers and recording dates of the Miles Davis recordings, see pages 235–236.
14. Listen to his trio rendition of his composition "The Sorcerer" on *Jazz Piano* (Smithsonian: 7002 [039], 4CD set).
15. *Death Wish* (Columbia: 36825 (33199), LP, 1974).
16. *Fat Albert Rotunda* (on *Mwandishi,* Warner Bros.: 45732-2).
17. *Taking Off* (Blue Note: 46506 [84109], 1962).
18. *Sextant* (Columbia: CK 64983 [32212], 1972).
19. *Crossings,* 1971 (on *Mwandishi,* Warner Bros.: 45732-2).
20. *Maiden Voyage* (Blue Note: 46339 [84195], 1965).
21. *Empyrean Isles* (Blue Note: 84175, 1964).
22. *Head Hunters* (Columbia: CK 65123 [32731], 1974).
23. *Thrust* (Columbia: CK 64984 [32965], 1974).
24. Hancock had led groups in recording studios before and during his years with Davis, but they were not usually working bands. Most were put together solely for the recordings.
25. *Future Shock* (Columbia: CK 38814, 1983).
26. Jan Hammer, Richard Beirach, Jeff Lorber, Andy LaVerne, and Mulgrew Miller were among the many who exhibited Corea's influence.
27. The mid-1960s recordings that Corea made with Blue Mitchell show the influence of Bud Powell and Horace Silver. His work with Herbie Mann and Cal Tjader points up his use of Evans and Tyner as sources. (See *Instructor's Resource Manual* for discography of Mitchell, Mann, and Tjader records featuring Corea.) Though drawing from Tyner, Corea's style differs from Tyner in several respects. For example, in Tyner's reharmonization of popular-song chord progressions, his use of fourths simplifies the movement of harmonies, whereas Corea's delineates the movement of harmonies. Though both Tyner and Corea occasionally venture outside their harmonies, Corea's "outside" lines

usually return to the harmonies in a more systematic way where Tyner uses his outside playing more for its coloristic value alone. Though both improvisers use pentatonics, Tyner tends to use them more against pedal points, whereas Corea employs them as much in lines that are set atop moving chords.

Though similar in many ways to Bill Evans, Corea devotes a very large portion of his output to voicing in fourths, whereas Evans tends toward a balance of quartal and tertial harmonies. Though both Evans and Corea play notes in a very marked manner, Evans is more legato and Corea more staccato. To hear Corea's resemblance to Evans, listen to Evans on the final selection of Miles Davis, *Kind of Blue,* or on "Peace Piece" on *Everybody Digs Bill Evans;* then listen to the title track from *Return to Forever,* "Where Have I Known You Before" (Polydor: 825206-2 [6509], 1974), or "Song for Lee Lee" on Chick Corea, *Piano Improvisations, Vol. 2* (ECM: 78118-21020-2, 1971). Also listen to other Evans solos on those albums, then to Corea's solos on Stan Getz, *Sweet Rain* (Verve: 815054-2 [V 8693], 1967). Corea's compositions, "Tones for Joan's Bones" (Chick Corea, *Inner Space,* Atlantic: 305-2 [Vortex 2004], 1966) and "Windows" (Getz, *Sweet Rain*), reflect the Evans style of chord voicing.

28. See pages 222, footnote 27 above, and 417–418 for more about sounds created by fourths. Fourths are used extensively in the melody line of his tune "Litha" and his left-hand comping on *Now He Sings, Now He Sobs.* The chord voicings in *Now He Sings, Now He Sobs* are reminiscent of music by Paul Hindemith. *Now He Sings, Now He Sobs* (Blue Note: 90055 [Solid State 18039], 1968).

29. Corea demonstrated a few of Silver's devices on Blue Mitchell, *The Thing to Do* (Blue Note: 84178, 1964), which was recorded by the Horace Silver quintet with Corea in Silver's place. Even Corea's compositions on the album are in Silver's style.

30. Corea played with the bands of Willie Bobo, Cal Tjader, Herbie Mann, and Mongo Santamaria, all of which featured Latin American music.

31. *Now He Sings, Now He Sobs* (Blue Note: 90055 (Solid State 18039), 1968). Some musicians learned to play its music note for note, and we are indebted to a few of them for transcriptions of his piano part. Bill Dobbins prepared *Chick Corea: Now He Sings, Now He Sobs* (Advance Music, 1988), and a number of observations about Corea's style that appear in this chapter were made originally by Dobbins in personal communication with the author. Scott Reeves transcribed and analyzed Corea's solo on "Matrix" in his *Creative Jazz Improvisation, 2nd ed.* (Prentice-Hall, 1995), and a few of his ideas are presented in this chapter. Both these books are available from Jamey Aebersold, P.O. Box 1244, New Albany, IN 47151; phone 800-456-1388. The recording of "Matrix" is also in *Jazz Piano* (Smithsonian: 7002 [RD-039], 4CD set).

32. *Trio Music* (ECM: 78118-21232-2, 2CDs, 1981), and *Trio Music Live in Europe* (ECM: 78118-21310, 1984).

33. *Song of Singing* (Blue Note: 46401 [84353], 1970); *A.R.C.* (ECM: 78118-21009-2 [1009], 1971). During this time Corea also appeared on the Miles Davis albums: *In a Silent Way, Bitches Brew, Live at Fillmore,* and *Black Beauty. Black Beauty* is the only Davis album in which Corea solos at length, and it is well worth having since it constitutes some of the best work of his career. See pages 235–236 for album catalog numbers.

34. *Piano Improvisations, Vols. 1 & 2* (ECM: 78118-21014-2 & 78118-21020-2, 2CDs, 1971); all selections were spontaneously conceived and performed, with the exceptions of "Song for Sally," "Song of the Wind," "Some Time Ago," "Trinkle Tinkle," and "Masqualero."

35. *Return to Forever* (ECM: 78118-21022-2 [1022],1972); *Light as a Feather* (Polydor: 827148-2 [5525], 1972). See a transcription and analysis of Corea's solo on "Spain," from *Light as a Feather,* in John Rodby, *Solos for Jazz Piano* (Carl Fischer, 1989; from Carl Fischer Music Store, 54 Cooper Square, NY, NY 10003).

36. Stanley Clarke's *School Days* was a hit, as were Al Dimeola's *Elegant Gypsy* and *Casino.*

37. Listen to "Windows" and "Litha" on Stan Getz, *Sweet Rain* (Verve: 815054-2 [V8693], 1967).

38. For example, the bass lines that accompany his "Senor Mouse" (Gary Burton, *Crystal Silence,* ECM: 78118-21024-2 [1024], 1972) are central to the composition. Without them, the melody would not convey the same flavor.

39. John Patitucci's playing of the rapid melody line to Corea's "Got A Match" from *The Chick Corea Elektric Band* (GRP: 9535, 1986) dazzled listeners of the 1980s.

40. To detect Jarrett's debt to Evans, listen to "Shades of Jazz" on Keith Jarrett, *Mysteries* (Impulse!/GRP: IMPD4-189) and "Ellen David" on Charlie Haden, *Closeness* (A&M/Horizon: CD-0808 [SP710], 1976). For more about Jarrett, see Ian Carr, *Keith Jarrett: The Man and His Music* (Grafton, 1991).

41. Jarrett's style is a curious blend of influences. There is a hint of Wynton Kelly in his playing on Art Blakey, *Buttercorn Lady* (Emarcy: 822471-2 [Limelight 82034], 1966). Bill Evans and Ornette Coleman are obvious. Jarrett's piano style and quartet sound of the 1970s were based on the style of pianist Paul Bley and his group that included saxophonist John Gilmore, bassist Gary Peacock, and future Jarrett drummer Paul Motian. They are documented on Paul Bley, *Turning Point* (Improvising Artists: 123841-2, 1964); *New Music: The Second Wave* (Savoy: 2235, 2LP set), *Turns* (Savoy: 1192, LP, 1964). Jarrett has cited Bley's *Footloose* (Savoy/Denon CV78987 [12182], 1962–63) as a favorite.

Influences converged for Jarrett in a friendship he began with pianist John Coates around 1957. Coates's favorites included Paul Bley, Ornette Coleman, black gospel music, and early white American music. Both men eventually showed similar amalgams of them, though Coates was perfecting his first, and Jarrett listened to Coates. (A late example is *The Piano Sound of John Coates,* Omnisound: 1004, LP, 1974.)

42 Even though "Matrix" and "Steps" are 12-bar blues tunes, listeners do not usually recognize them as blues because of the fresh way Corea treats their form. Portions of his solos avoid traditional ways of announcing the significant chord changes that earlier pianists would make at the fifth, ninth, and eleventh measures. For some of Corea's solo passages, the arrival points are determined exclusively by the direction of the melodic line. Sometimes he leaves out those moves; other times he stretches the traditional time before playing them. In other words, he restructures the tension points. The ways bop pianists favored for adding chords to make more movement within the 12-measure progression are also missing. When Corea does add chords, their identity is not as pronounced, because voicing in fourths makes the origin of the chord ambiguous. Moreover, sometimes Corea phrases in ways that do not neatly fit the three 4-measure phrase organization his predecessors were inclined to use when playing the blues. He starts and stops his lines in nontraditional places, but the result does not sound odd. Incidentally, it is precisely the fact that it does not sound odd, coupled with the smoothness and finished quality of his constructions, that masks the music's adventuresome construction for some listeners. Many have failed to appreciate the newness of Corea's ideas because the presentation was so smooth that it failed to jar them.

The selection on *Now He Sings, Now He Sobs* called "Now He Beats the Drum, Now He Stops" also begins with a traditional foundation: the chord progression to "How Deep Is the Ocean?" But Corea takes that set of chords, combines it with a few ideas from a Bill Evans rendition, and composes a fresh and original piece that sounds like nothing ever heard before.

43. *In The Light* (ECM: 78118-21033-2 [1033/34], 1973).

44. Jarrett wrote melodies in Coleman's style as well as soloing in it. Redman soloed in the Coleman style, and Haden's unique approach was central to both the Coleman and Jarrett groups.

45. Listen to Jarrett's up-tempo piano lines on "Shades of Jazz" and his slow playing, with its sustained tones and chord voicings on "Rainbow," both on Keith Jarrett, *Mysteries* (Impulse!/ GRP: IMPD4-189, 4CD set, 1975-76). Compare this with Bill Evans *Sunday at the Village Vanguard* or *Everybody Digs Bill Evans.*

46. Listen to Jarrett's "In Front" on *Jazz Piano* (Smithsonian: 7002 [RD-039], 4CD set), or on Keith Jarrett, *Facing You* (ECM: 78118-21017-2 [1017], 1971).

47. *Staircase* (ECM: 78118-21090-2 [1090], 2CD set, 1976).

48. It helps us hear Jarrett's debt to Coleman when Jarrett omits left-hand playing and improvises lengthy, saxophone-like solos with his right hand. In fact, when accompanied only by drums and bass (especially Charlie Haden) and not playing in a two-handed pianistic style, Jarrett often sounds like Coleman transferred to the piano. For more comparisons between Coleman and Jarrett, listen to Jarrett's soprano saxophone playing on "Pocket Full of Cherry," originally on his *Bop-Be,* reissued on *Mysteries* (Impulse!/GRP: IMPD4-189); and "Encore (a-b-c)" on his *Eyes of the Heart* (ECM: 78118-21150-2 (1150), 1976). Jarrett's stylistic debt to Coleman is particularly evident in his solos on Jan Garbarek, *Belonging* (ECM: 78118-21050-2 [1050], 1974). Despite all the similarities between styles, even to employing the same sidemen, at least three differences between Coleman's and Jarrett's approaches are evident: (1) Coleman is more complex than Jarrett, more varied and unpredictable in his improvised lines, and he draws upon a wider selection of moods and tempos than does Jarrett; (2) Jarrett possesses very high-level technique, and, because of the uniformity in touch this affords, he plays more smoothly than Coleman, and his music is less jarring; and (3) the notes in Jarrett's lines usually seem more loyal to the original key that a given piece is in, and Coleman shifts pedal points more often.

49. In a substantial portion of Jarrett's unaccompanied solo improvisations, the musical vocabulary is classical. Much of this work sounds like piano pieces by Maurice Ravel. This sound might provide a bridge for listeners who are not accustomed to jazz but are acquainted with symphonic music, especially the familiar works of French composers Ravel and Claude Debussy. For many such listeners, the only aspect that separates Jarrett's work from classical music is that Jarrett's is largely improvised.

50. Lande's affinity for Jarrett is particularly evident on Art Lande, *Red Lanta* (ECM: 78118-21038-2 [1038], 1973).

51. Beirach's affinity for Jarrett is most noticeable on David Liebman, *Forgotten Fantasies* (A&M/Horizon: SP-709, LP, 1975). Note that his style has more resemblance to Chick Corea and Herbie Hancock and their mutual influence from Bill Evans. Beirach, however, can be identified for his own style, as well. He has, in turn, influenced other pianists.

Chapter Sixteen

Herbie Hancock **Photo by Grace Bell**

Jazz-Rock Fusion

The first group of jazz styles to attain widespread popularity after the swing era was called jazz-rock fusion. This collection of approaches became a dominant stream of jazz during the 1970s, and it spawned styles that became the main popular music for an entire segment of the music market in the 1980s and 1990s. The first portion of this chapter clarifies what is included in this category. The middle portion discusses the major contributions of **Miles Davis, Larry Coryell, John McLaughlin, Joe Zawinul, Jaco Pastorius,** and **Pat Metheny.** (The fusion styles of **Herbie Hancock** and **Chick Corea** were examined in chapter 15, and those of **Wayne Shorter** were mentioned in chapter 12.) The third portion discusses three light-weight variants and the reasons for their popularity: (1) **New Age music,** described in this chapter because sometimes it is marketed in the jazz category, even though its concepts are only peripherally related to jazz; (2) **Smooth jazz**, covered here because this radio format defined jazz for a significant portion of listeners during the 1980s and 90s; (3) **Acid jazz**, included because the term initially described a subset of fusion styles in the 1990s and eventually became applied to a broad assortment of jazz-rock and experimental mixtures. Keep in mind that hundreds of musicians have played in various fusion styles, but this chapter describes only a few of the most significant.

◆DISTINGUISHING JAZZ FROM ROCK AND FUNK

Jazz of almost any period can be distinguished from rock and funk music because rock and funk typically have:

1) shorter phrase lengths
2) less frequent chord changes
3) less complexity of melody
4) less complexity of harmony
5) less improvisation, especially in accompaniments
6) much more repetition of melodic phrases
7) more repetition of brief chord progressions
8) simpler, more repetitive drumming patterns
9) more pronounced repetition of bass figures

More is preset in rock and funk performances than in jazz performances. Not only does jazz ordinarily require solos to be improvised anew each time they occur; it also requires that the accompaniments for the solos be improvised. Even the accompaniments for the theme statements spontaneously differ from performance to performance.

Rhythmic feeling provides another means for distinguishing jazz from rock and funk music. Where jazz emphasizes flexibility and relaxation, rock stresses intensity and firmness. Rock and funk music seem to sit on each beat, whereas jazz projects a shuffling feeling. Jazz musicians describe the time sense of rock and funk musicians as "straight up and down." On the other hand, jazz attempts to put forth a lilting, bouncy feeling that seems to pull each beat along.

Instruments preferred by jazz musicians are often different from those of rock and funk musicians. Jazz musicians usually place less emphasis on electronic instruments and high amplification of acoustic instruments.

Jazz, rock, and funk music share similar roots in work songs, the blues, and gospel music, but they represent the products of two divergent lines of musical evolution (see Figure 16.1). For example, jazz employs aspects of formal European concert music and steers away from vocals; it is primarily instrumental music. Sometimes it is as intricate as twentieth-century symphonic music. Rock and funk music, on the other hand, emphasize vocals and stick largely to elementary compositional forms. Rock and funk favor the four-chord, twelve-bar blues and other brief chord progressions that repeat continuously. While rock and funk became a part of the popular music mainstream, jazz acquired a status like classical chamber music because its audience was small and specialized. While it is true that blues singers from early in the twentieth century, such as Leadbelly, Robert Johnson, and Bessie Smith, are routinely cited in jazz history texts, they are usually mentioned in discussions of the origins of jazz rather than the dominant course of jazz itself. The stream of stylistic evolution that runs from Leadbelly through B. B. King to Jimi Hendrix is essentially separate from the evolution of most jazz styles. Religious music had influenced blues singers such as Bessie Smith, and it continued to influence popular music, as exemplified by more recently popular singers such as Aretha Franklin and James Brown. However, it influenced jazz somewhat less.[1]

Prior to the 1950s, blues and gospel music were especially influential in popular music made by black performers who were marketed to black audiences. Ranging from Bessie Smith in the 1920s to Louis Jordan in the 1940s, these performers made music for what were called "race records." In 1949, this category acquired a new name—rhythm and blues

(R & B)—and it strongly influenced another style of popular music called rock and roll (see Figure 16.1). In addition to its R & B roots, much rock also reflects the predominantly white musical streams of country music or hillbilly music. One early form of rock was called rockabilly, and early Elvis Presley exemplifies this style. Rock also reflects western swing. This is a form that combines hillbilly music and jazz with a diversity of ethnic traditions that range from the dance music of Cajuns and Czechs to that of Mexicans, Germans, and Poles. Rock is distinctly removed from jazz, being less like jazz than R & B had been. Rock and R & B remain similar, however, because they both emphasize extremely simple melodies, extensive pitch bending, reliance upon ostinato, and strict adherence to steady tempo.

Some R & B in the 1960s contained accompaniment rhythms more complicated than those in rock. During the late 1960s, some styles which extended R & B became the source for intricately syncopated drum patterns and bass figures. Some of the musicians working for Motown recording artists[2] and for singer James Brown,[3] for example, devised accompaniment patterns which were more complicated than those used at the time by rock groups. The work of accompanists for Sly Stone[4] during the early 1970s was especially complex. By this time, many people were beginning to call this music "soul" and "funk" instead of R & B. However, this new pair of labels still served the same purpose: identifying a primarily African American form of popular music. It was the accompaniment style for this funk-soul category, more than rock, which influenced a number of jazz musicians during the 1970s (see Figure 16.1). Therefore, **the jazz-rock label itself is not entirely appropriate for the music that it identifies.** "Jazz-funk" might be a more accurate designation.[5]

Some jazz musicians remained unaffected by funk, and many funk groups continued unaffected by jazz. But much of the music produced by jazz groups during the 1970s and 1980s demonstrated a larger number of funk characteristics than had previously been used in modern jazz, and some funk groups attempted to incorporate more of the improvisation and advanced harmonies found in jazz.

◇FORERUNNERS OF JAZZ-ROCK

Mid-1960s forerunners of the "jazz-rock" approaches include the 1966 band called the Free Spirits[6] with guitarist Larry Coryell, the 1967 quartet of vibraharpist Gary Burton and Coryell,[7] and the Fourth Way, a 1968–1971 band with pianist Mike Nock and violinist Michael White.[8] The greatest popular acclaim did not go to these groups, however. It went to Blood, Sweat & Tears,[9] an eight-piece band featuring vocals in a James Brown and Ray Charles style with horn work similar to that of Brown and Charles. Next was the 1968 group called Chicago,[10] a seven-piece pop band featuring solo voice singing as well as four- and five-part harmony. Its horn parts were often voiced for trumpet, trombone, and saxophone, in the style of late-1960s Motown. After them was the 1970 group called Ten Wheel Drive,[11] a ten-piece band whose style was similar to that of the first two. These three groups were identified by music journalists as "jazz-rock" bands, and they were phenomenally successful with the record-buying public.

Journalists gave much attention to the horns and improvisation in Ten Wheel Drive, Chicago, and Blood, Sweat & Tears. Listeners and journalists assumed that such elements lent jazz character to the music, that it was innovative, and that it justified the "jazz" part of the "jazz-rock" label. Yet R & B bands, including those of soul singer James Brown, for example, had been using horns and improvisation since the 1950s. In other words, some elements presumed to be significant contributions by Chicago and Blood, Sweat & Tears merely reflected existing traditions within popular music (see Figure 16.1). Their horn parts were modeled after the James Brown and Motown brass style rather than jazz. And their singing style was patterned after soul singing. Admittedly, the harmonies written for their horns

Figure 16.1 **Chart of Parallel Streams Distinguishing Jazz from Rock and Jazz-Rock***

Jazz and rock share a few similar origins, but they are separate styles.

Their origins constitute musical streams that continued by themselves and remain alive today.

Chicago, BS&T, and Ten Wheel Drive are offshoots of soul music, more than offshoots of jazz.

Rythm & Blues evolved into soul music and already had a tradition including jazz improvisation before soul music influenced Chicago, BS&T, and Ten Wheel Drive.

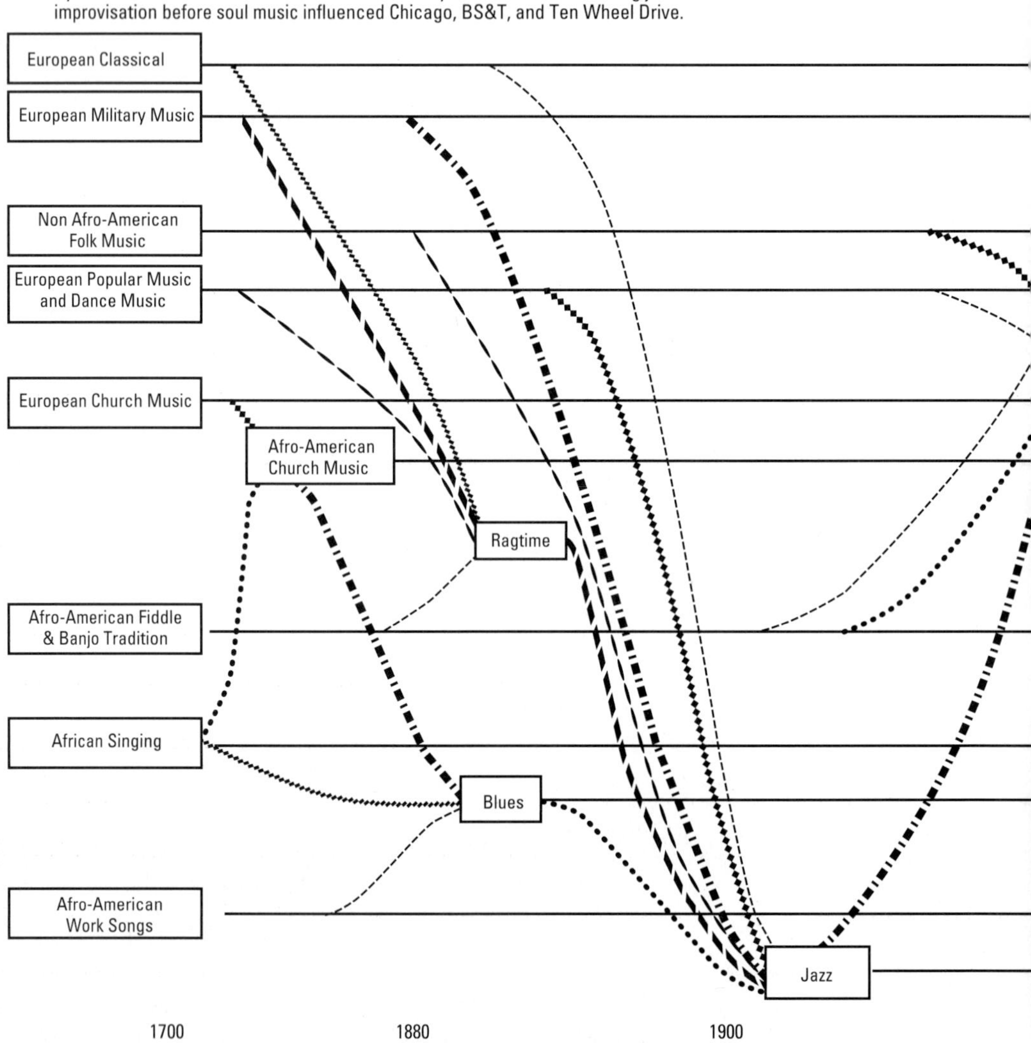

* There has been such a continual back and forth borrowing among the creators of the styles shown here that there is no way that we can trace all the sharing. To be completely accurate, this chart would have to include numerous feedback loops. To avoid creating such a tangled web, only a few major interconnections are portrayed here. To better understand the limitations of the chart, see pp. **305–307** and **310–312.**

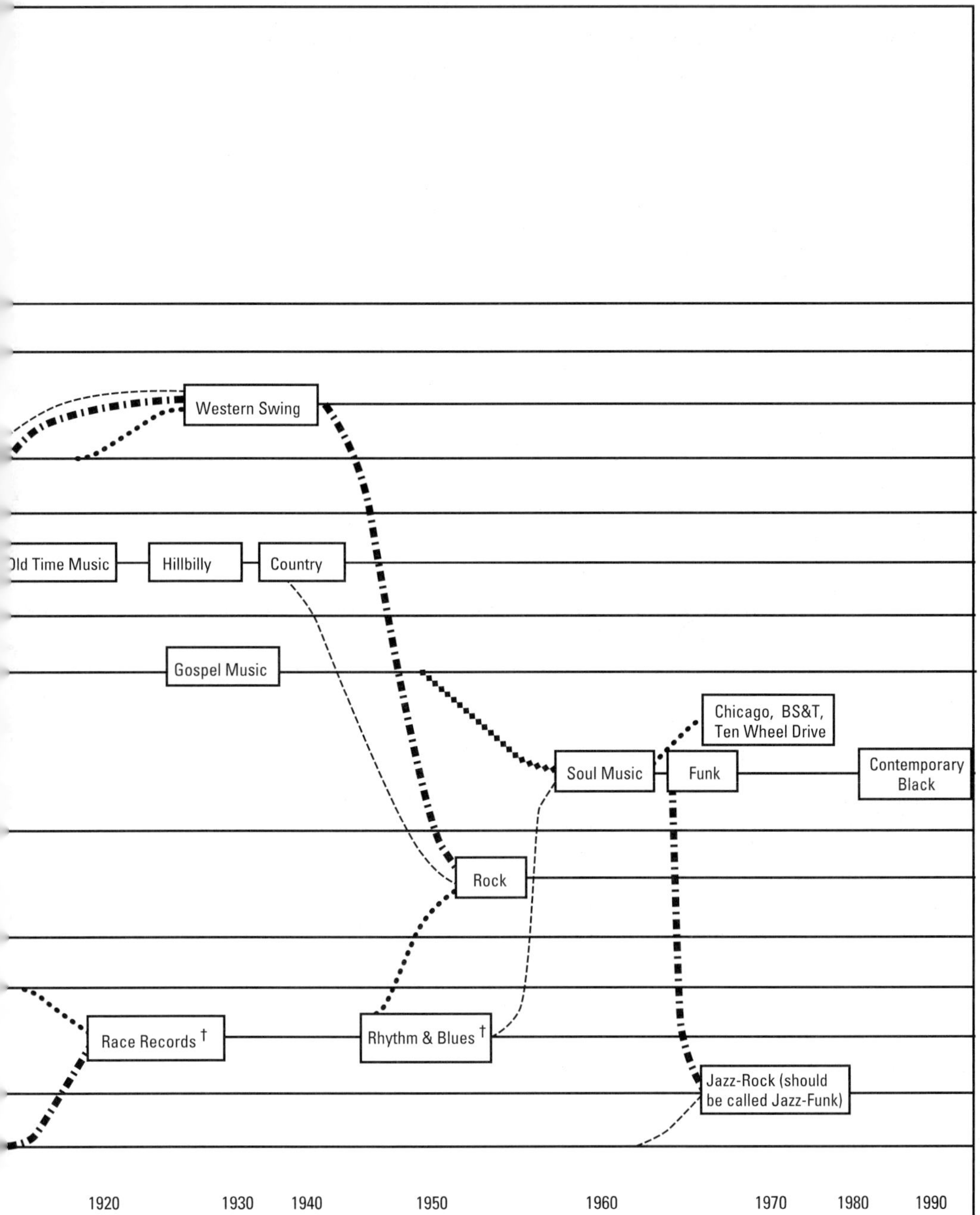

† These terms never designated particular styles. They served instead as a catchall category for many types of pop music performed by black artists.

were more advanced than Motown's and James Brown's, but such sophistication had already been common in pop music and was not exclusive to jazz, either. Almost the only element these bands had in common with jazz was the occasional presence of a brief, improvised solo. Yet this was something that R & B had long been known for.

Another line of reasoning was used in applying the jazz label to the most popular "jazz-rock" groups. This was the knowledge that some members of the groups had played jazz or had jazz aspirations. This colored the thinking of journalists who overlooked the traditions with R & B, James Brown, and Motown and instead assumed a primary connection with jazz. These journalists overlooked the long history of jazz musicians touring and recording with popular non-jazz groups. Jazz musicians had not made those groups into jazz groups any more than the presence of jazz hornmen in Blood, Sweat & Tears made that group into a jazz band. In other words, Blood, Sweat & Tears was a highly professional and creative group of musicians who performed several different styles of popular music; but, they did not necessarily demonstrate a fusion of jazz with rock. Bands which developed a new kind of music by fusing jazz with rock and funk were led by Larry Coryell, Gary Burton, and Mike Nock. The most lasting fusions were made in the bands of trumpeter Miles Davis and in bands led by his sidemen between 1968 and 1975.[12]

◇TRAITS OF FUSION MUSIC

Jazz-rock fusion mixed jazz improvisation with the instrumentation and rhythmic conception of R & B. The compositions, tone colors, and rhythms were adopted not only by musicians who were just then developing their own styles, but also by older, established players. Rhythm sections began replacing piano with electric piano and synthesizer, and they replaced acoustic bass viol ("string bass") with electric bass guitar ("Fender"). Pianists and guitarists often adopted repeating accompanying riffs in place of the spontaneous comping which had been customary since the 1940s. Bassists began accumulating the syncopated and staccato figures found in the Motown bands of the late 1960s and the backup groups for James Brown and Sly Stone of the early 1970s. (See page 19 for instrument photos and pages 426–427 for notations of rock bass figures.) Much as the early swing era bassists often had to play brass bass (tuba) as well as string bass viol, early fusion bassists often had to play bass guitar ("Fender") as well as string bass viol ("acoustic"), and many eventually abandoned bass viol altogether.

Drummers learned new timekeeping patterns which resembled those of R & B as well as Latin American styles. (See page 431 for notations of drumming figures used in recordings by Sly Stone and Herbie Hancock.) Jazz-rock drumming style was very full and active. Following the lead of Tony Williams, initially the high-hat was snapped shut sharply on every beat instead of every other beat. There was an increase in the use of drums, particularly the bass drum, and a decrease in the use of cymbals for timekeeping. The rhythms were stated insistently, not in the jazz manner which regularly alternated tension with relaxation. The jazz-rock style maintained a high level of tension for long periods. There was considerably less bounce and lilt than in jazz of the 1950s. Timekeeping was more strictly stated than during the exploratory years of jazz in the 1960s. The first models for jazz-rock drummers were Tony Williams and Billy Cobham; then, after the mid-1970s, Steve Gadd, and after the mid-1980s, Dave Weckl.

The jazz-oriented soloists in jazz-rock fusion tended to be inspired by John Coltrane's early-1960s style if they were saxophonists, Freddie Hubbard if they were trumpeters, and Herbie Hancock, McCoy Tyner, or Chick Corea if they were pianists. Bop melodic rhythms were not compatible with most jazz-rock accompaniment patterns, but the 1960s style of Coltrane's and Tyner's lines were. Pianists and guitarists often adopted repeating accompaniment riffs in place of the spontaneous comping that had been customary in jazz since the 1940s. Development of repeating patterns in a funk music style usually took higher priority than comping, though the more adventuresome accompanists played spontaneously and re-

TABLE 16.1 A Few of the Many Jazz-Rock Musicians and Bands

INSTRUMENTAL GROUPS AND THEIR LEADERS Lifetime (Tony Williams) The Head Hunters (Herbie Hancock) Return to Forever (Chick Corea) Mahavishnu Orchestra (John McLaughlin) Free Spirits (Larry Coryell) Fourth Way (Mike Nock) Eleventh House (Larry Coryell) Blackbyrds (Donald Byrd) Prime Time (Ornette Coleman) Spyro Gyra Word of Mouth (Jaco Pastorius) The Decoding Society (Ronald Shannon Jackson) Caldera Oracle Soft Machine Jeff Lorber Fusion The Crusaders Weather Report (Joe Zawinul and Wayne Shorter) Miles Davis Bob James Hiroshima Steps Ahead Yellow Jackets	**SINGER-BASED BANDS** Blood, Sweat & Tears Chicago Ten Wheel Drive Chase **TRUMPET** Randy Brecker Tom Browne Michael Lawrence Lew Soloff Miles Davis **SAXOPHONE** Michael Brecker Wayne Shorter David Liebman Steve Grossman Grover Washington Eddie Harris Ronnie Laws David Sanborn John Klemmer Kenny G Najee	**PIANO** Herbie Hancock Chick Corea Joe Zawinul Jan Hammer Jeff Lorber Milcho Leviev George Duke Bob James Lyle Mays **GUITAR** Pat Metheny Mike Stern Al Dimeola John McLaughlin Larry Coryell Steve Khan Blood Ulmer Larry Carlton John Scofield Bill Frisell Alan Holdsworth George Benson **VIOLIN** Michael White Jerry Goodman Jean-Luc Ponty Michael Urbaniak	**VIBRAHARP** Gary Burton Roy Ayers **DRUMS** Tony Williams Billy Cobham Steve Gadd Lenny White Leon Chancler Ronald Shannon Jackson Peter Erskine Al Foster David Weckl Omar Hakim Alphonse Mouzon **BASS GUITAR** Michael Henderson Stanley Clarke Jaco Pastorius Rick Laird Jeff Berlin Jamaaladeen Tacuma John Patitucci Victor Bailey Marcus Miller

sponsively. The less jazz-oriented pianists in fusion devised their own simpler styles or imitated players who leaned more toward the rock side of the jazz-rock mix. The less jazz-oriented saxophonists used models from R & B and R & B-oriented jazz such as King Curtis, Junior Walker, Wilton Felder, and Hank Crawford. Popular models during the 1980s were Dave Sanborn and Michael Brecker. Then Grover Washington, Kenny G, and Najee were the most imitated among young fusion saxophonists of the 1990s.

◇MILES DAVIS

In addition to developing many extensions of existing jazz styles, the 1964–1968 Miles Davis Quintet was one of the first established jazz groups to begin mixing the musical devices of rock and funk music with those of jazz. Rhythmic styles other than bouncy, swinging jazz patterns occur throughout their records. Drummer Tony Williams sometimes played straight, repeating eighth notes on the ride cymbal instead of playing the ching chick-a ching pattern. Occasionally, he also stated each beat by sharply snapping closed the high-hat, instead of closing it only on every other beat. Bassist Ron Carter sometimes complemented those drumming patterns with simple, repeating bass figures that did not fit traditional walking bass rhythms. All of this evoked a feeling that was similar to the rhythmic feeling of rock.[13] One album in particular, their 1968 *Filles de Kilimanjaro* (coming directly after *Miles in the Sky*), clearly signalled a trend away from jazz sound. It not only used electric piano and bass guitar, it also contained military-like drumming patterns that resembled the insistent playing of rock drummers more than the relaxed and lilting playing of modern jazz drummers.

The next two albums that Davis recorded became significant in directing modern jazz of the 1970s.[14] These records were *In a Silent Way* and *Bitches Brew,* both made in 1969. They contained a variety of musical approaches, but their dominant accompaniment style was a combination of jazz and funk. Their dominant melodic style was reminiscent of the floating, almost motionless feeling of Wayne Shorter's "Nefertiti"; and Shorter's tune "Sanctuary" was included on *Bitches Brew.*

Partnership with Joe Zawinul

In a Silent Way marked the beginning of Davis's important **partnership with pianist-composer Joe Zawinul,** who had been with the Cannonball Adderley quintet during the 1960s. Zawinul's ideas, compositions, arrangements, and keyboard playing helped lead the Davis band to a new style. In that way Zawinul played a role in the Davis career that was similar to those of Gil Evans in the late 1940s and late 1950s, Bill Evans on *Kind of Blue,* and Shorter from 1964 to 1969. Davis recorded Zawinul pieces of the "Nefertiti" style: "In a Silent Way" (*In a Silent Way*) and "Pharaoh's Dance" (*Bitches Brew*). Davis also used Zawinul's compositions on later albums, though Davis's name mistakenly appears as composer instead of Zawinul's on the album labels.[15]

Instrumentation

The post-1968 music of Davis differed in several respects from his 1963–1968 style. For example, **instrumentation** was altered as follows:

1) Electric piano and organ replaced conventional piano; and Davis often employed two or more electric keyboard instruments at once.
2) Electric bass guitar replaced acoustic bass viol (see page 19 for illustration).
3) Electric guitarists were more frequently employed; at one time, he had three in a single band.
4) The Davis saxophonists of this period played soprano sax more often than any other instrument. The soprano had the potential for penetrating and carrying its sound over drums and electric instruments, where a tenor might not cut through.
5) Davis usually employed two or more drummers. By the early 1970s, he had settled into the practice of using one player on conventional drum set and another on auxiliary percussion such as conga drums, shakers, rattles, gongs, whistles, and a large number of instruments native to Africa, South America, and India. Davis sometimes additionally used Indian musicians playing the sitar (a stringed instrument) and tabla (drums).

Rhythm Section Concept

The **rhythm section concept** was another way in which Davis's post-1968 groups differed from his 1963–1968 groups. The later groups featured elaborate configurations of colors and textures. His accompanists played with a very high level of activity. The beat was easily detectable, but it was surrounded by a mass of constantly changing sounds. Sometimes they were delicate and gentle. Sometimes they were turbulent. Textures often seemed to be created for their own sake rather than as accompaniments. For example, the textures on *In a Silent Way* and *Bitches Brew* were as much in the forefront as the written melodies and improvised solo lines. The textures were generated by several electric keyboard instruments (piano and organ), guitar, basses, and several drummers. Sources for the bass lines include rock formulas, a freely improvised nonwalking style, and figures borrowed from Latin American music. (See notated rock and Latin bass figures on pages 427 and 428)

Performance Format

Performance format and harmonies differed from previous jazz styles. Most post-1968 Davis music centered on a few repeated chords, a repeating bass figure, or a mode, rather than a sequence of frequently changing chords. The tunes reflected Wayne Shorter's composing style, particularly its departures from bop. Complexity was now concentrated in the rhythm section figures rather than in the melodies. This new format used medleys instead of the entire band stopping before going on to the next tune, everyone taking a turn soloing. Davis often set up a new mood and its harmonies by playing chords in a rhythmic fashion on an electric keyboard instrument. In this way he often dictated the tempo and rhythm for the next passage. Davis used this method to make transitions gracefully between moods within the medleys. Davis conducted the transitions between tunes, and his bassists led the way by changing the patterns of their repeating figures. The bass was the pivot in this music; **bass figures were as essential to the 1970s and 1980s style as complex chord**

The electric jazz-funk band that ended a five-year retirement for trumpeter Miles Davis in 1981: (left to right) soprano saxophonist Bill Evans (his tenor sax is sitting to his right), bass guitarist Marcus Miller, Miles Davis (wearing hat, holding trumpet), Mino Cinelu (playing conga drum), Al Foster (playing full drum set). Guitarist Mike Stern, a regular member of this group, is not shown.

Photo by Mark Vinei, 1982

changes had been to hard bop. The albums *Live-Evil, Black Beauty,* and *Agharta* documented this music.

Despite the marked simplification in rhythm section harmonies, improvising soloists tended to retain considerable harmonic complexity. John Coltrane had perfected techniques for spontaneously superimposing sequential patterns atop relatively static accompaniments. Such patterns were devised in ways that made them sound as though they possessed the direction that one ordinarily detects in a progression of chords. The listener would hear a coherence that is normally associated with melody lines that closely mirror an underlying set of chord progressions. This time, however, that coherence did not necessarily derive from any progression of chords. This approach provided harmonic interest without depending on the movement of chords we ordinarily require to attain a similar effect. Coltrane and his pianist McCoy Tyner had developed these approaches for improvising on mode-based forms and repeating bass figures. The saxophonists and guitar soloists who worked with Miles Davis during the 1970s and 1980s used these same approaches. It is important to note that these techniques replaced the bop concepts of jazz phrasing; none of Charlie Parker's or Dizzy Gillespie's pet phrases was used. In fact, much of the lyricism that had been associated with bop was not evident in this new style. Improvisers seemed more intent on creating moods than melodies.

Personnel

After 1968, Miles Davis changed sidemen more frequently than he had in his late-1950s and his mid-1960s bands. For example, each new album during the 1968–1973 period had new personnel. Also, the musicians on tour were not always the same as those on the album. John Coltrane had been with Davis on and off for five years; Wayne Shorter had also stayed approximately five years. But after Shorter left, Davis employed more than five different saxophonists in five years.

Personnel in the Davis rhythm sections were more stable, however. After various combinations of pianists, bassists, and drummers, Davis settled for several years on drummers Al Foster (conventional set) and M'Tume Heath (conga drums and auxiliary percussion) and bass guitarist Michael Henderson. Between the 1971 departure of pianist Keith Jarrett and the mid-1980s, the Davis band often appeared without a keyboard instrument. Davis did, however, occasionally use one himself to begin pieces by setting up a mood with chords and rhythms. After 1971 he almost always carried at least one guitarist, sometimes using three at the same time.[16] Beginning in the mid-1980s, Davis again carried two keyboardists, as he had done briefly during the early 1970s. He also added a guitarist and a saxophonist.

Trumpet Style

For the new jazz-rock idiom, Davis added new dimensions to his trumpet style. As he had done on many live recordings of the 1960s, he again played fast, sweeping runs in and out of his extreme high register. He wired his instrument to an amplifier and connected electronic attachments which simulated echo (by means of a tape loop device called an Echoplex, evident on the title track from *Bitches Brew*). Sometimes he created alterations of tone color by means of the wah-wah pedal (evident on "Sivad" in *Live-Evil*). He could be quite violent and sound much like a rock guitarist, or he could play in the tender, mournful manner he had displayed on *Porgy and Bess* and *Sketches of Spain.*

Sometimes most of the band would become silent while Davis quietly played with only one other musician, but that was rare. Usually the mood was very outgoing and full of unrelenting tension. The level of musicianship was very high, and the complexity of the music set it apart from rock. It was often quite similar, however, to the loud turbulence of many rock bands of the 1960s and 1970s. Admiration for such non-jazz musicians as Jimi Hendrix and Billy Preston was evident in Davis's music. The post-1968 Davis recordings displayed a blend of the jazz tradition, funk music, and the music of India and South America. It was infused with the spirit of Coltrane, but the tone colors were those of rock.

1980s Formula

The mid- and late-1980s recordings of Davis sometimes contained unimprovised accompaniments produced for him by Robert Irving III and Marcus Miller. Davis added his trumpet sound to funk vamps that had been prepared by computerized synthesizers. His formula for much of the 1980s was to employ a Jimi Hendrix disciple on guitar and a Coltrane disciple on saxophone, both of whom could play hot solos on demand. This was placed atop thick layers of sounds produced by electronic keyboards, a drummer playing in a funk style that had been adapted for the Davis bands by Al Foster, and a bassist playing in the funk style of Marcus Miller. Davis rarely allowed his keyboardists to solo. His music of this period was highly arranged and not as freewheeling and explosively daring as in the period of *Live-Evil*, *Black Beauty*, and *Agharta*. It was energetic, however, and its sound usually remained distinguishable from most pop music of the period.

◇JOHN MCLAUGHLIN

John McLaughlin (b. 1942) is a British guitarist who had been active in British rock bands[17] and jazz groups since the late 1950s. He first became known to American musicians during the period 1969–1971 when he began playing with Lifetime, the fusion band of drummer Tony Williams, and when he started recording with Miles Davis (see footnote 12).

McLaughlin is notable for his phenomenally high level of instrumental proficiency, and he has become one of the most prominent jazz guitarists since Wes Montgomery. Despite his being considered a jazz musician, McLaughlin used a tone which was unlike traditional jazz guitar quality. It was hard, not soft, cutting, not smooth, and metallic, not warm. In short, it had the color and texture preferred by rock guitarists, not jazz guitarists. Also, he frequently altered the size and shape of his tone by use of a wah-wah pedal and a phase shifter. (The phase shifter produces a subtle swirling of the sound.) Another point of contrast between McLaughlin and more traditional jazz guitarists is that most of his improvisations contain far less of the pronounced syncopation and the easy, relaxed, swing feeling that had previously typified jazz. Improvisations in McLaughlin performances were unlike the bouncy conception which was part of the Charlie Christian, Wes Montgomery, and Kenny Burrell styles. McLaughlin performances also lacked the gentle lyricism that characterizes improvisations by Jim Hall.

The syncopations in John McLaughlin's lines were more typical of rock than of jazz. And his solos were often composed of long strings of sixteenth notes periodically interrupted by held tones which McLaughlin expressively distorted in waveform and in pitch. The inflections he preferred were refinements of those customary in rock and in blues guitar playing. McLaughlin's rhythmic conception and his melodic conception had more in common with classical music and the 1960s improvisations of John Coltrane than with standard bop practice. In his long lines of sixteenth notes, he often chose sequences reminiscent of the patterns used by Coltrane. Both McLaughlin and Coltrane had studied the music of India and were fond of basing their solos on modes learned from this study.

During the early 1970s, McLaughlin played a custom-made electric guitar with two necks, one with six and the other with twelve strings. He also worked with the vina, a seven-string Indian instrument that has four playing strings and three accompanying strings. During the late 1970s, he played another specially built instrument inspired by the vina, with a form like an autoharp's, a scalloped fingerboard and accompanying strings.

McLaughlin's work in Lifetime and in his own Mahavishnu Orchestra projected unusually high intensity, partly due to high amplifier settings and a stress on rapidfire, multinoted themes with extremely busy accompaniment. The interaction and determination displayed by such Mahavishnu albums as his 1971 *Inner Mounting Flame* and his 1972 *Birds of Fire* come from a high level of cooperation and mutual inspiration between drummer

John McLaughlin, virtuoso guitarist-composer who led the Mahavishnu Orchestra, a top fusion band of the 1970s.

Photo by Bill Smith

Billy Cobham, electric bass guitarist Rick Laird, and electric pianist/synthesist Jan Hammer. Many listeners feel that these recordings remain benchmarks for ensemble cohesion and inspired jazz-rock improvisation. Feeling for this music was so high that *Birds of Fire* in 1973 reached the very high position of number 15 on *Billboard's* record sales chart in the popular album category. Most jazz albums never even reach position number 200. These two Mahavishnu albums are also distinctive for their use of irregular meters—time signatures which, though common to Indian music, had previously been rare in jazz and rock.[18] Many listeners consider this to have been the greatest of all fusion bands.

Not all of McLaughlin's 1970s output consisted of high-intensity electronic music. He also recorded on hollow-body guitar in his 1970 *My Goal's Beyond,*[19] an album which McLaughlin personally lists among his favorite works. It contains one side of overdubbed, self-accompanying, solo guitar improvisations and one side with saxophone, violin, acoustic bass, and drums. There is an expansive and exhilarated feeling in the solo side, especially in McLaughlin's rendering of his original composition "Follow Your Heart." Though he left the nonelectric approach for a few years right after this album, McLaughlin returned to it when touring and recording with Shakti, an Indian music ensemble comprised of violin, tabla, mrindagam, and ghatam. His fondness for the nonelectronic sound also emerged in what many fans consider to contain his best solo: "Rene's Theme," a duet with fellow guitarist Larry Coryell on

Coryell's *Spaces*[20] album of 1970. This pairing with Coryell recurred during the 1980s when McLaughlin toured in duo and trio with several other guitar giants, all playing hollow-body guitar: Coryell, Al Dimeola, Christian Escoude, and Spanish flamenco guitarist Paco de Lucia.

◇LARRY CORYELL

Guitarist **Larry Coryell** (b. 1943) is especially significant in jazz history because he was one of the first to blend the styles of country music, blues guitar, and rock with established jazz styles. He did this during the mid-1960s while playing in the bands of drummer Chico Hamilton and vibraharpist Gary Burton. Coryell's own group, the Free Spirits, was also active in 1966, well before the historic rise of rock-influenced jazz groups in 1969 and 1970 (see footnote 6). Burton had been attracted to Coryell's work with the Free Spirits and the possibilities that it suggested for jazz. The 1967 *Duster* album contains several passages in which Coryell solos in a style clearly drawn from rock (see footnote 7). Burton and his other sidemen follow Coryell's lead and manage to approximate the flavor and intensity of Coryell's work. Burton further pursued this avenue with guitarist Jerry Hahn on a 1968 album called *Country Roads and Other Places,* and then continued to employ excellent guitarists who were interested in combining country music, rock, and jazz. Along the way, Burton introduced Mick Goodrick and Pat Metheny.[21]

The Free Spirits, Foreplay (Coryell's 1969–1972 band), and the Eleventh House (a later band) were all jazz-rock groups, but Coryell was not strictly a rock guitarist. As early as his time with Chico Hamilton, Coryell had proven himself to be an unusually imaginative and technically proficient improviser of jazz lines. His playing could be distinguished from McLaughlin's because Coryell's note beginnings were more percussive; they had more "pop." In addition, he was given to greater variety in his solos than McLaughlin. The twists and

Guitarist Larry Coryell, one of the first musicians to devise original combinations of jazz, rock, and country music. He began a series of innovative bands during the late 1960s.

The Jazz Image

turns in Coryell's lines suggested more jazz roots. All these comparisons are easy to make because McLaughlin performed on Coryell's *Spaces* album, which documents a time when both guitarists were at a peak of creativity and technical prowess.[22]

◇JOSEF ZAWINUL

Joe Zawinul (b. 1932) is a pianist and composer who moved from his native Vienna, Austria, to the United States in 1959. His first great impact was made with the bands of saxophonist Cannonball Adderley between 1961 and 1970, during which time he authored two of the band's most popular funk hits, "Mercy, Mercy, Mercy"[23] and "Walk Tall." His next great success came when Miles Davis used his "In a Silent Way" as the title track for a 1969 album which pioneered the fusion of jazz improvisation with electronic instruments and funk accompaniment patterns. Davis also included Zawinul's "Pharaoh's Dance" on *Bitches Brew* and used Zawinul as chief arranger for *In a Silent Way* and *Bitches Brew.*

In 1971 Zawinul founded an innovative jazz-rock fusion band called Weather Report. With this band's 1977 *Heavy Weather*[24] album, he enjoyed his greatest record sales since "Mercy, Mercy, Mercy." (The album became a certified "gold" album because it sold more than 500,000 copies.) It contained Zawinul's "Birdland," an arrangement of catchy, syncopated phrases in extended repetition. This piece was inspired by the composer's memories of hearing the Count Basie band at the New York nightclub called Birdland. It epitomizes the danceable, riff-band style favored by Basie, though translated here into jazz-rock. "Birdland" received wide exposure in discotheques and in recordings by the Maynard Ferguson big band and the vocal group Manhattan Transfer. It was later redone for a Quincy Jones album called *Back on the Block.* (Listen to the original "Birdland" at the beginning of the *Jazz Classics CD.* It is positioned immediately following Count Basie's "One O'Clock Jump" so that listeners can compare Zawinul's approach with the music that inspired it. The complete recording is on the *Classics CD* for *Concise Guide to Jazz.*)

Wayne Shorter (soprano saxophone), Miroslav Vitous (bass), and Joe Zawinul (piano), founding members of Weather Report and masters of collective improvisation. Pictured here in the early 1970s. (Listen to these musicians play "Surucucu" on the *Jazz Classics CD.*)

Photo by Bill Smith

Listening Guide for

"SURUCUCU"

Composed by Wayne Shorter; recorded January 13, 1972 in Tokyo, Japan by Weather Report: Wayne Shorter (soprano sax), Joe Zawinul (piano), Miroslav Vitous (bass), Dom Um Romao (auxiliary percussion and vocal), and Eric Gravatt (drums); available on the *Jazz Classics CD;* also available on Weather Report, *I Sing the Body Electric* (Columbia: CK 46107 [31352],1971–72).

Weather Report originated numerous approaches in their fifteen-year career. (An excerpt from their biggest hit concludes the African American retentions sequence at the beginning of the *Jazz Classics CD.*) Though most famous for their funk music performed with electric instruments and their role as the premier jazz-rock fusion band, they are also historically significant for the way they loosened the roles of the rhythm section instruments and spontaneously devised collective interplay that was smoother and pleased more listeners than similar "free" jazz of the 1960s. Aside from the music on the band's first album (*Weather Report,* Columbia PC 30661), little of this loosely organized work is demonstrated in their studio recordings. We are therefore fortunate to have this concert recording available as documentation.

This performance draws partly upon a composed theme, Wayne Shorter's "Surucucu." But the musicians do not neatly divide their improvisations into a set number of beats that parallel the theme, nor do they use the theme to provide a chord progression that strictly prescribes the motion of harmonies for improvisation. The arrangement is spontaneous, and the theme is represented only in very fragmented form, a phrase here and there being played out of tempo by Shorter. Moreover, the sequence of sections here does not follow the traditional pattern of introduction, theme, solo choruses, theme, end.

Most of the sounds in this performance will be unfamiliar. The first sound was made by Dom Um Romao slapping his face and changing the shape of his mouth while making vocal sounds articulated by quick tongue movements. The zither-like sounds that accompany Romao's voice are produced by Joe Zawinul playing what is technically termed "prepared piano." Before the performance, he had prepared the piano strings by laying weights on top of some, wedging pieces of rubber between others, attaching clothes pins to others. Zawinul caused the piano strings to vibrate sometimes by plucking them himself and sometimes by depressing the piano keys in the conventional manner.

To appreciate how the music of Weather Report is unique, it is helpful to notice what is not heard: walking bass, ride rhythms, comping, and bop style horn solos. (Compare the "Surucucu" performance, for instance, with the playing of Chick Corea, Miroslav Vitous, and Roy Haynes on "Steps" on the *Jazz Classics CD.*) It is also important to recognize that the piece hangs together and has its own momentum without depending on many of the devices that propel standard jazz performances. There are exceptions. Vitous does briefly play repeating patterns on bass, as at 1' 25" into the piece, and Gravatt sometimes maintains long strings of repeated eighth notes distributed across different cymbals and drums, for example at 1' 33". Their most common practice, however, is to invent variations on steady rhythmic figures rather than strict repetitions of them.

Elapsed Time	
0' 0"	voice, accompanied by prepared piano and the sounds of Romao slapping his own face
0' 27"	chords on prepared piano (to 39")
0' 34"	the tinkling of a triangle
0' 45"	trills played on a wooden flute
0' 53"	Percussion enters; bass sustains deep-pitched tones.
1' 07"	wire brushes playing snare drum and cymbals (to 1' 15")
1' 10"	slide whistle
1' 18"	Bass interjects sporadic comments.
1' 20"	Timekeeping rhythms begin on cymbals struck with drum sticks.
1' 25"	resonant, low pitched tones of highly amplified bass viol, played pizzicato in a timekeeping manner, accompanied by cymbals
1' 27"	Zawinul strumming the strings inside the piano (to 1' 50")
1' 33"	a single squawk from Shorter's soprano sax steadily repeating eighth notes on drums and cymbals
1' 39"	chords played on prepared piano
1' 50"	a sequence of sustained sax tones (to 2' 32") (a paraphrase of the "Surucucu" melody) accompanied by acoustic piano
2' 17"	Zawinul strumming the strings inside the piano
2' 20"	"Surucucu" melody in ascending sax tones which are detached from each other, ending with a high, scream-like sound and fall-off at 2' 30"
2' 34"	Rhythm section unwinds, then resumes its pace.
2' 40"	strumming inside piano (to 2' 50")
2' 55"	high-pitched descending arpeggios on piano
3' 05"	stop-time
3' 07"	Zawinul plays highly amplified Fender Rhodes electric piano and makes it sound like the distorted tone of a rock musician's electric guitar (to 3' 35").
3' 30"	Sax and electric piano improvise against each other, accompanied by bass and percussion (to 3' 53").
3' 53"	Shorter acts as though a member of the rhythm section by producing an unaccompanied, repeating figure in a fast staccato manner.
4' 01"	Shorter's staccato figure accompanies Vitous, who has abandoned an accompanying role in favor of a melodic line played by bowing highly amplified upright bass.
4' 04"	duet between legato sax and bass (to 4' 36")
4' 15"	fade out

Zawinul has made significant contributions in the use of electronic instruments for jazz. He had used the Wurlitzer electric piano on Adderley's 1966 recording of "Mercy, Mercy, Mercy," and he subsequently employed a Fender Rhodes electric piano on tour. Singer-bandleader Ray Charles had previously carried electric piano, as had Sun Ra, but it was not common in jazz until Zawinul began using it. Miles Davis was so taken with the Fender Rhodes when he heard Zawinul playing it in Adderley's band that he required its use by three successive pianists in his own bands—Herbie Hancock, Chick Corea, and Keith Jarrett—thereby influencing subsequent work by those men with their own groups. The Rhodes became the most common keyboard instrument in jazz groups of the 1970s; even such non-fusion pianists as Bill Evans and Oscar Peterson recorded with it. Zawinul was also one of the first musicians to master the Oberheim Polyphonic[25] and the Arp and Prophet synthesizers, as well as the ring modulator.[26]

One of the leading composers of the 1970s, Zawinul demonstrated a creativity which parallels that of Charles Mingus in the 1950s and Duke Ellington in the 1940s. He generated a broader variety of melodic and accompaniment rhythms than possibly any other jazz composer of the 1970s. Zawinul wrote numerous pieces that touched highly diverse tone colors and moods. Throughout his albums with Weather Report run playful melodies with highly imaginative accompaniments.[27] His "In a Silent Way" and "Arrival in New York" are impressionistic tone poems.[28]

Zawinul encouraged the use of a wide assortment of exotic percussion instruments by his musicians. He himself produced unusual timbres and rhythms by playing clay drum, tambura, xylophone, steel drums, and African thumb piano. Gentle sounds are conjured by ocarina, hollow-body guitar, thumb piano, and tambura on his "Jungle Book."[29] And like Ellington, Zawinul arranged wordless vocals.[30] The breadth of timbral spectra in Weather Report's work might explain how Zawinul's music found its way onto the turntables of demonstration units in stereo equipment stores. Weather Report's creations had joined symphonic music as a vast source of varied timbres and loudnesses by which to judge the quality of sound systems.

◇WEATHER REPORT

When Joe Zawinul left Cannonball Adderley's quintet in 1971, he joined saxophonist Wayne Shorter and bassist Miroslav Vitous to develop new concepts in improvisatory music for a band they called Weather Report. Zawinul, Shorter, and Vitous were joined by two drummers. One played on conventional drum set, and one played exotic percussion instruments, creating sound effects for which Airto Moreira had become known in the bands of Miles Davis. It should be noted that Weather Report performed in a broad range of styles that combined jazz with non-jazz styles in original ways, thereby "fusing" assortments of different styles. In other words, they invented some of their own styles, but only a few of them qualify as jazz-rock fusion. **The collective improvisation of musical textures and the emancipation of rhythm section instruments from conventional roles were significant aspects of Weather Report's approach.**

Miroslav Vitous was a bassist uniquely able to improvise melodies as well as the average horn player, and he had already demonstrated his ability to alternate roles when he abandoned the timekeeping role in several selections on his own album *Infinite Search.*[31] Vitous had a sophisticated melodic sense that put him in a class with such outstanding bass soloists as Paul Chambers and Scott LaFaro. He was also very capable with bowed bass. Vitous had a keen sense of what to play for the sake of creating interesting rhythmic textures and how to keep his instrument's voice in sensitive musical conversations with other group members. Vitous did not merely break up walking bass lines or play in a decorative-two feeling. **The Vitous contributions to Weather Report included fragmented melody statements, bowed sustained tones, and syncopated interjections.** He could just as easily bow melody in unison with a sax line as feed rock-style bass figures into the group texture. Vitous could play in unison with a rhythm the drummer was stating on ride cymbal or underscore a pattern being played on piano. Or he could quickly go back and forth. Vitous had cast off the restraints of traditional bass playing and become a textural improviser in the Weather Report context. Moreover, his work made sense, too. It was not just the flashy playing of a gifted showoff. (Listen to Vitous on "Surucucu" on the *Jazz Classics CD.*)

Airto Moreira overdubbed percussion parts in the recording studio for Weather Report's first album. Though he never performed with the band, his imaginative, highly original use of Latin American percussion instruments provided a model for the unique combination of sounds that Weather Report refined. Dom Um Romao, another outstanding Brazilian percussionist, was the band's regular percussionist. Within a few weeks of the band's inception, Eric Gravatt became the band's regular drummer. The band then underwent numerous personnel changes, and, by the mid-1970s, bassist Miroslav Vitous was gone and the only founding members who remained were Shorter and Zawinul. Then after 1985, Shorter and Zawinul were leading separate groups.

Weather Report came on the scene with the standard instrumentation of saxophone, piano, bass, and drums. They also had an auxiliary percussionist, but that was not unusual; many 1950s and 1960s jazz groups had employed conga drummers or other auxiliary percussionists to add a Latin American flavor to their sound. What was unusual is that in its earliest albums, **Weather Report did not use its conventional instrumentation in conventional ways.** It was rare for bassist Miroslav Vitous to play walking lines, or for the drummer to play standard ride rhythms or snap the high-hat closed sharply on every other beat. Zawinul usually did not comp for Shorter, and the auxiliary percussionist was not restricted to the conga drum.[32]

Collective Improvisation

Weather Report explored an unusual approach to combo improvisation on their first three albums.[33] (On the *Jazz Classics CD,* this approach is exemplified in "Surucucu," from Weather Report's *I Sing the Body Electric.*) **Instead of adhering to roles consistent with bop traditions, the instruments in Weather Report performed a variety of different roles.** Spurts of melody might come from any member, not just from the saxophone. Rhythmic figures and fills could come from any member, not just from a bassist or drummer.

The kinds of interaction between members were so varied that **in some pieces there was no distinction between soloist and accompanist.** One player's sound might stand out momentarily from the ensemble texture, but it soon blended into the overall texture again. In this situation, every member had to be capable of playing melodically as well as merely adding to the overall texture of the group sound in a nonmelodic fashion. Weather Report's members developed special techniques for managing such tasks. (See chapter 3 for an explanation of standard jazz solo and accompaniment roles.)

The swing and bop convention of solo choruses was not evident on Weather Report's first album. One particular voice such as saxophone, piano, or bass did often hold the focal point for a few moments. However, it maintained much more continuity with the entire piece than did conventional jazz solos. Swing and bop style soloists had adhered to fixed chorus lengths and they were improvising without much regard for whether mood or color was developed or continued from the preceding solo.

In Weather Report's first three albums, each member's work contributed to the prevailing mood and color rather than to a solo concept. They did not usually feature themselves. They played primarily to serve the group sound. This produced a variety of consistently maintained musical feelings and flavors. Weather Report offered a greater variety of moods and sound textures than most bop, cool, and hard bop groups. Only bands led by such versatile composers as Duke Ellington, Charles Mingus, and Sun Ra had achieved comparable breadth.[34]

Away from Improvised Textures

Weather Report did not entirely abandon collective approaches, but much of their work after their 1973 *Sweetnighter* album left collectively improvised approaches in favor of more repeated, prewritten themes and preset rhythm section figures. Many of these rhythms were freshly devised by Zawinul, not borrowed from Latin American or funk music models. With *Sweetnighter,* Weather Report began including more compositions constructed of brief phrases repeated continually and accompanied by a more repetitive, funk-influenced rhythm section style. With this new emphasis on repetition and funk, Zawinul sought to capture a larger segment of the record-buying market. And, as exemplified by "Boogie Woogie Waltz" on *Sweetnighter,* this music departed from the style of the band's earlier innovations. Their discotheque hit "Birdland" on their 1977 *Heavy Weather* album exemplifies these methods. The new strategy led to wider popular acceptance of the band. Much of Weather Report's music during the 1980s, especially the pieces without Shorter, is essentially party music. It was conceptually less daring than the group's earliest efforts. When we consider Weather Report's music, we must distinguish between the collectively improvised and the preset-highly repetitive phases.

Historical Significance

In summary, Weather Report is significant in jazz history for a number of different reasons.

1) Their first three albums
   a) brought simultaneous collective improvisation to a new level of refinement
   b) offered collective improvisation that was rhythmically compelling at the same time as it was rich with wide-ranging tone colors;
   c) demonstrated the improvisation of textures more than jazz solo lines and did this in a way that was palatable to much larger audiences than previous attempts had attracted.
2) Their group concept afforded a unique opportunity for emancipation of the bassist from bop roles.
3) The band evolved a form of jazz-funk that featured more improvisation than most other fusion bands used.
4) It was one of the first fusion bands to achieve popular recognition without using vocals.
5) It made more original and extensive use of exotic rhythms than previous jazz groups.
6) The band combined the talents of several jazz giants and gave them a unique platform for creative composing and improvising.

◇JACO PASTORIUS

In 1976, bass guitarist **Jaco Pastorius** (1951–1987) joined Weather Report. To understand the roles he assumed in the band, note the four ways Zawinul called upon his bassists to perform. First is the standard jazz technique of **walking bass** (as demonstrated by Miroslav Vitous on "Eurydice" in Weather Report's first album, CBS 30661). Second is a **nonrepetitive, interactive approach** (exemplified by Scott LaFaro's work with the 1961 Bill Evans trio in "Solar" on the *Jazz Classics CD*). This was demonstrated by Miroslav Vitous in his improvisations within "Waterfall" on Weather Report's first album. This technique requires that the bassist second-guess his colleagues, discreetly omit many notes, and play only when it will do the most good. It also demands considerable imagination. Third is what is commonly called **funk bass** (see page 427 for notations). This is the repetition of highly syncopated bass figures, often filled with staccato notes, that are played with a contagious feeling that moves people in a way peculiar to funk music. These types of figures were common in the popular dance music of the 1970s and 1980s. This technique was not a specialty for Miroslav Vitous, though it was for his replacement, Alphonso Johnson. The fourth role of the bassist in Weather Report was to **solo.** This was, however, not a high priority for Weather Report bassists until Pastorius joined the group. Pastorius was outstanding in all four bass roles. He walked persuasively.[35] He played in the nonrepetitive, interactive style.[36] He played funk style with great naturalness.[37]

Pastorius appreciably altered the character of Weather Report's sound and the rhythmic feeling that went with it.[38] The bassist's fluid tone, his use of vibrato at the end of some notes, and his ease of playing all combined with his high energy and playful spirit to propel the band in a lighthearted way not previously part of the group's sound. In Pastorius, Zawinul found an enticing soloist with all the other qualities he had originally sought from Miroslav Vitous and Alphonso Johnson. And he discovered a versatile and original composer who contributed "Barbary Coast," "Teen Town," "Havona," "Punk Jazz," "River People," and "Three Views of a Secret" to the Weather Report repertory.

Weather Report concerts during the late 1970s always featured an unaccompanied Pastorius solo. The bassist drew upon electronic means for altering sound in ways reminiscent of guitarist Jimi Hendrix. Pastorius used playback echo to provide spontaneous accompaniments for his improvisations. He extracted chords from his instrument and capitalized on overtones to orchestrate his performance as though he had an entire band behind him. He demonstrated the same prodigious speed that had impressed listeners who heard his 1976 recording of the intricate bop melody "Donna Lee."[39]

In 1982, Pastorius left Weather Report and launched his own unique group called Word of Mouth. Using no keyboard instruments or guitars for chording, Pastorius employed trumpet and saxophone paired with steel drum and his bass to state melody lines. On this band's first album,[40] he employed the sound of harmonica as well as thick-textured ensemble writing at times reminiscent of Gil Evans and Thad Jones. Like Zawinul, Pastorius used the gentle sound of children's voices as an additional seasoning in his timbral repertory.[41] Diversity was the byword of his presentations. Pastorius explored a unique spectrum of tonal textures. He tapped orchestral music and the music of the Caribbean as well as American pop styles such as soul music.

Pastorius set the pace for a new generation of jazz bassists. He became the most imitated bassist after Jimmy Blanton, Paul Chambers, and Scott LaFaro. Many talented bassists entered the jazz scene during the 1970s and 1980s. And because electric bass guitar was the instrument most preferred in jazz and jazz-rock fusion groups of the 1970s, there was a great need for an inspiring model to imitate. Pastorius became that model, in part because he received wide exposure as a result of Weather Report's wide popularity. Pastorius also became a model because the speed and grace with which he played were almost hypnotizing. Practice rooms were soon humming with the sounds of bass guitarists attempting to duplicate the Pastorius rendition of "Donna Lee." However, Pastorius held the attention of new bassists not just with his speed. He impressed them also with a special tone quality comprised of overtones that were not associated with funk bassists or jazz bassists. It had a high center of gravity and a slippery texture. He capitalized on overtones that allowed his instrument to project a delicacy that had not been associated with it before. The way he used it also departed from tradition. He played his rhythmic figures with a very graceful legato quality that any classical orchestra player would be proud to produce. He imparted a singing quality to his solo lines and to many of his accompanying lines as well. By the mid-1980s, numerous fusion records were being issued which made fans listen very closely before they knew the sound was not Pastorius but merely a facile Pastorius disciple. However, even if the disciples succeeded in replicating his tone and speed, their playing could be distinguished from the model by the boldness and vigor of Pastorius's ideas and the swaggering character with which he carried them out.

◇PAT METHENY

Pat Metheny (b. 1954) is a guitarist-composer-bandleader who became one of the biggest names in jazz of the 1970s and 1980s. His initial exposure came as a featured soloist with vibraharpist Gary Burton's group from 1974 to 1977 (see footnote 21). He then formed his own group with keyboardist Lyle Mays and continued with it throughout the 1980s. Originally influenced by Wes Montgomery, Metheny also incorporated elements of country music and the approach of Ornette Coleman in the process of developing his own unique style. Many of his compositions and solo improvisations have a twangy, loping, country-music flavor. Known for his good taste and excellent sense of balance, he plays with an inspired lyricism that makes his solos flow gracefully and naturally. There is a remarkable evenness to his playing. In fact, Metheny plays syncopated rhythms in such a smooth way that they don't sound syncopated. His lines are nearly always legato, and his facility is so good that each note is cleanly played and linked smoothly to the next. Among guitarists, Metheny is also known for popularizing a sound that depends partly on electronic means for reverberating his notes by means of studio-quality equipment that he carried with him. (Listen to examples on the *Demo CD* Track 97.)[42] His affinity for Ornette Coleman and for Keith Jarrett, who has roots in Coleman, make Metheny's style especially compatible with that of his pianist, Lyle Mays, a Jarrett disciple. Together, Mays and Metheny have pioneered lush combinations of electronic alterations of keyboard and guitar sounds and integrated them rhythmically into an original quartet concept.[43] Their group sound is remarkably spacious and uncluttered. The music conveys a clear sense of openness. Though some of his music from the late 1980s falls into the "new age" category, Metheny might best be viewed as a fusion player who is sufficiently versatile and creative to play well in a number of different jazz styles. In fact, he even recorded an extremely turbulent album of free jazz with Ornette Coleman.[44]

◇NEW AGE

During the 1980s a new idiom of popular music surfaced. Record stores initially did not have bins for displaying it. So clerks placed it in the jazz bins because they thought it sounded more like jazz than like classical music or rock. Even after this music earned a bin of its own, much of the public continued to call it jazz. Record store clerks sometimes described it as a mixture of jazz and classical music, or "classical jazz," and it was found in the jazz bins of many stores even at the end of the decade.

Though new age music employs improvisation as one of its methods, that is about all it has in common with most jazz. It does not swing. In fact, its rhythms are purposely designed to avoid creating any of the tension that jazz swing feeling requires. The methods for creating this music prevent evoking tension in other ways, too. Harmony is not dissonant. Tone qualities are soft and smooth. Changes are made only in the most gradual ways. Often the same chord or mode remains in effect for an entire performance. Sound levels are usually low and remain that way for long stretches. Changes in loudness are rarely sudden. Models for this music were provided by modern classical composers Lamonte Young, Terry Riley, Philip Glass, and Steve Reich. Those composers, in turn, had been influenced by Gregorian chant music as well as the sounds of nature—wind and waves, for example—and such continuous industrial sounds as an air conditioner's steady hum. Since these composers reduced music to a bare minimum of materials and activity, their musical approach was called "minimalism." Some of their music superficially resembled some of the unaccompanied piano improvisations of Keith Jarrett during the 1970s, as well as the solo piano pieces of French impressionist composers Claude Debussy and Maurice Ravel that had inspired some of Jarrett's work. Both products were calm and soothing. Neither projected jazz swing feeling. Much of it explored the sonorities of a single chord or brief chord progression.[45] The Paul Winter Consort and its spin-off group, Oregon, made music like this. Harpist Andreas Vollenweider promoted a similar sound and gained considerable popularity for it during the 1980s. Pianist George Winston imitated Jarrett's long, vamp-based improvisations that meander and seem soothing. Winston's records sold millions of copies, his concerts packed auditoriums, and his style was dubbed "new age."[46]

◇SMOOTH JAZZ

Many of the radio stations that had broadcast New Age format during the 1980s gradually introduced music having more active and louder drumming, more intrusive bass lines, and rougher sounding saxophones. This is quieted, refined funk music. It lacks the intensity of major jazz styles, such as hard bop, for instance. Improvised solos are stylized rather than adventuresome. Many listeners choose to have this music around them because they find it pleasant and just as easy to ignore as to hear. In other words, it is background music with a beat. Musicians dubbed it "fuzak" because it is jazz-rock fusion as soft and pleasant as the highly processed music that was once piped into office buildings' elevators, marketed by the Muzak company, informally termed "elevator music." Most styles of jazz have had their easy-listening variants, and this is fusion's.

A few of the bands making such music had jazz backgrounds: The Crusaders, Yellow Jackets, and Spyro Gyra, for example. (Only some of their work fit this style.) Several established jazz musicians appeared in a variety of contexts playing this style, among them: pianist Bob James,[47] guitarists Lee Ritenour, Larry Carlton, Earl Klugh,[48] and George Benson.[49] For them, it was an additional style in which to become fluent. Bob James had already recorded avant-garde jazz and accompanied singer Sarah Vaughan during the 1960s and then composed for movies and television in the 1970s. George Benson had toured with hard bop groups in the 1960s. Like Louis Jordan, Earl Bostic, and King Curtis, their pop jazz predecessors of the 1940s and 50s, these musicians chose not to play the intricate and extended improvisations they were capable of. Instead they played simpler music whose improvisations were more obviously melodic. These improvisations were consequently more accessible to most listeners. This was done to ensure musicians their livelihoods, and it worked as well for them as it had for their predecessors.

During the late 1980s and early 1990s, some radio stations characterized this fare as "light jazz and soft rock." By the mid-1990s, most New Age radio formats had been replaced by this refined funk music, now called "smooth jazz" and "cool jazz." Historically these terms were unfortunate designations because the music sounded no smoother than ballads of the swing era, and it had nothing in common with cool jazz of the 1950s. Furthermore, a portion of the programming was music not derived from jazz. So omitting the "and soft rock" designation during the late 1990s further confused the classification.

Smooth jazz became quite popular. By the late 1990s it was the fastest growing radio format. Among the most prominent saxophonists who specialized in this style were Grover Washington, Jr., Kenny G, and Najee. Each of these men also had a number of imitators. Between 1986 and 1995, sales of some Kenny G albums ran into the millions of copies.[50] This means, for example, that sales of just one of his albums (as many as four to seven million copies) would exceed all the recordings ever sold by Charlie Parker and John Coltrane combined. *Though perceived by many musicians as more decorative than substantial, the music of Kenny G and smooth jazz defined jazz for a very large segment of American listeners during the 1980s and 90s.* Unlike other modern jazz, this sound was not relegated to small nightclubs and limited-range radio stations, but heard frequently in airports and banks, auditoriums, and arenas.

During the 1950s and 60s, background music radio stations and the Muzak company offered instrumental pop music, partly derived from sounds of the swing era from a decade or two earlier. Then during the 1980s and 90s, many background music stations became dedicated to smooth jazz, modelled after some pop music of a decade or two earlier. Models include 1965–68 recordings of Wes Montgomery,[51] the 1972–1980 work of Grover Washington, Jr.,[52] some of the more subdued approaches within the late 1970s output of Weather Report,[53] and the most refined of Motown. But unlike its Muzak/background music antecedents, this radio format programmed selections which usually contained improvised solos. *The extent of improvisation was one element which qualified smooth jazz as jazz, rather than merely a continuation of the instrumental pop tradition of background music.*

◇ACID JAZZ

The term "acid jazz" was coined during 1987 by English disc jockeys Gilles Peterson and Chris Bangs at a weekend-long party in England where each room provided a different kind of music. One was a type of dance music originating in Detroit and Chicago called "house music." Some of it was intended to accompany the effects of taking the drugs called "ecstasy," and LSD, nicknamed "acid." So it became known as "acid house music." Announcing the availability of jazz in one of the rooms, Peterson reportedly remarked to the partiers, "Now that you've had your fill of 'acid house,' we're going to give you acid jazz." Though originally offered as a joke, the term was soon applied whenever disc jockeys combined current pop dance music with excerpts from old jazz albums. Gilles Peterson and other British disc jockeys particularly liked funky hard bop recordings of the 1960s from the Blue Note and Prestige firms, sometimes by Art Blakey, Horace Silver, Lou Donaldson, Herbie Hancock, and Grant Green. Gilles Peterson's firm, in turn, founded a subsidiary called Acid Jazz, and some of the groups they hired thereby defined the genre.[54] Like the swing style of the 1930s and 40s, acid style first functioned primarily as dance music. Some of it later came to serve just as well for "easy listening," and some acid jazz recordings found a place on "smooth jazz" radio broadcasts.

At the same time, rap groups were beginning to borrow jazz sounds. They had at least two reasons. First, they needed a new way to get accompaniments cheaply. So they were excerpting the introductions, during which the pace and feeling of the original selections were established. In the early years, they borrowed accompaniment riffs from the funkiest of jazz records because the riffs helped provide a continuous pattern of repeating rhythms under their rap. Second, some rappers believed that their performance would gain a jazz flavor if any element associated with jazz were incorporated. This might consist of a brief part of a trumpet or saxophone improvisation, a few piano chords that typified jazz of the 1960s or 70s, a walking bass pattern, or a jazz drummer's ride rhythm. Some rappers felt that just naming famous jazz musicians within the rap itself would make their product more hip.

Within some acid jazz selections, even those without rap, jazz horn work is overdubbed in a way that merely decorates whatever else is happening. It is not the main focus of attention.[55] For example, sometimes horn sounds provided only minor coloration, while the drum beat remains the most prominent aspect of the sound. This reversed the roles traditionally occupied in most jazz. Drums were background, while horns were foreground. *Though using jazz solos as decoration reversed the trend for jazz, it continued a long tradition in popular music.* "Hot solos," as they were called, had been added to otherwise nonjazz pieces as early as the 1920s. They were commonly included in performances by rhythm and blues singers of the 1940s and 50s. Rock and roll bands frequently carried a saxophonist for this purpose in the 1950s. Soul and funk bands of the 1960s and 70s had used brief jazz improvisations.

Sampling

Much of acid jazz depends upon electronically excerpting portions of old albums. This procedure is called "sampling." Among producers, the term is used in two slightly different ways. The older meaning refers to recording samples of a given instrument's tone from each pitch range. The result remains stored in a computer to be altered according to the programmer's wishes. Entire melodies and accompaniments can be pasted together by electronically changing the pitch and rhythms of that tone. The synthesizers can even determine the ways that tones begin and end. In this way, the programmer can give them the character of a live hornman or human voice. This had been common in pop music products since at least the early 1980s.

The newer meaning for "sampling" is the one that applies more to acid jazz. Entire phrases from an old album are recorded into a computer. Then they are re-synthesized into another recording apparatus if a new album is being created. Or they are resynthesized into playback facilities if a disc jockey is using them spontaneously at a dance party. In some of the earliest acid jazz mixtures, disc jockeys sampled more than just accompaniment phrases. They excerpted a few moments of intact music from an old jazz album.[56] The particular way the phrases were mixed was determined by the creativity of the disc jockey. Performing these procedures became a career for disc jockeys who termed themselves **mixers.** When devised during a dance party, the resulting mixtures were not usually saved. When devised in the studio, however, the mixtures often became part of CDs that the disc jockey copyrighted and marketed as new material. Often he took credit for what he called "programming."

Looping

In many acid jazz selections, the instrumental phrase that was sampled came from the accompaniment portion of an old recording. It was then repeated continuously by a process called "looping." This produced an accompaniment groove. On top of this was placed (1) an assortment of additional sounds from samples or (2) electronically synthesized sources. Often the additions included (3) a loud snare drum sound on every other beat.[57] This is known as a "back beat" if it happens on the second and fourth of every group of four beats. Sometimes the addition was (4) a closed high-hat cymbal struck twice for each beat, thereby providing a continuous pulse. (5) A strong bass drum rhythm was also added in some mixes. Usually all these elements were combined. Then a collection of (6) new raps and (7) jazz improvisations were placed on top of that foundation.[58] In other words, *acid jazz was not invented by musicians. It was invented by disc jockeys and rap artists.*

Overdubbing

The methods for creating acid jazz were not entirely new. For instance, overdubbing had been used already for several decades in pop music. But among most jazz musicians and purist fans, it was considered cheating. Though it was uncommon in jazz until the 1970s, guitarist Wes Montgomery's popular recordings of the 1960s had expanded the practice.[59] By the 1980s, most of Miles Davis's albums used at least some overdubbing.[60] Also for more than a decade already, disc jockeys had been devising original mixtures by adding sound effects to recordings and by taking sounds from one recording and adding them to another.

Sampling was not new, either. For example, *by the mid-1980s, composer-arrangers owned electronic samples of most musical instrument sounds. This conveniently allowed composers to excerpt and reprocess sounds to create complete performances without hiring musicians. Producers had assumed the role of performers several years before the emergence of acid jazz. What was new with acid jazz was the extent to which disc jockeys became involved in making the music themselves, instead of only playing the work of others.* Musicians were hired by disc jockeys to record fresh improvisations on top of accompaniments prepared by synthesizer, drum machine, and loops.[61] Occasionally a disc jockey actually toured, as though a bandleader. He would plug in his playback equipment and allow one or two musicians to perform live music over the recorded sounds.

The converse of this situation had been presented by jazz musician Herbie Hancock when he added a disc jockey to his touring band to contribute his own original sounds. Some were made by scratching records with the stylus while the system was connected to loudspeakers. Some were achieved by mixing various sounds electronically. Hancock's hit recording "Rockit" had incorporated such sounds.

From selection to selection, the amount of improvised jazz that could be found in acid jazz varied widely. The term eventually became applied to hip hop music that was only slightly jazzy and usually did not have fresh jazz improvisation. In the mid1990s, "Acid Jazz" appeared on the labels of some recordings that contained only rap music.

Categories of Acid Jazz

As it evolved, acid jazz came to be applied to a wide assortment of music. Some, but not all, music under this umbrella can be loosely classified into three categories. (1) **Fusions devised by disc jockeys of jazz elements with various pop dance music styles** current from the mid-1980s into the 1990s, such as hip hop[62] techno,[63] trip hop,[64] and rap. Medleys were devised spontaneously by disc jockeys during parties in England. Some medleys and mixtures were prepared in studios and issued for sale. Some of their mixture incorporated excerpts from the funkiest hard bop albums of the 1960s and 70s, particularly the selections that maintained a groove and had tempos similar enough to loop into the continuous medleys. Selections featuring organ and guitar were particularly welcome. Though most music in this category is described above, a slice of their programming somewhat overlapped smooth jazz which contained improvisation but rarely swung in the jazz manner. Tempo and rhythmic feeling were stiffer in most acid jazz than in most smooth jazz. Statement of tempo was more elastic in smooth jazz because machine-made rhythms that typify acid jazz are perfectly constant, whereas a group of musicians, as live performers in smooth jazz, do not keep absolutely perfect time when they are playing. Their rhythms are more elastic. Though many listeners do not realize when they are hearing a drum machine, real drumming has an organic quality not conveyed by electronic imitations. A drum machine supplies neither the richness and depth of tone qualities nor the spontaneous variations in rhythms. The most important missing feature is the subtle ebb and flow of tensions. Incidentally, smooth jazz recordings that employ drum machines more closely resemble acid jazz. (2) **Fresh music** made specifically for this audience by bands around the world, not just England and America. Their music exhibited a range of styles, some made by musicians using drum machines and loops themselves, some not much different from early 1970s jazz-rock fusion.[65]

(3) **Renamed music from earlier recordings.** Several U.S. and British record companies during the mid-1990s applied the "acid jazz" designation to their old recordings and resold them. This succeeded as long as the selections were sufficiently funky and sustained a groove. Record companies reclassified several of their previous recording artists as "legends of acid jazz," for example, Ahmad Jamal, Roy Ayers, Houston Person, and Don Patterson. Some companies used the term "roots of acid jazz" to designate their old music by Wes Montgomery and Jimmy Smith. They sold it in different combinations of selections, with new album covers and new commentary. In other words, "acid jazz" served more as a marketing term than a musical style. But it was so loosely applied in music stores that a customer might have to seek the "rap music" bins to find it.

Dominant Aspects of Acid Jazz

Despite the diversity of sounds that have been called "acid jazz," at least three aspects of acid jazz make all but category #3 something more than a mere marketing term. (1) The most dominant aspect is the accompaniment rhythm and the way it feels. This is termed "the groove." It is important because much of this music was meant to stimulate dancing. (2) Another aspect is that few chord changes occur. Often an entire selection revolves around two chords that continuously alternate with each other. Much of it borrows the introduction from some other funky recording, for instance, soul music, disco, or boogaloo. Then the selection repeats that introduction continuously, with occasional variations. Based almost entirely upon an introduction, the harmonic content of most acid jazz selections is understandably limited because the function of an introduction is to set the pace, not offer harmonic development. (3) Melodic development is less elaborate than in any other style of jazz. In fact, many acid jazz selections have no melody at all.

In these three respects, acid jazz is more African than any other jazz style because much African folk music is focused primarily on rhythm and tone quality, not melodic or harmonic development. It is no coincidence that one category of pop music from the mid-1990s that was being incorporated into British acid jazz around 1996 was called "jungle jazz."

◇BUT IS IT JAZZ?

After fusion had arrived, many musicians and jazz fans did not consider it to be a form of jazz. Most of them eventually softened in their view, but some still consider fusion styles to be separate from the descendants of dixieland, swing, and bop. Keep in mind, however, that before fusion, many reacted to the avant-garde of Ornette Coleman and Cecil Taylor by saying that it was not jazz, either. But despite the views of some musicians and purist jazz fans, both the avant-garde of Coleman and Taylor and the fusion of Miles Davis, Weather Report, and Kenny G continue to be found in the jazz bins of music stores, not in the classical or rock bins. This indicates that—at least to the outsider—these styles sound more like jazz than like anything else. Were the outsiders missing the distinctions? Or were the insiders missing the commonalities? Incidentally, big band swing had been classified as nonjazz by many dixieland fans during the 1930s and 40s. They felt that it was not true jazz, partly because it represented a dilution of jazz traits. Collective improvisation did not occupy as much of each performance as it did in early jazz, for instance. Swing big bands emphasized refinement more than spontaneity.

Different people use different criteria for deciding whether a given performance is jazz. For those whose definition requires both improvisation and jazz swing feeling, much music by Weather Report fails to qualify because its rhythmic properties do not resemble the swing era or bop grooves, though they do achieve their own infectious groove. The piano music of New Age stylist George Winston would not qualify because it fails to swing. Music stores, on the other hand, use much looser criteria and display both Weather Report and George Winston in their jazz bins.

Jazzy Pop

Let us examine three other labelling dilemmas. (1) For those who find jazzness in music whenever it uses saxophones and a particular accompaniment style, music by Kenny G qualifies as jazz, even though it would not qualify by a strict definition that requires swing era or bop rhythmic properties. *Musicians might be more specific, though, and call music of Kenny G "jazzy pop."*

Rap

(2) Classification procedures are so loose that jazz journalists once contemplated including rap in the jazz category. Perhaps this was suggested by the African American origins they share. However, (a) most rap does not have melody. It is poetry recited atop a repeating funk rhythm. Though rhythmically compelling, (b) most rap does not swing in the jazz sense, and (c) not much of it is freshly improvised for each performance.

Jazzness in Acid Jazz

(3) If a personal perception of jazzness increases with the number and obviousness of aspects that remind a person of jazz, then acid jazz performances would qualify to the extent that they featured instruments and harmonies associated with jazz, even without improvisation or swing feeling. If any passages conveyed swing feeling, for instance, they would bear more jazzness.

Watered Down Jazz

There is another motive for saying something is not jazz despite its roots in the jazz tradition: rejection of pop jazz. To say a style is not jazz is merely another way that some jazz fans recognize that (1) improvisation does not occupy as much of each performance as in more serious jazz and/or that (2) improvisations in it are not as elaborate or (3) as well-crafted or (4) as rhythmically compelling as in other styles. Or it is a way these fans say (5) they do not like it and are refusing to give it their stamp of approval by calling it "jazz." Some dislike it because of reasons 1–4. Some dislike it for other reasons. *There has long been a reluctance among musicians and purist fans to include within the jazz category any watered-down variants of a style that derives from the jazz tradition.* This was why distinctions were made between swing bands and sweet bands during the 1940s. (See page 99.) Count Basie fit the former category, and Glenn Miller fit the latter, for instance. During the 1990s, the same distinctions could be made between saxophonists Michael Brecker and Kenny G. So you see that to be fair in classifying styles, we need to consider the actual characteristics of the music, not just the reactions of listeners. When one listener dislikes a style, this does not necessarily mean that another listener will also consider it bad music. We have also learned that if one listener does not consider a musical style to be jazz, this does not necessarily mean the style will not qualify as jazz for another listener.

◇POPULAR APPEAL

By 1990, rock had been popular twice as long as swing in the mainstream of American music, and jazz-rock fusion itself had been popular for more than two decades. Fusion became the first jazz style since the swing era to gain popular acceptance anywhere near the level accorded swing, and it lasted at least as long as the swing era. By incorporating elements of R & B and rock into their music, several established jazz figures achieved popular success that rivaled all the peaks of recognition accorded to jazz players since the end of the swing era's wide appreciation of jazz-oriented band music.[66] Though jazz instrumentals ordinarily sold fewer than 10,000 to 20,000 copies, jazz-rock albums of the 1970s and 1980s frequently sold more than 100,000 copies.[67]

This new success for jazz musicians did not depend so much on jazz character as on jazz-rock character. As with swing era, big band recordings, those pieces presenting the least improvisation tended to enjoy the most popular acclaim. And, as with the hits of the swing era, jazz-rock hits were identifiable by simple, repeating riffs syncopated in a catchy way. Much of what went by the jazz-rock label consisted of little more than funky rhythm vamps, elementary chord progressions, and an improvised solo riding on top.[68] This music was so popular that, in addition to the "jazz-rock" and "jazz fusion" labels, it also acquired the label of "crossover" music because sales of the records crossed over from the jazz market into the popular market.

There are several possible explanations for the new popularity of jazz and jazz-rock in particular. First, rock had already been popular for more than fifteen years by the time that Herbie Hancock's *Head Hunters* was released. So perhaps when **jazz adopted the electric instruments and the accompaniment rhythms associated with rock,** and rock was so familiar already, the instruments and rhythms provided a bridge of similarity for listeners that eased them into a music that had otherwise been strange and difficult to listen to. A second possibility is that the **increased prominence of drums was more inviting to dancers.**

Herbie Hancock's first fusion band: Hancock (Fender Rhodes electric piano), Buster Williams (bass guitar; his acoustic bass is lying on its side, between him and the drums), Bennie Maupin (bass clarinet), Billy Hart (drums), Eddie Henderson (fluegelhorn), and Julian Priester (trombone; only partially shown). This photo was taken during the early 1970s, near the time the band recorded *Sextant*, *Mwandishi*, and *Crossings*.

Courtesy of the Cleveland Press Collection/Cleveland State University Archives

Third is the **relative simplicity of chord progressions** found in jazz-rock. The new music was more involved than rock had been, but it was harmonically less complex than other jazz styles. A fourth explanation involves the **extensive use of repetition for a single accompaniment pattern.** Technically it is known as *ostinato,* which means that a particular rhythm or brief melodic figure is repeated continuously. It was fundamental to most of the jazz-rock hits of the 1970s, and its use might explain the enormous popularity of the boogie woogie style of jazz piano playing during the 1940s. Many of the largest-selling recordings in any category of music are distinguished by their simplicity, rhythmic vitality, and extensive use of repetition. This combination of features could also account for much of jazz-rock's commercial success.

CHAPTER SUMMARY

1) Jazz and rock represent separate streams in African American music which have occasionally overlapped.
2) Jazz differs from rock in its smaller amount of repetition, larger amount of improvisation, greater complexity, and higher musicianship.
3) Chicago Transit Authority (Chicago), Blood, Sweat & Tears, and Ten Wheel Drive ought not to be called jazz-rock because they used little improvisation and had more roots in soul music than in rock and roll.
4) These three groups represent amalgamations of existing trends, such as the band styles of James Brown, rather than a fresh style.
5) The most original fusions of funk and jazz occurred in bands of Larry Coryell, Gary Burton, Miles Davis, and the bands launched by their sidemen.
6) The most prominent jazz-rock guitarists were John McLaughlin, Larry Coryell, and Pat Metheny.
7) Their tone color and rhythmic conception departed from jazz guitar tradition and drew more from urban blues and rock practices.

8) John McLaughlin plays with phenomenal speed and precision, and draws from the music of India and John Coltrane.
9) McLaughlin led several innovative bands containing musicians who were themselves important jazz-rock bandleaders.
10) Pianist Joe Zawinul wrote the funk hits "Mercy, Mercy, Mercy" and "Walk Tall" while with Cannonball Adderley's band.
11) Zawinul's arrangements formed the basis for the important 1969 Miles Davis jazz-rock albums *Bitches Brew* and *In a Silent Way.*
12) In 1971, Zawinul and Wayne Shorter founded Weather Report, an innovative fusion band which lasted until 1985.
13) Weather Report originally began with much collective improvisation.
14) Weather Report eventually adopted approaches employing extensive repetition and the feeling of soul music, culminating in Zawinul's riff-based hit "Birdland." Their later approaches influenced "smooth jazz."
15) Jaco Pastorius was the bass guitarist with Weather Report from 1976 to 1982, and his sound became an important model for bassists.
16) The post-1968 work of Miles Davis displayed a blend of the jazz tradition, funk music, and the music of India and South America.
17) New Age music features soft tone qualities, few changes of chord and texture, non-jarring rhythms. Pianist George Winston is its best known practitioner.
18) Smooth jazz is a quieted, refined funk music. Guitarist George Benson, pianist Bob James, and saxophonist Kenny G are its best known practitioners.
19) Acid jazz was created initially by disc jockeys who excerpted accompaniment vamps from funky hard bop recordings and overlaid synthesized sounds, raps, and new jazz improvisations. It later became a style that was also produced live, not just through sampling.

◇BOOKS ABOUT ROCK AND JAZZ-ROCK

For more information about rock and jazz-rock, see:

Carl Belz. *The Story of Rock, 2nd ed.* New York: Harper and Row, 1987.

Charles T. Brown. *The Art of Rock and Roll, 3rd ed.* Upper Saddle River, NJ: Prentice-Hall, 1992.

Mike Clifford, ed. *The Illustrated Encyclopaedia of Black Music.* New York: Harmony Books, 1982.

Julie Coryell and Laura Friedman. *Jazz-Rock Fusion: The People, the Music.* New York: Dell, 1978.

Anthony DeCurtis, et al. ed., *The Rolling Stone Illustrated History of Rock and Roll.* New York: Random House, 1992.

Charlie Gillett. *The Sound of the City, 2nd ed.* New York: DaCapo, 1996.

Lee Hildebrand. *Stars of Soul and Rhythm & Blues.* New York: Billboard, 1994.

H. Wiley Hitchcock and Stanley Sadie, eds. *The New Grove Dictionary of American Music.* New York: Grove, 1986.

Stuart Nicholson. *Jazz-Rock: A History.* New York: Schirmer, 1998.

Joe Stuessy. *Rock and Roll: Its History and Stylistic Development, 3rd ed.* Upper Saddle River, NJ: Prentice-Hall, 1998.

For background on blues styles and their history see:

Lawrence Cohn, ed. *Nothing But the Blues: The Music and the Musicians.* New York: Abbeville, 1993.

David Evans. *Big Road Blues.* Berkeley: University of California, 1982.

Paul Oliver. *The Story of the Blues.* Boston: Northeastern University, 1997.

Robert Palmer, *Deep Blues.* New York: Penguin, 1981.

The following reference works by Joel Whitburn catalog comparative popularities:

Top Pop Singles: 1955–1996
Top Pop Albums: 1955–1996
Bubbling Under the Hot 100: 1959–1997
Top R&B Singles: 1942–1995
Pop Memories 1890–1954

Record Research Inc., P.O. Box 200, Menomonee Falls, Wisconsin 53052-0200; phone 800-827-9810.

NOTES

1. The impact gospel music had on modern jazz was usually felt in the simplest styles, those containing characteristics similar to the African American popular music known as rhythm and blues. These jazz styles were created by commercially successful players who, although possessing jazz skills, remained on the periphery of important jazz developments: the Earl Bostic and Eddie Vinson bands of the 1940s and 1950s; organ and saxophone combinations beginning in the late 1950s, such as those of Jimmy Smith and Stanley Turrentine; the piano trios of Les McCann, Ramsey Lewis, and the Three Sounds; the combos led by King Curtis; pianist Ray Charles and the saxophonists he employed, including Hank Crawford, David "Fathead" Newman, and James Clay.

2. Listen to the bass figures and drum patterns on "Reflections" (1967) or "Love Child" (1968) by the Supremes. Or listen to "I Heard It Through the Grapevine" (1967) by Gladys Knight & the Pips or "Cloud Nine" (1968) by the Temptations (all available on *Hitsville USA: The Motown Singles Collection,* Motown: 37463-6313-2, 4CD set, 1959–71; or see various *Greatest Hits* or *Anthology* compilations by Motown artists).

3. Listen to the rhythm section style on James Brown's 1967 "Cold Sweat," available on James Brown, *20 All Time Greatest Hits* (Polydor: 314 511 326-2 [King] 1956–74, or Brown, *Star Time* (Polydor: 849 108-2 [King], 4CD set, 1956–74).

4. Listen to Sly Stone's "In Time" on Sly & the Family Stone, *Fresh* (Epic: EK 32134, 1973); see page 431 for a transcription of the drum part.

5. The style, which during the late 1970s and early 1980s was called disco, is a blend of funk and Latin American rhythms played at the tempos most conducive for dancing (usually about 120 beats per minute, the standard march tempo). It refers mostly to an accompaniment style which has been heard under almost every kind of solo line, from the singing of Donna Summer to swing era melodies to excerpts from Beethoven compositions. This style of music should also be removed from the umbrella category of rock.

6. Free Spirits, *Free Spirits* (ABC: 593, LP, 1966).

7. Gary Burton, *Duster* (Koeh Jazz: 3-7846-2H1 [RCA LSP 3835], 1967).

8. The Fourth Way, *Sun and Moon Have Come Together* (Harvest/Capitol: SKAO 423, LP, 1969).

9. Blood, Sweat & Tears, *Blood, Sweat & Tears* (Columbia: CK 9720, 1969).

10. Chicago, *Chicago Transit Authority* (Columbia: CGK 8, 1968); *Chicago's Greatest Hits* (Columbia: CK 33900, 1969–75).

11. Ten Wheel Drive, *The Best of Ten Wheel Drive* (Polydor 314 527 420-2, 1969–71).

12. Miles Davis, *Bitches Brew* (Columbia: C4K 65570 [GP 26], 4CD set, 1969–70); Weather Report (Joe Zawinul & Wayne Shorter), *Weather Report* (Columbia: CK 48824 [30661], 1971); Tony Williams Lifetime (with John McLaughlin & Larry Young), *Emergency!* (Polydor: 314 539 117-2 [25-3001], 1969); Mahavishnu Orchestra (John McLaughlin), *The Inner Mounting Flame* (Columbia: CK 65523 [31067], 1971) and *Birds of Fire* (Columbia: CK 31996, 1972); Return to Forever (Chick Corea), *Hymn to the Seventh Galaxy* (Polydor: 8253362 [5536], 1973); and Herbie Hancock, *Head Hunters* (Columbia: CK 65123 [32731], 1974).

13. Listen to hints of rock in the accompanying patterns on "Eighty-One" on *E.S.P.,* "Freedom Jazz Dance" on *Miles Smiles,* "Masqualero" on *Sorcerer* (and the *Jazz Classics CD*), and "Frelon Brun," "Tout de Suite," and "Filles de Kilimanjaro" on *Filles de Kilimanjaro.* See pages 235–236 for catalog numbers of all Miles Davis recordings cited in this chapter.

14. For these sessions, Miles Davis drew from a pool of drummers—Tony Williams, Jack Dejohnette, Lenny White, Charles Alias, and Jim Riley. His pool of keyboard players included Herbie Hancock, Chick Corea, Joe Zawinul, and Larry Young. Wayne Shorter played tenor and soprano saxophones, Bennie Maupin played bass clarinet, John McLaughlin played guitar, and the bassists included Dave Holland and Harvey Brooks.

15. Most Davis recordings made after 1969 list Davis as sole composer despite the fact that usually he was performing the compositions of others. Zawinul's "Orange Lady," which is the last third of "Great Expectations" on *Big Fun,* is wrongly credited to Davis. Hermeto Pascoal's "Little Church" and "Selim" are wrongly credited to Davis on *Live-Evil.*

16. For details on the many changes of personnel and instrumentation in this period, see Jack Chambers, *Milestones: The Music and Times of Miles Davis* (DaCapo, 1998).

17. McLaughlin had collaborated in 1963 with bassist Jack Bruce and drummer Ginger Baker, both of whom later joined Eric Clapton in the well-known rock group, Cream.

18. Over the years, McLaughlin's groups also offered fine examples of jazz-rock violin playing: first Jerry Goodman; then, in 1974, Jean-Luc Ponty, whose recordings with his own bands have been among the best selling in all of jazz-rock.

19. John McLaughlin, *My Goal's Beyond* (Rykodisc: RCD 10051 [Douglas 9], 1970).

20. Larry Coryell, *Spaces* (Vanguard: VMD 79345 [6558], 1970).

21. Gary Burton features Goodrick and Metheny on his albums *Ring* (ECM: 78118-21051-2, 1974); and *Dreams So Real* (ECM: 78118-21072-2, 1975).

22. Like McLaughlin, Coryell also demonstrated considerable interest in nonrock playing during the late 1970s and early 1980s. He performed as an unaccompanied solo guitarist and played duets with guitarists Philip Catherine, Steve Khan, McLaughlin, and violinist Michael Urbaniak.

23. Cannonball Adderley, *Mercy, Mercy, Mercy* (Capitol: 29915 [ST 2663], 1966).

24. Weather Report, *Heavy Weather* (Columbia: CK 65108 [34418], 1977).

25. This is exemplified on side one of Weather Report, *Heavy Weather.*

26. Zawinul first recorded with ring modulator in 1971 on "Seventh Arrow" on Weather Report's first album, *Weather Report* (Columbia: CK 48824 [37616], 1971).

27. "Man in the Green Shirt" (*Tale Spinnin'*, Columbia: CK 57905 [33417], 1975) and "The Juggler" (*Heavy Weather*).

28. Both are on Joe Zawinul, *Zawinul* (Atlantic: 1579-2, 1970).

29. "Jungle Book" is on *Mysterious Traveler* (Columbia: CK 32494, 1974). During a period of jazz history when electric instruments dominated the sound of most albums, Zawinul used strains of unamplified piano on the recording of Wayne Shorter's "Blackthorn Rose" (*Mysterious Traveler*), precisely sounding each tone, paced as though to savor its every vibration. He also used it in combination with sustained organ tones in his "Five Short Stories" (*Tale Spinnin'*).

30. Zawinul used his own voice in this capacity on his "Badia" (*Tale Spinnin'*) and "Jungle Book" (*Mysterious Traveler*), and that of bassist Jaco Pastorius on "Birdland" (*Heavy Weather,* the *Jazz Classics CD* for *Concise Guide to Jazz* and excerpted on the *Jazz Classics CD for Jazz Styles* Track 6). Zawinul combined Wayne Shorter's tenor saxophone tone with the soft texture of a children's choir on "The Orphan" (*8:30,* Columbia: CK 57665 [36030], 1979).

31. Miroslav Vitous, *Infinite Search* (Embryo: 524, LP, 1969).

32. "Eurydice," on Weather Report's first recording (*Weather Report,* Columbia: CK 48824 [30661], 1971), drummer playing ride rhythms and closing high-hat on every second and fourth beat, sax solo followed by piano solo, etc. Even in such a conventionally formatted performance, there are portions which deviate from the standard bop roles. For example, drummer Alphonse Mouzon often closed his high-hat on all four beats and interjected musical comments to the point where, instead of just keeping time and coloring the sound, he is heard in the forefront of the group. Bassist Miroslav Vitous often abandoned the walking role and instead contributed embellishments to the ensemble. Pianist Zawinul did not always comp behind saxophonist Shorter, but set up delicate flourishes, played counter-melodies, and sometimes did not play at all. Airto Moreira overdubbed interjections of colorful, speech-like sounds throughout the proceedings with his cuica, an instrument in which the player gently slides his fingers along a stick which in turn alters the tension of a specially connected drumhead and causes it to vibrate.

33. *Weather Report* (Columbia: CK 48824 [30661], 1971); *I Sing the Body Electric* (Columbia: CK 46107 [31352], 1971–72); and *Sweetnighter* (Columbia: CK 64976 [32210], 1973).

34. Representative examples of such collective improvisation are "Seventh Arrow" and "Umbrellas" on Weather Report's first album, *Weather Report,* and "125th Street Congress" on *Sweetnighter.* The music seems spontaneous except for the rehearsed figures that occur at the beginning, end, and occasionally within the pieces.

35. "Crazy About Jazz" on Weather Report's eleventh album, which bears the same title as their first: *Weather Report* (Columbia: CK 37616, 1981).

36. "Dara Factor One" (*Weather Report,* Columbia: CK 37616, 1981) and "Dream Clock" (*Night Passage,* Columbia: CK 36793, 1980).

37. Listen to the funk bass style Pastorius used in accompanying soul singers Sam and Dave on his own album (*Jaco Pastorius,* Epic: EK 33949, 1976), and the dancing feeling he lent Weather Report's "Barbary Coast" (*Black Market,* Columbia: CK 34099, 1976), "Palladium" (*Heavy Weather,* Columbia: CK 65108, 1977), and "River People" (*Mr. Gone,* Columbia: CK 46869 [35358], 1978).

38. Pastorius's effect on Weather Report will reveal itself if you compare the sound of the band's *Heavy Weather,* on which Pastorius is prominent, with the sound of *Sweetnighter* or *Mysterious Traveler,* which are earlier albums without him.

39. Jaco Pastorius, *Jaco Pastorius* (Epic: EK 33949, 1976).

40. Jaco Pastorius, *Word of Mouth* (Warner Bros.: 3535-2, 1981) was sufficiently popular to penetrate the *Billboard* "top 200" in album sales during 1981.

41. On "John and Mary," Pastorius used the same children's choir that Zawinul used on "The Orphan."

42. Among the phase shifters, Metheny used a combination of a Chorus (which takes the harmonics of the note and reinforces some and cancels others in a continuous motion) and Lexicon digital delay (which repeats the note at a delay of about 20 milliseconds—this contrasts with ordinary reverb because this is just one simple repeat, and it contrasts with concert hall reverb, which is thousands of repeats at various delays). Chorus effect acts as a detuner, takes the signal, detunes it and gives it a fatter sound, shifts the pitch. Flanging, chorusing, and echo are all time-delay techniques. Flanging is very small delay, 30–40 milliseconds; Chorusing is from 40 ms to where the human ear can detect it, 90 ms. Where the ear can discern between original signal and the delay is called an echo. In chorusing, you increase the feedback (the number of repeats); typically the repeats will tend to fade in intensity, the more there are. This makes it sound like many players, nonsynchronized, because of the slight imperfections in timing and pitch, thereby increasing the harmonics. The device will modulate the time delay slightly. It sweeps the time back and forth, from 1 or 2 ms away from 60 ms delay to 20 ms away from 60 ms—this is called the depth of modulation. It also adjusts for speed of modulation. The device mixes the direct signal with the repeated signal. Chorusing was originally de-

vised to synthesize the Leslie organ effect. Digital delay converts the signal to a code via sampling, whereas an analog system will color the sound and degrade it.

43. Pat Metheny, *The Pat Metheny Group* (ECM: 78118-21114-2, 1978); *Offramp* (ECM: 78118-21216-2, 1981). Two Metheny albums sold more than 500,000 copies apiece: *Still Life* (Geffen: 24145) and *Secret Story* (Geffen: 24468).
44. Pat Metheny/Ornette Coleman, *Song X* (Geffen: 24096-2, 1985).
45. Jarrett's unaccompanied solo improvisations are far more varied, far more dynamic, and should not be confused with either minimalism or the popular idiom it spawned. And his jazz work is not related at all to this movement.
46. George Winston, *December* (Windham Hill: WD 1025, 1982).
47. Bob James & Earl Klugh, *One on One* (Warner Bros.: 45141-2, 1979). James also leads Fourplay: *Fourplay* (Warner Bros.: 26656, 1991); *Between the Sheets* (Warner Bros.: 45340, 1993). Each of these three albums sold more than 500,000 copies.
48. Earl Klugh, *Low Ride* (Capitol: 12253 [46007], 1983).
49. George Benson, *In Flight* (Warner Bros.: 2983, 1977) sold more than one million copies.
50. Among Kenny G's albums, *Breathless* (1992) sold more than 10 million copies. *Miracles* (1994) sold more than 6 million copies. *Silhouette* (1988) sold more than 4 million copies.
51. *Bumpin'* (Verve: 314 539 062-2, 1965) is typical of Montgomery's hits that influenced smooth jazz. *A Day in the Life* (A&M: 75021 0816-2, 1967) sold more than 500,000 copies. For a sampler, see Wes Montgomery, *Greatest Hits* (A&M: 31454-0519-2, 1967–68).
52. Grover Washington, Jr., *Winelight* (Elektra: 305-2, 1980) sold more than a million copies and became a model for Kenny G and music on smooth jazz radio. For a sampler, see *Grover Washington, Jr.'s Greatest Performances* (Motown: 3746.35307-2, 1972–78).
53. "Harlequin" on *Heavy Weather* (Columbia: CK 65108, 1976, 1977) exemplifies the slice of Weather Report's output that was imitated for smooth jazz formats.
54. U.S.-issued samplers of London-based groups include *This Is Acid Jazz, Volume 1* (Instinct: EX 225, 1991), and *Volume 2* (Instinct: EX 244-2, 1992). *The Best of Acid Jazz: A Five Year Retrospective* (Instinct: EX 317, 1995) represents several nations.
55. "Keep On" on *This Is Acid Jazz, Volume 2* (Instinct: EX 244-2, 1992) uses saxophone as decoration. "Move y'all" on *A New Type of Jazz* (New Breed: 020-2, 1994) uses fragments of muted trumpet and piano as decoration for a rap.
56. US3, *Hand on the Torch* (Blue Note: 80883, 1993) was created by British disc jockeys and musicians who excerpted old jazz albums, added raps and new instrumental jazz improvisations. It sold more than 2 million copies worldwide. *The New Groove* [The Blue Note Remix Project–Volume 1] (Blue Note: 36594, 1996) excerpted old jazz albums, added drum machine and new raps.
57. "Cutting Loose" on *This Is Acid Jazz, Volume 2* (Instinct: EX 244-2) uses loud back beat from snare drum, steady bass drum (synthesized), and synthesized bass guitar. "Racial Facial" on *A New Type of Jazz* (New Breed: 020-2, 1994) has loud back beat by synthesized snare drum, with loops, using horns as occasional decoration.
58. GURU, *Jazzmatazz, Volume 1* (Chrysalis: 21998, 1993) began each selection with an electronically created rhythm track, then had a jazz musician record a new solo improvisation over that, and a fresh rap was then overdubbed atop it.
59. See footnote 51.
60. Miles Davis, *doo-bop* (Warner Bros.: 926938-2, 1991) uses overdubbing of Davis trumpet solo improvisations as well as a rapper.
61. "T.S.O.J." on *A New Type of Jazz* (New Breed: 020-2, 1994) uses drum machine, synthesizer, and loops and has fresh jazz improvisations overdubbed.
62. One hip hop compilation is *The Source Presents: Hip Hop Hits, Vol. 1* (Polygram: 314 536 204-2, 1997).
63. One techno compilation is *Rave 'Til Dawn: Techno's Finest* (SBK: 27018-2, 1993).
64. One trip hop compilation is *Red Hot Trip Hop* (Street Beat: 1021, 1996).
65. Prominent touring bands are Jamiroquai, James Taylor Quartet, The Brand New Heavies, The Groove Collective, Ronny Jordan, Incognito, the 11-piece Count Basic (not a typographical error) from Austria (represented twice on *This Is Acid Jazz, Volume 3: New Voices* (Instinct: EX 338-2, 1996) and the 10-piece Liquid Soul from Chicago. Some music of these last two (particularly Count Basic's "Sweet Luis" and Liquid Soul's "Ricky's Hat") differs little from typical jazz-rock band fare of the 1970s, thereby furthering the breadth of music which store clerks of the late 1990s were told to "file under acid jazz." Instrumentation differs somewhat, however, in that rapper, turntable operator (for scratching), and extra percussionists are often included.
66. It had been unusual for jazz instrumentals to be within the top hundred best-selling albums for any given year; yet Herbie Hancock's Sly Stone-influenced *Head Hunters* reached position 13 on the *Billboard* chart, selling over a million copies, and Miles Davis had the greatest success of his career with his rock-flavored *Bitches Brew.* The album reached position 35, selling more than 500,000 copies, far more than any of his previous albums which had reached "the top 100."
67. Trumpeter Chuck Mangione's rock-flavored *Feels So Good* (A&M: 75021-3219-2 [SP4658], 1977) sold about 2.2 million copies. Spyro Gyra's *Morning Dance* (Amherst: AMH-8008-2 [9004], 1979) sold over a million copies. Kenny G's *Duotones* (Arista: ARCD-8496, 1986) sold over 6 million copies, as did George Benson's *Breezin'* (Warner Bros.: 3111-2 [2919], 1976). After the Jazz Crusaders dropped "jazz" from their group name and began playing rock-oriented material, "The Crusaders" enjoyed hit after hit. Their *Southern Comfort, Images,* and *Street Life* albums each sold over 500,000 copies.
68. This was the formula for several hits by saxophonists Grover Washington (*Mr. Magic,* Motown: 37463-5175-2 [Kudu 20],1974), and Kenny G ("Songbird"); guitarist Earl Klugh (*Living Inside Your Love,* Capitol: 48385 [Liberty 667], 1976); and the bands of Jeff Lorber (*Soft Space,* Inner City: 1058, LP, 1978) and Spyro Gyra (*Spyro Gyra,* Amherst: AMH 8002-2 [1014], 1977).

Chapter Seventeen

Wynton Marsalis, 1991   Courtesy of Jack Vartoogian

Contemporary Jazz: 1980 to the Early 2000s

The contemporary period of jazz has seen many developments and a tremendous amount of activity. No other era can boast the sheer diversity of styles that were explored in the 1980s and 1990s. Players probed all earlier formats of jazz, from the predecessors of early jazz to jazz-rock fusion, carrying on the many traditions that emerged prior to that period. As could be expected, this era also saw the development of many new styles and playing innovations. Some of these relied on older jazz concepts and principles, but added modern devices to create something that sounded fresh and new. Others drew from an increasingly wide array of influences, incorporating classical, folk, popular, and world music elements into the already jammed and eclectic musical language. Some contemporary players even borrowed from drastically different approaches on a regular basis, tackling new musical scenarios with each recording or concert, constantly reinventing themselves.

◇NEO-TRADITIONALISM

During the 1970s, music relying heavily on electronics became so popular that acoustic jazz was almost abandoned altogether. Major record labels refused to sign acoustic jazz artists, fearing they would not sell enough albums for the venture to be profitable. There was even speculation that acoustic jazz might completely die away. However, during this decade a number of musicians became interested in preserving earlier styles of jazz through concerts and recordings. During the early 1980s, Dexter Gordon, and other old timers, returned to the United States after a period of working in Europe, rekindling an interest in hard bop. In 1981, a 20-year-old trumpeter named Wynton Marsalis gained fame and popularity following the release of his early recordings. Within a few years, an explosion of young musicians playing acoustic jazz erupted. The performers, who became known as **young lions,** were interested in **preserving various elements of older jazz styles while incorporating their own voices.** Called **neo-traditionalists,** these young lions often composed and improvised in styles recalling Jelly Roll Morton, Duke Ellington, Thelonious Monk, and a host of other figures. The following trends were common among neo-traditionalists:

1) Traditional jazz instruments were employed (trumpet, trombone, sax, rhythm section).
2) Many groups performed compositions from earlier periods.
3) Other ensembles composed pieces drawing on elements of previous styles.
4) Rhythm sections played the traditional role of comping behind the melody and soloists.
5) Bop and hard bop concepts were the most important influence on soloists.
6) Swing feel was emphasized.
7) Collective improvisation was avoided.

◇POST-MODERNISM

At around the same time the neo-traditionalists were coming into public view, a contrasting school of jazz was also evolving. The players from this movement incorporated anything their imaginations could conjure: new instruments, new timbres, and new influences. For this reason, they are called **postmodernists,** mirroring trends in contemporary philosophy. While bands perfecting a single way of playing characterized earlier periods, the **postmodernists were driven by eclecticism.** Each recording project, concert, or individual section of a single composition might reference an entirely different style of playing. Though various musicians and bands found unique approaches, most of the music from this school employs some of the following:

1) Unusual instruments for jazz (flute, violin, cello, oboe, bassoon, etc.)
2) New instrumental combinations
3) New sounds, timbres, and techniques for all instruments
4) Highly arranged and written-out sections combined with solo and collective improvisations
5) Sections during which all the players are rhythmically "in sync" with each other, contrasted by moments of rhythmic dissonance and conflict
6) Highly interactive textures
7) Jazz fused with classical music
8) Jazz fused with music from around the world (Klezmer, Middle Eastern, Indian, African, etc.)
9) Jazz fused with many forms of popular music (country, rock, hip hop, film music, etc.)
10) Different styles of jazz fused together

TABLE 17.1 COMPARING FREE JAZZ WITH POSTMODERNISM

FREE JAZZ	POSTMODERNISM
Avoidance of traditional jazz harmonies	Inclusion of many types of harmonies from jazz and other sources
Avoidance of singable melodies at all costs by most players	Often presents simple, even familiar melodies in fresh contexts, or contrasts singable melodies with non-melodic passages
Avoidance of regular, clear beats and grooves in favor of unpredictable rhythms	Inclusion of a wide variety of beats and grooves, including but not limited to unpredictable rhythms
Avoidance of clear, easy to understand structures; sometimes completely improvised music	Often very clear structures, serving as foundations for a great deal of improvisation
Avoidance of obvious reference to earlier types of jazz by most players	Reference to many types of music, jazz or nonjazz
Often serious demeanor	Often humorous demeanor
Concern for new and interesting sounds on all types of instruments	Concern for new and interesting sounds on all types of instruments

Many of the musicians involved with postmodernism perform frequently at a club in New York called the Knitting Factory, resulting in the term **Knitting Factory musicians.** These players have expanded concepts from free jazz of the 1960s and 1970s, a period that went all but ignored by the neo-traditionalists. However, music from the postmodernists differs significantly from the earlier free jazz movement.

◇NEO-TRADITIONALISM AND POST-MODERNISM

Ironically, as time progressed, the chasm between neo-traditionalists and postmodernists began to diminish. The neo-traditionalists began to take greater risks while reflecting on music of earlier times, making the music more personal and current. The postmodernists have become increasingly interested in fusing, sometimes shocking, unusual and new sounds with jazz from the past. Some players even divide their activities between both of these communities. However, the significant differences between the goals and musical output of the two contrasting groups are still substantial.

◇WYNTON MARSALIS

The most discussed trumpet player of contemporary jazz, and the most controversial, is **Wynton Marsalis** (b. 1961). A child prodigy, by age 22 he became the first musician to win Grammy awards for both jazz and classical recordings. Imagine being considered the heir-apparent to all great jazz trumpeters of the past. Marsalis's virtuosic technical command and extraordinary tone control convinced many that he would become the natural successor to Clifford Brown. His promise as a musician led people to believe he would extend the great trumpet legacy of Louis Armstrong, Dizzy Gillespie, and Miles Davis.

When Marsalis was still a youth, he performed with Art Blakey's *Jazz Messengers* and with pianist Herbie Hancock, bassist Ron Carter, and drummer Tony Williams, the famous rhythm section that accompanied Miles Davis in the 1960s.[1] While his early recordings demonstrated the brilliance of his trumpeting, it was uncertain in which direction Marsalis would push the music. Clarification began with two albums he recorded in the late 1980s.[2] Both featured a quartet playing a collection of standards. Some of the significant contributions of these albums were:

1) A highly interactive rhythm section
2) Frequent changes of meter, and the superimposition of various rhythms
3) Aggressive and forward-looking playing
4) A certain amount of dissonance
5) A good deal of blues influence

These techniques resembled investigations by Miles Davis's sextet from the 1960s. Following these recordings, Marsalis embarked on a sudden change of direction. He focused his efforts on the study and emulation of earlier jazz forms, most specifically the music from his hometown, New Orleans. Since most neo-traditionalist jazz musicians of this time were primarily influenced by hard bop figures, this action marked a significant departure. His projects since this time have featured the use of many mutes, growling sounds reminiscent of Bubber Miley and Cootie Williams, sparse and soulful playing, and heightened attention to the blues.[3]

Marsalis's focus then shifted to composition, sometimes even downplaying his trumpet mastery. He reintroduced the clarinet as a vital jazz instrument, worked with trombonists (whose role had diminished greatly over the previous several decades), and began writing for larger ensembles. His opera *Blood on the Fields,* an extended work dealing with slavery, was the first jazz composition ever to win the Pulitzer Prize (1997). It features gospel sounds, blues-inflected forms, two-beat struts, and other structures suggesting early jazz. It explores techniques of arranging characteristic of Duke Ellington, including specifically writing for his players' personal sounds, Ellingtonian harmonies, and the use of cross-section voicings.[4]

Marsalis's Impact

In the entire history of jazz, few musicians have earned as much recognition and fame in such a short time as Wynton Marsalis. After the 1970s, a time when acoustic jazz was on the verge of extinction, Marsalis almost single-handedly turned the industry around. Following his success and example, major record labels signed scores of young lions, hoping they would garner similar popularity. Hundreds of musicians were influenced not only by Marsalis's playing, but also by his historical consciousness. He has been an active teacher, self-appointed spokesperson, and concert organizer, educating the public about the music he loves. In 1987, Marsalis became the artistic director of "Jazz at Lincoln Center," where he has commissioned many new works and directed numerous high-profile concerts.

Marsalis's Controversy

Marsalis' fame is rivaled only by the controversy that surrounds him. Especially in his early career, he was outspoken about what qualified as "real jazz" and what did not. He felt, for example, that jazz-rock fusion was not jazz. He once stated, referring to Miles Davis's funk band, that "Bird would roll over in his grave if he knew what was going on." He discounted or downplayed music with too much European classical influence, instead emphasizing the need for jazz to return to its African American roots such as the blues. His attitudes raise some interesting questions. Must music swing for it to be jazz? Does it need to be blues-inflected? Does it have to include specific "jazz" instruments? Does music that sounds so connected to the history of jazz, at the expense of evolving it, forward the spirit that has been present since the earliest days of the music? Such questions have sparked serious debate.

John Zorn
Courtesy Jules Photographe/SIPA Press

◇JOHN ZORN

John Zorn (b. 1953) epitomizes the concepts and principles of the postmodernists and is responsible for developing many of these ideas himself. While far less recognized than Wynton Marsalis, he is an example of a contemporary player who has taken jazz in a diametrically opposed direction to that of the neo-traditionalists. An exploration of his approach can give a great deal of insight into the postmodernist aesthetic. His sound on the alto sax is abrasive and harsh, reminiscent of a screaming child. While the ferocity of his playing has earned him respect in jazz circles, his most significant contributions have come through his compositions and philosophies built around music.

Zorn's output is first and foremost eclectic. His music borrows from everything he has experienced: hard bop soloists, classical composition techniques, punk-rock bands, Latin grooves, Klezmer dances, spaghetti western film soundtracks, R & B hits, Japanese traditional melodies, and nature sounds. He has composed for a wide variety of ensembles, combining jazz and orchestral instruments with electronics, turntables, train whistles, duck calls, instruments from around the world, and many other sound-making mechanisms. Much of Zorn's music is violent, shocking, and relentless. His overriding goal is to "shock" his listeners into a higher state of awareness, forcing the audience to listen to his music actively rather than passively (as background music), the way so much music is heard today.

Many of his compositions are organized around what Zorn calls **alternating "blocks" of sounds.** He cites Igor Stravinsky and cartoon composer Carl Stalling (Warner Brothers) as his major influences for this technique. An early piece, entitled *Cobra*, demonstrates this approach. It lacks a traditional score. Instead, it is approached like a game with "rules" laid out for the players. The 12 musicians switch abruptly between various blocks of sound, following the instructions. By doing this, Zorn gives some guidelines to the piece without actually determining the outcome.[5] This approach is analogous to playing a game of baseball. The guidelines are set in stone before the game begins, but the resultant experience is vastly different in every game. Later works include shifting blocks of various styles. For example, he might have 15 seconds of punk rock interrupted by a short blurb of free jazz followed by an extended passage of swing.

Zorn has worked with a punk band called *Mr. Bungle,* his own rock band *Naked City,* the *Kronos Quartet* (a string quartet devoted to the performance of contemporary classical music), and many Knitting Factory musicians. His compositions for his ongoing project *Masada,* which explores Jewish culture, number several hundred. Viewing himself as a product of the Information Age, he uses the recording studio as a compositional tool, often adding electronic sounds to his music, mixing and splicing to get the desired result. Zorn continues to investigate many types of music, breaking new ground, and redefining the role of composers, performers, and musicians.[6]

Zorn's Impact

Though not nearly as well known as Wynton Marsalis, Zorn's impact on musicians from many genres has been substantial. By refusing to fit into any category of music, he challenges others to break down the barriers of style. Many have followed his lead, making overt references to a variety of genres. His interest in Jewish culture has contributed to the recent resurgence of interest in Klezmer music. His work with punk rock bands has influenced artists in that world, as well as connecting him with new audiences. In 1995, Zorn became the executive producer of a record label called *Tzadik.* Dedicated to the exploration of new sounds, this label seeks bands with unconventional and unusual concepts. John Zorn is a figure, like Ornette Coleman, who gives musicians permission to take enormous risks. Many of the important Knitting Factory musicians, such as guitarist Bill Frisell and drummer Joey Baron, began with Zorn and went on to make significant contributions of their own.

Zorn's Controversy

Some argue that Zorn is not a jazz musician at all. Though many of his compositions make direct reference to "jazzy" sounds, others could not be further from it. Several of his albums will never find their way into jazz bins at a CD store, and those that do sound quite different from the Wynton Marsalis model and aesthetic. But others argue that his approach embodies the jazz experience. Improvisation does play an enormous role in all of his output. He borrows from what came before him, mixes it with a variety of influences, and looks for ways to make his music personal, fresh, and forward-looking. Is this any different than what Duke Ellington, Thelonious Monk, and Charles Mingus were striving to accomplish? In fact many similarities can be drawn between Ellington and Zorn. Both wrote specifically for the musicians who played their music, both collaborated frequently with others, both melded new sounds with more familiar ones, both shocked as well as pleased audiences. But there are also obvious differences between the way the music sounds, bringing into question the legitimacy of the claim that Zorn's music is "jazz."

◇ECM RECORDS

Since the first jazz recording in 1917, many record labels have been largely responsible for exposing and promoting new jazz innovations and artists. Without record labels such as Blue Note, Verve, and Columbia, jazz would certainly not have developed as quickly as it did. One record company deserves special mention here. The **ECM record label** (Edition of Contemporary Music) has not only produced a multitude of important and influential recordings, it also created its own unique audio picture. It is not uncommon to speak about the ECM "style" or "sound."

The ECM label was founded in 1969 by **Manfred Eicher** (b. 1943). During the 1970s, when many record companies neglected or abandoned outright their support for jazz players, favoring instead rock musicians, this company worked with a great many innovative

Product or Process?

Comparison of the music of Marsalis and Zorn raises some interesting questions about which one best fits the jazz tradition. Both Marsalis and Zorn share some commonalities with Duke Ellington, considered the greatest jazz composer of all time. For example, Marsalis's compositions often *sound like* those of Ellington. His music certainly sounds like "jazz" to our ears. It is built around swing feel, the blues, traditional jazz harmonies, and many other musical elements associated with Ellington and jazz. His output fits the stereotype perfectly. **But is jazz defined by the product or the process?** What Marsalis hopes to accomplish is a far cry from Ellington. Ellington always pushed the music forward, sounding like nobody before, and incorporating as many influences as possible. He refused to acknowledge that his music was jazz, instead insisting that it was "beyond category." In fact, the attitude, or process, of going beyond what jazz had done in the past has defined the leaders of this tradition from its inception. Armstrong, Parker, and just about every artist identified in this book had one thing in common: they all created music with a product that sounded *unlike* what had preceded it. When observing *process,* this attitude describes Zorn much more accurately than Marsalis. However, Zorn's *product* doesn't sound the way most of us imagine jazz should sound. We must then ask ourselves again: what defines the jazz tradition, the product or the process?

acoustic jazz improvisers. Eschewing the commercial bent of other labels during this era, Eicher focused instead on producing recordings of the highest level of integrity. Since then, and throughout contemporary jazz, many of the most important European and American artists have recorded for this label, including pianists Keith Jarrett, Chick Corea, and John Taylor; saxophonists Jan Garbarek and John Surman; trumpeter Kenny Wheeler; guitarist Pat Metheny; bassists Jaco Pastorius and Eberhard Weber; vocalist Norma Winstone; the Art Ensemble of Chicago; and dozens of others. The recordings on this label range from extremely beautiful, melodic compositions with rich, luscious harmonies, to free and experimental performances with strange instrumental combinations and techniques. Yet somehow, all these recordings are linked. Eicher manages to get a unique, open sound from all of his disks. The special type of reverb he adds can make even the most adventuresome and experimental performances sound beautiful and never harsh. Even artists who work with other labels often attempt to emulate the sound that is so easily identifiable with ECM records.[7]

◇M-BASE AND STEVE COLEMAN

Several other approaches to jazz developed during the final two decades of the twentieth century. In the early 1980s, alto saxophonist **Steve Coleman** (b. 1956) and a group of musicians based in Brooklyn formed a movement called **M-Base** (Macro-Basic Array of Structural Extemporization). Frustrated with the celebrity status of Wynton Marsalis and the conservative viewpoints he proclaimed, the M-Base collective fused jazz with hip-hop and other types of rhythm-driven music. By blending these styles, they forwarded concepts first explored by Miles Davis and other jazz-rock fusion artists. **They wanted to play music accessible to dancers.** However, M-Base does not represent a style of music. Rather, it denotes a philosophy about how musicians can think about what they are doing. It is an ideology that allows all styles to enter the music. M-Base preaches that any label, such as "jazz," limits creative expression, dictating what would or would not be appropriate to play. The premises behind the M-Base mentality derived largely from non-Western concepts, specifically musical perceptions present in the African Diaspora. M-Base has been influential on a significant number of players. As the official M-Base Collective roster continues to grow, this philosophy has influenced not only the mindset of performers, but also the style of music they perform, giving credibility to those who combine jazz with current dance grooves.[8]

◇JAM-BANDS AND MMW

In the 1990s, a new type of ensemble, called **jam-bands,** began to gain popularity. These groups did exactly as the term implies—they jammed. Working with nonchanging or slowly morphing rhythms, these bands featured extended improvisations over grooves intended for dancing. The most famous jam-band, *Phish,* has a huge variety of influences, swimming in and out of jazz and nonjazz approaches. Other jam-bands, such as the "avant-rock-jazz-hop" group **Medeski, Martin, and Wood (MMW),** come directly out of the jazz tradition.

The bassist and drummer of MMW, Chris Wood and Billy Martin, lay down various dance grooves, while the band's driving force, John Medeski, explores a host of inventive, creative improvisations. One of the most talked about pianists and organists of contemporary jazz, Medeski melds chord clusters, angular post-bop lines, aggressive octave passages, repetitive minimalist patterns, and Jimmy Smith-like funky, bluesy organ fills. Straddling the outer limits of organ, electronics, and acoustic piano playing, he alternates freely between tonal and nontonal harmonies and completely free improvisations. By combining sometimes unrestricted and bizarre elements with the regularity of dance grooves, MMW has been able to reach beyond jazz audiences. Their popularity demonstrates that if the beat is strong enough, dancers can be wooed regardless of what is played on top. This is a significant accomplishment, representing one of the few times such a creative and experimental band has acquired an extensive following.[9]

◇ ◇ ◇ ◇

Most of the artists discussed throughout this text have been influential innovators. In discussing contemporary jazz, with the availability of recordings today, it is possible to quickly assess who is composing and performing innovative and fresh music. Determining who will profoundly influence history is another story. With time, this will become clear. The musicians listed below are a combination of innovators who have "pushed the envelope" of the jazz world in contemporary times and those who have already become extremely influential.

◇TRUMPET

Trumpet players have acted as bandleaders, innovators, and driving forces of jazz since the early 1900s. The contemporary period is no exception. A number of young trumpet players have developed personal voices, often in conjunction with the exploration of earlier styles of jazz. Many players have developed staggering technique and brilliance in their playing. Of exceptional note is **Dave Douglas** (b. 1963). Douglas is representative of a growing number of players who can play just about anything. His innovative approach avoids jazz clichés as he attempts to expand and challenge his own vocabulary. With playing that runs the gamut he moves from fast, angular, bebop lines to slow, expressive passages. Inserting dramatic eruptions, he alternates intelligently developed phrases with clearly articulated punctuations. Douglas inflects his pitches in a variety of ways, including scoops, wide vibrato, and pinched attacks.

In addition to performance, Douglas is revered as a composer and bandleader. He has worked with a number of stylistically diverse ensembles, each opening new compositional and improvisational environments. One group stretches Balkan-inspired music in unexpected directions.[10] Another includes violin and accordion, both unusual jazz instruments. As a reg-

TABLE 17.2 A FEW OF THE MANY MUSICIANS ACTIVE IN CONTEMPORARY JAZZ

TRUMPET

Wynton Marsalis
Dave Douglas
Tom Harrell
Terrence Blanchard
Marlon Jordan
Nicholas Payton
Randy Brecker
Kenny Wheeler
Roy Hargrove
Wallace Roney
Ryan Kisor

TROMBONE

Steve Turre
Robin Eubanks
Curtis Fowlkes
Josh Roseman
Wycliffe Gordon
Conrad Herwig
Hal Crook
Ray Anderson
Roswell Rudd
Curtis Fuller

SAXOPHONE

John Zorn
Branford Marsalis
Joshua Redman
Chris Potter
Tim Berne
David Murray
James Carter
Michael Brecker
Joe Lovano
Jerry Bergonzi
Tim Ries
Rick Margitza
Jane Ira Bloom
Jan Garbarek
Lee Konitz
Greg Osby
Steve Coleman
Bobby Watson
Henry Threadgill
Kenny Garrett
James Carter

CLARINET

Don Byron
Todd Williams
Chris Speed
Ken Peplowski
Eddie Daniels
Buddy Defranco
Marty Ehrlich

PIANO

Uri Caine
Wayne Horvitz
Myra Melford
Mulgrew Miller
Kenny Kirkland
Geri Allen
John Taylor
Gonzalo Rubalcaba
Joey Calderazzo
Stephen Scott
Marcus Roberts
Brad Mehldau
Fred Hersch
Benny Green
Michel Petrucciani
Kenny Werner
John Medeski
Kenny Barron
Keith Jarrett
Chick Corea
Matthew Shipp

GUITAR

Bill Frisell
John Scofield
Jim Hall
Pat Metheny
Mike Stern
John Abercrombie
James "Blood" Ulmer
Ralph Towner
Vernon Reid
Marc Ribot
John McLaughlin
Stanley Jordan

BASS

Mark Dresser
Dave Holland
Charlie Haden
Robert Hurst III
John Patitucci
Steve Swallow
Gary Peacock
Victor Wooten
Marcus Miller
Lonnie Plaxico
Christian McBride
Charnett Moffett

DRUMS

Joey Baron
Jeff "Tain" Watts
Bobby Previte
Matt Wilson
Billy Kilson
Marvin 'Smitty' Smith
Terri Lyne Carrington
Peter Erskine
Jack DeJohnette
Bill Stewart
Paul Motian
Jon Christensen

VOICE

Cassandra Wilson
Dianne Reeves
Shirley Horn
Mark Murphy
Bobby McFerrin
Diana Krall
Kurt Elling
Norma Winstone

COMPOSER-ARRANGER

Jim McNeely
Maria Schneider
Django Bates
Bob Brookmeyer
Bob Mintzer
Matt Darriau
Vince Mendoza
Bill Holman
Claire Fischer
Manny Albam
Carla Bley

ular contributor to John Zorn's *Masada,* he pushes that ensemble as it reflects upon Jewish music. He has even recorded an album devoted entirely to the exploration of music by the innovative jazz pianist and composer Mary Lou Williams.[11] Douglas has also done interdisciplinary work with dance, visual art, and film.

◇TROMBONE

Quite a few interesting trombonists have appeared on the scene since 1980. Taking the lead from J.J. Johnson, many contemporary players find ways to navigate this awkward instrument. A favorite trombonist of contemporary jazz is **Steve Turre** (b. 1949). Having performed with diverse musicians, including Dizzy Gillespie, Art Blakey, and Woody Shaw, he has been a member of *Saturday Night Live's* house band since 1984. Though Turre does not play as quickly or cleanly as J.J. Johnson, he has extraordinary control over his horn, allowing him to expand the upper range on the instrument. His approach has led him to experiment with:

1) many types of mutes
2) growls and fluttertongueing
3) circular breathing (a technique of inhaling through the nose while exhaling through the mouth, allowing longer passages to be played than would be possible in one breath)
4) a wide dynamic range
5) several styles of music, including hard bop, Afro-Cuban, Brazilian music, and jazz-rock fusion

Steve Turre performing in 1998.

Courtesy of Tom Zaccareno/Stage Image

Of note, Turre's primary innovation lies with his accomplished conch and seashell playing. While blowing into one end of the shell, he controls the pitch by inserting his hand into the opening. Just as moving a slide controls the amount of air that must be blown through a trombone, this process enables him to determine how much air needs to be sent through the shell. Able to evoke a surprisingly wide range of clear pitches, Turre has opened a new world for trombonists. His group *Sanctified Shells* features several trombonists who double on shells, creating a shell choir.[12]

◇SAXOPHONE

Following the lead of Charlie Parker and John Coltrane, saxophonists possessing laser-fast fingers seem to be the rule rather than the exception. Many players have extended the range of the sax upward, by playing in the altissimo register. While most specialize on either alto or tenor sax, many double on soprano and other woodwinds, such as flute, clarinet, and various wind instruments from around the world. Although playing with traditional ensembles is still common, some saxophonists choose to work with unusual instrumental combinations. The most notable of these is **Henry Threadgill** (b. 1944). His group, *X-75,* had four basses; his *Sextette,* actually made up of seven players, included two drummers and cello; a more recent group, *Very Very Circus,* involves multiple tubas and a French horn in addition to guitars and percussion.

Joe Lovano (b. 1952) has emerged as one of the most versatile, mature, and emulated tenor saxophonists of contemporary jazz. His extraordinary command and ability to elicit fast lines is stunning. Yet, he often opts to play short and simple phrases, focusing more on the beauty of his sound than on the mastery of his technique. His tone is smooth and smoky, though he often turns up the fire, evoking a raw growl. Drawing upon a wide variety of influences, he is equally comfortable in swing, post-bop, or experimental settings. Often Lovano will incorporate modal and free jazz devices while improvising over standards. Most known for his tenor playing, he also makes appearances on alto and soprano saxes, clarinets, flutes, gongs, and drums.

Lovano constantly searches for new settings to surround his dynamic and vital playing. First finding recognition with several big bands, including that of Mel Lewis and Woody Herman, he has also appeared with many smaller ensembles that showcase different features of his playing. Some of his albums as a leader have explored a retro side, featuring Broadway show tunes and music of his heroes ranging from Frank Sinatra to Thelonious Monk. He has also recorded with pianoless quartets and trios (which have become the proving ground for saxophonists, following the lead of Sonny Rollins). Other projects place him in extremely adventurous settings. One of his groups, *Universal Language,* prominently features his wife, Judi Silvano, singing wordless vocals. The compositions performed by this ensemble are endlessly inventive and interactive. Lovano's versatility and creativity have made him one of the most respected jazz musicians to emerge at the end of the twentieth century.[13]

While a large majority of saxophonists in the past thirty years have focused on tenor sax, **Kenny Garrett's** (b. 1960) mastery of the alto has made him one of the most exciting players on his instrument to emerge in decades. Though he has not invented any new genres or a completely unique approach to playing, he is simply the most technically gifted player around, bringing the virtuosity of John Coltrane to the alto sax. Stunningly fast fingers, perfect intonation, and vibrant rhythms characterize many of his solos, combined with asymmetrical, playful, and superb phrasing. His tone is clean but intense, with little vibrato. Garrett's expansive vocabulary and vast variety of musical statements always keep the listener guessing what will come next.

Garrett's talents were groomed while performing with the likes of the Duke Ellington Orchestra (under Mercer Ellington) and Art Blakey, but it was his five year engagement

Joe Lovano playing tenor saxophone.

Courtesy of Jack Vartoogian.

with Miles Davis that brought him widespread visibility and prominence. Since then he has explored many different styles. His most representative playing reflects a neo-traditional approach, but he has also worked with fusion and hip-hop artists. Like Lovano, one of his outstanding recordings features him with a pianoless trio, showcasing some of the most exhilarating music ever to come from this ensemble. Regardless of the setting, his dazzling improvisations are sure to be scrutinized by aspiring musicians for a long time to come.[14]

◇CLARINET

The clarinet, which lost its popularity after the swing era, has once again become an important instrument in contemporary jazz. While still not as common as the saxophone or trumpet, a handful of players have revitalized this instrument. Wynton Marsalis and others have included clarinets in their compositions to suggest music of an earlier time. Some players set out to expand its musical possibilities. The most innovative clarinetist of contemporary jazz is **Don Byron** (b. 1958). Byron's approach to playing is a far cry from the Benny Goodman model most people recall as the standard for jazz clarinet. Instead of mimicking Goodman's clean, even, and consistent sound, Byron inflects almost every note differently. At the core of his style is contrast. His tone ranges from airy and warm to harsh and raspy, and he often reaches for notes well above the usual range of the clarinet, straining to articulate these pitches. A single phrase might switch abruptly between beautiful lyrical expressions, honky low notes, out-of-tune pinched squeaks, exaggerated sense of vibrato, and slides between pitches. He occasionally tosses off fast lines, but opts more often for shorter, deliberate statements, sometimes even fighting against the pulse. At times, he purposely gives the impression that he is struggling to make the clarinet speak. Byron's playing is like a game, whose purpose is to constantly surprise the listener.

Beginning as a classical clarinetist, Byron's early inclinations toward creative settings led him to improvise with ragtime and Klezmer bands. Klezmer, unlike jazz, has consistently involved the clarinet from its inception. The first album that brought him widespread acclaim was based on the music of Mickey Katz, a Klezmer bandleader and musical comedian from the 1950s.[15] Other projects have been extremely diverse in nature, recreating works by such artists as Ellington, cartoon composer Raymond Scott, Robert Schumann, and Stevie Wonder. He has taken excursions into Latin rhythms, free jazz, and other styles. Some of his recordings feature him reciting politically charged narrations on top of the music. Byron, who also plays bass clarinet, has not only created opportunities for his instrument to be included in jazz groups, he has been a leading force in forwarding jazz in new directions.[16]

◇PIANO

While many contemporary pianists have downplayed the importance of standard jazz compositions, **Brad Mehldau** (b. 1970) has made it a priority to find fresh ways to approach these familiar tunes. Combining the introspective melodic style of Bill Evans and Keith Jarrett with the sensibility of Schubert and Schumann, Mehldau often uses these pieces to frame his improvisations. Within this context, he finds various ways to make the material new and fresh. Standards are often placed in unusual keys, odd meters, or supplanted with adventurous and fresh-sounding harmonies. Mehldau uses the original melody as a point of departure. In addition to playing quick, single note lines in his right hand, he often adds a second melody, achieving a contrapuntal effect reminiscent of a modern-day Bach. His left hand emerges prominently, developing melodic or chordal motives, ostinatos, or arpeggiations, while streaming eighth notes graciously glide out of his right hand. He focuses most of his energy on the art of playing with a trio, recording standards, original compositions, and even versions of the pop tunes like "Blackbird" by The Beatles and "Exit Music (For A Film)" by Radiohead.[17]

Uri Caine (b. 1956) is unquestionably one of the most eclectic and versatile pianists and composers today. He has performed with hard bop musicians such as trumpeter Freddie Hubbard and saxophonist Benny Golson, as well as many Knitting Factory players. His style ranges from fast, driving lines to a more percussive chordal method, and everything in between. He has even explored a version of stride piano that recalls James P. Johnson, adding cluster chords and "wrong notes" to evoke a feeling that the music is exploding. Caine combines a variety of synthesizers with his piano playing.

Growing up as a student of classical and jazz piano, many of Caine's projects marry these two interests. His first such venture was organized to accompany a silent film about the life of Romantic composer Gustav Mahler (1860–1911). Several of Mahler's pieces are reworked by Caine. Instead of using an orchestra as Mahler had, Caine's versions showcase traditional jazz instruments alongside violin, cello, and turntables. Some moments are rather literal transcriptions, while others bear little resemblance to the original. He mixes diverse styles with Mahler's own, adding significantly new rhythms, uncharacteristic improvisations, and free textures. Following the success of this project, Caine cut several albums reflecting on other classical composers, including Johann Sebastian Bach (1685–1750), Robert Schumann (1810–1856), and Richard Wagner (1813–1883). Other explorations are devoted to Middle Eastern music, Klezmer, Tin Pan Alley, funk, and various forms of jazz.[18]

◇GUITAR/BANJO

Many guitarists have excelled in contemporary jazz, but none has had as unique a voice as **Bill Frisell** (b. 1951). Frisell's sound is cool, sentimental, and reflective. His notes often fade in and out of one another. Combining the influence of guitarists such as Jim Hall and Jimi Hendrix with a hint of country twang, he uses a number of electronic devices and distortion techniques to manipulate his tone, creating timbres unlike those of any other guitarist. He takes a minimalistic and understated approach to playing, always avoiding clichés. Mystical sounding melodies compliment chords that often feel a little weird and off kilter. He is the consummate accompanist, supporting soloists with sensitivity and grace. Frisell performs on several types of guitars, bass, banjo, ukulele, and even makes a rare appearance on clarinet.

Frisell has worked extensively with John Zorn, and like Zorn, his list of influences is eclectic. He organically blends pop, rock, soul, bluegrass, worksongs, jazz, and world music in his performances and compositions. One extraordinary album, *Have a Little Faith,* displays his simple yet quirky style over a number of pieces by American composers as diverse as Copland, Sousa, Sonny Rollins, Bob Dylan, and Madonna.[19] Other projects include the reworking of music from Buster Keaton films and a collaboration with rock singer Elvis Costello.[20] Frisell's imaginative approach to sound and style set him apart from other guitarists, each project bringing new innovations and exciting music.

For the first time since early jazz, a banjo player has shown not only that this instrument is jazz compatible, but that it can be a vital voice in pushing the tradition forward and synthesizing styles. **Bela Fleck** (b. 1958), whose roots were in bluegrass, began exploring bebop on the banjo early in his career. Since then, he has combined bluegrass, jazz, pop, and funk to derive a unique sound. Interestingly enough, Fleck has not explored early jazz. His style is usually busy, favoring finger picking lines over strumming chords, often at quick tempos. Most of his work has been with a band called *The Flecktones.* This group features other unusual instruments and techniques of playing alongside the banjo. The electric bassist, Victor Wooton, plays like no one else. His unique, innovative, and breathtaking approach features exciting displays of popping and slapping. His brother, who calls himself "Future Man," performs on an instrument he invented called the *SynthAxe Drumitar.* Shaped like a guitar, this contraption allows him to electronically trigger various drum and percussion sounds with just a few fingers. The band has also featured Howard Levy, a harmonica and keyboard virtuoso, and multi-instrumentalist Jeff Coffin, who plays everything from two saxophones at a time to flutes, throat singing, and singing bowls.[21]

◇BASS

If one generalization can be made about contemporary jazz bassists, it is that an unprecedented number possess an extraordinary level of technical fluency. Players with comparable techniques to saxophonists and trumpeters are active in all styles. Depicting memorable and imaginative solos in addition to functional bass lines, players combine techniques taken from all previous periods while stretching their instrument's capabilities. Acoustic bass, which was all but abandoned in the 1970s, has made a strong recovery. Dave Holland and Charlie Haden (see chapter 14, Free Jazz) continue to make important contributions. Many others focus on electric bass. **Steve Swallow** (b. 1940), the most distinct contemporary personality on bass guitar, has created an expressive style. Always using a pick, he plays his instrument more like a guitar than a bass. His compositional approach to improvisation exudes beautiful harmonies and superb solos.

◇DRUMS

While many drummers continue performing in the post-bop style, others have made great efforts to create new and personal ways of playing. Some drummers prefer an extremely interactive and busy approach even while keeping a strict pulse. Others aim to free up the music, yielding a transparent, floating feel. Drummers often incorporate non-traditional colors and instruments into their sonic palate, including percussion instruments from around the world.

Joey Baron (b. 1955) can make his drum set sound like an orchestra. Though he typically plays a relatively small kit, he evokes hundreds of sounds from these instruments. Baron strikes the drums and cymbals in different places with a variety of beaters. He plays on the rim and sides of drums, cymbal stands, and anywhere else he can find to create unusual sonorities. Sometimes he strikes a cymbal violently, immediately choking (muting) it with his hand. At other times, he focuses solely on the drums. Unlike many drummers who repeat or slightly vary a limited number of patterns, redundancy is rarely heard from Baron for extended periods of time. He favors an approach in which he constantly surprises the listener with new sounds and rhythms. Familiar with a wide variety of styles, he switches freely between them. His inclusivity has placed him in high demand, demonstrated by his extensive work with postmodernists like John Zorn and Bill Frisell, more mainstream musicians such as trumpeters Dizzy Gillespie and Chet Baker, vocalists Carmen McRae and Tony Bennett, and rock star David Bowie.

◇BIG BAND COMPOSERS/ ARRANGERS

After almost vanishing in the 1970s, big bands have had a strong resurgence in the past few decades. Many cities house professional big bands that play everything from old swing favorites to new experimental compositions. **Jim McNeely** (b. 1949) has emerged as one of America's most imaginative and influential big band composers and arrangers. An active pianist, many compositions use the rhythm section as the foundation for his work, layering the winds on top to create interesting textures, jarring harmonies, and plenty of surprises. He has experimented with organizational techniques uncommon to jazz, including the use of 12-tone rows, unusual sets of pitches, complex forms, and other developmental techniques more often employed by classical composers. When arranging standards, McNeely takes the concept of reharmonization to extremes. His own compositions match a sense of creativity and adventure with a deep respect for the jazz tradition.[22]

Despite the fact that she does not perform on any instrument, **Maria Schneider** (b. 1960) is one of the few jazz musicians who has achieved recognition exclusively as a composer, arranger, and conductor. Her studies with trombonist and arranger Bob Brookmeyer inspired a desire to work on large-scale compositions, and her apprenticeship with Gil Evans has profoundly influenced the way she approaches blending various instrumental colors. Schneider's music is extremely beautiful. It utilizes lush harmonies, long, fluid melodic lines, and sensitive combinations of instruments. Her music recalls Impressionism as much as it does jazz. While her compositions can be aggressive, they all seem to capture delicate and lyrical qualities few have been able to duplicate.[23]

One of the most creative European jazz musicians of late is British composer-arranger-performer **Django Bates** (b. 1960). While Bates is a phenomenal keyboard and tenor horn player, his most significant contributions have come as a composer, arranger, and bandleader. He has written for string quartet, orchestra, his chamber group *Human Chain* (which has included auctioneers, newsreaders, harpsichord, and electric tuba in addition to traditional jazz instruments), and big bands. Many of his works combine electronic and acoustic instruments. His own big band, *Delightful Precipice,* was originally formed to accompany one of Europe's leading circuses. Since then, Bates has been involved with several cross-media collaborations.

Bates has an outrageous sense of humor and wit. His compositions are often sophisticated parodies, flirting with everything from jingles to heavy metal to funk. However, the musical substance of his compositions is quite new, original, and serious. His creations are complex, driven with relentless energy. Often many layers of activity occur simultaneously. Some pieces quickly contrast several different styles or moods, reminiscent of the "alternating cells" concept explored by John Zorn. While Bates's reputation is just starting to grow outside of Europe, he is truly an innovative force of the jazz world today.[24]

◇MISCELLANEOUS INSTRUMENTS

While trumpets, trombones, saxophones, clarinets, rhythm section, and voice have been the most common instruments in jazz, others have made infrequent appearances. Several flute players have enjoyed recordings as soloists; Duke Ellington worked with a trumpet player (Ray Nance) who doubled on violin; Gil Evans often used French horn and tuba in his arrangements; Sun Ra called for oboes, bassoons, and orchestral percussion instruments in some compositions. Recently, a growing number of players on unusual jazz instruments have made significant contributions. Flutist **James Newton** (b. 1953) combines a pure, classical sound with special effects and extended techniques. Sometimes he sings while playing, and uses multiphonics (overblowing to produce more than one pitch at the same time), glissandos, fluttertonguing, and wide, airy tremolos.[25] A number of string players have emerged in contemporary jazz. Two of the most exploratory and virtuosic performers are violinist **Mark Feldman** (b. 1955) and cellist **Erik Friedlander** (b. 1960). Both have worked with Knitting Factory musicians, share classical and jazz backgrounds, and play with traditional jazz groups in addition to more experimental ones. Feldman combines bowed passages with plucked ones, dazzling leaping double-stops, rapid flights in squeaky registers, and harsh attacks. He often augments his sound with electronic effects, adding distortion, echo, and other manipulations.[26] Friedlander, arguably the first star cellist of jazz, combines his beautiful classical tone with a sophisticated linear approach to improvisation. He pushes the limits of what the cello can do.[27]

Some musicians have incorporated non-Western instruments into jazz contexts. One such artist is **Rabih Abou-Khalil** (b. 1957), an oud player from Lebanon. The oud is a traditional, short-necked Arab lute quite popular in the Middle East. Abou-Khalil mixes original Arabic-like melodies with a variety of jazz-inspired concepts, mingling East with West.[28] A number of other players on unusual instruments have expanded the language of jazz, including oboist Paul McCandless, bassoonist Michael Rabinowitz, French hornist Tom Varner, accordionist Guy Klucevsek, and tuba player Howard Johnson.

◇SINGERS

The most creative, distinctive, and popular jazz vocalist to emerge in contemporary jazz is **Bobby McFerrin** (b. 1950). He has developed a large following among jazz, classical, and pop audiences. His enormous range allows him to reach deep bass notes, intense soprano pitches, and everything in between. Finding fame with a style that allows him to leap quickly between different registers, he creates the illusion of two or three vocalists singing simultaneously. He often imitates the sound of instruments with his voice, such as trumpet or violin. Just as comfortably, he impersonates soaring classical sopranos, rugged rock singers, children screaming, or birds chirping. McFerrin can produce notes even while inhaling, and uses his hands, feet, and chest, to simulate the sound of percussion instruments. His voice was the featured instrument on the theme from the television sitcom *The Cosby Show.*

When McFerrin began giving solo concerts, he lent new meaning to the term "one man band." Finding creative ways to sing melodies while accompanying himself, his concerts have included interpretations of J.S. Bach's piano music and imaginative scat solos over jazz

Singer Bobby McFerrin performing on stage in 1982.
Courtesy of Deborah Feingold/Getty Images Inc.

standards. He dreamed up a full-blown performance of *The Wizard of Oz,* performing the role of *all* the characters in addition to the orchestra. Sometimes he simply improvises on the names of people in the audience. His recording *The Voice* was the first solo jazz vocal album without accompaniment to be released on a major recording label.[29] A series of collaborations has included jazz pianist Chick Corea, classical cellist Yo Yo Ma, comedian Robin Williams, and the Muppets.[30] McFerrin's interest in *a capella* (unaccompanied) vocal music led him to explore the potential of various all-vocal groups. He made several recordings where he sang all the vocal parts, including his hit single "Don't Worry, Be Happy."[31] The group *Voicestra,* his vocal orchestra, explores uncharted territories. In addition to written arrangements, they experiment with collective improvisation, each singer bringing individual experiences to the music while responding to the others. McFerrin has also conducted symphony orchestras around the world. It is no surprise that such a talented and versatile musician, possessing wonderful communication skills and a friendly sense of humor, has found so much popularity.

One of the biggest challenges for jazz vocalists has always been selecting what music to sing. What can be performed that will evolve the jazz vocal tradition while staying true to its roots? **Cassandra Wilson** (b. 1955), the most daring and revered female jazz vocalist in

Cassandra Wilson, contemporary female jazz vocalist.

Courtesy of Herman Leonard Photography LLC

contemporary times, is finding fresh answers to this perplexing dilemma. She has reinterpreted jazz standards such as Billie Holiday's *Strange Fruit,* a ballad about the lynching of blacks in the South, spoken (not quite rapped) on top of sophisticated hip hop grooves, and even scatted over a tune originally performed by the Monkees. Her projects often tackle unusual themes, presented within challenging and creative musical environments. When singing familiar material, she alters the tempo, changes the harmonies, or adds fresh accompanimental textures. Her own compositions mix politics and humor.[32] Such diversity is represented by the vast array of communities in which she has worked. She is a rare spectacle, venturing into worlds as different as Steve Coleman's M-based, groove-oriented ensembles on one extreme, to that of Wynton Marsalis on the other (starring in his opera *Blood on the Fields*).

Wilson's voice is deep and sultry. She can hit extraordinarily low notes with an amazingly full and unforgettable tone. Though her alternation of whispered intimate expressions and belted cries is captivating, her most significant vocal achievement is the **attention she pays to expressing the words.** Her clear diction, superb phrasing, and emotional declamations follow the lead of Billie Holiday. When she sings, she tells a story. Her scatting focuses on enhancing the mood of the piece, rather than showing off her technique. Occasional affectations to her sound, such as growls or slides, strengthen the message of what she sings.

❖POPULAR APPEAL

Contemporary jazz appeal has paralleled trends illustrated by earlier periods. The more danceable and simple the music, the more popular it has become. More sophisticated and abstract music attracts smaller audiences with esoteric tastes. A handful of artists, including Cassandra Wilson, Bobby McFerrin, Bela Fleck, and jam-bands such as Medeski, Martin, and Wood have found ways to tap into popular music audiences not normally exposed to jazz through their unique and accessible approaches. Wynton Marsalis, with his dual career in classical and jazz music, possesses exceptional communication skills and charismatic demeanor, reaching a remarkably large audience for a "straight-ahead" jazz artist. While most other contemporary jazz profiles are far from household names, many make their entire livelihood through performance. Many cities have clubs that attract local and national acts, larger-scale jazz festivals, and jazz radio stations. Most of these concentrate on neo-traditional, post-bop, and retro bands, often excluding postmodernists. Nonetheless, there are dedicated, underground, cult followings for even the most abstract work of John Zorn and his disciples, especially at college campuses and progressive clubs in New York. While many contemporary jazz artists struggle to find mass appeal, they can usually count on a slowly growing support network of dedicated fans.

CHAPTER SUMMARY

1) Several genres developed in contemporary jazz from 1980 to 2000.
2) Since the extreme limits of technical possibility had been explored by earlier figures, contemporary jazz musicians often expand their language by playing multiple styles reflecting the past and combining jazz with many other types of music.
3) Many performers are also composers.
4) The neo-traditionalists, represented by trumpeter Wynton Marsalis, reflect on styles from earlier eras while incorporating their own voices. Although not innovative, these players revitalized acoustic jazz after a period where it almost died out.
5) The postmodernists draw from a vast array of influences, including jazz, rock, classical, and world music.
6) John Zorn, one of the most influential postmodernists, composes using alternating "blocks" of music, creating shocking sounds.
7) A group of musicians, led by Steve Coleman, created the idea of M-Base. They wanted to reach new creative heights while performing music that would welcome dancers. Some of these bands have performed with rappers.
8) The ECM record label created a unique, warm sound that is sometimes referred to as its own style. This label recorded many of the leading jazz musicians from 1969, when it was founded, to the present.
9) Medeski, Martin, and Wood, a jam-band, explores a variety of jazz oriented textures on top of techno and other dance beats.
10) Players like saxophonist Joe Lovano, trumpeter Dave Douglas, pianist Uri Caine, and vocalist Cassandra Wilson are extremely versatile, performing in traditional and experimental settings with equal comfort.
11) The clarinet and banjo have been reintroduced in contemporary jazz with fresh roles. New territory is being covered by Don Byron and Bela Fleck respectively.
12) Many unusual instruments have been seriously explored as solo voices in contemporary contexts. Many players utilize unusual instrumental combinations for their ensembles.
13) Big bands have resurfaced in recent times. Some important composers for this ensemble are Jim McNeely, Maria Schneider, and Django Bates.

NOTES

1. Wynton Marsalis with Art Blakey and the Jazz Messengers, *Straight Ahead* (Concord: CCD-4168, 1981).
2. Wynton Marsalis, *Marsalis Standard Time, Vol. 1* (Columbia: CK 40461, 1987); *Live at Blues Alley* (Columbia: G2K-40675, 1988).
3. Listen to Wynton Marsalis, *Crescent City Christmas Card* (Columbia: CK 45287, 1989); *Tune in Tomorrow* (Columbia: CK 47044, 1990); *Citi Movement* (Columbia: C2K-53324, 1992).
4. Wynton Marsalis, *Blood in the Fields* (Columbia: 57694, 1997).
5. John Zorn, *Cobra* (Avan: 049, 1995).
6. John Zorn, *The Big Gundown—John Zorn Plays the Music of Ennio Morricone* (Nonesuch: 9 79139-2, 1985); *Naked City* (Elektra Musician: 979238-2, 1989); *Kristallnacht* (Tzadik: 33005).
7. Some excellent ECM recordings are: Keith Jarrett, *My Song* (ECM 1115 821 406-2, 1978); *Still Live* (ECM 1360/61 835 008-2, 1988); Jan Garbarek, *I Took Up The Runes* (ECM 1419 843 850-2, 1990); Peter Erskine, *Time Being* (ECM 1532 78118-21532-2, 1994); Kenny Wheeler, *Music for Large & Small Ensembles* (ECM 1415/16 78118-21415-2, 1990). For more information on ECM records, visit the website: www.ecmrecords.com.
8. Some interesting M-Base recordings are: Steve Coleman, *Black Science* (Novus: 3119, 1990); *The Tao of Mad Phat/Fringe Zones* (Novus: 63160-2, 1993); Greg Osby, *3-D Lifestyles* (Blue Note: B2-98635, 1992). For more information on M-base, visit the website: www.m-base.com.
9. Medeski, Martin, and Wood, *Friday Afternoon in the Universe* (Gramavision: 79503, 1994); *Shack-Man* (Gramavision: 79514, 1996).
10. Tiny Bell Trio, *Songs for Wandering Souls* (Winter & Winter: 910 042-2, 1988).
11. Dave Douglas, *Soul on Soul* (RCA Victor, 63603); Also listen to *Witness* (Bluebird: 09026-63763-2, 2001).
12. Steve Turre, *Sanctified Shells* (Antilles: 314 514 186-2).
13. Joe Lovano, *Worlds* (Label Bleu: ECD 22132-2, 1989); *Rush Hour* (Blue Note: CDP 7243 8 29269 2 4, 1995); *Flights of Fancy, Trio Fascination Edition Two* (Blue Note: 7243 5 27618 2 1, 2001).
14. Kenny Garrett, *Introducing Kenny Garrett* (Criss Cross: 1014, 1984); *Triology* (Warner Brothers: 9 45731-2, 1995).
15. Don Byron, *Don Byron Plays the Music of Mickey Katz* (Elektra Nonesuch: 9 79313-2, 1993).
16. Don Byron, *Tuskegee Experiments* (Elektra Musician: 9 79280-2, 1992); *Music for Six Musicians* (Nonesuch: 9 79354-2, 1995); *Bug Music* (Nonesuch: 79438-2, 1996).
17. Brad Mehldau, *The Art of the Trio, Vol. 1* (Warner Brothers: 9 36260-2); *Art of the Trio, Vol. 4* (Warner Brothers: 9 47463-2, 1999).
18. Uri Caine, *Primal Light, Music of Mahler,* (Winter & Winter: 910 004-2, 1997); *The Goldberg Variations,The Music of Bach* (Winter & Winter: 910 054-2, 2000); *The Philadelphia Experiment*(Ropeadope: 93042-2, 2001).
19. Bill Frisell, *Have a Little Faith* (Elektra Musician: 9 79301-2, 1993).
20. Bill Frisell, *This Land* (Elektra Musicians: 9 79316-2, 1992); *Quartet* (Nonesuch: 79316, 1996).
21. Bela Fleck & the Flecktones, *Flight of the Cosmic Hippo* (Warner Brothers: 9 26562-2, 1991); *Left Of Cool* (Warner Brothers: 9 46896-2, 1988).
22. Jim McNeely with the Stockholm Jazz Orchestra, *Jigsaw* (Dragon: DRCD 213, 1991); with the Village Vanguard Orchestra, *Lickety Split* (New World: 80534-2, 1997).
23. Maria Schneider Jazz Orchestra, *Evanescence* (Enja: ANJ-8048 2, 1994).
24. Django Bates, *Summer Fruits (and Unrest)* (JMT: 697 124 052-2, 1993).
25. James Newton, *The African Flower* (Blue Note: CDP 7 46292 2, 1986).
26. Mark Feldman, *Music for Violin Alone* (Tzadik: 7006, 1995).
27. Erik Friedlander, *Topaz* (Siam: 50003, 1999).
28. Rabih Abou-Khalil, *The Sultan's Picnic* (Enja: ENJ-8078 2, 1994).
29. Bobby McFerrin, *The Voice* (Elektra Musician: 60366-2, 1984).
30. Bobby McFerrin with Chick Corea, *Play* (Blue Note: CDP 7 95477 2, 1992); with Yo-Yo Ma, *Hush* (Blue Note: B2-95477, 1990).
31. Bobby McFerrin, *Don't Worry, Be Happy* (IEMI: 50146, 1988).
32. Cassandra Wilson, *Blue Light 'Til Dawn* (Blue Note: CDP 0777 7 81357 2 2, 1993); *New Moon Daughter* (Blue Note: CDP 7243 8 32861 2 6, 1995).

Chapter Eighteen

American jazz pianist, singer, songwriter, Fats Waller (1904–1943). Courtesy Getty Images

So, What Is Jazz?

In chapter 2, four definitions of jazz were suggested. This chapter showed that while all four theories aid in an understanding of this music, none of them defines it completely. The first view, **music need only be associated with the jazz tradition to be called jazz**, has consistently been tested throughout history. Some musicologists argue that dance music from the swing era was not jazz, but popular music. Louis Armstrong rejected bebop, calling it instead "Chinese music." The harsh reaction against free jazz by many bop and hard bop musicians demonstrated their insistence that this style had nothing to do with *their own* tradition. And Wynton Marsalis refused to accept the placement of jazz-rock fusion under the umbrella of jazz. What one person assumes is jazz often is disputed by others.

The remaining definitions also prove both helpful and problematic. The concept that the music must **convey jazz swing** feeling ignores much important literature from the jazz canon. Adherence to this view eliminates Latin jazz, jazz-rock fusion, much free and contemporary jazz, and a host of other critical works. If music **must be improvised** to be jazz, many of the highly arranged suites of Duke Ellington, as well as a large body of first-class but written-out solos from the swing era, would be eliminated. The fourth view, combining the second and third definitions, states that jazz requires **improvisation *and***

conveys a jazz swing feeling, eliminating even more names from the jazz roster. Yet, the presence of improvisation and swing feeling have undeniably played a major role in the evolution of jazz styles and in characterizing this music.

So, what is jazz? Is there more to it than that? The qualities described in chapter 2 speak to the musical characteristics that are most often associated with jazz. But jazz means more than simply the performance of a particular style of music. It takes more than simply improvising over a swinging groove with jazz sounding melodies, harmonies, and phrases. Jazz artists also seem to possess a certain type of attitude. It is the combination of this attitude with the musical characteristics that has defined this tradition from its earliest days. While the characteristics listed below may not apply exclusively to jazz, each of the points seems to be present in every era and genre of this quickly evolving and ever-changing tradition.

1) **Jazz is a music concerned with looking forward.** Throughout history, no other music has evolved so quickly and so often. In the classical world, the Romantic style of composing lasted around a century; the Renaissance period existed for two. Music from other cultures, such as parts of Africa or India, has remained virtually unchanged for hundreds upon hundreds of years. But the jazz tradition is one of constant flux and evolution. With every generation, or even decade, at least one new genre and many sub-genres were introduced. In this sense, **leading jazz musicians from every era have been avant-gardists,** creating something new with the language they inherited.

2) **Jazz is a music concerned with looking back.** At every point in its history, players found influence from musicians who preceded them. Some, like Louis Armstrong, Charlie Parker, and Miles Davis, were predisposed to their immediate predecessors and mentors. Others, such as Wynton Marsalis, look much further back, to styles played well before these musicians were born. Even Cecil Taylor, whose harmonic and rhythmic language seemed unique, was influenced by Bud Powell, Duke Ellington, and Dave Brubeck. In this sense, **leading jazz musicians from every era have been neo-traditionalists,** influenced significantly by jazz movements of the past.

3) **Jazz is a music concerned with looking around.** This has always been the case with jazz. Even at its inception, jazz was influenced by both African and European elements within the context of America. Dave Brubeck borrowed from the music of Turkey, Dizzy Gillespie from Cuba, John Coltrane from India, Weather Report from rock, Stan Getz from Brazil, John Zorn from Klezmer, Gunther Schuller from classical, Duke Ellington from the Far East. With a music that incorporates so many sources, claims that jazz is an "African American" art form simply do not do the experience justice. In this sense, **leading jazz musicians from every era have been fusionists,** borrowing freely from any kind of music within reach, mixing it with personal ideas about jazz and the jazz tradition.

Several other points can be made as well. Jazz responds to events in the society that surrounds it and reflects on these events. Jazz is creative, and jazz mirrors the individual personality of the musicians who perform it. It challenges, inspires, and delights. Most of all, jazz is a legacy that will be with us for a long, long time. However, after all is said and done, do we really have a clear definition of jazz? Perhaps Louis Armstrong said it best, after being asked by an admiring fan, "just what exactly is jazz?" His reply summed it up in only seven words. "If you gotta ask, you'll never know."

◇WHY HASN'T JAZZ BECOME MORE POPULAR?

This text has examined the popular appeal of various jazz styles. Jazz found its zenith of popularity during the swing era. The free jazz movement was the least popular. Today, while fans live almost anywhere around the globe, jazz cannot boast widespread and unencumbered popularity. Currently jazz accounts for a relatively insignificant percentage of CD sales in this country. Why is music with such a vibrant and exciting history not more popular?

There are several reasons. First of all, **understanding jazz requires a certain amount of knowledge about jazz and sophistication.** Much of the music employs intricate harmonies, complex melodic statements, and highly syncopated rhythms. Jazz can be quite varied and unpredictable. Often solos sound abstract to the untrained listener who may be more comfortable with literal presentations of a clear melody. History has shown that simpler styles of music have found more popularity than complex ones. Within the jazz tradition, swing, jazz-rock fusion, and smooth jazz enjoy the greatest popularity. Swing presents catchy melodies, uncomplicated solos, and straightforward rhythms. Jazz-rock fusion often consists of few harmonies, repeated bass figures and drumming patterns, and short phrase lengths. Some smooth jazz is so uncomplicated it has been described as "easy listening" music.

A second reason for the lack of popularity is that **much jazz is inaccessible to dancers.** The most popular styles have been dance music. Flappers danced to jazz during the 1920s Jazz Age, a host of moves were invented to fit swing, and dancing was possible with jazz-rock fusion. Even current artists who present their music with danceable grooves, such as the jam-band Medeski, Martin, and Wood, receive more popularity than those without this element. The general population tends to prefer "functional" music (in other words, music that has some function other than the sheer sound of it) over "listening" music.

A third explanation is that **some jazz requires a long attention span.** Many jazz performers, such as John Coltrane and Sonny Rollins, play extended solos spanning lengthy intervals of time. Ellington and other composers have written extended suites, lasting ten, twenty, or thirty-plus minutes. Such lengthy performances can be overwhelming for the average radio listener raised on the three-minute pop tune model. (This explanation holds true in the classical world as well. For example, many symphonies last thirty minutes to an hour, or even longer.)

A final possibility is that **people listen to music that is readily available to them.** For a variety of reasons, American television and radio stations tend to focus on rock, country, rap, and other popular types of music, rather than jazz. Most jazz radio in this country is operated by public stations, supported more by fans than advertisers. It seems logical that if people have a lower level of exposure to a particular genre, the music will have less popularity. Take, for example, music that seems unlistenable to most Westerners, such as Chinese opera or Javanese Gamelan. These sounds, so unusual to our ears, are widely cherished by their respective communities, places where they can be heard around the clock. Some of the most popular jazz artists have been those who maintained regular radio or television appearances: Benny Goodman, Duke Ellington, Nat "King" Cole. When a jazz musician appears in or scores a popular film, CD sales often skyrocket. (Take, for example, the enormous following that pianist/singer Harry Connick, Jr. received after performing for the blockbuster hit *When Harry Met Sally.*) People gravitate towards music they are used to hearing, feeling comfortable and safe with familiar material.

Regardless of its popularity, jazz has much to offer to anyone willing to investigate it. Jazz tells a story. It represents a wide range of emotions: joy, anger, sorrow, elation, frustration, rebellion, freedom. Through jazz, a history of collaborators, risk takers, and striking individual personalities has emerged, yielding a tradition of great and uncompromised art. Jazz, whether popular or not, has been a deep and honest musical expression from its earliest moments to its most recent descendants.

◇SO, WHAT NOW?

Currently it is possible to enjoy music from any period of jazz. Recordings from any style are plentiful, from the *Original Dixieland Jazz Band* to the latest innovations of Knitting Factory musicians. Dixieland festivals are hosted across the country; swing orchestras play dances for a variety of occasions; repertory bands perform the music of Duke Ellington, Count Basie, among others; bop and post-bop influenced musicians headline jazz festivals worldwide; free musicians continue to create new and exciting ways to approach jazz; jazz, rock, and contemporary dance forms continue to be fused by many artists.

This is a very exciting time for jazz musicians. They can play any way they choose. In the future, some musicians will explore simpler styles. Others will delve into new harmonies, grooves, improvisational techniques, unusual timbres, and fresh instrumental combinations. Some players will combine their work with artists from different disciplines, including dance, visual art, and film. As the world becomes smaller, jazz will become bigger, borrowing more and more from any exotic styles that can be assimilated and encapsulated. It will continue the traditions of looking forward, looking back, and looking around, and will not stop capturing the feeling of "jazz" that, after completing this entire text, we still haven't been able to define.

What will the next movement be? Where will it begin? Who will develop the freshest innovation? How popular can it become? The future is difficult to predict, but one thing is certain. Jazz will not stand still. If history is any indicator, this music will continue to grow, evolve, and mutate. It will reflect the state of a changing world and continue to react to it. Jazz is vibrant and jazz is alive.

Appendix

A Very Abbreviated Outline of Jazz Styles—Not strictly chronological; many styles overlap the same time periods, and most have continued long after their inception. Many innovators continued playing for decades after their style emerged.

Time	Style	Hornmen	Pianists	Composers-Arrangers	Rhythm Section Musicians
1920s	*Early Jazz*	Louis Armstrong Sidney Bechet Bix Beiderbecke	James P. Johnson Earl Hines	Jelly Roll Morton	Baby Dodds Zutty Singleton Pops Foster
1930s	*Swing*	Coleman Hawkins Roy Eldridge Johnny Hodges Benny Carter	Art Tatum Teddy Wilson	Duke Ellington Fletcher Henderson Sy Oliver	Chick Webb Dave Tough Sid Catlett Walter Page Gene Krupa
Late 1930s	*Transition to Bop*	Lester Young Don Byas	Nat Cole		Count Basie Rhythm Section 1937–43 Jimmy Blanton
1940s	*Bop*	Charlie Parker Dizzy Gillespie Dexter Gordon Stan Getz	Thelonious Monk Bud Powell Al Haig	Thelonious Monk Tadd Dameron Dizzy Gillespie	Kenny Clarke Max Roach Oscar Pettiford Roy Haynes
Late 1940s	*Transition to Cool &* West Coas	Lee Konitz Miles Davis	Lennie Tristano	Claude Thornhill Gil Evans	
1950s	West Coast	Gerry Mulligan Chet Baker Art Pepper	Dave Brubeck	Gerry Mulligan Shorty Rogers Jimmy Giuffre	Chico Hamilton

Time	Style	Hornmen	Pianists	Composers-Arrangers	Rhythm Section Musicians
1950s	*Hard Bop*	Clifford Brown Sonny Rollins Thad Jones John Coltrane Cannonball Adderley Miles Davis	Tommy Flanagan Horace Silver Red Garland	Horace Silver Benny Golson Cannonball Adderley Jackie McLean Gigi Gryce	Art Blakey Philly Joe Jones Paul Chambers Sam Jones Wilbur Ware
Late 1950s	*Transition to Modal Jazz & Free Jazz*	Miles Davis John Coltrane Ornette Coleman	Bill Evans Cecil Taylor	Charles Mingus Miles Davis	
Early 1960s	*Coexistence of Hard Bop, Free Jazz, & Modal Jazz*	Eric Dolphy	Bill Evans McCoy Tyner Cecil Taylor	John Coltrane Ornette Coleman Wayne Shorter Charles Mingus Don Cherry	Elvin Jones Bill Evans Trio with Scott LaFaro Cecil Taylor with Sunny Murray
Mid-1960s		Freddie Hubbard Joe Henderson Wayne Shorter Don Cherry	Herbie Hancock	Wayne Shorter John Coltrane Herbie Hancock	Miles Davis's 1963–68 Rhythm Section
Late 1960s	*Transition to Jazz-Rock*	Miles Davis	Joe Zawinul	Joe Zawinul	Tony Williams
1970s	*Coexistence of AACM, Jazz-Rock, & Modal Jazz*	AACM players	Keith Jarrett Herbie Hancock Chick Corea Joe Zawinul	Chick Corea AACM Joe Zawinul John McLaughlin	Miroslav Vitous Airto Moreira Jaco Pastorius

Elements of Music

In describing the nature of jazz and the characteristics of different styles, several basic musical terms are quite helpful. This chapter is devoted to defining some of these terms, and I urge all readers, including those who are musically knowledgeable, to examine them carefully.

When people think of jazz, they usually think of rhythm first. But because the word rhythm is often used to describe a large variety of musical characteristics, some uses convey inaccurate or contradictory meanings. Much of the confusion can be avoided by first understanding three related terms for which rhythm is often mistaken: beat, tempo, and meter.

Beat Music is often said to have a pulse. The unit of pulse is called a beat. When you tap your foot to music, you are usually tapping with the beat. Here is a visualization of the pulse sequences we call beats.

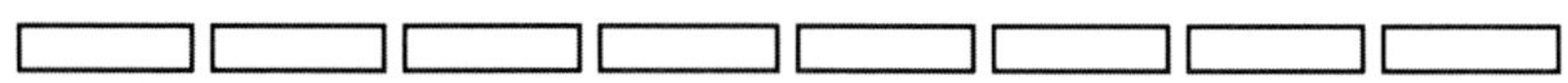

Tempo Tempo refers to the speed or rate at which the beats pass. If you describe a piece of music as fast, you probably mean it has a rapid tempo, not that it occupies a short time span. When the beats continue at a regular rate, we say the tempo is constant. A clock's ticking is a good example of constant tempo. If the passage of beats is rapid, the speed is called "up tempo."

Meter The beats in music are rarely undifferentiated. They are usually heard as being grouped. Meter describes the type of grouping. Our perception of grouping results when sequences of beats are set off from each other. This occurs in several ways. Every third or fourth beat may be louder or longer than the others. It may be distinctive because it has a different pitch or tone quality. Those differences are perceived as emphasis or accent. If we hear a sequence of beats grouped in fours, it may be due to a pattern of accents which creates this effect: ONE two three four ONE two three four. That pattern represents a meter which musicians simply call "four."

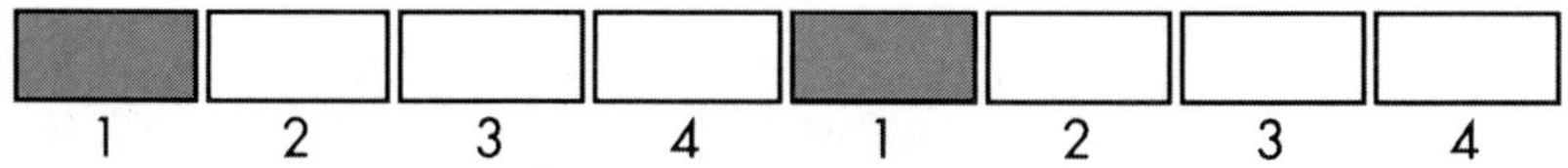

If the beats fall into the pattern, **ONE** two three, **ONE** two three, **ONE** two three, musicians say that the music "is in three" or in "waltz time."

Meters of four and three are quite common, but there are also meters of five, six, seven, and others. A meter of five might sound like **ONE** two three four five **ONE** two three four five, **ONE** two three four five, with a large accent on the first beat and no other accents. Or there may be a strong accent on the first beat and a smaller accent on the fourth: **ONE** two three FOUR five **ONE** two three FOUR five **ONE** two three FOUR five; or a smaller accent on the third beat: **ONE** two THREE four five **ONE** two THREE four five **ONE** two THREE four five. A meter of six usually feels like **ONE** two three FOUR five six **ONE** two three FOUR five six.

Each group of beats is called a **measure.** When the meter is three, there are three beats in a measure; when the meter is four, there are four beats in a measure.

Rhythm In the broadest sense, rhythm simply refers to the arrangement of sounds in time, and therefore encompasses beat, tempo, and meter. But rhythm has come to mean something more specific than these features. In fact, beat, tempo, and meter furnish the framework in which rhythm is described.

Imagine a continuous sequence of beats occurring at a constant tempo, with four beats to a measure. The steady beat which in musical notation is represented by a string of quarter notes can also be visualized as a series of boxes, representing equal amounts of time. Our meter would be called "four." Each beat is called a quarter note, and each unit of four beats constitutes a measure.

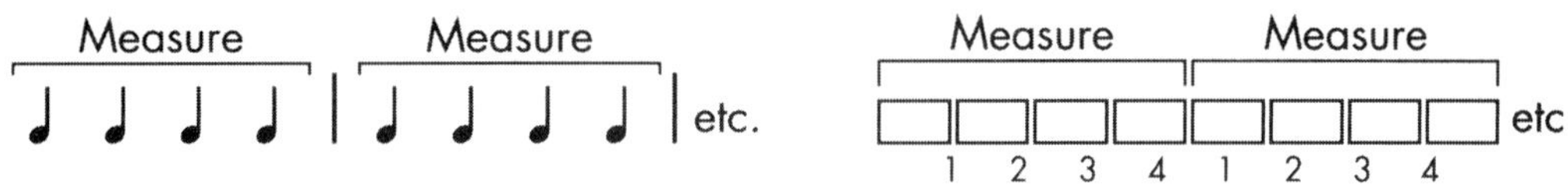

The sound within a measure can be distributed in an infinite number of ways, one of which includes "filling" the measure with silence. Rhythm is the description of how that measure or a sequence of measures is filled with sound.

Let us take a few examples, numbering the four parts of the measure one, two, three, and four, respectively. We shall create rhythms by using a single sound mixed with silence. First, divide a measure into four equal parts, filling only the first and third with sound.

We have a rhythm. It is not complex, but it does what a rhythm is supposed to do: it describes the distribution of sound over time. In fact, this is the bass drum part in numerous marches, and it is the string bass part in many slow dance pieces.

Now, instead of taking just one measure, take two measures as a unit of repetition. In other words, the rhythm is two measures long.

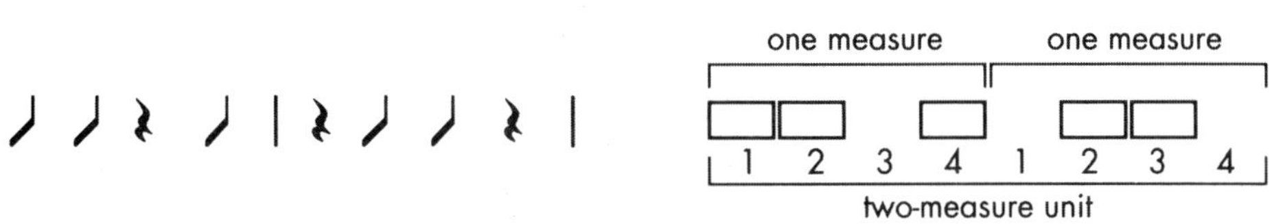

Finally, repeat a one-measure rhythm to fill two measures' worth of time. This might be heard as a two-measure rhythm or as two one-measure rhythms.

Rhythm is the distribution of sound over time, but rhythm also refers to the way sounds are accented. Usually, the first beat of a measure is accented. An example would be the typical OOM pah pah accompaniment for a waltz. In a measure of four, the first and third beats are often accented, as in the BOOM chick BOOM chick drum pattern used in much popular music.

Syncopation

Examining our use of accents can lend understanding to a rhythmic element called *syncopation*, a crucial aspect of jazz feeling. For example, if we expect to hear a sound on every beat but only hear it in a few odd places, the upset we feel is the result of syncopation. This upset can be very stimulating and contribute a prime component of jazz feeling.

Examine this manner of filling two measures.

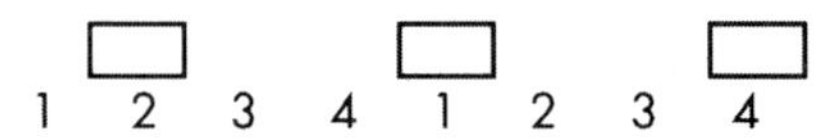

Note that the sounds which occur, bordered by silence, in positions other than on the first and third beats seem to stand out. They seem to be self-accenting. If we additionally stress these odd positions by making the sounds in those positions louder than the sounds in other positions, syncopation is enhanced: one TWO three four ONE two three FOUR.

The concept of syncopation partly depends on a listener's expectations. For example, if we are expecting to hear *ONE* two THREE four, but we actually hear one *TWO* three FOUR, we are experiencing syncopation. Jazz drummers often keep time by playing boom CHICK boom CHICK (one TWO three FOUR) instead of BOOM chick BOOM chick. This syncopation is part of what makes a performance sound like jazz. Another frequently used syncopation occurs when we hear one two three FOUR when we are expecting to hear ONE two three four. So you see that rhythm involves the arrangement of stresses in addition to just describing the arrangement of sound over time. We have also seen that a phenomenon called syncopation results when the sounds are arranged or stressed in unexpected ways. Of course, what is expected depends on what the listener is accustomed to hearing. Therefore, the statement that syncopation consists of unexpected accent is inadequate. Perhaps a more useful definition involves the accent of beats other than the first and, in a measure of four beats, also the third beat. Silence can also be syncopating. For example, if we encounter silence at a time when we are expecting to hear ONE, the feeling of syncopation results.

Eighth Notes

To understand more complex syncopations and another essential element of jazz feeling, the swing eighth note, requires an acquaintance with ways in which beats are divided into smaller units. Here is a measure in four, with four quarter notes to the measure. We can divide each quarter note in half to produce eighth notes.

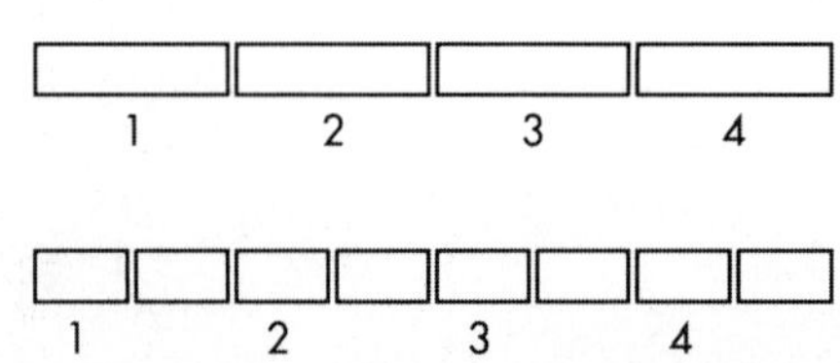

There are two eighth notes for every quarter note. If we place accents on the eighth notes according to the way we previously accented the measure of quarter notes, we have *ONE* two three four FIVE six seven eight. The time span for a measure of eight eighth notes is identical to that in a measure of four quarter notes, but keeping track of eight eighth notes is cumbersome. So we express the eighth notes in terms of subdivided quarter notes, saying "and" for the second half of each quarter note (every other eighth note): one and two and three and four and. Each word, whether it is the name of a number or the word "and," represents an eighth note.

Syncopation occurs when any of the "ands" receives more emphasis than the numbered units. Accenting the "ands" is essential to rhythms frequently employed in jazz. The final two beats in a measure are often divided into eighth notes with the last one accented the most: three and four AND. Many notes which appear in written form on the first beat of a measure are played on the "and" of the fourth beat in the preceding measure when given a jazz interpretation. The practice of playing a note slightly before or slightly after it is supposed to be played is a syncopating device which jazz musicians apply to pop tunes in order to lend jazz feeling to a performance.

Triplets

The quarter note can also be divided into three equal parts to produce what are called eighth-note triplets.

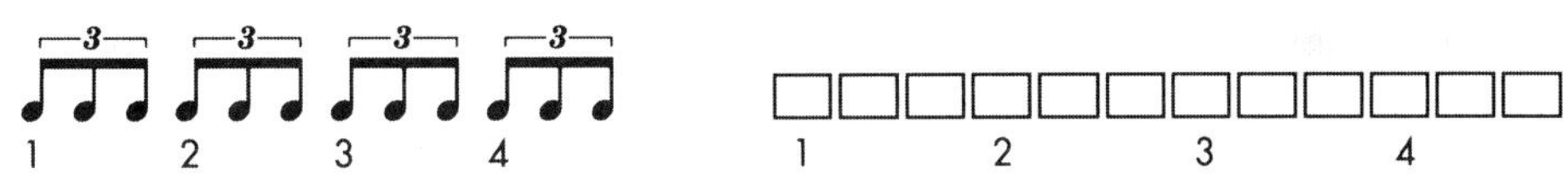

Sixteenth Notes

Here, each quarter note is divided into four equal parts, called sixteenth notes.

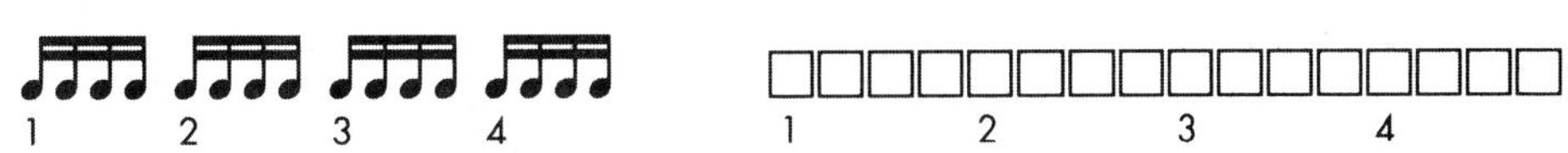

Dotted Eighth-Sixteenth Note Pattern

So far we have examined equal divisions of the quarter note. But it is also possible to divide it into notes of unequal value, for instance, a long note and a short note. One such pattern consists of a dotted eighth note followed by a sixteenth note. A dot after a note means that the note receives one and a half times its usual value; therefore, the dotted eighth note has the combined value of an eighth note and a sixteenth note.

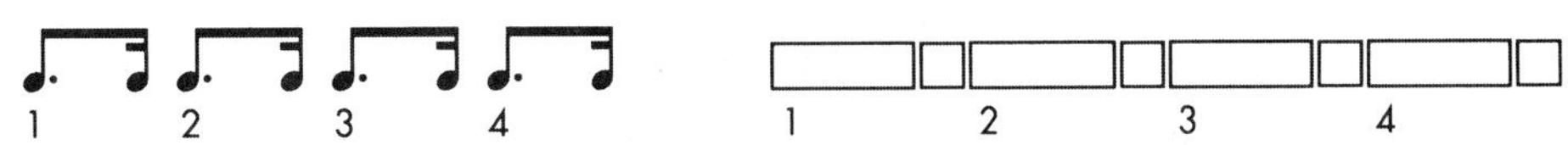

Tied Triplet Figure

Another long-short pattern is based on the triplet division of the quarter note. The pattern is called a tied triplet figure. Here, the first note has the value of two-thirds of a quarter note, and the second has the value of one-third.

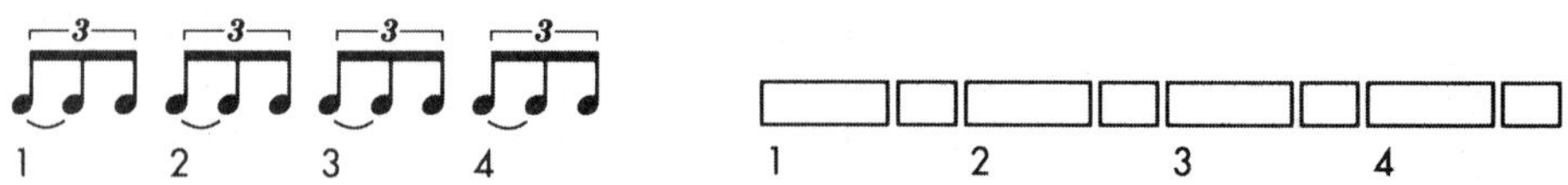

Jazz has one rhythmic quality which, to my knowledge, is not found in any other kind of music: jazz swing feeling. A discussion of it appears in the "What Is Jazz?" chapter, but that discussion hinges on the *swing eighth note* which is examined next.

Having heard the term "swing eighth note," you might wonder how, if an eighth note is simply half the duration of a quarter note, we can have different types of eighth notes, swing eighth note being one of them. Strictly speaking, you cannot have different types. An eighth note is an eighth note. Our descriptive language is loose enough, however, that we can use the term to label notes of slightly more or less duration than the eighth note is understood to receive.

Legato and Staccato

This looseness in applying the term "eighth note" is not exclusive to jazz musicians. Non-jazz musicians often use terms such as **legato**, which means long or slurred together or connected. They use the term **staccato**, which means short, abruptly separated. A legato eighth note equals a full-value eighth note. A staccato eighth note, on the other hand, has variable duration. Its length depends on the style of performance, and its value may actually be less than half of a legato eighth note. It can be called an eighth note only because it is immediately followed by silence which fills up the remaining time that a full-value eighth note requires. Perhaps a staccato eighth note should be called a sixteenth note, or it should bear some designation that is more precise than the label of "staccato eighth note."

(Listen to examples on *Demo CD* Tracks 44-45.)

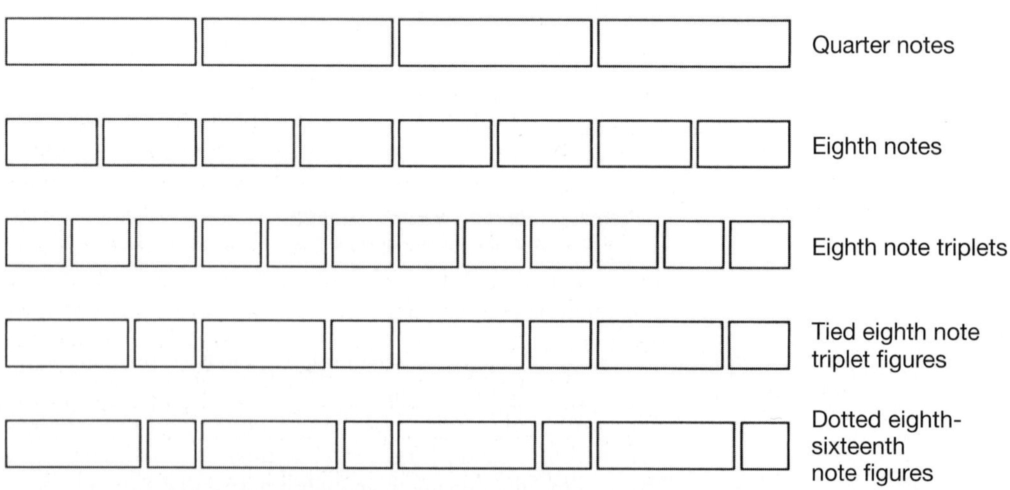

Swing Eighth-Note Pattern

A wide assortment of eighth note durations and stresses are found in jazz styles. There are no jazz musicians who divide the beat in only one way. But there is a pattern that is more common than any other. It is a long-short sequence which is close, but not identical, to the pattern of durations found in the tied-triplet figures. The tied-triplet figure, you may remember, consists first of a long sound, then a shorter sound which is half the duration of the first sound. The two sounds together fit the duration of a single beat in the manner of a quarter-note triplet. The duration pattern most commonly employed by jazz musicians, the **swing eighth-note pattern,** falls somewhere between the tied-triplet figure and a sequence of eighth notes having identical durations. In other words, the first member of the pair is shorter than the first member of a tied-triplet pattern, and the second member is somewhat longer than a triplet eighth note. But neither member's duration is truly equal to an even eighth note, what musicians call "a straight eighth."

(Listen to examples on *Demo CD* Track 43.)

The stress patterns for swing eighth-note patterns are distributed differently from player to player. Sometimes within the work of a given player, the stresses are distributed differently from performance to performance, sometimes from passage to passage. Basically, however, the first in a group of such swing eighth notes is louder than subsequent notes which occur on upbeats.

There is considerable confusion about notation of swing eighth notes. Such lack of uniformity exists in this regard that about the only accurate statement is that, when reading eighth notes, the desired choice of duration patterns usually depends upon the particular band and the style of arrangement being played. A little history might make this point a bit clearer. In countless written arrangements of jazz-oriented pieces which were published before the 1960s, dotted eighth-sixteenth figures appeared whenever the arranger wanted a swing eighth sound. (The arranger did not want true dotted eighth-sixteenth note patterns in which long-short meant the long member sounded three times the duration of the short one.) The notation appeared as even eighths thereafter in most arrangements, but the intention was for those notes to also be played as swing eighths. (If an arranger of this period wanted *truly even* durations, a written message appeared above the notes: "even 8ths." The musician's assumption was to otherwise play all the written eighth notes in a swing rhythm.)

Polyrhythm

To appreciate the rhythms which typify jazz, we should keep in mind the fact that several rhythms are usually played simultaneously. *Polyrhythm* (meaning *many rhythms*) is very important to jazz. When you listen carefully to a modern jazz performance, you should be able to hear several different rhythms at the same time. These include the rhythm in the melodic line, that of the bassist, the rhythm played by each of the drummer's four limbs, and each of the pianist's two hands.

Polyrhythms are often created by patterns which pit a feeling of four against a feeling of three. In other words, two measures can be played at the same time, with one being divided by multiples of two and the other being divided by multiples of three. In addition to that, the onset of one pattern is often staggered in a way which results in something less than perfect superimposition atop another pattern. Pitting three against four and staggering the placement of rhythms can project the feeling that the rhythms are tugging at each other. The resulting combination of stresses can be extremely provocative, and it can produce new syncopations in addition to those already contained in the separate patterns.

You can now understand why to say that jazz is quite rhythmic is to make an almost meaningless statement. All music has rhythm, and most music has syncopated rhythms. What sets jazz apart from many other types of music is the preponderance of syncopated rhythms, the swing eighth-note sequences, and the frequent presence of polyrhythm.

SCALES, KEYS, TONALITY, AND MODALITY

Understanding scales is basic to appreciating chord progressions, and an acquaintance with scales and chord progressions aids our knowledge of the rules which guide jazz improvisation. Everyone is familiar with musical scales. No one has been able to live very long without hearing a friend, neighbor, or family member practice "his scales."

Scales comprise the rudiments of beginning practice routines for singers and instrumentalists alike. Even people who cannot read music are familiar with the sequence *do* (pronounced "dough"), *re* (pronounced "ray"), *mi* (pronounced "mee"), *fa, sol, la, ti* (pronounced "tee"), *do.* Those eight syllables do not represent exact pitches as C, D, E, F, G, A, B, C; they are only the names of acoustic relationships. (Do not let that term, acoustic relationships, scare you. It is one of the simplest concepts in music. It means only that no matter what frequency of so many vibrations per second is assigned to *do,* the remaining seven pitches are determined by set multiples of it, for example twice the frequency, 1½ the frequency, and so forth.)

"*Do re mi fa sol la ti do*" numbers eight elements, the eighth element carrying the same name as the first, *do.* Its relationship to the first is exactly double the frequency of the first. For example, if the first *do* were 440 vibrations per second, the next higher *do* would be 880. It is no more complicated than that. That last *do* ends one sequence and begins another. The relationship between the bottom *do* and the top *do,* the first and eighth steps of the scale, is called an *octave.* The sound of two notes an octave apart is so similar that if they are played simultaneously, you can easily mistake the pair for a single tone. Most naturally produced tones contain an octave as one component of all the frequencies that combine to give a tone its own characteristic color or quality. The octave is called a harmonic or an overtone of the tone's fundamental pitch. That is the reason two tones an octave apart sound like one when they are played at the same time. Since the interval of an eighth, from *do* to *do,* represents a doubling of frequency, you have probably guessed that those intervals between the first and the eighth must be fractions. You guessed correctly. The ratio of the fifth step (*sol*) to the first step (*do*) is 3/2; that of the third (*mi*) to the first (*do*) is 5/4, etc.

The seven-note scale has many labeling systems. We have already used three of them: a) do, re, mi, fa, sol, la, ti, do; b) first, second, third, fourth, fifth, sixth, seventh; and c) the frequency ratios: re/do = 9/8; mi/do = 5/4; fa/do = 4/3; sol/do = 3/2; la/do = 5/3; ti/do = 15/8. Next is the system which uses alphabet letters A, B, C, D, E, F, and G.

Look at the diagram of the piano keyboard printed here.

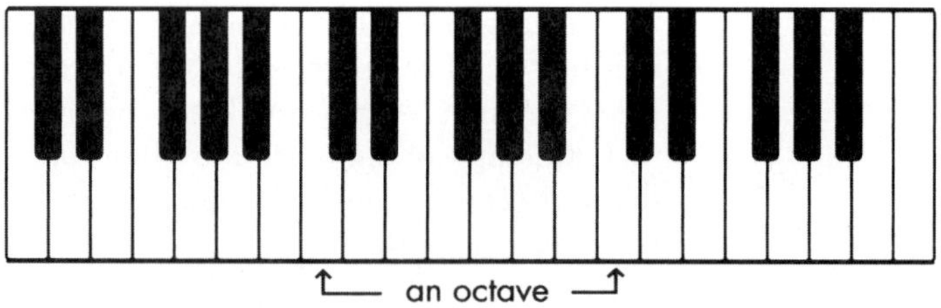

It is constructed so that the pattern of eight white keys and five black keys recurs again and again. The distance, or interval, between the beginning of one pattern and the beginning of the next is called an "octave." The scale which beginners usually learn first is the C scale; the C scale is obtained by playing eight of the white keys in succession, starting with the one labeled C. That scale, C, D, E, F, G, A, B, C, contains the same note relationships which we know as do, re, mi, fa, sol, la, ti, do. Play the notes of the C major scale in the order in which they are numbered in the diagram.

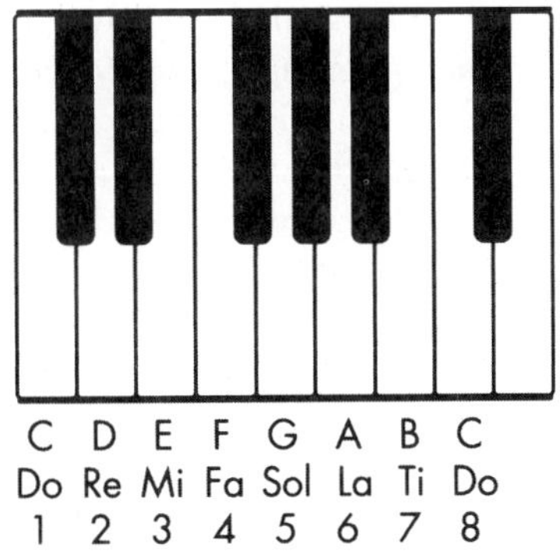

Look again at the piano keyboard.

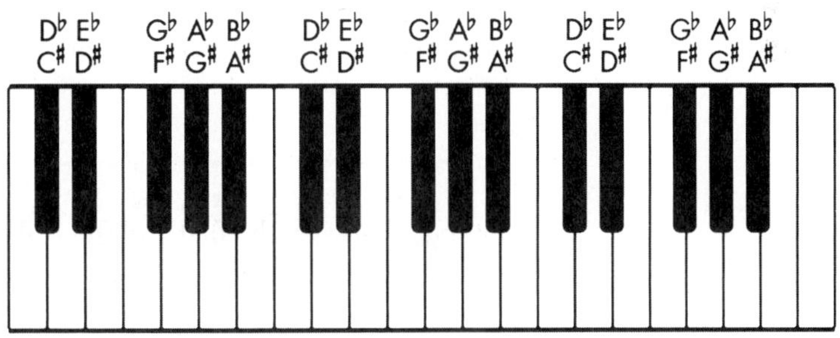

The black keys are known as sharps and flats. Sharp is symbolized # (like the number sign on a typewriter) and flat is symbolized ♭ (like the lower case b on the typewriter). The black keys derive their names from the white keys which are next to them. The black key to the right of A is called "A-sharp" because it is slightly higher than A. But it is also referred to as "B-flat" because it is slightly lower than B. If we want only a C scale, going up an octave from C to C, we use none of the black keys. But if we want scales which begin on any note other than C, we have to employ at least one (and sometimes all) of the black keys. For instance, to play a major scale on D, it is necessary to make use of two sharps, F-sharp and C-sharp.

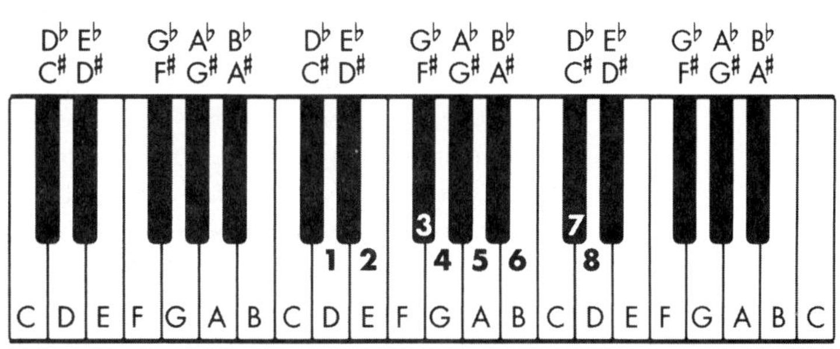

D Major Scale

A scale may be played starting from any black or white key. Altogether there are twelve such scales. Going up (moving left to right) from C, they are the scales of C, C-sharp, D, D-sharp, E, F, F-sharp, G, G-sharp, A, A-sharp, and B. Or, naming them in descending order, C, B, B-flat, A, A-flat, G, G-flat, F, E, E-flat, D, and D-flat.

When musicians say that a tune is in a certain key, for instance, the key of C, they mean that the song is played with the notes of the major scale beginning on C.

The relationship of the notes of the major scale gives a song a particular kind of sound and structure, which is called **tonality.** Although tonality is a complicated idea, it can be understood as the feeling that a song must end on a particular note or chord. A key defines a scale which, in turn, defines that key. If a piece of music has the feeling of reaching for the same note, the key note, or it seems loyal to some note more than to any other, the overall harmonic character of the piece is called **tonal.**

There is another term like the term "scale" that is not interchangeable with "key." The term is **mode.** Like a scale, a mode describes a sequence of acoustic relationships. Some modes even have the same number of elements as the scales we just explored. In fact, the C scale has a mode name: Ionian. But if we use the notes in the C scale and start the sequence on D, we produce another mode, Dorian. In other words, if we go from D to D in the key of C, we have constructed the Dorian mode. (See page 418.)

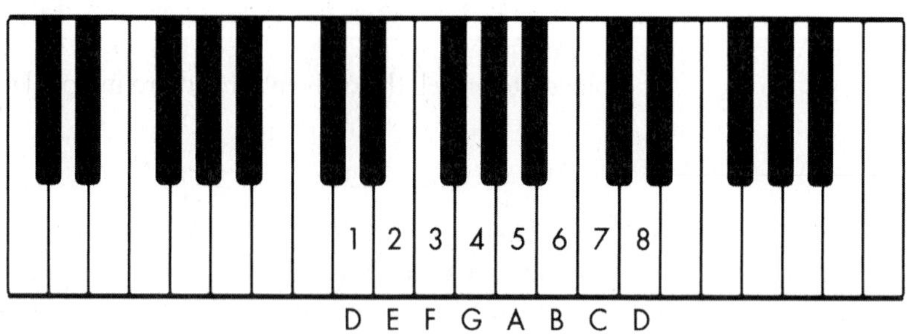

Dorian mode

For each of the seven scale steps in a key, there is a corresponding mode. The major scale itself has a mode name: Ionian; beginning on the second step produces the Dorian mode; the third step, the Phrygian mode; fourth, the Lydian mode; fifth, the Mixolydian mode; sixth, the Aeolian mode; and seventh, the Locrian mode. Each has a different sound because each has a different sequence of acoustic relationships which results from starting on different steps of the scale. I urge you to find a keyboard and play these modes. The concepts outlined here mean little without the sounds they describe.

We have seen that there are twelve keys, C, C# (or D♭), D, and so forth. We also know that for each key there is a corresponding seven-note scale starting on the note which bears the name of the key (C D E F G A B for the C scale). Within each key there are modes, one mode beginning on each of the seven steps. The mode constitutes an octave of its own. Scales (modes) of fewer than seven notes and greater than seven notes also exist. (See pages 417–418.) The most common scale constructed of more than seven notes is the chromatic, simply that sequence of all the piano keys in an octave, white ones and black ones. Scale is a poor name because **the chromatic scale is actually just another way of dividing an octave into twelve equal parts.** It does not indicate a key as the C scale and the B♭ scale do. *The chromatic scale is only a sequence of very small intervals called half steps.*

The chromatic scale has twelve steps: C, C#, D, D#, E, F, F#, G, G#, A, A#, and B. Unlike the modes, which have to be started on certain scale steps to guarantee their unique qualities, the chromatic scale can be started on any note, proceed through an octave and create the same identifiable chromatic quality no matter what note is chosen for its starting position. That means the C chromatic scale is identical to the C# chromatic scale (and all others). Perhaps it should be called "chromatic scale starting on C" or "chromatic scale starting on C#," specifying exactly what tone is to be the reference note.

The chromatic scale is very important because it expands the number of acoustic relations possible. Given twelve different tones in place of only seven, we have the option of raising and lowering (sharping and flatting) virtually any note we wish. Most Western European music of the past two centuries uses the chromatic scale instead of limiting itself exclusively to notes within one key at a time or, what is even more restrictive, only one mode at a time. Music was produced during the twentieth century which used all twelve tones equally and discarded the feeling of particular keys. Tonal music, you remember, is simply music which seems to be loyal to a certain note, always reaching for that note. Music without tone center is called *atonal.*

Most music has key feeling even when employing all twelve tones in the chromatic scale. This is just another way of saying that most music has tonality. During improvised music, tone centers might shift, but they usually remain long enough for their effect to be perceived. Most jazz employs tone center. It is extremely difficult to improvise without at least implying temporary tone centers and key feelings. The twelve tones are usually employed to enrich the conventional do re mi tonal orientation instead of providing a harmonic orientation all their own, one of atonality. Keep in mind that some music employs more than one key at once, but this type of music is not generally termed atonal. It is called *polytonal,* which means many keys.

If you play within the do re mi scale and enrich your melody with chromatic tones, the character of your playing can be partly described by how often you employ certain chromatic tones. Many people consider *bluesy quality* essential to jazz. A central component of bluesy quality is the frequent use of chromatics, three chromatics in particular: the *flat third, flat fifth,* and *flat seventh* notes of the scale. In other words, chromatic scale tones are employed to enrich the seven tones already available.

In the key of C, the blue notes are E-flat, G-flat, and B-flat. Remember the C scale consists of C, D, E, F, G, A, and B; there are no sharps or flats (none of the piano's black keys). To create a blue note, we lower the third step of the scale. In the key of C this means changing E (a white key) to E-flat (a black key). We use both E *and* E-flat in constructing jazz lines, but the E-flat stands out because it is not one of the notes in the C major scale.

(Listen to *Demo CD* Track 55 to hear these sequences.)

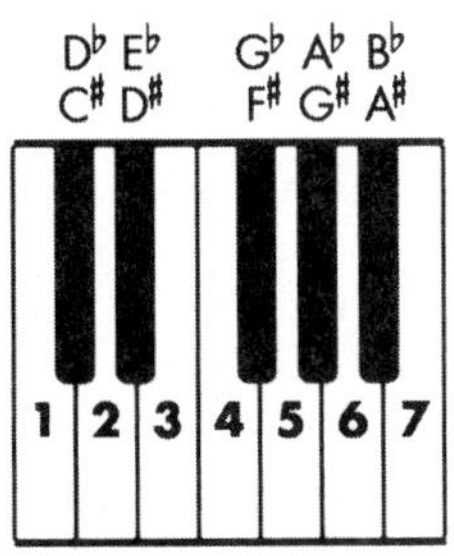

C scale without any blue notes

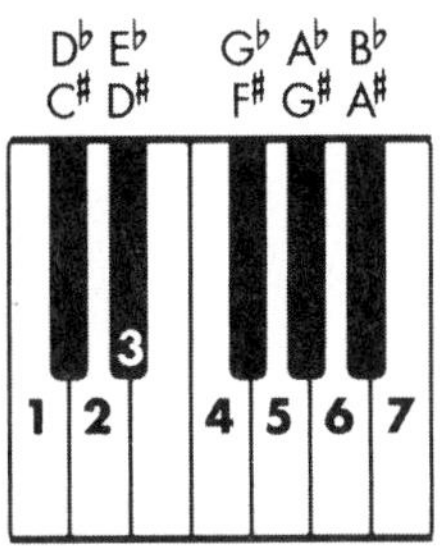

C scale with the flat third blue note

The second most common blue note is achieved by lowering the seventh step of the scale. In the key of C, this means changing B (a white key) to B-flat (a black key). Again we use both B *and* B-flat for our lines, but the B-flat is more distinctive because it is not in the key of C.

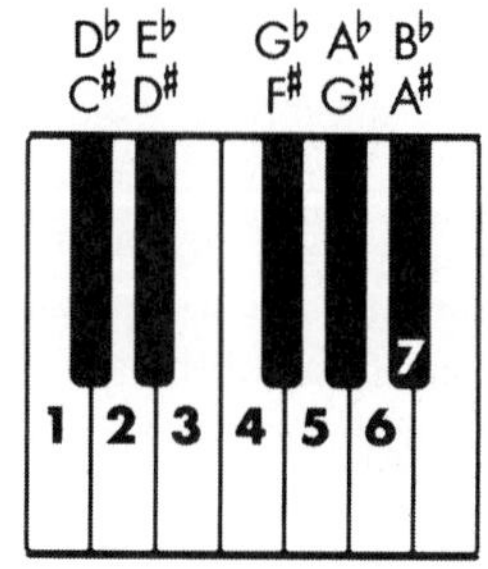

C scale with the flat seventh blue note (B-flat)

Note that the concepts of regular third step and blue third step are like the concepts of major chord and minor chord (the sounds of which you can demonstrate for yourself, using the following keyboard diagram as a guide to positioning your first, third, and fifth fingers).

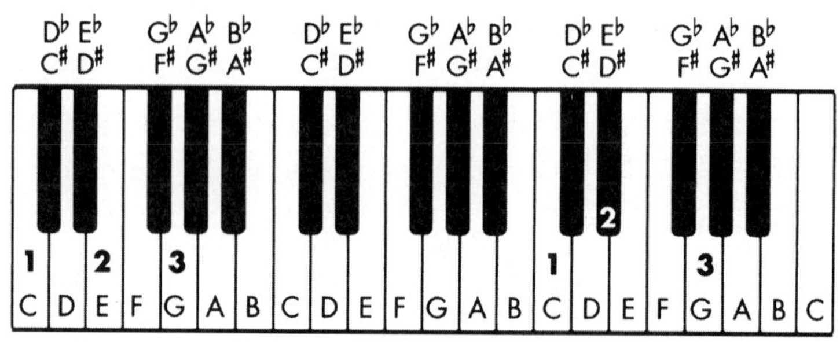

Major chord Minor chord

The third most used blue note is the lowered fifth. Its use was not frequent until modern jazz began in the 1940s, but thereafter it became a standard device to convey a bluesy feeling, much as the lowered third and seventh had been in early jazz. In the key of C, a flat fifth is achieved by lowering G (a white key) to G-flat (a black key).

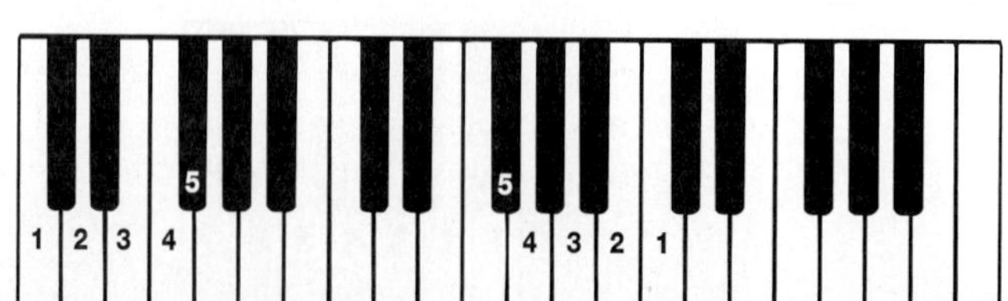

Going up to the flat fifth (G-flat) Coming down to the flat fifth (G-flat)

BLUE NOTES

The term "blue note" does not have a single, universally accepted use. Some writers use it to designate the flat third and flat seventh that were discussed above. These sounds might best be termed "chromatically lowered" pitches because they are lowered by one step of the chromatic scale, the interval known as a "half step," a "chromatic semitone." Some writers use the term "blue note" to designate any pitch that is not completely a half step below another. This makes its classification "indeterminate" because, instead of being a clearly identifiable pitch of the chromatic scale, it is a pitch we might obtain only if we could play a note from the region within the cracks between the piano keys, so to speak. Musicologists variously call such pitches "neutral thirds;" "heptatonically equidistant;" or "indeterminate pitches." (For a closer examination, see "Blue Notes and Blue Tonality" by William Tallmadge, *The Black Perspective in Music,* 1984, Volume 12, Number 2, pages 155–165.) These pitches cannot be produced on the piano, but that does not mean that pianists have not wanted to produce them. The recent proliferation of synthesizers in the hands of jazz-rock pianists saw the molding of numerous solos employing this second kind of blue note, apparently because synthesizers are capable of generating pitches that represent fine gradations between those found on the piano. Playing with pitches is termed "pitch bending." (See page 42, and listen to Track 58 of the *Demo CD* for examples.)

The attraction that jazz musicians have for out-of-tune thirds and sevenths might be the result of differences between European and African preferences for tuning. One origin is suggested here. The European seven-tone scale (do, re, mi, fa, sol, la, ti, do) is not based on equal divisions of the octave. It is a sequence of whole steps and half steps (the "diatonic" system) in which each half step represents about one twelfth of an octave. (The interval between C and D is a whole step, as is that between E flat and F. The interval between B and C is a half step, as is that between E flat and E.) A mix might have resulted between the European seven-tone approach and a West African seven tone (heptatonic) approach in which the interval separating each successive scale tone is equal, not the unequal pattern we find in whole steps and half steps. This African "equidistant heptatonic" scale has pitches that coincide fairly closely with those in the European diatonic scale. However, the third and the seventh steps are flat in relation to their counterparts in the European scale. This means that if an African sang his own pitch in a European piece, the third and seventh steps would sound "blue" or not perfectly in tune to the ears of a listener who was accustomed to the European scale. If African American singers and musicians retained their taste for this particular kind of tuning, and seasoned European music to suit their tastes, then they performed European-style music in the "blue" manner we today associate with jazz.

CHORDS AND CHORD PROGRESSIONS

Familiarity with the concept of scales allows us to explore the concept of chords and chord progressions, which, in turn, is essential to appreciating the harmony that jazz improvisers follow. These concepts are quite simple, but they have far-reaching applications, not only in jazz, but in all music that uses harmony.

A chord is obtained by sounding three or more notes simultaneously. Although chords can be constructed from any tones, they are usually described in terms of scale notes and given Roman numeral names. The most common chord, one alternately described as a tonic chord, a major triad, the key chord, or a I (Roman numeral for 1) chord, employs the first, third, and fifth notes of the scale: *do, mi,* and *sol.* In other words, this chord is produced by simultaneously sounding do, mi, and sol in any key, any register, with any loudness or tone color. Try these:

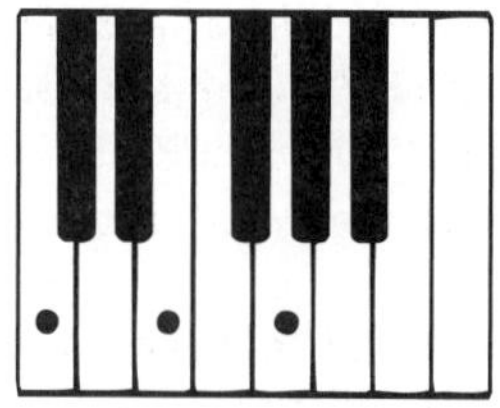

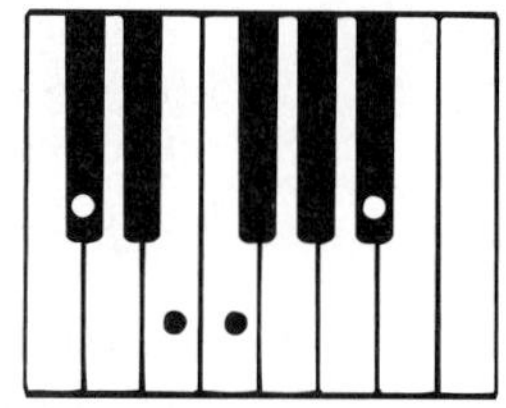

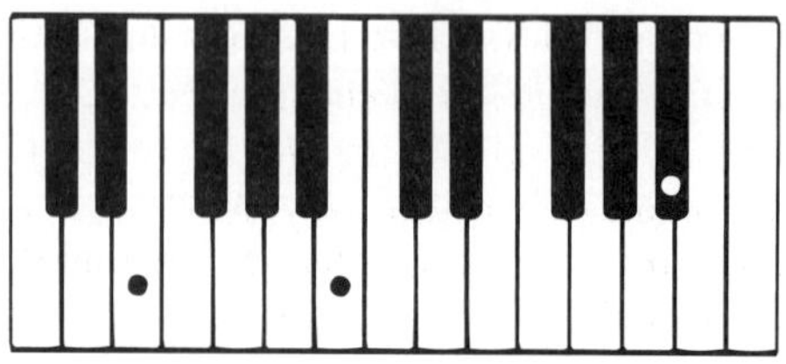

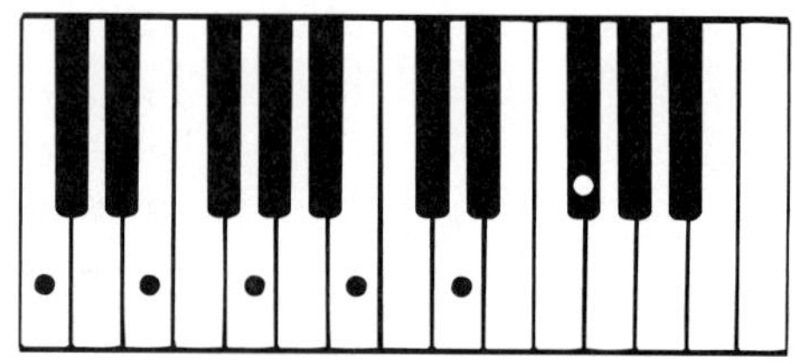

Chords are named for the scale step on which they are based. A I chord is based on the first step of the scale, do; a II chord is based on the second step, re; a III chord on the third step, mi; a IV chord on fa; a V chord on sol; a VI chord on la; and a VII chord on ti. This system of naming is very handy for describing chord progressions. (See page 415 for notations.)

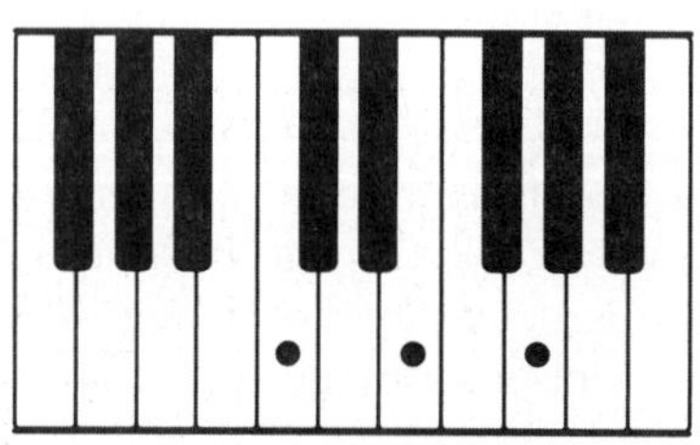

I chord in key of C

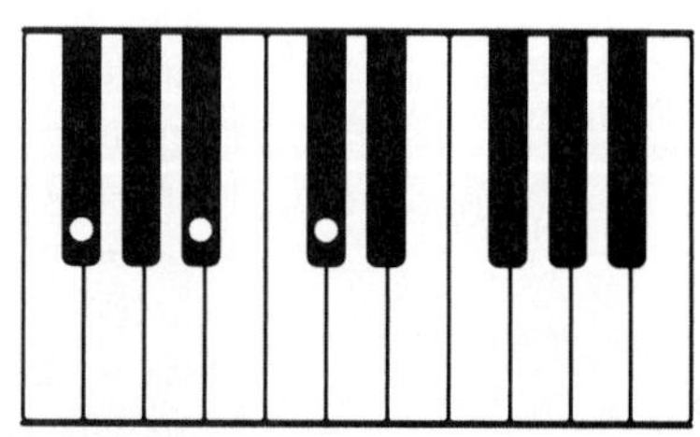

I chord in key of F-sharp

I chord in key of B-flat

A chord change is simply what it says, changing a chord. If we move from one chord to another, we have executed a **chord change.** We have moved forward, progressed, from one chord to another. In other words, a **chord progression** has been made. If the chords involved are those based on the first and second steps of the scale, respectively, we could describe the chord change as a I-II progression. If we move from a chord based on the first step to a chord based on the fourth, we create a I-IV progression. The reverse of that is a IV-I. If we move from the I chord to the V chord, and then back to the I chord, we create a I-V-I progression.

To hear the sound of a very common chord progression, the I-IV-I-V-I blues progression, find a piano, an organ, an accordion, or any other keyboard instrument and strike all the keys simultaneously, the number of counts (1234, 2234, etc.) indicated in the diagram below. You need not worry about what fingers to place on what keys. In fact, go ahead and use fingers from both hands if necessary. Try to keep a steady rate for striking the keys. If you can keep a steady rate, you may find that you are sounding like you have heard pianists and guitarists in rhythm and blues bands sound.

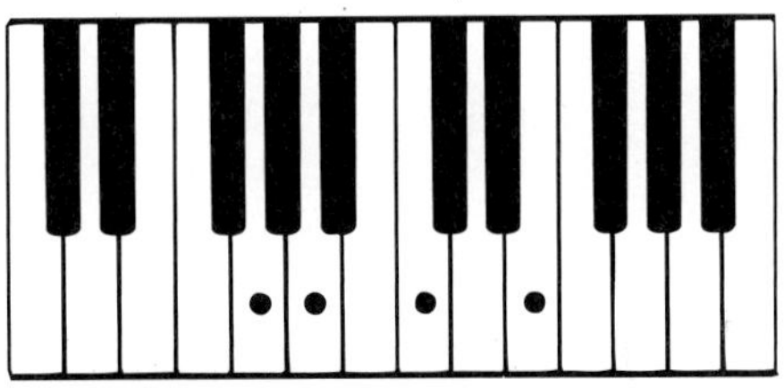

1234 2234 3234 4234 (I chord for 4 measures)

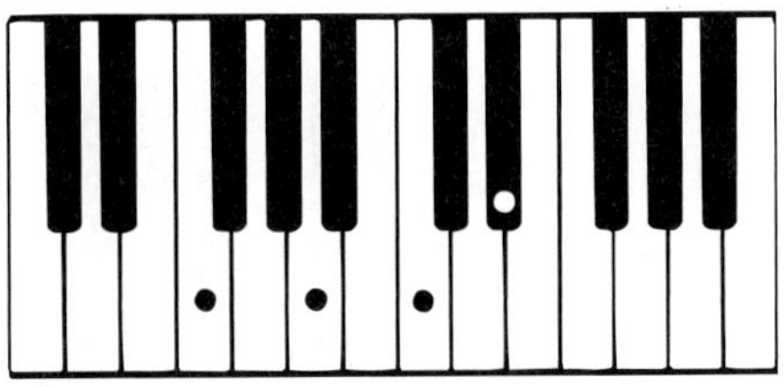

1234 2234 (IV chord for 2 measures)

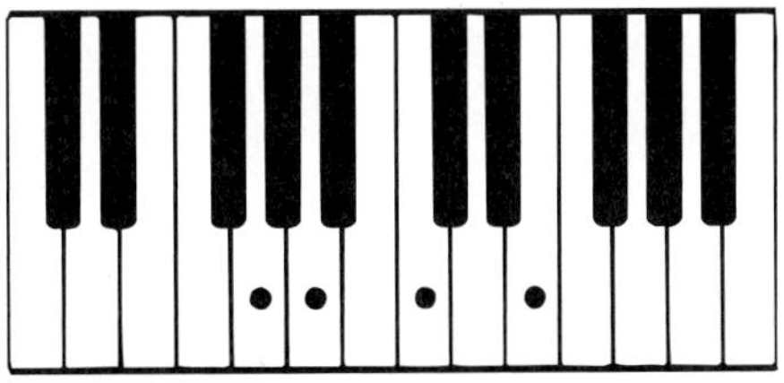

1234 2234 (I chord for 2 measures)

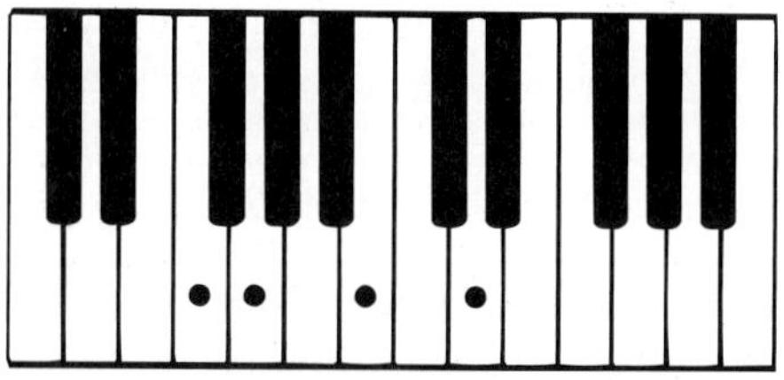

1234 2234 (V chord for 4 measures)

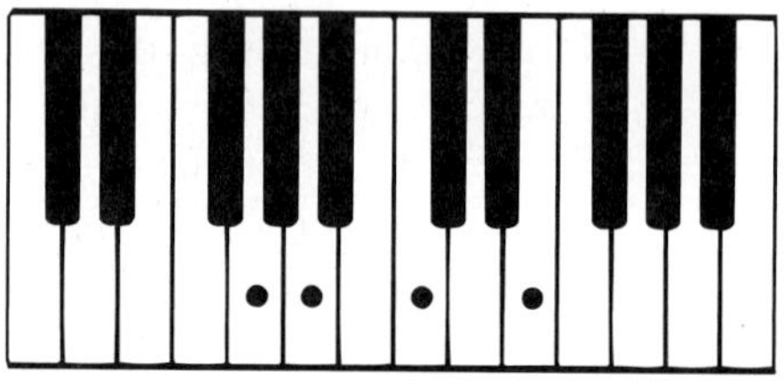

1234 2234 (I chord for 4 measures)

(demonstrated in *Demo CD* Track 19)

Chord Voicing Most music uses chords that have been **voiced.** (For notated examples, see page 417.) The concept of voicing is a very simple one. It involves the fact that the keyboard is a succession of repeating octaves.

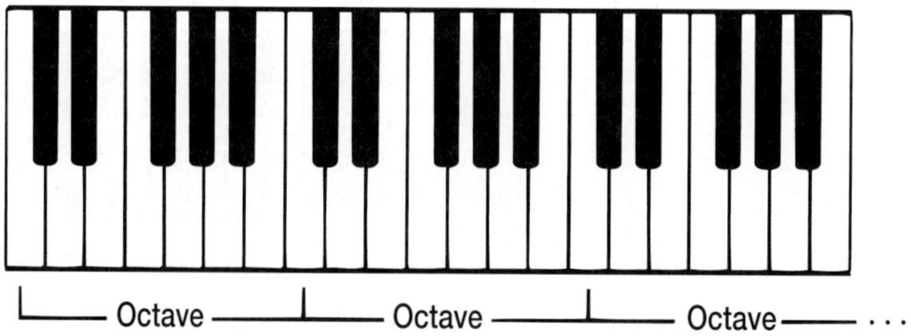

With the resulting repetition of notes available, we can pull each chord note away from the position it holds within a single octave and spread the chord over the range of the keyboard. We can also include additional notes and/or omit some of the original notes. All these manipulations fall under the heading of "voicing."

The same chord (three notes) arranged in different positions across the keyboard.

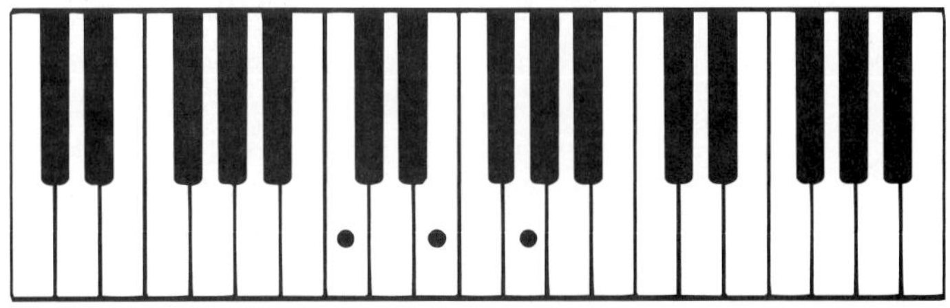

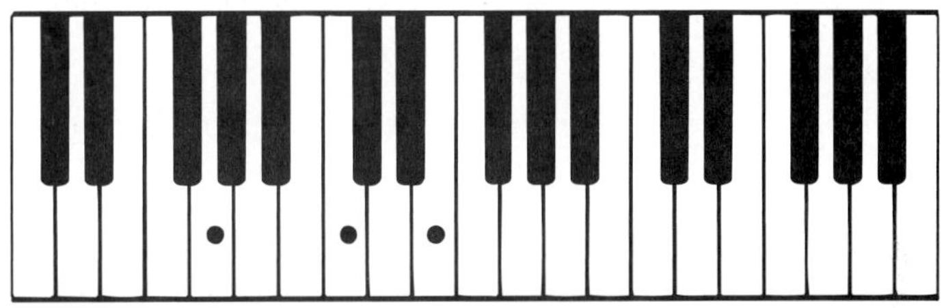

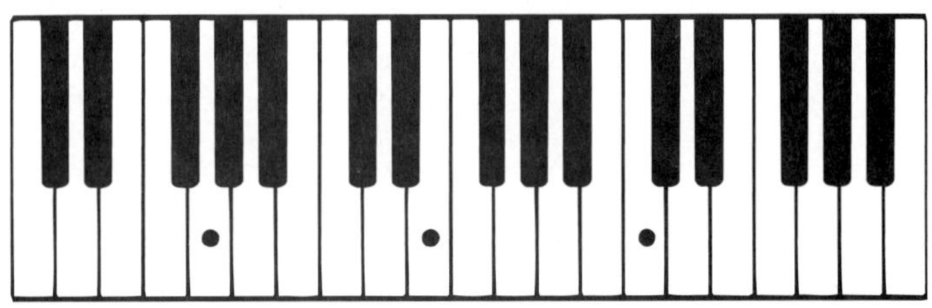

Jazz pianists can often be identified by the way they voice chords, and characteristic preferences in piano voicing are important components of the style in almost every period of jazz. In recent jazz, for example in the work of pianists McCoy Tyner and Chick Corea, **voicing in fourths** is quite common. Voicing in fourths means that chords are made up of notes four steps away from each other. In other words, a chord voiced in fourths might contain do, fa, and ti instead of do, mi, and sol. (The interval between do and fa is called a perfect fourth. To create a perfect fourth between fa and ti, the ti must be flatted. In building a chord composed of perfect fourths, each successive note is considered do of a new scale and the fourth note, fa, in that scale is used.) You can hear the sound of a chord voiced in fourths by playing this:

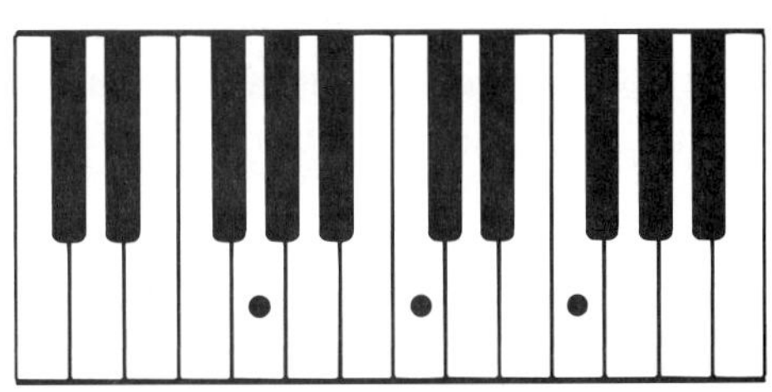

Voicing in fourths

The term "voicing" also refers to how the notes of a chord are assigned to instruments in an orchestra or band. The ranges of the instruments as well as their tone colors are taken into consideration in voicing chords. Characteristic voicings serve to identify the work of different arrangers. Duke Ellington, for instance, voices chords in a manner distinguishable from Stan Kenton. Both Ellington's chords and his choice of instruments differ.

Voicing is also a term used to identify the instruments playing a melody. For example, we might say Duke Ellington "voiced the lead (the melody) for clarinet, trumpet, and tenor sax," meaning that those instruments played a unison passage in a particular Ellington arrangement.

The Blues

The term "the blues" has several meanings. It can describe

1) a sad feeling, or music which projects a sad feeling;

2) a rhymed poetic form;

3) a slow, funky, earthy type of music;

4) a type of chord progression, usually contained in twelve measures, which has certain predictable chord movements in the fifth, seventh, ninth, and eleventh measures;

5) any combination of the above.

Blues poetry is so common in popular music that a technical description of the positions of accent and rhyme is not necessary in order for you to recognize the form. A single, very characteristic example can serve to illustrate the structure of blues poetry:

> My man don't love me, treats me awful mean. (pause)
>
> My man don't love me, treats me awful mean. (pause)
>
> He is the lowest man I've ever seen. (pause)

The I, IV, and V chords are basic elements of harmony used in the blues. In the twelve-bar blues, which is the most common blues form, these chords are distributed over twelve measures in a particular way. Although many variations are possible, the basic form is always the same. The chords and their respective durations are shown in the following chart. Each slash (/) indicates one beat. Perhaps it is helpful for you to think of a chord played on each beat by a rhythm guitarist. Note that the principal chord changes occur in the fifth, seventh, ninth, and eleventh measures.

I				IV		I		V		I	
////	////	////	////	////	////	////	////	////	////	////	////

Although the chord relationships of the fifth, seventh, ninth, and eleventh measures usually hold, the remaining measures are the scene of countless alterations. Modern jazz blues progressions often employ more than one chord in a single measure and at least one change every measure. It is not unusual to have ten to twenty chord changes in the space of twelve measures. Sometimes the principal chords of the fifth, seventh, ninth, and eleventh measures are also altered. When the blues is sung, the words are often distributed in a standard way over the twelve-bar progression (see page 382).

A blues can be fast or slow, happy or sad. It may have lyrics, or it may be a purely instrumental piece, and its chord progressions may be simple or complex. For a piece to be a blues, the only requirement is that the I-IV-I-V-I chord progression or a variant of it be presented in a twelve-measure form.

The Thirty-Two-Bar A-A-B-A Tune

Another form on which jazz musicians often improvise is the thirty-two-bar A-A-B-A tune. The thirty-two bar tune is made up of four eight-measure sections. The opening eight measures, called the A section, is repeated in the second section. The third part is the B section, sometimes referred to as the bridge, release, inside, or channel. The last eight bars bring back the material of the first eight. So the tune falls into what is called A-A-B-A form. Thousands of pop tunes composed during the 1920s, 30s, 40s, and 50s were thirty-two bars long in A-A-B-A form.

Listening for the Twelve-Bar Blues and Thirty-Two-Bar Forms

To gain a practical familiarity with chord progressions, glance at the list of tunes on page 383. These are categorized as twelve-bar blues or thirty-two-bar tunes in A-A-B-A form. Go to a record collection and find performances of tunes on the list, and choose one of them. Listen to approximately the first thirty seconds to determine whether this rendition has an introduction or begins immediately with the tune itself. Also determine how fast the beats are passing. A clue can often be found in the bass playing. If the bass is walking, there is a bass note for every beat, four beats to the measure. Listening to that sound, you should be able to hear the pulse as though the bassist were a metronome. The sound of the drummer's ride cymbal may also be a good indication of where the beats lie.

Having listened long enough to determine the tempo, you will also have discovered whether there is an introduction, and the point at which it ends and the tune begins. If you are not sure whether the beginning of the piece is an introduction or part of the tune itself, wait a while and listen for it to recur. If it does not recur, it is probably an introduction. In A-A-B-A form, the first part, A, is immediately repeated, A-A, before a new section, B, occurs. The routine for most twelve-bar blues tunes consists of repeating the entire twelve bars before beginning improvisation. Musicians occasionally use the same music for an ending that they used for the introduction. So if you hear something familiar at the end which does not seem to fit exactly in twelve or thirty-two bars, it may be the introduction attached for use as an ending.

By now you should know both the tempo at which to count beats and the moment to begin counting. Start when the tune itself starts (right after the introduction, in most cases). For a twelve-bar blues count: "1234, 2234, 3234, 4234, **5**234, 6234, **7**234, 8234, **9**234, 10 234, **11**234, 12 234." Listen and count until you can detect the chord changes in measures five, seven, nine, and eleven:

```
I                        IV         I          V          I
//// //// //// //// //// //// //// //// //// //// //// ////
```

If your counting is accurate, you will eventually be able to anticipate these important chord changes. That should provide some insight into harmonies that the jazz musician uses in his improvisation.

Count like this for a thirty-two-bar A-A-B-A tune:

(Listen to examples on *Demo CD* Track 33.)

	"1234, 2234, 3234, 4234, 5234, 6234, 7234, 8234,
repeat	234, 2234, 3234, 4234, 5234, 6234, 7234, 8234,
bridge	234, 2234, 3234, 4234, 5234, 6234, 7234, 8234,
back to A	234, 2234, 3234, 4234, 5234, 6234, 7234, 8234."

Listen and count over and over until you can not only hear the bridge and the repeated sections, A-A, when they occur, but anticipate them. Do not become discouraged if you find it necessary to start and stop many times. Counting beats and measures requires practice. It is very important because it may be your only clue to the tune's form once a soloist

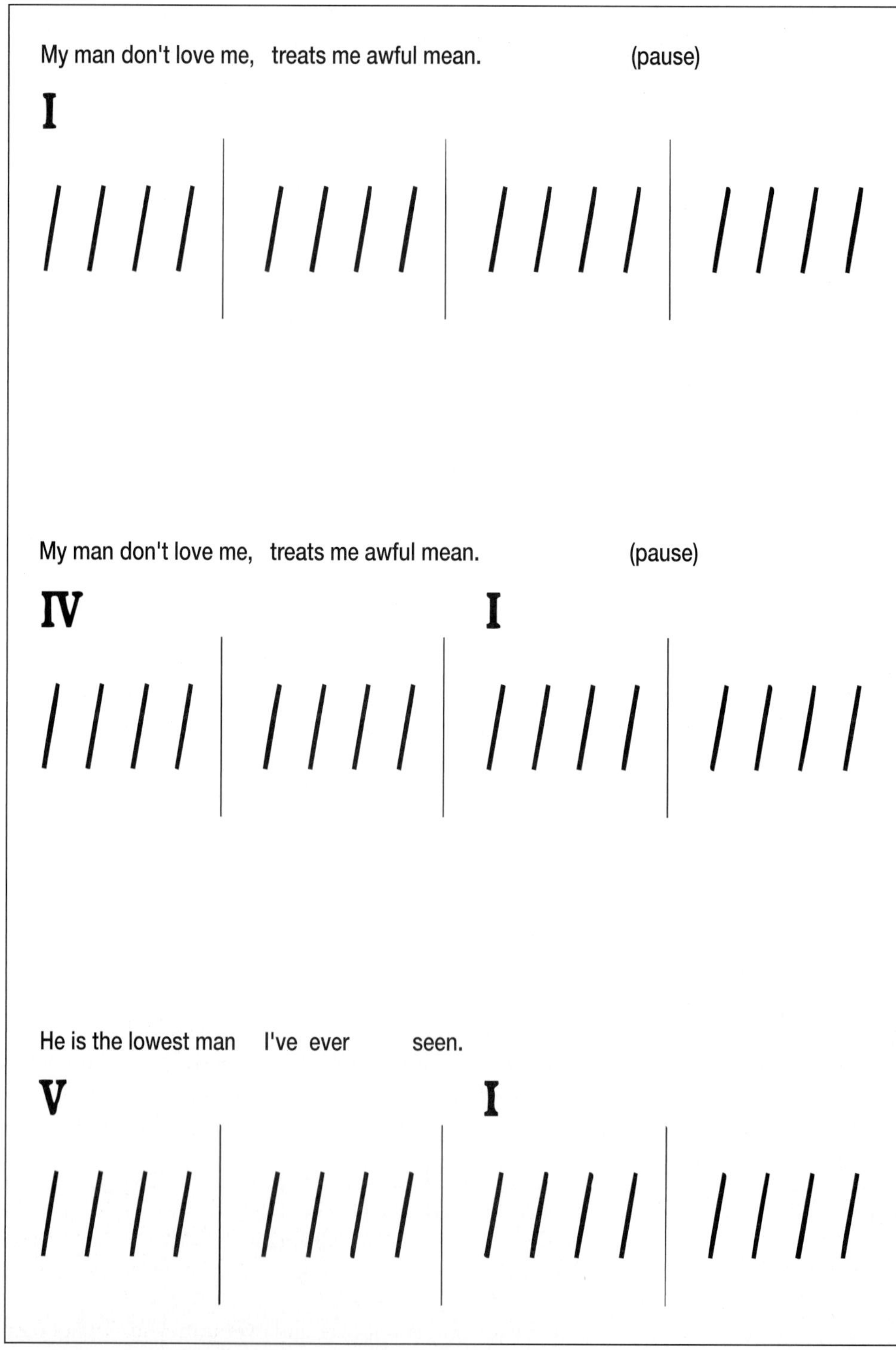

Blues poetic form in relation to the twelve-bar blues chord progression. the lyrics shown are from Billie Holiday's "Fine and Mellow." Available on *The Sound of Jazz* (Columbia: CK 45234, 1957).

Compositions in Twelve-Bar Blues and Thirty-Two-Bar A-A-B-A Forms

Twelve-Bar Blues Compositions

"Bags' Groove"
"Barbados"
"Billie's Bounce"
"Bloomdido"
"Bluesology"
"Blue Monk"
"Blue 'n' Boogie"
"Blues in the Closet"
"Blue Trane"
"Cheryl"
"Cool Blues"
"Cousin Mary"
"Footprints"
"Freddie the Freeloader"
"Goodbye Porkpie Hat"
"Jumpin' with Symphony Sid"
"Mr. P. C."
"Now's the Time"
"One O'Clock Jump"
"Sid's Ahead"
"Soft Winds"
"Straight, No Chaser"
"Walkin'"
"Woodchopper's Ball"

Compositions with Thirty-Two-Bar A-A-B-A Construction

"Ain't Misbehavin'"
"Angel Eyes"
"Anthropology"
"Birth of the Blues"
"Blue Moon"
"Body and Soul"
"Budo" ("Hallucinations")
"Darn That Dream"
"Don't Blame Me"
"Don't Get Around Much Anymore"
"Easy Living"
"52nd Street Theme"
"Flamingo"
"Four Brothers"
"Good Bait"
"Have You Met Miss Jones"
"I Can't Get Started"
"I Cover the Waterfront"
"I Love You"
"I'm Beginning to See the Light"
"It's Only a Paper Moon"
"I Want to Talk About You"
"Jordu"
"Lady Be Good"
"Lover Man"
"Lullaby of Birdland"
"Makin' Whoopee"
"Man I Love, The"
"Midnight Sun"
"Misty"
"Moten Swing"
"Move"
"Oleo"
"Over the Rainbow"
"Perdido"
"Robin's Nest"
"Rosetta"
"'Round Midnight"
"Ruby, My Dear"
"Satin Doll"
"September Song"
"Take the 'A' Train"
"Well, You Needn't"
"What's New?"
"What Is This Thing Called Love?"

has begun improvising. Learning to count accurately may take a few minutes, a few hours, or even a few days, but it is essential to an understanding of jazz improvisation. It will be well worth the effort. You might get especially good at anticipating the B section. If you know the tune, or can learn it by listening a few times, try humming it while listening to the soloists improvise on its chord changes. This will help clarify the relationship between the improvisation and the original tune. It will also help you keep your place.

Detecting Other Forms

Not all tunes fit into the twelve-bar blues form or the thirty-two-bar A-A-B-A form. "I'll Remember April" is a forty-eight-bar A-B-C-D-A-B form. "I've Got You Under My Skin" is a fifty-six-bar A-B-A-C-D-E-F form. Together, the twelve-bar blues form and the thirty-two-bar A-A-B-A form probably describe more tunes than any other single form, but they actually describe less than forty percent of all tunes written between 1910 and 1960. Let us examine a few other forms.

The twelve-bar blues is a particular set of chord progressions (I-IV-I-V-I) in a twelve-measure package. There are twelve-bar forms which are not blues simply because they do not follow the I-IV-I-V-I progression or any variation of it. For example, Richard Rodgers's "Little Girl Blue" is an A-A-B form in which each section is twelve bars long, but it is not a blues. It is also not uncommon in pop tunes to find a twelve-bar section which is actually an eight-bar progression with an extra four-bar progression connected to it.

The word "blues" in a song title does not necessarily signify the twelve-bar blues form. Both musicians and nonmusicians use the term "blues" to describe any slow, sad tune regardless of its chord progression. "Birth of the Blues" is a thirty-two bar A-A-B-A tune and "Sugar Blues" is an eighteen-bar tune. The "St. Louis Blues" is actually a twelve-bar blues plus an eight-bar bridge and an additional twelve-bar blues. Performers sometimes choose to repeat, delete, and reorder sections of "St. Louis Blues" when they play it.

Some people use the terms "eight-bar blues" and "sixteen-bar blues." Usually the tune they are describing has the I-IV movement in the first five bars and deviates from the twelve-bar I-IV-I-V-I progression thereafter. Some tunes of lengths other than twelve bars sound very much like twelve-bar blues simply because they contain the I-IV-I-V-I progression, but the durations of a few chords may be changed, and certain sections may be repeated. Herbie Hancock's "Watermelon Man," for example, has been called a "sixteen-bar blues."

Unlike the twelve-bar blues, the thirty-two-bar A-A-B-A form is not always based on the same basic chord progression. Many different chord progressions have been used in the A-A-B-A form. Fats Waller's "Honeysuckle Rose" and Erroll Garner's "Misty" are both thirty-two-bar A-A-B-A tunes, yet they have almost completely different chord progressions.

The form A-A-B-A does not always contain thirty-two bars nor does each section necessarily have the same number of measures. In "Girl from Ipanema," which is A-A-B-A, the A section has eight bars while the bridge has sixteen. In "Secret Love," another A-A-B-A tune, the A section has sixteen bars while the bridge has only eight.

There are also elongated versions of the basic twelve-bar blues and thirty-two-bar A-A-B-A forms. Lee Morgan's "Sidewinder" is a twenty-four-bar blues: each chord lasts twice as long as it would in a twelve-bar blues. Another example is the sixty-four-bar A-A-B-A form in which each section is sixteen bars long instead of eight. Ray Noble's "Cherokee" and Lerner and Loewe's "On the Street Where You Live" are both sixty-four-bar A-A-B-A tunes. Charlie Parker's "Ko-Ko" is based on the chord changes of "Cherokee"; consequently it is also a sixty-four-bar A-A-B-A tune. There are shortened versions of the thirty-two-bar A-A-B-A, too. Sonny Rollins's "Doxy" is a sixteen-bar A-A-B-A tune; each section is only four bars long.

A-A-B-A is not the only common thirty-two-bar form for pop tunes. Numerous tunes fit an A-B-A-C form (both the C section and the B section differ from the A section). "My Romance," "On Green Dolphin Street," "Indiana," "Sweet Georgia Brown," and "Out of Nowhere" all fall into a thirty-two-bar A-B-A-C form. In addition to the thirty-two-bar A-A-B-A and A-B-A-C, there is also the thirty-two-bar A-B-A-B. "How High the Moon" is an example. There are shortened versions of these, also. "Summertime" is a sixteen-bar A-B-A-C tune.

Hundreds of tunes fit into sixteen measures. "Peg o' My Heart" is a sixteen-bar pop tune. Horace Silver based his "The Preacher" on the sixteen-bar pop tune "Show Me the Way to Go Home." Wayne Shorter has written many sixteen-bar tunes, including "E.S.P.," "Nefertiti," "Prince of Darkness," etc. Some chord progressions are used in sixteen-bar tunes almost as often as the I-IV-I-V-I progression appears in the twelve-bar blues. Certain sixteen-bar progressions have become standard.

Verse and Chorus. It is important to note that the forms we have been examining refer only to chorus length. A large number of tunes consist of two major parts, a verse followed by a chorus. The verse traditionally differs from the chorus in tempo, mood, and harmony:

1) The chorus might be played at a faster tempo than the verse.
2) Verses are often performed freely, with accelerations and decelerations of tempo.
3) The verse might feel as though it is leading up to something, whereas the chorus usually has the stamp of finality to it.
4) There may be little similarity between chord progressions used in the verse and those in the chorus.
5) The key of the verse is sometimes different from that of the chorus.
6) Choruses are repeated, but once a verse is played, it is usually over for the entire performance.
7) The chorus is the section of the tune jazz musicians usually choose as a basis for improvisation.

Breaking into Multiples of Two. When you are listening to performances and trying to detect forms, be aware that arrangements of thirty-two-bar A-A-B-A, A-B-A-C, and A-B-A-B tunes sometimes depart from strict repetition of those thirty-two bars. Arrangements sometimes contain four-, eight-, and sixteen-bar sections, formed by omitting or adding to portions of the original thirty-two-bar tune. Note also that many tunes, especially pre-1930s Dixieland tunes, have long, elaborate forms similar to those of marches and of nineteenth-century European dance music (such as the quadrille). Forms for many tunes in pre-1920s jazz were derived from march music. A piece might have a series of sections consisting of multiples of eight bars. Designating each section by a letter of the alphabet, a piece might conceivably follow a pattern like this:

A – A – B – B – C – D – E – F – C – D – E – F
16–16–16–16–16–16–24–32–16–16–24–32

When listening for form, keep in mind that even in the most intricate pieces, forms can usually be broken down into two-bar segments. So if you are unable to divide a piece neatly into either four-bar or eight-bar sections, try using a few two-bar sections. "Sugar Blues" can be heard as 18 or as 8+10 or as 8+8+2. That form poses problems for the improviser because it tends to break the flow of ideas conceived in four- and eight-bar melodic units. It is like being forced to walk left, right, left, right, left, left, right. The form of the original "I Got Rhythm" is:

A—A—B—A + tag
8—8—8—8 + 2 or
8—8—8—10

When jazz musicians improvise on its chord progression, they omit the two-bar tag. If included, the tag would interrupt the flow of the improvisations and again be like having to take two steps with your left foot before going back to an alternation of right with left. Another popular tune that has an unusual structure is "Moonlight in Vermont." It follows the form:

A—A—B—A + tag
6—6—8—6 + 2

Modal Forms

During the late 1950s and especially during the 60s and 70s, modal forms practically eliminated the "change" part of "chord change." In modal music, improvisations are based on the extended repetition of one or two chords. Those chords contain so many notes that they either include or are compatible with all the notes in a scale. The term mode is synonymous with scale, hence the term "modal music." Although this is not the definition of modal employed by classical composers and in textbooks on classical music, it is what jazz musicians and jazz journalists have come to mean by "modal." In most instances, jazz musicians also employ notes which are not contained in the mode or in the repeated chords. Some of John Coltrane's work, for example, is not strictly modal, but has the flavor of music that is.

In modal music, the entire improvised portion of the performance is often based on a single chord and scale. Usually the chord and its scale are minor, Indian, Middle Eastern, or in some way more exotic-sounding than the chords used in most pop tune progressions. Because it is based on a single scale, the music has no real chord changes, just a drone.

Sometimes a melody containing chord changes of its own precedes the improvised section of a modal performance. John Coltrane's recordings of the Rodgers and Hammerstein tune "My Favorite Things" are good examples. Coltrane played the original melody while his rhythm section played the appropriate chord changes. Then the entire group improvised only on the primary chord of the tune (and the scale compatible with that chord). Near the end of their improvisations, they switched to another chord, which lent the piece a slightly different character. Coltrane could have retained the chord progressions of the tune and used them as the basis for improvisation, but he chose not to.

Some modal music does have chord changes, or "mode changes." One rich chord (or scale, depending on how one cares to conceive it) is the basis for four, eight, or perhaps sixteen measures. Then a different chord is in effect for another similar duration. The Miles Davis tune "Milestones" is based on one mode for the first sixteen bars, a different mode for the second sixteen bars, and a return to the original mode for the final eight bars. The melody has the form A-A-B-B-A, and each section is eight bars long. Herbie Hancock's "Maiden Voyage" has a thirty-two-bar A-A-B-A construction; here each mode lasts for four bars. The A section is based on two different modes, each lasting only four bars. The B section makes use of another two modes also lasting four bars each. If each mode were labeled by letter name, "Maiden Voyage" could be described as X-Y-X-Y-Z-W-X-Y. "So What" (on the Miles Davis album *Kind of Blue*) has a melody in thirty-two-bar A-A-B-A form, and the use of modes corresponds to that form: there are sixteen bars of one mode, eight of another, and a return to the original mode for the last eight bars. John Coltrane's "Impressions" not only takes the same form as "So What" but also uses exactly the same modes. (See page 421–423 for modes on "Milestones," "Maiden Voyage," and "So What.")

Much jazz of the 1960s and 70s was based on infrequent chord changes (another way of saying modal) instead of the frequent chord changes found in most twelve-bar blues and thirty-two-bar forms. Many groups abandoned both the blues form and the thirty-two-bar forms. Some groups used complex melodies and intricate rhythm section figures, yet their improvisations were based almost exclusively on one or a small number of chords ("Freedom Jazz Dance," for example).

The Effects of Form on Improvisation

Song forms of four- and eight-bar sections tend to break improvisations into small segments of similar length. Divisions of form, in other words, can influence the flow of improvised lines. This is not necessarily a disadvantage, however. The divisions in form can frame well-chosen melodic figures, and they can provide a means of transition from one figure to another. This creates more continuity than a solo might contain without chord progressions. Forms based on single modes sounding indefinitely tend to free the improviser, enabling him to create lines that are as long or short, tense or relaxed as he desires. No preset tension-relaxation devices in the form of chord progressions are there to suggest construction patterns for his improvised lines.

Bridges. The B section of an A-A-B-A tune is called the bridge. It bridges the gap between repetition of the A sections, and it usually provides a contrast to the material in the A sections. The bridge can break up or lift the mood established by repeated A sections. Many bridges are placed a few keys higher than the A section. A key change can be a boost in any situation, but is especially effective after the repeated A sections.

The bridge is important to improvisers because a good improviser can capitalize on the bridge's natural capacity to provide contrast. Some of the greatest solo segments in jazz are those improvised over the chord progressions of a tune's bridge. The rhythm section also takes advantage of the bridge and is often especially active just before the bridge is entered and just before it is exited. Heightened rhythmic activity can announce the arrival or departure of the bridge.

Combos often use the bridge as a container for solo spots. Sometimes a tune's melody will be played for the final time in the performance, and when the bridge occurs, everyone stops playing except the drummer. It becomes his feature. Then the entire band returns precisely on the first beat of the final A section.

In some jazz tunes the bridge consists only of chord changes. Such pieces require improvisation during the bridge but return to the written melody when the final A section is reached. Sonny Rollins's tune "Oleo" is an example. Many groups also use that approach on "The Theme," a popular up-tempo number for jazz combos of the late 1950s and early 60s.

Turnarounds. Another important part in the construction of standard tunes is the turnaround (also known as the turnabout or turnback). In many, perhaps in most songs, the seventh and eighth measures of each section are occupied by a single sustained tone or two long tones (see page 388). That part of the tune might be considered dead space due to the lack of melodic movement, but the jazz musician uses that space. He fills it with chord changes which lead directly to the beginning of the next section. Jazz musicians are expected to know a variety of chord progressions common to turnarounds. The manner in which they fill that space with chord changes and improvised lines is the art of the turnaround. (See page 416 for common progressions.)

The whole combo digs in when a turnaround comes up. Drummers tend to kick more and, thus, tie together the musical statements of one section and bring in the next. Those bassists who almost invariably walk are more likely to vary this pattern in a turnaround. Tension can be built during a turnaround and resolved by the onset of the next section of the piece.

Turnarounds in 32-bar A-A-B-A pieces and 12-bar blues pieces.

In 32-bar A-A-B-A form:

A ———— A ———— B ———— A ————

8 ———— 8 ———— 8 ———— 8 ————

6 ———— 2 – 6 ———— 2 – 8 ———— 6 ———— 2 –

(turnaround) (turnaround) (turnaround)

In 12-bar blues form:

———— 12 ———— 12 ———— 12 ————

———— 10 ———— 2 – 10 ———— 2 – 10 ———— 2 –

(turnaround) (turnaround) (turnaround)

Phrasing in Relation to Form

Jazz musicians prior to the mid-1940s tended to improvise phrases which coincided with the tune structure. Most progressions consist of two- and four-bar units, and improvised solos often proceeded in phrases of similar length. Furthermore, soloists tended to make larger silences at or near the end of an A section or B section. They rarely connected tune sections by continuing phrases through the turnarounds. They stopped at or before the turnarounds, and then started anew at the beginning of the next section. They treated the eighth bar line as a barrier. Twelve-bar blues solos often contained phrases which started at the beginning of each chorus regardless of what happened at the end of a previous chorus, thus treating the twelfth bar line as a barrier.

One characteristic of modern jazz (beginning in the 1940s) and the music of the players who most influenced it was the use of phrases which began somewhere within an eight-bar section and continued into the next section without a pause. There was no lull during the turnaround.

A characteristic of some modern jazz during the 1960s and 70s was the absence of preset chord progressions. That free approach significantly loosened the tendencies of jazz phrasing. Although players retained patterns common to preceding jazz eras, they were free to phrase with greater variety due to the lack of underlying chord movements. Some jazz of this type projects a feeling of expansiveness quite unlike the crowded feeling often projected by modern jazz of the 1940s and 50s.

Some tunes which appeared during the 1960s, especially those of Wayne Shorter, were sixteen or more bars without any repeated sections. The A section was not repeated, there was no bridge, no turnaround. These tunes were "all A." That form enabled improvisers to play with great continuity yet without the crowded, segmented feeling which sometimes characterizes improvisations based on standard A-A-B-A and A-B-A-C forms with the usual turnarounds and bridges. Sometimes a free, floating feeling could be projected by improvisers using these "all A" forms.

TONE COLOR

An important element of music, usually the first to be perceived, is tone quality or tone color. This element is also known as timbre (pronounced tamm´ burr).

How can you tell the difference between the sound of a flute and the sound of a trumpet if they each play only one note, and it is the same note? The difference is tone color, the spectrum of frequencies generated by each instrument in its own unique way. This definition is an oversimplification of a complex situation in which many factors come into play.

The spectrum of frequencies produced by an instrument is not fixed. The spectrum varies depending on the pitch and the forcefulness with which it is played. The ways in which a player starts and stops a note, the attack and release, also are important in determining tone color. The attack and release are accompanied by temporary changes in a tone's frequency spectrum.

Another complication arises from our tendency to associate an instrument's tone color with the aggregate effects of all the notes being played on it rather than the spectrum of frequencies present in a single note.

Finally, when sounds come to our ears, they are modified by room acoustics and by recording and playback techniques. The way our ears deal with that variability is quite involved.

Tone color varies greatly from one instrument to another, and there are also especially discernible differences in tone color among jazz musicians playing the same instrument. For example, to speak of the tenor sax tone color of John Coltrane or Stan Getz is to describe sounds so unique that some inexperienced listeners could differentiate them as easily as they could distinguish flute from trumpet. The evolution of jazz tenor saxophone playing reflects not only changes in the phrasing and rhythms, but also changes in tone color.

Tone color is a very personal characteristic of a player's style. Jazz musicians place great emphasis on creating the particular tone colors they want. A jazz musician's attention to tone color is comparable to an actor's concern for costume, make-up, and voice quality combined. Tone color is so important to saxophonists that many spend lifetimes searching for the perfect mouthpiece. They also experiment with different methods of blowing and different ways of altering the vibrating surface of the cane reeds that are attached to their mouthpieces.

Because the tenor saxophone is capable of producing an exceptionally wide variety of tone colors, it is easier to differentiate jazz tenor saxophonists by tone color alone than it is to recognize a particular trumpeter or pianist. That is not to say that differences are absent from trumpeter to trumpeter or from pianist to pianist. The differences are just more subtle.

Two pianists can play the same piece on the same piano and produce quite different sounds. No two pianos have the same tone color, and one piano can produce distinctly different tone colors, depending on how hard the keys are struck. The use of the pedals and a pianist's timing in releasing one key and striking the next are crucial to the sound. A key may be released before, after, or at the same time as the next is struck. When a note is short and ends well before the next note begins, we call it a staccato note. If one key is released after the next is struck, the two sounds overlap in time. Notes played smoothly one after the other are said to be legato. The amount of overlap influences the clarity of attack and the dimension of legato-staccato. Our ears hear sounds in combined form rather than as single tones. Whatever is left in the air from a preceding sound mixes and colors the subsequent sound. The relationship between consecutive sounds, ranging from complete separation to extreme overlapping, are resources which contribute to the personal character of a pianist's style. Count Basie's touch and tone color differ remarkably from Duke Ellington's. Perhaps you will perceive Basie's touch as lighter than Ellington's. No matter how you describe the sound, you will notice a difference if you listen carefully.

Guitarists' interest in tone color is manifested by their search for different types of picks, guitar strings, and amplifiers. Guitar amplifier dial settings are essential to the control of tone color. Bass players are also concerned with many of the same factors.

Mutes. (Listen to examples on *Demo CD* Track 63.)

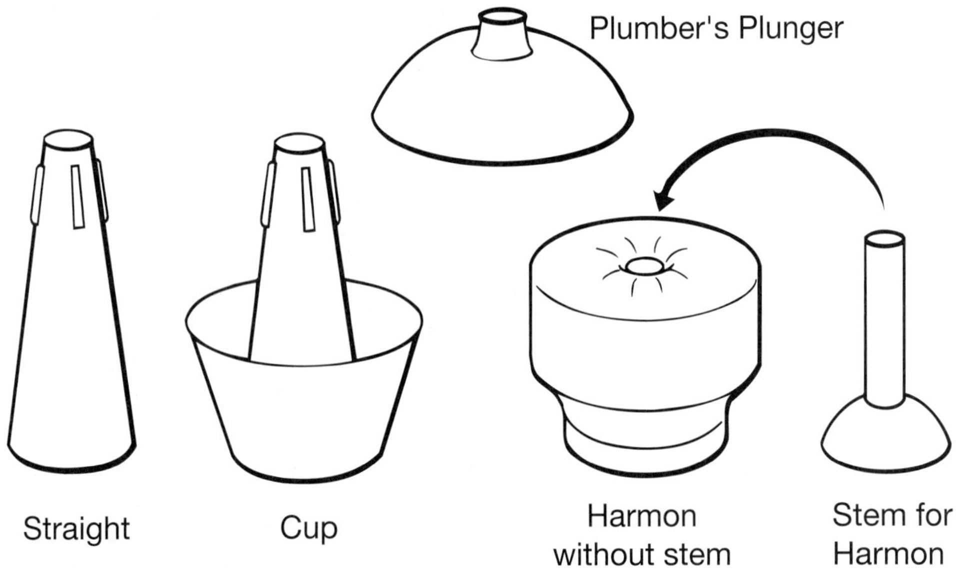

Trumpeters and trombonists explore available tone colors by experimenting with mouthpiece changes, methods of blowing, mutes, and instruments which represent different manufacturers and models.

Intonation is also an important aspect of tone. Intonation refers to playing in tune, playing sharp or flat. Playing sharp means playing at a pitch level somewhat higher than the average pitch of the ensemble. Playing flat refers to playing a pitch somewhat lower than that

Trombonist Quentin Jackson playing into plunger mute.

Photo courtesy of John Richmond

Miles Davis playing into cup mute.
Courtesy of Frank Driggs

of the ensemble. Do not confuse the terms sharp and flat with words describing actual note names such as C-sharp and B-flat. These notes are raised (sharped) and lowered (flatted) by a larger amount than is usually the case in out-of-tune playing. That is, the interval between C and C-sharp is greater than the interval between C and that of a performer playing C a bit sharper than his fellow ensemble members. Small deviations of pitch occur all the time even in the best ensembles, but larger deviations lead listeners to comment "someone is playing out of tune."

Miles Davis playing into Harmon mute without its stem.

Courtesy of Bill Smith

Trombonist Dicky Wells playing into straight mute.

Photo courtesy of William Gottlieb

Why is intonation described in this section on tone color? Intonation affects the tone color of both the soloist and the ensemble as a whole. If a group of musicians played the same piece twice, once without listening or adjusting to each other's pitch (perhaps by pretuning their instruments and then wearing ear plugs for the performance), and then a second time, listening carefully to each other's pitch and continuously adjusting accordingly, you would hear two performances, each having distinctly different tone colors. Ensembles that lack precision tuning have a thicker, rougher sound than precisely tuned ensembles. One element of a slick ensemble sound is careful and consistent tuning.

For tone color reasons, some soloists systematically play a little "high," meaning a bit sharp. Intonation is a musical resource for them. This is common in most types of music, including symphonic, but it is especially true for jazz soloists. A tone cuts through an ensemble if it is a bit sharper than the average pitch of that ensemble. Some jazz soloists, Johnny Hodges, Stan Getz, and Paul Desmond, for instance, play at the average pitch, whereas Charlie Parker and John Coltrane, for instance, tend to various degrees of sharpness. That is another component of tone color which helps us identify a particular player's work.

Buying Strategies

One key to being a happy jazz fan is finding the right albums. This section of the book provides guidelines and shortcuts to help you.

Minimizing Risk in Selecting Albums

1) **Beware of endorsements in newspapers and magazines.** They represent knowledge and understanding no greater than that of one individual. The reviewer might not be knowledgeable or perceptive. Moreover, his tastes might differ from yours. For instance, staples in the record collections of musicians are sometimes unknown by many critics, and some of these masterpieces were given only lukewarm reviews by the critics who did notice them. Albums that win Grammy awards are not necessarily outstanding, either. They are merely among the albums that a small committee of journalists has heard and voted upon within the preceding twelve months. (Over a thousand albums are issued each year in the U.S. alone.) A parallel might be helpful. You probably remember a few Academy Award-winning movies you did not find enjoyable. Conversely, you might have also found yourself liking a few movies that received bad reviews. You may have been impressed by a few movies that no one was talking about, too. Similarly, *albums receiving the most press and airplay are not necessarily the highest quality.* Extent of press and airplay is determined largely by the record company's promotional budget, luck and persistence, plus the tastes of disc jockeys and journalists. Some of the best albums never get publicized.

2) **Listen to the music before you buy it.** Try to avoid album buying as an impulse purchase. Unless you want a record for purely academic reasons or historical perspective, you might realize too late that you spent your money on something you don't enjoy. This is worth keeping in mind unless you can afford to experiment expensively. Friends, libraries, jazz courses, and radio programs can often expose you to new albums. If there is a jazz radio station near you, don't hesitate to phone and ask them to play a particular album. (College radio stations not only broadcast more jazz than commercial stations, but they are also more likely to be interested in your requests.) And when you hear something you like, you could also phone the station and ask for its album title and record company name.

3) **Use a broad sampling of recordings before forming your opinion of a particular player.** One good reason is that *few jazz improvisers are extremely consistent in producing inspired recordings.* Some of even the greatest jazz musicians have had whole strings of unexciting albums. This means that, if the only recording you hear is from an off day for that player, you derive a nonrepresentative view of his talent. You are not fair to the musician.

   Another reason for using a broad sampling is that, *if the player had more than one style period in his career, you cheat yourself if you draw a conclusion from sampling only one of them.* For instance, Sonny Rollins had a creative peak in the middle 1950s, and another in the 1990s with a different style. This means that, if you heard a few recent Rollins records and did not like them, you might not seek any mid-1950s Rollins material, even though you might have liked it. The converse would also be true.

4) **Don't accept substitutions.** The quality and character of improvised music can vary drastically from album to album, even if made by the same band during the same

period as the music you seek. So once you decide which albums you really want, don't get others first, merely because they are available and look similar.

5) **Don't wait for your desired albums to appear in stores.** They probably won't appear. Quality of music and availability often seem inversely related. Try mail-order sources, and stick to what you really want. See page 400 for such mail order firms as Cadence Record Sales and The Public Radio Music Source.

Confusing Album Titles

Be suspicious of titles for compilations. Let's examine reasons for caution with two categories of compilations: (a) *Greatest Hits* and (b) *The Best of, The Indispensable,* and *The Essential.* **Problems for both categories often occur when the compilation comes from only one company's recordings,** and that particular company did not record the artist during his creative peak (invalidating *The Best of* designation) or during his height of popularity (invalidating the *Greatest Hits* designation). Another company did. For example, a Verve album of 1950s recordings called *The Essential Lester Young* is probably "essential" only to those Lester Young collectors who already have much of Young's creative peak represented in his 1930s Count Basie recordings, reissued by Columbia/SONY and Decca/MCA/GRP.

A second set of problems arises **when musicians have had several different styles during their careers** and a creative peak for each. They may have been recording for a different company during each important period. For example, John Coltrane made important recordings as a bandleader for three different companies (Prestige, Atlantic, and Impulse). Each company documented a stylistically different stage in his career. (And some of his best work was recorded with Miles Davis's bands for Columbia, a *fourth* record company.) This means, for example, that an Atlantic album called *The Best of John Coltrane* cannot contain Coltrane's best work from all three periods—although it could sample some of his best Atlantic sessions if the compiler knew what he was doing.

A third set of problems results **when musicians made their best recordings as sidemen in the bands of others,** not as bandleaders, yet the compilation draws only from recording sessions where they were bandleaders. For instance, Lester Young's best work was done as a sideman with the 1936–41 combos and big bands associated with Count Basie. The music on his combo recordings as leader does not sound like his music on the Basie recordings. This means that an Emarcy album called *Pres at His Very Best,* containing music from 1943–44 in which Young was bandleader, is probably not his "very" best recorded improvisations, though it might represent the best playing he recorded as a bandleader. The Emarcy album title is misleading.

Here are some other examples of the confusion arising from album titles not coordinated with varied careers. In the 1960s, pianist Herbie Hancock and saxophonist Wayne Shorter both recorded for Blue Note as bandleaders. During much of that time they were also recording for Columbia as sidemen in the Miles Davis Quintet. Most of their playing on the Davis recordings is superior to that on their own records. But since they were bandleaders for Blue Note, the Blue Note recordings, not the Columbia recordings, provide the pool for albums titled *The Best of Herbie Hancock* and *The Best of Wayne Shorter.* Hancock's and Shorter's work on Blue Note is excellent music, and it also features the outstanding composing for which Hancock and Shorter are distinguished. But when heard strictly as piano and saxophone improvising, their work on Blue Note may not be the absolute best of either man's career, as claimed by an album title. Incidentally, a Columbia album called *The Best of Herbie Hancock* (JC 36309) contains neither his innovative playing with the 1963–69 Miles Davis groups nor his distinguished composing within the Blue Note work. The album samples a third facet: Hancock's jazz-rock material of the 1970s.

A fourth reason for approaching compilation titles with caution is that **sometimes compilers are not qualified for their task.** This means that, even if an artist recorded solely for one company during his creative peak, a *Best of* album might omit his *best* work because the person in charge of preparing the compilation was not familiar enough with all the artist's work for that firm. The compiler might not have had sufficiently developed taste, either, or he did not realize how much he needed to call upon the taste and knowledge of consultants. This may explain why a number of single-company compilations of several jazz giants, which emerged on compact disc during the 1990s, had knowledgeable consumers wondering why so many unremarkable selections had been included while outstanding performances remained untapped in the company's vaults. It might also explain why even a few multi-company compilations have had knowledgeable jazz fans puzzled about odd choices.

Greatest Hits can be misleading as an album title because, in addition to all the previously mentioned problems, a player's best-selling material might not even appear on it. For example, the largest-selling Miles Davis recording for Columbia was his 1969 *Bitches Brew* (GP 26). Yet it is not represented on the Columbia album *Miles Davis's Greatest Hits* (PC 9808). The 1964 recording of "Girl From Ipanema" for the Verve company was the highest selling recording of Stan Getz's career. Yet there is an album titled *Stan Getz's Greatest Hits* (Prestige 7337) drawn from 1949 and 1950 sessions made for the Prestige company. The Prestige material is excellent, perhaps better than the Verve material, yet it does not include his largest-selling hits, as the album title deceptively implies.

To avoid being misled by compilation titles, first learn about the musician's career. Then check details on the album wrapper or box insert to confirm that recording dates, titles, and personnel match what you seek. It is also wise to consult authorities to determine what companies were recording the artist during critical portions of his career and what selections are deemed outstanding.

By seeking prescreened items such as the types of anthologies discussed above, rather than making impulse purchases, you lessen risks in finding music you will want to keep. Ultimately you need to remember, however, that the main reason for buying compilations and samplers is to become familiar with a wide range of music for a small price. But also bear in mind that just because selections on the samplers are critically acclaimed or generally popular does not guarantee you will like them.

While you are pursuing this strategy, you will rarely see a desired album in the stores. Jazz fans have become accustomed to the fact that *most current jazz albums must be special-ordered, and all out-of-print albums must be obtained through special sources.* So-called out-of-print material frequently becomes available in repackaged formats, discussed below as reissues. Sources are listed on page 400.

Locating Albums

Many people think certain albums are available only in big city stores. But no matter where you live, **most albums can be obtained by mail.** In fact, many of them will never surface in big city stores. It might be more practical to get albums by mail even if you live in or near a big city that has many music stores, such as New York or Los Angeles, for instance. The cost of getting there could exceed the price of an album. When you arrive at the store, the clerk may end up ordering your request by mail anyway. The main point is that *most of the jazz albums mentioned in this book will not be found in average stores.* If they are available to a store, they will probably require a special order. You therefore ought to phone ahead to determine whether traveling an inconvenient distance will be worthwhile. Some stores accept special orders over the phone. You then need only call the store periodically, and find out whether your order has arrived. Some will mail them to you, also. Keep in mind, however, that most stores are not interested in your special order business. It is an unprofitable hassle for them, though they will often fail to admit this to you. They will take forever to fill your order or never bother to notify you when they give up trying to find a particular item. Perhaps the most expedient path is to use the mail order method. A few reliable sources are listed at the end of this section. Incidentally, out-of-print records can be obtained by getting your name on the mailing lists for jazz record auctions. You merely scan their fliers, then bid by mail on what you want. The addresses for jazz magazines and specialty record stores on page 400 can be used to begin this process. Note that auctioneers advertise in jazz magazines.

About Reissues

When seeking out-of-print recordings, there are several things to keep in mind. Many jazz recordings which have disappeared from catalog listings return later in altered form. This includes the category known as *reissues*, *re-releases*, and *repackages*. Before we discuss them, here is some relevant history. Prior to the widespread use of twelve-inch, 33⅓ rpm (revolutions per minute) LP (long play) records, most jazz was issued on ten-inch, 78 rpm records. Twelve-inch 33s were not common until the 1950s, so many bop and cool style bands—in addition to Dixieland and swing bands—were initially presented on 78s. Due to the size of the record and the speed of rotation, most 78s could accommodate only about three minutes of music per side. An *album* consisted of several records packaged much like a photo album. Each record had its own pocket or sleeve. The set was bound in cloth or leather. Then when the LP arrived, many of the three-minute selections originally on 78 were issued again (reissued) as compilations within 33⅓ rpm albums. This time, the word *album* meant one disc containing many selections. All the recordings in this book's premodern section and a few modern items are to be found in this kind of "reissue." Later on, LPs themselves began to be reissued, re-released, and repackaged as "new" LPs. Then when compact disc technology emerged, the contents of old LPs began appearing in CD format. Sometimes additional selections were included when the album was reissued on CD because the CD could accommodate up to about 77 minutes of music instead of the 50-minute limit that was common for LPs. Sometimes two LPs were represented on one CD. This is the altered form in which you can often find music originally available on recordings which have "disappeared" from the catalog.

Many albums that are no longer marketed by U.S. firms are available in foreign countries under the same titles they carried before they went out of print in the U.S. For instance, Japanese and European distributors have been repackaging out-of-print American albums, sometimes selling them with the original album jacket art and liner notes intact. Because of this, a list of importers and their addresses appears on page 400. More can be found advertised in jazz magazines. Relying on imports is not always dependable. So first match tune titles, personnel, and recording dates to determine whether a foreign release is the same as the American original you seek. There is something else to consider when searching for a reissue of a particular recording. *It is common for jazz groups to record several versions of the same tunes, and some players record the same tunes with different groups.* Since you are a jazz fan, you are seeking recordings of particular improvisations, not merely the tunes they are based on. So you must find the actual performances you want. A musician's improvisations on other versions of the tune might not even resemble what you want.

When you are trying to locate music from a recording that has gone out of print, you will be looking for it in new compilations of old material. For these new packages, album titles are sometimes changed, and material from the original album is scattered over several different compilations. Another common problem is that the recordings may have belonged originally to companies which later sold their material. The original company's name helps you identify reissued material. For instance, one group of important Charlie Parker recordings was originally made for the Dial company, and its reissued form is called *The Dial Masters.* However, when record companies are bought and sold, sometimes the music is reissued intact, causing you no headaches. For example, Impulse was bought by ABC, then by MCA, then GRP, but many of the important albums John Coltrane made for Impulse during the 1960s continued to be distributed intact, though with GRP catalog numbers.

Another key to locating material in reissued form is that it is often identified by where it was recorded. For example, the pivotal Bill Evans-Scott LaFaro music originally made at New York City's Village Vanguard nightclub for Riverside record company, originally issued on albums titled *Sunday at the Village Vanguard* and *Waltz for Debby,* has been reissued by Fantasy-Prestige-Milestone as *The Village Vanguard Sessions.* Recordings from an outstanding 1953 concert by Charles Mingus, Charlie Parker, Dizzy Gillespie, Bud Powell, and Max Roach are frequently identified only by recording site: Toronto's Massey Hall (*The Massey Hall Concert*).

When seeking music that you think is out-of-print, you need a complete listing of the musicians, the pieces, the recording dates, the original album title, and the name of the record company. It also sometimes helps to have the original catalog numbers. Personnel listings can be especially useful because material is sometimes reissued under the name of a musician who was a sideman on the original recording session but has now become more significant than the leader. It is packaged as though he were leader at that original session. For example, a 1956 Tadd Dameron album called *Mating Call* was reissued under John Coltrane's name and called *On a Misty Night.* Coltrane was a sideman on it but is now in much demand in his own right. Several reissues of Joe Oliver's Creole Jazz Band have come out under Louis Armstrong's name, even though Armstrong was a sideman, not the leader, on Oliver's recordings. Much pre-1940 Lester Young material is available in reissues under Young's name, though it was originally recorded under Count Basie's leadership.

There are several ways you can keep up with what is being reissued. Reading jazz magazines is the most efficient. This will allow you to keep up with material that won't be broadcast on radio. Some magazines that attempted to announce most new albums and reissues were *Jazz Times* (8737 Colesville Road, Silver Spring, MD 20910-3921) and *Cadence* (Redwood, NY 13679). You can also phone or visit music stores to track listings in their *Phonolog, Spectrum,* or *Muse.* Several mail-order services give information and take orders by phone. The Public Radio Music Source is one (800-75MUSIC). If you do not want to wait for an album to be reissued (and some never are), watch for it in the bins of cut-outs and used albums at music stores, garage sales, house sales, and flea markets. *Or contact rare record dealers and auctioneers, advertised in the back pages of jazz magazines.*

Many Versions of the Same Tune

The problem of a single tune recorded many times by the same artist increased substantially during the past forty years. This was due to increases in: (1) legitimate reissue programs by major firms, (2) illegitimate releases (called bootleg or pirate records) by numerous small firms, and (3) the discovery, or rediscovery, of a seemingly endless variety of broadcast performances, called *air shots* or *air checks.* (Music of the 1930s and 1940s, unlike that of the 1950s and 1960s, is well documented by air checks because most jazz groups made live radio broadcasts in those days.)

Beginning in the 1960s, record companies began massive distribution of repackaged material. Hundreds of albums with new titles were introduced. Many contained music originally on 78s. Other albums had music originally available on LPs. Some of the albums featured alternate, but originally rejected, versions of tunes. These are called *alternate takes.*

(Some are labeled as alternate takes, but for others, you have to hear both versions to know whether they differ. They sometimes have improvisation equal or superior to the versions originally issued.)

Albums flooded the market from companies, both American and foreign, which operated without the consent of the recorded artists (or of their estates, in the case of deceased artists). Those albums constitute the illegitimate releases mentioned earlier as *bootlegs.* The companies were small and disappeared quickly. Some of their material had appeared previously on other records, but much of it had never been available before. A lot of it came from homemade recordings of nightclub appearances and radio broadcasts. Many albums have incorrect tune titles. Few contain complete personnel listings and recording dates. Many display poor sound fidelity. But if you can tolerate all those weaknesses, you might be well rewarded by the music itself. It is also worthwhile to be aware of bootleg recordings because their appearance and distribution is very common and likely to continue.

With the bootleg material added to the legitimate releases and reissues, it became possible to own, for instance, more than eighty albums of Charlie Parker, or more than one hundred of Duke Ellington. The record collector might be confronted with five to ten Parker versions of "Confirmation" and "Ornithology" and just as many Ellington versions of "Mood Indigo" and "Sophisticated Lady." Keeping track of recording dates and personnel became essential to discussing particular performances of these frequently recorded tunes.

A few Charlie Parker classics illustrate the usefulness of having personnel, tune titles, recording dates, and original record company name before you begin seeking a particular recording. The much praised music that Parker originally made in the form of 78s for Dial Record Company has been sold in numerous forms, some of them offered by tiny, obscure record companies that worked without the consent of Parker's estate. Take "Embraceable You," for example. Parker recorded many different versions of it. But if you want his famous Dial recording of it, remember that he made two different versions at the same session in 1947 with pianist Duke Jordan, bassist Tommy Potter, and drummer Max Roach. Any deviation from that particular combination of identifiers will indicate that you are holding another version of the tune instead of the famous one. It is also essential to note the record company name and recording date if you want to locate Parker's famous 1945 "Now's the Time," which was made for Savoy record company with the Miles Davis trumpet solo that was later adapted and recorded by pianist Red Garland on the Miles Davis *Milestones* album. It is especially easy to become confused in this instance because another version of the same tune was also recorded by Parker without Davis in 1953 and released on a Verve album called *Now's the Time.* There are instances in which historic figures recorded only one version of a given tune, but the more you study jazz, the more you will find it beneficial to **keep track of details to ensure you're buying what you originally set out to buy.**

One final example is offered to illustrate the usefulness of having complete information about an improvisation you seek. If you have a transcription of a Miles Davis trumpet solo from a performance of "Joshua," and you want to hear the original or play along with it, you cannot just run out and buy the correct album, even if you already have the personnel listing and the year of recording. Miles Davis recorded "Joshua" at least three times with saxophonist George Coleman, pianist Herbie Hancock, bassist Ron Carter, and drummer Tony Williams. Two out of the three times were in the same year, 1963. One version was released on *Seven Steps to Heaven,* an album which was issued with two different catalog numbers:

Columbia CS 8851 and CL 2051. Another version was released on *Miles Davis in Europe* (Columbia CL 2183 and CS 8983). Then Davis recorded another version in 1964 that was released in *Four and More* (Columbia 9253 and CL 2453) that was reissued on CD under a new title and new catalog number in 1992.

Rare Record Dealers, Importers, and Auctioneers

Worlds Records
P.O. Box 1992
Novato, CA 94948
800-742-6663

Cadence Record Sales
Cadence Building
Redwood, NY 13679
315-287-2852

Roots and Rhythms
P.O. Box 837
El Cerrito, CA 94530
The Public Radio Music Source
800-75-MUSIC

Memory Lane Out-of-Print Records
1940 East University Drive
Tempe, AZ 85281
800-326-5343

International Association of
Jazz Record Collectors
P.O. Box 518
Wingate, NC 28174

(Write for a membership listing, then determine who specializes in the style you seek, and write that member.)

Mosaic Records runs a broad-ranging program of reissuing hard-to-find items. Their reissue packages are prepared in a very intelligent and conscientious manner with excellent annotation. In the past, Mosaic carried material by Stan Kenton, Duke Ellington, Louis Armstrong, Maynard Ferguson, George Shearing, Miles Davis, Nat Cole, Don Cherry, Charlie Parker, and others. Mosaic also was running a subsidiary, called True Blue, which distributed Blue Note recordings, a source for pivotal music from the 1950s and 60s that has become difficult to locate. Request a catalog from Mosaic Records, 35 Melrose Place, Stamford CT 06902-7533; phone 203-327-7111.

A Small Basic Collection of Jazz Videos

Listening to Jazz by Steve Gryb (Prentice Hall) 60 minutes; demonstrations of instruments and their combo roles, corresponding to the audio illustrations in the *Demonstration CD* for the *Jazz Styles: History and Analysis* textbook by Gridley; ISBN 0-13-532862-4; phone 800-947-7700.

The Sound of Jazz (Vintage Jazz Classics) 58 minutes; an unedited copy of the 1957 kinescope of the CBS broadcast with performances by Count Basie, Lester Young, Coleman Hawkins, Ben Webster, Billie Holiday, Roy Eldridge, Thelonious Monk, Jimmy Giuffre, and others.

Trumpet Kings (VAI) 60 minutes; hosted by Wynton Marsalis; includes Louis Armstrong, Bunny Berigan, Roy Eldridge, Red Allen, Dizzy Gillespie, Miles Davis, Freddie Hubbard, and others.

Piano Legends (VAI) 63 minutes; hosted by Chick Corea; includes Earl Hines, Fats Waller, Art Tatum, Thelonious Monk, Bill Evans, Cecil Taylor, and others.

Reed Royalty (VAI 69072) 58 minutes; hosted by Branford Marsalis; includes Johnny Hodges, Charlie Parker, Gerry Mulligan, Eric Dolphy, Lee Konitz, Sidney Bechet, Ornette Coleman, Benny Goodman, Sonny Stitt, and others.

Tenor Titans (VAI 69073) 60 minutes; assorted tenor saxophonists: Coleman Hawkins, Lester Young, Stan Getz, John Coltrane, Wayne Shorter, Sonny Rollins, Dexter Gordon, and others.

Jazz Masters Vintage Collection, Vol. 2: 1960–61 (A-Vision 50-239-3) 45 minutes; Ben Webster, Ahmad Jamal, Miles Davis Quintet with John Coltrane, Miles Davis with Gil Evans Orchestra.

One Night With Blue Note, Vol. 1 (SVS) 55 minutes; Bobby Hutcherson, Herbie Hancock, Ron Carter, Freddie Hubbard, Joe Henderson, Tony Williams, Stanley Jordan, Art Blakey, Curtis Fuller, Johnny Griffin, Walter Davis, and Reggie Workman.

One Night With Blue Note, Vol. 2 (SVS) 60 minutes; Kenny Burrell, Grover Washington, Grady Tate, Reggie Workman, McCoy Tyner, Jackie McLean, Woody Shaw, Cecil McBee, Jack DeJohnette, Charles Lloyd, Michel Petrucciani, Lou Donaldson, Jimmy Smith, and Cecil Taylor.

Sun Ra: A Joyful Noise (RHAP) 60 minutes; documentary and much live music.

Satchmo (CBS) 86 minutes; documentary on the career of Louis Armstrong.

Duke Ellington and His Orchestra (JCVC-101) film clips of the Ellington band, 1929–52.

After Hours (RHAP) 27 minutes; 1961; featuring Coleman Hawkins, Roy Eldridge, and Cozy Cole.

Thelonious Monk: Straight, No Chaser (Warner Bros.) 89 minutes; performances and recording session, some dialog.

Bill Evans: The Universal Mind (RHAP) 45 minutes; Evans talks and plays.

The Coltrane Legacy (VAI) 61 minutes; John Coltrane, Eric Dolphy, Elvin Jones, McCoy Tyner, Reggie Workman, Jimmy Garrison; performances; interviews with Jimmy Cobb, Elvin Jones, Roy Haynes, Reggie Workman.

Note: These videocassettes can sometimes be found in video stores, libraries, and music stores. To keep up with new and reissued videocassettes, watch for reviews and advertisements in the jazz magazines listed on pages 409 and 410. Some of the above videocassettes and several others may be available by mail from these distributors:

Rhapsody Films (RHAP)
P. O. Box 179
NY, NY 10014
212-243-0152

Spectrum Music Videos
P.O. Box 1128
Norristown, PA 19404
800-846-8742

Jamey Aebersold
P.O. Box 1244
New Albany, IN 47151
800-456-1388

Cadence Record Sales
Cadence Bldg.
Redwood, NY 13679
315-287-2852

Jazzland
Box 366
Dayton, Ohio 45401
513-222-2413

GLOSSARY

acid jazz usually the creation of a disc jockey who takes funky accompaniments that have been synthesized electronically and/or sampled from jazz recordings, then repeats them continuously with raps and/or jazz improvisations superimposed atop them (see page 326).

antiphonal an adjective describing a common pattern of interaction between improvisers or between sections of a band, taking the form of a question and answer or a call and response.

arco the technique of playing a stringed instrument with a bow.

atonal the character and organization possessed by music that has no key (see page 373 for further explanations and illustrations).

attack the very beginning of a sound (opposite of release).

back beat strong accent on the second and fourth beats of every four-beat measure; a term usually applied to the work of a band's drummer.

ballad a slow piece (though not applied to slow blues).

big band an ensemble of ten or more players.

blue note 1) a pitch somewhere between a major third and minor third or between a major seventh and minor seventh step of the scale (see page 373).
2) minor third or seventh scale step (see page 374).

blues 1) a simple, funky style of black music separate from but coexistent with jazz; beginning at least as early as the turn of the century, probably much earlier; exemplified by such performers as Blind Lemon Jefferson, Leadbelly, Lightnin' Hopkins, Muddy Waters, T-Bone Walker, and Robert Johnson. It has been and continues to be an influence on jazz and rock. The majority of blues compositions employ the I-IV-I-V-I chord progression or a variation of it.
2) a piece characterized by any one or any combination of the following:

a) the I-IV-I-V-I chord progression or some variation of it in a twelve-measure package

b) a sad feeling

c) a slow pace

d) poetry in the form of paired couplets in iambic pentameter

e) many lowered third, fifth, or seventh intervals (see page 373 for further explanation).

bomb a pronounced accent played by the drummer.

boogie woogie a premodern jazz piano style associated with Meade Lux Lewis and Albert Ammons. It is characterized by a repetitive left-hand bass figure that states almost every beat by dividing it into dotted-eighth sixteenth-note patterns.

bop (bebop) the style associated with Charlie Parker, Dizzy Gillespie, Thelonious Monk, Bud Powell, Dexter Gordon, and Sonny Stitt (see page 136).

break 1) the portion of a piece in which all band members stop playing except the one who improvises a solo. The tempo and chord progressions are maintained by the soloist, but, because the band has stopped, it is called a stop-time. Rarely do such breaks last longer than two or four measures (see page 15 for detailed explanation).
2) the solo itself.

bridge the B part of an A-A-B-A composition; also known as the channel, the release, or the inside (see page 13 for further information).

broken time 1) a style of rhythm section playing in which explicit statement of every beat is replaced by broken patterns which only imply the underlying tempo, exemplified by the 1961 Bill Evans trio with Scott LaFaro and Paul Motian.
2) the manner of playing bass or drums in which strict repetition of timekeeping patterns is not maintained, but constant tempo is; exemplified by the 1960s and 70s playing of Elvin Jones.

chart the jazz musician's term for what is written as musical arrangement. This is distinguished from the classical musician's "score" because not all the notes are present. Many spaces in the chart are filled only by symbols indicating the chord progression that guides improvisation. Often the drum "parts" are almost blank.

chops instrumental facility.

chord progression 1) when one chord changes or "progresses" to another chord.

2) a set of harmonies in a particular order with specified durations; for example, the twelve-measure I-IV-I-VI blues progression (see pages 375–380).
3) the sequence of accompaniment chords intended for a song but used instead as the basis of a jazz improvisation.

chorus 1) a single playing through of the structure being used to organize the music in an improvisation.
2) a jazz solo, regardless of its length.
3) the part of a pop tune performed in constant tempo and repeated several times after the verse has been played, usually the only portion of a tune's original form used by the jazz musician (see page 385 for further explanation).

collective improvisation simultaneous improvisation by all members of a group together.

comping syncopated chording which provides improvised accompaniment for simultaneously improvised solos, flexibly complementing the rhythms and implied harmonies of the solo line (see page 20 for further explanation and pages 424–425 for musical notation).

cool 1) an adjective often used to describe the subdued feeling projected by the music of Bix Beiderbecke, Lester Young, Claude Thornhill, Gil Evans, Miles Davis, The Modern Jazz Quartet, Gerry Mulligan, Lee Konitz, and Jimmy Giuffre (see pages 167–185).
2) sometimes used as a synonym for West Coast style.
3)sometimes used to denote modern jazz after bop.

counterpoint two or more lines of approximately equal importance sounding together.

Creole 1) French- or Spanish-speaking individual born in the New World.
2) a person who has both French and African ancestry and was born in the New World (also known as "Creole of Color," as opposed to the white-skinned Creole defined above).

decay the very end of a sound; also known as a release. Opposite of attack (see pages 40–42 for discussion).

Dixieland style 1) Chicago combo style that was prominent during the 1920s.
2) a synonym for all preswing-era combo jazz.

double-stop sounding two bass strings at the same time.

double-time the feeling that a piece of music or a player is going twice as fast as the tempo, although the chord progressions continue at the original rate.

Fender bass electric bass guitar, used to play bass lines instead of chords; common in jazz rhythm sections after 1970.

fill in general, anything a drummer plays in addition to basic timekeeping patterns; in particular, a rhythmic figure played by a drummer to
1) fill a silence
2) underscore a rhythm played by other instruments
3) announce the entrance or punctuate the exit of a soloist or other section of the music
4) stimulate the other players and make a performance more interesting.

free jazz an approach associated with Ornette Coleman and Cecil Taylor, in which the music contains improvised solos that are free of preset chord progressions, and sometimes also free of preset meter (see pages 257–266).

front line musicians appearing directly in front of the audience, not blocked from view by another row of musicians. This designation is sometimes used to separate hornmen (because they stand in the front of a combo) from accompanists (who usually appear to the rear of the hornmen).

funky an adjective describing rhythms as well as melody, harmony, and tone color characteristics that evoke an effect perceived as
1) earthy or dirty
2) mean, "low down," evil, or sexy
3) bluesy
4) gospel-flavored.

fusion a synonym for jazz-rock style (see pages 305–336).

fuzak music that blends the characteristics of jazz-rock fusion styles with the characteristics of Muzak. It tends to stress electric instruments, steady funk rhythms, smooth textures, without many surprises. Used as background music during the 1980s and 90s by listeners who liked the softer variants of fusion and funk. Often used to designate music of Kenny G, Grover Washington, Earl Klugh, and Najee (see **smooth jazz**).

growl style a method used by some trumpeters and trombonists in which by unorthodox use of mutes, lips, mouth, and blowing techniques a sound is produced that resembles the growl of an animal. Despite the odd assortment of sounds that the growl includes, recognizable melodic figures can be played with this alteration of tone quality. (See Bubber Miley, Cootie Williams, and Joe "Tricky Sam" Nanton.)

hard bop the jazz style associated with Horace Silver, Art Blakey, and Cannonball Adderley (see page 186 for further explanation).

head the melody or prewritten theme for a piece.

head arrangement a band arrangement that was created extemporaneously by the musicians and is not written down.

high-hat (sock cymbal) an instrument in the drum set which brings two cymbals together by means of a foot pedal (see page 23 for illustration).

horn general label for any wind instrument; sometimes includes stringed and percussion instruments as well (the most general term for all instruments is ax).

jam session a musical get-together where improvisation is stressed and prewritten music is rare (jam means to improvise); may refer to a performance that is formally organized or casual, public or private, for profit or just for fun.

jazz-rock a variety of styles beginning in the late 1960s that use electric instruments, funk rhythm accompaniments, and jazz improvisation; also known as fusion music; often applied to the post-1968 music of Miles Davis, Spyro Gyra, Weather Report, the Crusaders, John McLaughlin, the electric music of Herbie Hancock and Chick Corea (see pages 308–330.)

laid back an adjective used to describe a feeling of relaxation, laziness, or slowness; often describes the feeling that a performer is playing his rhythms a little later than they are expected, almost after the beat or "behind" the beat.

lay out to stop playing while other players continue.

legato a style of playing in which the notes are smoothly connected with no silences between them (opposite of staccato).

lick a phrase or melodic fragment.

locked-hands style a style of piano playing in which a separate chord parallels each note of the melody because both hands are used as though they are locked together, all fingers striking the keyboard together; also known as block chording, playing the chord notes as a block instead of one at a time. (See sections on Milt Buckner, Lennie Tristano, George Shearing, Ahmad Jamal, Red Garland, and Bill Evans.)

modal music in which the melody and/or harmony is based on an arrangement of modes. In jazz, the term can mean music based on the extensive repetition of one or two chords or music based on modes instead of chord progressions (see page xxx for further explanation).

mode 1) the manner of organizing a sequence of tones, usually an ascending sequence of an octave.
2) the arrangement of whole steps and half steps common to scales.
(See page 372 for further explanation.)

mute an attachment which reduces an instrument's loudness and alters its tone color (see page 390 for illustrations).

new age music that is soft and soothing, lacks variety in rhythm, loudness, and chords. Often applied to the work of George Winston, selected works of Pat Metheny and others who recorded for Windham Hill, Narada, and ECM record companies. It tends to combine characteristics of

a) the minimalist style associated with nonjazz composers Philip Glass, LaMonte Young, and Steve Reich.

b) the style that Keith Jarrett developed for his unaccompanied solo piano improvisations of the 1970s and 80s.

c) music of classical musicians, including members of the Paul Winter Consort and Oregon, who improvised soft, smooth sound textures that did not swing.

pedal point low-pitched, repeated, and/or sustained tone. It usually retains its pitch despite changes in chords and improvisations occurring around it; common in the 1960s work of John Coltrane and McCoy Tyner.

pitch bending purposeful raising or lowering of a tone's pitch; usually done for coloration or expressive purposes (see pages 40, 41, and 42 for illustrations and explanation).

pizzicato the method of playing a stringed instrument by plucking instead of bowing.

polyrhythm several different rhythms sounding at the same time (see page 369).

progressive jazz music associated with Stan Kenton (see pages 174–177).

ragtime 1) a popular turn-of-the-century style of written piano music involving pronounced syncopation.
2) a label often applied to much pre-1920 jazz and pop music, unaccompanied solo piano styles as well as band styles, improvised as well as written music.
3) the style of music associated with composers Scott Joplin and Tom Turpin.

release 1) the manner in which a sound ends or decays (opposite of attack).
2) the bridge of a tune.

rhythm section the group of players whose band function is accompanying. This role is particularly common for pianists, bassists, and drummers, but it is not exclusive to them (see pages 18–24 for explanations and illustrations, see pages 415–418 and 424–431 for musical notations).

ride cymbal the cymbal suspended over a drum set, usually to the player's right, struck by a stick held in the drummer's right hand; used for playing timekeeping patterns called ride rhythms (see page 21 for illustration).

ride rhythm the pattern a drummer plays on the ride cymbal to keep time, the most common being ching-chick-a-ching-chick-a (see notations on page 430).

riff 1) phrase
2) melodic fragment
3) theme.

rim shot the drumstick striking the rim of the snare drum at the same time as it strikes the drum head.

rip an onset ornament in the form of a quick rise in pitch directly preceding a tone. (Listen to Bix Beiderbecke or Louis Armstrong.)

rubato free of strict adherence to constant tempo.

scat singing jazz improvisation using the human voice as an instrument, with nonsense syllables (dwee, ool, ya, bop, bam, etc.) instead of words.

sideman a designation for each musician in a band except the leader.

smooth jazz a designation for the styles of music played on radio stations subscribing to "The Wave" format of the 1980s and 90s: a blend of Kenny G, Grover Washington, Earl Klugh, Lee Ritenour, Larry Carlton, George Benson, Bob James, and their disciples (see page 325).

sock cymbal see **high-hat**.

staccato brief and separated (opposite of legato).

stride 1) left-hand style used by early jazz pianists. It usually employs a bass note on the first and third beats of each measure and a chord on the second and fourth.
2) the piano style of James P. Johnson and Willie "The Lion" Smith.

swing 1) a word denoting approval—"It swings" can mean it pleases me; "to swing" can mean to enjoy oneself; "he's a swinging guy" can mean he is an enjoyable person.
2) the noun indicating the feeling projected by an uplifting performance of any kind of music, especially that which employs constant tempo (see page 5 for further explanation).
3) the feeling projected by a jazz performance which successfully combines constant tempo, syncopation, swing eighth notes, rhythmic lilt, liveliness, and rhythmically cohesive group playing (see page 6 for further explanation).
4) the jazz style associated with Count Basie, Duke Ellington, Jimmie Lunceford, Benny Goodman, Art Tatum, Roy Eldridge, and Coleman Hawkins, as in the "swing era" (see pages 79–80).

syncopation 1) stress on any portion of the measure other than the first part of the first beat (and, in meter of four, other than the first part of the third beat), i.e., the second half of the first beat, the second half of the second beat, the fourth beat, the second half of the fourth beat, the second beat, etc.
2) stress on a portion of the measure least expected to receive stress (see page 366 for further explanation).

synthesizer any one of a general category of electronic devices (Moog and Arp, for example) which produces sounds or alters the sounds created by other instruments.

Third Stream a style that combines jazz improvisation with the instrumentation and compositional forms of classical music (see page 145 for further explanation).

tonal inflection alteration of a tone's pitch or quality, done purposefully at the beginning, middle, or end of a sound (see **pitch bending**, and see pages 40–42 for illustrations and explanations).

tone color (timbre, tone quality) the characteristic of sound which enables the listener to differentiate one instrument from another, and, in many cases, one player from another.

tremolo 1) fluctuation in the loudness of a sound, usually an even alternation of loud and soft.
2) a manner of playing a chord by rapidly sounding its different notes in alternation so that the chord retains its character, but also sustains and trembles.
3) the means of sustaining the sound of a vibraharp (see page 146).
4) an expressive technique for use by instruments in which vibrato is very difficult (flute, for example) or in which the variation of pitch necessary for vibrato may not be wanted (some styles of oboe playing, for example).
5) the rapid reiteration of the same note.

turnaround (turnback, turnabout) a short progression within a chord progression that occurs just prior to the point at which the player must "turn around" to begin another repetition of the larger progression (see page 373 for further explanation and page 416 for musical notation).

two-beat style a rhythm section style which emphasizes the first and third beats of each four-beat measure, often leaving the second and fourth beats silent in the bass; sometimes called boom-chick style.

vamp a short chord progression (usually only one, two, or four measures long) which is repeated many times in sequence. Often used for introductions and endings. Much jazz and pop music of the 1960s and 70s used vamps instead of more involved chord progressions as accompaniment for melody and improvisation.

vibrato the slight fluctuation of a tone's pitch, alternating above and below its basic pitch; used as an expressive device, varied in speed and amplitude by the performer to fit the style and feeling of the music (see page 41 for further explanation).

voicing 1) the manner of organizing, doubling, omitting, or adding to the notes of a chord (see pages 378, 379, 416–418).

2) the assignment of notes to each instrument (see page 106 for further explanation).

vocalese the practice of singing lyrics set to the notes of a recorded instrumental jazz improvisation, as in lyrics composed by Eddie Jefferson for the saxophone improvisation on the James Moody recording of "I'm in the Mood for Love," released as "Moody's Mood for Love," and in lyrics composed by Jon Hendricks for Count Basie hits, performed by the singing group Lambert, Hendricks and Ross, and in lyrics set by Annie Ross to the melody and saxophone improvisations recorded by Wardell Gray for his piece "Twisted"; not to be confused with scat singing (nonsense syllables improvised by singers acting as jazz instrumentalists).

walking bass a style of bass line in which each beat of each measure receives a separate tone, thus creating a moving sequence of quarter notes in the bass range.

West Coast style the jazz style associated with Gerry Mulligan and Chet Baker during the 1950s (see **cool** and page 174 for further explanation).

Supplementary Reading

Biographies

ARMSTRONG, LOUIS. *Satchmo: My Life in New Orleans.* Upper Saddle River, NJ: Prentice-Hall, 1954; New York: Da Capo, 1986.
Louis Armstrong's autobiography.

CARNER, GARY. *Jazz Performers: An Annotated Bibliography of Biographical Materials.* Westport, CT: Greenwood, 1990.

CARR, IAN. *Miles Davis: A Biography.* New York: Morrow, 1982.
An intelligently written and knowledgeable biography of Davis by fellow jazz trumpeter Carr. Contains discography as well as transcriptions of solo improvisations.

CARR, IAN, FAIRWEATHER, DIGBY, and PRIESTLEY, BRIAN. *Jazz: The Essential Companion.* Upper Saddle River, NJ: Prentice-Hall, 1988.
The single most intelligently written biographical reference work to be published during the 1980s. Contains hundreds of biographies of jazz musicians written by jazz musicians.

CASE, BRIAN, and BRITT, STAN. *The Harmony Illustrated Encyclopedia of Jazz.* 3rd ed. New York: Harmony, 1986.
Over 400 biographical entries.

CHARTERS, SAMUEL B. *Jazz New Orleans 1885–1963, An Index to the Negro Musicians of New Orleans.* New York: Oak, 1963; Da Capo, 1983.
A valuable source of biographical and musical information on the first jazz musicians.

CHILTON, JOHN. *Who's Who of Jazz: Storyville to Swing Street.* 4th ed. New York: Da Capo, 1985.
Biographies of hundreds of musicians born before 1920.

DANCE, STANLEY. *The World of Count Basie.* New York: Scribner, 1981; Da Capo, 1985.
Covers Basie and his sidemen in profile and interview formats.

DANCE, STANLEY. *The World of Duke Ellington.* New York: Scribner, 1970; Da Capo, 1980.

DANCE, STANLEY. *The World of Earl Hines.* New York: Scribner, 1977; Da Capo, 1983.
Includes reminiscences by numerous Hines associates, historical accounts in Hines's own words, an exclusive chronology of Hines's life, plus excellent bibliography and discography.

DANCE, STANLEY. *The World of Swing.* New York: Scribner, 1975; Da Capo, 1979.
Vignettes of swing era figures with an emphasis on interview material.

ELLINGTON, DUKE. *Music Is My Mistress.* Garden City, NY: Doubleday, 1973; New York: Da Capo, 1976.
Duke Ellington's autobiography.

ELLINGTON, MERCER. *Duke Ellington In Person.* Boston: Houghton-Mifflin, 1978; New York: Da Capo, 1979.
A biography by Duke Ellington's son, sideman, and road manager.

FEATHER, LEONARD. *The Encyclopedia of Jazz.* rev. ed. New York: Bonanza, 1960; Da Capo, 1984.
Leonard Feather and Ira Gitler's monumental compilation with over 2,000 biographies arranged alphabetically.

FEATHER, LEONARD. *The Encyclopedia of Jazz in the Sixties.* New York: Horizon, 1966; Da Capo, 1986.
A follow-up to the above including 1,400 biographies.

FEATHER, LEONARD, and GITLER, IRA. *The Encyclopedia of Jazz in the Seventies.* New York: Bonanza, 1976; Da Capo, 1987.

FEATHER, LEONARD. *From Satchmo to Miles.* New York: Stein & Day, 1972; Da Capo, 1984.
Chapters on Louis Armstrong, Duke Ellington, Count Basie, Lester Young, Charlie Parker, Dizzy Gillespie, Miles Davis, and others.

FOSTER, GEORGE MURPHY. *Pops Foster: The Autobiography of a New Orleans Jazzman.* Berkeley: University of California Press, 1971.
Contains numerous details of New Orleans jazz history from the turn of the century plus much on the history of jazz in Chicago. The musical information in the book is indispensable to understanding the history of jazz rhythm section playing, and is not limited to the bass style of its author.

GARA, LARRY. *The Baby Dodds Story.* Los Angeles: Contemporary Press, 1959.

Contains a peek into the techniques used by early jazz drummers. Also has much on New Orleans and Chicago jazz history.

GILLESPIE, DIZZY. *To Be or Not to Bop.* Garden City, NY: Doubleday, 1979; New York: Da Capo, 1985.
Reminiscences by Gillespie plus interviews with his colleagues done by Al Fraser.

GITLER, IRA. *Jazz Masters of the Forties.* New York: Macmillan, 1966; Da Capo, 1982.
One of the most intelligently conceived jazz history books, it includes musical and biographical discussions of Charlie Parker and the alto and baritone saxophonists; Dizzy Gillespie and the trumpeters; Bud Powell and the pianists; J. J. Johnson and the trombonists; Oscar Pettiford and the bassists; Kenny Clarke, Max Roach, and the drummers; Dexter Gordon and the tenor saxophonists; Lennie Tristano and Lee Konitz; and Tadd Dameron and the arrangers.

GOLDBERG, JOE. *Jazz Masters of the Fifties.* New York: Macmillan, 1965; Da Capo, 1980.
A chapter each on Miles Davis, Thelonious Monk, Gerry Mulligan, Charles Mingus, John Coltrane, Sonny Rollins, Ornette Coleman, and Cecil Taylor.

HADLOCK, RICHARD. *Jazz Masters of the Twenties.* New York: Macmillan, 1965; Da Capo, 1986.
A chapter each on Armstrong, Beiderbecke, Earl Hines, Fats Waller, James P. Johnson, Fletcher Henderson, Eddie Lang, and The Chicagoans.

HITCHCOCK, H. WILEY, ed. *The New Grove Dictionary of American Music.* New York: Groves Dictionaries of Music, 1986.
Contains numerous biographies as well as different jazz styles summaries.

JEWELL, DEREK. *Duke: A Portrait of Duke Ellington.* New York: Norton, 1977, 1980.
Biography by a British jazz critic who knew Ellington.

PORTER, LEWIS. *Lester Young.* Boston: G. K. Hall, 1985.
A scholarly and technical study of Young written by a saxophonist and jazz historian.

PORTER, LEWIS, ed. *A Lester Young Reader.* Washington: Smithsonian, 1991.
A collection of articles and papers on Lester Young.

REISNER, ROBERT. *Bird: The Legend of Charlie Parker.* New York: Citadel, 1962; Da Capo, 1975.
A biography in the form of recollections and documents.

RUSSELL, ROSS. *Bird Lives: The High Life and Hard Times of Charlie Parker.* New York: Charterhouse, 1973.
Charlie Parker biography in the style of a novel.

SHAPIRO, NAT, and HENTOFF, NAT. *Hear Me Talkin' to Ya.* New York: Rinehart, 1955; Dover, 1966. Interviews with famous jazz musicians.

SHAPIRO, NAT, and HENTOFF, NAT. *Jazz Makers.* New York: Rinehart, 1957; Da Capo, 1979.
A chapter each on Jelly Roll Morton, Baby Dodds, Louis Armstrong, Jack Teagarden, Earl Hines, Bix Beiderbecke, Pee Wee Russell, Fats Waller, Art Tatum, Coleman Hawkins, Benny Goodman, Duke Ellington, Charlie Parker, Fletcher Henderson, Count Basie, Lester Young, Roy Eldridge, Charlie Christian, and Dizzy Gillespie.

SIMPKINS, C. O. *Coltrane: A Biography.* New York: Herndon House, 1975; Baltimore: Black Classic, 1989.
Contains transcriptions, work sheets, interviews, and analyses in addition to biographical details.

SPELLMAN, A. B. *Four Lives in the Bebop Business.* New York: Pantheon, 1966; Limelight Edns, 1985.
Biographical interviews with Ornette Coleman, Cecil Taylor, Jackie McLean, and Herbie Nichols.

STEWART, REX. *Jazz Masters of the Thirties.* New York: Macmillan, 1972; Da Capo, 1980.
A chapter each on Ellington, Hawkins, Henderson, Basie, Art Tatum, and Benny Carter.

SUDHALTER, RICHARD M., EVANS, P.R., and MYATT, W.D. *Bix: Man & Legend.* New York: Arlington House, 1974.
An exhaustive biography of Bix Beiderbecke. Written by trumpeter Sudhalter, this book includes technical analyses and a chronology of Beiderbecke's life with explanations for almost every mystery surrounding it; also contains transcriptions of solos and an excellent discography.

SUMMERFIELD, MAURICE J. *The Jazz Guitar: Its Evolution & Its Players.* Gateshead, Tyne and Wear, England: Ashley Mark, 1978; Milwaukee: Hal Leonard, 1986.
Biographies of almost all the prominent guitarists in jazz history.

TAYLOR, ARTHUR. *Notes and Tones.* New York: Perigee Books, 1982.
Interviews by drummer Taylor with musicians including Miles Davis, Ornette Coleman, Philly Joe Jones, Don Byas, Ron Carter, Max Roach, Erroll Garner, Dizzy Gillespie, Tony Williams, Sonny Rollins, Don

Cherry, Kenny Clarke, Freddie Hubbard, Elvin Jones, and Art Blakey.

THOMAS, J. C. *Chasin' the Trane: The Music and Mystique of John Coltrane.* Garden City, NY: Doubleday, 1975; New York: Da Capo, 1976.
Impressionistic biography interwoven with quotes from Coltrane's colleagues; excellent discography.

ULANOV, BARRY. *Duke Ellington.* New York: Creative Age, 1946; Da Capo, 1975.

WILLIAMS, MARTIN. *Jazz Masters of New Orleans.* New York: Macmillan, 1970; Da Capo, 1978.
A chapter each on King Oliver, Jelly Roll Morton, Sidney Bechet, Louis Armstrong, and the Original Dixieland Jazz Band.

Jazz Magazines

Cadence
(ISSN 0162-6973) 1976–.
Cadence Building
Redwood, NY 13679

Coda
(ISSN 0010-017X) 1958–.
The Shire
Hornby Island, British Columbia
VOR IZO, Canada

Crescendo & Jazz Music
(ISSN 0962-7472) 1991–.
Limelight Publishing
28 Lamb's Conduit St.
London
WCIN 3LE, England;
previously *Crescendo International*
(0011-118X) 1962–1990.

Down Beat
(ISSN 0012-5768) 1934–.
P.O. Box 906
Elmhurst, IL 60126-0906; ph: 800-535-7496

Jazz Educators Journal
(ISSN 0730-9791) 1969–.
P.O. Box 724
Manhattan, KS 66502

Jazz Journal International
(ISSN 0140-2285) 1948–.
1/5 Clerkenwell Road
London EC 1M 5PA
England

Jazz Times
(ISSN 0272-572X) 1980–.
8737 Colesville Road, Fifth Floor.
Silver Spring, MD 20910-3921; ph: 888-279-7444

Jazziz
1983–.
3620 NW 43rd St.
Gainesville, FL 3260; ph: 800-742-3252

Jazzletter
(ISSN 0890-6440)
1981–.
Box 240, Ojai, CA 93023

Jazz Improvisation
491 Old York Road
Jenkintown, PA 19046; ph: 888-472-0670

Sources for Information About Jazz Records

ALLEN, DANIEL. *Bibliography of Discographies, Vol. II: Jazz.* New York: Bowker, 1981.

HEFELE, BERNHARD. *Jazz-Bibliography.*
Haimendorfstr. 8, D-91126
Schwabach Wolkersdorf, Germany

IAJRC Journal.
(ISSN 0098-9487)
International Association of Jazz Record Collectors
P.O. Box 518
Wingate, NC 28174

Basic Jazz Discographies

Discographies are books that tally information about recording sessions, the formats and catalog numbers in which the recordings have been issued. They indicate how many versions ("takes") of each piece were made, the date, place, and musicians. Some list all the recording sessions for a given player or company.

RUST, BRIAN. *Jazz Records: 1897–1942.*

JEPSEN, JORGEN GRUNNET. *Jazz Records 1942–[1969]: A Discography.*

BRUYNINCKX, WALTER. *Jazz: Traditional Jazz, 1897–1985: Origins, New Orleans, Dixieland, Chicago Styles, Swing, Modern Jazz, Progressive Jazz.*

LORD, TOM. *The Jazz Discography: 1898 to Present.*

Note: North Country Distributors carries many discographies, rare jazz books, and imported jazz books. Write them at 7 Cadence Building, Redwood, NY 13679; phone 315-287-2852.

Contact your interlibrary loan librarian to locate discographies of particular musicians. The Providence, Rhode Island Public Library maintains a vast collection of such items, some of which might be available for loan via your library.

Texts for Readers Familiar with Musical Notation

HODEIR, ANDRE. *Jazz: Its Evolution and Essence.* New York: Grove, 1956; Da Capo, 1975.
Technical analyses of various styles and recordings including an essay on trombonist Dicky Wells and one on Ellington's "Concerto for Cootie."

JOST, EKKEHARD. *Free Jazz.* Vienna, Austria: Universal Edition, 1974; New York: Da Capo, 1981.
Technical analyses and notations of work by John Coltrane, Miles Davis (*Kind of Blue*), Charles Mingus, Ornette Coleman, Cecil Taylor, Archie Shepp, Albert Ayler, Don Cherry, the Association for the Advancement of Creative Musicians (AACM), Sun Ra, and the Art Ensemble of Chicago.

OWENS, THOMAS. *Bebop: The Music and the Players.* New York: Oxford Press, 1995.
Scholarly and technical examination of bebop, its origins, techniques, and the differences between styles of its players; goes all the way from Charlie Parker to John Coltrane and Freddie Hubbard, and their disciples.

OSTRANSKY, LEROY. *The Anatomy of Jazz.* Seattle: University of Washington Press, 1960; Westport, CT: Greenwood, 1973.

Schuller, Gunther. *Early Jazz: Its Roots and Musical Development.* New York: Oxford Press, 1968.
Scholarly and quite technical examination of the earliest jazz known, its possible sources in African music and nineteenth-century American popular music. Detailed analysis of Louis Armstrong, Jelly Roll Morton, other pre-swing players, Fletcher Henderson, Ellington's earliest recordings, Bennie Moten and territory bands during the 1920s and early 1930s.

TAYLOR, BILLY. *Jazz Piano: History and Development.* Dubuque, IA: Wm C Brown, 1983.
Discussion by a well-known jazz pianist and teacher. Interspersed with musical notations and technical examples, the book is still useful for nonmusicians.

Technical References

BAKER, DAVID. *Jazz Improvisation: A Comprehensive Study for All Players.* Chicago: Maher, 1969; rev. ed. Van Nuys, CA: Alfred Publishers, 1988.
A helpful instruction manual for intermediate and advanced as well as beginning jazz improvisers.

COKER, JERRY. *Improvising Jazz.* Upper Saddle River, NJ: Prentice Hall, 1964; Touchstone Bks, 1986.
Excellent explanation of chords, chord progressions, how to swing, and how to improvise melodically.

MEHEGAN, JOHN. *Jazz Improvisation 1: Tonal and Rhythmic Principles.* New York: Watson-Guptill, 1959.

MEHEGAN, JOHN. *Jazz Improvisation 2: Jazz Rhythm and the Improvised Line.* New York: Watson-Guptill, 1962.

MEHEGAN, JOHN. *Jazz Improvisation 3: Swing and Early Progressive Piano Styles.* New York: Watson-Guptill, 1964.

MEHEGAN, JOHN. *Jazz Improvisation 4: Contemporary Piano Styles.* New York: Watson-Guptill, 1965.
Mehegan's textbooks provide a scholarly instruction series for the serious jazz student who has solid knowledge of the piano. The series is not exclusively for pianists, but any nonpianist using it must have some acquaintance with the keyboard.

REEVES, SCOTT D. *Creative Jazz Improvisation.* Upper Saddle River, NJ: Prentice Hall, 1989, 1995.

SUDNOW, DAVID. *Ways of the Hand: The Organization of Improvised Conduct.* Cambridge: Harvard University Press, 1978.
A difficult-to-read narrative on how one man learned how to play jazz piano. Filled with useful photographs and drawings of hand positions on the keyboard.

ZINN, DAVID. *The Structure and Analysis of the Modern Improvised Line.* New York: Excelsior Music Pub Co, 1981; available through Theodore Presser Company, Bryn Mawr, PA 19010.
A very formal, technical instruction manual for musicians. It should also interest music theorists because it represents an intelligent analysis for the construction of melodic lines from rhythmic and harmonic perspectives.

Note: To keep up with the currently available technical references, seek the catalogs of Jamey Aebersold, P.O. Box 1244, New Albany, IN 47151-1244; phone: 800-456-1388.

General References

BASCOM, WILLIAM R., and MELVILLE J. HERSKOVITS, ed. *Continuity and Change in African Cultures.* Chicago: University of Chicago Press, 1959, 1962.
Contains an excellent chapter on African music by Alan Merriam and several other studies of African art and culture that should be helpful for readers interested in the roots of jazz.

BEBE, FRANCIS. *African Music: A People's Music.* Westport, Conn: Lawrence Hill, 1975.
African music, its forms, musicians, instruments, and place in the life of the people; well illustrated.

BERLIN, EDWARD A. *Ragtime: A Musical and Cultural History.* Berkeley: University of California Press, 1980.
Scholarly evaluation of ragtime; includes musical notations.

COKER, JERRY. *Listening to Jazz.* Upper Saddle River, NJ: Prentice-Hall, 1978, 1981.
One of the best guides to appreciating the playing of jazz improvisers. Loaded with insights about how musicians develop solos. Keyed to the *Smithsonian Collection of Classic Jazz;* contains numerous, detailed analyses that often require musical background from the reader.

COLLIER, JAMES LINCOLN. *The Making of Jazz.* Boston: HM, 1978; New York: Delta, 1979.
If you can get past the author's attempts at psychoanalyzing musicians, you will find some interesting musical analyses here. This is probably the longest American history of jazz, and it integrates a large assortment of styles in an easy-to-read manner.

FEATHER, LEONARD. *The Book of Jazz.* New York: Horizon, 1957, 1965, 1976.
An instrument-by-instrument history of jazz plus discussions of the origins of jazz and the nature of jazz improvisation. This book, in all its revisions, remains the best compact guide to jazz and summary of the perspectives of this exceedingly knowledgeable and insightful musician-journalist.

NKETIA, J.H. KWABENA. *The Music of Africa.* New York: Norton, 1974.
Nontechnical description of African musical traditions, training of performers, musical instruments; technical analyses of vocal and instrumental music; richly illustrated with music, photographs, maps, and song lyrics.

SOUTHERN, EILEEN. *The Music of Black Americans: A History.* 2nd ed. New York: Norton, 1983.
Covers popular, classical, folk, and religious music, and jazz.

Women in Jazz

DAHL, LINDA. *Stormy Weather: The Music and Lives of a Century of Jazzwomen.* New York: Pantheon, 1984; Limelight Edns, 1989.

GOURSE, LESLIE. *Madame Jazz: Contemporary Women Instrumentalists.* New York: Oxford, 1995.

HANDY, D. ANTOINETTE. *Black Women in American Bands and Orchestras.* Metuchen, NJ: Scarecrow, 1981.

KOENIG, KARL. "Women Pianists in Early New Orleans Jazz." In *Jazz Research Papers,** ed. Charles Brown, 115–121. Manhattan, KS: National Association of Jazz Educators, 1986.

LEDER, JAN. *Women in Jazz: A Discography of Instrumentalists, 1913–68.* Westport, CT: Greenwood, 1985.

MCCORD, KIMBERLY. "The Conceptualization of Women in Jazz." In *Jazz Research Papers,** ed. Charles Brown, 93–105. NAJE, 1985.

MCCORD, KIMBERLEY. "History of Women in Jazz." *Jazz Educators Journal,** 18, No. 2 (1986): 15.

MCCORD, KIMBERLEY. "All-Women Jazz Groups." In *Jazz Research Papers,** ed. Charles Brown, 134–140. NAJE, 1986.

PLACKSIN, SALLY. *American Women in Jazz.* New York: Wideview Books, 1982.

UNTERBRINK, MARY. *Jazz Women at the Keyboard.* Jefferson, NC: McFarland & Co, 1983.

**Jazz Educators Journal* and *Jazz Research Papers* are available from the International Association of Jazz Educators, Box 724, Manhattan, KS 66502 (phone 913-776-8744).

Sources for Notated Jazz Solos

There are hundreds of books filled with transcriptions of famous jazz improvisations. Catalogs and ordering information for them are available in *Jazz Educators Journal,* the official journal of the International Association of Jazz Educators. You can get back issues from school band directors who belong to the organization. Or you can join the organization yourself by sending only a small fee, and the information they distribute is well worth it. Just write International Association of Jazz Educators, P.O. Box 724, Manhattan, Kansas 66502.

Many jazz books and magazines include notations of jazz improvisations. The Mehegan books, listed on page 410 under "Technical References," contain numerous solo transcriptions. *Down Beat* magazine, listed on page 409 under "Jazz Magazines," includes transcriptions or instructional aids in almost every issue. Going through back issues of *Down Beat* can reveal a treasure trove of notations.

James DaPogny has transcribed several Jelly Roll Morton piano solos and added them to published works and music from the rolls of player pianos for a total of 40 numbers in *Ferdinand "Jelly Roll" Morton: The Collected Piano Music,* published by Smithsonian Institution Press/G. Schirmer.

The most dedicated of all solo transcribers is Andrew White. From him, you can order more than 600 John Coltrane solos, more than 300 Charlie Parker solos, and several Eric Dolphy solos. Just write Andrew's Music at 4830 South Dakota Avenue, N.E., Washington, D.C. 20017.

Jamey Aebersold distributes numerous books of solo transcriptions. One series is by David Baker, and it includes one book each for Clifford Brown, Miles Davis, John Coltrane, Sonny Rollins, Cannonball Adderley, and Fats Navarro. Aebersold also distributes transcription books by Ken Slone and Don Sickler. Slone has prepared a book of Clifford Brown solos. Sickler has one of Joe Henderson's solos. There are also some fairly elaborate books of transcriptions from a series originally published under the auspices of *Down Beat* magazine. It includes *Jazz Styles and Analysis: Guitar* by Jack Petersen (74 solos from 64 guitarists), *Jazz Styles and Analysis: Alto Sax* by Harry Miedema (125 solos from 103 saxophonists), and *Jazz Styles and Analysis: Trombone* by David Baker (157 solos). Aebersold distributes so many more such books, you should just write for his catalog. Aebersold has been known to carry books of solos by Stan Getz, Chick Corea, Louis Armstrong, Bill Evans, Horace Silver, Benny Goodman, Art Tatum, J. J. Johnson, Charlie Parker, Thelonious Monk, Bud Powell, Paul Chambers, Dexter Gordon, and others. Write Jamey Aebersold at P.O. Box 1244, New Albany, IN. 47151-1244.

Carl Fischer Music, Inc. (62 Cooper Square, NY, NY 10003) has published several books by Stuart Isacoff that contain solo transcriptions, accompanied by useful analyses and comments about the styles of major players. *Solos for Tenor Sax* contains analyses of improvisations by John Coltrane, Stan Getz, Coleman Hawkins, Oliver Nelson, and Sonny Rollins. *Solos for Jazz Trumpet* contains analyses of improvisations by Louis Armstrong, Dizzy Gillespie, Miles Davis, Lee Morgan, and Freddie Hubbard. *Solos for Jazz Alto Sax* contains analyses of improvisations by Cannonball Adderley, Paul Desmond, Eric Dolphy, Johnny Hodges, Charlie Parker, and Phil Woods.

Hal Leonard Publishing Corporation has published Greg Fishman's transcriptions of nineteen solos by Stan Getz, Tim Price's transcriptions of twenty-five solos by Cannonball Adderley, Mike Barry, and Kevin Carberry's transcriptions of twenty-four solos by Freddie Hubbard, Bob Leso's transcriptions of twelve solos by McCoy Tyner, Sanford Marten's transcriptions of twenty-five solos by Wayne Shorter, and Lennie Niehaus's transcriptions of twenty-two solos by Dexter Gordon. The books may be obtained through Aebersold or directly from Hal Leonard, 7777 West Bluemound Road, Milwaukee, Wisconsin 53213.

Many solo transcriptions can be found in doctoral dissertations, which are written to earn a doctoral (Ph.D.) degree. Most are never commercially published. However, when the degree is granted, most dissertations are automatically deposited with a company called University Microfilms, which permanently retains one copy and then makes and sells additional copies on demand. This has been occurring only since 1956, so do not contact University Microfilms for work completed before then. (Note that University of Chicago, Harvard University, and Massachusetts Institute of Technology are among the few institutions that do not contribute to this repository.)

To get a dissertation, write University Microfilms International, 300 Zeeb Road, Ann Arbor, Michigan 48106. Tell them the author's name (it helps to have the middle initial), the first two words of the title, the college where the dissertation was done, and the year it was completed. This information helps them identify the dissertation when you lack the catalog number. When you correspond with them, tell them your college affiliation because they extend a discount to students and faculty. You can phone them at their toll-free number: 800-521-3042 (from Michigan, Alaska, and Hawaii: 313-761-4700; from Canada: 800-268-6090). They also accept credit card orders.

You will probably come across many titles of books, articles, and dissertations that you just want to glance at, not necessarily own. (Most cost more than $20.) For that reason, it is handy to know about interlibrary loan services. If you have never used such a service, ask the staff at your college library's reference desk. The staff should have a computer that will tell what nearby library is holding the book, article, or dissertation you want. The staff can put in a request. Then you need wait only a few weeks before your library receives it for you. You can check it out just as you would check out one of your own library's holdings. Note that if you want only a single article from a periodical, your interlibrary loan staff can sometimes arrange for a distant library to copy the article and send it for you to keep. (This can be quite convenient when you want a particularly good transcription that lies in an old jazz magazine that no one in town seems to have.)

To keep up with new dissertations that are being added to the literature about jazz, you could scan the music listings in your library's current copies of *Dissertation Abstracts.* This is a periodical that publishes summaries of dissertations that have just been completed.

Here are a few dissertations that have many transcriptions in them:

Charlie Parker: Techniques of Improvisation, by Thomas Owens, 1974, University of California
Catalog Number 75-1992
(Contains about 250 Parker solos)

A History and Analysis of Jazz Drumming to 1942, by Theodore Dennis Brown, 1976, University of Michigan
Catalog Number 77-7881
(Contains numerous drum solos and timekeeping rhythms as well as analyses.)

The Improvisational Techniques of Art Tatum, by Joseph A. Howard, 1978, Case Western Reserve University
Catalog Number 78-16468

Structural Development in the Jazz Improvisational Technique of Clifford Brown, by Milton Lee Stewart, 1973, University of Michigan
Catalog Number 73-24692

John Coltrane's Music of 1960 Through 1967, by Lewis R. Porter, 1983, Brandeis University
Catalog Number 83-18239

Jazz, 1920 to 1927: An Analytical Study, by Launcelot Allen Pyke, II, 1962, State University of Iowa
Catalog Number 62-4988
(Contains transcriptions of 1926 "Perdido Street Blues" with Kid Ory, Johnny Dodds, and Baby Dodds, 1923 "Snake Rag" by King Oliver's Creole Jazz Band, 1942 "Down By the Riverside" by Bunk Johnson's Original Superior Band, 1927 "Keyhole Blues" by Louis Armstrong and His Hot Seven, the 1923 Gennett recording of "Dippermouth Blues" by King Oliver's Creole Jazz Band, 1924 "Cake Walkin' Babies" by Armstrong and Bechet, 1926 "Big Butter and Egg Man From The West" by Louis Armstrong and His Hot Five, 1923 "Sweet Lovin' Man" by King Oliver's Creole Jazz Band minus Oliver, 1925 "Papa De-Da-Da" by Armstrong and Bechet, and 1923 "Southern Stomps" by Oliver's Creole Jazz Band.)

For Musicians

You have now entered the technical part of the appendix. This section is designed to give musically literate readers a chance to experience some of the musical elements discussed in the main body of the text. Keep in mind that it is possible to learn more by playing the examples at the piano than by merely reading the attached explanations. Once you have played these demonstrations yourself, the principles will be more obvious to you when they occur in jazz recordings.

Chords and Chord Progressions

One way to understand how chords can be constructed is to imagine them as being built from tones in the major scales. For instance, in the key of Bb, tones for the chords can be drawn from the notes in the Bb major scale (Bb C D Eb F G A Bb). In the key of C, they can be drawn from the notes in the C scale (C D E F G A B C). Beginning with a single tone, the chord is made by adding every other tone in the scale. In other words, the first, third, and fifth tones are used when the beginning tone is the key note (first tone of the major scale). The second, fourth, and sixth tones are used when the chord is based on the second step of the scale. The third, fifth, and seventh tones are used when the chord begins on the third step of the scale.

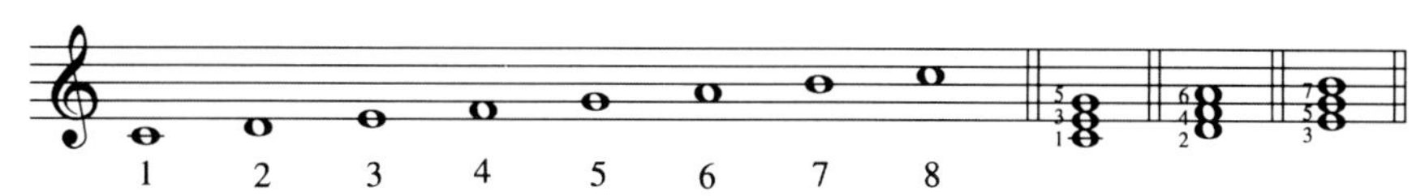

If a chord is based on the first tone of the major scale, it is called the "one chord," symbolized by the Roman numeral for one, I. The chord based on the second step of the major scale is a II chord. The labeling system continues through the VII chord.

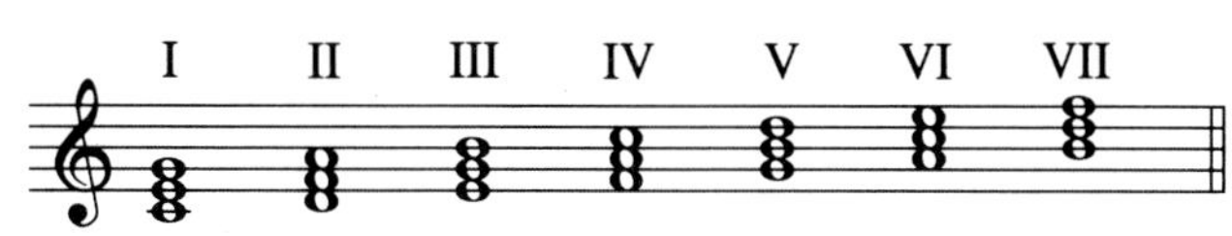

The system is more involved than what we have discussed. Before you can apply chord knowledge to studying improvisation, you must become acquainted with construction of many types of chords: dominant sevenths and major sevenths; major, minor, diminished, and augmented chords; chords with added ninths, elevenths, and thirteenths; chords with added fourths and sixths, flat fifths, raised ninths, etc. You will also need to confront a collection of different chord labeling systems.

Twelve-Bar Blues Progressions

Though basically a I-IV-I-V-I progression, the twelve-bar blues may contain a huge assortment of chord progressions. Here are three possibilities for a blues in the key of C.

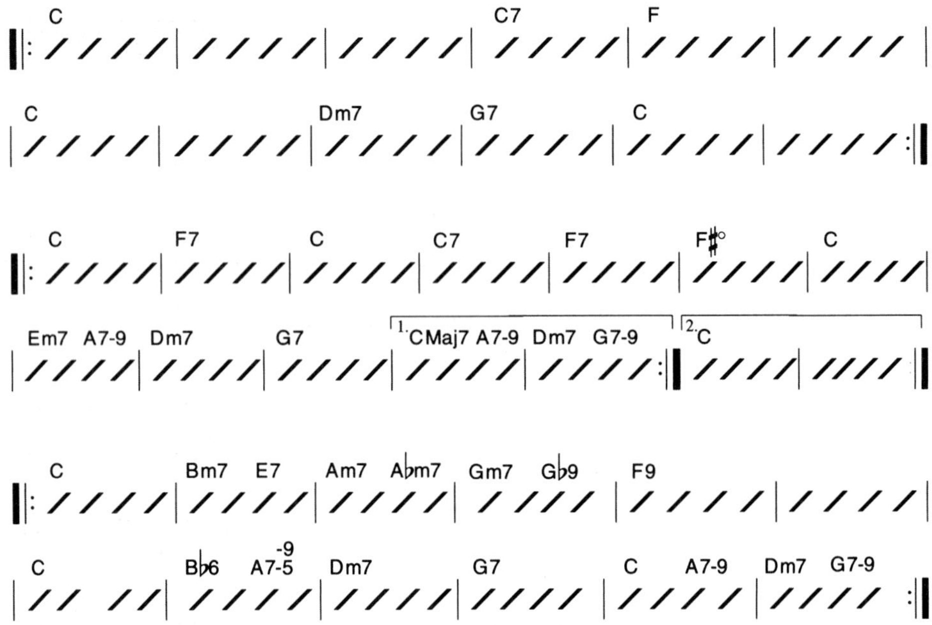

Turnarounds Turnarounds are the sets of chord progressions occurring in the seventh and eighth, fifteenth and sixteenth, thirty-first and thirty-second bars of a thirty-two-bar chord progression and in the eleventh and twelfth bars of a twelve-bar blues progression. Some turnarounds occupy more or less than two measures, however. Turnarounds provide an opportunity for numerous variations, all of which depend on the preferences and era of soloist and accompanists.

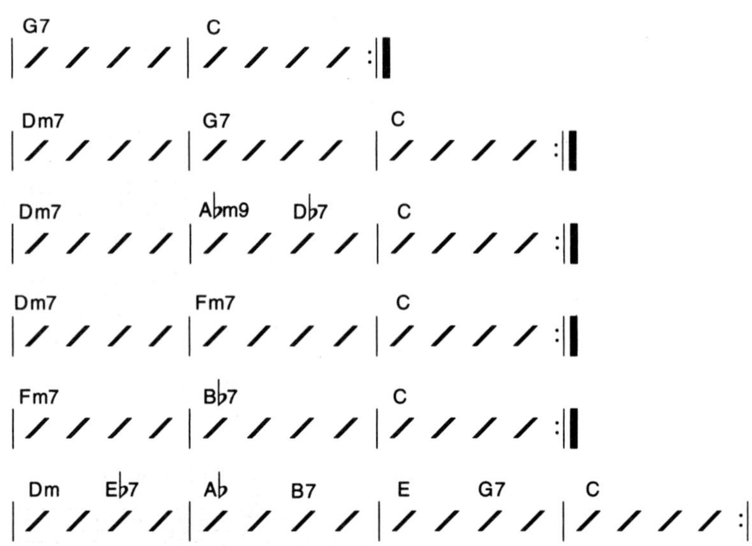

Voicing Rarely is a chord played with its tones contained in a single octave, the root on the bottom, the third in the middle, and the fifth on the top.

Usually chords are voiced. This means that the positions of a chord's tones are scattered over the keyboard; the tones may be altered, doubled, added to, or missing. For instance, instead of having the root on the bottom and the fifth on the top, a chord might have its root on top and fifth on the bottom.

Or perhaps the third is on the bottom, the fifth in the middle, and the root on top.

In some voicings, the root is doubled by being duplicated in different octaves.

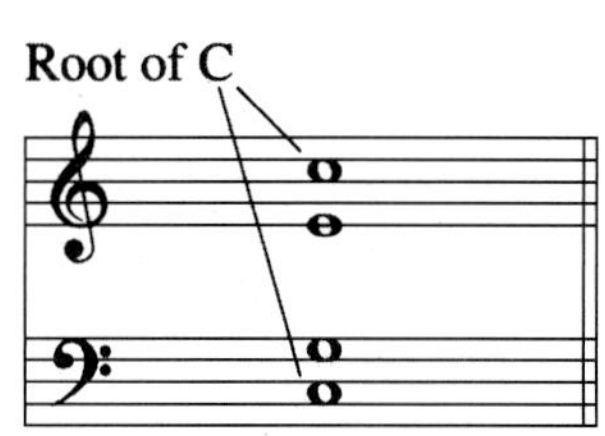

Quite frequently the sixth is added to enrich major triads.

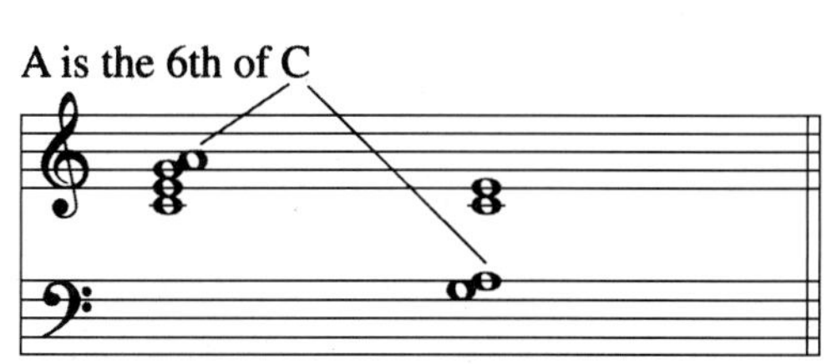

Instead of being voiced in thirds (every other step in a major scale), some chords are voiced in fourths.

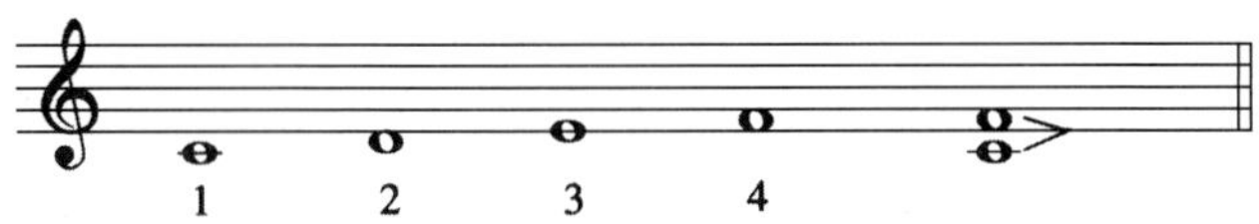

Many other possibilities are available for voicing chords. Only a few simple examples have been cited here as an introduction. Voicings are important partly because, in addition to striking force, phrasing, speed, and precision, an identifying characteristic of a jazz pianist's style is his preference in voicings. For instance, McCoy Tyner often uses an interval of a fifth in his left hand and a chord voiced in fourths in his right hand.

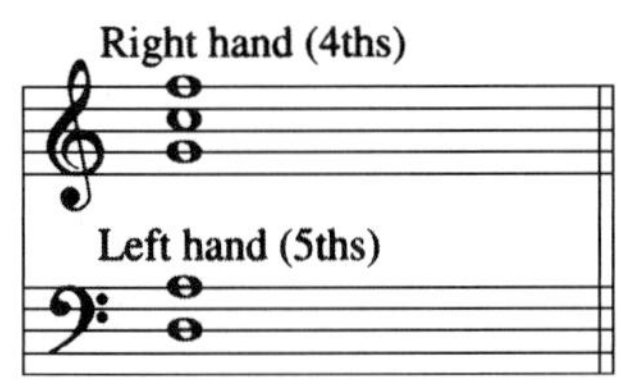

Modes Though used for centuries in classical music, modes just recently became popular harmonic bases for jazz improvisation. To get a rough idea of what is meant by the term "modes," we can use the tones of the major scale to produce different modes if we play ascending sequences, starting on different steps of the scale. Each mode's unique sound is the result of its particular arrangement of whole steps and half steps. For example, in the Ionian mode (also known as the major scale), half steps occur only between the third and fourth steps and the seventh and eighth steps. (The eighth step is an octave up from the first step.)

The Dorian mode is constructed from the same tones as the Ionian, but it begins on the second tone of the major scale. The Dorian mode has half steps between its second and third and its sixth and seventh tones.

There is a mode for each step of the major scale. Each mode has a distinct musical personality because its half steps fall in different places.

Examine the following modes. Play them, and listen carefully while you play them. Find the positions of the half steps in each mode. Once you know a mode's pattern of whole and half steps, you should be able to begin it on other notes. Remember that the interval between Bb and C is defined as a whole step, as is that between E and F#. Remember also that the interval between B and C is a half step, as is that between E and F.

Ionian (also known as major scale)

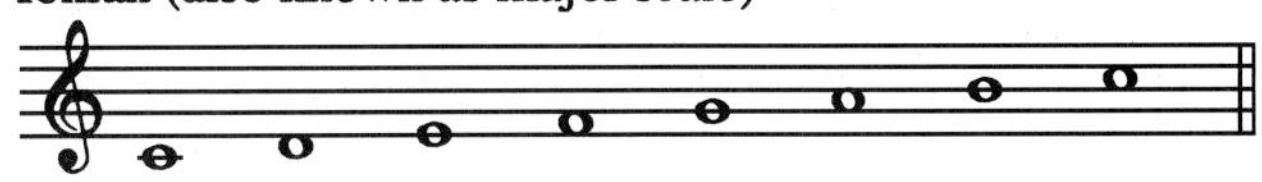

Dorian

Phrygian

Lydian

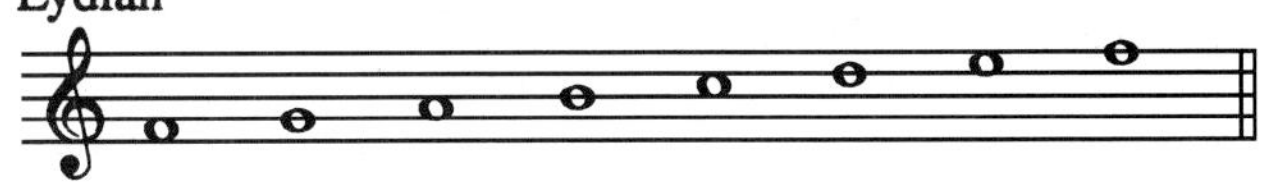

Mixolydian

Aeolian (also known as ancient, minor, pure, natural)

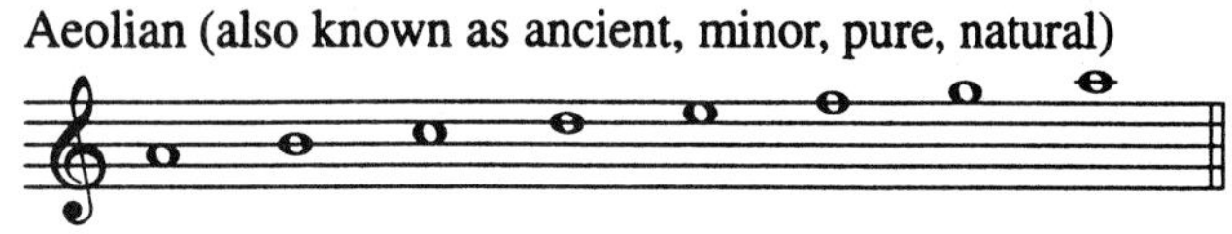

Locrian

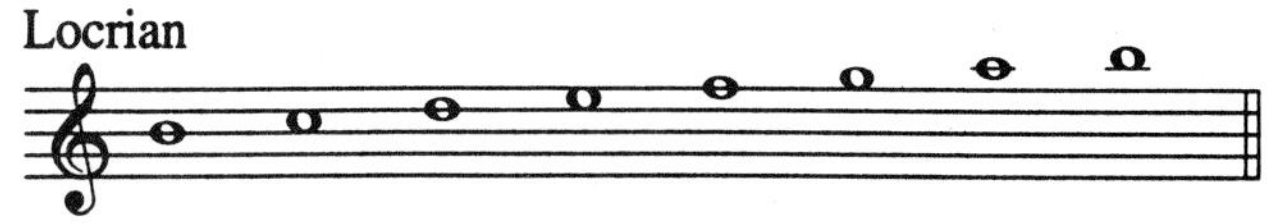

Kurd (Arabic)

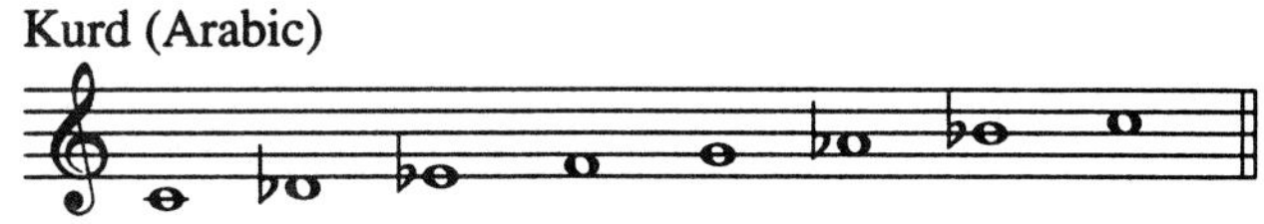

Gypsy

Hungarian

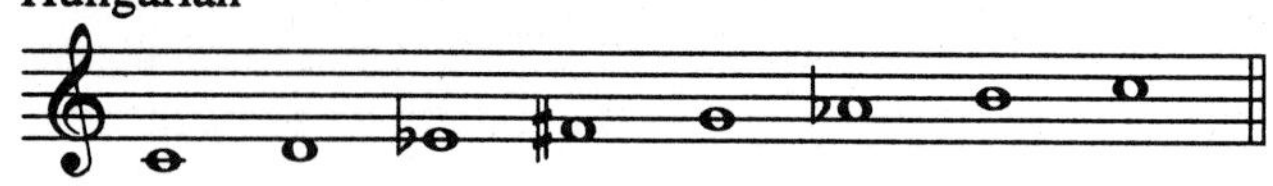

Byzantine

Charhargah (Persian)

Balinese

Spanish

Chinese

Ahavoh Rabboh (Jewish)

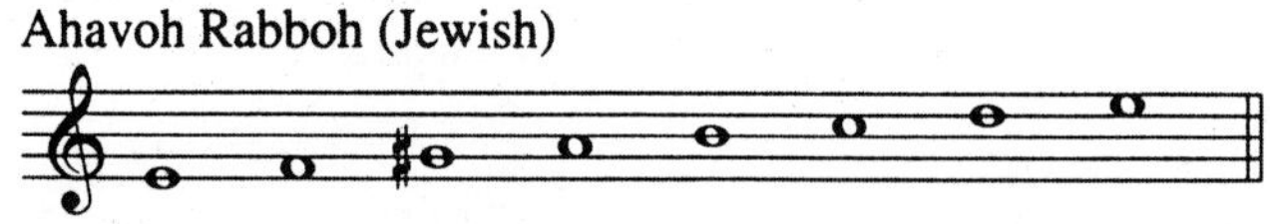

Pentatonic

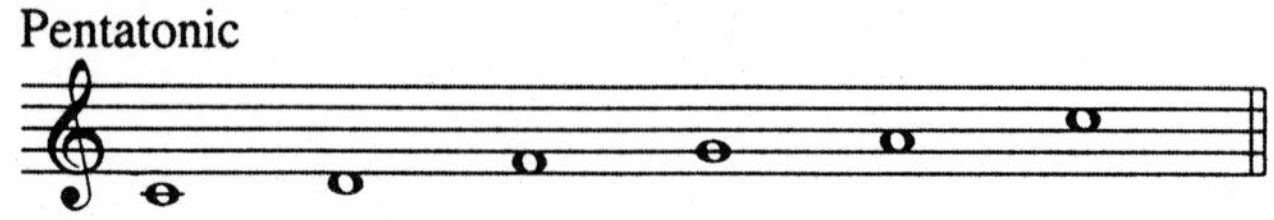

Whole Tone

Diminished

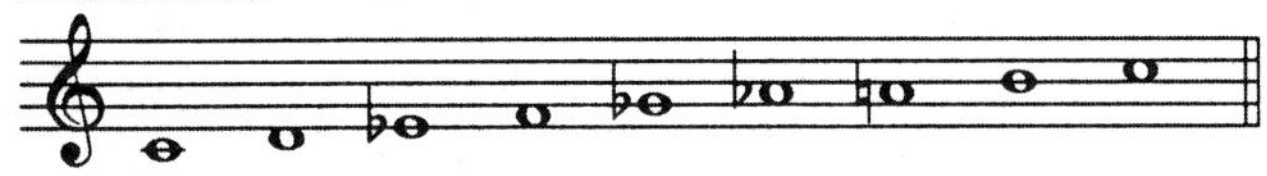

Inverted Diminished

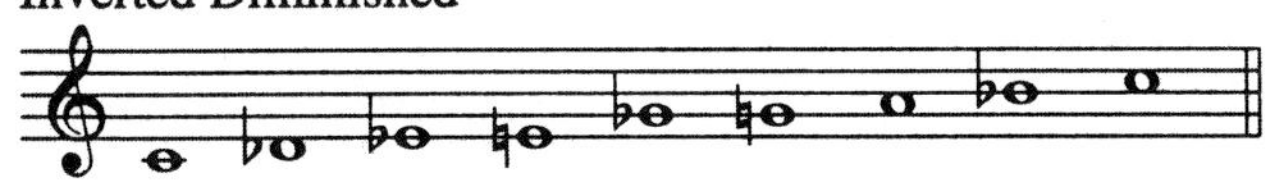

Modal Construction of "Flamenco Sketches"

The piece "Flamenco Sketches" on the Miles Davis album *Kind of Blue* follows the modal construction illustrated below. Note that the piece was labeled "All Blues" on many copies of the album. It is the final selection in the LP, cassette, and CD formats of the album, no matter what it is called on the label. It is also available on the *Jazz Classics CD.*

mode 1

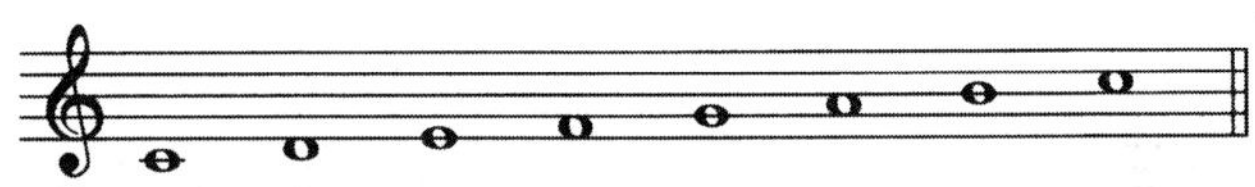

mode 2

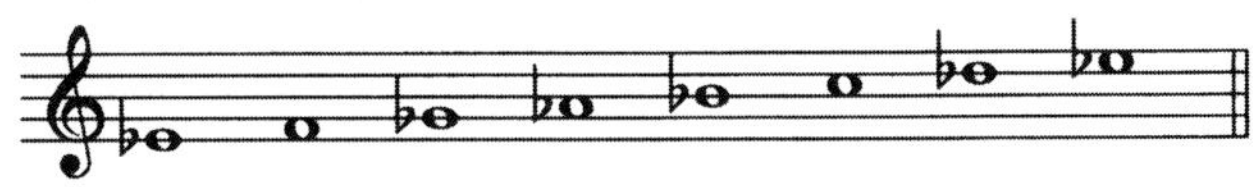

mode 3

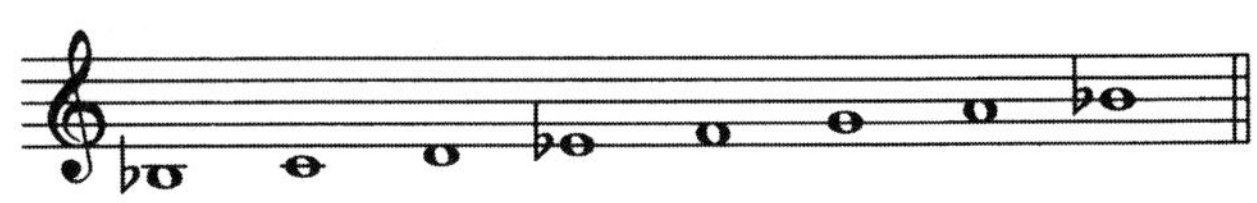

mode 4

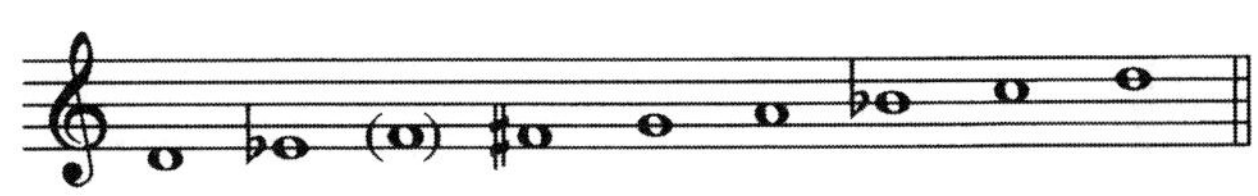

mode 5

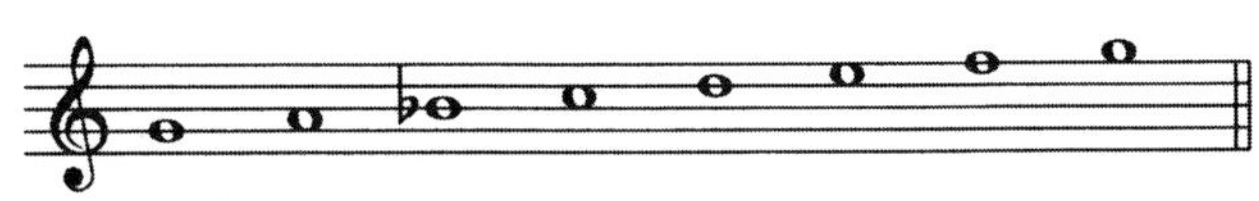

Modal Construction of "Maiden Voyage"

Am7/D "D" Mixolydian mode **4 bars**	Cm7/F "F" Mixolydian mode **4 bars**
B♭m7/E♭ "B♭" Dorian mode **4 bars**	C♯m7/F♯ "C♯" Dorian mode **4 bars**
Am7/D "D" Mixolydian mode **4 bars**	Cm7/F "F" Mixolydian mode **4 bars**

"D" Mixolydian, first mode for A section of "Maiden Voyage"

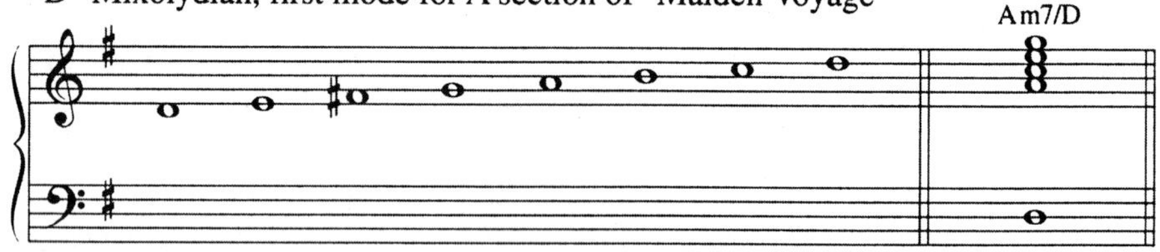

"F" Mixolydian, second mode for A section of "Maiden Voyage"

"B♭" Dorian, first mode for bridge of "Maiden Voyage"

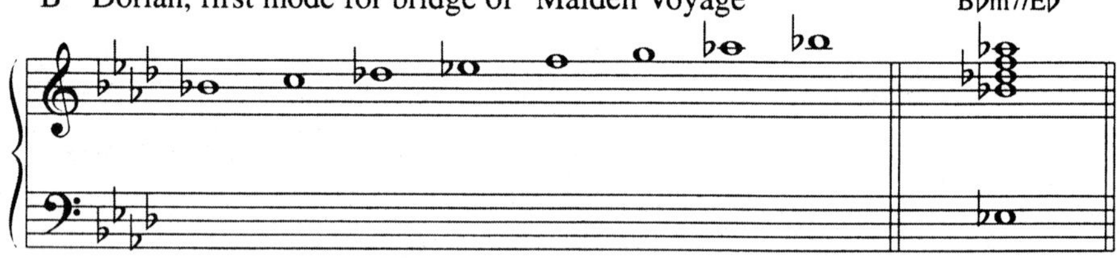

"C♯" Dorian, second mode for bridge of "Maiden Voyage"

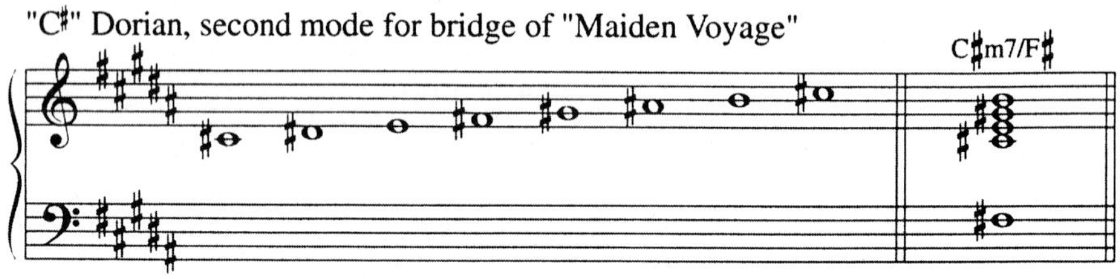

Modal Construction for "So What" and "Impressions"

Dm7	E♭m7	Dm7
"D" Dorian mode	"E♭" Dorian mode	"D" Dorian mode
‖: **8 bars** :‖	‖ **8 bars** ‖	‖ **8 bars** ‖

"D" Dorian mode for first sixteen bars of "So What" and "Impressions"

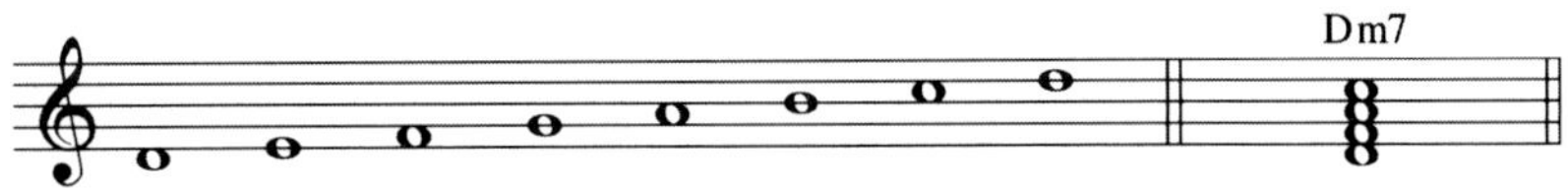

"E♭" Dorian mode for bridge of "So What" and "Impressions"

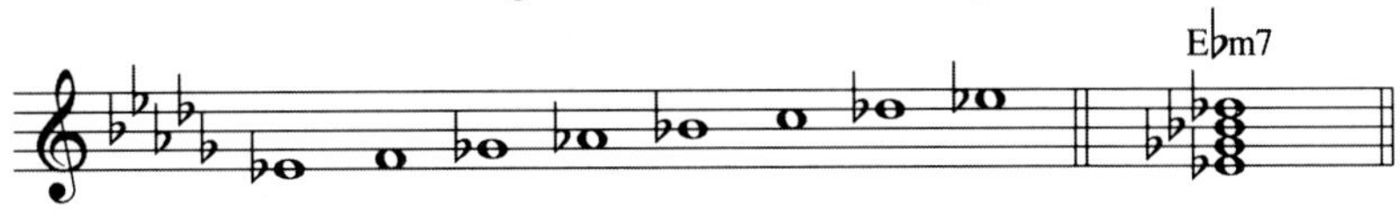

Modal Construction of "Milestones"

Gm7/C	Dm7/E	Gm7/C
"G" Dorian mode	"A" Aeolian mode	"G" Dorian mode
‖: **8 bars** :‖	‖: **8 bars** :‖	‖ **8 bars** ‖

"G" Dorian mode for first sixteen bars of "Milestones"

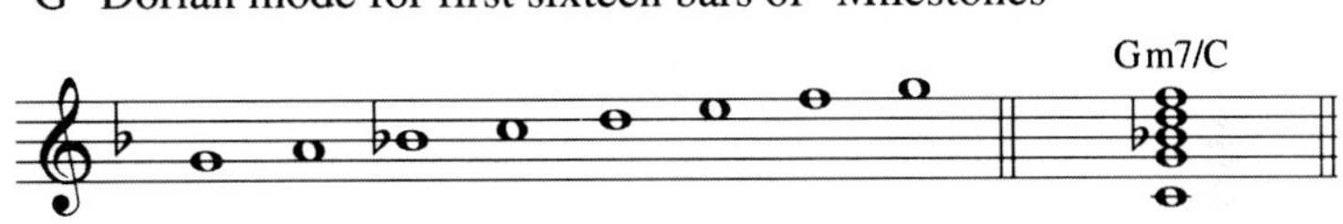

"A" Aeolian mode for bridge of "Milestones"

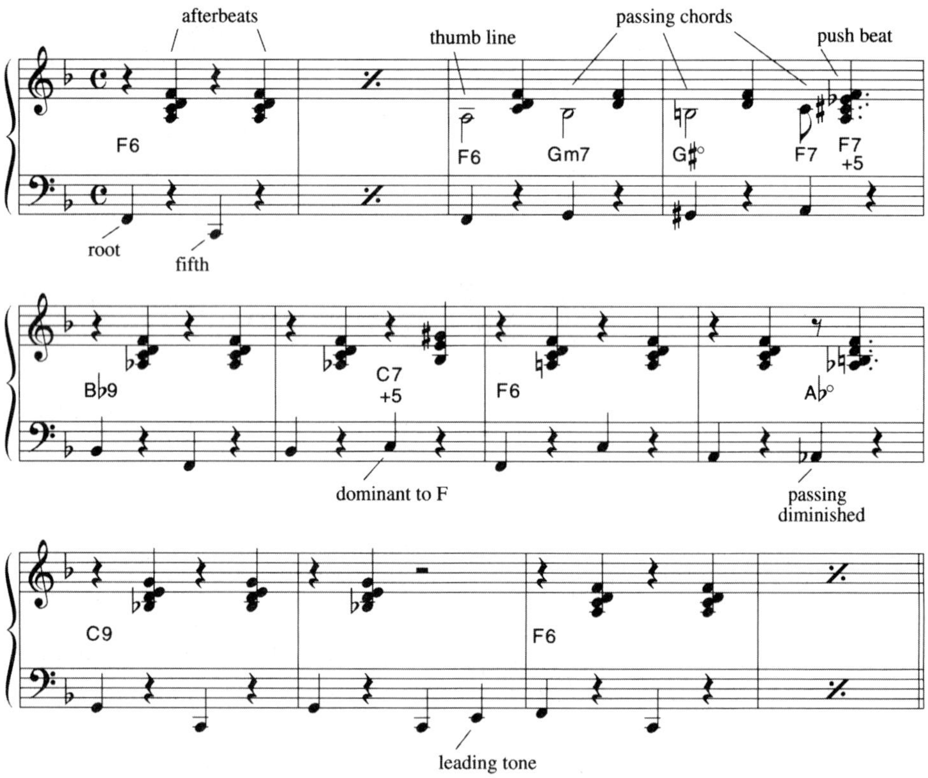

"Boston" or Two-Handed Stride-Style Comping (notated by David Berger)

Comping Here are two examples of piano accompaniments, or comping, for a jazz twelve-bar blues solo. Comping is accompaniment that is simultaneously composed and performed to fit the style of a piece and the directions in harmony, rhythm, and melody that are taken by the soloist. Comping usually contains pronounced syncopation.

Note that these chords have been voiced. Comping involves a seemingly endless variety of ways to voice chords, alter chord progressions, and design rhythms. But basically, comping is meant to accompany and complement the solo line by producing syncopated, unpatterned bursts of chords. Prepatterned chording, by definition, cannot flexibly enhance a spontaneously conceived solo line. Rehearsed patterns (and accompaniment figures that sound written) cannot sensitively interact with solo improvisation. The improvising soloist

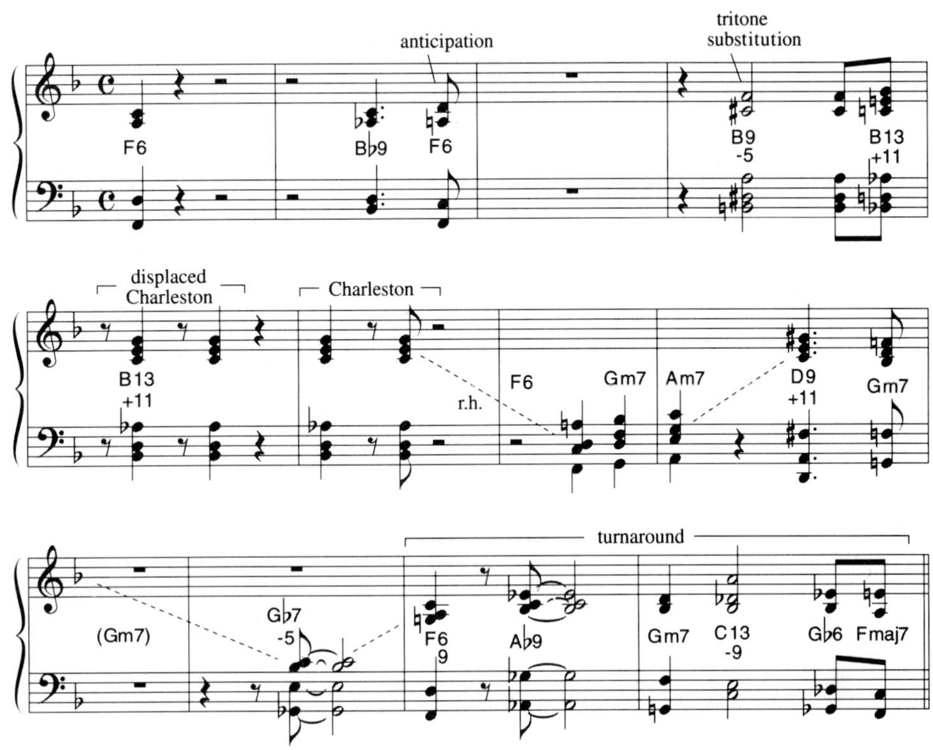

Bebop-Style Comping (notated by David Berger)

might just as well be playing with a big band and its written arrangements. To understand what this means, listen first to Tommy Flanagan's accompaniment work on any of the recordings he made during the 1950s and 1960s or any of the accompaniment work that Herbie Hancock did during the 1960s. Then listen to Horace Silver's accompaniment work of the 1960s with his own bands or John Lewis's with the Modern Jazz Quartet. The Flanagan and Hancock examples interact with the soloists, whereas the Silver and Lewis examples often sound more like worked-out material, even if they were spontaneous.

Walking Bass Lines

Walking is meant to provide timekeeping in the form of tones chosen for their compatibility with the harmonies of the piece and style of the performance. Ideally, the walking bass complements the solo line.

Three choruses of walking bass are shown here. They display three increasing levels of complexity for walking bass lines for the twelve-bar blues in the key of C (conceived and notated by Willis Lyman).

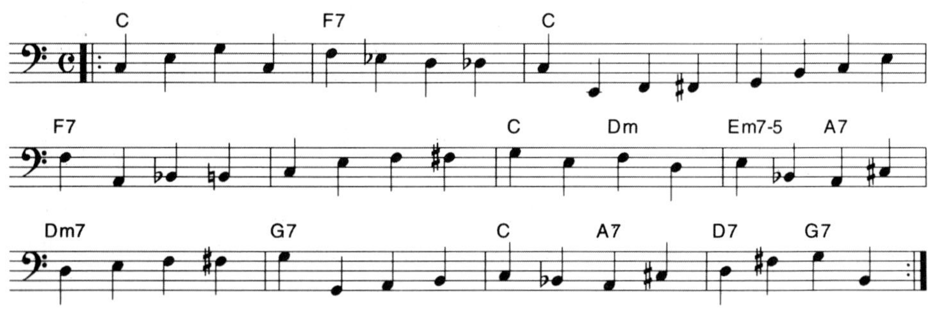

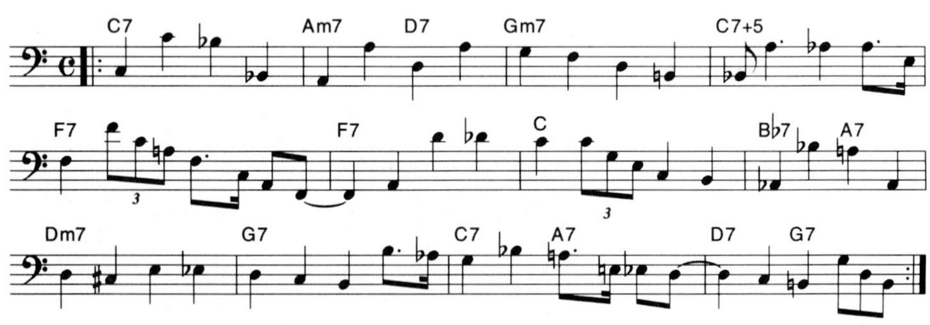

Rock Bass Lines

Jazz bassists of the 1970s incorporated many devices that were previously used mainly by rock and funk bassists. A number of rock and funk bass figures are notated here to illustrate the material from which many 1970s jazz bassists drew (notated by Richard Straub).

Latin American Bass Line

During performances of many jazz pieces during the 1950s and 1960s, including the first eight measures of "On Green Dolphin Street" and "I'll Remember April," bassists employed a figure like the one below. Musicians called it a "Latin bass figure."

Syncopations

The rhythms common to jazz contain many syncopations. Here are a few examples.

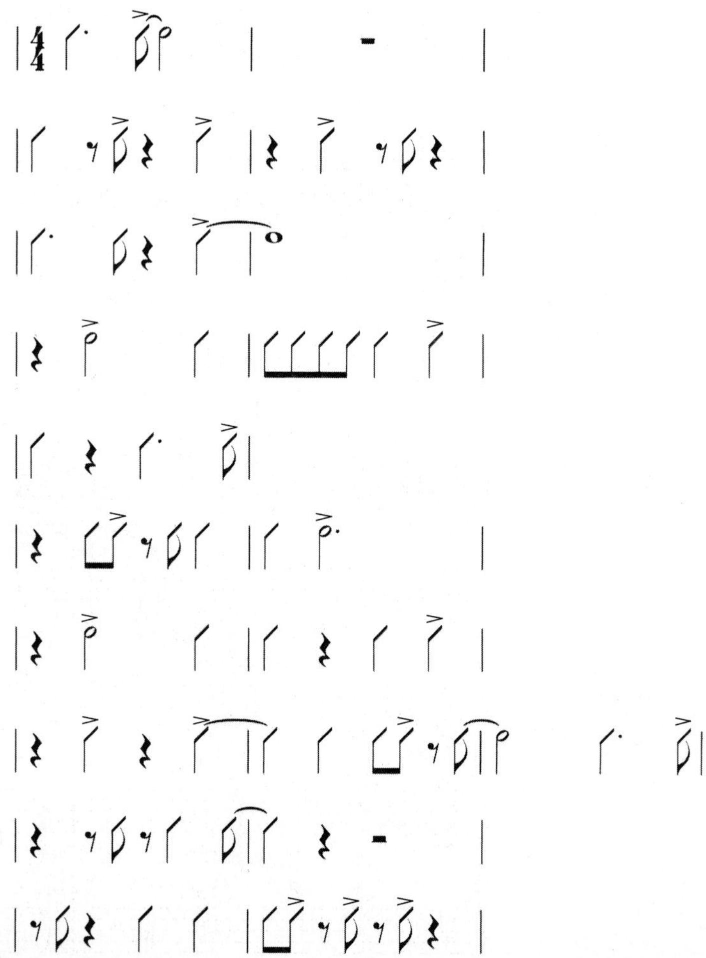

Comping Figures for "Rhythm Changes"

This is a typical example of piano comping for improvisations that follow the chord changes used by George Gershwin to accompany his melody "I Got Rhythm." This would also fit "Cottontail," "Shaw Nuff," "Lester Leaps In," and "(Meet the) Flintstones." Comping examples for Flintstones can be heard on the *Demo CD,* with and without the Flintstones melody. (Comping composed and notated by Jerry Sheer.)

Ride Rhythms

Ride rhythms are used by drummers to keep time and propel a performance. These rhythms contribute to jazz swing feeling, accomplishing in the high register, on the cymbals, what the walking bass does in the low register. (These were all transcribed and notated by Chuck Braman.)

Basic Jazz Ride Rhythm Common in Slow and Medium Tempos (4-beat Feel)*

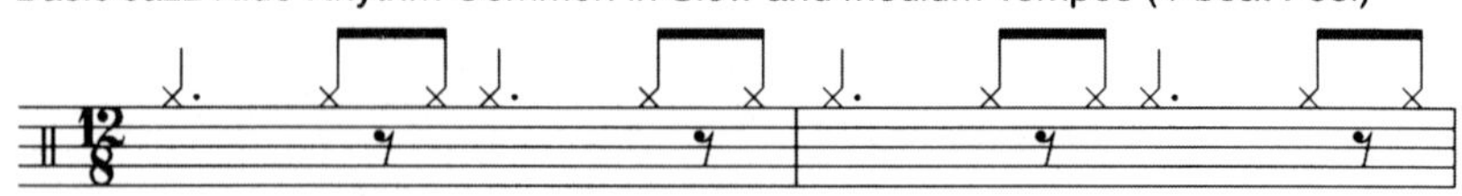

Basic Jazz Ride Rhythm Common in Fast Tempos (4-beat feel)

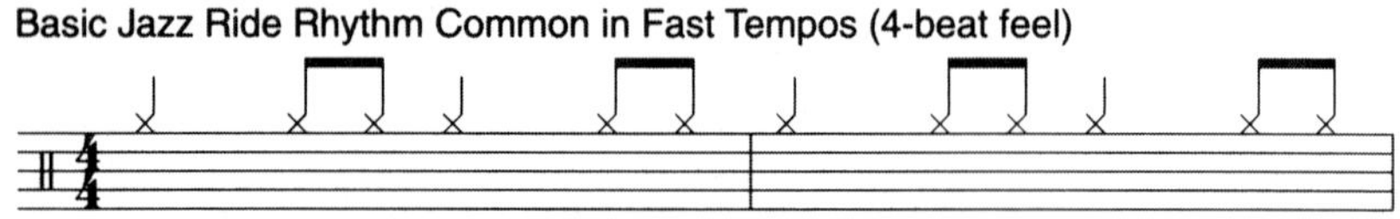

VARIATIONS:

Medium Tempos - Elvin Jones

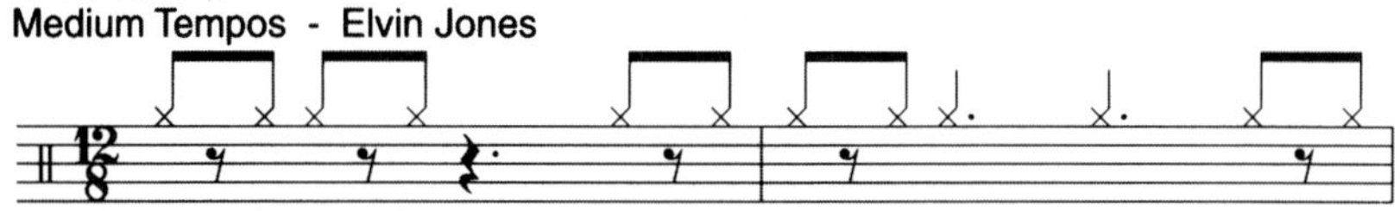

Medium Tempos - Roy Haynes

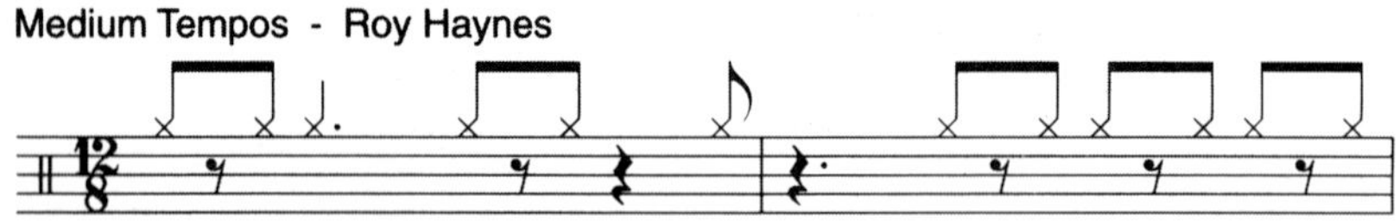

Fast Tempos - Billy Higgins

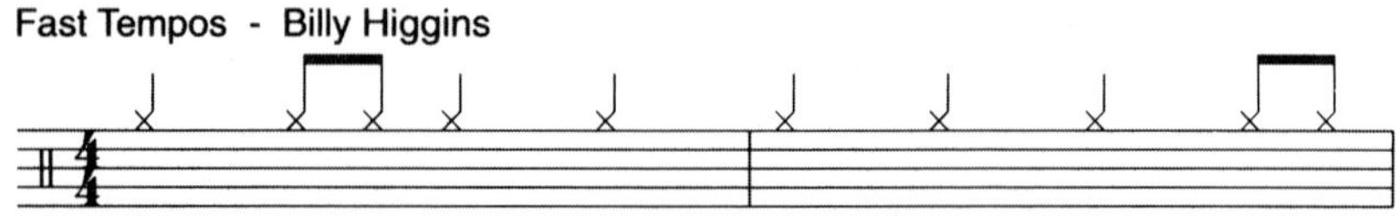

Fast Tempos - Roy Haynes

Basic Jazz Ride Rhythm Used to Imply 2-Beat Feel

*NOTE: The 12/8 figures are notated from 4/4 tunes. (Transcribed by Chuck Braman.)

Jazz-Rock/Jazz-Funk Drumming

Drummers of the late 1960s learned new timekeeping patterns that resembled the materials of rhythm and blues bands as well as Latin American styles. Below is a comparison that illustrates what Herbie Hancock's drummer learned from Sly Stone's drummer. (These were all transcribed and notated by Chuck Braman.)

Andy Newark - "In Time" from Sly Stone's *Fresh* 1973

Mike Clarke - "Butterfly" from Herbie Hancock's *Thrust* 1974

KEY (for this page only):

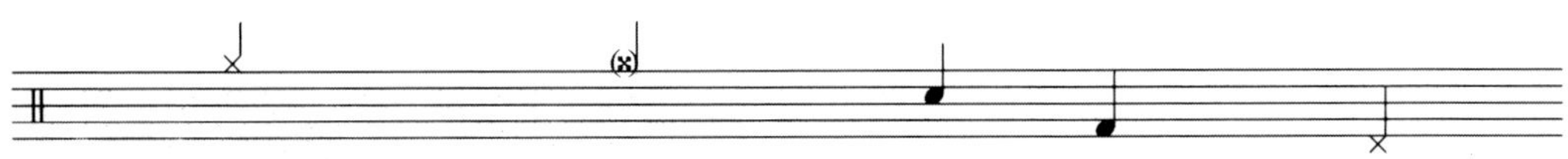

CLOSED HIGH HAT STRUCK WITH STICK

OPEN HIGH HAT STRUCK WITH STICK

SNARE DRUM

BASS DRUM

HIGH HAT SHARPLY CLOSED WITH FOOT

INDEX